THIS GUIDEBOOK

The Berlitz Travellers Guides are designed for experienced travellers in search of exceptional information that will enhance the enjoyment of the trips they take.

Where, for example, are the interesting, out-of-the-way, fun, charming, or romantic places to stay? The hotels described by our expert writers are some of the special places, in all price ranges except for the very lowest—not just the run-of-the-mill, heavily marketed places in advertised airline and travel-wholesaler packages.

We indicate the approximate price level of each accommodation in our description of it (no indication means it is moderate in local, relative terms), and at the end of every chapter we supply more detailed hotel rates as well as contact information so that you can get precise, up-to-the-minute rates and make reservations.

The Berlitz Travellers Guide to Portugal 1993 highlights the more rewarding parts of the country so that you can quickly and efficiently home in on a good itinerary.

Of course, this guidebook does far more than just help you choose a hotel and plan your trip. *The Berlitz Travellers Guide to Portugal 1993* is designed for use *in* Portugal. Our writers, each of whom is an experienced travel journalist who either lives in or regularly tours the city or region of Portugal he or she covers, tell you what you really need to know, what you can't find out so easily on your own. They identify and describe the truly out-of-the-ordinary restaurants, shops, activities, and sights, and tell you the best way to "do" your destination.

Our writers are highly selective. They bring out the significance of the places they do cover, capturing the personality and the underlying cultural and historical resonances of a city or region—making clear its special appeal.

The Berlitz Travellers Guide to Portugal is full of reliable and timely information, revised and updated each year. We would like to know if you think we've left out some very special place. Although we make every effort to provide the most current information available about every destination described in this book, it is possible too that changes have occurred before you arrive. If you do have an experience that is contrary to what you were led to expect by our description, we would like to hear from you about it.

A guidebook is no substitute for common sense when you are travelling. Always pack the clothing, footwear, and other items appropriate for the destination, and make the necessary accommodation for such variables as altitude, weather, and local rules and customs. Of course, once on the scene you should avoid situations that are in your own judgment potentially hazardous, even if they have to do with something mentioned in a guidebook. Half the fun of travelling is exploring, but explore with care.

ALAN TUCKER
General Editor
Berlitz Travellers Guides

Root Publishing Company
330 West 58th Street
Suite 504
New York, New York 10019

"The strength of the [Berlitz Travellers Guides] lies in remarks and recommendations by writers with a depth of knowledge about their subject."
—*Washington Times*

"The most readable of the current paperback lot."
—*New York Post*

"Highly recommended."
—*Library Journal*

"Very strong on atmosphere and insights into local culture for curious travellers."
—*Boston Herald*

"The [Berlitz Travellers Guides] eliminate cumbersome lists and provide reliable information about what is truly exciting and significant about a destination.... [They] also emphasize the spirit and underlying 'vibrations' of a region—historical, cultural, and social—that enhance a trip."
—*Retirement Life*

"Information without boredom.... Good clear maps and index."
—*The Sunday Sun* (Toronto)

CONTRIBUTORS

JEAN ANDERSON, a recognized authority on Portugal and on Portuguese food and wine, is the author of *The Food of Portugal*. She is a frequent contributor to *Travel & Leisure, Travel/Holiday, Food & Wine, Bon Appétit,* and *Gourmet* magazines, among others, and has received awards from the Portuguese government for her writing. She has worked on many *Reader's Digest* books and is the editorial consultant for this guidebook.

THOMAS DE LA CAL grew up in Portugal and returns there regularly from his current home in California. He has contributed articles to *Connoisseur, European Travel and Life, Travel/Holiday,* and other magazines. He has worked on documentaries about Portugal for the National Geographic Society, the BBC, and NBC, and has written the screen adaptation of a Portuguese novel for a European miniseries.

JEAN TODD FREEMAN first visited Lisbon 27 years ago and has been in love with it ever since. A novelist and freelance travel writer, she has written for *Travel & Leisure, Venture,* and *Diversion* magazines, and for Reader's Digest Books.

MARVINE HOWE, on the staff of the *New York Times* since 1972, has covered Portugal and the Portuguese-speaking world extensively. She also contributes articles about Portugal to the *Times* travel section.

MARION KAPLAN spent 20 years in Africa as a freelance photojournalist working for *Time* and *National Geographic,* among other magazines. In Portugal after 1980, she contributed to such publications as *Reader's Digest* and the *New York Times.* Now based in France, she is the author of *Focus Africa* and *The Portuguese.*

INGEBORG LIPPMANN, a freelance photojournalist, was based in Africa and the Middle East for the *New York Times* and *Time* magazine for 20 years, contributing to the *Christian Science Monitor, Newsweek,* and other publications as well. She has also covered much of South America. Over the past two decades she spent a few weeks each year covering Portugal, especially for the *New York Times* travel section. She now lives just outside Lisbon.

THE BERLITZ
TRAVELLERS GUIDES

THE AMERICAN SOUTHWEST

AUSTRALIA

BERLIN

CANADA

THE CARIBBEAN

ENGLAND & WALES

FRANCE

GERMANY

GREECE

HAWAII

IRELAND

LONDON

MEXICO

NEW ENGLAND

NEW YORK CITY

NORTHERN ITALY AND ROME

PORTUGAL

SAN FRANCISCO &
NORTHERN CALIFORNIA

SOUTHERN ITALY AND ROME

SPAIN

TURKEY

THE BERLITZ TRAVELLERS GUIDE TO PORTUGAL 1993

ALAN TUCKER
General Editor

BERLITZ PUBLISHING COMPANY, INC.
New York, New York

BERLITZ PUBLISHING COMPANY LTD.
Oxford, England

THE BERLITZ TRAVELLERS GUIDE
TO PORTUGAL 1993

Berlitz Trademark Reg U.S. Patent and Trademark Office
and other countries—Marca Registrada

Published by Berlitz Publishing Company, Inc.
257 Park Avenue South, New York, New York 10010, U.S.A.

Distributed in the United States by
the Macmillan Publishing Group

Distributed elsewhere by Berlitz Publishing Company Ltd.
Berlitz House, Peterley Road, Horspath, Oxford OX4 2TX, England

ISBN 2-8315-1785-0
ISSN 1057-4646

Designed by Beth Tondreau Design
Cover design by Dan Miller Design
Cover photograph by Guy Marche/FPG International
Maps by Volti Graphics
Illustrations by Bill Russell
Copyedited by Candace Lyle Hogan
Fact-checked by Doram Tamari
Edited by Patricia Fogarty

Printed in the United States of America
1 3 5 7 9 10 8 6 4 2

CONTENTS

This Guidebook	v
Travelling in Portugal in 1993	4
Overview	5
Useful Facts	21
Bibliography	37
Lisbon	45
Getting Around	79
Accommodations	81
Dining	89
Bars and Nightlife	97
Shops and Shopping	98
Day Trips from Lisbon	104
Costa do Estoril	108
The Sintra Area	120
Northern Estremadura	133
South of the Tagus River	145
The Ribatejo	160
The Alentejo	200
The Algarve	239
Beira Litoral	282
Beira Alta and Beira Baixa	313
Porto and the Douro Valley	343
The Minho	388
Trás-os-Montes	437
Madeira	464
The Azores	501
Historical Chronology	528
Index	543

MAPS

Portugal   3
Lisbon   52
The Alfama   58
Lisbon Environs   106
Northern Estremadura   134
The Ribatejo   162
The Upper Alentejo   202
The Algarve West   249
The Algarve East   264
Beira Litoral   284
Coimbra   292
Northern Beira Alta   316
Beira Baixa and Southern Beira Alta   332
Porto   350
The Douro Valley   371
The Minho   390
Guimarães   397
Trás-os-Montes   438
Madeira   465
The Azores   502

THE
BERLITZ
TRAVELLERS
GUIDE
TO
PORTUGAL
1993

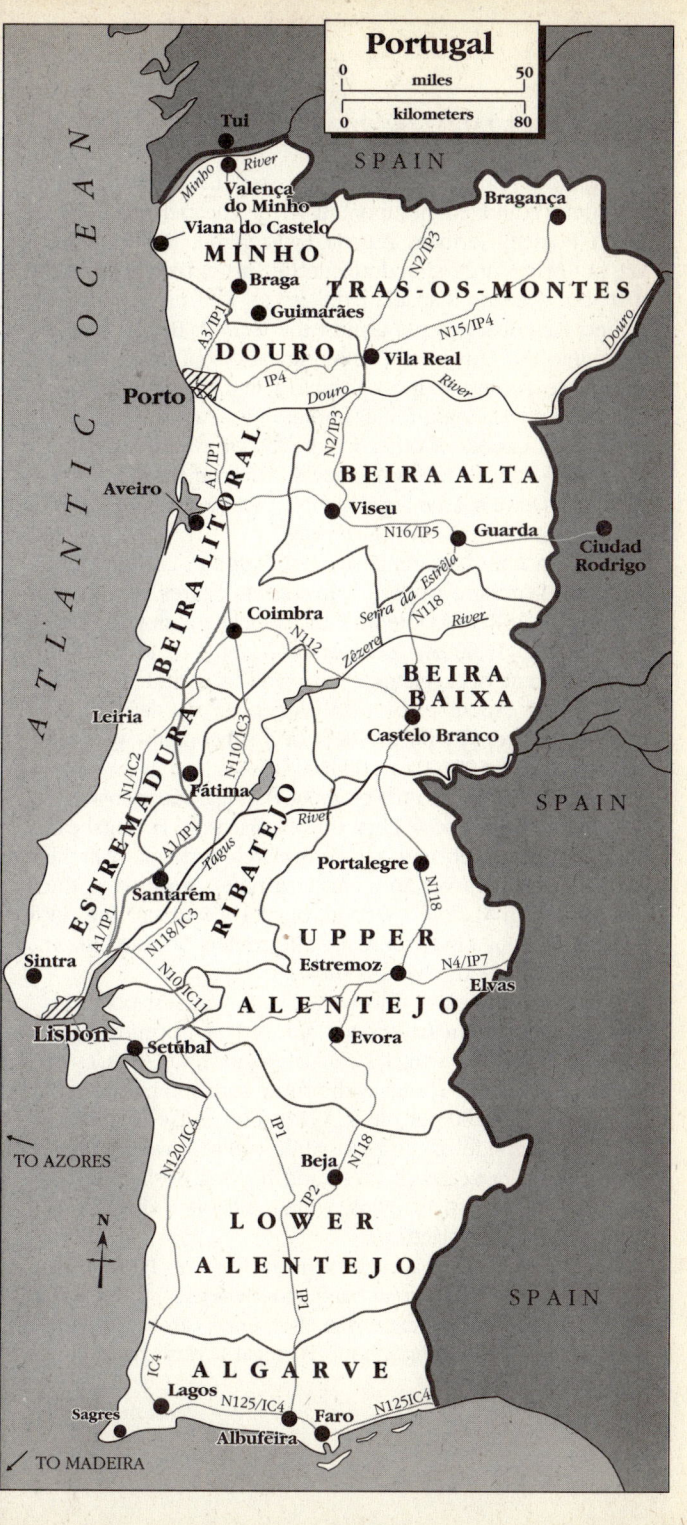

TRAVELLING IN PORTUGAL IN 1993

For decades Portugal was the one Western European bargain travellers could count upon. It's still cheaper than Italy, Spain, France, Germany, Austria, Switzerland, and Scandinavia, but prices are rising dramatically. Part of the problem is that the U.S. and Canadian dollars as well as the British pound have lost ground against the *escudo*. But Portugal's entry into the European Community also sent prices flying.

Double rooms at five-star hotels in Lisbon, Porto, the Algarve, and Madeira, for example, now fetch the kinds of prices you expect of other major European cities. Even at many of Portugal's lovely *pousadas* (government inns) double rooms have soared beyond the 12,500$00-a-day (US $88) mark—not the buys they once were.

Meals in fine restaurants such as Tagide in Lisbon, Dona Filipa de Lencastre in Porto's Infante de Sagres Hotel, and Les Faunes in Reid's Hotel in Funcha, Madeira, now average 12,000$00 to 15,000$00 per person (US $84 to $105 at the press-time rate of exchange, service and tax included). Gasoline, always expensive by North American standards, costs more than ever. To fill the tank of a subcompact you can expect to pay 4,500$00 to 5,000$00 (US $32 to $35).

Is it still possible to travel about Portugal inexpensively? Absolutely. Here's how: First, travel off-season. Portugal can be lovely in late February and early March, particularly in the Alentejo and Algarve. And—make a note—*summer* is the low season in Madeira. Second, opt for a four-star big-city hotel instead of a five (there are choice new ones in Lisbon and Madeira, as our chapters show).

Other ways to save: Choose the more modest pousadas (nearly all of them have been spruced up recently), and make the most of Portugal's palatial manor houses, many of which offer double rooms with private bath and breakfast at less than 12,500$00 per night. As for food, make up picnics to eat by the side of the road while you're travelling. And choose big-city *tascas* (bistros) and regional restaurants in small to medium-size towns, which still offer rib-sticking fare at reasonable prices.

Instead of renting a car, try using the fine Portuguese trains and buses (still great bargains). Better yet, travel with friends to spread the expenses of a rental car—by far the best means of poking about Portugal's very rewarding boonies.

—*Jean Anderson*

OVERVIEW

By Jean Anderson

Jean Anderson, a recognized authority on Portugal and on Portuguese food and wine, is the author of The Food of Portugal. *She is a frequent contributor to* Travel & Leisure, Travel/Holiday, Food & Wine, Bon Appétit, *and* Gourmet *magazines, among others, and has received awards from the Portuguese government for her writing. She has worked on many* Reader's Digest *books and is the editorial consultant for this guidebook.*

And if Spain is the head of Europe, Portugal, set at its western extremity, where land ends and sea begins, is as it were the crown on the head." (Luís Vaz de Camões, *The Lusiads,* 1572)

Thus wrote Portugal's great epic poet. And yet to see Portugal on the map of Europe today is to suspect that this pint-size country can't offer much of interest. It's a mere sliver on the face of Iberia, a piece of real estate about the size of Indiana or Ireland enveloped by Spain on the east and north and pummeled by the Atlantic on the west and south.

Compared to Spain, Portugal is minuscule, which no doubt explains why travellers so often give it short shrift. Usually it's the add-on to a tour of Spain, a two-day dip that includes a dash across the Algarve or Alentejo before or after a day in Lisbon.

A huge mistake. Portugal has more to show than most countries ten times its size: some of the world's sugariest beaches... tumbles of Roman ruins... medieval walled towns that, except for a moped or two, look much as they did 700 years ago... castles galore... vineyards so steeply terraced they might be Tibetan tea plantations... exuberant country festivals . . . red-brown plains scribbled with a calligraphy of cork oaks and olives . . . women sashaying down the road balancing everything on their heads from baskets of laundry to crates of chickens . . . shepherds in black sheepskin cutaways tending clouds of sheep . . . old men bending over nets . . . fishing villages so quaint they might have been knocked together by the folks at Disney.

To be sure, the Portugal you see today has been shaped down the millennia by a parade of invaders, aggressors, and occupants from shores as distant as Phoenicia, Greece, Rome, northern Europe, and North Africa. And, not least, from England. English blood flows in the veins of many Portuguese, which explains why you often see tall, blue-eyed blonds among these mostly small, olive-skinned, brown-eyed people. Even Prince Henry, the great navigator who in the 15th century slew forever the Atlantic's "demons of the deep" and launched Portugal's great Age of Discovery, was half British.

Who were the original Portuguese? No one knows. But some manner of men and women were living in the vicinity of Lisbon before the dawn of history, and in the Alentejo province directly east as well. They were probably simple hunter-gatherers; crude hand axes have been unearthed here, together with tools and weapons shaped of flint and bone. Scarcely 30 years ago a small "painted" cave was discovered about a half-hour's drive southwest of Evora, a district capital in the Alentejo, and the scribblings on its walls are believed to date back as far as 18,000 B.C.

Portugal abounds with menhirs (tall standing stones), dolmens (upright stones topped by horizontal slabs of rock, thought to be prehistoric tombs), and cromlechs (clusters of upended stones arranged in circles or squares). So many of them are scattered about the Alentejo that some archaeologists now suspect that it may be the birthplace of a megalithic society that gradually moved northward, leaving in its wake the great standing stones of Brittany and, quite possibly, Stonehenge.

Unfortunately, the Portuguese have been rather haphazard about archaeology, so hundreds and possibly millions of valuable shards have probably been lost. Only recently have they begun to probe in earnest for the riches that may lie underneath the farmer's plow. The story is told of how three archaeologists—amateurs at that—while poking about in the fields of Medobriga, near Portalegre in the northeastern Alentejo, found three Roman bridges joined by a Roman road, two streets of Roman houses, and an imposing villa—all of this less than 50 years ago. And, even more astonishing, all in a single afternoon.

Although dates can only be sketchy at best, it is known that Portugal was overrun and/or influenced by such diverse peoples as the Phoenicians, Greeks, Celts, Romans, Vandals, Alani, Suevi (Swabians), Visigoths, Moors, and Spaniards, in more or less that order (see the Chronology at the end of the book).

It was the Roman presence that 19th-century English explorer Richard Burton sensed most strongly. The Romans developed the system of large farms that persists today in the Alentejo, introduced the secrets of wine making, and built towns and aqueducts, not to mention an elaborate network of roads.

"Portugal, the western terminus of Rome's conquests, remains to the present day the most Roman of Latin countries," Burton wrote in 1869. "Her language approaches nearest to the speech of the ancient mistress of the world. Her people still preserve the sturdiness and perseverance.... Even in the present day, the traveller in Portugal sees with astonishment the domestic life of Rome, her poetry and literature, her arts and sciences."

Today's visitor to Portugal, however, is more likely to feel the presence of the Moor—understandable given the fact that Muslims occupied much of the country for more than 500 years and weren't finally driven from it, in the Algarve, until 1249. You see the Arabic influence in the squat, square houses of the Algarve and Alentejo forever being whitewashed, in the brightly patterned glazed tiles that face buildings all over Portugal, in the arcaded streets and lacy wrought-iron grills. You hear it in the plash of fountains and trickle of water gardens, smell it in the orange blossoms, and taste it in the golden egg-and-almond sweets of the Algarve.

The extraordinary thing about 20th-century Portugal is that it's so unspoiled, so much itself despite the fact that it lies scarcely five and a half jet hours east of New York, significantly nearer than London or Paris. Still, if you want to see the Portugal of picture postcards, the Portugal of old, you'll have to hurry. Now that it has joined the European Community things are changing fast. Tractors are replacing teams of long-horned oxen, olive trees are being axed to make room for wheat, and *veiculos longos* (16-wheelers) from Germany, France, and Italy are barreling down the blacktops, smudging some of Europe's cleanest air.

Lisbon

The logical place to begin any tour of Portugal is Lisbon, the country's capital and the point of entry for most travellers. We all have images of this seaport on the Tagus river, thanks to Hollywood spy movies. The Lisbon they showed us was decidedly *chiaroscuro,* a city full of sinister types skulking through dimly lighted alleys, of dethroned royalty being smuggled aboard freighters, of spies courting counterspies in grimy basement *tascas* (bistros).

The real Lisbon couldn't be more different. Although it's a proper metropolis pushing 1.5 million in population, it's just an overgrown country town, a sunstruck place of low-rise, pastel buildings sprawled across seven hills, a city of broad palmy boulevards and jungly gardens. In what other world capital can you be awakened by a cock's crow? Where else can you see goats nibbling bits of grass, as you sometimes do on the slopes of the **Alfama** (the old Moorish quarter)? Or round a corner to find women grilling a lunch of fresh-caught sardines on little sidewalk braziers?

That notwithstanding, Lisbon is a cultural town with enough museums and galleries to keep you busy for days. And its proximity to the museums, castles, convents, and cathedrals of Belém, Queluz, Sintra, and Mafra, not to mention the beaches of Estoril and Cascais and the scenic attractions of the Arrábida peninsula just across the Tagus, makes it a perfect base for day trips.

All of these places are in the province of **Estremadura,** which in one direction spills south across the Tagus from Lisbon to the port of Setúbal 47 km (30 miles) away. On its way north from Lisbon to Leiria, where the Beira Litoral (West Central Portugal) begins, the other part of Estremadura ripples along the cliffy west coast for approximately 170 km (106 miles), embracing vineyards, orchards of espaliered fruit trees, and cloth-sailed windmills whistling in the wind. From Lisbon, it's possible to loop deep into Estremadura to the south one day, to the north the next, and make it home before dark (see the Day Trips from Lisbon chapter).

Touring Portugal

Most people allow too little time for Lisbon. Too little, too, for the rest of the country. How long should you stay in Portugal? A week is the absolute minimum, two weeks better. Even then, you'll only be hitting the high spots.

Rental car is the best—some say *only*—way to go, especially if you stick with the scenic back roads. They're narrower than the primary roads, and more tortuous as well, but you do miss much of the heavy traffic. You also miss most of the crazy drivers who love to floorboard it on wider, straighter highways, passing on hills and riding your rear bumper if you're not travelling fast enough to suit them (you never are).

Every aspiring Mario Andretti loves to bomb up A 1/IP 1, the four-lane *auto-estrada* at long last linking Lisbon and Porto, 317 km (197 miles) north, without unwelcome *desvios* (detours) onto the old two-lane segments of N 1. (Tolls for the Lisbon–Porto drive total 2,590$00; shorter runs cost less).

But in truth the zigzag coastal route—via Ericeira, Peniche, Obidos, Nazaré, Marinha Grande, Figueira da Foz, and Aveiro—is more rewarding in every way. A good rule of thumb, unless for some reason you're in a tearing hurry: Stick with the secondary roads (these are the yellow routes on Michelin map number 440, which is far and away the most detailed map of Portugal, although, as of the 1992 edition, not the most up to date on the many new, larger roads and their new designations).

Because distances look so small on the map, people assume they can just zoom around Portugal. Not true. First of all, you can't average more than 100 to 125 miles a day on Portugal's twisting, two-lane blacktops. Nor would you want to, unless you're a kamikaze driver willing to view everything on fast forward. You should focus instead on two or three areas, pick a headquarters for each, then, once ensconced, set forth each morning in a different direction, returning to your home base at night so you don't waste time checking in and out, packing and unpacking. You might choose Lisbon and the Algarve or Alentejo, for example. Or Lisbon plus Madeira. Or Lisbon plus Porto and the Douro (or Minho).

In Portugal, perhaps more than in any other country, where you go and what you should do depends on your particular interests. You may be a sports enthusiast, for example. Or a history buff. Or a connoisseur of food and wine. Or an architecture nut. Or a nature lover. Or a collector of folk art. Or someone who just needs to get away from it all, escape the pressure of too many problems and too many people. Portugal can accommodate all of these interests—but each involves a slightly different Portugal.

Fun in the Sun

If all you want to do is thwack tennis balls, play golf, or deliver yourself to the sun, the **Algarve** is the place for you. The southernmost province, this skinny band of rumpled shore turns its back on the rest of Portugal and faces southward into the Atlantic, toward Morocco, which it resembles. Wind and wave have battered its 184-km (115-mile) coastline—from the *fim do mundo* (land's end) at Cabo de São Vicente on the west to the Guadiana river and the Spanish border on the east—reducing its rugged orange cliffs, here and there, to crescents of sand. Inland, mountains fence off the Algarve, separating it, body and soul, from the Alentejo directly north, and blocking much of the weather that blows down across it. The result: a "Mediterranean" climate that attracts the winter-weary of northern Europe by the jumbo-jet load.

The Algarve is Portugal's Riviera, an alternately creamy and craggy shore where golf courses, marinas, and fancy resort hotels and condos, sleek white boxes lined up along the sea cliffs like outsize refrigerators, have gobbled up farms and villages. In other words, a strip. Fortunately, vestiges of the old Algarve remain, and to find them you need only head for the hills. In the hillside almond groves above Almancil, for example, it's strictly business at the market town of Loulé, where natives outnumber tourists three to one. And westward, above the gridlock of Portimão, the red sandstone citadel of Silves doesn't seem far removed from its glory days as a Moorish capital—at least on slow tourist days.

Then there's the land's-end promontory of Sagres, where Prince Henry the Navigator retreated 574 years ago to plan his voyages of discovery. You can't help wondering what he'd think of the campers and caravans that have come to roost on his wild, heathery peninsula, not to mention the souvenir vendors at the gates of Cabo de São Vicente lighthouse.

There are other Algarve must-sees: the pottery at Porches, where you can watch artisans paint bowls and plates with ancient Algarve designs; the old Moorish town of Olhão, which might be a chunk of Tangier; and the cliffs at Ponta da Piedade, where great sandstone monoliths, red as iron rust, lounge in offshore waters like prehistoric beasts.

Two other choices for sun worshipers: Estremadura's **Estoril-Cascais-Guincho coast**, which begins 22 km (14 miles) west of Lisbon (no shortage of golf, tennis, sailing, riding, and beaches here, although these last can be crowded), and the **Madeira islands**. Madeira itself boasts everything *except* beaches (you'll have to settle for hotel pools or sorry stretches of gravel). Neighboring **Porto Santo** island has a beach that will forever be the envy of Madeira: six miles of sand the color of country cream. It also has a few small, comfortable beachfront hotels—but very little else, unless you count the house where Christopher Columbus is said to have lived.

Architecture and History

For these you should combine Lisbon and Estremadura with the Beira Litoral and Alentejo or Minho provinces. You'll find dolmens and menhirs here, Celtic *castros* (fortified towns), Roman ruins, and at least a dozen living walled towns stuck in a medieval mindset.

Lisbon itself is an architectural confection, a mostly 18th-century city, rebuilt after the cataclysmic earthquake of 1755. Its roots, of course, go deeper. You can find the fallout of centuries past at Castelo de São Jorge atop the city's highest hill (Roman, Visigothic, Moorish), in the narrow winding streets and stairs of the Alfama that lead up to the castle, and in the alfresco archaeological museum housed in the skeleton of the 14th-century Igreja do Carmo (Carmelite Church) toppled by the great quake. You can also stride back across the centuries at suburban **Belém**, whose cache of museums includes the sugary Tower of Belém, a masterpiece of Manueline ("wedding cake") architecture and the spot from which Vasco da Gama sailed; the Jerónimos monastery, where the ornately carved marble cenotaphs of da Gama and Camões, the 16th-century poet who immortalized da Gama's triumphant voyage in *Os Lusíadas (The Lusiads)*, are dwarfed by the 82-foot ceilings; and, adjoining the monastery, the Museu Nacional de Arqueologia e Etnologia (National Museum of Archaeology and Ethnology), filled with fascinating fragments of prehistory.

Near enough to Lisbon for an easy day's outing in **Estremadura** are the castles and palaces at Queluz, Sintra, and Mafra. On a more northerly day trip you can easily visit Obidos, a cubistic walled town so perfect that the kings of Portugal made a practice of presenting it to their queens, plus the imposing cathedrals at Alcobaça (12th century) and Batalha (14th century; Prince Henry the Navigator's marble tomb is here). On the return to Lisbon there should even be time to detour 50 km (31 miles) east from

Leiria to Tomar in the **Ribatejo** (it adjoins Estremadura to the east) to see the 12th- to 16th-century convent and chapel of the Knights Templars. Its convoluted "rope window," now encrusted with lichen, is by most accounts Portugal's most elaborate example of Manueline architecture.

The most extensive Roman ruins are those at Conimbriga (in the coastal **Beira Litoral**), a red-brick town of fountains, reflecting pools, and mosaics of stunning detail just south of the university town of Coimbra—itself worth a look, especially the 12th-century *Sé* (Cathedral) and the 18th-century gilded, muraled, and inlaid old library on the upper campus. You'll find more Roman ruins in the sprawling **Alentejo** province, which begins only 82 km (51 miles) east of Lisbon, occupies more than a third of Portugal, and butts up against Spain all along its eastern boundary. There's a doll-size second-century Roman temple at the provincial capital of Evora (about a third of the temple still stands) and, in the regional museum just a few steps away, a courtyard of Roman relics.

Portugal's greatest cluster of prehistoric and megalithic artifacts can be found in the Alentejo, too: the primitive, painted Escoural Cave, 30 km (19 miles) southwest of Evora (it may date as far back as 18,000 B.C.), and the scatter of dolmens, menhirs, and cromlechs all about the central Alentejo.

There are also dolmens in the **Minho**, Portugal's most northerly province, notably the splendidly preserved Dolmen de Barrosa near the mouth of the Lima river. But the Minho's most significant sites are Celtic: Citânia de Briteiros and the nearby Castro de Sabroso (Portugal's oldest settlements), both located 12 km (7½ miles) southeast of Braga. Celtic ornaments, implements, and pottery unearthed at these ancient towns are on display in Guimarães (see also below) at the Martins Sarmento Museum. While you're at Braga or Guimarães you may want to circle east into Portugal's remotest province, the **Trás-os-Montes** (Behind the Mountains), to see the mighty rock at Outeiro Machado, which is completely covered with early Neolithic carvings. It stands 3 km (2 miles) northwest of Chaves, an old Roman town 129 km (80 miles) east of Braga.

Medieval fortress towns perch atop buttes and mounts all across the **Alentejo**. The most imposing of them face the Spanish border, hardly surprising given the fact that Spain and Portugal have squabbled for centuries. Two walled towns almost untouched by time—Marvão and Castelo de

Vide—cling to rocky scarps within 8 km (5 miles) of each other and about a half hour north of the textile town of Portalegre. Farther south but still on the Spanish border, there's Monsaraz, an old Moorish citadel gripping a pedestal of rock 10 km (6 miles) east of the busy agricultural center of Reguengos de Monsaraz. There are other Alentejo walled towns, too: Evora, Elvas, Estremoz, Arraiolos, Avis, Evoramonte. Two beauties exist in the **Minho** as well, both high above the Minho river, Portugal's northern frontier with Spain: Valença do Minho and Monção. Every one of these is worth a visit.

So, too, is the Minho town of **Guimarães**, 52 km (32 miles) northeast of Porto, which is known as "the Cradle of Portugal." It was here, in the 11th century, that the tiny county of Portucale (named for Portus and Cale, two towns on opposite banks of the Douro river that are known today simply as Porto), the territorial dowry of a Galician princess, began to splinter off from León and become a kingdom in its own right. The final break occurred some years later, in 1139. Portugal's first king, Afonso Henriques, was born in Guimarães's ninth-century castle, a brooding pile of stone with sawtooth crenellations and seven fortress towers. (He was christened in the little Romanesque chapel of São Miguel on the castle slopes.) The castle stands on a hill outside Guimarães, a town that remains largely medieval at heart and is thus itself of more than passing historical interest.

Religious Sites

Like every Roman Catholic country, Portugal abounds with cathedrals; every town of consequence has its Sé. And, as if to underscore the piety of this nation, convents and monasteries of architectural and historical significance as well as of religious interest loom everywhere about the countryside (see the preceding discussion of historic sites).

Portugal's most famous religious site, the one to which hundreds of thousands of pilgrims come each year, quite literally on bended knee, is **Fátima**, in the **Ribatejo** province some 145 km (90 miles) northeast of Lisbon. On this desolate plateau rimmed by dour crags of granite, the Virgin of the Rosary appeared to three small shepherd children on May 13, 1917. She reappeared five times, on the 13th of every month thereafter, except for August, when she appeared to the children on the 19th in Valinhos. By October 13, the date of her last appearance, 70,000 people had gathered, among them cynics ready to refute the children's story of the visions. They did not see the Blessed Virgin, but they do admit to watching strange celestial pyrotechnics: Storm clouds parted, then the sun seemed to spin toward the earth.

Today millions of faithful dream of visiting Fátima at least once before they die, and there's no denying that it has become Portugal's shrine of shrines. To the less-than-faithful it exemplifies the tawdry commercial side of religion. Fátima's Neoclassical basilica (begun in 1928 and consecrated in 1953), great colonnades arching toward a 215-foot central tower of white stone, is oddly clinical-looking. A strict dress code prevails; no shorts, halters, or minis allowed inside the hallowed shrine. And yet the souvenir shops lining Fátima's sprawling esplanade (it's bigger than St. Peter's Square in Vatican City) sell gimcracks of the most appalling taste. On the 12th and 13th of each month, from May through October, pilgrims converge on Fátima. The two biggest pilgrimages are always the first and last.

Portugal claims a number of additional pilgrimage sites, the two most important of which are **Bom Jesus do Monte** near Braga in the Minho and **Nossa Senhora dos Remédios** at Lamego in the Beira Alta. Both are exuberant examples of the Portuguese Baroque, walls of almost blinding whiteness trimmed with flourishes of granite. These two 18th-century shrines consist of steep double flights of stairs that go switchbacking up the face of mountains in crisp black and white. Pilgrims climb up on their knees, pausing to pray at the little wayside chapels all along the way. There are several annual pilgrimages in Braga; the largest takes place during Pentecost. Lamego's is held in early September.

Folk Art and Country Fairs

No one should leave Lisbon without touring the **Museu de Arte Popular** in suburban **Belém**, which showcases Portugal's finest handicrafts. Indeed, to stroll through its exhibits, arranged province by province, is to make a mini arts tour of Portugal. There's no quicker way to decide what pottery you like best, what embroideries and baskets, which hand-hammered metal cookware, which tapestries. Certainly, there's no better preview of the provinces, and no surer way to plan a crafts-oriented tour outside Lisbon.

The more rural the province, the more likely you are to see potters bending over their wheels, women seated in doorways making lace or embroidering linens, men weaving straw into baskets or hammering copper into caldrons. And the greater your chance of happening upon a country market or harvest festival. The Portuguese National Tourist Offices (see "Further Information" in the Useful Facts section, following) can mail you a list of the major fairs and festivals, together with their dates.

Portugal's biggest and best country fair takes place every Thursday in downtown Barcelos in the **Minho** province, about an hour's drive north of Porto. Here you can buy cotton blouses, aprons, placemats, and tablecloths embroidered in hot colors, many from the nearby coastal town of Viana do Castelo, which specializes as well in such things as delicately filigreed gold jewelry. You can buy the nubby, hand-knitted fishermen's sweaters of Vila do Conde and the lace of Trofa and Guimarães, all three Minho towns known for their handicrafts. There are flocks of brightly painted clay Barcelos roosters, renowned as the emblem of Portugal, and acres of brown pottery fancifully trimmed with hearts and flowers— immense dough bowls, tureens, casseroles, platters, and plates, all hand decorated in shades of yellow and white. And all absurdly cheap. Among the farm implements you'll find *cangas,* the intricately carved wooden ox yokes for which the Minho is famous. They're collector's items now, and they're being snapped up by decorators, who have discovered that they make dandy headboards.

The Saturday fair at Estremoz in the heart of the **Alentejo** is no slouch either, especially if it's pottery you're after. Laid out on the ground you'll find mounds of *tachos de barro,* the terra-cotta casseroles beloved by every Portuguese cook, as well as dozens of unglazed clay water jugs of classic Roman design, piles of crude hand-painted earthenware, and platoons of the little festival figures unique to Estremoz. You can see more of these—shepherds, soldiers, and assorted saints—at the little Museu Municipal de Estremoz directly opposite the palatial Pousada da Rainha Santa Isabel at the top of the town, and you can even watch sculptors shape them in the atelier behind the museum.

To see country potters at work you've only to peek in the open doors of any *olaria* (pottery) at Redondo or São Pedro de Corval in the Alentejo (you can identify them by the huge terra-cotta amphoras placed at their entries, or by the racks of gaily painted plates). Portugal's most famous earthenware comes from Caldas da Rainha, 88 km (55 miles) north of Lisbon (see Day Trips from Lisbon). The 100-year-old Bordalo Pinheiro factory here is big time, employing 150 workers to turn out the cabbage-leaf plates, duck tureens, and honeybee honeypots prized by hosts the world over. Visitors are welcome at the company's ceramics museum, its shop, even in the pottery itself, where you can watch "slip" being poured into molds, then the individual pieces being glazed and fired.

For rugs and tapestries make your way to the white castle town of Arraiolos, some 30 km (20 miles) north of Evora in the **Alentejo**. These gros-point tapestries with curiously Oriental motifs are Portugal's finest, and most famous. But they aren't cheap. Still, you can beat the prices of Lisbon at any of the *fábricas* lined up along the main street (look for the *tapête* signs).

The island of **Madeira** has cornered the market on wicker and intricately embroidered linens. Both are very much cottage industries, so it's not unusual to see men near the village of Camacha peeling osiers (willow shoots) by the side of the road or piling baskets onto bicycles, motor scooters, or pickup trucks. Or, deep in the island's interior, to come upon a circle of women, shy and giggly, embroidering and gossiping the afternoon away. Once they've finished a respectable stack, the linens will be picked up, trucked to Funchal, washed, pressed, and packaged for sale in the boutiques you see everywhere around town.

The **Alentejo** (and especially the provincial capital of Evora) is headquarters for copper cookware, cork ice buckets and coasters, and bright wooden trays, boxes, and furniture strewn with hand-painted flowers. All are astonishingly cheap.

As for the decorative tiles (*azulejos*) you see facing buildings all over Portugal, the best place to buy them is **Lisbon**. There are half a dozen shops selling faithful replicas of antique tiles—and, of course, antiques stores where you can buy the real thing. See our Shopping section for Lisbon or ask the Portuguese National Tourist Office for a list of shops (see "Further Information" in Useful Facts, below).

Most tourists become so smitten with Portugal's folk art that they buy and buy, giving little thought to how they'll get all their treasures home. Luckily, there's a Lisbon shipper geared to solving just such problems (see "Packing and Shipping" in the Useful Facts section).

Food and Wine

No doubt about it: Portugal's best restaurants are in **Lisbon**, some of them nothing more than neighborhood *tascas* where

Mama presides over the stove and Papa waits table. The best way to get a gastronomic fix on Portugal is to visit Lisbon's morning market, the rollicking Mercado da Ribeira near the waterfront and the Cais do Sodré station. If it's seafood you seek, do as the Lisboetes do and drive west out to **Cascais** or **Guincho** beside the Atlantic. Lisbon, they insist, is too far "inland"—all of 25 km (16 miles)—for saltwater fish to be fresh.

Porto ranks second for food, but first for wine (although **Madeira** may dispute that because its wines are equally noble and its lodges just as adept at showing visitors about). You can visit any of the Port wine lodges on Porto's (the Douro river's) left bank at Vila Nova de Gaia, pausing at tour's end to sample the four basic types of Port: white, ruby, tawny, and vintage.

If Port wine is of particular interest, you'll surely want to drive up the **Douro river** as far as **Pinhão**, about 132 km (82 miles) east of Porto. This little village deep in the heart of the vineyards is devoted altogether to the production of Port. The stately *quintas* (wine estates) are here, many of them perched high in vineyards that stairstep up near-perpendicular slopes of buff-colored schist. The best time to visit is late September or early October, when the *vindima* (grape harvest) is on and folk songs ring from hill to hill. But you'd better make sure you have overnight reservations somewhere nearby. The best place, hands down, is the stylishly rustic 11-room **Pousada do Barão de Forrester** at Alijó, a half-hour's drive beyond Pinhão. Although you *can* drive from Porto to Pinhão and back in a day, it's dangerous to try. The roads are roller coasters, pitch-dark after sundown, and murderous to navigate.

The Portuguese table wines best known outside of Portugal are the rosés of Mateus and Lancer's and the Aveleda *vinhos verdes*. Each of these wineries can be visited. The Lancer's (José Maria da Fonseca) operation occupies a good chunk of the little town of Vila Nogueira de Azeitão on the **Arrábida peninsula** across the Tagus from Lisbon, and both its old and new wineries welcome tourists. The other two wine companies are way up north: Aveleda at Penafiel, in the **Douro Litoral** (Lower Douro) about an hour east of Porto (a marvelous, gingerbready estate engulfed by subtropical gardens), and Mateus at Vila Real, some 77 km (48 miles) farther east at the edge of the **Trás-os-Montes** province. Its Baroque white manor house edged in black basalt looks just the way it does on every wine label, and it can be toured (as can its formal gardens). But the manor house today is a museum only.

Mateus wine is now made several miles away in a modern plant as full of ducts, pipes, and tanks as an oil refinery.

One of the curiosities of Portugal is the little town of **Mealhada**, in the **Beira Litoral**, 19 km (12 miles) north of Coimbra. It's nothing more than a wide place in the road, but gourmets converge here from all over Portugal to feast upon suckling pig, the town's specialty. There are no fewer than a dozen restaurants serving it, most of them lined up along N 1, the old Lisbon–Porto highway.

For what may be the most Portuguese of Portuguese food, you must spend time in the **Alentejo** province, where the hog reigns supreme, where the olive oil is deeply fruity, where markets sell bunches of coriander as big as bridal bouquets, and where most dishes contain enough garlic to blow a safe. Evora is pig heaven (especially a little back-street restaurant called **Fialho**). And Estremoz isn't far behind.

Portugal's main epicurean event takes place each autumn at the little farmer's town of Santarém in the **Ribatejo**, 70 km (43 miles) up the Tagus from Lisbon. It's the annual Festival Nacional de Gastronomia (National Gastronomy Festival), during which Portugal's best provincial cooks show their stuff. It lasts for days, brings folk dancers out in regional costume, and attracts artisans from all over the country.

Great Gardens

The Portuguese have the greenest thumbs on earth, and if you doubt that you've only to visit one of the country's famous gardens. **Lisbon** can claim three of them, and the surrounding countryside three more. A good place to begin is the Estufa Fria (Cool House) in the city's Eduardo VII park, an extraordinary collection of botanical exotics under canopies of lattice or glass. Next there's the Jardim Botânico (Botanical Garden), with its stately avenue of royal palms and neatly labeled specimens from the former Portuguese colonies. Then, in suburban **Benfica**, Palácio dos Marqueses de Fronteira (see the North Lisbon section in the Lisbon chapter), an opulent 17th-century mansion (private) and gardens (open) that are as famous for their panels of antique *azulejos* as for their geometric plantings. Hans Christian Andersen, who spent some time here in 1866, described Fronteira as "lively and quite unusual . . . Italian in style and comfortably old-fashioned." From the main building, he continued, "a high terrace leads through the garden" where gallery walls "are covered with quite remarkable mosaic pictures—all of female figures representing, for example, Geometry, Astronomy, Poetry, etc."

You could probably spend half a day wandering through the extensive formal and informal gardens at the 18th-century pink palace at **Queluz** (Portugal's Versailles), 15 km (9 miles) west of Lisbon, where showers of bougainvillaea spill over walls paved with blue-and-white tiles. And another half-day at Monserrate, about 3 km (2 miles) west of Sintra on the mountainous road to Colares.

Sintra has been called "Byron's Eden," because the great English poet, while staying in this mossy hideaway, wrote, "I must observe that the Village of Cintra in Estremadura is the most beautiful, perhaps, in the world." Thirty years later, another Englishman, Francis Cook, vowed to make a private Eden of **Monserrate**, his estate just west of town. Today, its steep slopes strewn with jungly plants remind you more of a tropical rain forest. But they *are* impressive.

The formal boxwood gardens at the Quinta da Bacalhôa at Azeitão on the **Arrábida peninsula** south of the Tagus are famous for their pavilions of early *azulejos* and botanical symmetry. Quinta da Bacalhôa, now owned by Americans, has another claim to fame: Its smooth, well-balanced red table wine is Portugal's only true cabernet sauvignon.

Portugal's most spectacular garden is actually a forest, the 250-acre **Parque Nacional de Buçaco** (also known as Bussaco Forest) located 28 km (17 miles) northeast of Coimbra in the Beira Litoral province. The old royal hunting "lodge" here has been turned into a hotel. A good thing, too, because you could spend days strolling Buçaco's secluded paths, marveling at the *Green Mansions* majesty of a place where 400 native and 300 exotic species flourish among the waterfalls and reflecting pools.

In the north of Portugal there are two more important gardens, both at well-known wine quintas: the free-form floral groupings at Quinta da Aveleda at Penafiel in the **Douro Litoral**, and at Mateus, near Vila Real in the **Trás-os-Montes**, a meticulously pruned topiary separating two broad parterres, one worked out in great arabesques of greenery, the second in rigid geometrics. These two gardens are altogether different, and if you're in the vicinity of Porto or, better yet, Guimarães in the Minho, you can see them both in a day.

When the 15th-century Venetian explorer Cadamosto visited **Madeira** he exclaimed, "The whole island is a garden!" And so it is, an outsize nosegay that seems to float upon the sea. Because of the island's rich volcanic soil and near-perpendicular terrain, there are dozens of microclimates, some hospitable to orchids, birds-of-paradise, and poinsettias, some to calla lilies and hydrangeas, some to heather and gorse. In addition, there are two dreamy gardens shelved in the hills above the capital city of Funchal: the Botanical Gardens, devoted mostly to indigenous flora, and the Quinta do Palheiro Ferreiro. Here, among some 12 hectares (30 acres) of woodlands, Madeira's own spiky dragon trees and stately mahoganies coexist with South African proteas, Japanese loquats, Mexican blood lilies, and New Zealand fern trees, plus dozens of other botanical exotics imported from around the world.

To Get Away from It All

The ultimate retreat has to be the **Azores**, which have barely entered the 20th century. Or so it seems, even though there are modern hotels, with all the expected amenities, on most of the islands. Out in the countryside, however, even on the big island of São Miguel, life snoozes along in an earlier, easier mode. São Miguel is terrific for just poking around, inhaling the clean Atlantic air, and eating your fill of fish so fresh it all but swims to your table. So are Terceira, São Jorge (its sharp ivory cheese is superb), Faial, and Flores. All of the Azores, in fact, will please nature lovers—indeed, anyone who craves peace and quiet instead of a bouncy brand of nightlife.

The mountains of **Madeira** are almost as quiet, especially the two isolated *pousadas* (government inns) perched high in the interior—just the place to catch up on your reading or maybe simply watch the clouds sail by. Well-marked trails lead across this dramatic roof of the world, and you needn't be an Olympic medalist to negotiate them with ease.

Honeymooners love **Bussaco Forest** in the Beira Litoral (see Great Gardens, above); the otherworldly Serra da Estrela in the **Beira Alta** in eastern Portugal's mountainous midriff; also the 175,000-acre **Parque Nacional de Peneda-Gerês**, created in 1970 to preserve the natural beauty of this gentle green "Switzerland of northern Portugal" (see **Minho**); and the elegantly enlarged and renovated **Pousada de Santa Maria** in the old walled town of **Marvão** (see **Alentejo**).

The hulk and the height of the Beira Alta's **Serra da Estrela** (6,539 feet) startles many travellers. Skiers whiz down its slopes in winter, but for pure, unadulterated bliss you must come to these hardscrabble heights in late spring, summer, or early autumn. You'll be above the tree line, indeed often on top of the clouds, surrounded by a brutal beauty of barren crags, snowmelt lakes, and shingly fields of granite. In certain light at certain times of day it's easy to imagine that you're strolling across the moon.

There are several places to stay up here (notably the sky-high **Pousada de São Lourenço**), but it's equally pleasant to perch across the western valley, and halfway up the facing slope. The best choice is chalet-like **Pousada de Santa Bárbara**, deep in a pine woods a few kilometers north of the village of Oliveira do Hospital (covered in our Beira Litoral chapter). Every bedroom has a balcony, and every balcony frames a view of this mighty "Mountain of the Star."

This overview gives you some notion of the riches that await you in Portugal. But there's an additional treasure: the Portuguese people, who are quick to greet every friend, every stranger with a hearty *"Bom dia!"*—"Good day!" Portugal may be tiny, but its welcome is as big as all outdoors.

USEFUL FACTS

Climate and Seasons

If you were to draw a line straight across the Atlantic from Washington, D.C., you'd hit Lisbon. And that surprises many people, because Lisbon *feels* like Florida. Palms, oleander, and bougainvillaea grow as far north as Porto (on a parallel with New York City), and, thanks to the warm, moist breath of the Gulf Stream, oranges and olives thrive along the banks of the northerly Douro river together with Port wine grapes.

As millions of visitors have discovered, summer is glorious everywhere in Portugal, so you'll have to fight for room at the inn (not to mention the beach). Sunny midday highs range from the upper 30s Celsius (95 and up Fahrenheit) in the Algarve and Alentejo to a few degrees cooler around Lisbon and points north. Even February can be balmy in the Algarve and Alentejo, with noon temperatures in the 20s Celsius (70s to 80s Fahrenheit). But don't count on it. Rain may swoop down from the north and lock you in for days, especially in the Alentejo.

The best seasons to visit mainland Portugal are late spring (mid-April to mid-June), although there is some chance of rain, and autumn (mid-September through October), when every village seems to stage some sort of harvest fair or festival. Portugal's rainy season begins in November and lasts throughout the winter, dreary days (or weeks) alternating with sudden bursts of sunshine. Only the Algarve, Portugal's southernmost province, is blessed in winter by a more Mediterranean climate, but here, too, it can—and does—rain.

On Madeira weather changes less from June to January than from seashore to mountaintop. Not for nothing is it called the "Isle of Perpetual June." Days are always sunnier on the south shore than on the north because the island's mountainous spine blocks most of the storm clouds rolling off the ocean from the north. Funchal and its big resort hotels, sprawled along a sheltered south-shore bay, enjoy a singularly mild microclimate. Here midday temperatures hang in the 20s Celsius (mid-70s to mid-80s Fahrenheit). Funchal's high season (more for social than climatic reasons) runs from December 15 to April 30. The busiest times of all are the Christmas holidays and Easter, when reservations must be made months in advance. The smaller, semi-arid island of Porto Santo, located just 37 km (23 miles) northeast of Madeira, is flatter, hotter, and sunnier than Madeira, even in winter.

The Azores are another story altogether. These nine mid-Atlantic islands, scattered across 650 km (400 miles) of open ocean, are colder and rainier than the Madeiras. You can be pretty sure of sunshine and shirt-sleeve weather with midday temperatures in the 20s Celsius (75 to 85 Fahrenheit) between May and September. The rest of the year, however, the islands can be buffeted by wind and rain, and local waters often grow so turbulent that even Azoreans shun the inter-island boats.

Entry Requirements
Nothing more than a valid passport is required of U.S., Canadian, British, and Australian citizens. There are no vaccination requirements.

Flying to Portugal
TAP Air Portugal jets daily from New York (or Newark) to Lisbon during the high summer season (June until late October), less often in winter. TWA flies five times a week between New York and Lisbon in summer, four times each week in winter, but because the line has been in bankruptcy, cutting costs, and reorganizing, the schedules may change. Delta, which bought Pan Am's routes last year, serves Lisbon four times a week in the high season, three times a week off season.

There are also four TAP flights each week to Lisbon, year-round, from Boston, and two nonstops each week between Boston and Ponta Delgada and Boston and Terceira, both in the Azores. During the high season, TAP Air Portugal also flies nonstop to Lisbon from Montreal twice a week, and from Toronto three times a week. Service is less frequent between November and June.

British Airways and TAP Air Portugal maintain several daily nonstops to Lisbon from London's Heathrow Airport. In addition, British Airways jets twice daily, nonstop, from Gatwick to Faro in the Algarve, while TAP has a daily service from Heathrow. Both TAP and British Airways offer daily London–Porto service, and TAP also has three weekly nonstops to Funchal from London's Heathrow and four nonstops from Porto. Finally, TAP now jets twice a week between Manchester, England, and Lisbon. There is also direct service to Faro in the Algarve from a dozen European cities.

At present there is no direct service from Australia to Portugal. Other major carriers serving Lisbon and/or Porto include Air France, Alitalia, Finnair, Iberia, KLM, Lufthansa, Sabena, SAS, South African Airways, Swissair, and Varig.

At this writing, the standard taxi fare from Lisbon airport into the city center was 1,500$00 (without tip), but for luggage weighing more than 50 kilos (110 pounds) many cabbies add a 50 percent surcharge.

Flying around Portugal
and to Madeira and the Azores

There are no direct flights to Madeira from the United States or Canada, so you must change planes in Lisbon; but thanks to TAP's rapidly expanding routes, it is now possible to fly nonstop twice a week from London, Madrid, and Paris to Madeira and once a week direct, if not nonstop, from Frankfurt, Milan, Rome, and Zurich. There are also four weekly nonstops from Porto to Madeira.

From Lisbon there are daily nonstops via TAP Air Portugal (sometimes several a day) to Faro, Porto, and Madeira, also to Terceira and Ponta Delgada in the Azores; in addition, there are four nonstops each week to Horta on the Azorean island of Faial. There are frequent Aerocondor flights via small prop planes between Madeira and neighboring Porto Santo, as well as among all the major Azorean islands, via SATA, the Azorean airline. In addition, the domestic airline, Portugália, operates several flights each day between Lisbon and Porto and Lisbon and Faro, and, as of this year, service several times a week between Lisbon and such European cities as Cologne, Strasbourg, Madrid, and Turin; there are even once-a-week flights between these cities and Porto. Finally, LAR Transregional, a TAP subsidiary, is now building a mainland network that already connects such medium-size cities as Bragança, Chaves, Covilhã, Faro, Portimão, and Viseu with Lisbon and, in the case of Bragança, with Porto as well. LAR is now even flying internationally: between Porto and Bordeaux, in France, and between Porto and Lisbon and four Spanish cities (Bilbao, Málaga, Seville, and Santiago de Compostela).

Customs

Lisbon International Airport, at long last modernized and enlarged, is far more efficient than it used to be. Still, if you should arrive the same morning as the overnight flights from Africa (on a Sunday, for example), the passport line creaks because the papers of every visitor from a former Portuguese colony are carefully scrutinized. Some Americans have shortcut the hours of waiting by switching to the European Community passport lines and have been waved right through. It's worth a shot.

There are two different main exits from the baggage area of each international airport in Portugal: one for those who have nothing to declare and another for those who do. Visitors over 17 years of age may bring in, duty free, two bottles of table wine, one bottle of liquor, 400 cigarettes or 250 grams (about 8 ounces) of tobacco, ¼ liter (about 8 ounces) of toilet water, and 50 grams (about 1½ ounces) of perfume. You may also bring in small quantities of tea or coffee for personal use.

Getting Around by Train and Bus

From Lisbon there are six crack trains a day to Porto (the Alfa service, approximately three hours one way) as well as morning, afternoon, and evening *rápido* service to Albufeira and Faro in the Algarve, with connections for points east and west. In Portugal the only way to travel by train is first class, but fares are low. If you can prove you're over 65 or can produce a Eurorail Senior Card, you can travel by train in Portugal for half fare.

Like London and Paris, Lisbon has several different train stations, and the one you use depends on your destination. Santa Apolónia (Tel: 01-87-75-09), down on the waterfront just below and to the east of the Alfama at the corner of avenida Infante Dom Henrique and largo dos Caminhos de Ferro, is Lisbon's central station, where international trains arrive and depart; it's the one you'll want if you're north-bound to Coimbra or Porto. Sul e Sueste, often called Terreiro do Paço station (Tel: 01-87-71-79 or 01-87-86-31), your point of departure if you're headed for the Algarve or lower Alentejo, is actually a ferry slip on the left side of praça do Comércio as you face the water. You must board a ferry here, baggage and all, and cross the Tagus to Barreiro on the south bank of the river, where your train awaits. From the Art Nouveau Rossio (Tel: 01-346-5022), on praça Dom João da Câmara next door to the Avenida Palace hotel, trains shuttle back and forth to Sintra, some 25 km (16 miles) west. Cais do Sodré (Tel: 01-347-0181), located on Lisbon's riverfront praça Duque da Terceira (four blocks west of praça do Comércio), is the spot from which three- and four-car electric "interurbans" whiz along the river Tagus to and from Belém, Estoril, and Cascais with commuter frequency. The Portuguese railway company Caminhos de Ferro (CF) also now maintains an Information Services number that tourists can call for details about routes and schedules: (01) 888-4025.

The Rodoviária Nacional, Portugal's national bus network, no longer exists. But its big, streamlined, orange-and-white buses with air-conditioning still rocket along Portugal's high-ways. They follow the old RN routes, use the old RN depots (in Lisbon it's at avenida Casal Ribeiro, 18B; Tel: 01-54-54-39), but they now belong to nine private, regional bus companies named according to the areas they serve: Rodoviária do Alentejo, for example, runs from Lisbon to Evora, Beja, Elvas, Portalegre, and other Alentejo towns; Rodoviária da Beira Interior connects Lisbon with Castelo Branco, Guarda, and other towns of the Beira Baixa and Beira Alta. The "orange-and-whites" now zooming back and forth between Lisbon and the Algarve are Eva Transportes, and the one serving Porto is Rodoviária Entre Douro e Minho.

In addition, other privately owned, even more luxurious air-conditioned buses with on-board toilets (and sometimes multilingual hostesses) ply daily between Lisbon and Porto and Lisbon and the Algarve. There's Mundial Turismo, a strictly top-of-the-line private company that maintains fre-quent express service between Lisbon and Porto (four and a half hours) and Lisbon and Faro in the Algarve (three and a half hours). Its state-of-the-art buses offer about every amen-ity you could want (cushy reclining seats, air-conditioning, picture windows, hostesses, toilet). The company's main Lisbon office is at avenida António Augusto Aguiar, 90B; Tel:

(01) 52-77-13. Three other top lines making frequent Lisbon–Porto–Lisbon runs, all working out of a terminal at Campo Pequeno, 42, directly opposite the bullring (you can buy tickets here, too) are: Avic (Tel: 01-76-72-27), Turilis (Tel: 01-797-0309), and Rapide-Auto Viação do Minho (Tel: 01-793-6527).

Renting a Car

At Lisbon, Porto, Faro, and Madeira, all major car-rental firms maintain offices both at the airport and in town. It's also possible to rent a car in some of the mainland district capitals such as Aveiro, Coimbra, and Evora, on Porto Santo island (in the Madeira group), and throughout the Azores. For most travellers, driving is the only way to tour Portugal effectively: You can set your own pace and poke around the back roads, visiting the towns time forgot. Although gasoline is very expensive, especially by North American standards, there's no shortage of modern service stations (more and more of them manned by English-speaking attendants), no lack of places to eat or sleep, and no dearth, certainly, of panoramas where you'll want to stop to "ooh" and "aah."

After decades of construction, the Lisbon–Porto *auto-estrada*—the A 1/IP 1—finally opened in September 1991. For years this major national route was an on-again, off-again combination of the old two-lane N 1 (maddeningly thronged with trucks, cars, motorbikes, vans, even donkey and ox carts rumbling along the rights of way) and pristine stretches of the new four-lane A 1 (mostly empty because the tolls were too steep for the average Portuguese).

The newly completed A 1/IP 1 is a two-toll road (the first toll is for the Lisbon–Vila Franca de Xira section; the second toll is for Vila Franca to points north. And the tolls aren't cheap. The full Lisbon–Porto run, for example, costs at this writing 2,590$00. Shorter trips are cheaper. On entering the new *auto-estrada* near Vila Franca, some 23 km (14 miles) north of Lisbon (the Lisbon–Vila Franca stretch is also four-lane, just not so new) or the Arrábida bridge in Porto, you're given a ticket, then charged according to the number of miles you travel. A drive to the university town of Coimbra, located about midway between Lisbon and Porto, will cost about half as much as whizzing the full length of the road. Still, for people in a hurry, A 1/IP 1 is a bargain, considering the time it saves and traffic it avoids. The new highway with a speed limit of 120 kilometers per hour (74 mph) and a way of bypassing even medium-size towns, has trimmed the Lisbon–Porto driving time from four or four and a half hours to two and a half (well, maybe three hours for non-Portuguese drivers). Of course, that's from city limit to city limit.

The A 1/IP 1 may now zoom you right up to the outskirts of Lisbon or Porto, but traffic invariably screeches to a halt around both cities. Getting in or out of Lisbon you must contend with airport traffic as well as the usual suburban overload. Porto is ten times worse, maybe because it's Portugal's big industrial city and most of its factories are right on the highway, disgorging hundreds of vehicles onto it morning, noon, and night. So far, alas, highway engineers haven't figured out how to break the bottleneck.

Similar problems exist on the *auto-estrada* linking Lisbon and Setúbal on the Arrábida peninsula across the Tagus river. At rush hour, it is backed up all the way across the April 25 bridge. There's an easy explanation for this. Some 200,000 new automobiles are sold each year in Portugal, and half of them remain in the Lisbon area. According to one recent news report, 350,000 cars come jamming into Lisbon from the suburbs on any given weekday. There's already talk of flinging a second bridge across the Tagus at Lisbon—from the airport area on the northern fringes of the city over to the eastern shore near the little town of Alcochete or perhaps to the fishing village of Montijo, nearby. But this project isn't even on the drawing boards yet. Meanwhile, the best way to beat the traffic is simply to avoid the rush hour or to plan your itinerary so that you drive against the traffic.

All Portuguese roads, you'll be pleased to know, whether superhighway, primary, or secondary, are well marked and maintained. Still, many road signs confuse foreign drivers. For example, the arrows indicating that you should drive straight ahead often aim off toward the right—not sharp right, mind you, but vaguely. The logical conclusion, of course, is to turn right. Wrong! You should continue dead ahead. *True* right turns also point to the right, but the signboard itself is at strict right angles to the road. After a few wrong turns you'll get used to the Portuguese system of signposting, but in the meantime you can waste a lot of time retracing your steps. Here's a method that may help: Each day before you set out, study your route carefully, noting whether there are any major turns along the way. Then jot down in big bold letters the names of upcoming towns and keep the list handy so you don't have to keep stopping to consult your map.

Here's another problem you'll encounter on the back roads. Village houses and shops open directly onto highways (no sidewalks), and cats, dogs, chickens, and especially children burst into the street without looking. They seem to have no fear of automobiles, so you must keep your wits about you at all times. Worse still, few secondary roads are lighted at night, and many donkey carts, bicycles, motorbikes, even cars, have no taillights or reflectors. Whole families, moreover, often dressed in black (half the country, it seems, is in mourning), stroll the highways after dark, walking *with,* instead of facing, the traffic. So it's risky to drive·after sundown, at least for now. But things may soon improve. Many highways are being straightened and widened thanks to recent infusions of funds from the European Community, which Portugal joined in 1986. Meanwhile, don't be afraid to drive throughout Portugal. Just exercise plenty of caution. Portugal's accident rate is one of the highest in the world, mostly because the Portuguese are new to driving and because their personalities undergo an awesome change the minute they slide behind a wheel. Normally courteous to a fault, the Portuguese go "macho" in their cars, passing on hills and curves, riding your rear bumper when they can't pass, and shaving your left front fender when they can.

Although few Portuguese seem to obey them, there are speed limits: 60 kph (37 mph) in built-up areas unless signs indicate otherwise; 90 kph (56 mph) on two-lane highways in open country; 120 kph (74 mph) on *auto-estradas.* By law, seat belts must be worn outside of towns and cities, and children less than 12 years old must ride in the back seat.

Always book a rental car well in advance (your credit card guarantees your reservation). As for licenses, all that's needed for Americans, Canadians, British, and Australians is a valid national license.

The latest trend is the rental RV (recreational vehicle, called a *motorhome* in Portugal). These come fully equipped (heat, hot and cold water, toilet, shower, stove, refrigerator, and radio/cassette player—color TV and telephone extra). One Lisbon firm that rents modern *motorhomes* is Deltacar, avenida São João de Deus, 17B, 1000 Lisbon; Tel: (01) 848-1428; Fax: (01) 80-03-36. A small RV (comfortable for two) ranges in price from an off-season low (November through March) of 11,000$00 per day to a peak-season high (June through September) of 130,000$00 per week. Rates do not include 17 percent V.A.T. (value-added tax). Portugal has no shortage of campsites; the Portuguese National Tourist Office can provide you with a list of them.

Note: The Portuguese word for "gasoline" is *gasolina,* not

gasóleo, which is diesel fuel. And if you want lead-free *gasolina,* look for the pump that says *"sem chumbo."*

Pousadas (Government Inns)

"Government inn" has an ominous ring, but this is no cot-and-candle operation. Portugal's *pousada* (po-ZAH-da) program, begun in 1942 both to provide local employment and to create a model other innkeepers might emulate, has grown into an impressive network of first-class hostelries. Today there are 32 inns scattered around the mainland, the newest of which, the 28-room, four-suite Pousada de São Miguel, opened in November 1992 in the centrally located Alentejo town of Sousel (see Choosing an Alentejo Base, in the Alentejo Chapter). Six more pousadas are in the works. The two expected to open first (perhaps as early as 1993) are a 45-room inn at Condeixa near the Roman ruins at Conimbriga 15 km (9 miles) south of Coimbra, and a 12-room town house in the perched stone village of Monsanto in the Beira Baixa. In addition, the Convento de Tibães at Braga is on its way to becoming a pousada, as are three historic Alentejo properties: the old castle at Alvito and the monasteries at Crato and Beja.

There are two additional pousadas on the island of Madeira, but these now operate independently of ENATUR (Empresa Nacional de Turismo), the Portuguese government agency responsible for the pousadas (see below in this section for address). In 1993 the pousadas are being partially privatized, the better to fund future properties. But the Portuguese government will retain 51 percent of the stock and total control of the pousada program.

Some of the pousadas are truly palatial. The largest (the Santa Marinha da Costa at Guimarães in the Minho province) has 55 rooms and suites, but some pousadas offer no more than a dozen, so you must make reservations well in advance. You should also know that there are four basic pousada categories:

- B: Small, snug, basically rustic inns located, for the most part, in out-of-the-way places. Although they have no delusions of grandeur, these pousadas offer nearly every amenity you could want (the government has renovated the older ones so that every room now has a private bath, and some pousadas now even boast swimming pools). Most are appointed with simple country furniture and local handicrafts. They often boast eye-popping views, gutsy home-cooked regional dishes, and wine lists featuring the best of the local output.

- **C:** There's a hunting-lodge look to many of these somewhat more elegant pousadas: beamed ceilings, terra-cotta tile floors, blazing stone hearths, wall-to-wall windows framing something of historic or scenic significance. Rooms tend to be small (and sometimes sleekly modern), but they can all claim private baths and sometimes balconies and swimming pools as well. Here, too, the cooking is done by good local cooks who have a way with soups, stews, and the devastating egg sweets for which Portugal is famous.

- **C Superior:** This new category, added in 1991, designates pousadas that are special in some way though not opulent enough to make the CH category. They include pousadas of historic significance, those located in resort areas, and a number that have recently undergone massive renovation.

- **CH:** You'll find these strictly top-of-the-line pousadas in historic castles (Obidos, Palmela, Setúbal, Estremoz, Vila Nova de Cerveira) and in convents or monasteries (Evora, Guimarães). All have been painstakingly renovated and modernized without sacrificing any of their architectural integrity, and many are furnished with rare antiques and pride themselves on their baronial dining rooms. In the past year, the quality of the cooking has improved significantly at many pousadas, mostly because the focus is once again upon regional specialties, not on "Continental classics," which few Portuguese country cooks ever mastered.

There has been an all-out effort, too, to enlarge and upgrade several of the humbler pousadas. The Pousada de Santa Maria at Marvão, with 27 beautifully furnished new rooms, has now doubled in size; 16 rooms have been added to the Pousada do Infante at Sagres and ten to the Pousada de São Bento at Caniçada. In addition, ten palatial new rooms are being carved out of third-floor attic space at the Pousada da Rainha Santa Isabel in Estremoz and should be ready some time in 1993 (this castle pousada will now have 33 individually decorated, antiques-filled rooms).

For details about pousadas contact the Portuguese National Tourist Office (see "Further Information," below) or your local travel agent. For reservations, contact: ENATUR, Avenida Santa Joana Princesa, 10, 1700, Lisbon; Tel: (01) 848-1221 or (01) 848-9078; Fax: (01) 80-58-46. In the United States or Canada you can book pousada rooms directly through Marketing Ahead, 433 Fifth Avenue, New York, NY 10016; Tel: (212) 686-9213; Fax: (212) 686-0271. Note: *Estalagems* (esh-ta-LAH-zhems), which often resemble pousadas, are privately owned inns, and some of them are very good, too.

The Manor House Program

Within the past few years it has become possible to stay at the *solares* (town houses), *quintas* (estates), *paços* (palaces), and *casas* (simple country houses) of Portugal's nobility, aristocracy, and just plain rich. It all began with a need for hotel rooms in isolated areas, in combination with a move to save historic properties from neglect or ruin. The Portuguese government made low-interest loans available to the owners of important houses if they would modernize them and make rooms available to travellers. Today there are dozens of fine private homes where you can stay in antiques-filled rooms (many with baths *en suite*) in areas that you might not otherwise see. Many families participating in the manor-house program speak English, and a few have been so caught up with the idea that they will, if you request it, serve lunch and dinner as well as breakfast, arrange tours of their area, even provide introductions to families whose interests you might share.

Most of the manor houses belong to one or more of four main associations, which handle bookings. These manor-house associations, which also publish booklets describing the properties and their locations, are:

- ANTER (Associação Nacional de Turismo no Espaço Rural), Quinta do Campo, Valado dos Frades, 2450 Nazaré, Portugal (Tel: 062-57-71-35 or 57-71-26; Fax: 062-57-75-55)
- P.I.T. (Promoções e Ideias Turísticas), Alto da Pampilheira, Torre D-2, 8º A., 2750 Cascais, Portugal (Tel: 01-486-7958 or 01-284-4464; Fax: 01-284-2901)
- PRIVETUR (Associação Portuguesa de Turismo de Habitação), Rua João Penha, 10, Sala 15, 1200 Lisbon, Portugal (Tel: 01-69-05-49)
- TURIHAB (Associação do Turismo de Habitação), Praça da República, 4990 Ponte de Lima, Portugal (Tel: 058-94-27-29; Fax: 058-74-14-44)

In the United States and Canada, it is possible to reserve rooms in P.I.T. manor houses through E & M Associates, 211 East 43rd Street, Suite 1404, New York, NY 10017; Tel: (212) 599-8280; Fax: (212) 599-1755; they can also supply P.I.T. brochures. You can also obtain details about the manor-house program by contacting the Portuguese National Tourist Office (see "Further Information").

The Direcção-Geral do Turismo publishes an annual four-color directory to the principal manor houses, quintas, and farms that take paying guests. The latest edition, with commentary in English, contains 256 pages but is compact enough to carry in your purse or car glove compartment. It costs 1,500$00 (about US $11) and can be bought in Lisbon at Divisão do Turismo no Espaço Rural, Direcção-Geral do Turismo, avenida António Augusto de Aguiar, 86.

Room Rates

Room rates provided in this book are for double rooms and are based on double occupancy. Rates are projections for 1993 and, unless otherwise stated, include Continental breakfast. As prices are subject to change, always double-check before booking.

The rates given have been provided directly by the establishment concerned. If you reserve rooms through a travel service or booking agency, you may pay a surcharge of 5 to 10 percent or more.

What to Wear

Casual dress is acceptable during the day throughout Portugal, but this doesn't mean shorts, except at the beach. Miniskirts, tights, and tank tops may raise a few eyebrows, too, although Portugal's dress code isn't as staid or stuffy as it once was. At elegant restaurants in Lisbon, Porto, and Funchal, Madeira, coat and tie are usually de rigueur for both lunch and dinner. In the old days women were expected to cover their arms and heads when entering church. While this is no longer the case, it is still improper to enter skimpily clad.

In spring, summer, and fall you'll need lightweight clothes plus a sweater and raincoat (more for cool nights than for rain). Layering is the trick when travelling in Portugal, because there are often abrupt drops of temperature at night. And don't forget your sunglasses and sunscreen. You'll need them everywhere, not just at the beach.

Local Time

Mainland Portugal, formerly on Greenwich mean time betwen the last Sunday of September and the last Sunday of March, will keep daylight saving time throughout 1993, which puts it one hour ahead of Great Britain, five or six hours ahead of New York, Montreal, and Toronto, and eight or nine hours ahead of California and Vancouver, depending on whether or not they are on daylight saving time. Madeira will keep Greenwich mean time in fall and winter, just as mainland Portugal used to, and adopt daylight saving time in spring and summer. The Azores are now two hours behind Lisbon, except between the last Sunday of March and the last Sunday of September, when they too are on daylight saving time. When it's noon in Lisbon, it's 9:00 P.M. in Sydney.

Language

Portuguese may look like Spanish, but it *sounds* nothing like it because the Portuguese slur so many syllables with *shhs* and *zhhs*. The *nh* in Portuguese is somewhat similar to the *ñ* in Spanish; Minho province, for example, is pronounced "Mean-yo." And to English-speakers, who've been drilled with "i-before-e-except-after-c" lessons, it's startling to see so many *ei* combinations in Portuguese words: *pinheiro* (pine tree), for example, or *Madeira*. The Portuguese *ei* is pronounced exactly like a long *a* in English; thus *pinheiro* becomes peen-YAY-ro, and *Madeira,* ma-DAY-ra. The most difficult Portuguese sound to master, however, is the *ão*, which is drawn through the nose. It occurs everywhere, it seems—*pão* (bread), *Dão* (a popular wine), and so on. The *ão* sounds something like *ow* (as pronounced in *town* or *crown*). But it's more nasal. Here's a trick that helps: Add an *ng* to the *ow* so that *pão* sounds something like *powng* and *Dão, downg.* That's close enough for the Portuguese to understand.

Until recently, French was Portugal's second language, and it's still widely spoken in the north, but English is fast gaining ground. The waiters and receptionists at every inn and eatery of consequence speak English, as do many bank tellers and shopkeepers. Whether or not they speak a word of English (or you of Portuguese), however, the Portuguese are unusually accommodating, and you can usually make do with sign language. Many Portuguese don't much like being addressed in Spanish (given their long and uneasy relationship with the Spaniards, it's easy to understand why). And one last word of advice: When touring the wine lodges of Porto or Madeira, remember that "Sherry" is a dirty word.

Telephoning

The country code for Portugal is 351. The city code for Lisbon is 01; for Porto, 02 (eliminate the zero when telephoning from outside Portugal). In case of emergency when travelling about Portugal, dial 115. The equivalent of the U.S. 911, it connects you with an emergency operator who will summon the police, fire department, or an ambulance straightaway.

Many Portuguese telephone numbers have recently been changed or will be changed during the next few years. Expect to encounter difficulties in placing calls. Sometimes, but not always, a recording provides a new number. Some new numbers have resulted from the addition of a single digit, while others are completely changed, and in some cases both old and new numbers work. In case of difficulty with telephone numbers, dial 118 (the national information service) for assistance. Operators now often speak English.

Electrical Current

Throughout Portugal it's 220-volt, 50-cycle AC. Americans and Canadians will need adapters plus assorted plugs.

Currency

The *escudo* (pronounced ish-KOO-doe and divided into 100 *centavos*) is the official monetary unit of Portugal. As if to bedevil North Americans, the decimal point is written as a dollar sign. Thus 1,000$00 means 1,000 escudos (called a *conto*). Portugal sets no limit on the amount of cash or traveller's checks that you can bring into the country, but does on what you're allowed to carry out: It's 100,000$00 in Portuguese escudos and 500,000$00 in foreign currency, but the regulations change frequently and it's advisable to check what the current limits are.

At press time, 1$00 was valued at US $.007; conversely, US $1 was worth 141$00.

Credit Cards

Access, American Express, Diner's Club, Eurocard, MasterCard, and Visa are widely accepted throughout Portugal. If you should use a credit card for gasoline, you may find that your purchase is limited to 5,000$00 and that you are also slapped with a 100$00 surcharge.

Business Hours

As a rule, banks are open from 8:30 to 3:00 P.M., Monday through Friday; in Lisbon, certain branches are open again from 6:00 to 11:00 P.M. In the Algarve, the bank at the Vilamoura Marina is open daily from 9:00 A.M. to 9:00 P.M. The bank at the Lisbon airport is open round the clock.

Shops open at 9:00 A.M. and close for lunch at 1:00 P.M., then reopen at 3:00 and remain open until 6:00 or 7:00 P.M., Monday through Friday. On Saturdays the shops are open only from 9:00 A.M. to 1:00 P.M. Most big shopping centers are open seven days a week from 10:00 A.M. to 11:00 P.M. or midnight. In every community, at least one drugstore (*farmácia*) is open 24 hours a day, seven days a week; check the hotel concierge or local newspaper for the listing.

As for restaurants, lunch is served from noon to 3:00 P.M. (although fancier Lisbon establishments may not open until 12:30 or 1:00 P.M.) and dinner from 7:30 to 10:00 P.M.

Most museums are closed on Mondays.

National Holidays

All of Portugal observes New Year's Day, Liberty Day (April 25), Labor Day (May 1), Camões's Day (June 10), Assumption (August 15), Republic Day (October 5), All Saints' Day (November 1), Restoration Day (December 1), Immaculate Conception (December 8), Christmas Eve, and Christmas Day. Shrove Tuesday, Good Friday, Easter, and Corpus Christi, dates that change from year to year, are also celebrated.

Packing and Shipping

It's easy to get so carried away with Portuguese folk art that you buy more than you can possibly lug home. The rug, tile, and linen shops will probably pack and ship what you buy. But how do you transport all that heavy, breakable country-market pottery? You'll be happy to know that there's a first-class shipper in Lisbon who will pack things meticulously, then send everything to your door. It's the International Travel Service, at rua Castilho, 61B, near the Ritz hotel (Tel: 01-386-3830; Fax: 01-386-0879). But expect to pay plenty for their services, possibly five times what you spent for the folk art. And, if you've managed to travel all through Portugal without buying everything you wanted, you will surely find it at the Centro de Turismo e Artesanato, which, as luck would have it, is run by the friendly people who operate the International Travel Service. It occupies the same quarters on rua Castilho and is one of Lisbon's biggest and best handicrafts shops.

Cautions

The Portuguese say it's safe to drink the water everywhere (unless signs indicate otherwise), but they themselves always drink one of the fine local bottled waters. The most popular is Luso, a nonsparkling, mineral-rich water from the spa of the same name just north of Coimbra.

The surf in the Algarve is rarely rough, but along the west coast of Portugal, particularly at Guincho near Cascais and Estoril, it pounds in with awesome force and the undertow can be lethal.

Portugal is being industrialized and motorized at such a clip that no one's paying much attention to the fallout. Much of the time industrial fumes enshroud Lisbon and Porto, and even such medium-size towns as Aveiro, Guarda, and Covilhã. In addition, Portuguese motorists drive about blithely tossing plastic potato-chip bags, styrofoam cups, beer tins, even glass bottles from their car windows with nary a backward glance. For a people always known for neatness, the litter is shocking. Indeed, some remote stretches of road have become garbage dumps and/or automobile graveyards. What the Portuguese need in the worst way is a highway beautification program like the one Lady Bird Johnson launched in the United States in the 1960s. A series of community improvement contests would work wonders in cleaning up the country. It's singularly blessed with scenic splendor and deserves all the "t.l.c." the Portuguese can muster.

Finally, alas, with progress come additional problems. Traditionally a safe country for travellers, Portugal is now having to deal with car break-ins and purse- and camera-snatchings. Joining the European Community meant wide-open borders for member nations; from the outset, the Portuguese worried that the bands of thieves operating so freely in Spain would expand their turf to include Portugal. Perhaps they already have. Whatever the reason, thievery is on the rise—especially in Lisbon's Rossio and Alfama, also on its buses, subways, and ferries. The moral: Carry only what you can afford to lose. And leave nothing locked in a car, day or night, town or country.

Further Information

Contact the Portuguese National Tourist Office at these addresses: in the United States, 590 Fifth Avenue, New York, NY 10036-4704 (Tel: 212-354-4403/4/5/6/7; Fax: 212-764-6137); in Canada, 60 Bloor Street West, Suite 1005, Toronto, Ontario M4W 3B8 (Tel: 416-921-7376; Fax: 416-921-1353); in

Great Britain, 22–25A Sackville Street, London W1X 1DE (Tel: 71-494-1441; Fax: 71-494-1868). In Australia, contact your travel agent.

BIBLIOGRAPHY

H. WARNER ALLEN, *The Wines of Portugal* (1963). Discussions of the demarcated and undemarcated wines, many of them unknown outside Portugal.

HANS CHRISTIAN ANDERSEN, *A Visit to Portugal, 1866;* translation from the Danish by Grace Thornton (1972). Portugal through the eyes of the famous Danish storyteller. Not among his best works, but fascinating nonetheless.

JEAN ANDERSON, *Henry the Navigator, Prince of Portugal* (1969). A biography of Portugal's visionary 15th-century scholar-prince and the story of Portugal's conquest of the Atlantic.

————, *The Food of Portugal* (1986). Recipes from Western Europe's most original and least known cuisine (worked out using American measures, ingredients, and implements), with advice for travellers about Portuguese inns, menus, wines, and foods.

W. C. ATKINSON, *A History of Spain and Portugal* (1960). A highly readable account of the two Iberian nations, often at odds with one another.

CARLOS DE AZEVEDO, *Churches of Portugal* (1985). The Visigothic, Romanesque, Gothic, Manueline, Renaissance, and Baroque churches of Portugal captured in all their splendor by photographer Chester E. V. Brummel. Azevedo provides the narrative.

SAM AND JANE BALLARD, *Pousadas of Portugal* (1986). Profiles of Portugal's famous *pousadas* (government inns), many of them housed in historic castles and convents.

ANTÓNIO ALÇADA BAPTISTA, ED, MARIA DEOLINDA ESTUDANTE, SOFIA MANTUA AND ANISIO FRANCO (text) AND NUNO CALVET (photographs), *Pousadas de Portugal* (1992). To celebrate the 50th anniversary of the founding of its pousadas, the Portuguese government published this handsome, four-color volume showcasing one dozen pousadas, from the very first one (Santa Luzia, at Elvas) to some of the more recent and more opulent. The text is in English as well as Portuguese and French.

MARCUS BINNEY, *Country Manors of Portugal* (1987). Binney's text plus the lush four-color photographs of Nicolas Sapieha and Francesco Venturi add up to a voyeur's tour of Portugal's great houses, built over the past seven centuries.

DANIEL J. BOORSTIN, *The Discoverers* (1983). This history of man's quest to know the earth and its peoples includes an important section on the Portuguese discoveries.

MANUEL BORRALHO, ED., *Alentejo: Hidden Treasure of Portugal* (1990). The regional tourist offices of Evora, São Mamede, and Planície Dourada jointly produced this colorful profile of what may be Portugal's least appreciated province. Richly illustrated chapters survey the archaeological riches, architecture, major handicrafts, industries, and, not least, that largely unknown-to-tourists stretch of Atlantic coastline.

PATRICK BOWE (text) AND NICOLAS SAPIEHA (photographs), *Gardens of Portugal* (1989). This 223-page stroll through tropical gardens, palace grounds, tightly clipped topiary, and parterres of stunning symmetry proves that the Portuguese are blessed with the greenest thumbs on earth.

C. R. BOXER, *The Portuguese Seaborne Empire, 1415–1825* (1969). A straightforward political, economic, and cultural history of the Portuguese part in the great expansion of the European powers; written by a leading historian.

ERNLE BRADFORD, *Southward the Caravels* (1961). A sailor follows the routes of the great 14th- and 15th-century navigators.

ANN BRIDGE AND SUSAN LOWNDES, *The Selective Traveller in Portugal* (1949, revised edition 1967). Shunpiking in Portugal with two women who love it and know it well. Bridge's husband was the British ambassador to Portugal; and Lowndes, the niece of Hilaire Belloc, was married to Luiz Marques, a writer and correspondent in Portugal for major English and American newspapers.

L. A. BROWN, *The Story of Maps* (1949). How cartography evolved through the centuries; the Portuguese have of course been one of the major forces.

ROBIN BRYANS, *The Azores* (1963). A highly personal introduction to these mid-Atlantic Portuguese islands.

LUÍS VAZ DE CAMÕES, *The Lusiads,* translated by William C. Atkinson (1952). Camões, the "Virgil of Portugal," wrote this epic poem in the late 16th century to immortalize his country's voyages of discovery, particularly those of Vasco da Gama, to whom he was related and who died the year he was born. But *The Lusiads* is also the story of Portugal itself.

SUZANNE CHANTAL, *Portugal, The Land and Its People,* translated by F. R. Holiday (1943). Personal impressions of each of the Portuguese provinces.

RUPERT CROFT-COOKE, *Madeira* (1961). The definitive story of Madeira wine.

G. R. CRONE, ED., *The Explorers* (1962). Profiles of the world's great navigators and explorers, including Magellan, da Gama, and other Portuguese.

C. DERVENN, *The Azores* (1956). A detailed look at this mid-Atlantic archipelago discovered by the Portuguese early in the 15th century.

JOHN DOS PASSOS, *The Portugal Story: Three Centuries of Exploration and Discovery* (1969). This important American writer of Portuguese ancestry turns his attention to the tiny land of his forefathers and details its role in leading Europe out of the Middle Ages and in opening up the world to Europe. His carefully researched history traces the evolution of Portugal from its earliest days through its Golden Age in the 15th century.

JOSÉ MARIA DE EÇA DE QUEIRÓS, *The Maias* (1986). An entertaining and perceptive novel of 19th-century Portuguese society and manners.

JOHN AND SUSAN FARROW, *Madeira, Pearl of the Atlantic—The Complete Guide* (1987). This British couple, now living on the island of Madeira, have written the most complete guide yet available to the "Isle of Perpetual June."

A. MOREIRA DA FONSECA, A. GALHANO, E. SERPA PIMENTEL, AND J. R.-P. ROSAS, *Port Wine: Notes on Its History, Production & Technology* (4th ed., 1991). Detailed, lavishly illustrated, and highly technical, this prizewinning book published by the Instituto do Vinho do Porto in Porto is aimed at wine makers and connoisseurs of one of Portugal's noblest wines.

JÚLIO GIL (text) AND AUGUSTO CABRITA (photographs), *The Finest Castles in Portugal* (1986). Richly illustrated capsule histories of more than 100 of Portugal's most famous castles, which dot the landscape from the Minho and Trás-os-Montes in the north through the great central sweep of the Alentejo to the southernmost Algarve.

————, *The Loveliest Towns and Villages in Portugal* (1991). The writer-phtographer team who profiled *The Finest Castles in Portugal* have focused their pen and lens on villages in mainland Portugal, Madeira, and the Azores that are blessed with particular beauty. Most lie deep in the countryside and are unknown to any but the most dedicated traveller.

FRANCISCO ESTEVES GONÇALVES, *Portugal, A Wine Country* (1983). The most detailed book available on the wines of Portugal. Lavishly illustrated.

LAWRENCE S. GRAHAM AND DOUGLAS L. WHEELER, EDS., *In Search of Modern Portugal: The Revolution and Its Consequences* (1983). Fifteen scholarly essays analyze the domestic and international conditions that led to Portugal's 1974 revolution, the postrevolutionary chaos, and the present republic.

JOHN L. HAMMOND, *Building Popular Power* (1988). The story of Portugal's 1974 "Flower Revolution," especially the role of the workers and neighborhood movements.

RICHARD J. HARRISON, *Spain at the Dawn of History* (1988). How the Iberians, Phoenicians, and Greeks helped to shape Spain and Portugal.

WILLY HEINZELMANN, *Azores* (1980). Swiss writer-photographer Heinzelmann not only trains his lenses on the nine islands of the Azores but also examines their history, geography, economy, legends, and lore.

————, *Madeira* (1971). A portrait in photographs and words of the two inhabited islands in the Madeira archipelago: Madeira and Porto Santo.

ANTHONY HOGG, *Travellers' Portugal* (1983). Off the beaten path in Portugal.

BEN HOWKINS, *Rich, Rare & Red: A Guide to Port* (1982; revised ed., 1987). Just the book for anyone seriously interested in Port wine.

A. C. INCHBOLD, *Lisbon and Cintra* (1907). A romantic description of Portugal around the turn of the century, with watercolor illustrations and sound historical background on places of interest in Estremadura.

MARION KAPLAN, *The Portuguese* (1991). A wide-ranging look at the land and its people, past and present. Describing a nation that is once again on the move, the author focuses on the new Portugal, with all its incongruity and paradox.

MARY JEAN KEMPNER, *Invitation to Portugal* (1969). A well-written and informative exploration of the country, with evocative sections on bullfighting and *fado,* Portugal's soul music.

WILLIAM KINGSTON, *Lusitanian Sketches* (1845). A tour of the north of Portugal during the mid-19th century, with particular references to the Anglo community in Porto.

CYNTHIA AND RALPH KITE, *Karen Brown's Portuguese Country Inns & Pousadas* (1987). A close look at more than 50 Portuguese inns and small hotels.

BJÖRN LANDSTRÖM, *The Quest for India* (1964). A profusely illustrated history of exploration from an expedition to the Land of Punt in 1493 B.C. to the discovery by Portuguese navigators of the Cape of Good Hope in A.D. 1488.

ALEX LIDDLE AND JANET PRICE, *Port Wine Quintas of the Douro* (1992). This coffee-table book offers fascinating peeks over the walls and behind the gates of Portugal's rich and famous Port-wine barons.

ROSE MACAULAY, *They Went to Portugal* (1946). This classic chronicles the journeys of celebrated travellers—Lord Byron, Tennyson, Palgrave, English royalty, William Beckford, and others—who went to Portugal, and tells what they found there and how the country affected them.

MAITE MANJON, *The Gastronomy of Spain and Portugal* (1990). The facts, legends, and lore of Iberian food and drink, neatly catalogued from A through Z.

FREDERIC P. MARJAY, *Portugal and the Sea* (1957). This picture book with blocks of text documents Portugal's long-standing love affair with the sea.

A. H. DE OLIVEIRA MARQUES, *History of Portugal* (1976). A solid historical account of the formation of the Portuguese nation and the rise and decline of the empire.

JOSÉ MECO, *The Art of Azulejo in Portugal* (1988). A four-color photo-history of the decorative glazed tiles that face so many buildings in Portugal. It begins with the earliest examples (used in Coimbra's Sé Velha and Sintra's Paço Real, among other places), includes the Renaissance, Baroque,

Rococo, and Neoclassical styles, then concludes with a look at the tiles of today.

MARIA DE LOURDES MODESTO, *Traditional Portuguese Cooking*. Now available in English, this masterwork by Portugal's Julia Child is so profusely illustrated that flipping through its pages amounts to a culinary tour of Portugal.

GUIDO DE MONTEREY, *Madeira, Isle of Flowers* (1987). A field guide to the extraordinary flora of Madeira.

SAMUEL ELIOT MORISON, *The Great Explorers* (1978). This abridged edition of Morison's classic history of the European discovery of the Americas acknowledges the valuable contributions of such Portuguese scholars and explorers as Prince Henry the Navigator, Bartolomeu Dias, Magellan, and Pedro Alvarez Cabral.

R. R. PALMER, *Atlas of World History* (1957). World history told via maps.

MAGDELAINE PARISOT, ED., *Portugal, Madeira, Azores* (1956). A hamlet-by-hamlet, museum-by-museum, stone-by-stone journey through Portugal, Madeira, and the Azores that is heavy on the history.

J. H. PARRY, *The Age of Reconnaissance* (1963). The story of how Europe discovered the rest of the world, from Prince Henry the Navigator onward.

————, *The Discovery of the Sea* (1974). The principal events of the great Age of Discovery (in which the Portuguese played a major role), covered with clarity and elegance.

RICHARD PATTEE, *Portugal and the Portuguese World* (1957). A useful study of the Portuguese principle of "biracialism" as a means of managing the far-flung empire.

WERNER RADASEWSKY AND GUENTER SCHNEIDER, *Porto*. Portugal's "second city" lovingly profiled in prose and pictures.

ELAINE SANCEAU, *Henry, the Navigator* (1947). A well-researched and well-written biography of Portugal's most famous prince.

DON GLEN SANDY, *Madeira Wine at Home* (1988). The story of the Madeira wine industry, plus tips for serving and cooking with these noble wines.

ROBERT C. SMITH, *The Art of Portugal, from 1500 to 1800* (1968). A comprehensive survey of Portuguese architecture, sculpture, paintings, ecclesiastical art, ceramics, silver, furniture, and textiles, illustrated in color and black and white and with many floor plans of monasteries, cathedrals, and churches.

MURAT GEOFFREY TAIT, *Port, from the Vine to the Glass* (1936). Still the definitive guide to these fine wines.

LUÍS FORJAZ TRIGUEIROS (literary director) AND RAÚL CONSTÂNCIO (photographer), *A Tradição de Portugal: Portuguese Manor Houses* (1990). A glamorous photo album (with brief histories in English as well as Portuguese) of 54 noble estates, little palaces, and country houses that now accept paying guests. These properties are part of the P.I.T. network (see "The Manor House Program" in the Useful Facts section).

JOHN AND PAT UNDERWOOD, *Madeira* (1987). John Underwood's photographs capture the many moods of Madeira.

NELSON H. VIEIRA, ED., *Roads to Today's Portugal* (1983). To provide the English-speaking world with an understanding of contemporary Portugal, Portuguese and non-Portuguese scholars examine the work of 20th-century Portuguese artists, dramatists, poets, and novelists whose voices were heard despite persistent suppression.

FRANK VILLIER, *Portugal* (1963). A frank, sometimes dour, profile of the country and the people.

CAROLYN WALKER AND KATHY HOLMAN, *The Embroidery of Madeira* (1987). Two American teachers of needlework synopsize the history of the Madeira embroidery industry, then teach the essential stitches and techniques through the use of detailed how-to photographs and diagrams.

DOUGLAS L. WHEELER, *Republican Portugal: A Political History, 1910–1926* (1978). A broad, unbiased, illuminating analysis of Portugal's ill-timed (and ultimately unsuccessful) first attempt at democracy.

HELMUT AND ALICE WOHL, *Portugal* (1983). Travels through Portugal recorded in photographs and text. The accent is both architectural and historical.

DAVID WRIGHT AND PATRICK SWIFT, *Algarve* (1965). Two insiders share the sights, sounds, and scents of the southernmost Portuguese province.

LISBON

By Jean Todd Freeman and Marvine Howe

Jean Todd Freeman first visited Lisbon 27 years ago and has been in love with it ever since. A novelist and freelance travel writer, she has written for Travel & Leisure, Venture, *and* Diversion *magazines, and for Reader's Digest Books. Marvine Howe, on the staff of the* New York Times *since 1972, has covered Portugal and the Portuguese-speaking world extensively. She also contributes articles about Portugal to the* Times *travel section.*

Lisbon is a city that inspires poetry and creates its own mythology. Luís Vaz de Camões, in his great Portuguese epic *The Lusiads,* described it as "Princess of the world . . . before whom even the ocean bows." Legend holds that its Roman name, Olisipo, derives from that of the Greek hero Ulysses, who paused here on his voyage long enough to seduce the nymph Calypso. Heartbroken at his departure, she changed herself into a serpent whose coils formed the seven hills of the city.

Today those hills, rising from the broad Tagus river and stacked with tile-roofed houses and pastel palaces like a child's village of blocks, form a fine natural setting for a city of unusual character and charm. Lisbon has undergone occupation by the Romans, the Visigoths, and the Moors, a disastrous earthquake, and the shock of finding itself, in the golden Age of Discovery, the richest city in Europe. A world capital with a country manner, Lisbon harmoniously balances its formal squares, palm-lined boulevards, and classically proportioned buildings with crowded, colorful neighborhoods where old women grill sardines at the doorsteps, laundry flaps from lines strung between balconies brightened with geraniums and caged finches, and children play games in cobblestone churchyards.

Such contrasts are common throughout Lisbon: A narrow, dark, and twisting alley opens abruptly onto a *miradouro* (lookout), presenting a sweeping view of the city below; a shabby house tucked away in a cul-de-sac reveals a wall splendidly paneled with 17th-century pictorial *azulejos* (tiles); an unmarked door opens into a major museum. Pleasant surprises like these captivate first-time visitors and sometimes cause them to exaggerate the city's assets, like the 12th-century Crusader who wrote of Lisbon's Tagus, "This noble river was most abundantly fishy, and there was gold on its banks." He might, of course, have simply been dazzled by the sunlight reflected off the Tagus. The marvelous light of Lisbon, suffusing all its buildings and monuments with a tawny radiance, is what most visitors first notice about the city, what they best remember, and what beckons them to return.

MAJOR INTEREST

Neighborhoods
The Baixa and the Rossio
The Alfama: old Moorish quarter
The Chiado shopping district
Bairro Alto *tascas* (bistros)
Belém's museums and monuments

Sights
Praça do Comércio
Avenida da Liberdade
Castelo de São Jorge
Aqueduto das Aguas Livres
Torre de Belém
Mosteiro dos Jerónimos

Museums
Museu Nacional de Arte Antiga
Museu Nacional do Azulejo (tile museum)
Fundação Calouste Gulbenkian (Gulbenkian Foundation)
Centro de Arte Moderna
Museu de Arte Popular (Folk Art Museum)
Museu da Marinha (Maritime Museum)
Museu Nacional dos Coches (Coach Museum)

Churches
The Sé (Cathedral)

São Vicente de Fora: *azulejos*
Santa Engrácia
Ruins of Carmo
São Roque: chapel of Saint John the Baptist
Basilica da Estrela

Parks and Gardens
Jardim Botânico
Parque Eduardo VII: Estufa Fria (Cool House)
Jardim Zoológico
Palácio dos Marqueses de Fronteira
Parque Florestal de Monsanto

Lisbon's earliest visitors were probably Phoenicians, who arrived by sea around 1100 B.C. to found a port they called Alisubbo (Serene Harbor), settling above it on the hill where the Castelo de São Jorge stands today. Later came Greeks, Carthaginians, and, in 206 B.C., the Romans, who fortified the hill, built roads, bridges, and stone houses with tiled roofs, and cultivated fruit and olive trees. More important, they laid the foundation for the gradual development of the Portuguese language, spoken today by nearly 200 million people.

When the Romans withdrew, Lisbon was invaded by various barbarian tribes, most notably the Visigoths. Then in swept the Moors in the eighth century, bringing with them a rich, exotic culture that is strongly felt in the city even today. Although strongly resented and resisted, the Muslims improved the economy, beautified the growing city, encouraged education, arts, and crafts, and practiced sophisticated methods of irrigation and agriculture. They introduced new foods: rice, oranges, lemons, saffron, and lettuce—called *alface* in Portuguese and so relished by the Lisboetes that they were later nicknamed *alfacinhas* (lettuce-eaters). Far from being ruthless oppressors, the Moors allowed both Christians and Jews to practice their faiths openly (though in separate ghettoes) within the Muslim state.

In 1147 young Afonso Henriques, who had recently proclaimed himself king of Portugal (which at that time consisted of only the northern part of the country), resolved to drive the Moors out of the south. With the help of a motley crew of English, French, and German Crusaders who providentially had been blown ashore by a storm, he besieged and captured the Moorish stronghold. This decisive victory cleared the way for Lisbon to emerge as the capital of the rapidly growing country and the center of its social, cultural,

and political life. By the late 15th century Lisbon had become the richest and most cosmopolitan city in the west,
with merchant ships from near and far bringing rare and
costly goods to her harbor. The Renaissance spirit then
flaming through Europe inspired the Portuguese not only to
achievements in art and literature but to daring exploration
of the physical world. Prince Henry, nicknamed "the Navigator," founded a unique school in the Algarve where eager
young men could learn all that was then known about
sailing, geography, and astronomy. Wide-hulled caravels,
equipped with innovative devices such as the compass and
the portolan chart, set forth to challenge the limits of the
known world and came back loaded with spices and gold
from India, Africa, and Brazil. Neither the Inquisition nor the
Black Plague could quench the tremendous excitement gen-
erated by this Age of Discovery, an excitement most clearly
expressed in the exuberant Manueline architecture of the
day.

A few old etchings and tile panels, still to be seen in
Lisbon's museums, show the city as it looked during its
Século de Ouro (Age of Gold), when João V was king. In the
foreground is Terreiro do Paço (Palace Square, today also
known as the praça do Comércio and as Black Horse
Square) with its handsome three-story palace, from which
an earlier king, Manuel I, used to ride an elephant down to
the Tagus to watch the boats unload their riches. In the
background is a skyline gleaming with towers, castles, and
convents, most of which disappeared in the cataclysmic
earthquake of 1755.

That quake, which shook all of Europe, occurred on All
Saints' Day when most of Lisbon was at mass. Falling candles
ignited fires, and when those terrified people who were not
crushed by the crumbling walls fled from the flames they
were engulfed by a tidal wave rolling up from the Tagus.
Tens of thousands died in the disaster, and nearly all the
lower town was destroyed.

Quickest to take charge in the crisis was the powerful
and arrogant marquês de Pombal, then prime minister,
who put the paralyzed city back in running order and
oversaw its rebuilding along Neoclassical lines. All that
hadn't fallen down was torn down, the rubble swept away
for a fresh start. The new avenues were straight, wide, and
crossed at strict right angles; squares and statues were carefully balanced; even houses were matched in height and
style. The resulting Baixa (pronounced BYE-sha and mean-

ing Lower Town) was strikingly modern for its day and is still aesthetically pleasing.

In fact, the central Lisbon of today is not so very different from that of Pombal's time, although automobiles have replaced carriages and cows are no longer kept in the Alfama. The spread of the city to the suburbs, which began in the 17th century, has engulfed many more forested hills than the original seven. People who admired the old Lisbon deplore the enormous apartment complexes on its fringes, the glass-fronted office buildings beginning to invade the avenida da Liberdade, the skyscraper hotels springing up beyond Parque Eduardo VII, and especially the Disneyesque shopping center that recently opened in Amoreiras, where Pombal once founded a silk factory. Yet many (though not all) of these new buildings blend in well enough with Lisbon's simple style of architecture, and a number of fine old homes are being restored rather than replaced.

During the 20th century Portugal, like many countries, has undergone major political upheavals, and Lisbon has felt their effects. In 1908 King Carlos and his son, Crown Prince Luís Filipe, were assassinated in the praça do Comércio, the city's main square; two years later the monarchy ended as a republic was declared. But government after government failed to solve the country's problems, and in 1932 António de Oliveira Salazar took over as virtual dictator, repressing the people through censorship and secret police, and exploiting the African colonies.

On April 25, 1974, young army officers with carnations stuck in their rifles staged a bloodless coup in Lisbon, so delighting the people that they renamed the new Salazar suspension bridge Ponte 25 de Abril. A year later the new government granted independence to the colonies. Almost immediately Lisbon, deluged with more than a half million *retornados* (refugees) from these colonies, was plunged into an acute housing shortage from which it is only now recovering. While temporarily unsettling, the sudden infusion of African culture has given Lisbon a new vitality most evident in the city's music, fashion, and cuisine.

As Portugal's capital, Lisbon sets the tone and takes the heat for the rest of the country. Yet it doesn't seem to take itself too seriously. There's an air of frivolity in the flowery gardens and splashing fountains and curlicuing mosaic sidewalks that makes you suspect that Lisbon offers, most of all, fun. It makes you want to get out and explore this charming and accessible city, block by block and hill by hill.

Getting Oriented

Grasping the central plan of Lisbon is, thanks to Pombal, rather easy. With map in hand, stand in the praça do Comércio facing north. Behind you is the Tagus river with its ferry slips, tram terminals, and market areas. Before you is a grand triumphal arch (Arco Triunfal da Rua Augusta) opening onto the Pombaline grid of shopping streets that lead into the praça de Dom Pedro IV, which everyone calls the Rossio and which is in effect three squares in one, spilling over into the praça da Figueira to the east and the praça dos Restauradores to the northwest. The Rossio, lined with shops and sidewalk cafés and always thronged with people, is the heart of the Baixa.

From the Rossio, the imposing avenida da Liberdade runs northwest almost a mile up into the new part of town to the praça Marquês de Pombal, which is actually a breakneck traffic circle presided over by a large statue of the prime minister stroking a ferocious-looking lion. Beyond lies the green oasis of Parque Eduardo VII. Running off to the right from the entrance to the park is avenida Fontes Pereira de Melo, which leads to another circle, off which a second main avenue, da República, extends to the north past the bullring and up to the vicinity of the airport. A burgeoning new business quarter of corporate headquarters and hotels is centered around the avenida da República.

On a hill to the west of the Baixa is the Bairro Alto (Upper Town), a 17th-century residential area known today for its Chiado shopping district, excellent restaurants, and nightlife. High above the city to the east, the Castelo de São Jorge looms over the Alfama, the old Moorish maze of houses, courtyards, stairs, and alleys.

Most of the sights of interest to visitors lie within these neighborhoods, or farther west in the suburb of Belém. Once you get the neighborhoods straight, it's fun—and helpful—to go to one of the city's many *miradouros* to locate their major landmarks. On the western side of town, one of the most pleasant *miradouros* is São Pedro de Alcântara, easily reached by the Elevador da Gloria, a cable-car departing from the praça dos Restauradores. From this tree-shaded lookout you can see the Castelo de São Jorge, the twin towers of São Vicente de Fora, one of Lisbon's famous churches, and the large dome of another church, Santa Engrácia. By consulting the pictorial tile table on the belvedere's balustrade you can locate numerous other landmarks in the city. For an opposite view, take a taxi to the

Castelo de São Jorge, where a spectacular overlook and a similar pictorial guide allow you to pick out the broad green avenida da Liberdade, the ruins of the Carmo convent, the belfries of Estrela basilica, the impressive Ponte 25 de Abril suspension bridge linking Lisbon with the expanding towns across the Tagus river, and beyond it the striking Cristo Rei (Christ the King), inspired by Rio de Janeiro's Christ the Redeemer.

Knowing the relative positions of a few key landmarks will help you to orient yourself when walking about the city, but be prepared to get lost occasionally. Because of the extreme steepness of the streets and their complicated twists and turns, it's possible to glimpse a familiar statue or steeple at one intersection and lose it at the next. Furthermore, streets often change names in midcourse and are frequently labeled at one end only—invariably the end you have not yet reached. Bear in mind that an hour or two of steep climbs and tricky descents on uneven cobblestones or mosaics can prove more tiring than you might expect. Wear comfortable shoes, try to start at the top of hills and work your way down, and stop often to rest—at a sidewalk café, in a public garden, or even in the lobby of a convenient hotel.

Finally, you'll be glad to know that visitors can still venture into just about any neighborhood of Lisbon (and the rest of the country) without fear of violent crime. While you might hear of an occasional holdup in a deserted park or dark alley, Portuguese parks are still places where people can relax and enjoy themselves during the day. But a word of caution: People can no longer leave valuables in automobiles in downtown Lisbon with impunity. Parked cars, particularly rentals and those with foreign license plates, have become prime targets for larcenists. Lisbon's underground parking lots, convenient as they may be, are notorious for break-ins. Pedestrians, too, who appear at a loss in a crowd, whether it's at a beach, bus stop, or street fair, and particularly in the subway, are popular quarry for larcenous urchins and other pickpockets. And we've recently heard reports of purse and camera snatchings in the Alfama.

CENTRAL LISBON

The obvious place to begin touring Lisbon is the **praça do Comércio** (which is really the government square; there's very little commerce here), distinguished not only for its beauty but for its superfluity of names. Locally known as

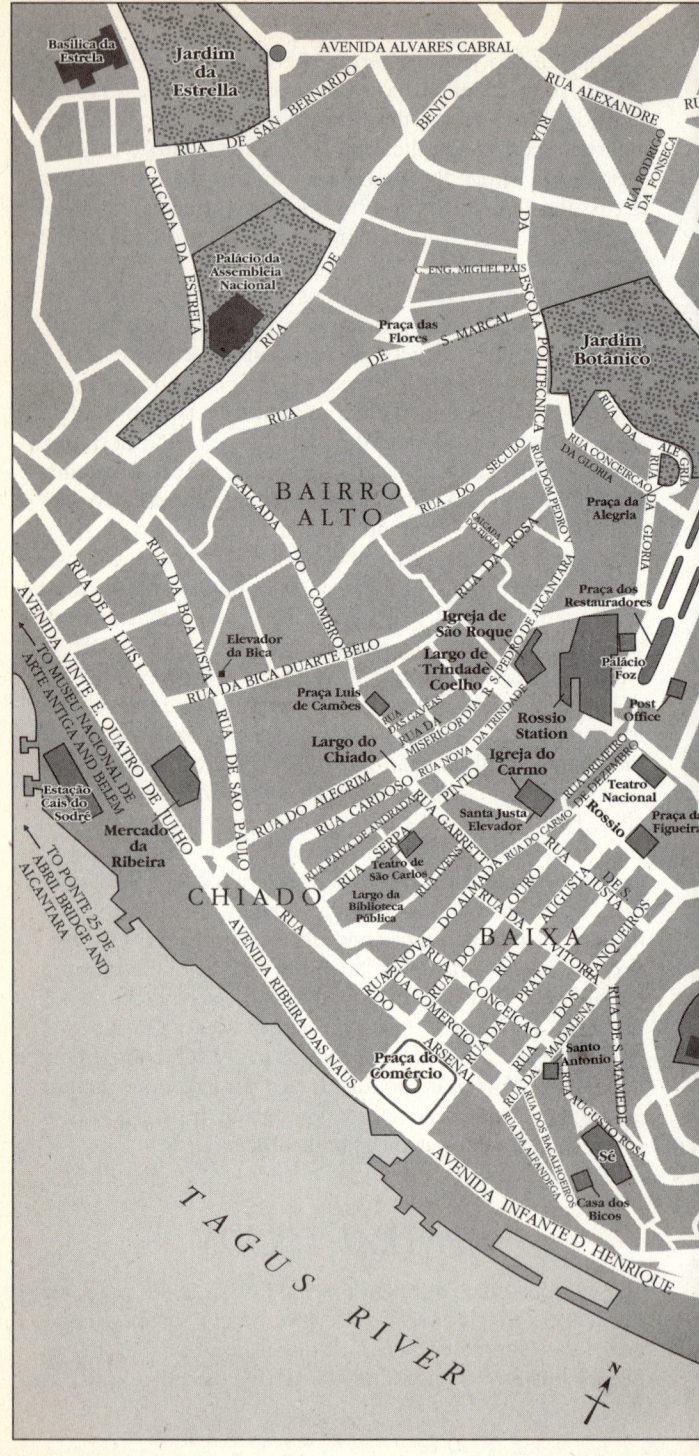

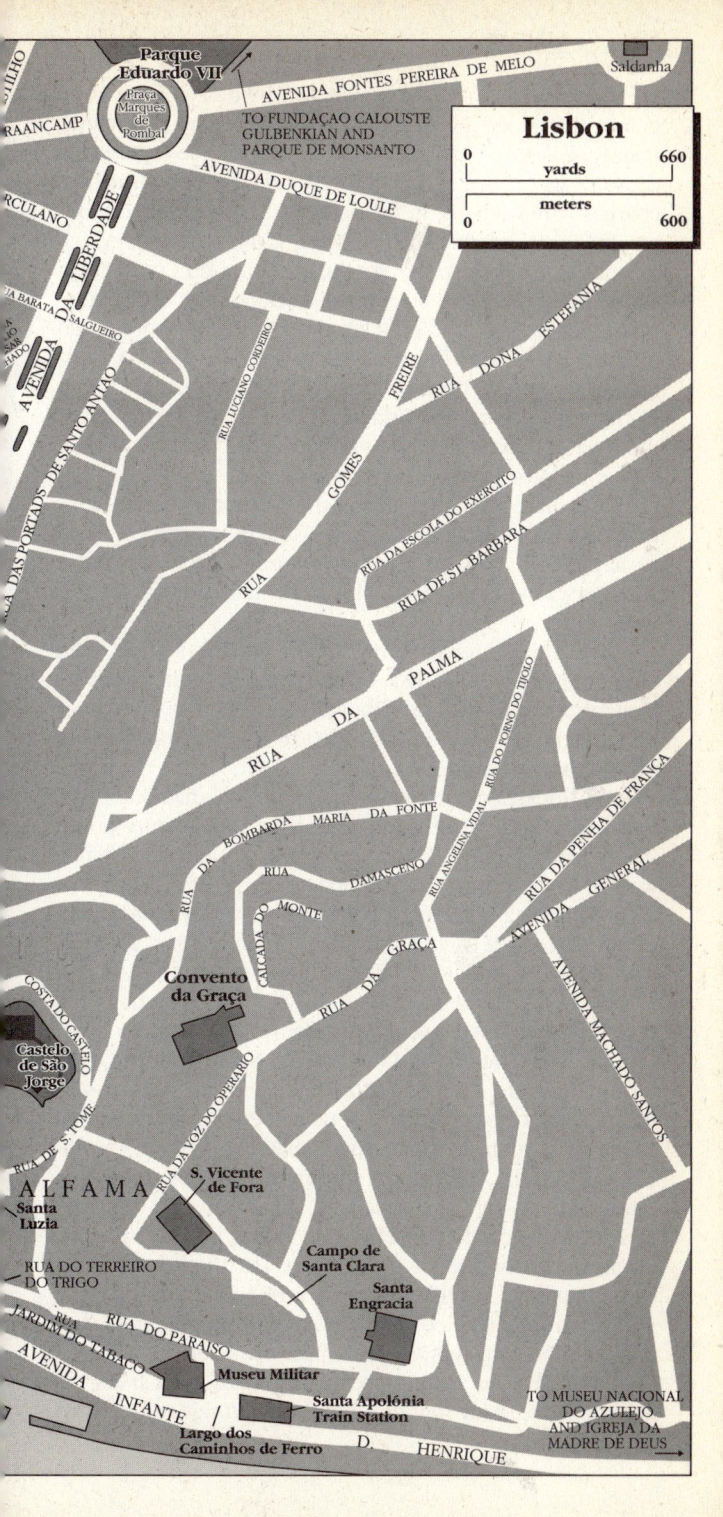

Terreiro do Paço (Palace Square) in memory of the royal palace that stood here until destroyed by the 1755 earthquake, it is also frequently called Black Horse Square because of its bronze statue of José I astride a fine Lusitanian charger (the horse is, in fact, green). The southern anchor for the area known as the **Baixa** (Lower Town), which extends northward to the Rossio, the praça do Comércio is surrounded on three sides by tall arcades supporting Neoclassical buildings with pink façades; on the fourth it is open to the Tagus, which here broadens into the Mar da Palha (Sea of Straw), the tidal wetlands of the river's estuary. South of the square, near the Estação Fluvial where ferries cross the river and excursion boats are docked, a marble staircase descends into the water between graceful columns, relics of the lost palace. Much praised in the past for its harmonious proportions and spaciousness, the square is presently used as a parking area by government employees and Baixa shoppers, but plans are afoot for its revitalization as a pedestrian center.

From the northeast corner of the square, a short walk along the rua da Alfândega brings you first to the **Igreja da Conceição Velha** with its elaborately carved Manueline door dating from about 1520, and then to the remarkable **Casa dos Bicos**, its façade completely covered with diamond-shaped stones, once thought to contain real diamonds. Partially destroyed by the earthquake, this 16th-century house that once belonged to the important Albuquerque family was recently restored according to early engravings that showed in detail the upper balustraded windows and balconies. Currently it is used for offices of the national commission for the celebration of the Portuguese discoveries.

West of the praça do Comércio, take a stroll through the recently landscaped riverside garden to the Estação do Sul (South Ferry Station) and the Cais do Sodré (Sodré Quay) terminal where commuter trains depart for Estoril and Cascais. Just beyond is the chaotic and colorful **Mercado da Ribeira**, a farmers' and fishermen's market open every morning but Sunday. If you get there by 7:00 A.M. you'll see mountains of cabbages, bananas, peaches, and tomatoes arriving by truck, donkey cart, or in wicker baskets balanced on the heads of girls or old women. The market, enclosed today in a huge barnlike building, is not as picturesque as it was when gaily painted fishing boats unloaded their catches and *varinas* (fishwives) scaled slippery hake on the wharves, but it's still a fascinating scene when observed from the gallery above, with vendors shouting out their wares while buyers from the best hotels and restaurants in Lisbon scurry about securing the freshest sole and the most aromatic herbs. What's left over will be peddled door to door in the streets of the Alfama and the Bairro Alto.

From the market it's a half hour's walk west to the **Museu Nacional de Arte Antiga** (National Museum of Ancient Art), partly housed in a 17th-century palace at rua das Janelas Verdes, 95, where Pombal once lived. It's wiser to go there by taxi—and perhaps to save this important museum for a rainy day when you won't be tempted to rush through its impressive collections. The emphasis here is on Portuguese artists of the 15th and 16th centuries; most of the works are religious in theme, although other periods and other painters are included, among them Raphael, Dürer, and Rodin. The Age of the Discoveries is richly represented by Portuguese-African ivory statues and Portuguese-Indian furniture and embroidery. There's also a small but fascinating display of Japanese Namban screens portraying the arrival of the Portuguese at Nagasaki in 1571. The Japanese, who had never seen Portuguese before and referred to them as *namban-jin* (barbarians from the south), were apparently so amazed by their clothing, features, and accoutrements that they hastened to capture these curiosities in their paintings. As a result, we have a strikingly detailed record of an important historical moment.

Among the museum's many treasures are Hieronymus Bosch's *Temptation of Saint Anthony,* Cranach the Elder's *Salome,* a possible portrait of Vasco da Gama by an anonymous artist, and another quite charming anonymous painting of Saint Anthony preaching to the fishes. Finally, there's Nuno Gonçalves's masterpiece, *The Adoration of Saint Vincent,* a polyptych showing the saint surrounded by many recognizable historical figures, among them the duke of Bragança and his family, Prince Henry the Navigator with a moustache, and the artist himself.

The Rossio

Heading north from the praça do Comércio by way of the rua Augusta, you will find yourself in the heart of the Baixa, a bustling commercial area of shoe stores, perfume shops, jewelers, watchmakers, specialty boutiques, food and wine shops, and souvenir stands. According to Pombal's plan, these streets were named for the various crafts in the area—thus rua do Ouro was the goldsmiths' street, rua dos Sapateiros was where cobblers worked, and so on. While these nice distinctions have blurred with time, quite a few businesses still operate in streets that bear the name of their craft. Some of the cross streets are pedestrian malls, as is rua Augusta; some have benches or clusters of tables shaded by parasols where shoppers may enjoy a *bica* (espresso) or *agua mineral* (bottled water, available with or without carbonation, or "gas," as the Portuguese say in English) while watching the crowds, the street vendors, and occasional strolling musicians. All this activity intensifies as rua Augusta merges with the Rossio (officially the praça de Dom Pedro IV).

The hub of city life since the 13th century, the Rossio is a large oval space punctuated by two Baroque fountains and a statue of Dom Pedro, and surrounded in three directions by Neoclassical buildings, their ground floors devoted to cafés and shops. The entire north side is taken up by the restored **Teatro Nacional Dona Maria II** (National Theater), built in the 1840s on the site of the former Palace of the Inquisition. In the 16th century it was in the Rossio that suspected heretics were condemned, tortured, and sometimes burned at the stake. More pleasant public events were also held here: bullfights, banquets, parades, and carnivals. Today the Rossio is very noisy and crowded, and it seems perpetually spinning with yellow buses, green-topped taxis, white rock doves, and surging people. In the center of this kaleidoscope are flower stalls massed with chrysanthemums and roses, street vendors peddling postcards and lottery tickets, newspaper kiosks, taxi queues, and a few weary backpackers grouped around the fountains. On the outer edges, shoppers stand and wait for sidewalk tables at the briskly busy **Pastelaria Suíça** and **Café Nicola**.

Just northwest of the Rossio lies the **praça dos Restauradores**, named for the "restorers" who, in 1640, revolted against Spanish rule and placed a Portuguese king on the throne. On the south side of this square is Estação do Rossio (Rossio Station), a fantastic mock-Moorish/Manueline edifice with horseshoe-shaped doorways, regarded by Lisboetes with mixed embarrassment and pride. On the west, in the 18th-century Palácio Foz, is Lisbon's main Turismo (Tourist Office).

The praça dos Restauradores opens into the capital's prime boulevard, the **avenida da Liberdade**. Both the square and the initial section of the avenue were built as a promenade in the 18th century, when the Rossio had become crowded with beggars and Gypsies. To keep out undesirables the promenade was enclosed by walls and a gate, within which fine ladies, perfumed, coiffed, and dressed in silks, strolled the tree-lined paths among the rosebushes, statues, and fountains. After the Liberals came to power in 1821 the walls were torn down and the promenade became a public space, gaslit for dances and other festivities. In 1879 it was lengthened into a double avenue, lined with palms, and planted with a continuous stretch of water gardens. Because of its inherent elegance the street is often compared to the Champs-Elysées. Although in recent years sleek office buildings have replaced some of the handsome town houses that once lined the Liberdade, it is still an avenue on a grand scale, shaded by stately trees, dotted with outdoor cafés, and passing such hotels as the Pullman, the Tivoli, and the Fénix. Walking along it is a pleasure, if only to see the street mosaics of loops, dolphins, arabesques, and other motifs, among the best in Lisbon. British writer Brigid Brophy describes their "abstract curlicues of high fantasy, as though some very dotty but very grand duchess had dipped her train in ink and gone swishing down the hill."

THE ALFAMA

The Alfama, overlooking the Baixa from a hilltop east of the town center, is the poorest but also the most picturesque neighborhood in Lisbon. Although it has a Moorish name (which translates roughly as "warm springs" and refers to the waters once found near the largo das Alcaçarias) and certainly a Moorish atmosphere, the quarter itself probably predates the Romans. Under the Moors and through the medieval period the Alfama was the city's most desirable district, full of fine homes, palaces, and churches. Though built on solid rock and not as much damaged by the earthquake as other parts of the city, the Alfama gradually deteriorated as fashionable people moved westward, and was eventually abandoned to fishermen and the poor. Today the Alfama is a jumble of stone and stucco houses crowded into narrow cobbled lanes that twist, cross, climb steeply, turn into staircases, or end in blank walls. Finding your way through this labyrinth is not easy even with a good map in hand; you'll enjoy it more if you resolve in advance not to mind being a little lost.

Because the Alfama's hillsides are so steep, it's wise to take a taxi up to the Castelo de São Jorge and then, after exploring the castle, wend your way slowly down through the old quarter. It's also a good idea to take this walk unencumbered

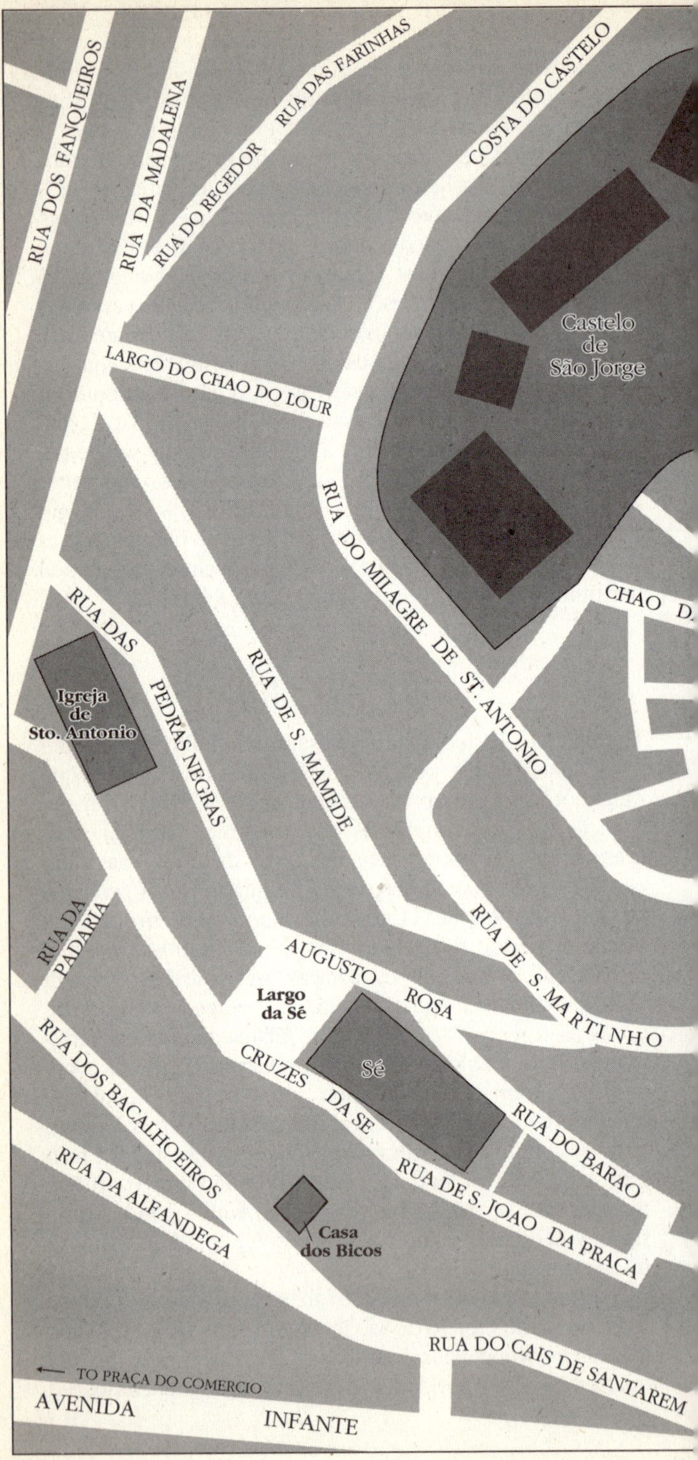
RUA DOS FANQUEIROS
RUA DA MADALENA
RUA DO REGEDOR
RUA DAS FARINHAS
COSTA DO CASTELO
Castelo de São Jorge
LARGO DO CHAO DO LOUR
RUA DO MILAGRE DE ST. ANTONIO
CHAO D
RUA DAS PEDRAS NEGRAS
Igreja de Sto. Antonio
RUA DE S. MAMEDE
RUA DA PADARIA
RUA DE S. MARTINHO
AUGUSTO ROSA
Largo da Sé
Sé
CRUZES DA SE
RUA DO BARAO
RUA DOS BACALHOEIROS
RUA DE S. JOAO DA PRACA
RUA DA ALFANDEGA
Casa dos Bicos
RUA DO CAIS DE SANTAREM
TO PRAÇA DO COMERCIO
AVENIDA INFANTE

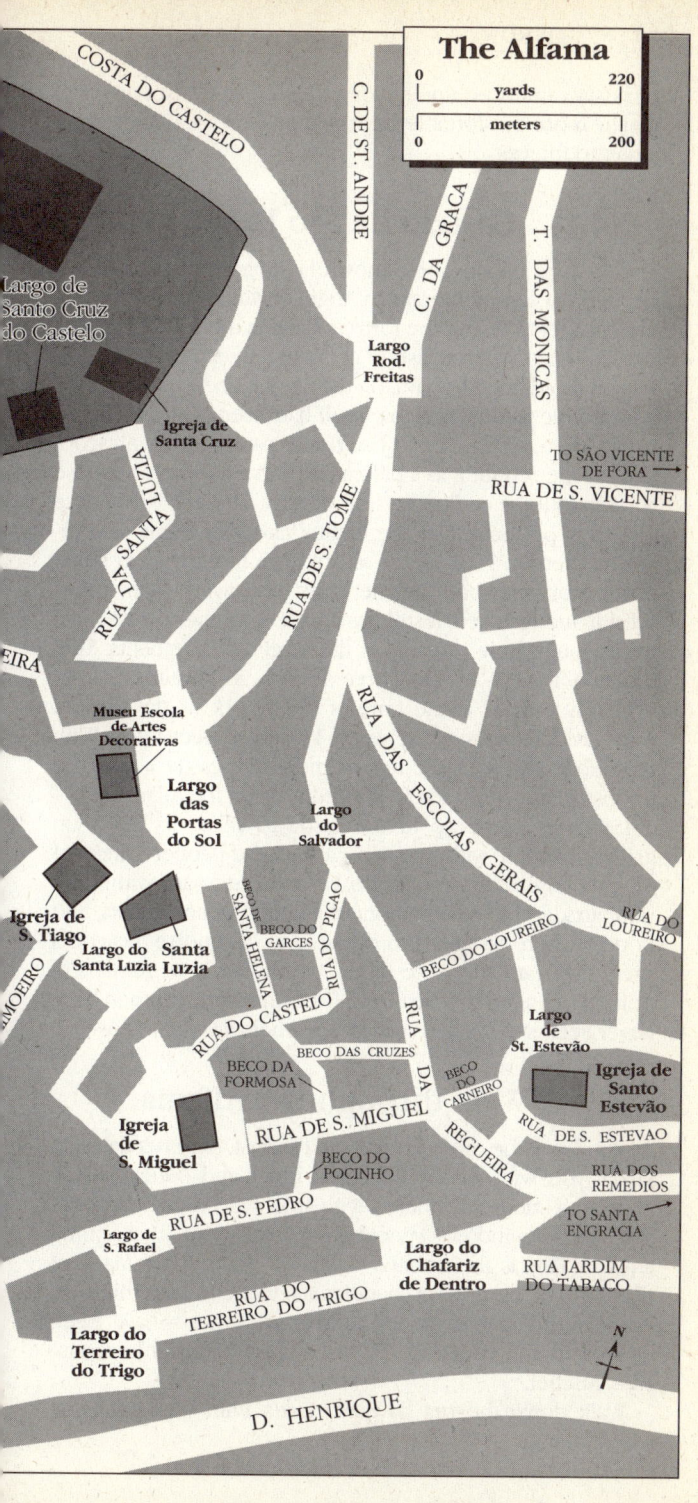

by heavy camera equipment or a weighty wallet. Not only will you be more comfortable, but you'll present a less interesting target to thieves.

Castelo de São Jorge

The *castelo,* Lisbon's best-known landmark, was named "St. George" to commemorate an Anglo-Portuguese alliance dating back to 1371, but the fortress itself is much older. When the Moors conquered Lisbon in the eighth century they built a stronghold, the Alcaçova, on the city's highest hill on top of a Visigothic fortification that itself had been built on Roman ruins. Then, when Afonso Henriques captured the Alcaçova in 1147, he rebuilt it as a palace that was used by Portuguese royalty until the end of the 16th century. The first Portuguese play was performed at the castle; Vasco da Gama was received there in 1503 on his return from India; the city's first observatory was built in one of its ten towers. Many times rebuilt and restored, it still has a look of medieval authenticity, although little remains of the original battlements. Still, the two towers of the Porta de Traição (Traitor's Gate) probably existed at the time of the Moors, as did the old walls, which measure between 15 and 30 feet thick. With their sheer drop of 100 feet or more, the castle walls offer unobstructed views across the red roofs of the Alfama.

Lisboetes come up to the castle to relax, to lunch on grilled prawns with *piri-piri* (a hot red-pepper sauce of African origin) at the **Casa do Leão**, a restaurant within the ramparts, and to stroll among the cool gardens, moats, and ponds where swans and white and turquoise peacocks preen beneath the olive trees. A Lisboete once remarked, pointing to a flurry of feathers, "The children of Lisbon have never seen snow. These peacock feathers are their snow."

A Walk through the Alfama

As you leave the castle grounds to the east, onto rua da Santa Luzia, you will see, between the inner and outer walls, a cluster of medieval houses with iron balconies and doors with judas windows (peepholes), set about a charming square. This is the artisans' village of Santa Cruz. Many of the houses here have handicrafts to sell, and three—a blacksmith's, a barbershop, and a wineshop—have been converted and combined to make a delightful little restaurant, **Michel**.

Walk down the rua da Santa Luzia until you reach the

largo das Portas do Sol, so called because it was once the city gate facing east. On this square are **Cêrca Moura**, an inviting terrace restaurant serving light lunches and drinks overlooking the Alfama, and the **Museu Escola de Artes Decorativas**, housed in a 17th-century palace. The museum-school is part of the Ricardo Espírito Santo Silva Foundation, which seeks to preserve Portugal's tradition of fine craftsmanship by training young men and women in woodcarving, bookbinding, repairing antique carpets, and applying gold leaf. More than 20 workshops are in daily operation here; they may be visited with special permission from the secretariat next door (Tel: 01-886-2183; closed Sundays, Mondays, and holidays). You may tour the house itself without prior arrangement, accompanied by a guide (speaking Portuguese and French only). The large and handsome rooms, overlooking an inner courtyard, are filled with beautiful Portuguese furniture, silver, and gros-point tapestries collected from the provinces and the former colonies. Particularly impressive is a marquetry gaming table of jacaranda and walnut. The late founder of the museum lived here with his family for many years, and the children's rooms are especially appealing.

Before heading down into the Alfama, take time to pause at the *miradouro* of the **Igreja da Santa Luzia**, just around the corner and down the hill from the museum. Santa Luzia is a small neighborhood church with a pretty garden and an arbored promenade, shaded with bougainvillaea and grapevines, built on the remains of the old Visigothic walls. The church's exterior is covered with *azulejos,* one panel depicting Lisbon as it was before the earthquake and another illustrating the heroic death of Martim Moniz, who, in the battle of 1147, held open the castle gates so that Afonso Henriques and his Crusaders could enter. In the summer, neighborhood children splash in the big, shallow pool outside the church, while tourists lean on the tiled balustrade enjoying the view.

If you continued walking downhill from Santa Luzia (along the rua do Limoeiro) you would come to the *Sé* (Cathedral). To reach the Alfama you must return to the largo das Portas do Sol. Almost any random route you take from here will lead you through twisting streets and steep staircases opening into unexpected courtyards, past children and cats playing on almost every doorstep, and women doing their wash at outdoor fountains. You will see houses whose front walls are entirely covered with blue-and-white *azulejos,* some with designs so delicate that the effect is like wallpaper. Often the limestone trim of the doorways and windows is further ornamented with borders of narrow tiles decorated with stars. The craftsmanship that has gone into these marvelous façades is endlessly rewarding to the eye. Windows, often at eye level, are sometimes provided with shutters painted in subtle contrast to the color of the wall tiles.

Even though the most haphazard route through the Alfama is interesting, you might want to seek out a few of the quarter's special houses. If so, leave the largo das Portas do Sol via the ramp just across the square from the museum. The ramp shortly turns into the beco (alley) de Santa Helena stairway; halfway down these steps turn left on the beco do Garcês and then, 150 feet or so later, left again on the rua do Picão. This route brings you to the largo do Salvador. At number 22 stands the superb 16th-century mansion of the counts of Arcos, with a splendid Baroque balcony. Leave the largo do Salvador by the rua da Regueira, a street lined with small shops and restaurants, and in about 300 feet you will come to the steps of the beco das Cruzes, on your right. At the corner is an 18th-century house whose upper floors are supported by carved ravens, those birds so important in the legends of Lisbon (see the description of the Sé, below).

Farther along the beco das Cruzes you will pass on your left a doorway with a fine panel of *azulejos* showing the Virgin of the Conception. At the top of the beco das Cruzes, where you pass beneath an arch surmounted by a cross, turn left down the beco da Formosa. In 150 feet you will come to the rua de São Miguel and, if you again turn left, after another 150 feet you will see ahead of you the steps of the beco do Carneiro (Sheep's Alley), so narrow that the houses on either side almost meet above your head; in order for someone to pass you must duck into a doorstep. At the top of the steps is another breathtaking vista of tiled rooftops. Continue to wander down any of the streets, and when you reach the foot of the hill you will be able to hail a taxi to get to your next destination.

Every June, during the Festas dos Santos Populares (Festivals of Popular Saints), the Alfama explodes with revelry. Celebrations begin, as they have for centuries, on June 12, the eve of Saint Anthony's feast. (Born in the Alfama, Saint Anthony is considered its patron saint.) First there's a huge costumed parade, sweeping exuberantly down the avenida da Liberdade to the praça dos Restauradores. Then, around midnight, everyone heads for the Alfama to dance, drink, and sing or listen to *fado,* that strange, emotional, and fatalistic folk music so characteristic of Lisbon. The festivities continue every night till dawn and then begin again, almost without interruption until the feast of Saint Peter on June 29. During this time the streets of the Alfama are brightly festooned with streamers and paper lanterns, and every corner, patio, and little square is turned into a makeshift café with music and dancing. The air is filled with the smell of roasting sardines, and everywhere women sell pots of fresh basil, believed to bring luck in love.

Lisbon's Great Churches

If you end your walk on the Alfama's main market street, the rua de São Pedro, as you are likely to do, you will soon arrive at the largo de São Rafael, a small square surrounded by 17th-century houses and the remains of a Moorish tower. From here it's only a short walk along the rua de São João da Praça and the rua do Barão to Lisbon's Romanesque cathedral, the **Sé**. Built in the late 12th century, it was damaged in the earthquake and has been extensively remodeled. Its two low towers are softened by a large rose window, and in the transept Gothic arches have been imposed over Romanesque. The ambulatory dates back to the 14th century, and in the chapels opening off it are some interesting tombs. Lopo Fernandes Pacheco, a companion at arms to Afonso IV, lies with his bright-eyed little dog at his feet, while nearby his wife reads forever from her prayerbook. In the sacristy is a small museum of religious treasures, including a casket containing the relics of São Vicente, patron saint of Lisbon. Legend has it that after this saint was martyred his body was protected by ravens, and that two ravens escorted the boat in which Afonso Henriques had his remains brought to Lisbon in 1172. Until its regrettable demise, an ancient bird thought to be descended from those very ravens lived in the cathedral's ruined cloisters, from which it occasionally emerged to be photographed by tourists.

Tucked behind the cathedral is the little **Igreja de Santo António da Sé**, built on top of the room where the saint, usually associated with Padua in Italy, is believed to have been born. The city's most popular saint, he is venerated here not for his knack of finding lost articles, as in other Catholic countries, but for his matchmaking skills.

From the cathedral it's a confusing route and a steep climb but only a five-minute taxi ride to two more important churches, São Vicente de Fora (St. Vincent Outside) and Santa Engrácia. **São Vicente de Fora**, which derives its name from its position outside the city walls, was designed by the

Italian architect Filippo Terzi and built between 1582 and 1627 on the site of an earlier monastery. With its white limestone exterior and twin towers the church is imposing enough, but most visitors come here to see the cloisters, covered with 18th-century *azulejos* illustrating the *Fables* of La Fontaine. Just off the cloisters, the former monks' refectory serves as a mausoleum for Portuguese kings and queens, princes and princesses from João IV to King Manuel II, who abdicated in 1910.

Across the campo de Santa Clara (just to the east of São Vicente) is **Santa Engrácia**, Portugal's great Baroque church, which is also its national pantheon. It is actually the third church on the site, and took so long to complete—almost 300 years—that a popular saying grew up around it: Anything that takes a long time to do is called *uma obra de Santa Engrácia* (a work of Santa Engrácia). The limestone used to build Santa Engrácia is so white it looks like marble, and the church's four façades trace the architectural development of the Baroque style. The interior, covered in multicolored slabs of polished marble set in contrasting patterns, is shaped like a Greek cross and topped by a giant dome with semicircular vaults above deep alcoves. All around the walls are cenotaphs of Portugal's great historical figures: Prince Henry the Navigator, Vasco da Gama, Camões, and others. You can take an elevator to the upper gallery of the church and to the roof to see all of Lisbon spread out below.

In the campo de Santa Clara between the two churches, the **Feira da Ladra** (Thieves' Market) takes place every Tuesday and Saturday. You probably won't find a great bargain here, but it's fun to look—at everything from antique brass coach lamps and sheep bells from Serra da Estrela to videocassettes and flashlight batteries.

A short taxi ride east from Santa Engrácia, just off avenida Infante Dom Henrique on rua Madre de Deus, is the **Igreja da Madre de Deus**, one of Lisbon's real treasures, and the adjoining **Museu Nacional do Azulejo** (National Tile Museum). Anyone who has admired the decorative tiles used so flamboyantly throughout Lisbon and indeed throughout Portugal—on churches, schools, houses, terraces, garden walls, even train stations—will thoroughly enjoy this museum and especially its wonderful location. The church was built in 1509 by Queen Leonor to house the relics of Santa Auta, a Portuguese saint who was one of the so-called 11,000 Virgins of Cologne slaughtered by Huns as they were returning from a pilgrimage to Rome. A Manueline doorway, its twisted columns embellished with carved pelicans and fishnets, leads into the church, suggesting the opulence that awaits. Inside, walls are lined halfway up with blue-and-white *azulejos,* the upper walls and ceiling are adorned with ornately framed paintings, and surfaces throughout are rich in carved and gilded woodwork. At the center of the choir is a splendid lectern surmounted by a lamb, head held erect, bearing a waving pennant. The effect is literally staggering.

The adjoining cloisters house the museum. When the Portuguese captured Ceuta in Morocco from the Moors in 1415, they apparently saw and appreciated the beauty of Moorish tiles and, when they returned to Portugal, brought with them the art of making them. While the earliest dated Portuguese tiles, those at the Quinta de Bacalhôa on the Arrábida peninsula across the Tagus (see Day Trips from Lisbon), go back only to 1565, by the 17th century they were all the rage, in such demand that they were even being imported from Holland. Blue-and-white Delft tiles were considered more desirable than the earthier local ones.

In the museum you can see a dazzling display of four centuries of Portuguese tile making, including excellent examples of huge floor, or "carpet," tiles. Among the museum's finest exhibits are two tiny tiles depicting King Charles II of England and his Portuguese queen, Catherine of Bragança; and an enormous wall of blue-and-white tiles that runs the entire length of the gallery on one side of the large cloister. Here is a panoramic view of pre-earthquake Lisbon, with the royal palace, the pointed towers of the cathedral, and many other early landmarks. The museum also has an interesting selection of Art Deco tiles, tiles by modern Portuguese painters (including Maria Keil, Manuel Cargaleiro, and Jorge Barradas), a charming restaurant, and a shop where you can buy books about *azulejos.*

To visit two more of Lisbon's great churches, Igreja de São Roque and Basílica da Estrela, you must cross to the western side of the city, as we do now.

WEST OF THE BAIXA
The Chiado

The Chiado, to the west and uphill from the Baixa, is Lisbon's most fashionable shopping area; it forms a natural link between the shopping streets of the lower town and the Bairro Alto (see Shopping, below). The unlikely sobriquet Chiado, which means "squeaking sound," refers to the 16th-century poet, António Ribeiro, who was known to his friends as "O Chiado" and whose statue stands in the neighborhood's main square.

The main shopping street, rua Garrett, is named for another poet, the Visconde de Almeida Garrett, and is lined with outdoor cafés and shops. **A Brasileira**, one of the oldest coffeehouses in Lisbon and still a gathering spot for artists and writers, has an amusing life-size statue of one of its former patrons, poet Fernando Pessoa, seated at one of the sidewalk tables. And just next door is **Benard's**, the smartest place in the area for tea and pastry. Try the *duchesses,* refined whipped-cream cakes. **Bertrand's** is a long-established bookstore here much frequented by English-speaking visitors. There are also shops where you can buy Vista Alegre china, embroideries from Madeira, or a tailor-made suit, or get a shoeshine. Some of Lisbon's best-known restaurants—Tavares, Tagide, and Aviz—are in the area.

A terrible fire swept through the lower Chiado in 1988, gutting four blocks and destroying a number of large stores. Rebuilding is now under way, but shops have been forced to relocate, and it will be some time before the district fully recovers. Meanwhile, covered walkways have been built through the ruins, enabling people to stroll by and see the disaster area close up. Macabre though it sounds, the walkways make a convenient shortcut and are usually crowded and cheerful, and street musicians and beggars find the location a profitable one.

Just south of rua Garrett is the Museu Nacional de Arte Contemporânea, closed for renovation, and a little farther downhill (on rua Serpa Pinto) is the city's opera house, **Teatro de São Carlos**. This handsome building, built in 1792, was modeled after the Teatro San Carlo in Naples and also suggests, in its imposing façade, Milan's La Scala. Here, according to tradition, Lord Byron was struck by an outraged husband for making advances toward his wife.

If you continue walking west along rua Garrett, you come first to the largo do Chiado and then to the **praça Luís de Camões**, where a statue of the poet stands on a tall pedestal in a pretty garden, surrounded by lesser literary figures. **Igreja do Loreto**, north of the square, has an impressive 17th-century doorway, and **Igreja de Encarnação**, on the south, has an exterior wall decorated with *azulejos*. A third church, farther downhill on the calçado do Combro, is **Igreja de Santa Catarina**, worth seeing for its decorative Italian sculpture and woodcarving, and its Baroque organ.

An easy way to visit these and other sites in the Chiado is

to join a guided walking tour sponsored by the Centro Nacional de Cultura and held weekday mornings during June, July, and August. Participants meet at 9:30 A.M. at largo do Picadeiro, 10 (south of the Teatro de São Carlos), for a three-hour stroll that includes historic and cultural sites, a refreshment stop, and commentary in English (Mondays, Wednesdays, and Fridays) or French (Tuesdays and Thursdays). For reservations and information about other cultural activities, Tel: (01) 347-8654.

The Bairro Alto

The Bairro Alto (Upper Town), northwest of the Chiado, overlooks central Lisbon from the west just as the Alfama overlooks it from the east. Not greatly damaged by the earthquake of 1755, it is one of the older parts of the city. Many of its houses open onto broad steps with stone risers and smooth terrazzo treads, shaded by fruit trees carefully placed down the center, one at each landing, and by overhanging grapevines or morning glories. The 17th-century houses and urban palaces that once stood here have deteriorated or disappeared, but here and there doorway and window decorations remind you of their more elegant past. Everywhere there are cats, just as in Princess Maria Leticia Rattazzi's day, when this great-niece of Napoleon remarked, "The cat is an indispensable adjunct in Portuguese homes."

During the day the Bairro Alto is primarily a commercial neighborhood, teeming with the bustle of small businesses, the hum of newspaper presses, and the clatter of kitchen work in the area's restaurants. But Lisboetes know the Bairro Alto for its *tascas,* mom-and-pop restaurants, usually no larger than one room, with the kitchen tucked somewhere behind a counter in the back and a smoking brazier set on the sidewalk outside the front door. While a grandmother tends the grill, the men and children of the family wait on tables, and the younger women work in the kitchen. Around lunchtime it is always easy to tell which are the best of these *tascas:* Inside they are jammed with regular customers, while outside eager customers line up to get in (see Dining, below). By evening, the *tascas* are closed, but other doorways light up as the Bairro Alto shifts gears to become the center of Lisbon's nightlife.

Most streets leading up to the Bairro Alto are dauntingly steep, like those of the Alfama, but there are three novel approaches to the district that every visitor should try. Two are funicular-like trams. One of these, the **Elevador da**

Gloria, departs from just behind the Turismo in praça dos Restauradores and deposits you at the São Pedro da Alcântara *miradouro;* the other, **Elevador da Bica,** climbs from the rua da Boa Vista (a few blocks northwest of the Cais do Sodré) to calçada do Combro, a few blocks west of the praça Luís de Camões.

The third and most popular method of ascent is from rua de Santa Justa in the Baixa aboard the **Santa Justa Elevador,** one of the world's great cast-iron whimsies. Often mistakenly assumed to be the work of Gustave Eiffel, it was in fact built by the Portuguese engineer Raoul Mesnier de Ponsard and inaugurated in 1901. The city is built here on a virtual precipice; the rear entrances of some buildings are a full seven stories above their front doors.

The elevator lifts you a hundred feet and delivers you to a little bridge. You walk through a succession of open galleries, their slender iron shafts and arches displaying a heady mixture of Gothic and Moorish styles, to an observation plaza from which you get a thrilling bird's-eye view of Chiado and Baixa rooftops. A narrow iron bridge leads from the top almost to the front door of the ruins of the 14th-century **Igreja do Carmo** (Carmelite Church), once a vast church with three richly decorated naves. The vaulting fell in the 1755 earthquake, and now only the façades and roofless Gothic arches remain, open to the sky. The ruins are floodlit at night and serve as a dramatic reminder of how much Lisbon lost in that awful event. Within the ruins is a small archaeological museum with ill-assorted but individually interesting pieces, such as Visigothic columns carved with gryphons, an Etruscan skull, and the fourth-century tomb of an unknown Roman poet.

Leaving Carmo, walk two blocks west on the rua Trindade, then turn north on the rua nova da Trindade. You will soon come to the **Cervejaria da Trindade**, an enormous beerhall-and-restaurant that is always crowded. Inside are *azulejo-*covered walls and good food; it's said that this vast hall was once the dining room of the Convento da Trindade, the first headquarters of the Inquisitor General.

Just ahead, at the end of the largo de Trindade Coelho, is the **Igreja de São Roque** (Church of Saint Rocco or Saint Rock). Rather plain on the outside, this 16th-century church is magnificent within, from the high altar with ornamented panels and double Corinthian columns to the *trompe l'oeil* ceiling of flat wood painted to look vaulted and depicting the Apocalypse. Most remarkable, though, are the richly decorated side chapels, successively and dramatically revealed as the sacristan illuminates them one by one. The most striking is the 1750 **Capela de São João Baptista** (Chapel of Saint John the Baptist), originally commissioned and constructed in Rome. After being set up for mass and blessed by the pope, it was dismantled and transported to Lisbon in three ships. Said to be the most costly structure of its kind ever built, it is composed of white Carrara marble, porphyry, amethyst, ivory, lapis lazuli, alabaster, gold, and silver. What appears to be an oil painting of the Baptism is actually a fine mosaic by Mattia Moretti.

From here it is only a short distance along São Pedro de Alcântara to the **Solar do Vinho do Porto**, the perfect place to take a break. Operated by Portugal's official Port Wine Institute as a pleasant spot where visitors may acquaint themselves with the country's most famous wine, the Solar offers comfortable, oversized leather chairs and sofas, in a room with a massive fireplace, vaulted ceilings, and polished terracotta tile floors—for all the world like a foreign version of an English men's club. Here, choosing from a menu that lists a staggering array of white, tawny, ruby, and rare vintage Ports, you can sample a glass or two and begin to appreciate this wine's complexities and delights.

The easiest way to get back down to the center of town from the Solar is via the Elevador da Gloria cable car. You can catch it just across the street and within minutes be whizzed down an alarmingly steep hill to the praça dos Restauradores. If you'd rather continue exploring the Bairro Alto, take a taxi or bus or walk up the rua Dom Pedro V, which becomes the rua da Escola Politécnica, to the **Jardim Botânico** (Botanical Garden). On foot it's a strenuous 15-minute climb, but the street is lined with fascinating antiques shops where you can window-shop while catching your breath.

The Jardim Botânico, opened to the public in 1873, has one of the finest collections of botanical specimens in southern Europe. You enter through a courtyard surrounded by the rather shabby buildings of the Faculdade de Ciências, then descend a flight of stone stairs into a cool, hilly, luxuriant garden of winding paths, boxwood mazes, lily ponds, and streams crossed by bridges and stepping stones. Set liberally about are benches where you can sit listening to the chaffinches and robins and looking at the stately or surprising trees—jacaranda, giant ficus, frangipani, araucaria, tipu, cork oak, eucalyptus, olive, and strange Australian and African species with grotesquely twisted trunks or enormous air roots. There are also tree-size camellias and floods of flowers, all neatly labeled. Along one side runs a grand avenue of magnificent palms, at least 50 different varieties. If you follow this path to its end you'll arrive at the park's second entrance, emerging on the rua da Alegria just a few blocks from the avenida da Liberdade and a few steps from the charming little hotel **Príncipe Real**. If you happen to be staying there, the garden offers a convenient downhill approach.

At the western edge of the Bairro Alto, at the foot of avenida Alvares Cabral, is another garden worth visiting, the **Jardim da Estrela** (Garden of the Star) adjoining the **Basílica da Estrela**. The basilica, with its imposing twin belfries and high dome, is one of Lisbon's most visible landmarks; from almost any *miradouro* looking west you can see it looming over the city. It was built in the late 18th century to fulfill a vow made by Maria I in the hope of bearing a male child. (She did have a son, Prince José, but he died at age 27, and the devout Maria later went mad.) The Baroque interior of the church is impressive in its use of pale multicolored marble, but what most visitors come to see is the delightful Nativity scene created by sculptor Machado de Castro. Contained in a gigantic glass case, the scene shows the Holy Family surrounded by terra-cotta figures of villagers going about their daily tasks of farming, cooking, drawing water, eating, gossiping, and playing games, all set against a green and hilly background.

The public gardens adjoining the church have lakes, statuary, terraces, pleasant walks, a children's playground, and a fanciful gazebo-like bandstand where concerts are often held on Sunday afternoons. Nearby are the Anglican church of St. George and the English cemetery where novelist Henry Fielding is buried.

From the Estrela quarter, follow the calçada da Estrela down several blocks until you reach the Palácio da Assembleia Nacional (parliament building). Originally constructed as a monastery in the 17th century, the Convento de São Bento da Saúde has housed the Portuguese congress since 1834 and is commonly called the **Palácio de São Bento**. The grandiose façade, with five arches and slender columns above, dates from the turn of the century. The chamber of deputies is a vast amphitheater, decorated with sculpture by Teixeira Lopes, and in the gallery are splendid murals by Columbano and other artists. Visitors wishing to attend one of the lively sessions should enter through the side door off rua de São Bento.

NORTH LISBON

At its northern end the avenida da Liberdade flows into the praça Marquês de Pombal, a dizzying rotunda into which cars funnel from seven directions. Secure on a lofty column high above the honking horns and carbon monoxide fumes, Pombal and his lion friend seem to survey the scene with supercilious detachment. In real life, the marquês was always in the thick of the action.

In addition to masterminding the rebuilding of Lisbon after the great earthquake and putting into action what was in effect the first large-scale urban construction program in preindustrial Europe, Pombal reformed the university, reorganized the army, and set up the Royal Bank. These extraordinary achievements were accomplished with such cruelty and vindictiveness that he was feared and hated throughout Portugal. He persecuted, imprisoned, and executed whoever opposed him, and even installed his brother as Grand Inquisitor so that he could use the Inquisition as a weapon against his enemies. When Pombal's protector, King José I, died in 1777, his successor, Maria I, stripped the marquês of all his powers and banished him to his estates in the Beira. It was a time of national rejoicing—hundreds of political prisoners were released and Pombal's effigy was burned in the streets of Lisbon.

The **Parque Eduardo VII**, named to commemorate that English king's visit to Lisbon in 1903, stretches nearly a mile uphill from the north of the praça Marquês de Pombal. Lisbon was the destination of Edward VII's first state visit abroad after his coronation, and he arrived in great pomp aboard the royal yacht *Victoria and Albert,* which anchored in the Tagus. Seven thousand Portuguese troops lined the shore as King Carlos I was rowed out in the royal barge to welcome the English monarch. An endless round of celebrations marked the royal visit, culminating in the official opening of the new park.

The park provides a welcome expanse of green and an opportunity for charming walks among formally clipped box-wood trees and quiet ponds. Two boulevards paved with black-and-white mosaics and connected by crosswalks run by the sloping lawns of the park to a lookout sided by large columns. Within the park are a sports pavilion, a terrace restaurant, and two horticultural wonders, the **Estufa Fria** (Cool House) and the **Estufa Quente** (Hothouse). The Estufa

Fria is a jungle of ferns and foliage entirely enclosed by bamboo slats designed to keep out the sun but let in the air. In this protected Eden flourish exotic flowers, plants, and trees from Australia, Africa, India, and China along with more familiar European species and recognizable houseplants grown to giant size. The flower beds are connected by winding paths; miniature bridges and stairways lead to an upper level. Everywhere there is flowing water—waterfalls, fountains, ponds, and streams. The air smells damp and rich, and the stillness is interrupted only by the sound of goldfish and carp breaking the surface of the water. The Estufa Fria leads to the Estufa Quente, a glassed-in garden supporting quite a different plant community. Here among orchids and fuchsias are lotus-filled pools where flamingos stalk, aviaries of finches and doves, and a separate section of fantastic and gigantic cacti.

After the extreme humidity of the Estufa Quente, it's refreshing to stop for a drink at the Ritz or the Méridien hotel, both on the park's western edge. Then get a taxi to the Fundação Calouste Gulbenkian (Gulbenkian Foundation), a wonderful museum northeast of the park at the juncture of the avenida de Berna and the praça de Espanha.

The Gulbenkian Foundation

It's easy to be overwhelmed by the Gulbenkian. This large and handsome museum complex, showplace of a foundation that influences and contributes actively to virtually every branch of Portuguese art, is set in its own park and has its own orchestra, choir, ballet company, concert halls, library, and two permanent art collections. In addition, it sponsors cultural events not only in Lisbon but throughout Portugal. Calouste Gulbenkian, the Armenian oil tycoon and art patron who created all this, came to Lisbon late in life. When he died in 1955, Portugal inherited one of the finest art collections in the world along with a generous endowment to support it. Eclectic and idiosyncratic, the collection ranges from a 2,700-year-old alabaster bowl from Egypt to Art Nouveau jewelry by René Lalique.

The museum is divided into two main sections, one for Eastern art and the other for Western. Explanatory notes in several languages are available for every subsection; you can ask for a complete set in advance. A cheerful café in the basement, lounge areas, and restorative views of the museum garden through windows in almost every gallery offer visitors partial protection against culture shock.

The first room you enter contains a small but choice collection of Egyptian art; look for the exquisitely detailed cats and the silver-gilt mummy mask. The Graeco-Roman exhibit is largely devoted to coins—Gulbenkian is said to have developed his passion for collecting as a child while bargaining for old coins in the markets of Constantinople. Next come Persian carpets, illuminated Armenian and Arabic manuscripts, Japanese screens and lacquer boxes, Chinese porcelain and carved jade. The extensive European wing contains furniture, porcelain, tapestries, and many impressive paintings, some of which Gulbenkian acquired from the Hermitage soon after the Russian Revolution. Among these is Rubens's full-length portrait of his sister-in-law, Hélène Fourment, in a black satin gown. Other knockouts are Rembrandt's helmeted *Pallas Athene,* a marble statue of Diana by Houdon, and a terra-cotta bust of Molière by Caffieri. Portraitists of the English School are well represented by Gainsborough, Romney, and Lawrence, and the Impressionists by Degas, Monet, Renoir, Cassatt, and others. Finally, there's a stunningly displayed collection of exciting jewelry and ornaments by Lalique, a personal friend of Gulbenkian, along with his less familiar book illustrations. Most memorable among these is Kaa from Kipling's *Jungle Book.*

On the south side of the landscaped gardens behind the Gulbenkian Museum is its **Centro de Arte Moderna**, with a large permanent collection documenting the development of modern art in Portugal, from such turn-of-the-century artists as Almada Negreiros and Amadeu de Sousa Cardoso to contemporary artists working in Portugal today. The Gulbenkian's garden, with romantic walks, a lake and ponds, and a fine collection of modern sculpture, is one of Lisbon's most popular parks.

Northeast of the Gulbenkian, past the end of the avenida de Berna and across the wide avenida da República, where so many new hotels and corporate headquarters are going up, is the **Campo Pequeno**, Lisbon's bullring. Portuguese bullfights differ sharply from Spanish (see the Ribatejo section); in Lisbon the season runs from Easter to mid-October. If you want to see a bullfight, your hotel concierge can arrange for tickets. Beyond the bullring, at the end of Campo Grande, is the **Museu da Cidade**, interesting chiefly for its many views of the city from different historical periods. There's an engraving of Catherine of Bragança departing from Terreiro do Paço (now praça do Comércio) to marry Charles II in 1662, several views of Lisbon before the 1755 earthquake, watercolor plans for the city's reconstruction afterward, and a number of fascinating city scenes showing landmarks both existing and long vanished.

About a mile and a half northwest of the Gulbenkian, on the estrada de Benfica at avenida das Forças Armadas, is the **Jardim Zoológico**, Lisbon's zoo. As might be expected in a city where people are both fond of gardens and kindly disposed toward animals, the zoo is a pleasure to visit, with wonderful flowery walkways, beds of roses and bright annuals, and attractive, spacious enclosures for the wildlife. For children there are elephant and pony rides, a miniature train and miniature village, rowboats, and puppet shows.

Still farther west, off the rua de São Domingos in Benfica (take bus number 46 or a taxi), is the **Palácio dos Marqueses de Fronteira**, a beautiful late-17th-century house set in terraces and formal Italian Renaissance gardens. The box hedges of the main garden are laid out in such a dense pattern that they appear to be a green carpet punctuated only by statuary and privet topiary. Beyond rise the red-and-white walls of the palace, its garden front a crazy quilt of panes, arches, and pilasters. At one side of the garden is a long water tank set against a backdrop of blue-and-white *azulejos* and a balustraded walk lined with marble busts in alcoves, large pyramids at each end.

The lower walls of the palace are covered with 17th-century tile panels depicting banquets, boats, houses, and, most particularly, cats—cats of all kinds, some staring quizzically at you as you pass, others offering you a fish. Perhaps the most memorable is a large panel showing a cat musicale—cat conductor, cat musicians—and, just next to this, a wonderful scene of a cat at the barber's, having a shave. And don't miss the grotto covered entirely in bits of Gaudí-esque broken china. (These are reminders of a visit by a king, long ago, who ordered that the china on which he had been served be broken so that no one else could ever eat from it.) Inside the palace is a huge library and more tile panels, these showing famous battles of Portuguese history in great detail. Fronteira is open only at the most unusual hours, so be sure to call before going; Tel: (01) 778-2023.

The Fronteira estate is folded into a corner of the extensive carpet of greenery that sprawls over the hills on the western side of Lisbon and that is called the **Parque Florestal de Monsanto**. This protected park, with its shady drives, riding trails, lookouts, old fort, and campsite, is a welcome respite from the frenzy of building that is taking place on the rest of Lisbon's periphery. Residents, however, fear the inroads into Monsanto being made by road builders who are busy cutting up the surrounding countryside.

If you have driven to Fronteira or are returning to town by cab, leave by the avenida 24 de Janeiro and then go left on the caminho das Pedreiras until you see, rising up in front of you, the other great sight in northern Lisbon, the **Aqueduto das Aguas Livres**. This huge water project, its 109 pointed arches spanning a distance of 11 miles, was built between 1729 and 1748. It survived the earthquake seven years later and is still in use, as impressive as ever.

BELEM

Two of Portugal's most extraordinary examples of Manueline architecture, the Torre de Belém and the Mosteiro dos Jerónimos, are located in Belém near the mouth of the Tagus river about 8 km (5 miles) west of downtown Lisbon. You'll need a full day, if possible, to see these and the many other museums and monuments clustered in this small settlement. The best way to get to Belém is by taxi (a 20-minute ride from the Rossio). A tram (number 13, 27, or 49) from the praça do Comércio takes about 45 minutes, depending on the time of day. Once there you can walk from place to place.

Almost every building, garden, cul-de-sac, and fountain in Belém has a history closely linked with the Portuguese Age of Discovery. It was from the harbor of Belém, where the Tagus meets the sea, that King João II and King Manuel I sent ships into the uncharted Atlantic on voyages that would turn Portugal into a major economic power and change the maps of the world. In 1487 Bartolomeu Dias sailed south from Lisbon, was blown off course by a storm, and realized when he at last sighted land that he had unknowingly rounded the tip of Africa, and so discovered a new sea route to India. In 1497 King Manuel sent Vasco da Gama with three ships to sail around the Cape of Good Hope to India, and on May 18, 1498, the expedition reached Calicut (now known as Kozhikode) on the southwestern coast of the Indian subcontinent.

These voyages were made possible by Portuguese development of the skills of ocean navigation and by the invention of the caravel, a three-masted vessel with a roundish hull, a high bow and stern, and lateen rigging. The heavier, square-rigged ships used at that time could sail only with the wind, but the sails of a caravel could be manipulated to catch the wind more flexibly. Because the prevailing winds along the west coast of Africa were from north to south, square-rigged ships could sail down the coast but couldn't return to Portugal, lending credence to the myth that the world was flat and that ships sailing too close to the edge would drop off. Only when Prince Henry the Navigator's designers at Sagres and Lagos perfected the caravel were the explorers able to sail against the wind and thus reach home. Their success enabled Portugal to take the lead among Western nations in exploring the African coast.

During this period Lisbon became Europe's richest capital and Manuel I its richest ruler. At the same time a distinctive form of architecture developed in Portugal, seeming to spring spontaneously from late Gothicism and expressing the heady excitement of the times. This style, called Manueline after the king, was characterized by dramatically twisted stone columns, a Moorish delicacy, and a profusion of decorative ornamentation using motifs that suggested the sea: waves, nets, tropical foliage, fruit, anchors, sea creatures, shells, and sextants.

The **Torre de Belém** (Tower of Belém), built between 1515 and 1520, has been a beacon to sailors for centuries and is perhaps Portugal's most distinctive landmark. Originally it stood well out in the water, but the Tagus has retreated and now just laps the tower's base. Though the tower is made of stone, its openwork balconies, ornamented loggia, and turrets topped with Moorish domes give it a wonderful lightness and elegance, like a storybook fortress. Along the battlements are stone crosses of the Order of Christ (formerly the Knights Templars), and on the terrace is a niche with a statue of the Virgin holding the Child and a bunch of grapes. On either side are columns and an armillary sphere, King Manuel's personal device. The interior of the tower is sparsely furnished, but you can look down into the dungeon and climb the spiral staircase to the top for a fine view of the Tagus and the sea beyond.

Several blocks east of the Belém tower, on the avenida Brasília, diagonally across from the praça do Império park is the **Museu de Arte Popular** (Museum of Folk Art), interesting because it displays the folk art of the provinces and gives a clear picture of the diversity of Portugal. The museum is arranged so that, when strolling through the rooms, you feel as if you are actually moving from province to province. Near the museum stands the **Padrão dos Descobrimentos** (Monument to the Discoveries), a modern (but not too inspiring) memorial depicting Prince Henry the Navigator poised at the prow of a caravel, with explorers, painters, and poets behind him. Within the monument is a multilevel museum with changing exhibits keyed to the discoveries (pottery from the Cape Verde islands, lace from Madeira); via elevator and stairs you may ascend to a long, narrow walkway atop the monument for a spectacular view of the Tagus.

The major piece of architecture in Belém is the **Mosteiro dos Jerónimos** (Monastery of Jerónimos), a white limestone structure embellished with richly sculpted Manueline decorations. The monastery was built in the early 16th century on the site of the little chapel where Vasco da Gama prayed before setting out into the Atlantic. Because the money to build it came from the profits of the spice trade, it was said to be "built of pepper." The first of its architects was Diogo Boytac, who worked in the Manueline style. After 1516 the work was carried on by the Biscayan stonemason João de Castilho, who completed the vaults and columns, the cloister, and the sacristy. He was succeeded by Portugal's greatest Renaissance architect, Diogo de Torralva, who worked on the chancel, the choir stalls, and the upper galleries. The final architect of the monastery was the classicist Jerónimo de Ruão (son of João de Ruão), who completed his work on the church in 1572.

Like the Belém tower, the Jerónimos monastery has an airy exuberance that transcends and transforms the stone of which it is made. You enter through a magnificent portal that is ornately decorated with many small statues and surmounted by a cross, and find yourself in a vast, silent space, under a vaulted ceiling that seems infinitely high and is supported by lofty, slender columns flaring out at the top like trees. The columns are intricately carved with spiraling foliage and faces, and the pulpits are similarly ornate. In the main chancel are the marble sarcophagi of Manuel I and João III and their queens, all borne by marble elephants, and on either side of the lower chancel are the marble effigies of Vasco da Gama and Camões, da Gama's cenotaph supported by lions and Camões's crowned with a laurel wreath. Especially beautiful are the monastery's cloisters, a double tier of columns with marvelous detail on every arch and each column differently ornamented with symbols of the sea.

The west wing of the Jerónimos monastery houses the **Museu Nacional de Arqueologia e Etnologia**, with an outstanding collection of ancient jewelry and some interesting prehistoric carvings, along with Iron Age and Bronze Age artifacts. The **Museu da Marinha**, adjacent, contains a wealth of nautical history—maps, paintings, charts, artifacts, and models tell the story of a great seafaring nation with a rich maritime history. Next door is Lisbon's planetarium. Most of the presentations at the **Planetário Calouste Gulbenkian** are organized for local school children. Public sessions on different aspects of astronomy, however, are given in English and French on Saturday and Sunday afternoons (Tel: 01-362-0002).

Just west of Jerónimos is an enormous new building that looks like a misplaced desert fortress but is in fact the controversial new **Centro Cultural de Belém**. Opened at the beginning of 1992, when Portugal assumed the presidency of the European Economic Community for six months, the convention and cultural center has been devoted largely to European and other international meetings. The small auditorium, which seats 400, has been designed for all kinds of theater, concerts, films, and lectures. Opera, ballet, and other grand spectacles are to be presented in the large auditorium, which seats 1,500 and is scheduled for completion by mid-1993. Work is also being completed on the exhibition hall, which includes a large zone of open space and galleries with natural light. The main criticism leveled against the new cultural center is that it was not necessary, particularly at a time of budgetary duress when the state cannot find the funds to restore many of its finest historical monuments.

The rua de Belém, leading from the monastery to the Palácio de Belém, is lined with little restaurants, many with outside terraces. Even if you don't have a sweet tooth, don't leave Belém without tasting the celebrated *pasteis de Belém,* crispy custard tarts sprinkled with sugar and cinnamon. The best place to get them is the popular café **Pastelaria de Belém**, a few paces from Jerónimos. Nearby, behind the Dionísios restaurant, there is a small cul-de-sac called **beco do Chão Salgado** (Alley of Salted Earth). A pillar here dated 1759 marks the spot of one of the cruelest executions in Portugal's history: The duke of Aveiro and other nobles, accused of attempting to assassinate King José I, were publicly hanged and then burned, as were their families and servants. The marquês de Pombal had their Belém palaces razed and the ground covered with salt to kill all vegetation.

The Palácio de Belém, now the official offices for the president of Portugal, was built in the 17th century and used as a summer palace by the kings of Portugal. If you're in the vicinity on the third Sunday of the month, don't miss the formal changing of the Guarda Nacional Republicana (GNR) at 10:00 A.M. The palace gardens are open to the public only on that day. The **Museu Nacional dos Coches** (Coach Museum) in the old riding school of the palace is one of the famous sights in Lisbon. Constructed in Louis XVI style, it has a painted ceiling that is handsomely decorated with allegorical paintings and a gallery from which the court would watch skilled riders put Lusitanian horses (see the Ribatejo chapter) through their paces. Founded by Queen Amelia in 1905 (her pink riding cloak, presented to the museum long after she had been exiled, is displayed near the entrance), the museum has what is probably the finest collection of coaches in Europe. The most magnificent, such as one made in Rome in 1716 for the Portuguese ambassador to the Vatican, are extremely ornate and carved with writhing Baroque figures. The most charming is a miniature carriage used by King Carlos I as a child.

At the left of the praça de Afonso de Albuquerque, which lies in front of the palace and museums, you can take a boat across the river to Porto Brandão, a small village where the **Mare Viva** restaurant specializes in fish and shellfish fondue and has a splendid view.

North of Belém, up the calçada da Ajuda—not far but a steep enough route to warrant a taxi—is the enormous **Palácio Nacional da Ajuda**. Begun in 1802 on the site of an earlier wooden palace that had burned, it was never completely finished. A significant part of it, though, is open to visitors. Though the lavishly decorated interior is ostentatious and often highly artificial (there is furniture made of Saxe porcelain), the state dining room and some of the sculpture, tapestries, and portraits are genuinely impressive.

GETTING AROUND

Lisbon is a walker's delight. Most sights you will want to see are concentrated in small areas, permitting you to stroll from one to another without expending too much time and energy. Occasionally you will need to use a bus, tram, or taxi to get from one neighborhood to another. A word of caution: When walking, or when travelling by public conveyances, carry a minimum of cash, camera equipment, and jewelry. Once considered among the safest of foreign capitals, Lisbon today is having to deal with incursions of street thieves and pickpockets. Even in the daytime, dark and narrow streets in the Alfama and in some parts of the Bairro Alto should be traversed with care.

The airport is close to the city, about 20 minutes by bus and half that by taxi, except during rush hours. A taxi from the airport to the city center costs around 1,500$00, without tip, but including a reasonable amount of baggage. If you are carrying more than 50 kilos (110 pounds) of luggage, you may be hit with a 50 percent surcharge.

Taxis. Green-topped taxis are plentiful and cheap; within the city they charge a metered rate, and outside the city limits a flat rate. You should tip about 10 percent. Drivers are courteous and skillful, although they sometimes seem to make a game of seeing exactly how narrow a space they can squeeze through. During rush hours taxis are scarce; if you can't flag one down, go to a taxi stand (the most central is in the Rossio), where you queue in a long but fast-moving line. You may also telephone for a radio cab or have someone call for you. A final taxi hint: A driver may not understand your pronunciation of the name of a given hotel, museum, or street; if this happens, rather than hurt your feelings by asking again, he may simply drive around at random, hoping for the best. Avoid this predicament by printing the name of your destination on a slip of paper or marking it on a map.

Buses and Trams. Lisbon has an extensive system of buses, trams, and cable cars. Bus stops are clearly marked (Paragem), and all display small route maps. You can buy tickets and get information from the orange-and-white Carris information booths scattered about the city; Carris (the city transport company, which operates buses, trams, and funiculars) has an excellent map, showing all routes, available at the Santa Justa Elevador and elsewhere. Tourist passes are available, as are packs of 20 prepaid tickets. Otherwise you pay a flat fee as you board. The brightly colored trams, covered with advertising, provide extremely efficient service. Many of them were made in England and predate World War I. Often the narrow streets they navigate are not much wider than they are, and from the open windows a passenger can almost touch the buildings. Bells ringing, people hugging the storefronts to get out of the way, goods almost within reach—a ride on a Lisbon tram is one of the city's chief charms, and a great way to window-shop. Don't worry about getting taken somewhere you can't get back from. Just get on the waiting tram at the end of the line and come back to wherever you started.

Subway. The Metro system has only two dozen stops and is easy to navigate. Stations are designated by large M signs. A tourist pass is valid on the Metro, or you can buy a book of tickets from a booth in one of the stations.

Car Rental. The major American rental companies have offices in Lisbon, and there are scores of local agencies. For a number of reasons, however, renting a car for getting around in Lisbon is not recommended. First, although on a map the layout of Lisbon looks simple, this is deceptive; the city's hilliness and its many levels make it difficult for newcomers to find their way. Second, traffic is extremely heavy—it's estimated that as many as 350,000 cars drive into the city each weekday from the suburbs, and during rush hours the congestion is fierce. Parking is virtually impossible, even at some of the big hotels. Finally, both drivers and pedestrians ignore traffic rules to a degree that seems downright suicidal. For day trips out of Lisbon a rental car is convenient, but within the city itself the excellent public transportation system is far preferable.

ACCOMMODATIONS

Hotel, residência, and *pensão* are the three general categories used to describe accommodations in Portuguese cities. (An *estalagem* is a privately owned country inn, and a *pousada* an inn run by the government, often in a converted monastery or castle.) The Portuguese Tourist Office gives hotels starred ratings; these are listed in an annual guide available at any Turismo. Rated hotels tend to be larger and offer such amenities as restaurants and room service. *Residênciais* (bed-and-breakfast type accommodations) and *pensões* (modest pensions, that may or may not serve breakfast), also rated on a star system, are smaller and offer few extras, but most are clean and sometimes more personal than the larger hotels.

Prices given for the accommodations discussed below are either actual prices established for 1993 or projections based on 1992 rates. They span the lowest rate for the low season to the highest rate for the high season. All prices given are for double room, double occupancy. Unless otherwise indicated, all rates include Continental breakfast (assorted breads and cakes, yogurt, frozen orange juice or Tang, coffee or tea) or the increasingly popular "American buffet" (cereals, juices, rolls, cheeses, and cold cuts).

Right now the hotel business in Lisbon is booming. A number of new hotels, both large and small, have recently opened or are soon to open, especially in the rapidly developing area northeast of Parque Eduardo VII. With so much variety in price and location, where you choose to stay will depend on personal inclination and convenience. As a rule, older neighborhoods have more charm but also more noise, while the newer areas of the city, beyond the praça Marquês de Pombal, are quieter and more up-to-date but lack the atmosphere of the old city. Many hotels, both old and new, have some rooms with balconies and some without; if fresh air and wonderful views sound appealing, ask for a balcony when reserving.

The telephone area code for Lisbon is 01.

Luxury Hotels

At the **Ritz Intercontinental**, still considered the pinnacle of sophistication and comfort, all 310 rooms have large private balconies, about half overlooking the Parque Eduardo VII. The rooms are spacious and elegant (and virtually sound-proof), with marble baths reputed to be the most luxurious in Europe. Now managed by an energetic, visionary French-man named Jacques Chevasson, the Ritz is engaged in a discreet but complete renovation of all its rooms, starting at the top and working down. At press time, about a third of the rooms (including those on the eighth and ninth floors) had been redone—literally from the inside out, with new plumbing, wiring, automatic climate control—and redeco-rated by French and Portuguese designers in crisp new schemes of blue or beige and cream, at a cost of about $65,000$00 per room. All rooms are expected to be refur-bished by 1994. The hotel has two restaurants, the lobby-floor **Varanda**, offering Portuguese specialties both indoors and out (weather permitting), and the downstairs, candlelit **Ritz Grill**, considered by some to be Lisbon's best, where dinner is served to the tune of classical guitar. The Ritz Snack, on the park side of the hotel, is busy at all hours.

Rua Rodrigo da Fonseca, 88A, 1093 Lisboa; Tel: 69-20-20; Fax: 69-17-83; in U.S. and Canada, Tel: (800) 327-0200; in U.K., Tel: (081) 847-2277 or (0345) 58-14-44. 44,000$00–54,000$00 (does not include breakfast).

The less expensive **Tivoli** is the first choice for many visitors because of its enviable location on the avenida da Liberdade midway between the old and new parts of town, its big swimming pool and tennis court set in lovely gardens, and its top-floor terrace grill overlooking the city. Rooms are smallish, simply but attractively decorated, and the large and comfortable lobby is a popular meeting spot.

Avenida da Liberdade, 185, 1200 Lisboa; Tel: 53-01-81; Fax: 57-94-61; in the U.S. and Canada, Tel: (800) 223-5652. 28,500$00–44,000$00.

The **Méridien**, just north of the Ritz and on the park, is perhaps Lisbon's most dramatic luxury hotel, using great sweeps of glass, marble, and mirrors for a bold contempo-rary look. This member of the French chain offers bou-tiques, a health club, a ground-floor brasserie, and the **Atlan-**

tic restaurant serving Portuguese cuisine. Compared with those at the Ritz, the 318 bedrooms here are rather small and less than soundproof.

Rua Castilho, 149, 1000 Lisboa; Tel: 69-04-00; Fax: 69-32-31. 31,000$00–41,000$00.

The **Altis**, situated on a quiet street a few blocks west of the avenida da Liberdade, was built 17 years ago but looks newer. Business travellers like it for its helpful and efficient staff and its many amenities: indoor pool and sauna, conference rooms, and easy parking. The rooftop restaurant, **Dom Fernando**, has a wraparound terrace and a reputation for good Portuguese food; the **Girassol** downstairs offers a buffet. The smallish rooms have large windows and contemporary, rather masculine decor.

Rua Castilho, 11, 1200 Lisboa; Tel: 52-24-96; Fax: 54-86-96; in U.S. and Canada, Tel: (800) 528-1234. 30,000$00–35,000$00.

An extravagant newcomer to the Lisbon scene, **Hotel da Lapa** is a restored 19th-century mansion in the heart of the diplomatic quarter directly west of the Basílica da Estrela. The hall looks like a grand ballroom with black, rose, and gray marble floors, a pink marble fountain, and decorative tiles. The gourmet restaurant, suitably named **Embaixada**, presents such subtle delicacies as crayfish and baby leeks gratinéed in mustard-seed sauce, and sea bass wrapped in lettuce leaves, served in a butter sauce with caviar. A new wing makes a total of 94 rooms, each with its own large terrace, elegant decor, mirrored gray marble baths, and modern conveniences galore. In addition, eight apartments in the original building have been meticulously restored with appropriate furnishings. But the hotel's particular charm is the site, an isle of tranquillity in the center of Lisbon, with views that encompass the city and the river beyond. The grounds take up most of a hillside and include a stream, pool, esplanade, and landscaped garden with two gnarled trees that have been declared national monuments. An underground garage holds 100 cars.

Rua do Pau de Bandeira, 4, 1200 Lisboa; Tel: 395-0005; Fax: 395-0665; in U.S., (800) 526-8539 or (212) 226-9056. 28,000$00–40,000$00 (does not include breakfast).

The **Avenida Palace** is the *grande dame* of Lisbon, built on the Rossio a cenury ago and retaining its 19th-century opulence despite recent major renovations. The reception rooms glitter with crystal chandeliers, polished wood, and silk brocade; a marble staircase spirals up to beautiful salons and card rooms on the mezzanine; and the 95 guest rooms are furnished with good reproductions of antiques. The dining room serves breakfast only.

Rua 1 de Dezembro, 123, 1200 Lisboa; Tel: 346-0151; Fax: 342-2884; in U.S. and Canada, Tel: (800) 448-8355. 25,000$00–50,000$00.

The sleekly modern **Alfa Lisboa,** part of the Madrid-based Occidental Hotels chain and located near the praça de Espanha north of Parque Eduardo VII, also appeals to business travellers because of its up-to-date comforts and services. The **Pombalino** grill serves elegant meals in 18th-century surroundings, while **A Aldeia** specializes in Portuguese fare.

Avenida Columbano Bordalo Pinheiro, 1000 Lisboa; Tel: 726-2121; Fax: 726-3031; in U.S. and Canada, Tel: (800) 843-3311. 28,000$00–33,000$00.

The tallest and largest of Lisbon's luxury hotels, with nearly 400 rooms, swimming pool, health club, and two restaurants, the **Lisboa Sheraton Hotel and Towers** overlooks a major boulevard a few blocks east of Parque Eduardo VII and about ten minutes by taxi from the airport. Rooms in the tower section are most desirable and most expensive, and the rooftop **Panorama Room** offers drinks, banquet buffets, and stunning views.

Rua Latino Coelho, 1, 1097 Lisboa; Tel. 57-57-57; Fax: 54-71-64; in U.S. and Canada, Tel: (800) 325-3535; in U.K., Tel: (0800) 35-35-35. 18,500$00–45,000$00 (does not include breakfast).

First-Class Accommodations

The **Holiday Inn Crowne Plaza** is only five minutes from the airport, ten minutes from downtown, and just around the corner from Campo Grande, a broad green promenade where Lisbon University and several museums are located. The decor and furnishings are ultramodern, the 221 rooms and 16 suites equipped with high-tech charm such as computerized minibars. But there have been complaints about the roar and rumble of low-flying planes and the racket of frequent landings and take-offs.

Avenida Marechal Craveiro Lopes, 390, Campo Grande, 1700 Lisboa; Tel: 759-9639; Fax: 758-6949; in U.S. and Canada, Tel: (800) 465-4329. 41,000$00–43,000$00 (does not include breakfast).

The **Holiday Inn Lisboa,** another member of the American chain that offers many amenities but, like the Holiday Inn Crowne Plaza, does not fall within the luxury class, is a good choice for North American tourists who like familiar surroundings. Located near the Campo Pequeno bullfight ring a few blocks off the avenida da República, the hotel has all the comforts of home (including hair-dryers in the marble-and-tile bathrooms) plus rooftop health club and swimming pool, parking facilities, and the **Vasco da Gama** restaurant.

Avenida António José de Almeida, 28A, 1000 Lisboa; Tel: 793-5222; Fax: 793-6672; in U.S. and Canada, Tel: (800) 465-4329. 34,000$00–56,250$00 (does not include breakfast).

Hotel Lisboa Plaza, family owned and operated since 1953, has been imaginatively redecorated in soothing beige and olive colors, with charming touches of Art Nouveau in both public and guest rooms. Its lovely **Quinta d'Avenida** restaurant specializes in Portuguese cuisine.

Travessa Salitre/Avenida da Liberdade, 7, 1200 Lisboa; Tel: 346-3922; Fax: 347-1630; in U.S. and Canada, Tel: (800) 528-1234. 19,500$00–29,500$00.

Opened in the spring of 1992, the **Hotel Pullman Lisboa** is delightfully located on the avenida da Liberdade, midway between the Tivoli and the Avenida Palace. Its 170 carefully soundproofed rooms enjoy panoramic views of either the avenue or praça da Alegria behind. The restaurant, with its turn-of-the-century decor, has a direct entrance on the avenue. And private parking is available for a modest fee in this area where parking is difficult because of congestion and a lack of garages.

Avenida da Liberdade, 123/125, 1200 Lisboa; Tel: 342-9202; Fax: 342-9222; in U.S. and Canada, Tel: (800) 221-4542. 27,500$00 (does not include breakfast).

Opened six years ago, the **Hotel Lisboa** is notable for its splendid location half a block off the avenida da Liberdade about midway between the Rossio and the praça Marquês de Pombal. Rooms are tastefully decorated in soft earth shades, and the more expensive of these are quite large, with wonderful geranium-lined terraces. The dining room offers breakfast only, but the popular piano bar serves sandwiches and light meals.

Rua Barata Salgueiro, 5A, 1100 Lisboa; Tel: 355-4131; Fax: 355-4139. 23,000$00–28,000$00.

The **Tivoli Jardim** is under the same management as the Tivoli (see Luxury Hotels, above), and visitors have access to the Tivoli's pool and tennis court. Set behind its parent hotel, it is a newer building and slightly less grand.

Rua Júlio César Machado, 7, 1200 Lisboa; Tel: 53-99-71; Fax: 355-6566; in U.S. and Canada, Tel: (800) 223-5652. 21,500$00–26,500$00.

Conveniently near the Gulbenkian Foundation, in the

heart of the new hub of modern hotels and office buildings around the avenida da República in northeastern Lisbon out toward the airport, the **Hotel Continental** is a 14-story sweep of curved glass enclosing 220 rooms, suites, and conference rooms. Portuguese-owned, the hotel has a pleasant lobby opening onto tropical gardens.

Rua Laura Alvez, 9/13, 1000 Lisboa; Tel: 793-5005; Fax: 797-3669; in U.S. and Canada, Tel: (800) 528-1234. 20,300$00–22,350$00.

The **Príncipe Real**, with 24 rooms, is a classic example of the fine small hotel whose devotees return year after year. Only a half block from the Jardim Botânico but hidden away in a rather confusing tangle of streets, it has the intimacy and charm of a private home, and for that very reason may not appeal to travellers used to large, full-service hotels. The public rooms are quiet and inviting, the service is excellent, there are fresh flowers in every room, and a tea tray is delivered to your door every afternoon. The menu in the top-floor dining room is limited, but the food is good. The Ritz sends its overflow guests to this hotel.

Rua da Alegria, 53, 1200 Lisboa; Tel: 346-0116; Fax: 342-2104; in U.S. and Canada, Tel: (800) 223-5695. 19,000$00.

The **Hotel Carlton**, quite new and, like the Continental (above), near the Gulbenkian Foundation, is small but elegant; its lobby is decorated in black-and-white checkerboard marble with wrought-iron furniture and luxuriant plants in terra-cotta amphoras, and its rooms have a Persian delicacy. The restaurant, serving breakfast only, overlooks a pretty courtyard.

Avenida Condé de Valbom, 56–62, 1000 Lisboa; Tel: 795-1157; Fax: 795-1166. 15,000$00–20,000$00.

The **Fénix**, at the top of the avenida da Liberdade, is 30 years old but has just undergone a radical renovation that makes it one of the most appealing hotels in its class. The reception area, refreshingly decorated in cool greens and whites, makes imaginative use of glass, luxuriant foliage plants, and contrasting woods. Of the 120 pleasing rooms, those on the top floor have private balconies. At present the dining room serves breakfast only.

Praça Marquês de Pombal, 8, 1200 Lisboa; Tel: 386-2121; Fax: 386-0131. 16,600$00–19,500$00.

For many people, **York House** is without doubt the most charming place to stay in Lisbon, despite its location quite a distance west of the city's center, near the Museu Nacional de Arte Antiga. Called a *residência* even though it has an excellent restaurant and offers full service, it is housed in a well-restored 16th-century monastery. You enter off an ordinary-looking street, go up a flight of stairs bordered on either side by trailing vines, fruit trees, and shrubs, and find yourself in one of the most delightful courtyards in all of Lisbon. In good weather, breakfast is served here. York House has long been a favorite of the British: Graham Greene always stayed here, as did the hero of John Le Carré's *Russia House*. Ask for a room overlooking the courtyard.

There is a 12-room annex in an old town house down the street, known as **Residência Inglêsa**. It is attractively furnished but extremely noisy, and unless you can get a room facing the garden it is not an acceptable alternative to the main building.

Rua das Janelas Verdes, 32, 1200 Lisboa; Tel: 396-2435; Fax: 397-2793. 16,000$00–21,000$00.

The **Hotel Veneza,** a 38-room *residência* that opened in 1990 next door to the Tivoli, is both convenient and comfortable. Set in an 1885 town house overlooking the avenida da Liberdade, it has balconied guest rooms attractively decorated with wicker furniture and light colors, and a pleasant small restaurant serving breakfast only. The main staircase is lined with marvelous murals of city scenes by artist Pedro Luiz-Gomes.

Avenida da Liberdade, 189, 1200 Lisboa; Tel: 352-2618; Fax: 352-6678. 17,400$00.

Albergaria Senhora do Monte is perched atop a hill near the Alfama. Originally a small apartment house, it was converted to an inn in 1969 and in 1990 was completely and skillfully remodeled. Its 28 rooms, some with their own balconies, are decorated in Portuguese provincial style, and bathrooms are lined with *azulejos*. The top-floor dining room serves breakfast and light meals, and affords a breath-catching view of Lisbon.

Calçada do Monte, 39, 1100 Lisboa; Tel: 886-6002; Fax: 87-77-83. 14,000$00–17,500$00.

The **Zurique** opened recently, a stone's throw from the Hotel Continental (see above), in the growing new neighborhood of hotels and office buildings in northeastern Lisbon. Portuguese-owned and run by an unusually helpful staff, the 13-story hotel has a modern look, with a striking spiral staircase curving from lobby to mezzanine, and imaginative use of lighting and exotic plants. The smallish rooms have double-glazed windows to cut out noise, ample closet space, and attractive baths.

Rua Ivone Silva, 18, 1000 Lisboa; Tel: 793-7111; Fax: 793-7290. 13,000$00–17,000$00.

The three-year-old **Amazónia Hotel**, not far from the Ritz (see Luxury Hotels, above), shows strong Brazilian influence in the decor of its public rooms, where Indian art and artifacts are displayed and lavish plantings suggest the rain forest. The nicely decorated bedrooms are airy, those at the back with large balconies, those at the front more spacious rooms without balconies. An underground garage, swimming pool, and inviting breakfast room are added features.

Travessa Fábrica dos Pentes, 1200 Lisboa; Tel: 387-7006; Fax: 387-9090. 16,100$00–21,000$00.

The **Hotel Rex**, two blocks north of the Ritz overlooking the Parque Eduardo VII, has recently been remodeled. Its 60 rooms are small and a bit spartan but clean, light, and cheerful. All have TV, radio, private bath, air-conditioning, and minibar. There's a rooftop restaurant with a wonderful view out over the park and the city.

Rua Castilho, 169, 1000 Lisboa; Tel: 388-2161; Fax: 388-7581. 10,000$00–21,000$00.

The new **Hotel Alif**, a dramatic shaft of sand-colored marble adjacent to the bullfight ring in northeastern Lisbon, boasts modern conveniences like satellite TV and automatic wake-up for an attractive price. The elevators are inadequate and the rooms are rather small but elegantly furnished with marble-topped built-in bureaus, luxurious carpets, double-glazed windows, and rose marble baths; some have ante-rooms leading to bath and bedroom. The top-floor breakfast room offers marvelous views.

Avenida João XXI, Campo Pequeno, 1000 Lisboa; Tel: 795-2464; Fax: 795-4116. 14,500$00.

Dom Manuel I, set on a quiet street near the Gulbenkian Foundation, is a little out of the way but offers considerable charm and atmosphere. Its downstairs lounge has comfortable double sofas flanking an open fireplace, Aubusson wall hangings, and a picture window framing a delightful interior garden. Guest rooms are spacious and restful.

Avenida Duque de Avila, 189, 1000 Lisboa; Tel: 57-61-60; Fax: 57-69-85. 14,500$00.

Travellers interested in an alternative to staying in Lisbon proper might try the **Hotel da Torre** in the suburb of Belém, adjacent to the Mosteiro dos Jerónimos on a quiet residential street. The rooms are currently being redecorated in floral patterns and sagey greens, and the lobby and restaurant are done in provincial style.

Rua dos Jerónimos, 8, 1400 Lisboa; Tel: 363-6262; Fax: 364-5995. 12,250$00–14,750$00 (does not include breakfast).

DINING

It's not surprising that Lisbon offers the greatest variety of dining experiences in all of Portugal. What is surprising is how great that variety is. As a seaport Lisbon enjoys the freshest of fish, and as a capital city it reaps the benefits of regional cuisines, such as *caldo verde* from the Minho and pork from the Alentejo. In addition, the glories of the former empire are reflected in the ethnic cuisines of former colonies in Brazil, the Atlantic, Africa, India, and China.

Restaurants in Lisbon are as diverse as the foods they serve. Popular not just in Lisbon but throughout Portugal are the *tascas,* little bistros, such as those concentrated in the Bairro Alto, that serve hearty meals at low prices. More specific to Lisbon are the restaurants where you can hear *fado*—songs of life and love, universally appealing and usually delivered by a sultry woman in black, supported by a band of deadpan male guitarists. Recently, a number of sophisticated places have opened whose chefs keep a close watch on international culinary trends. Finally, there are coffeehouses, *pastelarias* (pastry shops), and snack bars.

A full-course meal in a Lisbon restaurant might begin with olives, sausages, shrimp, *espadarte fumado* (smoked swordfish), or a plate of the delectable goose barnacles called *percêbes,* perhaps accompanied by an aperitif of beer or *vinho verde.* This might be followed by a regional soup, such as one of the local variations of *caldeirada* (fish stew) or the specialty of coastal Estremadura, *açorda de mariscos* (made with shellfish, bread, and eggs, and flavored with fresh coriander). A regional main course could be *pescada assada à Lisboeta* (hake baked with tomatoes, green pepper, and onion), accompanied by a dry table wine, or *lulas recheadas à Lisbonense* (squid with a stuffing that includes ham), washed down with a more full-bodied red wine. Although Lisboetes are nicknamed "lettuce-eaters," most main courses are served with rice and/or potatoes, as elsewhere in Portugal, though greens are increasingly available. Typical desserts include *torta laranja* (orange torte) and *pudim Molotov* (a poached meringue topped with caramel or apricot sauce). A tangy alternative is *azeitão,* a creamy ewe's-milk cheese, or fresh fruit.

Dinner may be followed by a tawny or vintage Port, a Madeira dessert wine, coffee (*bica* is espresso, *carioca* approximates American coffee, *café* is somewhere in between), the eau-de-vie *aguardente,* or the cherry-flavored liqueur *ginjinha.*

Whatever you choose to order, be forewarned that Portuguese portions seem as boundless and Old World to the contemporary palate as the old Portuguese Empire. Should you so desire, you can avoid excess by sharing one portion (*uma dose*) with your dining companion or by asking for a half-portion (*uma meia dose*) for yourself. No Lisbon restaurateur will insist that you gorge on a full-course meal.

Lisbon restaurants generally serve lunch between about 12:30 and 3:00 P.M. (1:30 is the most fashionable time for Lisboetes) and dinner from about 8:00 to 10:00 P.M. (the later the better for local atmosphere). If hunger strikes outside those hours, snack on a pastry at a *pastelaria* or buy a croquette, cold fish or meat, a roll, or a sandwich at a café.

Many restaurants are closed Sundays, and reservations are recommended at any time at the fanciest establishments, where jacket and tie are appropriate attire for men. Prices are much lower in Lisbon than in other capitals and usually include a service charge, but it is good form to add a 10 percent tip to the bill. Most larger restaurants accept credit cards.

The telephone area code for Lisbon is 01.

Portuguese Restaurants

Aviz (rua Serpa Pinto, 12B; Tel: 342-8391), on the southern edge of the Chiado, is the queen of Lisbon's restaurants, serving such rich dishes as *bacalhau à conde da Guarda* (salt cod and whipped potatoes au gratin), *migas à Minhota* (ham-and-garlic stove-top stuffing), and *arroz à pato* (duck, sausage, and rice fricassee) in an ornate, Empire-style setting. Reservations are vital, especially if you want to dine in the larger green-and-gold room.

Tágide (largo Academia das Belas Artes, 18; Tel: 346-0570), beautifully set on a high hill in the Chiado, overlooks the Tagus and offers refined versions of such Portuguese classics as sumptuous *sopa à Alentejana* (bread and garlic soup) and *rojões de porco à nortenha* (pork Minho style—browned, then dusted with paprika and simmered in red wine with pickled vegetables). It's worth visiting this lovely restaurant just to see its wonderful mythological scenes in blue-and-white *azulejos*. Reservations necessary.

Tavares (rua da Misericórdia, 37; Tel: 342-1112), also in the Chiado, is an old-guard establishment—the oldest, in fact, in the city (1784), with a long tradition of serving Lisbon's high society. In recent years, however, the restaurant's cuisine has not quite matched its elegant decor and steep prices.

Casa do Leão (Tel: 87-59-62) has a very special location in the Castelo de São Jorge at the top of the Alfama. A lunch favorite among knowledgeable Lisboetes, it's usually booked solid, so reservations are a must. From the French/Portuguese menu choose such Portuguese items as *presunto* (prosciutto) from Chaves, perhaps followed by *gambas grilhadas* (grilled prawns). This year the restaurant will be open for dinner, served to the music of classical piano and Portuguese guitar.

The French-inspired menu at **Michel** (largo de Santa Cruz do Castelo; Tel: 886-4338) has a loyal and well-heeled following in Lisbon. Its location just outside the Castelo de São Jorge is attractive, and its menu, based mainly on seafood, could be described as "nouvelle Portuguese." Owner Michel opened another, larger restaurant in the Alcântara district, just east of the Ponte 25 de Abril. But the new restaurant, Gare Maritima, did not live up to expectations and recently closed.

Gambrinus (rua das Portas de Santo Antão, 23; Tel: 346-8974), tucked away in a congested street just off the Rossio and behind the Teatro Nacional, is Lisbon's finest fish house, where you can sample sea bass prepared in the Minho way with bits of smoky ham, or baby clams gilded with olive oil, a recipe invented by 19th-century Portuguese poet Bulhão Pato. This well-known establishment is often crowded, and reservations are suggested.

Casa da Comida (travessa das Amoreiras, 1; Tel: 388-5376), located a ten-minute taxi ride northwest of the Bairro Alto near the new Amoeiras shopping center, is a lavishly decorated place serving trimmed-down Portuguese food to a crowd of Lisbon sophisticates. It's wise to reserve in advance.

More classic are the historic Portuguese recipes reinterpreted at **Conventual** (praça das Flores, 44; Tel: 60-91-96), in the Príncipe Real area on the northern edge of the Bairro Alto. Dishes once literally fit for kings are served amid ecclesiastical art.

Sua Excelência (northwest of the city center at rua do Conde, 42; Tel: 60-36-14) has no set menu, but owner Francisco Queiroz will tell you what he's found at the market that day and how the chef can prepare it, to order. One recurring dream is chicken Moambo, braised Angolan style with dendê oil (from palm-tree nuts), eggplant, and okra. Reservations a must.

Perhaps Lisbon's best regional restaurant, **Pap'Açorda** (rua da Atalaia, 57; Tel: 346-4811), located in the Bairro Alto, serves hearty, basically Alentejo food (besides its signature dish, *açorda de mariscos à Pap'Açorda,* a shellfish, bread, and egg porridge, loaded with fresh coriander, from coastal Estremadura) to an enthusiastic crowd of young professionals.

Opened in 1782, **Café-Restaurante Martinho da Arcada** (praça do Comércio, 3; Tel: 87-92-59) is a landmark institution, located in the handsome ensemble of government buildings laid out around Terreiro do Paço by the marquês de Pombal. The arches and chandeliers, sparkling white tablecloths, and cutlery give the place a pleasant resonance of bygone days. The food is excellent and quite reasonable. The grilled fish, for instance, could not be fresher or tastier.

Bonjardim (travessa Santo Antão, 7–11; Tel: 342-4389) has for years served the best chicken on the spit (and the best french fries) in town. Both the restaurant and its annex across the street are generally crowded. The service is brisk, and you may have to share your table.

An establishment simply called **Restaurante 33** (rua Alexandre Herculano, 33A; Tel: 54-60-79), located not far from Pombal circle, is popular with the business-lunch crowd. Among the specialties: fava beans with fresh coriander and duck with Champagne sauce.

Bachus (largo da Trindade, 8; Tel: 342-2828), in the Bairro Alto, has a sophisticated atmosphere, elaborate decor, and an interesting menu that includes such specialties as mountain goat and *salmonette à Setúbalense* (red mullet sautéed and served with a tart sauce of fresh oranges).

Escorial (rua das Portas de Santo Antão, 47; Tel: 346-4429), one of Europe's best seafood houses, is located just off the Rossio in a street crowded with interesting restaurants. Portuguese in atmosphere but Spanish in cuisine, it specializes in all kinds of shellfish.

Clara (campo dos Mártires da Pátria, 49; Tel: 355-7341) serves exceptionally good food in unusually appealing surroundings: a manor house dating to Pombaline times that's located in an old residential area eight to ten blocks east of the avenida da Liberdade. The big, cream-colored dining room overlooks a walled garden, tables are well spaced, and the atmosphere is that of a fine private home. The diverse menu includes steak with green peppercorns, grilled stone bass with shellfish butter, and imaginative Portuguese egg sweets.

Clube de Empresários (avenida da República, 38; Tel: 796-6380) sounds like some exclusive businessman's lodge; it isn't. Still to be discovered by foreign visitors, this restaurant, in a beautiful villa not far from the bullring, combines congenial atmosphere with quality Portuguese and international cuisine.

Porta Branca (rua do Teixeira, 35; Tel: 342-1024), a small and very chic Bairro Alto restaurant, is hard to find but worth the trouble for its regional and house specialties like *salmão do Rio Minho* (salmon served with bits of ham) and *entrecôte à la crème.* It offers the best steaks in Lisbon.

Much favored by young people is the Bairro Alto restaurant **Bota Alta** (travessa da Queimada, 37; Tel: 342-7959), tucked into an alley near the Igreja de São Roque. The bistro offers such Portuguese specialties as *bacalhau à bras* (salt cod scrambled with eggs, onions, and potatoes) and house wine in earthenware jugs.

Also near São Roque is the **Restaurante à Tipoia** (rua do Norte, 102; Tel: 346-8420), a small and spanking-clean establishment rather like an upscale *tasca* (see Tascas, below). The menu is in Portuguese and no English is spoken, but if you know that *frango* means chicken and *bacalhau* means salt cod you can enjoy an excellent meal for a reasonable price.

If you'd like to venture from strictly Portuguese cuisine, the **Ritz Grill** (Hotel Ritz, rua Rodrigo da Fonseca, 88; Tel: 69-20-20) is the place to go. Its menu is mainly French, but the uncommon quality of such locally produced dishes as smoked swordfish and *queijo da serra* (ewe's-milk cheese) are as good an argument as any for Portugal's inclusion in the European Community. Reservations are essential.

Tricana (Feira Popular de Lisboa, avenida da República, Entrecampos; Tel: 796-1612) is one of a number of restaurants in the amusement park just beyond the bullring that serve hearty, regional fare for reasonable prices. The park is open all day weekends and from 7:00 P.M. weeknights from April through October. A few of the park's restaurants, like Tricana, open for lunch weekdays; it can be very pleasant to sit under a linden tree in the uncrowded park, eating fresh grilled sardines or turkey steak and mushrooms.

Ethnic Restaurants

For a more exotic experience, take a taxi northwest of the Bairro Alto to the Rato district, where **Monte Cara** (rua Sol do Rato, 71A) serves the spicy, African-influenced cuisine of the formerly Portuguese Cape Verde islands, accompanied by the equally spicy strains of live Cape Verde music.

Comida de Santo (calçada Eng. Miguel Pais, 39; Tel: 396-3339), near the Jardim Botânico, offers such Brazilian dishes as *feijoada* (black bean and pork stew) and *vatapá* (a shell-fish porridge) in an intimate, tropical setting.

The food of Mozambique is the specialty of **Laurentina** (avenida Conde de Valbom, 71A; Tel: 796-0260), located a few blocks south of the Gulbenkian Foundation. Its robust seasonings are hopped up by a sauce made from *piri-piri*, explosive little chilies from neighboring Angola. (The fiery condiment has become a staple on Portuguese tables of every ethnic stripe.)

Velha Goa (rua Tomás da Anunciação, 41B; Tel: 60-04-46), in the Campo de Ourique section northwest of the Bairro Alto, serves the Indian-influenced specialties of the former Portuguese colony of Goa. Try *xacuti,* fried chicken served in a sauce of coconut milk laced with numerous spices.

Of the many Chinese restaurants in what is still, after all, the home capital of colonial Macao, **Tun Fon** (avenida Fontes Pereira de Melo, 6; Tel: 57-76-85), near the praça Marquês de Pombal, is perhaps the best, with *gambas doces* (sweet-and-sour prawns), a refreshing alternative to the usual sweet-and-sour pork and chicken.

Tascas

Lunch in a *tasca* is simple, usually delicious, and inexpensive. Typically it will begin with a plate of bread, cheese, and olives, then grilled fish—either *peixe espada* (scabbard fish—more on this in the Madeira chapter), *linguado* (sole), or *sardinhas* (Portuguese sardines are fat, meaty, and succulent, nothing like the skinny creatures packed tightly together in tins). Then comes a fresh green salad and a flan or piece of luscious ripe melon. The meal is almost invariably washed down with a bottle of the house *vinho verde,* that young, light Minho wine for which Portugal is famous. It all makes for a perfect light meal, one that is enjoyed every day by the vast majority of Lisboetes.

There are *tascas* all over the city, but some of the best are in the Bairro Alto, especially in the newspaper publishing district in and around the rua Diário de Notícias. Editors, journalists, lawyers, judges, and other professionals dine regularly in unpretentious little rooms where there may be only six or eight tables, each neatly set with spanking-white cloths and good flatware, frequently centered with a small bouquet of fresh flowers, and soon to be laden with good, inexpensive food. Four reliable *tascas* in the Bairro Alto are: **Tasca do Manel**, rua da Barroca, 24; **Baralto**, rua Diário de Notícias, 31; **Restaurante Cocheira Alentejana**, travessa do

Poço da Cidade, 19; and **Restaurante a Primavera**, travessa da Espera, 34. All but Baralto are closed for vacation in August.

Teahouses and Coffee Shops

According to the Portuguese, it was Catherine of Bragança who, after her marriage to Charles II in 1662, introduced the English to the tradition of afternoon tea. Many Lisboetes still cling to the custom, and a number of teahouses remain in the city, along with newer pastry shops and snack bars. The most elegant of the older teahouses is **Pastelaria Sala de Cha Versailles** (avenida da República, 15A), serving assorted cakes, *croissant com chocolate,* peach Melba, and such savory morsels as codfish balls, toasted cheese sandwiches, and toasted almonds. Almost as stylish is **Pastelaria Bénard** (rua Garrett, 104) in the Chiado, dating from the 19th century and remodeled ten years ago. Tea, sandwiches, and Portuguese confections made with eggs, sugar, and walnuts or grated orange peel are served either inside or on the mosaic sidewalk terrace. Another Chiado landmark, the **Pastelaria Ferrari**, was destroyed by the 1988 fire and is now operating in a renovated stable (calçada Nova de São Francisco, 2), where stone arches and cork ceilings offer a unique ambience and the macaroons are sheer bliss.

Of Lisbon's coffeehouses, **A Brasileira**, described above in the Chiado section, is probably best known. Even older, though, is **Martinho da Arcada**, next to the restaurant of the same name, dating from the 1700s and located beneath the arcades on the north side of the praça do Comércio. Recently renovated, it serves coffee and light meals both inside and out. On the west side of the Rossio, **Café Nicola** was once the meeting place for a Neoclassical literary society led by Manuel Maria Barbosa do Bocage; now anybody goes.

FADO

The Bairro Alto has been the spiritual home of *fado,* the local soul music, for a number of decades now, and most of the well-known houses are found here. Dinner usually begins around 8:00 P.M., the *fado* between 10:30 and 11:00 P.M. You can go after dinner and order just drinks, but there's usually a cover charge. In the more popular places it may be difficult to find a table unless you come earlier for dinner.

The most upscale of Lisbon's *fado* clubs is **Senhor Vinho** (rua de Meio à Lapa, 18; Tel: 397-2681), where some of the country's best-known Lisbon and Coimbra *fadistas* perform and the regional Portuguese cuisine is perhaps the best of the lot.

Lisboa à Noite (rua das Gáveas, 69; Tel: 346-8557) is another choice for *fado,* sung Lisbon-style by owner Fernanda da Maria, one of the leading exponents of the genre. The food here is also better than at most other *fado* places.

A Severa (rua das Gáveas, 51; Tel: 346-4006), named after the colorful and somewhat disreputable lady who was *fado*'s greatest idol until the appearance of Amalia Rodrigues, is one of the oldest traditional *fado* houses in the quarter. It also includes folk-dancing shows, so it is a good place for non-cognoscenti. A Severa is closed on Thursdays.

Adega Machado (rua do Norte, 91; Tel: 346-0095) is another Bairro Alto house where the classical *fado* is mixed with lighter folk dancing and other regional music in the interest of more general appeal. It is a big, cheerful place where the food is also quite good, but it tends to get crowded.

Restaurante São Caetano (rua de São Caetano à Lapa, 27; Tel: 397-4792) is not so commercialized as some of the better-known *fado* huses. The Portuguese come to this tiny, theatrically decorated upstairs restaurant for the cuisine as well as the music. In a break with tradition, *fadista* Maria de Lourdes is as likely to wear a white cocktail suit as the more traditional fringed black shawl.

Parreirinha (beco do Espírito Santo, 1; Tel: 886-8209) in the Alfama is the traditional tavern with hearty food and soulful music, but the modest old *taberna* prices are gone. It is still popular with Portuguese students, who drop in after dinner (around 10:00 P.M.) for a glass of wine, sausage, and guitar music.

Timpanas (rua Gilberto Rola, 24; Tel: 60-66-55) in Alcântara, near the docks where *fado* was born, presents a dinner show with good *fado* music and folk dancing, and is popular with tour groups.

Pátio Alfacinha (rua do Guarda Joias, 44; Tel: 364-2171) is located near the Ajuda Palace. The music is traditional and appeals to the Portuguese young and not-so-young alike.

CULTURAL HAPPENINGS
Lisbon's cultural calendar is rich and varied year-round. When the season ends in most other European capitals by the beginning of June, things go into full swing in Lisbon with an annual, multidimensional festival called **Festas de Lisboa**. There are all kinds of musical events, excursions, workshops, and plays. While most plays are in Portuguese, the concerts, opera, ballet, and recitals often feature international stars.

The best way to learn what is happening is to go to the Câmara Municipal (City Hall) on praça do Município, northwest of Terreiro do Paço, and ask for the monthly *Agenda Cultural*. Partly translated into English, this comprehensive booklet covers special events, theater, sports, exhibitions, cinema, museums, and cultural tours, and it is free.

Among the capital's main theaters are:

Grande Auditório, Fundação Calouste Gulbenkian, avenida da Berna, 45; Tel: 795-0236.

Teatro Nacional de São Carlos, rua Serpa Pinto 9; Tel: 346-8408.

Teatro Municipal São Luiz, rua António Maria Cardoso, 40; Tel: 347-1279.

Teatro Nacional Dona Maria II, Rossio; Tel: 347-2246.

Teatro Municipal Maria Matos, rua Frei Miguel Contreiras, 52; Tel: 849-7007.

Teatro da Trindade, largo da Trindade, 7A; Tel: 342-3200.

Coliseu dos Recreios, rua das Portas de Santo Antão; Tel: 346-1997.

BARS AND NIGHTLIFE

Bars of the Anglo-American type have established themselves as a feature of nightlife in Portuguese cities in recent years. They come alive around 11:00 P.M., as Lisboetes usually frequent them after dinner. **Procópio**, in a little cul-de-sac near largo do Rato, near the restaurant Monte Cara northwest of the Bairro Alto, is one of the oldest, catering to the thirsts of many of Portugal's leading politicians, artists, journalists, and their like. It is pub-like, with lots of bric-a-brac, and somewhat on the dark side (alto de São Francisco, 21; Tel: 365-2851). **Pavilhão Chines**, on the street where many of Lisbon's antiques shops cluster at the northern edge of the Bairro Alto, is another comfortable, civilized place for a drink, and has a billiards table in the back room beyond the magnificent mahogany bar (rua Dom Pedro V, 89; Tel: 342-4729). **Café Creme Piano Bar**, near the Gulbenkian Museum, caters to a rather loud clientele, but that doesn't seem to discourage people. The atmosphere is warm and the Italian specialties are tasty (rua Conde Valbom, 52A; Tel: 796-4360).

The most dynamic live-music bars in Lisbon are the ones that feature African music—quite often the Cape Verde variety, which blends Latin American rhythms with the African beat. Also in the Bairro Alto, the samba club **Grafieira** is the liveliest Brazilian bar in town, usually packed with expatriates from Lisbon's sizable Brazilian community (calçada do Tijolo, 8). At **Copo de Três**, near the restaurant Conventual in the

Príncipe Real district at the northern edge of the Bairro Alto, you get music of different sorts, from chamber to jazz, with an occasional poetry reading thrown in (rua Marcos Portugal, 1, at the corner of praça das Flores). Undiluted jazz can be heard in the **Hot Clube de Portugal** (praça da Alegria, 39), just off the avenida da Liberdade a few blocks north of the praça dos Restauradores.

Discos

The chic circuit consists of half a dozen places. They tend to be pricey and are sometimes exclusive when it comes to natives, but foreigners usually don't have any trouble getting in. **Ad Lib** (rua Barata Salgueiro, 18; Tel: 356-1717), near the praça Marquês de Pombal, is very expensive, fashionable, and smooth, but a bit on the staid side. **Primorosa de Alvalade** (avenida dos Estados Unidos da America, 128D, Tel: 797-1913) is the "in" place for teenagers, but 30-something is also acceptable. Stones (rua do Olival, 1) in the Lapa district west of the Bairro Alto, is now a private club and no longer open to the public, but **Springfellows** (avenida Oscar Monteiro Torres, 8), near the Campo Pequeno, equally chic, is still a popular spot.

Superchic in Lisbon at the moment means **Alcântara Mar** (rua da Cozinha Económica, 11; Tel: 363-6432), a converted factory in the Alcântara dock area. It can hold 2,000 people and usually does. You pay an entrance fee here that buys you the first drink. Closed Mondays and Tuesdays. **Bairro Alto** (travessa dos Inglesinhos, 50, in the Bairro Alto; Tel: 342-0238) is another huge place (a converted sawmill this time) and also very "in." The decor, created by architect Helder Oarita to reflect all of Lisbon's history, is imaginative, and so is the entertainment. In addition to disco you get live music and can expect anything from clowns to fire-eaters.

SHOPS AND SHOPPING

Lisbon is a wonderful source for traditional crafts and hand-made goods, and you will find prices reasonable in comparison with the rest of Europe.

Major Shopping Districts

The traditional shopping areas in Lisbon are the **Baixa**, the **Chiado**, and the streets around the **Rossio**, as well as Rossio station itself, which has an extensive mall. Major hotels, such as the Ritz, the Méridien, the Sheraton, and newer hotels northeast of the praça Marquês de Pombal, usually have interesting boutiques within or near their lobbies. Stores are generally closed between 1:00 and 3:00 P.M. but stay open till 7:00 P.M.

Rua Augusta, a pedestrian street with a small arts-and-crafts market at its southern end, is the main shopping street in the Baixa. **Madeira House** at number 131–135 is a good stop for cotton sheets, linens, and embroidery. Two of the better shoe shops are **Helio**, in the Chiado at the beginning of the rua do Carmo, and **Lisbonense**, at rua Augusta, 202. **Casa Canada** (rua Augusta, 232) and **Galeão** (rua Augusta, 196) both have a good selection of handbags and luggage.

Lisbon is not noted for its designer fashions, but you will find elegant, trendy clothes at **Ana Salazar**, Portugal's best-known designer, with shops at rua do Carmo, 87, and avenida de Roma, 16E. **Pitta** (rua Augusta, 195–197) and **Via Augusta** (rua Augusta, 282) have good-looking shirts, jackets, sweaters, and accessories for both men and women. **Santos & Nascimento** (avenida da Liberdade, 177) and **Lorenco & Santos** (praça dos Restauradores, 70) specialize in men's apparel.

The Chiado is considered Lisbon's most fashionable shopping area. Although the two main department stores were destroyed in the fire of 1988, **Ramiro Leão**, a small, old-fashioned department store on the rua Garrett across from the Hotel Borges, was not damaged and is worth a look. Be sure to ride in its hand-painted elevator, made in Paris at the turn of the century.

The huge new **Amoreiras shopping center**, on the western edge of Lisbon, is inescapable—its pink, blue, and yellow towers dominating the landscape—and with 350 shops, many restaurants, ten cinemas, and hours from 10:00 A.M. to midnight, it would seem to offer formidable competition to the older shopping areas. Indeed, many of the downtown shops have branches in the new center. Still, most Lisboetes remain loyal to their traditional shopping areas, and most visitors to Lisbon, certainly, will find the Baixa and the Chiado more interesting.

Artesanatos

Lisbon, unsurprisingly, has scores of souvenir shops selling bright Barcelos roosters and chrome Towers of Belém. For gifts and mementoes that are more than trinkets, stop in one of the *artesanatos* (crafts shops) offering good-quality handicrafts from the provinces. The **Centro de Turismo e Artesanato** (rua Castilho, 61B), a few blocks south of the Ritz hotel, is one of the biggest and best, and will also pack and ship your gifts, even if you bought them elsewhere. A

Bilha—Artesanato e Turismo (rua Milagre de Santo António, at the Castelo) and **Tourist House** (avenida da Liberdade, 159) are also good choices for souvenirs. **Artesanato Regional Português Arameiro** (praça dos Restauradores, 62–64) is the most convenient handicraft shop, located next to the main post office. It also has a broad range of crafts from all over the country, including copperware, *azulejos* and pottery, filigree and baskets.

Tiles and Pottery

Vista Alegre (largo do Chiado, 18) and **Casa Leonel** (rua do Carmo, 71), in the Chiado, offer good selections of Vista Alegre porcelain from the town of the same name near Aveiro. **Fabrica da Sant'Anna** (rua do Alecrim, 95), also in the Chiado, is the place to go for Sant'Anna *azulejos,* still made and painted by hand in the same way since this company was founded in 1741. You will find a large selection of samples to choose from, as well as hand-painted bowls, lamps, jars, jardinieres, and figurines. If you want to see how the tiles are made, the **Sant'Anna factory** in Belém (calçada da Boa Hora, 96) is open to the public.

Santa Rufina is another good source for handmade and hand-painted reproductions of traditional *azulejos.* The showroom (calçada Conde de Penafiel, 9A; Tel: 87-60-18) is near the Castelo de São Jorge. **Fabrica de Cerâmica Constancia** (rua Santo Domingos à Lapa, 8C) was founded in 1836 and specializes in hand-painted *azulejos* and ceramics. Too far north of the Castelo to walk but on the Metro line is **Viuva Lamego**, a tile shop at largo do Intendente Pina Manique, 25, that always has a wide selection of modern *azulejos* and pottery—plates, dishes, and planters.

Two other *azulejo* factories in the Lisbon vicinity that welcome visitors are **Cerâmica Artistica Isabel Garcia** (estrada de Ericeira, Terrugem, Sintra; Tel: 01-961-8509), which produces faithful copies of antique tiles as well as modern artwork; and **São Simão Arte** (rua Almirante Reis, 86, Vila Fresca de Azeitão; Tel: 01-208-3135), which specializes in hand-painted decorative *azulejos.*

Crystal and Jewelry

Portuguese crystal is much valued for its high quality. In the Chiado, **Casa Leonel** (rua do Carmo, 71) offers a good selection, as does **Atlantis**, a store with several branches, one of them in the same building as Vista Alegre (see Tiles and Pottery, above).

There are any number of jewelers and silversmiths in

Lisbon. **Eloy de Jesus** (rua Garrett, 45), in the Chiado, and **Sarmento** (rua do Ouro, 251), in the Baixa, are both noted for their silver filigree work; **Barreto & Gonçalves** (rua das Portas de Santo Antão, 17) offers a good selection of antique jewelry in a shop just off the Rossio, behind the Teatro Nacional.

Linens and Rugs

For fine linens and embroidered tablecloths visit **Lavores** (rua Aurea, 175–179), in the Baixa. **Casa Regional da Ilha Verde** (rua Paiva de Andrada, 4, just off the rua Garrett in the Chiado) has beautifully embroidered table linen as well as blouses and lace from the Azores.

Hand-embroidered rugs from the town of Arraiolos near Evora are treasured the world over. Known for their bold colors and Oriental motifs, they cost far less in Portugal than abroad. Several Lisbon shops specialize in Arraiolos rugs: **Casa Quintão** (rua Ivens, 34), in the Chiado, offers the largest selection of patterns and also takes orders for custom-made rugs. They can reproduce any design you choose and are familiar with the intricacies of shipping, insurance, customs, etc. **Casa dos Tapetes de Arraiolos** (rua da Imprensa Nacional, 116E), just off the rua da Escola Politécnica near the Jardim Botânico, displays its beautiful rugs on large flip-through hangers, and will also design carpets to order.

Traditional copperware is another popular Portuguese handicraft. The **Centro de Turismo e Artesanato** (rua Castilho, 61B) and **Francisco Ramos** (rua das Portas de Santo Antão, 3), behind the Teatro Nacional, stock a good selection of excellent copper cookware, priced from one-half to two-thirds lower than overseas.

Food and Drink Specialties

Two Chiado stores destroyed by the fire have now relocated: **Ferrari** sells the best chocolates in Lisbon and can be found on the escadinhas de São Francisco, and **Martins and Costa**, Lisbon's most exclusive gourmet food and wine shop, is now on the rua Alexandre Herculano, close to the praça Marquês de Pombal. Another excellent shop for coffee, tea, and chocolates is **Casa Macario** (rua Augusta, 272) in the Baixa.

Antiques

Antiques lovers are in for a treat in Lisbon. There are wonderful shops lining the long street that runs through the Chiado and the Bairro Alto, changing its name as it goes (in the confusing manner of Lisbon streets) from rua do Alecrim to rua da Misericórdia to rua de São Pedro de Alcântara to rua Dom Pedro V to rua da Escola Politécnica. Here you can find marvelous furniture, silver, paintings, and religious objets d'art as well as reasonably priced, particularly beautiful 18th- and early-19th-century hand-painted plates and *azulejos*. **Solar** (rua Dom Pedro V, 68–70) offers the best selection of antique tiles in all of Lisbon, many of them salvaged from monasteries and palaces. At the back of the shop and down a rickety flight of stairs is a real treasure trove: thousands of tiles sorted according to century. You can find everything from extremely rare 16th- and 17th-century examples to wonderfully colorful Art Nouveau and Art Deco pieces.

António Madeira (rua da Escola Politécnica, 97), in business since 1856, is Lisbon's oldest antiques store. Its cluttered rooms hold such treasures as a carved Portuguese bedstead, a 17th-century painted stone Madonna, Dutch Delft, Portuguese faïence, and 16th-century Moorish *azulejos*. Nearby is **Intermobilia** (rua da Escola Politécnica, 39), a well-lighted and well-arranged shop filled with Portuguese silver and early plates, pier mirrors, inlaid gaming tables, and church art. **Helena Simões Ferreira** (rua da Escola Politécnica, 53–55) has quality pieces: hand-carved wooden chests and chairs, 18th-century Portuguese tiles, a matched pair of Dona Maria (19th-century) inlaid wooden framed mirrors.

At rua Dom Pedro V, 111, is **Xairel**, with a fine collection of early Portuguese faïence, provincial furniture, brass, copper, and interesting folk art, including *cangas* (carved wooden ox yokes) from the Minho. **Luís L. Leal** (rua Dom Pedro V, 59) focuses on elegance and simplicity; for instance, a collection of 18th-century folding fans, intricately carved, painted, or decorated with peacock feathers.

Antiquariatum (rua do Alecrim, 107–109), considered one of Lisbon's top antiques stores, has an eclectic collection ranging from Oriental rugs to Portuguese silver services. **Abside** (travessa dos Fiéis de Deus, 14–16) has a knowledgeable owner, Dr. Carlos Penalva, and an unusual assortment of antiques: furniture from Portugal's Golden Age, church carvings, French porcelain, guns, swords, saints, jewelry boxes, and Portuguese paintings and drawings from the 19th century.

Books and Prints

Although interesting old maps, prints, and books may turn up at any antiques shop in the area, the rua do Alecrim is especially rich in *livrarias* (bookshops). **Amérigo Francisco Marques, Livreiro Antiquario** (rua do Alecrim, 40–42) has an outstanding collection of antique maps, prints, postcards, sheet music of Gregorian hymns in Latin, architectural drawings, autographs, and drawings by the 19th-century Portuguese caricaturist Rafael Bordalo Pinheiro. **Livraria Campos Trindade** (rua do Alecrim, 44) offers a somewhat less impressive assortment of old books, maps, magazines, and prints. **João Trindade Antiquario**, almost directly across rua do Alecrim (32) from the Sant'Anna tile showroom, is a pleasant shop with a good choice of books, prints, maps, photographs, postcards, and old aquatints, as well as clocks, small *santos*, and lovely painted screens.

Art Galleries

Two galleries of note are **Galeria São Mamede** (rua da Escola Politécnica, 167) and **Galeria Luis Serpa** (rua Tenenta Raul Cascais, 1B) a few blocks west. São Mamede, a handsome gallery with gray stone floors and vaulted ceilings with red-brick arches, displays contemporary Portuguese paintings and sculpture. Galeria Luis Serpa, the most avant-garde gallery in Lisbon, represents distinguished contemporary painters, sculptors, and constructionists from all over the world.

DAY TRIPS FROM LISBON
ESTREMADURA

By Marvine Howe

Lisbon is the center of its own private universe. Within a short radius, the rich diversity of landscapes provides many delightful excursions. Pampered gardens and parks cohabit with tropical forests and a profusion of wildflowers; Riviera-type playgrounds rub shoulders with untamed Atlantic shores. Roman walls, Moorish fortifications, and medieval castles and churches bear witness to a long and multicultural past. Noble manors and luxurious villas mingle with modest fishing ports and farm villages.

Despite the variety of sights, the distances between them and from Lisbon are not large, and so it is possible to visit many of these points of interest by taking day trips out of Lisbon. You may wish to stay overnight, however, in one of the seaside hotels, country manors, or converted castles along the way. These accommodations are generally good and often better than those in Lisbon. And there is always a good restaurant at hand, with hearty fare and wine.

The main drawback of day trips is that the traffic on the highways can be very heavy at rush hours and over weekends, and often extraordinarily reckless. The best way to avoid strained nerves is to take the train, a bus, or an excursion bus—but that doesn't give you much opportunity to get off the beaten track or do any spontaneous exploration.

If you want to explore the Lisbon region, Estremadura, on

your own by car, you can do it in several easy radial excursions, with Lisbon as the point of departure. Westward, there's the Costa do Estoril, a 30-km (19-mile) string of beaches and bays along the northern shore of the Tagus river and out along the Atlantic coast. Here is the cosmopolitan resort of Estoril, with its grand casino, international auto-racing track, golf courses, and fashionable hotel pools and bars. Nearby, the ancient fishing village of Cascais has become a popular vacation site, with sailing in the bay, a nightly fish auction, pleasant seafood restaurants, discos, and a bullring. Just to the northwest of Lisbon lies the Sintra mountain area, including the Colares valley and the plain of Mafra. Sintra itself is a fairy-tale town, often shrouded in mist, with mysterious palaces, dense forests, moss-covered walls, narrow winding streets, and antiques and handicraft shops. Mafra, to the north, is a modest town totally dominated by the massive 18th-century palace-monastery and basilica, which has splendid marble statuary, a museum of sacred art, and a magnificent library. Another track takes you farther north to Nazaré and other Atlantic fishing port–resorts, then inland to the medieval walled town of Obidos and the monument towns of Alcobaça and Batalha. South of the Tagus a circuit includes Caparica beach, the scenic Arrábida coast, and the developing Tróia peninsula.

MAJOR INTEREST NORTH OF THE TAGUS

Costa do Estoril
Beaches and dramatic scenery
Estoril (casino, golf, restaurants)
Cascais (fish market, shops, bullring)
Guincho (rugged cliffs and sandy beach)
Cabo da Roca, continental Europe's westernmost cape

Sintra
Castles and manors, music festival, parks
Palácio Nacional
Palácio da Pena
Moorish castle fortifications
Capuchos monastery
Monserrate botanical garden

Northern Estremadura
Beaches and fishing ports
Peniche (port, prison museum, islands)
The casbah-like town of Obidos
Nazaré beach

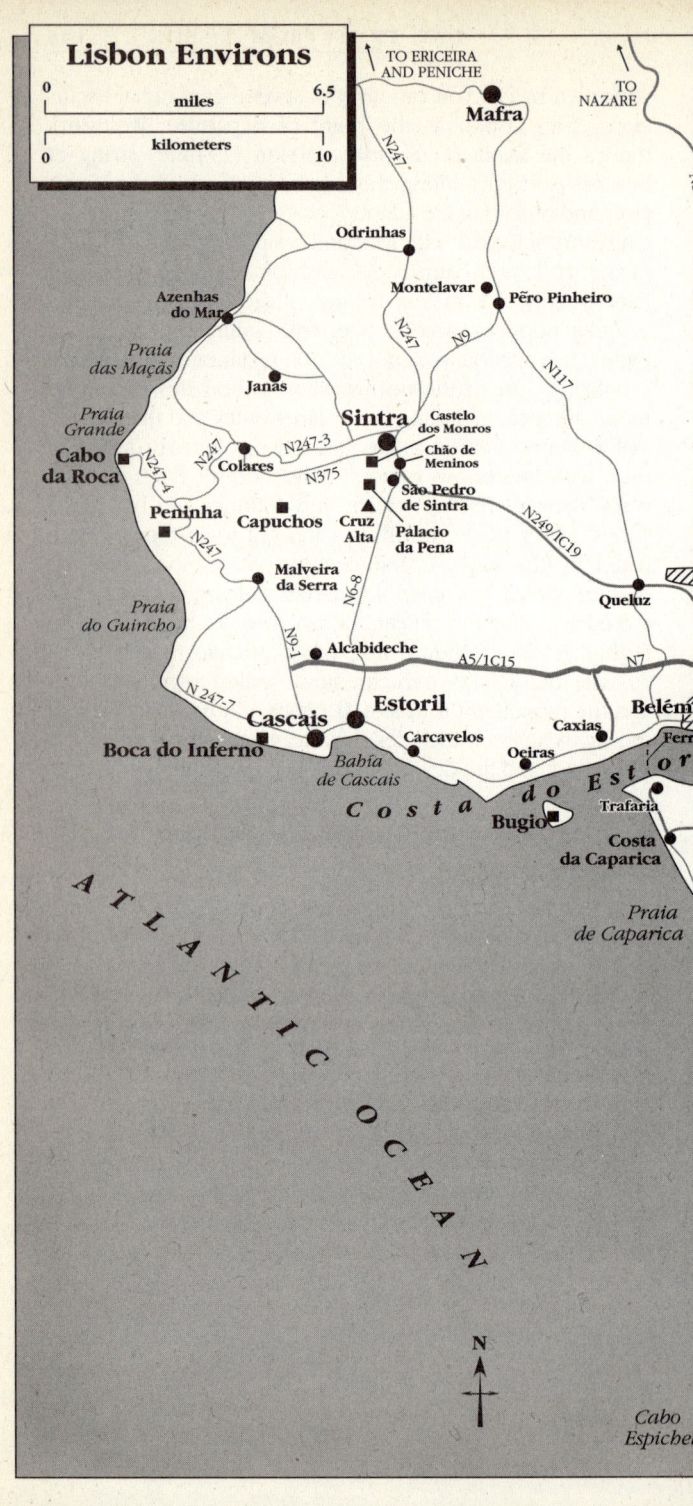

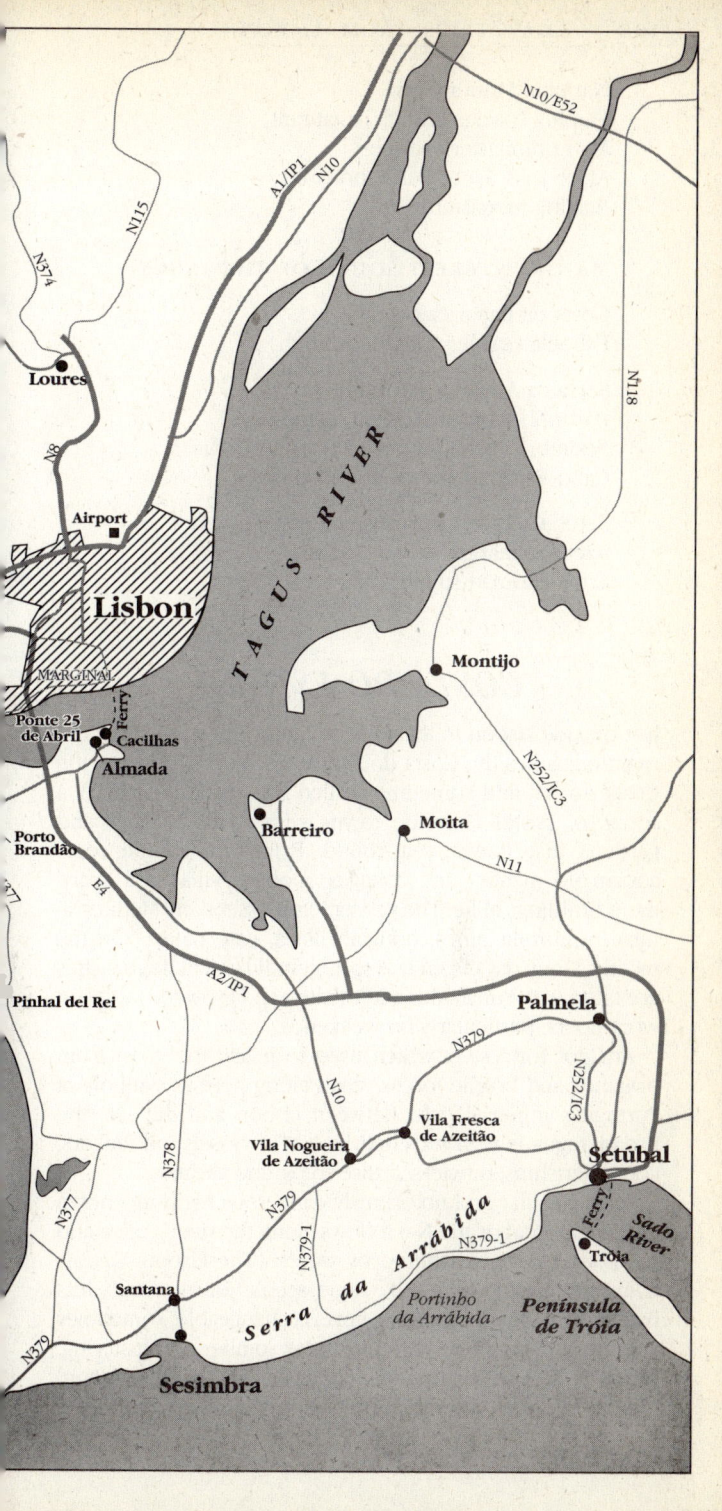

National Monuments
Queluz (palace and its restaurant)
Mafra monastery-palace
Alcobaça's Santa Maria monastery
Batalha monastery

MAJOR INTEREST SOUTH OF THE TAGUS

Costa da Caparica beach
Palmela (castle, pousada, church)

Serra da Arrábida corniche
Portinho da Arrábida (protected cove)
Sesimbra (fishing port, fort)
Cabo Espichel (sanctuary, chapel)

Setúbal's Igreja de Jesús and castle-pousada
Azeitão (market, winery, palace)
Tróia (Roman ruins, golf, beach)

COSTA DO ESTORIL

Just outside Lisbon to the west on the northern shore of the river Tagus lies the Costa do Estoril (formerly known as the Costa do Sol and sometimes called the Costa de Lisboa), a series of pastel riverside towns with small beaches and gardens that flower year-round. Bright-orange tile roofs adorn old manors and cottages, modern villas and apartment buildings alike. The vegetation is essentially Mediterranean: umbrella pines, bougainvillaea, date palms. On the mostly sunny days from late spring until late fall the beaches are lined with sunshades and cabanas and crowded with sun worshipers, particularly on weekends.

Ancient fortresses, which used to guard the coast from brigands and hostile forces, stand along here as symbols of Portugal's imperial past. Between Lisbon and the sea, the broad Tagus is well travelled by NATO vessels, oil tankers, container ships, trawlers, cruise ships, and yachts.

A spectacular and notoriously dangerous highway known as the Marginal or the N 6 follows along the river's edge and on stormy days is battered by waves. (The Lisbon–Cascais commuter train makes the same scenic journey with less hassle.) The river, very wide here, is changeable, sometimes shimmering and serene, other times somber or blustering. Beyond the Lisbon city limits there are few notable monuments, yet the ensemble of weathered rose- and olive-colored mansions, chipped tile walls, neat whitewashed apartments and villas, and evergreen gardens has a special beauty.

Leaving Lisbon, the Marginal first passes the suburb of **Belém**, generally treated as part of the city. (See the Belém section in the Lisbon chapter.) Here is the stately pink Presidential Palace; the impressive **Mosteiro dos Jerónimos**, Gothic in form, Renaissance in spirit and decoration (attached to it is a planetarium, a museum of Iberian antiquities, and the Museu da Marinha); the lavish little fortress called the **Torre de Belém**; and the famous landmark **Padrão dos Descobrimentos** (Monument to the Discoveries), honoring Prince Henry the Navigator. Inside the monument, there's an exhibition gallery worth visiting, and you may take an elevator up to the terrace for an admirable view of Belém and the river.

Just west of Jerónimos stands the vast new Centro Cultural de Belém, built to commemorate the establishment of a single European market in 1992. The fortress-like complex includes a 1,500-seat auditorium, opera house, and museum, with plans for two hotels and a shopping center. Although efforts were clearly made to reconcile the modern building with the majestic monastery, there are many critics who complain that the center tends to detract from the glory of Jerónimos and obscure its view from the west. Across the Marginal, overlooking the yacht club, is an attractive (but expensive) new restaurant, **Vela Latina**, with such seafood specialties as shrimp in a clay pot and *cataplana*—pork and tiny clams steamed in a kind of wok (closed Sundays). In the same complex, there's a health club, cafeteria/ice-cream parlor, and several boutiques.

Beyond Belém, you might pause to see the exotic fish and marine plants and ship models at the **Vasco da Gama Aquarium**, located in the small town of Dáfundo. In the neighboring village of Cruz Quebrada to the west, a slight detour takes you to the National Soccer Stadium, a lovely amphitheater built of stone, hidden in the wooded hills.

Just before the next village of Caxias, a road to the right now leads to the new six-lane inland motorway to Cascais, called the A 5/IC 15. This toll route is an extension of the N 7 four-lane highway (no toll) from Lisbon, which formerly went only as far as the National Stadium. On the Marginal at the entry to Caxias is the fashionable **Mónaco** restaurant, with good dining, dancing, and a river view. Reservations are recommended: Tel: (01) 443-2339.

Automobile enthusiasts should turn off the Marginal at Caxias, when they see the sign indicating the **Museu do**

Automóvel Antigo. Actually this new museum is located in the next town, Paço d'Arcos, at Quinta da Terrugem on alameda Calouste Gulbenkian. Organized by the Portuguese Antique Automobile Club, the museum contains an interesting array of vehicles, such as an 1860 Michaux bicycle with wooden wheels, an 1898 French Clement that goes 20 km (12 miles) an hour, and a 1956 navy-blue Jaguar convertible. Open daily; Tel: (01) 441-0633.

Worthy of a stop is **Oeiras** (pronounced WAY-rus), 17 km (11 miles) west of Lisbon, with its broad, sheltered beach. In the old part of town there's a charming 18th-century Baroque church. Nearby, the marquês de Pombal's fading pink *quinta* (estate), once the site of the Gulbenkian Museum, now belongs to the Agricultural Institute. It is not open to the public, but visitors can obtain authorization to see the formal gardens, inspired by Versailles, and the Cascata dos Poetas (Waterfall of Poets), with statues of Homer, Virgil, and Camões by Machado de Castro. You may take a chance and ask the guard to let you see the lovely gardens, but, better, write to the Presidente do Instituto Nacional de Administracão, Palácio Marquês de Pombal, 2780 Oeiras, Portugal. It is now also possible to arrange for a visit to the quinta itself, which is decorated with splendid stucco scenes, as well as the nearby Casa de Pesca (Fishing Pavilion) and Cascata da Taveira, a grand waterfall and fishing tank framed with romantic blue-and-white-tile scenes from Camões's poem "Ilha dos Amores," from his masterpiece, *Os Lusíadas*. For this, write to the Director da Estação Agrónoma Nacional, Quinta do Marquês, 2780 Oeiras, Portugal.

On the western outskirts of town is an austere, sand-colored 16th-century fortress, **São Julião da Barra**, built by Dom João III, the founder of Portugal's colonial system. Opposite the fortress, in the middle of the river Tagus, stands Torre de Bugio, a circular tower with a lighthouse marking the sandbar where the river waters meet the sea.

Between Oeiras and Carcavelos to the west, in a desolate field, is a low white building with a blue tile roof and flags usually in full sail: the headquarters for NATO's Iberian command. Special permission to visit the facilities, which are not open to the public, can be obtained by writing to the Public Affairs Officer, Cinciberlant, Reduto Gomes Freire, 2780 Oeiras, Portugal.

Now a popular seaside resort with a broad beach, **Carcavelos** used to be a farm town, surrounded by vineyards. In recent years the farms have been pushed inland by modern villas, apartment buildings, and hotels. Carcavelos is known for its "aristocratic" topaz-colored dessert wine, known as "Lisbon wine" by the English. A reminder of the town's bucolic past is the large weekly fair (on Thursdays), with displays of fruits and vegetables as well as household utensils, clothing, pottery, and basketware.

One of the rare old country estates open to overnight visitors near Lisbon is the **Quinta das Encostas**, located in the village of Sassoeiros, about a mile inland from Carcavelos. The 18th-century aristocratic farmhouse used to overlook rolling vineyards and olive groves but is today surrounded by high condominium blocks, supermarkets, and new highways. The walled manor, with private chapel and old water mill, has been classified as a national monument and enhanced with modern comforts. Four spacious bedrooms, each with period furniture and functional bathroom, have been set aside for guests, who are welcome to enjoy the mosaic-lined pool, box and pine gardens, and drawing rooms furnished with museum pieces. The owners, who live on the premises, sometimes join guests for breakfast on the terrace but do not serve other meals because there are so many appealing restaurants in the neighborhood.

All along the coast here are pleasant seafood restaurants where Lisboetes enjoy long working lunches on weekdays or take their families on weekends. For example, **Saisa**, at Praia de Santo Amaro de Oeiras on the cliff overlooking the sea, offers moderately priced fish that is fresher and tastier than that served at many luxury establishments in town. **Fateixa**, at nearby Carcavelos beach, serves a very presentable shrimp cocktail or oysters and sole meunière, with a splendid view of São Julião. One of the best restaurants on the coast these days is **Dom Pepe**, located unpretentiously over a gas station, at Parede, just off the Marginal, with a splendid view of the bay. Frequented mostly by Portuguese business and professional people, Dom Pepe serves an unusually tender beefsteak with mushroom sauce, a savory swordfish wrapped in ham and garlic, and a bittersweet chocolate mousse cake that is difficult to beat.

Estoril

There are at least four Estorils west of Carcavelos: Santo António de Estoril, São Pedro de Estoril, São João de Estoril, and Monte Estoril. But these distinctions need not normally concern you, because the four are grouped together and generally referred to by the generic name.

Estoril first came into prominence at the turn of the century as a winter resort for the rich and aristocratic. It was during World War II, when Portugal remained a neutral haven in Europe, that Estoril gained its international fame. The casino, the grand Hotel Palácio, and palatial villas made a perfect setting for espionage and other intrigues.

After the war this garden by the sea was discovered by exiled royalty seeking a refuge where they could live as they were accustomed. Estoril became known as the center of the Golden Triangle, home to such distinguished figures as Don Juan de Borbón, father of the present king of Spain; Umberto II, former king of Italy; the late King Carol II of Romania and his morganatic wife Magda Lupescu; Simeon II, former king of Bulgaria; the prince of Thurn and Taxis; Charles Hapsburg; and Henri, the count of Paris.

In recent times, however, royal or ex-royal residents have progressively been replaced by wealthy Portuguese and foreign visitors or retirees drawn by the relaxed, pleasant, affordable way of life here. Estoril today is not a playground where the rich and famous come to be seen, but rather a place to live well and *not* be seen. Monte Estoril, in particular, has managed to preserve a certain Victorian charm.

Lately, Estoril and southern Portugal have been discovered by a new sort of aristocracy, sportsmen attracted by the year-round good weather. There's an international championship golf course at the Estoril Golf Club north of town on the way to Sintra, another course at the Estoril Sol Golf Club (farther out toward Sintra), and a third designed by Robert Trent Jones, located in the Parque da Marinha, just west of Cascais.

Auto racing is a fairly new attraction at the Autódromo (Auto Racetrack) located on the road to Sintra from Estoril. The World Championship Formula One is held here every September. The Centro Hípico da Costa do Estoril in the Marinha area has horses for hire. Swimming pools and tennis courts are found in the main hotels.

Once famous for its white sand and calm waters, the Estoril beach—along with most of the beaches along the Costa do Estoril—has been badly polluted in recent years. Now, however, work is under way to reconstruct the sewers all along the coast. The Estoril beach, called the Praia do Tamariz, has been cleaned up and is now considered safe for bathing. The adjoining Praia Monte Estoril is the best beach in the area, but the Cascais beach is still way below standard. These beaches are so popular with local residents in summer that visitors usually prefer to stay by the hotel pool or drive to one of the wilder Atlantic beaches nearby to the west.

Nightlife revolves around the glittering casino complex and discreet hotel bars. Restaurants, and their clientele, are more formal than those in neighboring Cascais. One of the best-known landmarks here, the **Estoril Casino**, is open to anyone who has a passport or other identity card to prove he or she is over 18. This long, low, modern building is set in a flowering park with an illuminated fountain and mushroom lamps. The casino's roulette and baccarat tables are usually busy, as are the slot machines (in fact, they've brought in more machines recently). When bingo was the local craze, the Wonder Bar was turned into a bingo room, but casino sources say it will eventually revert to an after-hours club. For nongamblers there's a large restaurant with international entertainment (reservations recommended, as the dinner and show are popular with tour groups; Tel: 01-468-4521), a cinema (which frequently shows American films), shops, and several bars.

Yet to be discovered by international festival-goers, the Estoril Music Festival offers first-rate concerts at moderate prices from mid-July to mid-August. Concerts are held in the Estoril cathedral, the Cidadela (Fort) beyond the fishing port of Cascais, and other dramatic settings.

Because Estoril's hotels are known for comfort, good service, and amenities, some visitors prefer to make this their base and commute to Lisbon. The Old World **Hotel Palácio**, where royalty did reside at one time, still has great style. Facing the casino gardens, the Palácio was built in 1930 and is said to have served as an important base of operations for Allied agents during World War II. Today well-to-do Europeans and North Americans who want to impress Portuguese contacts tend to stay here. It is common knowledge that when in Estoril, the thing to do is to have a meal or drinks in the Palácio's gardens beside the heated pool. For elegant dining try the **Four Seasons** in the Palácio. The menu and the flowers change with the seasons. Reservations recommended; Tel: (01) 468-0400.

The **Hotel Atlântico** has wonderful sweeping views of the coast. This large hotel hasn't got the charm or snob appeal of the Palácio and is a little too close to the railroad, but it is conveniently situated on the border between Estoril and Cascais. It has a saltwater pool and a popular terrace bar, and many of the rooms have balconies overlooking the sea. Up the hill in a lovely park, the **Lennox Country club** is a very English hotel, with an understated elegance. Besides a great view, heated pool, and terrace garden, the Lennox offers its guests transport to and from Estoril's golf courses and special golfing packages.

Then there is the **Hotel Estoril-Sol**, a huge concrete-and-glass block, which is actually located within the town limits of Cascais. Old-timers say the late authoritarian ruler, António de Oliveira Salazar, drove past the Estoril-Sol while it was still under construction and lamented, "If I were the dictator they say I am, that monstrosity would not be going up here." While the hotel does mar the harmony of the coast, its guests enjoy a privileged position. From their private balconies *they* can't see the hotel, and they can view the river (as far as Lisbon), the bay of Cascais, and way out into the Atlantic. Conveniences include a restaurant with a great panoramic view, several bars and boutiques, an Olympic-size pool, a health club, sauna, bowling alley, and disco. Guests enjoy special rates at the Estoril-Sol golf course.

Restaurants in Estoril also attract many people from Lisbon. Somehow the sea air makes the fish seem fresher and the service better. Two fashionable retreats are frequented by people who want quality attention and are willing to pay prices comparable to those in London or New York: **A Choupana**, built into the cliff overlooking the sea at the entrance of São João do Estoril, serves splendid broiled lobster and *santola* (crab); reservations recommended (Tel: 01-468-3099). The **English Bar**, in a rock garden on the hill just off the Marginal at Monte Estoril, offers an admirable grilled sole. A recent arrival, **Furusato** (Tel: 01-468-4430) is located in a tastefully restored mansion overlooking the Estoril beach. Part of an international chain that extends to Hong Kong and Hawaii, the Japanese restaurant specializes in sushi and tempura, and has won a fervent local following.

Shopping is easy in Estoril because the main shops are located in the Arcadas do Parque, pleasant arcades on either side of the casino gardens. There are several good shops for women's clothing, and gifts for all the family can be found at either the **Bazar do Parque** or **Regionalia**.

If you are looking for something different in the way of gifts, you might try **Cerâmica de Bicesse**, a workshop where ancient tiles are restored and exact reproductions made. Take the road marked "Bicesse" from São João do Estoril and drive north about 5 km (3 miles).

Until not so long ago, the nearby village of Alcabideche was known only for a couple of country restaurants and a great view of Sintra mountain. In 1991 a vast shopping center called CascaiShopping changed the landscape. Located about a mile north of Estoril, CascaiShopping is open daily and has become a favorite hangout for Portuguese of all ages. There are regular shuttle buses from the Cascais and Estoril train stations, and free parking for 2,600 cars. This Portuguese-Brazilian venture is said to be the largest shopping center on the Iberian peninsula. Boasting the largest water clock in the world, CascaiShopping gave Portugal its first ice-skating rink and its first McDonald's (another has since opened in Lisbon). There are five cinemas, an amusement park, and some 160 shops. Most are clothing stores, like the French Printemps and the Dutch C & A, and are generally more expensive than their American mall counterparts. The real bargains are found at Continente, a super-hypermarket with 70 checkout counters.

Another shopping venue during July and August is Estoril's annual Handicraft Fair. Artists and craftspeople bring their works from all over the country. The stalls are set up outside, behind the Casino, and are open evenings from 5:00 P.M. to midnight. You can also dine here on grilled sardines and other regional specialties.

Cascais

A long stone's throw west of Estoril along the coast and 28 km (17 miles) west of Lisbon, Cascais (pronounced cask-EYE-sh) is altogether different in substance and spirit. Although it has become a popular holiday resort with fashionable boutiques, restaurants, and discos, it retains the flavor of a fishing village. In the old quarters, nonetheless, graceful mansions are a reminder of Cascais's former role as summer residence for Portuguese royalty. King Luís I actually resided in the **Cidadela**, an old fortress, rebuilt in the 17th century, that dominates the bay and is now used by the president of the republic for official receptions. It is open to the public only for occasional concerts, but there's a great view of the bay from O Passeio de Santo António, an esplanade under the Cidadela's walls. Many well-to-do Portuguese keep summer places in Cascais, and there is a substantial year-round foreign colony, mostly British. Some critics warn, however, that development is getting out of hand, with new high-rise buildings going up on the outskirts toward the lovely village of Malveira da Serra, north of Cascais.

The main attraction of Cascais is its little harbor, alive with bright-colored fishing boats and a bustling fish market, just off the main square. The best show in town is the nightly (except Sundays) auction at the market, where local fishermen and women present their wares.

At the end of the bay the Clube Naval de Cascais, a yacht club located at the base of the citadel, welcomes visitors, who may anchor their yachts in season (June to October) or rent a boat for the day. This is also the point of departure for half-day cruises of Cascais bay.

The beaches in Cascais are not recommended. The main beach, Praia da Ribeira, is for fishing boats, and the nearby Praia da Rainha and Praia da Conceicão are small and the water is not very clean.

Among the sights in Cascais is the **Igreja de Nossa Senhora de Assunção**, with a painted wood ceiling and walls lined with 18th-century tiles and paintings by Josefa de Obidos and José Malhoa. In the Parque Municipal da Gandarinha across the way the **Museu do Conde de Castro Guimarães**, formerly a private mansion, contains a good collection of Chinese porcelains, ancient maps, and tiles of the 16th and 17th centuries.

The town's main shopping area, near the railway station, is **rua Frederico Arouca**, now a pedestrian zone. It sports a number of fashionable dress shops, jewelry stores, and gift shops. One place to find an excellent gift is the **Atlantis** crystal boutique.

Another place for concentrated shopping is the **Jumbo** (Pão de Açucar), located just off the Marginal at the entry to Cascais, coming from Estoril. This shopping center is open weekends and evenings, when most other shops are closed, and includes specialty shops for cosmetics, leather goods, gifts, and the best country bread around.

One of the best shops for *azulejos* is **Isto e Aquilo**, on the largo de Misericórdia in old Cascais. Here you can find attractive hand-painted reproductions of 17th- and 18th-century tile panels or single tiles.

For modern tiles of traditional inspiration, there is **Ceramicarte** on the largo da Assunção, just opposite the church. The shop contains all kinds of ceramic tiles, jugs, plates, and vases decorated with fish and other sea motifs, as the local potters have done for some 4,000 years.

An open market is held on the fairground in the center of town every Wednesday. Itinerant vendors offer fruits, vegetables, flowers, clothing, and hardware. The market is not really geared to foreign visitors, but there is usually interesting pottery, woodcarving, and basketware for sale.

A popular afternoon pastime is to take tea at **Tagarela**, which is really just a pretext for relaxing and enjoying the finest view of Cascais bay and the Lisbon coast. There's a moderate prix-fixe menu that includes tea, scones or toast, butter, homemade jam, and freshly baked cake. The tearoom is located over the bay-side restaurant Baluarte (great views, fresh fish, but pricey), which is on avenida Dom Carlos I, but you have to enter from the back and you must ring a bell to get in. Open daily at teatime only, from 4:00 to 7:00 P.M.

Cascais's restaurants are usually noisier than those in Estoril, and less expensive. Tucked away behind the fire station on avenida Vasco da Gama, **Apeadeiro Restaurante** features succulent grilled lamb chops and pork chops, sardines, and sea bass at prices local people on holiday can afford. On the rua das Flores, just behind the fish market, there's a string of pleasant seafood places. The clientele is democratic: leaders of business and industry next to budget-conscious civil servants. **O Pescador**, for example, serves an outstanding sole meunière (Tel: 01-284-6037), and **O Batel**, nearby, specializes in shellfish paella (Tel: 01-483-0215); reservations are advised. On the main street, **João Padeira**, in an old bakery decorated with millstones, produces splendid roast goat.

The discos cater to Lisbon's golden youth. Currently in favor is **Coconuts**, a complex of disco, bars, and swimming pool cum ocean terrace, located on the road to the Boca do Inferno. Also popular is **Palm Beach**, perched on the hillside at Praia da Conceição, and **Van Gogo**, in an old fisherman's home on travessa de Alfarrobeia. There are also several *fado* (Portuguese folk song) houses, which seem somewhat out of context in modern villas, so far from Lisbon's old Bairro Alto—but the music isn't bad. The place to go for serious *fado* these days is **Forte Dom Rodrigo** on the road to Birre, a suburb of Cascais—most local taxi drivers know the spot. The show doesn't get started until after 10:00 P.M. And if you happen to be around in July, don't miss the Cascais Jazz Festival. Check with the local Turismo for exact dates.

If you feel like lingering in Cascais, try the charming **Casa da Pergola**. Located in the center of town, this private guest house has ten rooms. A typical summer mansion with brightly decorated façade and Mediterranean-style garden, it has been totally renovated. With its gray-and-white marble floors, sculpted stucco ceilings, mirrored doors, and antique furnishings, the Casa da Pergola has a special elegance not found in the usual first-class hotel, yet rates are lower. It serves only breakfast. Two hotels in Cascais should be visited, if only for lunch or tea, because of the view. **Hotel Baía**, a nondescript building on the noisy main square, has a terrace from which you can survey the action on the beach below. Although the Baía may lack the elegance of some hotels in the area, its rooms are comfortable, and most have a wonderful view of the bay. Recently added attractions are a rooftop swimming pool, café, and grill. On a nearby promontory stands the **Hotel Albatroz**, a small luxury inn that was once a private mansion. The hotel is beautifully furnished with antiques and has an elegant dining room, tile-paneled bar, and terrace, with a view of the entire coast as far as Lisbon (dinner reservations recommended; Tel: 01-483-2821). Try to get one of the rooms in the original villa; those in the new wing have less charm and character.

The **Hotel Village Cascais**, a huge, pink six-story rectangle with elongated arched balconies, is perched on a windy corner of the coast road just across from the Farol de Santa Marta lighthouse. This self-contained resort has 233 spacious apartments, each with kitchenette and satellite TV, two swimming pools, a health club, restaurant, and coffee shop, and a couple of bars. Part of the Occidental Hotels chain, it caters mainly to Spanish groups.

The Atlantic Coast

Around the corner from the protected bay of Cascais is the wilder Atlantic shore. Although civilization in the form of restaurants, hotels, and sports facilities has made inroads, the landscape along here has a desolate natural quality, and it is still possible to find an unpopulated beach.

Follow the coast road west out of Cascais to the **Boca do Inferno** (Mouth of Hell), a strange formation of arches and caverns carved out of the cliffs by fierce waves. A great place for a leisurely lunch is the **Furnas Lagosteira** here, overlooking the Boca, where you can select your own fresh lobster on the rocks and watch the waves battering the cliffs while you eat. (Lobster is expensive everywhere in Portugal, however; it might be wiser to settle for fish or the local specialty, barnacles.) Here at the Boca is a market that is increasingly popular, particularly with Spanish tourists (prices are often quoted in pesetas, so take care). Stalls lined up on both sides of the road are open all day, every day, and offer a wide variety of handicrafts and clothing at prices considerably lower than in shops. The style and quality are not always the best, but good buys can be found if you know how to look—and bargain.

Farther along the coast you will come to the Guia lighthouse on a rocky point and the lovely pine forest of the **Parque de Marinha**, with the spacious lodges and villas of the Quinta da Marinha, a large resort complex, mostly hidden by the trees.

At Quinta da Marinha itself there are a number of luxury villas with two or three bedrooms at what is called the **Quinta da Marinha Aldeamento Turístico**. Rooms here should be booked well in advance. In the middle of the woods, the Clube da Marinha offers horseback riding, tennis, and golf, and is open to visitors. Nearby, the Clube de Campo Dom Carlos also welcomes temporary members and has stables, tennis courts, and a good pool.

A couple of miles beyond the lighthouse, in a clump of umbrella pines, is the **Estalagem Senhora da Guia**. (An *estalagem* is a privately operated inn, whereas a *pousada* is government-run.) This large villa of the 1920s, with typical red-tile roof, white stucco façade, and high ceilings, was completely renovated and opened as an inn in 1984. There are 28 rooms, including four suites; every room has a spacious new bath decorated with attractive *azulejos*. A generous pool on the front lawn overlooks the sea. Many British and American guests come here to relax or enjoy the facilities of the Quinta da Marinha, a few hundred yards away.

Farther inland lies the Cascais bullring. Purists prefer Lisbon's Campo Pequeno, because, they say, the Atlantic coast is too windy for the bulls, but on hot summer days the spectators here at least enjoy the breeze.

The sea road, now heading north, continues on past large scattered boulders, rugged cliffs, sand dunes, and stretches of fine, uncluttered sand: This is **Guincho**, which means "scream" in Portuguese, referring to the almost continuous howling of wind and waves. Even on a calm day the breakers keep up a subdued roar. This is a favorite beach for windsurfers. The wind-surfing world championships are often held here. In summer the surf generally subsides enough for swimming or wave-jumping, but even the best swimmers must beware of the strong undertow.

An old favorite, the **Restaurante Porto de Santa Maria** has been completely rebuilt and was reopened in the summer of 1992, with a dining room three times the size of the original and wraparound windows overlooking the rocky Guincho shore and the Atlantic. It has a distinctly nautical feel—pickled woods and a color scheme of sea blues and grays. You can order nearly anything that swims, cooked at least a dozen different ways. Porto de Santa Maria specializes in such Portuguese classics as *açorda de mariscos* (made with shellfish, bread, and eggs, and flavored with fresh coriander) and *arroz de mariscos* (a casserole of rice with shellfish). Tel: (01) 285-0240 or (01) 285-1036. Just north of the Porto de Santa Maria, an imposing fortress on a rocky promontory has been converted into the **Hotel do Guincho**, an exclusive haven with 31 rooms decorated with old tiles and with balconies opening to the sea. Facilities include a medieval banquet hall, tearoom, bar, and restaurant.

On a nearby cliff the **Estalagem Muchaxo** overlooks a broad, sandy beach and a swimming pool. This inn, with two restaurants, is so popular that it seems to expand every year, now with a total of 60 rooms, plus a health club, squash court, and meeting rooms. Just a mile north of the Muchaxo take the dirt road on the left to the little Praia do Abano and the pleasant **Abano** restaurant, on the cliff. Try the *espetada de lulas* (squid on the spit), a favorite with Portuguese families who frequent the place.

From Guincho to **Cabo da Roca**, the westernmost point in Portugal and in continental Europe, the road winds north past bleak hills and along rocky cliffs overlooking the sea. It's a spectacular drive if you have time, but many people prefer to go to Cabo da Roca west from Sintra, across the gentle Colares valley. The remote and usually windy cape was best described by the Portuguese poet Luís Vaz de Camões as the place "where the land ends and the sea commences." Cabo da Roca is a wildflower sanctuary and remains unspoiled. There's a working lighthouse and a small Turismo (government tourist office), where certificates are available to testify that you have journeyed to the Continent's westernmost point. A recent addition is a large handicraft shop and restaurant. In the nearby village of Azoia, the restaurant called **Refúgio da Roca** serves excellent sea bass and a famous shellfish soup.

THE SINTRA AREA

Somehow Sintra, on a mountain northwest of Lisbon and north of Estoril, has not been spoiled by time or by its successive waves of visitors, from Roman and Moorish armies to English and German romantics—and Portuguese and North American vacationers. It is still a magic mountain with fairy-tale castles, thick forests, and abundant waterfalls, all generally veiled in mist.

Sintra's special charms have been celebrated by numerous well-known English writers who fell unabashedly in love with the place. Poet laureate Robert Southey lived here with his uncle for four months in 1796, returning in the spring of 1801 for another year. He wrote passionately of the landscape, calling it "my paradise—heaven on earth of my hopes." That diligent traveller Lord Byron spent only a brief time in Sintra but consecrated it in *Childe Harold* as "glorious Eden." He called the village "the most delightful in Europe." William Beckford, who felt quite at home among Portuguese nobility, had several lengthy sojourns in Sintra between 1787 and 1799, living first in Ramalhão Palace, at the base of the mountain, and later in Monserrate. His letters describe the gardens, woods, cataracts, and sea as "a Royalty of Nature."

The latest foreigners to discover the charms of Sintra are the Japanese. The Aoki Group recently opened the **Clube de Golfe da Penha Longa** on the craggy, woodsy, boulder-strewn Penha Longa estate, near Lagoa Azul at the base of Sintra mountain, including an 18-hole golf course; at a later date, a new 9-hole course is to be opened. Now under construction: a sleek, green's-edge hotel, scheduled to open in 1994, maybe even late 1993. Once the complex is completed, only hotel guests will be permitted to use the golf course; until that time, it is open to the public. The Japanese group has also bought the mansion in Cascais where former King Umberto of Italy lived in exile, and are said to be planning to build a luxury hotel complex there.

Some excursions combine Sintra with the lavish 18th-century palace of Queluz, and Mafra, the massive, austere palace and monastery (also 18th century). But it's best to devote at least one day to Sintra and another to its surroundings.

If you are driving from Lisbon, take the inland *auto-estrada* marked "Estoril" (the N 7) to get out of town. Just beyond Monsanto Park turn onto the N 117 and follow the signs for Sintra. The highway goes through rolling countryside, increasingly encroached upon by light industry and urban development. At Queluz take the N 249 for Sintra, which runs into a new highway, IC 19, that eventually will zoom from the Lisbon airport area direct to Sintra. Now after a couple of miles it runs into the old N 249, which leads to Sintra. Much of the countryside is currently being torn up, as a whole new network of highways is under construction in the Lisbon-Sintra-Cascais area. Pay close attention to the signs and drive slowly.

Queluz

A slight detour on the way to Sintra from Lisbon (follow the signs from the IC 19) will take you to the 18th-century Rococo **Palácio Nacional de Queluz**, 15 km (9 miles) northwest of central Lisbon, which began as a simple country lodge. Unfortunately, this beautiful rose-washed monument is surrounded by uninspired apartment buildings. Sometimes called Portugal's Versailles, the palace of Queluz was built by Pedro (who later became Pedro III), the future consort of Maria I, called the Mad Queen.

In modern times the palace has served as a guest house for state visitors, including Queen Elizabeth II and U.S. Presidents Eisenhower and Reagan, as well as a venue for special musical events. Generally, however, it is open to ordinary visitors. Perhaps more than the palace itself, the royal gardens, laid out by French architect Jean-Baptiste Robillon, evoke Versailles, with their neatly clipped box hedges, ponds, flower gardens, cypress trees, and statuary. Special points of interest inside the palace include the Music Room, with splendid crystal chandeliers; the Throne Room, with magnificent gilt woodwork and mirrors; and the Ambassadors Hall, decorated with fine marble.

If the palace proper is closed, at least visit the kitchen, which has a huge fireplace, giant spits, a 15-foot-long marble worktable, and a rich array of shining copper pans. Now known as **Cozinha Velha** (Old Kitchen), this is one of the most elegant restaurants in the area; open for both lunch and dinner, it serves the best of Portuguese cuisine. Among the many specialties is *linguado suado* (steamed sole) submerged in a velvety cream sauce with mushrooms, carrots, and onions. But the crowning glory is the pastry cart with its "royal sweets"—luxurious little cakes, made of egg yolks and sugar, whose secret recipe has been passed on from the royal chefs. Reservations are recommended; Tel: (01) 435-0232. The Cozinha Velha also operates a small cafeteria, for light refreshments, in the palace next to the gift shop.

Sintra

Back on the main road, N 249 heading west from Lisbon, you come first to Ramalhão, the pale-yellow former royal palace, where Beckford wrote his colorful letters; it's now a girls' school. Here you join the road from Estoril, N 9, and swing slightly to the right, joining the estrada Chão de Meninos and following the blue sign marked "Palacio." First you drive through **São Pedro de Sintra** (30 km/19 miles northwest of Lisbon) at the bottom of the mountain, where one of the best country fairs of Portugal is held on the second and fourth Sundays of every month. Good bargains are found in all kinds of pottery, woodwork, basketware, and other handicrafts, as well as clothing, leather goods, antiques, and imitation antiques. Popular with the fair crowd is **Adega do Saloio**, a typical tavern nearby at Chão de Meninos square in São Pedro, serving sausages, grilled goat, and other local specialties. For more cosmopolitan dining there is the **Solar de São Pedro**, also located in São Pedro de Sintra, on praça Dom Fernando II. Specialties include *coxas de rã à Provençal* (frogs' legs), the currently fashionable *filetes de tamboril* (monkfish), and especially tasty tournedos. Reservations are advised; Tel: (01) 923-1860.

The modern part of Sintra, farther up the mountain where the railroad station is located, is called Estefânia. Here, where the shops are less touristy than in old Sintra, is the place to get the best *queijadas* (cheese-and-almond tarts). Turn west at the largo de Afonso de Albuquerque, and follow the signs marked "Centro Histórico" leading to the Vila, the old part of town. You might wish to make a stop at the **Sapa** pastry shop, located at the beginning of the Volta da Duche, across the valley from the Palácio Nacional. Sapa's *queijadas* are reputed to be the best in the region, and its *nozes* (walnut sweets enveloped in crisp caramel) are beyond belief. This is also an excellent site for taking photographs of old Sintra and the valley. One exotic sight along the way is the Fonte Mourisca, an elaborate Neo-Moorish fountain. Volta da Duche, a horseshoe drive with a magnificent view of the countryside, leads to the Palácio Nacional, easily distinguished by its two immense cone-shaped chimneys (see below). Another almost permanent feature of the palace square is the fleet of tour buses, which exude obnoxious fumes and spoil the view. Almost everyone agrees that the buses are generally offensive, but no one seems to be able to do anything about them.

A little beyond the palace is the Turismo, located in a distinguished old mansion with a permanent museum and other exhibits. Turismo, open daily including weekends, is the best place to begin a visit of Sintra and find out about local events, which include concerts sponsored by the municipal council and Sintra's annual music festival. This last takes place in June and July, with concerts, recitals, and ballet presented in the Palácio Nacional, Seteais, Queluz, and some of the grand manors of the region.

The Turismo staff also provides information about restaurants, shopping, lodgings, and taxi and horse-carriage fares, and gives away maps for walking tours of the region. Walking about the cobblestone square and narrow alleys and stepped streets of the Vila is a delight, but, beyond that, Sintra's peaks are high and the roads steep and winding; most visitors would do well to take a carriage or car up to Castelo da Pena, Cruz Alta, the Moorish castle, and other lofty sights (see below for all these).

A few steps from the Turismo stands the Estalagem dos Cavaleiros (currently not open to the public). A small plaque notes that this is where Lord Byron stayed when he visited Sintra, and according to some people this is where he was inspired to write *Childe Harold*. This 18th-century inn has been bought by a Dutch entrepreneur, Jan Willem Bos, who has begun work to "restore it to its former glory." He planned to open the 16-room luxury inn and restaurant under its original name, the Lawrence Hotel, by early 1993, but the project has been delayed and he now hopes to open in 1994.

Behind the palace stands one of Sintra's most controversial buildings, the bulky, modern **Hotel Tivoli**, which seems out of character with the rest of the town. Sintra needed more hotel space, but there is a consensus that the hotel should have been designed to fit in with the old pastel palaces and manors, or at least should be enshrouded in greenery. The hotel's clients (who of course are spared having to look at the building when they're inside) have a superb view from private balconies and from the panoramic restaurant, and need only cross the street to visit the Palácio Nacional.

Also located next to the palace is the modest **Hotel Central**, built at the beginning of the century, with a lovely tile façade. The rooms are plain but perfectly adequate. Make sure you get one with a private bath. The terrace of the Central is a strategic place to view the goings-on of Sintra or to meet friends for a *galão* (café au lait) or a stronger drink. Another treat you can't leave town without tasting are *travesseiros* (pillows), egg and almond cakes you'll dream about. You'll find them at **Piriquita**, a coffee shop near the National Palace.

The Sintra district is known for its handicrafts: pottery, basket-weaving, stone- and marble-cutting. In Sintra, the **Central Bazaar**, next to the Hotel Central on the main square opposite the palace in Vila de Sintra, has a broad selection of local craftwork. A good place to find regional food at moderate prices is the **Alcobaça** restaurant, on the narrow street on the opposite side of the palace square, going up the hill. Another popular restaurant a little way down the hill from the palace is **Tulhas**, on rua Gil Vicente; try the veal cutlets or the codfish with heavy cream.

Continuing on foot down Gil Vicente to the largo Latino Coelho, you come to a small treasure of a museum that's too often neglected. This is the **Museu do Brinquedo**, the toy museum (Tel: 01-923-5079), a collection of some 20,000 toys from the 16th century to modern times. There are Dinky Toys, Meccanos, Tootsie Toys, and some rather remarkable items: a 1902 boat that moves with a clockwork system, a 1925 Citröen with headlights, springs, and brakes that work, a miniature Indianapolis racing car of 1930, Portuguese carriages in wood with papier-mâché horses from 1940, an Italian terra-cotta doll from the 17th century. The main focus of this private collection is automobiles, but there is an impressive display of toy soldiers through the ages, from the Roman armies to those of Napoleon and Hitler.

Palácio Nacional

The Palácio Nacional at Sintra (in the historic center) was built by King João I in the 14th century on the site of a Moorish palace and has subsequently undergone many alterations and additions, making it a fascinating conglomeration of Gothic, Moorish, and Manueline styles. (It is also known as the Palácio Real, the Paço da Sintra, and the Paço da Vila.)

With sharp eye and wit, Portugal's irreverent 19th-century novelist José Maria Eça de Queirós, in *The Maias,* paints a gracious, if devastating, tableau of "this massive, silent palace without fleurons or towers, seated patriarchally among the houses of the town, with those lovely windows that give it a noble and royal look, with the valley at its feet, leafy, dense and fresh, and on high its colossal chimneys, disparate, summing up everything as though that residence was all kitchen built on a scale to suit the gluttony of a king who daily devours an entire kingdom." Unfortunately there are no guides available, and only irregular tours accompanied by Portuguese-speaking guards.

Of special interest are the 15th-, 16th-, and 17th-century *azulejos* in the Sala dos Arabes, the Sala das Sereias (Sirens' Room), and the chapel, reputed to be among the finest tiles of the Iberian Peninsula. The marble fountain in the Sala dos Arabes is said by some to remain from the ancient Moorish palace, having been restored in the 15th century. Equally interesting is the Sala dos Brasões (Coats of Arms Room), whose walls are lined with blue-and-white-tile hunting scenes and battles. On the octagonal ceiling are painted 72 coats of arms of the most noble families of the 16th century. One has been effaced, that of the Tavora family, which was caught in a conspiracy against the throne. Also impressive is the Sala das Pêgas (Magpie Room), the ceiling of which is painted with little birds carrying standards in their beaks with the royal motto, "Por Bem" ("All for the Good"). As the story goes, Queen Philippa caught King João in the act of kissing one of her ladies-in-waiting, and he responded with bravado, "Por bem." As this incident was the subject of relentless court gossip, the king had the ceiling painted with magpies, symbols of gossip, to remind everyone of his motto.

Sintra's main churches were restored after being badly damaged by the 1755 earthquake. You might visit the **Igreja de Santa Maria** in the woods, on the rua da Trindade, the high road connecting Vila de Sintra to São Pedro, with a turnoff up the mountain to the Castelo dos Mouros. The church of Santa Maria was founded by Afonso Henriques in the 12th century and has been declared a national monument. Rebuilt in the 14th century, this Gothic temple has three naves with ogival (pointed) arches and beautiful capitals. The double entrance with a Classical column in the center was added in the 16th century.

Pena

The **Palácio da Pena** is located on top of one of the highest peaks of Sintra mountain on what was the site of a 16th-century Hieronymite monastery. From largo Ferreira de Castro in the upper part of Vila de Sintra, take the estrada da Pena, which twists up through dense greenery and rocky peaks. From a distance the building is quite imposing, but close at hand it resembles a Hollywood stage set, with its jumble of crenellated walls, forbidding dungeons, pointed turrets, and golden domes. It was rebuilt by the 19th-century German architect Baron von Eschwege as a summer residence for Queen Maria II's consort, Ferdinand of Saxe-Coburg-Gotha. The only authentic part of this ostentatious mock-medieval palace is a small chapel near the entrance, with 17th-century tiles and an alabaster altar by the 16th-century sculptor Nicholas Chanterene.

Without doubt, however, the best part of Pena is the 500-acre park and the view, which is overwhelming. Just below the Jardim das Camélias lies a forest of every kind of tree brought back from all over Portugal's erstwhile empire. Beyond, the green valley of Colares spreads out to the sea.

At the highest point of the Sintra range is **Cruz Alta**, a stone cross. The site can be reached by car, to provide a great view of Pena and the Costa do Estoril. Take the same road farther up until you reach the cross, first raised in 1522, later damaged by lightning and restored. Return by the calçada Pena, which comes out in São Pedro. On the crest of one of the lower mountains stands the **Castelo dos Mouros** (Moorish Castle), built in the eighth century and now largely in ruins. From its tower and crenellated walls you can get a different view of Sintra's great moss-covered granite boulders and of the gentle countryside below. To reach the Moorish castle take the caminho do Castelo dos Mouros from the Santa Maria church (see above).

Before going back down to the town, follow the estrada da Pena (also known as the N 247-3) westward along the mountain crest through thick forests to **Capuchos**, one of the most astonishing sights in the region. Deep in the woods, this 16th-century Franciscan monastery was built out of large boulders. The monks' cells were lined with cork against the extreme humidity, and their meager furnishings were also made of cork.

From Capuchos, you might want to make another slight detour a short distance to the southwest, but still in the mountains. Follow the sign for **Peninha**, another peak with a splendid panoramic view of the valley and the sea. There is a small chapel here whose walls are lined with handsome 18th-century tiles recounting the life of the Virgin.

You may wish to continue westward down and out of the mountains from Peninha to join the road to Colares (N 247) and circle back to Sintra from there. People generally prefer to backtrack to Capuchos and to the Pena road, N 247-3, which leads back down to Vila de Sintra.

Seteais and Monserrate

From Palácio da Pena, take the estrada da Pena, N 247-3, which twists its way down through the luxuriant park to largo Ferreira de Castro. Turn left onto the road to Seteais, past vine-covered stone walls, palatial mansions, and Moorish manors. This is the N 375, which leads to Seteais, a stately 18th-century palace built by a Dutch consul, Daniel Gildemeester. The royal arch of triumph marks the fact that King João VI once stayed here. This was long considered the site of the signing of the Treaty of Sintra between the duke of Wellington's forces and those of French Marshall Junot during the Peninsular War, but now it appears that the treaty was drafted here and signed in Lisbon.

Originally called the Quinta da Alegria, the estate later became known as Seteais (pronounced setee-EYE-sh), although it is not known why. According to local tradition, this is really two words in Portuguese, *sete ais,* meaning the "seven sighs" or "seven ayes," variously interpreted as either exclamations of sorrow or delight. Another school of thought, however, holds that this is the plural of the old Portuguese word *seto,* meaning "hedge" or "enclosure." In 1955 the palace was converted into the luxury **Hotel Palácio dos Seteais**, reputed to be one of the finest in Europe, with outstanding cuisine and service. Most of the rooms are decorated with murals, and the dining room and bar have landscapes said to be the work of Jean Pillement, an 18th-century French painter much appreciated in Portugal. All the furnishings are either antiques or replicas of antiques. The east wing has been tastefully restored, doubling the number of rooms to 38. A swimming pool and two tennis courts have been discreetly added without spoiling the beauty of the estate. The formal garden in front and the boxwoods in the back are meticulously kept. Prices match those of luxury hotels in other, more expensive, European countries. Nevertheless, the decor and the views of the mountain and valley are exceptional and worth a stopover, at least for tea.

Continuing on the N 375 (sometimes called the Estrada de Monserrate), you pass near several delightful quintas that have been opened to paying guests. A little way beyond the stone arch, at a sign on the left that says **Casa da Tapada**, you can take a winding dirt road for about a mile to a reconstructed manor in a clearing in the forest. This recently opened quinta has only four bedrooms but one of the best views of Sintra mountain, Pena Palace, and the Moorish walls. The long, low, whitewashed building with orange-tile roof and iron balconies looks something like a hacienda and is beautifully furnished with Portuguese antiques. It also has central heating and fireplaces. Just before you reach Monserrate Park, turn right down a steep dirt road to the **Quinta de São Tiago**, initially a 16th-century convent belonging to the monks of Pena. Tastefully decorated and furnished with antiques, the quinta has nine rooms with private baths, a suite, a music room, a swimming pool, and a tennis court. Elegant meals are served in the family dining room, built in the 1960s with an 18th-century–style painted ceiling and candelabra. The owners live at the quinta and willingly share their family stories with visitors. (Some guests note that the lady of the house can be somewhat overpowering.)

Some visitors to the region prefer the **Quinta da Capela**, which is located off the same road and just beyond Monserrate. This sprawling 16th-century country home has a lovely chapel, 11 rooms with baths, a conference room, and a minipool, gymnasium, and sauna. The owners do not live on the premises.

Monserrate itself is undoubtedly one of the finest parks in the country, with exotic trees and flowers from all parts of the world: cedars of Lebanon, African palms, mahoganies of Brazil, bamboo, and a profusion of local flora from camellias to rhododendrons. The original **Quinta de Monserrate**, where at the end of the 18th century English romantic writer William Beckford used to entertain his noble Portuguese friends, has been torn down. The present quinta is a Victorian version of an Arab fantasy, with arches and bulbous cupolas built by Sir Francis Cook, Viscount Monserrate, in the 19th century. It is closed, and no final decision has been made on plans for renovation.

The Monserrate road winds west along the side of the mountain through lush vegetation and then zigzags down to the valley of Colares. Along the way are several handsome old quintas. The finest is the **Quinta do Vinagre**, built in the 16th century and located on the outskirts of Colares. This quinta, restored in the late 19th century, has not been turned into a guest house but is used for some of the concerts in the Sintra music festival. If you wish permission to visit the manor and its lovely gardens, write to Quinta do Vinagre, 2710 Colares, Portugal.

Colares

Compared to the lush, dramatic Sintra mountain, the valley of Colares is a peaceful landscape of vineyards, narrow winding roads, and whitewashed villages, with an occasional ancient manor and a scattering of new villas. English poet and art critic Sacheverell Sitwell wrote that it could be part of Tuscany.

The village of Colares is a small rural center 6 km (3½ miles) west of Sintra, and its principal monument—the **Adega Regional de Colares** (local wine cellar)—is well worth visiting. Concerts are generally held in the *adega* during the months of May and June. Nobody knows when grape cultivation began in the Colares region, but as early as the 14th century the Portuguese were sending Colares wines to India for the royal tables. The grapevines are grown in a sandy soil that protected them against the phylloxera blight in 1865 and that gives the wine its distinctive aroma. Colares red wines are rich and full-bodied, ruby-colored and somewhat astringent when young, turning a velvety deep garnet with age. The white wines are straw-colored with a nutty flavor. A good place to test the local wine is the popular **Cantinho da Várzea**, a noisy riverside café that also serves palatable steaks and french fries, hamburgers, and pizza. If you take a half-day tour of the region from Sintra, you will generally end up at **Restaurante Várzea de Colares**, set in a lovely garden at avenida Dom Afonso Henriques, 6 (Tel: 01-929-2043), where group wine tastings are held at 5:30 P.M., except on Sundays and Mondays. If you're on your own, you might have a meal at this spacious, glassed-in restaurant with pleasant blue-and-white decor and local charm. A word of warning, however: As in many Portuguese restaurants, you'll get more than you asked for, like little dishes of tripe and pig's ears, for which you'll be charged unless you wave them away.

A short walk down the road is the old tram yard and the Banzão station, where you can catch the tram to the popular beach resort of Praia das Maçãs. The tram operates all day every day except Mondays, from June 1 until October 1, and is a very picturesque half-hour journey. In the old days, it used to run as far as Sintra.

It is only a few miles to Cabo da Roca (see the Costa do Estoril section, above) and several pleasant seaside resorts, frequented mainly by Portuguese families. **Praia das Maçãs**, northwest of Colares, has a broad sandy beach with relatively calm surf, a restaurant, and a place to change. Just to the south is the wide beach of Praia Grande, with the **Motel da Piscina** (formerly Motel das Arribas) built into the cliffs. It has family-size rooms (with five beds) and two big swimming pools, and is very popular with the Portuguese for summer vacations and weekends. **Azenhas do Mar**, to the north nearby, is a lovely little village built into the cliffs, with a natural swimming pool carved out of the rocks.

A mile or so inland lies the village of Janas and the 16th-century **Igreja de São Mamede**, an unusual circular building with Classical columns, said to have been built on Roman ruins. Little known and only partly excavated Roman ruins are found at **Odrinhas**, a village 10 km (6 miles) north of Sintra on the road to Ericeira (N 247). There are remnants of a fourth-century villa with a mosaic floor, a chapel, and strange monoliths. A small museum on the site, **Museu Arqueológico de São Miguel de Odrinhas**, contains Roman columns and tombstones found in the area.

An interesting expedition is to visit the pottery workshop and museum of **Eduardo Azenha** in the village of Santa Suzana, on the N 247 just north of the archaeological site at Odrinhas. A farmer-artist, Mr. Azenha has re-created Portuguese village life of 100 years ago in ceramic. He sells small figures, windmills, Nativity scenes, and the like for reasonable prices.

In the wooded region of Sabugo, near Pêro Pinheiro, the **Hotel de Vale de Lobos** is a moderately priced alternative to the luxury establishments in Sintra. Its 50 rooms are simply furnished, but all have private bathrooms and telephones. Vale de Lobos has all kinds of facilities, like disco, cinema, tennis court, and conference rooms, yet is just a few minutes' drive from Sintra.

Mafra

The rolling farmland between Sintra and Mafra used to be windmill country, but you'll be lucky to see any with their sails out. Although less poetical, machine-ground flour is more economical, so the windmills have been deserted or converted into smart summer homes. First take the N 247 to **Ericeira**, a beach resort popular among the Portuguese that has managed to retain its fishing-village atmosphere. In the town itself you can see cliffside dwellings, a lively harbor, and fine beaches. Since Ericeira is the home of that unusual Portuguese specialty *açorda de mariscos* ("dry" shellfish soup), you might want to stop at one of the fish restaurants in town, such as **Toca do Cabóz**, and give it a try. The basis for the soup is stale bread, soaked in shellfish stock and beaten well, then cooked with olive oil, garlic, and fresh coriander, to which eggs and shellfish are added. If the timing and technique are right, it all tastes like some heavenly soufflé. Ericeira is best known as the port from which the last king of Portugal, Manuel II, set sail for exile on October 5, 1910, when the monarchy was overthrown.

A 9-km (5½-mile) drive inland on the N 116 then takes you to the **Palácio Nacional de Mafra** (also called the Convento de Mafra), which looms over the surrounding villages like a proud monument to the lost empire. Indeed, Mafra rivals the Escorial in Spain in grandeur, but is very different. It reputedly took 50,000 workmen 18 years and a fortune from Portugal's former colony of Brazil to build this vast structure, completed in 1735. It was King João V who commissioned the German architect and goldsmith Friedrich Ludwig to undertake this ambitious work.

The Baroque monastery-palace is built of ivory-colored marble, darkened by lichen, time, and the elements. The basilica, crowned by a large cupola, stands in the center of two long wings, with a squat domed tower on each end. Giant marble statues of the saints stand guard at the entrance. The interior is richly decorated with marble statues and bas-relief. These works are by artists of the School of Mafra, a group of foreign and Portuguese sculptors specially commissioned for the project, among them Joaquim Machado de Castro, one of Portugal's finest.

The royal apartments, hospital, pharmacy, and monks' cells are open to the public, as is Mafra's jewel, the library. This splendid long gallery with vaulted ceiling contains some 35,000 books, many rare editions among them. The palace also has a small museum with works of religious art. Try to visit Mafra on a Sunday afternoon around 4:00 P.M., when the carillons are played. Dom João V ordered more than 100 carillon bells to be cast in Belgium for Mafra; they have recently been restored and have a beautiful sound.

Most of the **Tapada de Mafra**, the game reserve on the outskirts of town, is currently closed to the public; the northern part only is open from July through September. In this vast walled park, deer, foxes, wild boar, hare, and other game roam about freely.

Mafra is also known for its blue-and-white pottery, with delicate designs. Some of the most attractive tableware and other handicrafts can be found for reasonable prices at **José Medeiros** on the main square. There's also a pleasant café where you can gather strength before or after visiting the monastery.

Another rural handicraft center is the **Aldeia Saloia de José Franco**, located about 5 km/3 miles west of Mafra on the N 116. In this reconstituted village you may find some interesting ceramics and brasswork, as well as some pretty garish pieces. Not so easy to transport are the marble statues and tables for sale at a number of marble factories in Montelavar and Pêro Pinheiro on the N 9 road to Mafra from Sintra.

NORTHERN ESTREMADURA

Estremadura province is an extremely varied swath of land, stretching from the great pine forests and green hills of the Leiria region in the north to the cork oak and olive groves of the Árrabida peninsula in the south, bounded by the Atlantic cliffs and beaches on the west and the Tagus river estuary to the east.

A limited day tour of the northern reaches of Estremadura should include the medieval walled town of Obidos, the colorful fishing village of Nazaré, and the magnificent monasteries of Alcobaça and Batalha.

For those who travel by car and have more time, however, there is much more to see and enjoy in this area. Leaving Lisbon, take the N 8 route north to **Loures** (a road that used to wind through lovely old farms and vineyards but now goes through just another dormitory suburb). Stop at Loures to see the church with its fine 15th-century cross.

Continuing north on the N 8 through rolling farmland with defunct windmills, vineyards, and marble quarries, you will come to **Torres Vedras**, a busy industrial town and wine center 59 km (37 miles) north of Lisbon. An old fort stands on the hill here overlooking the Sizandro river, which has served as a natural defense since Roman times. Torres Vedras played an important role during the Peninsular War, when the duke of Wellington ordered the construction of fortifications that stretched from the Tagus river to the Atlantic near Mafra and successfully blocked the advance of the French army. Remnants of these fortifications are still visible here and there in the fields.

In town, the **Igreja de São Pedro** has a lovely Manueline doorway, 16th-century medallion-shaped tiles, and noteworthy primitive paintings in the chapel. The nearby Chafariz dos Canos, a Gothic fountain long since dry, dates back to the 14th century.

A short detour east along the river leads to the village of **Cucos** and the Termas do Vale dos Cucos, an *estação termal* (spa) with thermal waters and hot mud baths, good for rheumatism, arthritis, gout, and other ailments. There is an old-fashioned hotel on the site, but accommodations are better in Torres Vedras, which has several modest hotels and pensions.

Or you may wish to stay at the delightful **Quinta de São José** in the hamlet of Freiria, on the outskirts of the rail center of Sobral de Monte Agraço, 15 km (9 miles) southeast

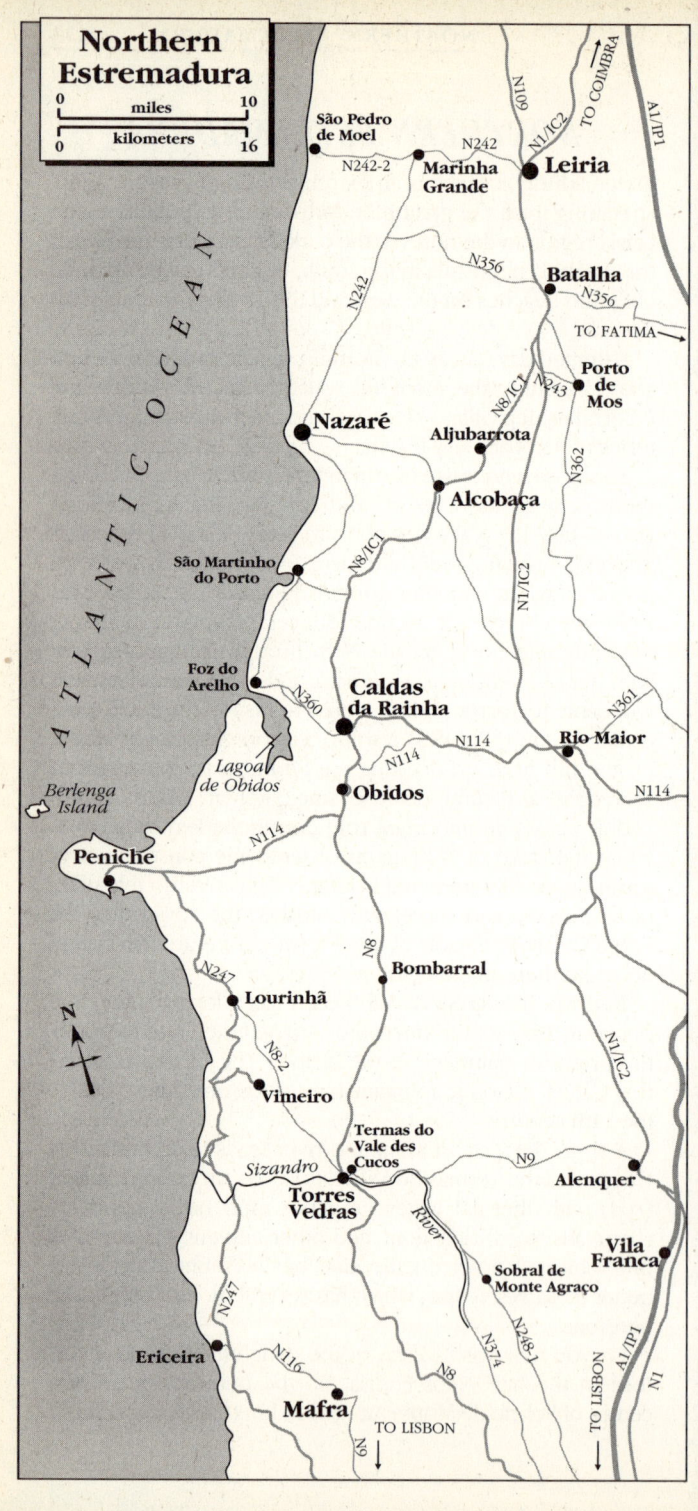

of Torres Vedras and 38 km (24 miles) north of Lisbon. This country estate used to produce wine but now only breeds sheep and greyhounds. The elegant 18th-century manor, built on the site of a 15th-century monastery, is open to paying guests. The eight bedrooms with private bathrooms are exquisitely furnished with antiques. Meals are served, often in the garden, and there's a swimming pool. Reservations should be made well in advance.

Also worthwhile is a visit to Arruda dos Vinhos, just 8 km (5 miles) southeast of Sobral. The town's fame comes not from its fine 16th-century churches but from its vineyards and dark, full-bodied red wines. The wine cellar–restaurant **O Fuso**, in the center of town, is known for its hearty regional cuisine and wines. It is especially pleasant on cool evenings to watch thick steaks, pork chops, and chicken being grilled in the huge fireplace. Servings are so generous that one shish kebab is ample for two people.

Another spa is located a few miles northwest of Torres Vedras at **Vimeiro**. The mineral water of Vimeiro is Portugal's Perrier, recommended for kidney diseases, digestive problems, and some skin ailments.

Take the road north from Torres Vedras to Peniche through **Lourinhã**, a farm center that goes back to Roman times. The parish church on the hill, built in the 14th century, is noted for its rose window and handsome tile balustrade. The 17th-century **Misericórdia** church contains some especially fine sculpture and religious paintings. The misericords were hospices, usually connected to a church, and were first established in the 15th century by Queen Leonor. Some continue their work as charitable institutions to this day, and many of the churches contain valuable works of art.

Peniche

An important fishing port today, Peniche stands at the end of a promontory 35 km (22 miles) north of Torres Vedras on route N 8-2/N 247 and 96 km (60 miles) north of Lisbon. Its steep cliffs made it a natural site for the **Fortaleza**, built in the 16th century to protect the coast. Later this fort was used as a prison, and only after the overthrow of the dictatorship in 1974 were the last of the political prisoners set free. Today the old prison cells have been turned into an antifascism museum, a school for lace making, and a ceramics workshop.

Among the fine buildings in Peniche is the parish **Igreja de São Pedro**, the fishermen's church, with such relics as a model of a sardine trawler, nets, and buoys. The 17th-century **Misericórdia** has some outstanding paintings by Josefa de Obidos, a remarkable artist of the time, and a fine series of paintings by her father, Baltasar Gomes da Figueira. The **Santuário de Nossa Senhora dos Remédios** near Cabo Carvoeiro has 18th-century tiles attributed to António de Oliveira Bernardes and a magnificent view of the cliffs.

The liveliest part of town is the newly built fishing port, located at the eastern part of the peninsula, where giant seagulls await their prey. The best time to see the action is early in the morning, when the trawlers return with their catch of tuna, sardines, or whatever is in season.

The sardine season runs from the end of May through October. You can find them almost anywhere in Portugal, but the sardine capital is Peniche. Stroll along the avenida do Mar, at the base of the fortress, and you'll see a dozen restaurants with charcoal grills outside, mainly for sardines. In Portugal, fresh grilled sardines are fat, juicy, and succulent, and except for the name have almost nothing in common with their small, pallid cousins in cans.

If you happen to be around on the first weekend in August, don't miss the festival of Nossa Senhora da Boa Viagem. On Saturday night a candlelight procession goes from São Pedro to the harbor, where a priest blesses the fishing fleet. The ceremony is followed by a fair. A regional fair is held in front of the fortress on the last Thursday of every month.

Should you wish to stay in Peniche, there is a comfortable modern hotel, the **Hotel da Praia Norte**, on N 114 at the entrance to town and not far from the beach.

Depending on the time and the weather, an excursion to the **Berlengas** can be delightful. This archipelago of extraordinary red rock formations, 12 km (7½ miles) out to sea, is a national bird sanctuary, and all kinds of migratory birds can be seen around its crags and caverns. Efforts are now being made to control tourism to protect the wildlife. During the season, from June though September, a regular ferry makes the trip of about one hour from Peniche harbor to the main island. On Berlenga get a good fish lunch at the **Mar e Sol** restaurant. Then take a walk along the rocky plateau to see the lighthouse, the magical rock formations, and the fishermen's cottages on the beach.

Obidos

Although Obidos now stands 10 km (6 miles) inland, this ancient walled town east of Peniche on N 114 (94 km/58 miles north of Lisbon) once guarded the coast; but over the centuries the shore silted up, leaving only the lagoon called the Lagoa de Obidos between the town and the sea. The Romans—and possibly the Celts before them—built a fortress here. In the eighth century the Moors occupied Obidos, and held it for more than 400 years. It was such a beautiful town in the 13th century that King Dinis presented it as a gift to his queen, Isabel, a pretty gesture that became a royal tradition.

Today Obidos retains the flavor of a Moorish casbah. Crenellated walls and towers surround the castle, the small whitewashed homes bedecked with geraniums and bougainvillaea, and the narrow cobblestone streets. The 16th-century castle itself has been converted into the elegant **Pousada do Castelo**, but reservations are required far, far in advance; there are only six rooms and three suites. The pousada's chef specializes in such Portuguese classics as *frango na púcara* (chicken baked in a terra-cotta pot with tomatoes, onions, ham, and lots of garlic) and *bacalhau à bras* (dried cod scrambled with eggs, onions, and potatoes and garnished with black olives). At least stop for a meal or take a walk along the ramparts to admire the view. Turned into a royal palace in the 16th century, the pousada has a spectacular carved Manueline doorway and windows. Inside, the furnishings are antiques or exquisite reproductions. There is an immense calm about the place that makes it easy to relate to times past.

If the pousada is full, as it usually is, there are several attractive inns here as well as some old houses that have been renovated and opened to the public. Just outside the ancient walls, the **Estalagem do Convento**, located in an old monastery, has 19 rooms with modern conveniences and old-fashioned charm. Nearby, the **Albergaria Residencial Josefa de Obidos** is a comfortable inn, with 40 rooms and a cozy bar. Also recommended are two attractive manors. Located inside the city walls, the **Casa do Poço**, with only four bedrooms, was built around a well in the patio, dating back to Moorish times. At the Portico da Graça, just outside the walls, the **Casa do Relógio**, named for the stone sundial in front of the house, has six rooms with baths.

Obidos is a natural tourist destination. It seems that every other house offers handicrafts or art work, some of it quite good. Specialties of the region include wrought-iron work, handwoven rugs and mats, and quilts.

On the shady main square stands a 15th-century fountain and pillory with the coat of arms of Queen Leonor. Here is the **Misericórdia** built by Queen Leonor, and beside it the **Museu do Município** (Municipal Museum) with archaeological discoveries, ancient arms, and paintings from the school of the extraordinary 17th-century primitive artist Josefa de Ayala, better known as Josefa de Obidos. Several of her finest paintings with their haunted faces can be seen here in the **Igreja de Santa Maria**, built on the foundations of a Visigoth temple. The tomb of Josefa de Obidos is located in the church of São Pedro. At the southern end of town is an impressive 16th-century **aqueduct**.

On the road north to Caldas da Rainha stands the vast and empty 18th-century Baroque sanctuary Nossa Senhora de Pedra, which was never completed.

While the Obidos area has not been designated specifically as a wine-growing region, it does produce some high-quality wines. The red Obidos is bright ruby and smooth, and the white is lemon-colored, with a fruity essence.

In the 15th century Queen Leonor found the sulfuric waters of Caldas da Rainha (Queen's Hot Springs) so therapeutic for rheumatism and respiratory diseases that she had a hospital built on the site. Today, people still flock to the Hospital Termal Rainha Dona Leonor to bathe in the curative waters. Also dating from Queen Leonor's time, the **Igreja de Nossa Senhora do Pópulo**, founded as the hospital chapel, is a good example of Manueline architecture, its inside walls lined with 17th-century tiles and its altars decorated with 16th-century Moorish tiles.

The spa's other claim to prominence is its pottery, the delightful green cabbage-leaf ware that makes such appetizing soup bowls and salad plates. There is also a line of oyster-white ware, particularly effective as fish platters. The daily market now has only a couple of pottery stands, but there are half a dozen shops with a wide selection on the rua da Liberdade in the center of town. The National Ceramics Fair is held in Caldas da Rainha in mid-July.

Some works of Rafael Bordalo Pinheiro, the talented, local, turn-of-the-century potter and caricaturist, can be found at the **Museu São Rafael Pequeno**, located on the street named for the artist. But the best place to go, on the same street, is **Faianças Artísticas Bordalo Pinheiro** (Tel: 062-84-23-53; Fax: 062-84-23-57), the original factory, which has set aside one of its buildings as a museum, containing ancient potter's tools, some of Rafael's most unusual pieces, and reproductions. The factory, which is open to visitors, continues its founder's tradition, turning out cabbage leaves and other nature ware and folk figurines, which can be purchased at the factory shop at good prices. A large pink building at the entrance to town is the headquarters of **Secla**, the country's main pottery exporters. Visitors can sometimes find bargains in garden ornaments, kitchenware, or candle-holders at the factory's sales office.

In the pleasant municipal park, the **Museu de José Malhõa** contains works by another outstanding native son, the turn-of-the-century naturalist painter Malhõa, whose murals and paintings of contemporary life and heroes of the past are found in many public buildings in Lisbon.

From Caldas da Rainha go west on N 360 to pick up the coastal road northeast to Nazaré at Foz do Arelho. The coastal road goes through the national park and several delightful resorts. Foz do Arelho is a village with a broad beach and the modern **Hotel Foz Praia** (formerly called the Foz Palace Motel), with modern comforts, restaurant, bar, tennis court, and boats for hire. A little farther up the road is São Martinho do Porto, which has a protected beach and a fine bay for sailing and other water sports.

Nazaré

Nowadays, Nazaré (122 km/76 miles north of Lisbon) should be visited *out of* season. This quintessential fishing village, with its fabulous long beach and an immense cliff blocking one end, its multicolored fishing boats, and its fishermen in plaid trousers and women in black, was discovered by sum-mer vacationers, especially the French, in the 1960s, and seems to have been posing for photographs ever since. But in the spring, fall, and even winter the town relaxes and seems genuinely glad to receive visitors.

There are really two Nazarés: the Praia, or beach area, and the Sítio, a 360-foot-high promontory, the cliff of which forms the northern end of the beach. The main part of town, with numerous cafés, restaurants, bars, hotels, and *pensões* (pensions), is located at the Praia. In season, the population of 15,000 increases tenfold; the hotels are generally medio-cre, and there are not enough rooms to go around. **Hotel da Nazaré**—located in town, set back from the beach—is the best known and the largest hotel, with 50 rooms and three stars. A popular seaside boardinghouse is **Pensão Ribamar**, located near the Turismo. There are no frills, and only 11 of the 19 rooms have a private bath, but the location and rates are difficult to beat. Local fishermen's wives also rent out rooms (and can be really quite intimidating as they assault visitors arriving at the bus station). Nearby, on the main square, praça Sousa Oliveira, are several good seafood restaurants that specialize in shellfish. Expect prices to be almost as high as in the Lisbon region. Two places where you can find the local specialty, *caldeirada* (seafood stew), for a reasonable price are **A Tasquinha**, largo da Independencia, 4, near the post office, and **S. Miguel** on avenida da República, with a great sea view.

Souvenir shops at the Praia offer attractive fishermen's sweaters and capes. The fishermen's quarter, just back from the beach, is a maze of small whitewashed houses and alleys. In the not-so-old days, the fishermen used to pull their Viking-style boats up on the beach with oxen—or, later, tractors—but this tradition was eliminated when a harbor at the southern end of town was built, where trawlers and flat-bottomed fishing boats are now anchored.

To reach the Sítio from the Praia, you can either take the funicular (in season) or drive up to the lookout, which has a magnificent view of the coast. Here are a minute white chapel, the **Capela de Nossa Senhora da Memória** and, nearby, a pillory with an inscription that says in Portuguese: "Before and after his first voyage to India, Vasco da Gama came to pray at Our Lady of Nazaré."

At the chapel near the edge of the cliff, somebody is bound to recount the story of the miracle of Dom Fuas: On one very misty day during the Middle Ages, Dom Fuas Roupinho, a local notable, was chasing a deer, which leaped off the cliff. Not aware of the danger, the horse and rider followed, but were saved by Our Lady of Nazaré. Believers even point out the horse's footprint on a rock overlooking the sea. At the far end of the promontory stands the São Miguel fort and lighthouse, built in the 16th century.

The **Igreja de Nossa Senhora da Nazaré**, a large 17th-century building with a handsome Baroque door, twisted pink marble columns, vaulted ceiling, and tile scenes of war and peace, dominates the main square of the Sítio. During the annual pilgrimage of Nossa Senhora da Nazaré, in the second week of September, worshipers carry a statue of the Virgin from the church down to the sea; the statue reportedly was brought back from Nazareth in the Holy Land by a pilgrim during the fourth century and was hidden in the hills during four centuries of Moorish rule. The statue's origin gave the town its name.

For travellers not addicted to the sea and crowds, an attractive alternative to lodgings in Nazaré is a room in a renovated monastic grange and school at Valado dos Frades, just 5 km (3 miles) inland on the road to Alcobaça. Part of a 14th-century monastery, the sprawling, lemon-colored **Quinta do Campo** was opened in 1991 to paying guests and is part of the Associacão Nacional de Turismo no Espaço Rural (ANTER; see "The Manor House Program" in Useful Facts). The owners, Mr. and Mrs. Collares Pereira, live on the property with their daughter Teresa and her husband, Pedro Silveira Botelho, who is secretary-general of ANTER. Each of the eight tastefully decorated rooms has a bath and garden view. Besides a swimming pool and tennis court, there's an *adega* (wine cellar), where barbecues with folk dancing can be organized for 40 to 300 people. Weather permitting, breakfast is served in the garden, and other meals can be arranged upon request. Valado dos Frades has another advantage as the railroad stop serving both Nazaré and Alcobaça. It is less than two hours to Lisbon's Entrecampos station on the Intercidades line.

Alcobaça

A few miles southeast of Nazaré is Alcobaça, located on the Alcoa and Baça rivers on route N 8. This is the site of the grandiose **Mosteiro de Santa Maria**, built in the late 12th century by King Afonso I to commemorate the capture of Santarém from the Moors earlier in the century. The vast abbey, which became the headquarters of the Cistercian order, was badly damaged during the 17th to 19th centuries and restored on several occasions, but the beautiful Gothic door and rose window are part of the original structure. The church, with three long aisles, massive walls, and pure lines, is considered a masterpiece of Cistercian architecture. Especially moving is the **Cloister of Silence**, dating from the 14th century, with vaulted ceiling and graceful columns. The most astonishing part of the abbey is the monumental **kitchen**, with a huge fireplace in which the monks could roast half a dozen oxen at once. They could also procure fish from the stream running right through the room—and enjoy a constant supply of fresh water.

The monastery of Alcobaça is best known for the tombs of Portugal's star-crossed lovers King Pedro I and his beloved,

Inês de Castro. As a young prince, Dom Pedro was bonded by a marriage of state to Constanza, Infanta of Castile, but he deeply loved her lady-in-waiting, the beautiful Inês. Learning of his son's illicit romance, King Afonso IV had Inês banished. When the Infanta died in childbirth, Dom Pedro sent for Inês and resumed the liaison openly, having several children by her. King Afonso, however, never accepted the liaison, fearing the influence of Inês's family and possible claims of Castile to the Portuguese throne. Unbeknownst to Dom Pedro, the king had Inês murdered at Coimbra, in her home, which is today called the Quinta das Lágrimas (Manor of Tears).

When Dom Pedro succeeded his father as King Pedro I, in 1357, he found the assassins and had them executed. Announcing that he had been secretly married to Inês, he had her body exhumed and carried in a torchlight procession to Alcobaça. There her corpse was crowned queen and members of the court were compelled to bow and kiss her hand. Dom Pedro had two magnificently carved tombs built with panels portraying their love story. Lifelike statues of Inês and the king recline on the tombs, which are placed so that on the Day of Judgment the two lovers will gaze into each other's faces when they rise.

Alcobaça is another pottery center, producing its own distinctive blue-and-white ware with floral designs. A number of shops and stalls on the square near the monastery offer everything from candlesticks and vases to statuary. The Casa Cisterciense, for example, has a wide variety of local pottery, as well as articles from other regions. The salespeople in the Casa are particularly helpful in gift-wrapping for travel. You can also visit the showrooms of the many pottery factories in the area. Vestal Faianças de Alcobaça, for example, produces a variety of cachepots, candleholders, garden ornaments, and miniatures.

Around the corner from Santa Maria is a Cistercian arch and, adjoining, a restaurant that appears to be part of the ancient monastery. Despite its solemn setting, the Celeiro dos Frades is a popular hangout with local youths and specializes in charcoal-grilled meat and fish; closed on Thursdays.

Batalha

There is not much to see in Aljubarrota, northeast of Alcobaça on the N 8/IC 1, except a small monument honoring the heroes of what the Portuguese call "the Battle." This was the decisive victory in 1385 of the poorly organized Portuguese forces against the much better equipped army of Castile, which saved the country from Spanish domination for 200 years. King João I had made a vow to construct the finest church in the realm to honor the Virgin if she helped him to defeat the forces of King Juan I of Castile. True to his word, King João had built what even today is the most magnificent monument in Portugal, the **Mosteiro de Santa Maria da Vitória da Batalha** (Monastery of Batalha) 20 km (12 miles) northeast of Alcobaça on N 8/IC 1 and then N 1.

Before reaching Batalha, take a 5½-km (3½-mile) detour east on N 243 to **Porto de Mós**, a picturesque medieval town built around a hill. Perched on top is an astonishing castle dating back to the 13th century (but restored a few years ago), with green cones and crenellated walls. Located at the tip of the **Parque Natural das Serras de Aire e Candeeiros**, Porto de Mós is the point of departure for anyone interested in visiting the many grottoes of the region. There are local buses to the **Grutas de Mira de Aire**, 14 km (8½ miles) southeast of Port de Mós on N 243. These caves, discovered in 1947, are said to be the deepest in Europe, reaching a depth of at least 360 feet. You can take an elevator down into this magical underground world of lakes and naturally sculpted limestone. Just a few miles south on a side road, the **Grutas de Santo António** were found in 1955. These marvelous rock formations are effectively displayed with light and sound effects.

Until a few years ago the road approaching Batalha passed at a respectful distance, giving a breathtaking view of the majestic building. Then, despite a clamor of protest, the new highway up to Leiria was built so close to the monastery that the perspective is lost. Nevertheless, Batalha is a notable sight, especially at sunset, when its burnished limestone turns to gold.

The flamboyant ensemble of towers, buttresses, vaults, columns, and arches is a masterpiece of Portuguese Gothic. A splendid portal, decorated with a statue of Christ and 100 other biblical figures, leads into the sober, beautifully proportioned church. Remarkable 16th-century stained-glass windows depict scenes from the lives of the Virgin and of Christ. In the **Capela do Fundador** (Founder's Chapel) the tombs of King João I and his English queen, Philippa of Lancaster, are placed so close that their reclining statues are holding hands. Lining the walls are the tombs of their six sons and a grandson, each bearing a motto. Among the sons is Prince Henry the Navigator, whose motto was "The talent to do well."

On the opposite side of the church, the **Claustro Real** (Royal Cloister) is a marvelous combination of Gothic arches and richly carved Manueline decoration. In the chapter house lie the tombs of two unknown soldiers from World War I, one of whom died in France, the other during the African campaign. The stained glass window, dating from the early 16th century, shows in vivid colors the Passion of Christ.

In the back of the church a Manueline doorway of the 16th century leads to the **Capelas Imperfeitas** (Unfinished Chapels). This large octagonal building with seven chapels, begun in 1435 by King Duarte, was to contain his tomb and that of Queen Leonor (Leonor of Aragón), but he died before the work was completed. Duarte's descendants seem to have lost interest in the chapels, and the columns and the passage to the church were never finished. Not to be overlooked on the vast square in front of the monastery is the imposing equestrian statue of the Portuguese hero Nuno Alvares Pereira, the chevalier who defeated the Spanish during the great battle.

Just across the square from Batalha is the pleasant **Pousada do Mestre Afonso Domingues**, named for the architect who designed the monastery. It has only 21 handsomely furnished rooms, so reservations are advised. There's also a first-rate dining room, which serves the best of traditional Portuguese fare like *caldo verde* (green soup), thin shreds of collards in a potato-onion broth with bits of sausage or pork. And if there's no room at the pousada, there's **Quinta do Fidalgo**, also in front of the monastery. This handsome 17th-century mansion is chock-full of classic period furniture. The owners live in the manor, speak English, and have opened five rooms, the gardens, and the family chapel to guests. Around the monastery can be found the usual assortment of souvenir shops and cafés. For a good coffee or tea with croissant or the local egg-and-almond sweet, you might try the **Pastelaria Oliveira**.

From Batalha you can return to Lisbon directly south on the N 1/IC 2 highway, a drive of only about an hour and a half, depending on traffic. Or continue north on the highway to Leiria and Coimbra, or even back to Lisbon. As the main north–south motorway (A 1/IP 1) is completed in this area, travellers in a hurry prefer going the extra distance (about 25 km/16 miles) to avoid the traffic on the mostly two-lane, winding N 1/IC 2.

SOUTH OF THE TAGUS RIVER

Southern Estremadura, or the Arrábida peninsula, is a gentle land of olive groves, vineyards, wooded hills, and many unsullied beaches and coves. There are splendid castles at Setúbal, Palmela, and Sesimbra. Setúbal has several fine churches, particularly the Igreja de Jesús, with its extraordinary twisted columns. And across the bay, at Tróia, a sophisticated new resort is growing up beside the Roman ruins.

Before the opening of the bridge over the Tagus river in 1966, going south from Lisbon was quite an adventure, and not really a one-day excursion. Although the ferry ride to the Arrábida peninsula took only 20 minutes, psychologically it was much farther, and the roads and tourist facilities were very poor. Even today the southern environs of Lisbon are less developed than the north, although some places, such as Almada, are catching up quickly—perhaps too quickly. Now, with the bridge, the Arrábida peninsula is so convenient to Lisbon that its sights are sometimes overlooked in the rush for the beaches and the warmer waters of the Algarve. If your time is very limited, there are some fine sheltered beaches just south of Lisbon. The principal attraction of the peninsula, however, is not its beaches but the **Serra da Arrábida**, a gentle mountain range located on the southern coast. The region's castles have been nicely restored, and the drive along the corniche is comparable in beauty to that of the Amalfi Coast in Italy.

At first the handsome suspension bridge was called the Ponte Salazar in honor of the dictator, who had ordered its construction. After the young captains launched the Flower Revolution on April 25, 1974, the name of the bridge was changed to the **Ponte 25 de Abril**.

Modeled after San Francisco's Golden Gate and built by U.S. Steel, the bridge has only five lanes—totally inadequate for weekend traffic. (There's serious discussion now about building another bridge from northeast Lisbon to Montijo, which would greatly ease the journey to Spain and provide better access to inland Alentejo province.) Originally planned to include a railroad bridge on the lower level, the bridge appears unfinished. Although vehicles cannot stop on the bridge, you can drive slowly and appreciate the spectacular view of Lisbon and its seven hills, particularly when approaching from the south.

Some people prefer the leisurely route by ferry. It is a pleasant minicruise and a good opportunity to take pictures of the Lisbon skyline and the assortment of boats plying the river. Ferries leave Lisbon from the Estação Fluvial (River Station) at the southeastern corner of Terreiro do Paço (praça do Comércio) and from the Cais do Sodré railroad station. They land at **Cacilhas**, a rather nondescript bedroom town with several popular restaurants overlooking the river. Many Lisboetes come here to eat fresh fish and gaze at Lisbon. You can also walk along the river to see the Cristo Rei statue in the neighboring town of Almada, or get a bus on the main square and go to Caparica beach, west on the Atlantic coast.

If you are driving, shortly after the toll gate on the southern end of the bridge you come to the turnoff for Almada and can drive right to the foot of the **Cristo Rei** (Christ the King). Inspired by the Christ the Redeemer of Rio de Janeiro, this statue is smaller and seems to be overwhelmed by its own pedestal. An elevator takes you up to the foot of the statue for an admirable view of the Tagus, Lisbon, and the entire Arrábida peninsula.

Two other ferry excursions, this time from Belém, will take you to either Porto Brandão or Trafaria, small fishing ports that have hitherto been rather neglected. But, more and more, Lisboetes are discovering the charms of the Outra Banda, or other side of the river. There's not much to see at Porto Brandão, a small nucleus of two-story pastel houses, but the restaurants have begun to make a name for themselves. **O Parafuso**, **A Doca**, and **Mare Viva** all offer good seafood at reasonable prices.

At the neighboring port of Trafaria, the **Antiga Casa Maritima** can produce a fish banquet that is difficult to match in quality and price. The Casa also has a rich wine cellar and at times can be cajoled into serving special vintages, like the Alentejo wine Rosado Fernandes of 1983. The nearby beaches are much better and much cleaner than the more famous ones across the river.

Caparica

Return to the main highway (A 2/IP 1) and continue a few miles to the exit marked "Costa da Caparica." (The name Caparica means "rich cape" and comes from a legend in which an old woman leaves the king of Portugal her greatest treasure—a cape decorated with golden coins.) Lisboetes flock to Caparica on weekends, because the long, crescent-shaped beach is more protected than the Atlantic beaches north of the Tagus and less polluted than the river beaches.

On weekdays you can find long stretches of sparsely populated beach and a number of restaurants where you can get a good fish meal. Try **Varanda do Oceano** or **Carolina do Aires**, both on avenida General Humberto Delgado. The gorgeous sea view is usually matched by the quality of the fish. The local specialty is *caldeirada,* a kind of bouillabaisse. There are several hotels and *pensões,* and most of the restaurants have modest facilities for changing.

If you prefer, take the little train that runs (daily in summer, weekends spring and fall) along half of the 20-km (12-mile) beach and ochre cliffs. You can get off at any one of a score of beaches, such as **Praia da Rainha**, where there's a good restaurant of the same name (Tel: 01-290-1099). Or get off at the southern end of the line and walk to where you can bathe or picnic in the privacy of sand dunes.

Families travelling with children, or even without, should visit **Ondaparque**, located just north of the highway before you reach Caparica. Opened in 1987, this vast water park has the latest things in aquatics, including toboggans, kamikazes, soft slopes, quick tubes, and swinging multislopes. There are also pools, playgrounds, solariums, and self-service snack bars. Open from the end of April to the end of September, the park gives special rates to groups and free admission for children under five and people over 60 years old.

On the outskirts of Caparica, make it a point to pause at the ruins of the 16th-century **Convento dos Capuchos** (Capuchin Monastery). Although the monastery is not particularly interesting, it is located high on a cliff in a forest of pines and has an extraordinary view of the coast, stretching from Sintra mountain south to the Arrábida range.

If you're a golfer, and even if you aren't, take route 377 about 20 km (12 miles) south to Pinhal del Rei (King's Pine Forest). Hidden away in the woods, you'll find **Aroeira— Clube de Campo de Portugal** (Portuguese Country Club), with an elegant bar and restaurant and a beautiful 18-hole course.

From Aroeira, it's best to return via route 377 to the IC 20, which takes you back to where you got off the A 2/IP 1. But if you go as far as the terminus of the Caparica beach train at the village of Fonte da Telha, you'll find a side road (no number) that will take you east to rejoin the A 2/IP 1 at Fogueteiro.

Leave the superhighway before getting to Setúbal, at the sign for Palmela (29 km/18 miles from Almada) and take route 379-2 for 3 more kilometers (2 miles) directly to the

Palmela castle. The **Castelo de Palmela** was already an important defensive post in the 12th century, when King Afonso Henriques captured it from the Moors. The Order of Saint James established its headquarters in the castle, later adding a church and monastery to the complex. Today the monastery has been turned into the **Pousada Castelo de Palmela**, which has 29 rooms, an attractive dining room in the old refectory, a comfortable lounge in the cloisters, and spectacular views of the mountains, Lisbon, and the broad Sado estuary. The church, restored, contains the tomb of Dom Jorge de Lencastre, son of João II and the last master of the Order of Saint James. At the foot of the castle wall, the **Igreja de São Pedro** is interesting for its lovely 18th-century tiles telling the story of Saint Peter's life.

From Palmela, it's not worth going back to the main highway; instead take the N 379 about 3 km (2 miles) and turn right on the N 252/IC 3, which leads straight into the center of Setúbal.

Setúbal

An important industrial town dating back to Roman times and always a busy fishing port, Setúbal (48 km/30 miles south of Lisbon) is today a center for fish canning, shipbuilding, auto assembly, and cement production.

This industrial aspect should not deter you; there are a number of interesting sights in and around Setúbal. The splendid 15th-century **Igreja de Jesús**, originally a part of the Convento de Jesús, is located on the praça Miguel Bombarda, just off the avenida 22 de Dezembro, which you run into if you're coming from Palmela, or a little to the right as you drive into the city from the eastern side, where the main highway from Lisbon, the A 2/ IP 1, joins the N 10. Designed in 1491 by Diogo Boytac, it is an outstanding example of Manueline art, with columns like twisted ropes, ribs crisscrossing along the high vaulted ceiling, and walls decorated with fine 17th-century tile panels. The Gothic cloister adjoining the church has been converted into a museum, the **Museu da Cidade**, with archaeological remains from the region and a good collection of tiles dating from the 15th to the 18th century. It also contains paintings by 15th- and 16th-century Portuguese and Flemish primitive artists, particularly one known simply as the Master of Setúbal. The cloister/museum has been closed for badly needed repairs, but the church is open.

Although difficult for driving, downtown Setúbal is a walking delight. Try to park near praça do Bocage, a grand mosaic-tile esplanade with palm trees and lovely old pastel houses, recently refurbished. In the center of the square a statue honors the city's best-known native son and poet, Manuel Maria Barbosa du Bocage. At one end stands the **Igreja de São Julião,** founded by fishermen nobody knows when and restored many times, particularly after the 1755 earthquake; it retains two beautiful 16th-century Manueline doorways and chimes that keep correct time. At the other end, the Turismo is located in the yellow-arcaded Câmara Municipal (Town Hall). Also on the plaza: a square clock tower, a lime-colored army recruitment center, and a number of pleasant cafés and snack bars.

Nearby on largo da Misericórdia you will find **O Beco** (Tel: 065-52-46-17; closed Tuesdays). This whitewashed restaurant with paneled walls and discreet music is popular with both Portuguese families and foreign visitors. Specialties include fresh fish daily, *caldeirada a fragateiro* (a lusty bouillabaisse with all kinds of fish), and wild boar and venison in season.

The **Museu Regional de Arqueologia e Etnologia** on the main promenade, avenida Luisa Todi, 162 (closed Sunday afternoons, Mondays, and holidays), presents archaeological displays from Paleolithic to Roman times. It also features local folk arts and crafts, as well as exhibits about the fishing, textile, and cork industries in the area. A **Municipal Gallery of Visual Arts** is installed in the Casa do Bocage, birthplace of the 18th-century poet, located on rua Bartissol near the Grilos church.

The **Igreja dos Grilos,** so named because of the crickets that still sing there in the summer, is part of an Augustinian monastery founded in 1566. This church is located on avenida Jaime Cortesão, just beyond the railway line. Its elaborate 18th-century Manueline altars are of rose-and-white marble. Tile panels depict the life of Saint Augustine.

It's not easy to find the **Pousada de São Filipe** (another castle-turned-inn), but the view from the top is worth the effort. Follow the signs scrupulously and you will reach the Estrada do Castelo de São Filipe on the western side of Setúbal. The road twists and turns upward to the castle, which is perched on a promontory high above the city. This fortified castle was built in 1590 by the Italian architect Felipe Terzi on the orders of King Philip II of Spain, when the country was under Spanish rule. His aim was twofold: to defend the estuary against the English, and to keep the Portuguese population in order. The old chapel is adorned with tiles recounting the life of Saint Philip.

From the terrace of the pousada you can watch the ferries scuttle back and forth across the Sado river to the Tróia peninsula, and on a clear day it seems you can see halfway to the Algarve. There are only 15 rooms, so reservations must be made well in advance. If you haven't got a room, make it a point to have lunch here anyway. The dining room is on the second floor, with a spectacular view of the sea and generally superb food and service. Try a local specialty like the grilled red mullet with oranges and olive oil (Setúbal style).

The Arrábida Area

Leave Setúbal by the avenida Luisa Todi, heading west to join the corniche road (the N 379-1). Shortly after leaving the city you will come upon an unsightly cement factory spewing fumes for miles around. But don't be deterred, because beyond this the road is breathtakingly beautiful.

After Setúbal, the road west climbs through the wooded foothills of the Arrábida range and proceeds along the mountain ridge. The thick pine and cypress forest, bright wildflowers, brick-colored ravines, and sapphire sea all have a Mediterranean luminosity. Down below, a cluster of white-washed buildings surrounded by forest is the 16th-century Convento Novo. A sign indicates the footpath to **Formosinho**, the highest peak of the range at 499 meters (1,637 feet).

Farther on, take the side road marked **Portinho da Arrábida**. This steep descent leads to one of the finest beaches in the area, with white sand and clear, clean water. There's a pleasant restaurant in a boardinghouse overlooking the beach, **Pensão Residencia Santa Maria da Arrábida**, where you can get a snack or a fish dinner. The nearby **Santa Margarida beach**, accessible only by boat, enchanted the English poet laureate Robert Southey at the end of the 18th century with its natural grottoes and transparent waters. In recent times, however, the grottoes have been badly defaced. From Portinho, go back the same way (there isn't any other) to the N 379-1, which now turns inland and makes a steep ascent, passing through pine and cypress woods. Then the landscape opens to vineyards and olive groves, and you come to the inland route, the N 379. Turn westward on this road past rolling hills, orchards, and farm hamlets. Just beyond the village of Santana you will see a sign for

Sesimbra, on a road to the left. As the road winds its way down to the sea, you get a magnificent view of the coast and the mountain range.

Sesimbra (32 km/20 miles south of Lisbon) has been an important fishing port since Roman times but is increasingly a holiday resort. The crenellated walls of the **Castelo de Sesimbra** dominate the town and provide a wonderful view of the coastline. Originally a Moorish fortress, the castle, which contains a 12th-century church, was badly damaged by the 1755 earthquake but has since been restored.

The main attraction of Sesimbra, however, is the fishermen's harbor at the foot of the cliff. Every morning and evening, trawlers bring in their catch of swordfish, eels, sardines, or whatever is in season, and a lively auction is held in the morning and in the afternoon. East of the port lies a protected bay with a swimming beach, water skiing, sailing, and other water sports.

The old part of town is built along the cliff, with steep alleys and steps leading to the port. It holds the **Igreja Matriz**, a parish church from the 16th century with a handsome marble pulpit and woodcarvings, halfway up the hill on rua João de Deus. The prison fort of **Santiago**, from the 17th century, is in the center of town by the sea. From the fort take the shore road, called avenida dos Naufragos, westward, and you will encounter several good seafood restaurants. **Alga-Mar**, for example, serves a copious *caldeirada* (fish stew) for two and tender squid stuffed with shrimp. The same road leads to the fishing port.

To leave Sesimbra you must go back up the hill. Take the road with the sign for the **Hotel do Mar**. Built into the hill on terraces, the hotel is tastefully decorated and has magnificent sea views; it is a favorite weekend abode for affluent Portuguese and foreign visitors, and a good place to try the specialty of the region, grilled swordfish.

From Sesimbra the road climbs north to the village of Santana, then winds west through country villages to **Cabo Espichel**. The landscape changes dramatically as you reach the windswept cape, which is covered with low brush and heath. In ancient times people used to make pilgrimages to the shrine of **Nossa Senhora do Cabo**, in a setting that looks like the end of the world. The two long rows of arcaded buildings where pilgrims used to stay, abandoned for many years, are now used on weekends by people from Setúbal (and occasional squatters). The church, built in the 17th century, is decorated with gilt wood carvings and a painted ceiling, now badly deteriorated. Beyond, standing on the edge of the cliff, is a small white seamen's chapel decorated with tiles depicting fishing scenes. A fishermen's festival is held here on the last Sunday in September to honor Our Lady of the Cape.

Azeitão

Back at Santana, take the inland route (N 379) northeast through vineyards and olive groves to the important wine center of **Vila Nogueira de Azeitão**. In the center of town stands the 16th-century Tavora Palace, which belonged to the dukes of Aveiro. The palace is now rather dilapidated, but there are plans to restore it, and part of the building is currently used as an art gallery.

On the first Sunday of every month Azeitão is the site of one of the best regional fairs in the country, offering a wide range of products from cattle and poultry to pottery and leather boots. The fair drew such crowds that it had to move from the central square to a large field on the outskirts of town.

Azeitão is also the home of one of Portugal's leading table-wine producers, José Maria da Fonseca. Visitors are welcome to tour the original factory cum residence and small museum, located in the center of town. The 20-minute free tour is led by guides speaking English, French, and Portuguese, and includes wine tasting. The factory, founded in 1834, still produces a delicate, honey-sweet muscatel, Moscatel de Setúbal. Here some of Portugal's best-known wines are produced. The soft, mellow, red Periquita wines, a favorite with Portuguese wine connoisseurs, are reasonably priced and increasingly popular abroad. Another outstanding Fonseca wine is the very dry white Branco Seco.

Just outside of town on the road to Setúbal you will see a modern winery, also open to visitors. This is J. M. Fonseca Internacional, which split off from the original Fonseca company several years ago and is totally different except for the similarity in name. Its wines are better known internationally: Lancer's red, white, and rosé wines, in their distinctive clay jugs, produced specifically for export. Two distinguished wines from the Setúbal region are João Pires, a dry white table wine from Pinhal Novo, and the Quinta da Bacalhôa, a rich red wine that is Portugal's only true cabernet sauvignon.

Nearby, on the outskirts of Vila Nogueira de Azeitão, is the 16th-century **Quinta das Torres**, which has been turned into an inn and is an ideal spot for a romantic weekend (although some have found it dreary).

After Vila Fresca, take the N 10 heading back to Setúbal and within a few minutes you will come to the **Quinta da Bacalhôa**, which dates back to the end of the 15th century and was once inhabited by Afonso de Albuquerque, viceroy of India. The manor, which now belongs to an American family, has been beautifully restored. Sitwell describes it as "a lovely half-caste of the East and West." The formal gardens, with clipped boxwoods, fountains, and bamboo and fruit trees, are open to the public. Here too is a pavilion lined with 16th-century tiles. One panel, dating from 1565 and depicting the story of Susannah and the Elders, is the oldest dated tile panel in the country.

It is possible to stay at the Quinta da Bacalhôa, but arrangements must be made well ahead of time because there are only three suites (six bedrooms). The owner lives in Washington, D.C., and rents the quinta, including its staff of seven, to families or groups for a fortnight or longer. Summer is usually heavily booked in this national landmark, but spring and fall can be even nicer. (Some guests have complained about the noise from the bus station across the road.)

Tróia

Portugal's newest holiday resort, on the peninsula of Tróia, can be a side trip or a day's excursion in itself. To get there, return to Setúbal port, where there are frequent ferries crossing the Rio Sado estuary to the narrow Tróia peninsula thrusting up from Lower Alentejo. Downtown Setúbal is a confusing maze, but if you follow avenida Luisa Todi eastward to the end, then turn right, you will come upon the Doca do Comércio, the commercial port. From here a car ferry (which also takes pedestrians, cyclists, and motorbikers) leaves every half hour for the 20-minute cruise to Tróia. Out of season the ferry goes every hour. You should note, however, that on Sunday afternoons (especially on holiday weekends) the queue of cars on the Tróia side stretches for miles and you may have to wait as long as three or four hours to board the ferry.

On the site of Tróia the Romans founded Cetobriga, an important fish-preserving town until it was swallowed up by the sea during the fifth century. Just a few years ago Tróia was the ultimate place for beachgoers seeking privacy. You had to have a private boat to get to the peninsula, where there was nothing but sand, pines, and intriguing glimpses of Roman ruins under the waters.

For those who loved the old Tróia, the high-rise apartments and hotels, the discos, cinemas, restaurants, and bars look like some kind of alien city that landed here in error. The new Tróia is for vacationers who enjoy a self-contained resort with modern comforts, entertainment, and sports facilities on a splendid, accessible site.

Generally called the Torralta Tourist Development, Tróia is really a family resort with two large aparthotels and several smaller ones. These are hotels that provide apartments—not rooms. Each apartment contains several beds, a private bath, a balcony, and a fully equipped kitchen. **Aparthotel Magnoliamar** and **Aparthotel de Tróia** have swimming pools and tennis courts, restaurants and nightclubs. The new Tróia golf course, designed by Robert Trent Jones, is one of the finest in the country. Also, every June there's an international film festival here.

Nature buffs can still get away from it all at Tróia. The developers have kindly concentrated their constructions, at least for now, at the northern tip of the peninsula. The **Roman ruins**, dating back to the beginning of the first century A.D., lie along the Sado, about 4 km (2½ miles) east of the tourist development. Archaeologists have uncovered the remains of a temple, a burial place, baths, numerous villas, and salting tanks, but much remains to be excavated.

And, thanks in part to the **Reserva Natural do Estuário do Sado**, there are still long stretches of sand dunes, pine forests, and secluded fishing villages in the area that are virtually untouched. Patient watchers can still sight dolphins, otters, wildcats, and all kinds of birds in the reserve area, including storks, herons, eagles, egrets, and flamingos. Anyone wishing to visit the reserve should first drop in at the head office, located in Setúbal port, next to the Naval Club, near the foot-passenger ferry station to Tróia. Here an exhibit shows the geography of the protected area and provides an idea of what to look for: the salt flats, rice fields, pine and cork forests, marshes, lakes, picturesque fishing ports, and traditional cane houses that have disappeared elsewhere.

GETTING AROUND

Because distances are short and many of Portugal's treasures are found off the beaten track, the best way to visit Lisbon's surroundings is by car. Cascais is normally only about 45 minutes from Lisbon along the scenic Marginal or a half hour on the new inland highway, but the trip can take a couple of hours during rush hour. Sintra takes about the same time, although the new roads have considerably reduced congestion during morning and evening rush hours (8:00 to 10:00 A.M. and 6:00 to 8:00 P.M.) and weekends. With the superhighway now reaching Setúbal, the trip there is about a half hour, except during the weekend rush, when it can take an hour just to get across the bridge. Even the drive to Nazaré and the northernmost reaches of the province takes less than two hours, not counting stops.

This said, there are several caveats. Except for the few superhighways, most roads are narrow and not very good. The local drivers are often reckless and seem oblivious of the country's appallingly high accident rate. Fuel and car-rental prices are high compared to those in North America or Britain.

But do not despair. Commuter trains run all day and late into the evening along the Costa do Estoril from Lisbon to the sea. It is a 45-minute ride from Lisbon's Cais do Sodré station, near the Ribeira central market, to the end of the line in Cascais. There are also frequent trains to Sintra from the Rossio station in downtown Lisbon, also about a 45-minute ride. The northern Leiria line goes from Santa Apolónia station near the Museu Militar (also called the Museu de Artilharia) in downtown Lisbon to Obidos and Caldas da Rainha, a journey of about two hours. But there are more trains from Lisbon to Caldas da Rainha and Obidos on what is called the Linha de Oeste (Western Line), leaving from Rossio station. A fairly new train, called Intercidades, is preferred by many Portuguese as faster and more comfortable than the regular trains to Porto and cheaper than the Rapidos or the express trains. The Intercidades line to Leiria, with a stop at Caldas da Rainha, also leaves Lisbon from Rossio.

In addition, Rodoviária regional buses go almost everywhere, and their rates are inexpensive. The bus terminal is located at avenida Casal Ribeiro, 18B, in central Lisbon (Tel: 01-54-54-39). There are also numerous private bus companies on intercity routes, and several companies also organize day tours of the Lisbon environs; check with your hotel.

Finally, hiking, climbing, canoeing, and jeep photo-safari tours are also available. Turnatur, Turismo de Natureza (rua Almirante Reis, 60, 2830 Barreiro, Tel. and Fax: 01-207-6886), has a team of mountaineering experts—all English-speaking—who accompany nature lovers on half-day and all-day tours to the loveliest natural zones in close range of the capital: the Sintra and Arrábida mountains, the Sado river estuary, and the Cabo da Roca coast.

ACCOMMODATIONS REFERENCE

Rates given are projected 1993 prices for a double room, double occupancy. Price ranges span the lowest rate in the low season to the highest in the high season. Unless otherwise stated, rates include Continental breakfast. As prices are subject to change, always double-check before booking.

Costa do Estoril

▶ **Casa da Pergola.** Avenida Valbom, 13, 2750 **Cascais**. Tel: (01) 284-0040. 14,000$00–17,000$00. Open April through October.

▶ **Estalagem Muchaxo. Praia do Guincho**, 2750 Cascais. Tel: (01) 285-0221; Fax: (01) 285-0444. 9,000$00–20,000$00.

▶ **Estalagem Senhora da Guia.** Estrada do Guincho, 2750 **Cascais**. Tel: (01) 486-9239; Fax: (01) 486-9227; in U.S., Tel: (212) 686-9213, Fax: (212) 686-0271. 14,000$00–31,000$00.

▶ **Hotel Albatroz.** Rua Frederico Arouca, 100, 2750 **Cascais**. Tel: (01) 483-2821; Fax: (01) 284-4827. 23,500$00–48,000$00.

▶ **Hotel Atlântico.** Estrada Marginal, 2765 **Estoril**. Tel: (01) 468-0270; Fax: (01) 468-3619. 10,000$00–30,000$00.

▶ **Hotel Baía.** Estrada Marginal, 2750 **Cascais**. Tel: (01) 483-1033 or 483-1034; Fax: (01) 483-1095. 8,000$00–16,000$00.

▶ **Hotel Estoril-Sol.** Parque Palmela, 2750 **Cascais**. Tel: (01) 483-2831; Fax: (01) 483-2280; in U.S., Tel: (800) 332-4872 or (212) 838-3322, Fax: (212) 935-9856. 25,000$00–35,000$00.

▶ **Hotel do Guincho. Praia do Guincho**, 2750 Cascais. Tel: (01) 285-0493; Fax: (01) 285-0431; in U.S., Tel: (800) 843-3311 or (212) 838-3322, Fax: (212) 935-9856. 18,000$00–34,000$00.

▶ **Hotel Palácio.** Parque do Estoril, 2765 **Estoril**. Tel: (01) 468-0400; Fax: (01) 468-4867; in U.S., Tel: (800) 223-6800 or (212) 838-3110. 39,000$00–43,000$00.

▶ **Hotel Village Cascais.** Rua Frei Nicolau de Oliveira, Parque de Gandarinha, 2750 **Cascais**. Tel: (01) 483-7044; Fax: (01) 483-7319; in U.S., Tel: (800) 843-3311 or (212) 838-3322, Fax: (212) 935-9856. 15,000$00–28,300$00.

▶ **Lennox Country Club.** Rua Eng. Alvaro Pedro de Sousa, 5, 2675 **Estoril**. Tel: (01) 468-0422; Fax: (01) 467-0859. 10,000$00–23,500$00.

▶ **Quinta das Encostas.** Largo Vasco D'Orey, **Sassoeiros,** 2775 Parede. Tel: (01) 457-0056; Fax: (01) 458-2647. 10,160$00–14,224$00.

▶ **Quinta da Marinha Aldeamento Turístico.** Quinta da Marinha, 2750 **Cascais.** Tel: (01) 486-9881; Fax: (01) 486-9032. 12,500$00–33,000$00.

Sintra

▶ **Casa da Tapada.** Tapada das Rocas, 2710 **Sintra.** Tel. and Fax: (01) 923-0342. 14,224$00–18,288$00.

▶ **Hotel Central.** Praça da República, 35, 2710 **Sintra.** Tel: (01) 923-0063 or 923-0963. 10,800$00–13,800$00.

▶ **Hotel Palácio dos Seteais.** Rua Barbosa do Bocage, 8, 2810 **Sintra.** Tel: (01) 923-3200; Fax: (01) 923-4277; in U.S. and Canada, Tel: (800) 448-8355. 23,000$00–45,000$00.

▶ **Hotel Tivoli.** Praça da República, 2710 **Sintra.** Tel: (01) 923-3505 or 923-3855; Fax: (01) 923-1572; in U.S. and Canada, Tel: (800) 223-5652. 10,500$00–27,500$00.

▶ **Hotel de Vale de Lobos.** Vale de Lobos/Sabugo, 2715 **Pêro Pinheiro.** Tel: (01) 927-3401 or 927-3419; Fax: (01) 927-4656; in U.S., Tel: (212) 686-9213. 9,000$00–11,000$00.

▶ **Motel da Piscina** (formerly Motel das Arribas). Praia Grande/Colares, 2710 **Sintra.** Tel: (01) 929-2145; Fax: (01) 929-2420. 7,500$00–10,000$00.

▶ **Quinta da Capela.** Estrada de Monserrate, 2710 **Sintra.** Tel: (01) 929-0170; Fax: (01) 929-3425. 21,000$00.

▶ **Quinta de São Tiago.** Estrada de Monserrate, 2710 **Sintra.** Tel. and Fax: (01) 923-2923. 16,000$00–25,000$00.

Northern Estremadura

▶ **Albergaria Residencial Josefa de Obidos.** Rua Dom João de Ornelas, 2510 **Obidos.** Tel: (062) 95-92-28; Fax: (062) 95-95-33. 7,000$00–9,500$00.

▶ **Casa do Poço.** Travessa da Rua Nova, 2510 **Obidos.** Tel: (062) 95-93-58. 7,500$00–9,000$00.

▶ **Casa do Relógio.** Rua da Graça, 2510 **Obidos.** Tel: (062) 95-92-82 or 95-93-58. 7,500$00–9,000$00.

▶ **Estalagem do Convento.** Rua Dom João de Ornelas, 2510 **Obidos.** Tel: (062) 95-92-17; Fax: (062) 95-91-59; in U.S., Tel: (212) 686-9213. 7,700$00–12,650$00.

▶ **Hotel Foz Praia.** Estrada Marginal, 2500 **Foz do Arelho.** Tel: (062) 97-94-13; Fax: (062) 97-94-60. 6,000$00–9,000$00.

▶ **Hotel da Nazaré.** Largo Afonso Zuquete, 7, 2450 **Nazaré.** Tel: (062) 56-13-11; Fax: (062) 56-12-38; in U.S., Tel: (212) 686-9213. 9,500$00–12,500$00.

▶ **Hotel da Praia Norte.** Estrada Nacional, 114, 2520

Peniche. Tel: (062) 78-11-66; Fax: (062) 78-11-65. 6,900$00–15,800$00.

► **Pensão Ribamar**. Rua Gomes Freire, 9, 2450 **Nazaré**. Tel: (062) 55-11-88; Telex: 43383. 5,000$00–8,000$00.

► **Pousada do Castelo**. 2510 **Obidos**. Tel: (062) 95-91-05; Fax: (062) 95-91-48. 15,400$00–25,200$00.

► **Pousada do Mestre Afonso Domingues**. 2440 **Batalha**. Tel: (044) 962-60; Telex: 42339. 9,700$00–18,000$00.

► **Quinta do Campo**. Valado dos Frades, 2450 **Nazaré**. Tel: (062) 57-71-35; Fax: (062) 57-75-55. 9,000$00–13,000$00.

► **Quinta do Fidalgo**. 2440 **Batalha**. Tel: (044) 961-14; Fax: (044) 76-74-01. 9,000$00–16,000$00.

► **Quinta de São José**. Freiria, 2590 **Sobral de Monte Agraço** (near Torres Vedras). Tel: (01) 284-4464 or (061) 94-11-33. 9,000$00–12,000$00.

South of the Tagus River

► **Aparthotel Magnoliamar**. Ponta do Adoxe, 2900 **Tróia**. Tel: (065) 442-21; Fax: (065) 442-56. 11,200$00–32,500$00.

► **Aparthotel de Tróia**. Ponta do Adoxe, 2900 **Tróia**. Tel: (065) 442-21 or 443-16; Fax: (065) 442-56. 6,000$00–16,500$00.

► **Hotel do Mar**. Rua do General Humberto Delgado, 10, 2950 **Sesimbra**. Tel: (01) 223-3326; Fax: (01) 223-3888; in U.S., Tel: (800) 421-3913. 11,500$00–23,200$00.

► **Pousada Castelo de Palmela**. 2950 **Palmela**. Tel: (01) 235-1226 or 235-1395; Fax: (01) 233-0440. 15,400$00–25,200$00.

► **Pousada de São Filipe**. Castelo de São Filipe, 2900 **Setúbal**. Tel: (065) 52-49-81 or 52-38-44; Fax: (065) 53-25-38. 15,400$00–25,200$00.

► **Quinta da Bacalhôa**. Vila Fresca de Azeitão. For information/reservations contact Thomas W. Scoville, 3637 Veazey Street, NW, Washington, D.C. 20008. Tel: (202) 686-7336. The quinta's six bedrooms and staff are rented by the fortnight or by the month.

► **Quinta das Torres**. 2925 **Vila Nogueira de Azeitão**. Tel: (01) 208-0001; Fax: (01) 219-0607. 9,000$00–15,000$00.

Pousadas can be booked through ENATUR, Avenida Santa Joana Princesa, 10, 1700 Lisbon, Portugal; Tel: (01) 848-1221 or 848-9078; Fax: (01) 80-58-46. But it is easier to make reservations through a travel agent. In the United States and Canada, pousadas can be booked through Marketing Ahead, 433 Fifth Avenue, New York, NY 10016; Tel: (212) 686-9213; Fax: (212) 686-0271.

Manor houses can be booked directly or through the manor-house associations—ANTER, P.I.T., PRIVETUR, and TURIHAB—listed in Useful Facts. Most of the houses belong to one or more of these associations, but because membership rosters change frequently we haven't attempted to spell out the associations for each house. Readers are advised to contact the manor-house associations for their current listings.

In the United States and Canada, it is possible to reserve rooms in P.I.T. manor houses through E & M Associates, 211 East 43rd Street, Suite 1404, New York, NY 10017; Tel: (212) 599-8280; Fax: (212) 599-1755.

THE RIBATEJO

By Thomas de la Cal

Thomas de la Cal grew up in Portugal and returns there regularly from his home in California. He has contributed articles to Connoisseur, European Travel and Life, Travel/Holiday, *and other magazines. He has worked on documentaries about Portugal for the National Geographic Society, the BBC, and NBC, and has written the screen adaptation of a Portuguese novel for a European miniseries.*

The Ribatejo is the geographical and agricultural heartland and spiritual center of Portugal. Sandwiched between the coastal province of Estremadura to the west and the Beira Baixa and the rolling expanse of the Alentejo to the east, this triangular region roughly to the northeast of Lisbon is known for its bulls and bullfighters, horses and horsemen, wines and large estates, shrines and religious militants.

The Ribatejo owes its name, economy, topography, and character to the river Tagus (Tejo, in Portuguese), which originates in Spain and runs in a southwesterly direction through Portugal before spilling into the Atlantic Ocean 16 miles west of Lisbon. Legend has it that on his epic journey Ulysses ventured up the Tagus. In the millennia that followed, the fertile banks of the river drew northern and southern settlers and invaders, including Crusaders from Cornwall, France, and the Rhineland, who were given lands in the Ribatejo in return for their help in liberating Lisbon from the Moors. Before the construction of dams in the 20th century to generate electricity and divert part of the flow to irrigate the surrounding farmland, the river was navigable all the way to the border with Spain, and served as an important commercial route between the two countries. Today, despite the dams, the Tagus continues to bring devastating floods that transform the small towns on the plain into mini-Venices. The people of the region have learned to live with the unpredictable Tagus, making the best of the good years and facing the bad with a graceful stoicism.

The Ribatejo is divided into three geologically distinct areas: the *campo,* the *bairros,* and the *charneca.* The *campo,* which includes the *lezirias* (marshlands) and is sometimes called the *borda d'água* (water's edge), is a rich alluvial plain northeast of Lisbon where irrigated fields of rice and wheat, vineyards, and vegetable gardens thrive. It also boasts vast pastures that bloom with a rainbow of colors in the spring, produce most of the country's beef, and serve as grazing land for the horses and wild bulls so dear to the heart of the typical Portuguese male. The bulls are tended by colorful *campinos* (herdsmen) usually dressed in white shirt, red cummerbund, scarlet waistcoat with silver buttons, green stocking cap, thick white stockings, black breeches, and a black wool jacket draped ceremoniously over the shoulders. These Portuguese cowboys are usually armed with *varas* (wooden poles) to help in handling the bulls. It was on the vast estates of the *campo* that Portuguese bullfighting had its origins. The wealth of the region has helped develop a basically happy people, as reflected in their lively folk dances and music.

The area called the *bairros,* on the hilly west bank of the Tagus, is wilder. Large areas, particularly in the north, are covered with sagebrush and ferns. Nonetheless, olives, figs, and grapes are grown where nature permits. Some of Portugal's best table wines are produced in the *bairros.* The people of this area are more serious, dress in darker colors, and have slower-paced dances than their neighbors in the *campo.* They are also more religious. This may be due in part to the fact that during the 12th century the *bairros* served as a critical line of defense for the Christians in the north against the Moors who controlled large tracts to the south. The remains of a string of castles and monasteries built by the Knights Templars, a military order that reached its peak of power and influence during the 12th through the 14th centuries, still dot its hills and rivers. And the fervor has not died down: One of the largest centers of religious worship in the world today—Fátima—is situated in the *bairros.*

The *charneca,* the flat southern fringe of the Ribatejo, borders the east bank of the Tagus estuary. Its poor, sandy soil sustains pine and eucalyptus trees and an occasional vineyard or grainfield. The *charneca* includes the Mar da Palha (Sea of

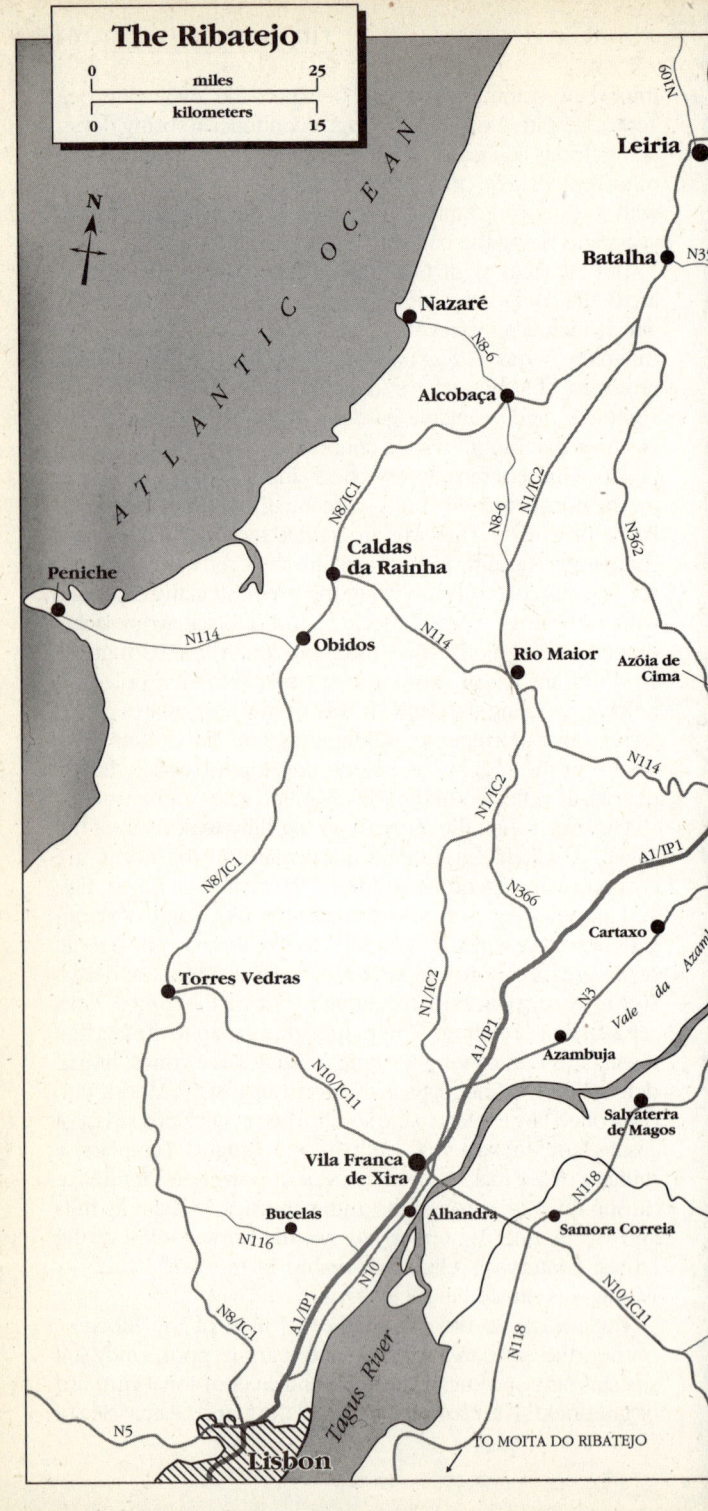

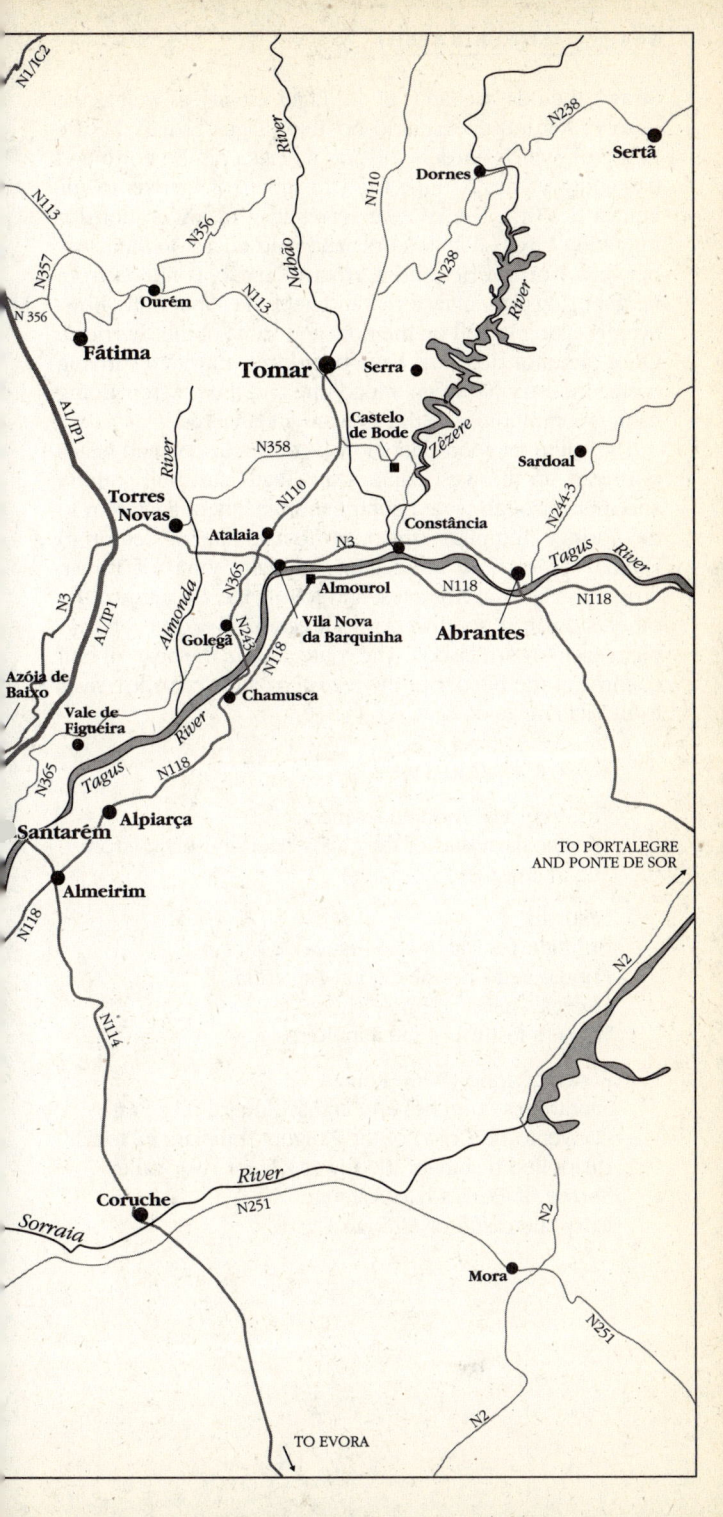

Straw), the tidal wetlands of the Tagus estuary, as well as the Reserva Natural do Estuario do Tejo (Tagus Estuary Nature Reserve), which borders the Mar da Palha on the north and east and stretches 20 miles from the mouth of the river to Vila Franca de Xira. The reserve serves as a resting station for migrating birds such as storks and wild ducks on their way between North Africa and northern Europe. Pollution from neighboring cement factories and steel and paper mills, however, is taking its toll on the flora and fauna of the *charneca:* Once-plentiful dolphins have been driven away, a thriving oyster industry has been wiped out, and the few remaining fishing communities in the area are endangered.

The route mapped out below begins in Lisbon and heads northeast up the west bank of the Tagus past bull country and then through wine country and the city of Santarém to the former Templars center of Tomar. After a detour to Fátima, we explore the region generally south of Tomar, cross the Tagus at Abrantes, and follow the river down the other side in a southwesterly direction over the Ribatejo plain back toward Lisbon. The route ends in the heart of bull country, at the border of the *charneca* and across the river from Vila Franca de Xira.

MAJOR INTEREST

Fine regional food and wine
Spectacular vistas of the Tagus river and plain (from Santarém and Abrantes)

Festivals
Bullfight festival at Vila Franca de Xira
Annual Feira do Ribatejo at Santarém
Golegã's national horse show
Tomar's festival of the Tabuleiros

Rota do Vinho (Wine Route)
Santarém's churches and archaeological museum
Convento de Cristo of the Knights Templars in Tomar
Unspoiled beauty of the lower Zêzere river valley
Shrine of Our Lady of Fátima
Fairy-tale castle of Almourol

The Food and Wine of the Ribatejo

The Ribatejo, the second-largest wine-growing region in Portugal, is known for its great selection of fine everyday wines. The British have known and drunk them since the 12th century. In fact, Shakespeare alludes to them in *King Henry VI, Part 2,* when Horner fortifies himself with a cup of *charneco* before fighting the tragic duel with his apprentice. The white Bucelas, whose grapes grow on the hillsides of the Trancão river valley just north of Lisbon, became popular with Wellington's officers during the Peninsular War against the French. It is not known for certain whether it was the Teutonic Knights, who settled the area in the 12th century, or the powerful marquês de Pombal, the country's prime minister from 1756 to 1777, who first introduced the Riesling-style grapes to the valley. What is certain, however, is that the soil and climate produce a wine that is quite different from that of their native Germany. The Arinto and Esgana Cão grapes, grown in a lime-and-sulfur-rich soil, yield a straw-colored, slightly acidic wine that goes well with fish and fowl. The older reserve Bucelas are less tart and more popular among connoisseurs. At the Camilo Alves cellars (which also bottle the heavier Dão and smoother Bairrada wines sold under the Caves Velhas banner) in the town of Bucelas, between Lisbon and Vila Franca de Xira, some of these finer wines are stored in large oak barrels.

Farther north, you will encounter full-bodied reds in the Cartaxo district of the *bairros* and smoother claret-style Serradayres wines from the slopes of the Serra do Aire (Mountain of the Air), which borders Estremadura. Fruitier wines can be found on the east bank of the Tagus around Alpiarça and Almeirim, while stronger spirits such as the wine-based *aguardentes* (brandies) and humbler *bagaços* are fashioned in the former Templars center of Tomar, located in the Nabão river valley northeast of Santarém.

The food of the Ribatejo is as varied and hearty as its wines. The river Tagus yields a bounty of fish, which is the principal ingredient of the delicious concoction known as *sopa de peixe* (fish soup). Regional delicacies include Cartaxo's *açorda de sável,* a shad soup laced with oil, garlic, and coriander and thickened with bread; and Golegã's *ensopado de enguias* (eel stew). Farther north, the Nabão and Zêzere rivers are known for their *lampreia* (lamprey), which is stewed in its own blood and red wine, with surprisingly tasty results.

Meat, of course, is popular in the southern ranch areas, where charcoal-grilled *entrecosto* (rib steak) and wood-fired *espetadas na vara de loureiro* (kebabs on laurel sticks) are the local favorites. The smoked *toucinho* (bacon) of the *charneca* graces all varieties of soups and bean dishes, as do the rice-filled *morcelas de arroz* (blood sausages) of the northeast. *Borrego* (young male lamb) and *cabrito* (kid), however, are the favorite meats, particularly in the *bairros,* where they are grilled, fried, stewed, and roasted.

Like their countrymen in general, Ribatejanos are addicted to sweets, a taste they inherited from the Moors and developed in the convents of the region. Some typical diet-wrecking delectables are *fatias de Tomar* (egg-yolk sponge shaped into little ovals, then bathed in cinnamon syrup), *tigeladas* (firm yet foamy custards baked in earthenware dishes and decorated with dustings of cinnamon), and *palha de Abrantes,* nuggets of almond paste covered with golden "thread eggs," beaten egg yolks formed into fine, hardened strands that resemble bits of straw (*palha*). The fruits of the *campo* are a less calorie-laden alternative, particularly the *morangos* (strawberries) of Almeirim and the green-and-black *tendral* melon and white-and-yellow Ribatejano melons, sold fresh from roadside stands during the summer months. Cheese lovers should try the goat and sheep varieties made in the mountain areas. The best known are the small cardamom-laced sheep cheeses of Tomar, which taste of wood smoke and nuts.

VILA FRANCA DE XIRA

Situated on the west bank of the river Tagus, 32 km (20 miles) northeast of Lisbon, this city of modern apartment blocks and smokestacks is bypassed by travellers most of the year. However, during the first weekend of July visitors flock to the Colete Encarnado—the major event of the Ribatejo's bullfighting season. The festivities, which are named after the scarlet waistcoat of the *campino,* the Ribatejo's colorful cowboy, include bull running and herding competitions in the streets, bullfighting in the town's arena, displays of the region's lively folk dancing, called *fandango* and similar to the Spanish *fandango,* and outdoor snacking on grilled sardines, pork steaks, and chicken.

Bullfighting existed on the Iberian Peninsula prior to the

Punic Wars. It developed during the rule of the Visigoths and was later modified by the Arabs. The *corrida* (bullfight) originated in both Portugal and Spain in the 16th century. Introduced by noble *cavaleiros,* or horsemen, bullfighting began as a way to train horses and men for battle. Over time, however, it became a popular spectacle. In the early 18th century the Portuguese and Spanish styles of bullfighting began to diverge after King Philip V of Spain, under papal threat of excommunication, took a dislike to the spectacle and frowned upon the nobility taking part in it. The Spanish public went on to lavish their attention on the *matador* (literally, "killer"), who was generally of the peasant class and who fought on foot. The Portuguese, meanwhile, kept the *cavaleiro* as their main attraction. By the late 18th century the first official bullrings began to appear in Portugal, and horsemen such as the marquês de Marialva became heroes of the national sport. (The word *marialva* later became a synonym for masculine pride and bravery.)

Portuguese bullfighting has not been without its controversies. In fact, ever since the late 18th century an always passionate and sometimes violent argument over whether or not to kill the bull in the ring has divided bullfighting aficionados. Since 1933 a ban on such killing has been in effect, and heavy fines are imposed on those who disobey the law. Critics argue that the ban deprives the bull of a noble death in the heat of battle, leaving him instead to be butchered in the slaughterhouse hours later. Bulls that distinguish themselves in the ring are allowed to live; their superficial wounds inflicted by the *farpas* (long darts) are treated, and then they are put to pasture in order to improve the breed.

The Portuguese bullfight is a lively and spectacular affair. In it, a *cavaleiro* dressed in 18th-century livery charges the bull and places the *farpas,* of varying sizes, in the back of its neck, all the while trying to avoid the horns of the enraged animal. Both horse and rider have to draw upon their tremendous skill and years of practice working together as a team. Once the *cavaleiro* has placed a minimum of four *farpas,* he turns the ring over to the *forcados,* a group of eight men dressed in rustic 19th-century garb—short jacket, breeches, white stockings, and green or red tasseled stocking caps—who confront the bull in single file. The *cara* (face) at the front of the line taunts the bull until it charges. When man and beast are about to collide, the *cara* leaps over the bull's horns, wraps his arms around its neck, and holds on for dear life. The other men then jump on the bull and try to bring the pair to a halt. More often than not, the bull manages to fling the *cara* into the air like a matchstick and pummel the rest of the crew. Developed in the 18th century by ranch hands and named after the pitchforks they used, *forcados* are unique to Portugal (those of Vila Franca, Santarém, and Lisbon are considered the best). They are not paid for their bone-breaking efforts, but being a *forcado* is the ultimate test of bravery for a young Portuguese male, a sort of coming-of-age ritual.

Bulls are raised in the salty marshlands of the Ribatejo (ocean tides push as far as 30 miles upriver) as well as in the wooded areas of the *charneca* and the Alentejo. The young *toiros bravos* (wild bulls) are separated from their mothers at an early age and, with a minimum of human contact so they don't become wise to the sport, are tested for their courage. At these *tentas* (trials), the bulls are prodded with long poles or challenged with a cape to see how they react. The most spirited bulls are selected and separated from the more docile ones that are then slaughtered for their meat.

Also of special interest in this area is the short, stocky Lusitano horse (named after the pre-Roman tribe of Portugal), which has been esteemed for its quick reflexes and courage. Its legendary maneuverability is due to the position of its hind legs, which are tucked well underneath the body axis. This gives the horse excellent balance and allows it to stop on a dime and accelerate quickly. Reputed to have been the first saddle horse in Europe, the Lusitano was prized by the Romans, who established remount depots in Portugal to supply their cavalry with the breed. In the 14th century King Fernando established laws regulating the breeding and raising of all Portuguese horses. When nobles were not off fighting their rivals or the Moors, they and their horses trained by pitting themselves against wild bulls. Less lethal equestrian games were also performed at court and on large estates throughout the country. The Napoleonic invasion in the early 19th century practically destroyed the Lusitano breed, which was reduced further with the coming of mechanized warfare. After World War I, horses were retired from the battlefield and the emphasis shifted to the bullring.

Today horse farms in the Ribatejo are spearheading a revival of the Lusitano. Enthusiasts can visit the **Centro Equestre da Lezíria Grande** at Povos, between Vila Franca and Alhandra. Coming north from Lisbon on the A 1/IP 1, get off at the first Vila Franca exit and swing back south on the N 10. The center is one kilometer (½ mile) from the exit. Recreating the elegance of the 18th-century Portuguese aristocracy, horsemen at the center dress in satin livery and perform beautiful equestrian ballets that combine both classical and popular dressage. The center, which also breeds and sells horses, offers typical Ribatejano lunches to groups and stages bullfighting spectacles in its outdoor bullring. For the schedule of events and to make reservations, Tel: (063) 227-81; Fax: (063) 240-23.

Portuguese horses can also be admired at the **Estação Zootécnica Nacional** (National Stud Farm) at Quinta da Fonte Bela, as well as at the annual national horse show in Golegã in November. At the latter you will also see patrician landowners dressed in traditional riding dress, which includes flat-rimmed hats and tight-fitting waistcoats and pants, competing in horse and carriage competitions.

You can ride Lusitano horses and take dressage lessons at the **Quinta de São Sebastião**, a sprawling estate at Arruda dos Vinhos, 11 km (7 miles) west of Vila Franca de Xira on the N 248. The 17th-century manor serves not only as a school but also as a stylish bed and breakfast, with one double and one triple in the main house (both with private baths and views of the surrounding countryside), and five doubles (three with private baths) in adjoining buildings.

Of historical interest in the Vila Franca de Xira area are the Torres Vedras defensive lines south of Vila Franca on the N 10 at **Alhandra**, which were built by Wellington to defend Lisbon against the French in 1810. At the end of the lines is a statue of Hercules, a tribute to the defenders who held against the French.

THE ROTA DO VINHO

This pleasant wine route from Vila Franca follows the A 1/IP 1 a few miles north to the N 3, which traverses a wide vine-combed plain flanked by the rolling hills and olive groves of the *bairros* on one side and the Vale da Azambuja and the river Tagus on the other. The town of **Azambuja**, 19 km (12 miles) from Vila Franca, was given to Childe Rolim, son of the count of Chester, in the 12th century by King Afonso I in return for his assistance in liberating Lisbon from the Moors. Today Azambuja is a prosperous farming town with a quaint main square.

About 13 km (8 miles) farther along the N 3, in the heart of the wine country, is the town of **Cartaxo**. Here you can park at the largo Vasco da Gama beside the bullring and walk to the other sights. Directly northwest, via rua Serpa Pinto, is the largo São João Baptista, a charming square where there is an ornate 16th-century Manueline cross and the **Capela do Senhor dos Passos,** which is all that remains of the former Solar dos Sousa Lobatos, where Wellington installed his headquarters during the winter of 1810–1811. Southwest of the chapel, behind rua de Batalhoz, is the **Museu Rural e do Vinho** (Rural and Wine Museum), on rua José Ribeiro da Costa, where you can savor (and buy) an assortment of regional wines, inspect traditional wine making and agricultural implements, and shop for regional handicrafts, including earthenware pottery with hand-painted wine motifs.

On the eastern outskirts of Cartaxo is the 17th-century **Solar dos Chavões** manor house and restaurant, the ideal spot to partake of the region's full-bodied, fruity wines and sample the regional cuisine—pork, fried eel, *sopa de peixe,* and Cartaxo's very own *açorda de sável* (shad soup). This former home of the counts of Unhão is surrounded by pines and vineyards. To get there, take the road to Santana for about 2 km (1¼ miles) before turning left toward Vila Chã de Ourique. The signposted property is on the right, or eastern, side of the road about 2 km north.

SANTAREM

Santarém is on the N 3, just 13 km (8 miles) north of Cartaxo. The unofficial capital of the Ribatejo, the town is also known as the *varanda* (verandah) of the region because it is built on seven hills overlooking the Tagus river and its fertile plain. It also has a number of interesting churches, has witnessed a host of miracles, and stages lively food and folk fairs.

The origins of Santarém are shrouded in legend. According to one account, Ulysses visited Lisbon in 1215 B.C., had an affair with Prince Gorgoris's daughter Calipso, and left before their son, Abidis, was born. The infuriated prince had the baby placed inside a basket and thrown into the waters of the Tagus. The high tide carried the basket upriver to the present site of Santarém, where it was discovered by a she-wolf who raised the child as her own. Years later, the boy was captured by royal hunters and taken to the court of the prince, where his true identity was revealed to his mother when she noticed the child's unique birthmark. Gorgoris, who had not been able to father a male heir, relented and welcomed Abidis back into the fold. Later still, after the youth had ascended to his grandfather's throne, he had a town built on the site where he had been found by the prince's hunters and named it Esca-Abidis (food of Abidis). Later, invaders from the north called the town Escalabis.

Santarém's current name dates from the seventh century. According to another legend, there lived north of Santarém, in present-day Tomar, a beautiful nun by the name of Iria. Her beauty was such that it caught the eye of Britaldo, the son of the governor. Failing to gain her love, Britaldo took to his bed with a high fever. When Iria visited the young man and cured him by placing her hand on his forehead, her reputation as a healer was made. Brother Remígio, her tutor, also could not control his passion for her. When his advances were rebuffed, he slipped the young nun a potion that swelled her stomach, making her appear pregnant. Hearing that the nun was pregnant, the enraged Britaldo had her murdered and her body thrown into the waters of the Nabão, where it eventually floated down into the Tagus and washed up at Escalabis. The monk eventually repented and confessed his sin. Hearing about the tragedy, the king changed the name of the town where she had washed up from Ecalabis to Santa Iria. The Moors altered the name to Xantarim, and the later Christians called it Santarém.

There is a statue of Santa Iria in the old riverside neighborhood of Ribeira, on the N 114 toward Almeirim. The statue, which stands on a pedestal, was commissioned by Rainha Santa Isabel (Queen Saint Isabel), the wife of Dom Dinis, in the 14th century. During floods it serves as a marker to gauge the water level. It was generally believed that if the waters reached the toes of the statue, everything downstream, including Lisbon, would be washed away. Flood waters reached the feet in 1979, but Lisbon was spared.

From the Phoenicians to the Romans, from northern to southern hordes, the strategic importance of Santarém has attracted traders and invaders. The Moors, who stayed the longest, were finally expelled in 1147 by King Afonso Henriques and a band of daring knights, who scaled the city walls under cover of night and surprised the sleeping garrison. From the 13th through the 16th century Santarém was popular with the Burgundian and Avis dynasties, who enjoyed the pleasures of the hunt in the surrounding area. Royalist and patriotic, it was the last city to lay down its arms in 1580, when Philip II of Spain invaded and captured Portugal. In 1810 it was taken by French forces under Masséna, who then plundered its churches and palaces. During the

Guerra dos Dois Irmãos (War of the Two Brothers, 1832–1834), the absolutist king Dom Miguel established his final headquarters in Santarém.

Most of the important sights in Santarém are within walking distance of one another. You can park in the northeastern corner of town beside the colorful tiled market across from the town hall and enter the old quarter through the remains of a Gothic tower to the south. The 17th-century **Igreja do Seminário**, a former Jesuit college that now serves as the city's cathedral, is the most prominent building on praça Sá da Bandeira. Vestiges of its palatial beginnings (it was built over a royal palace) can be detected in the elaborate cornices and windows above the Baroque façade. The interior, mostly marble, is cold and somber. The 19th-century Portuguese writer Almeida Garrett called it reactionary architecture: "There is no soul, no genius, no spirit in those heavy masses, devoid of elegance or simplicity; but there is a certain grandeur that imposes; a solid base, a calculated symmetry, cold proportions which reveal something of the century and the order which it characterized." Of a similarly cold nature was the 14th-century execution that took place outside the church: According to legend, King Pedro I oversaw the extraction of the hearts of two men who, following orders issued by Pedro's father, had murdered his beloved Galician mistress, Inês de Castro.

A more pleasant experience can be had directly south at the **Casa d'Avó**, rua Serpa Pinto, 62, a beckoning tea and snack establishment lodged in what was formerly a grand town house; here the city's doyennes meet to nibble on freshly baked Portuguese and English pastries. Farther down the street, on praça Visconde Serra do Pilar, is the elegant **Igreja de Marvila** with its ornate 16th-century Manueline doorway and lavish interior, which boasts walls covered with colorful 17th-century Neo-Mudejar tiles.

Veering east onto rua Conselheiro Figueiredo Leal, you'll come across the **Museu Arqueológico de São João de Alporão**, which is housed in a 13th-century Romanesque-Gothic church and contains treasures dating back to the days of the Roman occupation. The most impressive pieces, however, are the stone carvings taken from the churches, houses, and palaces of the area, particularly the beautifully carved balcony by Mateus Fernandes above the entrance and the Flamboyant Gothic tomb of Duarte de Meneses, count of Viana. It must have been these and other works that led Almeida Garrett to comment that "Santarém is a book written in stone." The tomb was built to house a tooth (item number 615)—all that remained of the count after he and a small band of Portuguese knights were hacked to pieces by the Moors. The knights were in the process of covering the retreat of King Afonso V during his disastrous campaign in North Africa.

Across the street is the 16th-century **Torre das Cabaças**, in which King Manuel had eight arches built to represent the eight senators, or *cabaças* (gourds), of the city who had, according to him, misused his funds on this nondescript clock tower. Farther east, at the end of the avenida 5 de Outubro, you come to the **Portas do Sol** (Gates of the Sun), which were part of the citadel walls from Moorish times. The gates open onto lovely gardens that overlook the river Tagus and the Ribatejo plain. Before entering the grounds, look for the stone crypt jutting out of the **Igreja de Santa Maria da Alcáçova**, which is the final resting place of the Jewish wife of a Christian knight who had asked to be buried beside her. The Catholic authorities granted the knight's wishes by placing her tomb beside his—but outside the church. On your left as you enter the gardens are the remains (two Gothic doors) of a former royal palace that was destroyed by the earthquake of 1755. Excavations in the southern corner of the gardens have uncovered what are believed to be the remains of Phoenician dye vats.

The snug **Portas do Sol** restaurant is lodged in the former wood-and-brick guardhouse overlooking the gardens. Its relaxed atmosphere and good food draw city officials and local intellectuals alike. Customers can enjoy grilled food on an outdoor patio during the summer.

The lovely 14th-century **Igreja da Graça**, northwest of the Portas do Sol, has an exquisite rose window, carved from a single piece of stone, that deftly makes use of the sunlight to give the appearance of glass. The church, which has been restored to its original Gothic appearance with the removal of all the extraneous elements added over the years, contains several important tombstones, including that of Pedro Alvares Cabral, the discoverer of Brazil. Cabral's discovery, made by accident in 1500 when his ship was blown off course on his way around Africa to India, was not deemed important at the time, in part because of a behind-the-scenes smear campaign by his archrival Vasco da Gama (which also explains why his simple, unassuming tombstone does not record his discovery).

On the other hand, the 15th-century tomb of Dom Pedro de Meneses is a sumptuous display of wealth and power, and contains the remains of Dom Pedro and his third wife surmounted by the carved reclining figures of the Dom and his first wife; his daughter by her paid for the tomb. The word *aleo*, inscribed in the stone, is significant. One day, while Dom Pedro was playing the cricketlike game of *truque* with the king, news arrived of a revolt in Ceuta in Morocco. Dom Pedro lifted his *aleo*, the club used in the game, and told the king not to worry; he would go to Ceuta and restore order there with the *aleo*. And so he did. Dom Pedro's *aleo* became a symbol of power in Ceuta and to this day hangs on the statue of Our Lady of Africa there.

The sacristy of the 14th-century **Igreja do Santíssimo Milagre**, next door on rua Braamcamp Freire, holds a crystal flask that is said to contain the blood of Christ. According to the 13th-century legend surrounding the flask, a young Catholic woman asked a Jewish *curandeira* (faith healer) how to stop her husband from beating her. Told to return with a holy wafer, the young woman feigned taking communion in church, wrapped the wafer in a cloth, and started back to the old *curandeira*'s home. Before she arrived, however, blood began to ooze out of the cloth. Terrified, the young woman rushed home and hid her bleeding bundle in a chest by her bed. But during the night, she and her husband were awakened by rays of light streaming from the chest. A priest was summoned, and he found, upon opening the bundle, that the wafer had been miraculously converted into a glass flask containing blood. During the French occupation of the early 19th century, the flask was taken to Lisbon for safekeeping. When the French departed, however, the people of Lisbon refused to return it, so a delegation from Santarém visited Lisbon and told its inhabitants that a man wearing boots with cork soles would walk across the Tagus at midnight. As all of Lisbon was at the dock waiting to witness this miracle, the delegation from Santarém took advantage of the opportunity to recover their flask.

The **Campo da Feira** is located near the bullring in the western corner of the town. It is here that the Feira Nacional de Agricultura, more commonly called the Feira do Ribatejo, is held. The one-week event, which begins on the first Friday in June, includes horse shows, riding competitions, bullfights, bull-herding meets by *campinos* (cowboys on horseback), and folk-dancing competitions. This is a colorful, popular fair, and accommodations are virtually impossible to find while it is running. But Lisbon is less than an hour away via the N 114 and A 1/IP 1 *auto-estrada*, so commuting is relatively easy.

Another popular event is the Festival Nacional de

Gastronómia (National Food Festival, scheduled in 1993 for the third weekend of October through the first weekend of November), at which you can savor regional cuisines as well as admire folk arts and handicrafts from all over Portugal, including the Azores and Madeira. The exposition is housed in one of the big fair buildings, where each province sets up its own elaborate booth. Most are decorated to look like a local town or house or country estate, and each showcases the area's most famous foodstuffs, wines, pottery, cookware, and other crafts. (Items are also for sale.) In addition, each day a different province prepares a regional feast for everyone at the festival. The Alentejo, for example, might bring the chef in from Fialho in Evora to prepare *açorda à Alentejana* (bread-thickened egg-drop garlic soup greened with fresh coriander), *porco à Alentejana* (braised pork and clams), and *queijadas de Evora* (little cheese tarts). Local folk dancers (in costume) and musicians perform throughout the meal, recipes are given out, and the local wines are served.

Two of Santarém's most popular restaurants are located on the fairgrounds. Don't be put off by **O Mal Cozinhado**'s name (Badly Cooked). This bistro, situated on the north side of the fairgrounds, is known for its regional menu (which includes fresh bull from the ring next door), rustic decor, thatched bar, and checkered tablecloths, and reflects the rural ambience of the area. Impromptu *fado* sessions are held on Friday evenings, when reservations are recommended (Tel: 043-235-84). The songs here are slightly more spirited than the mournful chants sung in the old quarter of Lisbon. The large air-conditioned **Restaurante Castiço** (the term for a local man) is next door to the equestrian ring. Decorated to look like the courtyard of a typical Ribatejo ranch, the restaurant has a mixed menu featuring such regional specialties as *caldeirada* (fish stew), *sopa de peixe,* and *feijão com entrecosto* (grilled steak and kidney beans).

Before leaving Santarém, you might like to see the 13th-century **Igreja de Santa Clara**, on avenida Gago Coutinho e Sacadura Cabral, in the northeastern part of the city. Apart from an elaborate Gothic tomb with Renaissance additions—the final resting place of Dona Leonor, the daughter of Afonso III—the former Franciscan convent contains interesting murals (said to depict part of the order's secret initiation rites) uncovered during restoration work in the 1940s. There was a tunnel from the convent to the former **Mosteiro de São Francisco**, but it has not been unearthed.

The 17th-century **Igreja de Santa Iria**, with its unusual

Gothic Cross, stands on a promontory overlooking the river-side neighborhood of Ribeira. Legend has it that a noble of the area convinced a young shepherdess to surrender her virginity by promising to marry her. When the nobleman failed to comply with his end of the bargain, the pregnant shepherdess presented her case to a magistrate, who proceeded to summon both parties to the church. The shepherdess asked the image on the cross for a sign to show she was telling the truth. Suddenly, the right arm of Jesus slipped from its position on the cross and pointed accusingly at the nobleman, who then agreed to the marriage.

Staying in the Santarém Area

Accommodations in Santarém proper do not do justice to its monuments. The **Hotel Abidis**, with 27 rooms in the old quarter near the praça Sá da Bandeira and the Casa d'Avó teahouse, is a modest exception. This clean, moderately priced establishment has an inn-like atmosphere and boasts pure country charm and service. Its ground-floor restaurant is decorated with regional pottery, tiles, farm implements, and bullfighting artifacts.

There are also two manor houses with guest rooms in the vicinity of Santarém. About 3 km (2 miles) northwest of town off the N 362 is the large estate **Quinta Vale de Lobos**, in Azóia de Baixo. It was here that the Portuguese historian Alexandre Herculano spent the last years of his life (1867 to 1877), running a farm. His room has been maintained as it was in his time and can be visited. The home and large grounds retain their 19th-century charm. There is also a pleasant pool surrounded by lawns and trees. The main house provides four bedrooms with private baths, furnished with rural touches. Baby-sitting and laundry services are available. Your charming English-speaking host, Joaquim Santos Lima, can direct you to nearby restaurants or, with advance notice, can have the kitchen prepare meals. The **Casa dos Cedros**, farther up the valley, in Azóia de Cima, has nice grounds and three comfortable bedrooms.

If you like horses, the **Estação Zootécnica Nacional**, the national stud farm at Quinta da Fonte Bela, 7 km (4 miles) southwest of Santarém via the N 3, will appeal to your equestrian fancies. The government-run farm lends out its stallions to horse breeders with registered mares, and also schools horses in the art of dressage. In addition to Portuguese breeds (Lusitano and Alter), the Estação raises Arab, Andalusian, and English thoroughbreds.

The towns of Almeirim and Alpiarça, on the east bank of the Tagus across from Santarém, are also possible excursions (see "The East Bank of the Tagus," below, for descriptions of both). Almeirim is about 7 km (4 miles) from Santarém via the N 114 and the Dom Luis I bridge. Alpiarça is 5 km (3 miles) north of Almeirim on the N 118/IC 3.

Golegã

This quaint town of whitewashed houses sits on a plain alongside the river Almonda, 31 km (19 miles) north of Santarém via the N 365. It was named, so the story goes, after a *galega* (Galician) woman who ran an inn where King Afonso Henriques stayed between military campaigns in the area. Some historians disputed the story, but that did not stop the town fathers from making a woman the centerpiece of Golegã's coat of arms.

The handsome 16th-century Manueline façade of the **Igreja Matriz**, on largo da Imaculada Conceição as you enter town from Santarém, was designed by Diogo Boytac, the genius behind the fabulous Manueline monasteries of Jerónimos in Belém and Batalha near Fátima. Across the street, on the western end of the square, is the charming, modern **Museu Martins Correia**. The two-story museum, housed in the town's former prison, holds a large collection of paintings and sculptures by its namesake. The native-born Golegã artist, whose work is largely inspired by Portuguese history and personages, uses oils, wood, iron, pottery, marble, and bronze to fashion his creations. Among the 600 works exhibited are busts of Portuguese greats such as epic poet Luís Vaz de Camões. The second-floor windows give onto the front of the Igreja Matriz, whose stone-carved ode to the Portuguese discoveries may have played a part in kindling Correia's patriotic passion as he grew up in the town.

Directly west, on largo Dom Manuel I, via rua Augustinho Macedo (in front of the law courts and town hall), is the **Atelier Fotográfico de Carlos Relvas**, in the elegant Victorian home of the former Portuguese statesman, farmer, and amateur photographer after whom the museum is named. In Relvas's former studio is a collection of early photographic equipment and some of his landscapes and portraits. The entrance foyer is lined with life-size, photographic self-portraits of the multifaceted Relvas in his various identities:

as a fireman, photographer, *cavaleiro* (bullfighter on horse-back), and country squire. A handsome, wooden spiral stair-case imported from Italy leads upstairs to the artist's studio, which contains ornate Victorian furnishings, intricate inlaid wood floors, photographs of Lisbon in the late 19th century, and a letter to Relvas from his friend, the Portuguese king Dom Fernando. Closed Mondays.

Golegã is also known as the equestrian mecca of Portugal. Its annual **Feira Nacional do Cavalo** (formerly called the Feira de São Martinho) is held during the first fortnight in November and draws horse enthusiasts, breeders, and bull-fighters from every region of the country. The horses are paraded around the fairgrounds and compete in all kinds of events, including carriage races. The riders wear tight-fitting Ribatejano riding clothes and flat-rimmed hats. Cool nights are made more appealing with roasted chestnuts and *água-pé* (foot water), which is derived from the skins and pulp left after the grapes have been pressed up to three times. Mixed with water and left to ferment for two or three days, this is a powerful drink.

If you want to mingle with the equestrian crowd and the local landowners, head for the **Central** restaurant adjacent to the Igreja Matriz at largo da Imaculada Conceição. Housed in the former residence of one of Portugal's premiere horse-men and bullfighters, Manuel dos Santos, the restaurant is known more for its bullfighting and equestrian decor and atmosphere than for its food. House specialties are large steaks with butter and mustard sauce, charcoal-grilled chicken, and *açorda de sável*, porridgy, bread-thickened shad soup spiced with coriander and garlic.

The **Quinta da Cardiga**, owned by the wealthy Sommer family, is a magnificent sprawling estate on the banks of the Tagus, 4 km (2½ miles) north of Golegã. Take the N 365 north toward Entroncamento and Tomar, veer right onto a small, unmarked road immediately past Golegã's cemetery, and turn left about 2 km (1¼ miles) down the road. You'll pass the simple, whitewashed homes of the estate's farm-hands and some farm sheds before entering a tree-lined drive that leads to the vine-covered estate. Famed for its beauty as well as its wine and cheeses, the estate is sur-rounded by forests and vineyards. The house has an elegant Italian façade and its own private chapel with a 16th-century door and several towers with glass-enclosed cupolas. The property was originally owned by the Knights Templars and came into private hands in the 19th century, when all monas-tic orders were banned after the War of the Two Brothers.

The public can visit the estate and, in season, buy its produce, which includes its own smooth Canto da Firlarga *aguardente*. Visits must be arranged in advance (written request required) through the estate's commercial offices in Lisbon at calçada da Tapada, 99, 5 Izquierdo; Tel: (01) 363-4072; Fax: (01) 362-1316.

Leaving Golegã for Tomar, take the N 365 north for 4 km (2½ miles) to the N 3 junction, where you connect with the N 110/IC 3. The steeple of the **Igreja de Nossa Senhora da Assunção** is to the north 2 km (1¼ miles) up the road at Atalaia. If you have time, stop and examine the arcaded doorway of this Renaissance church, along with its colorful tiled interior of figurative and geometric designs.

TOMAR

Tomar, with its cobbled medieval streets, ancient waterwheels, and parks, lies on the bucolic banks of the river Nabão, 135 km (84 miles) north of Lisbon. The crenellated battlements of a castle erected in 1160 by Gualdim Pais, grand master of the Order of the Knights Templars in Portugal, dominate a hill above the town. Behind the castle walls is the Convento de Cristo, the former stronghold of the Templars order and later the headquarters of its successor, the Portuguese Order of Christ.

The Knights Templars (a.k.a. the Poor Knights of Christ and of the Temple of Solomon) were established in Jerusalem in 1118 during the Crusades by French knights who vowed to defend the Holy Sepulcher, protect pilgrims, and fight the Muslims. At its peak the order had over 20,000 members and 9,000 castles, estates, and manor houses, and it was a major banking concern, lending money to kings and transporting bullion to the Levant. The Templars soon made enemies in the Church hierarchy; local prelates resented that the order was answerable only to the pope. The Knights' wealth and power were also viewed as a threat by various sovereigns in Europe. In 1307 Philip IV of France had the order's properties confiscated and its members arrested and accused of heresy, idolatry, and homosexuality. In 1312, when the order was disbanded by Pope Clement V under pressure from Philip, many of its members took refuge in Portugal. King Dinis, who was sympathetic to the banished order, found a way to circumvent the ban in 1320, by creating the Ordem de Cristo (Order of Christ). The new order assumed most of the trappings and properties of the disbanded Templars, and Tomar became the organization's headquarters.

The new Order of Christ played a significant role in the great discoveries of the 15th century. Prince Henry the Navigator, its most famous member, funded many of his explorations from the order's coffers, and the caravels under his command were emblazoned with its cross. In the 16th century King João III converted the Knights into monks and joined the three Portuguese orders (Cristo, Avis, and Santiago) under one banner. The 19th century saw the demise of the order. In 1810 the Convento de Cristo was sacked by Napoleon's armies. The final blow was delivered in 1834, with the disbanding of all monastic orders in Portugal. Squatters moved into the abandoned monastery and remained there until this century, when it was turned into a national monument. There are stories and books written about a lost Templars treasure buried somewhere on the grounds. The fortress convent and the Templars are described in Umberto Eco's novel *Foucault's Pendulum*.

The Convento de Cristo

The monastery (built over a period of six centuries, from the 12th to the 17th) is an impressive structure. The remains of this sprawling complex, which is surrounded by a 12th-century wall containing stones taken from the ruins of the town that had existed on the site, include a huge bell tower, a rotunda, seven cloisters, and a church. Although the lavish gold furnishings of the monastery have long since disappeared, the building still contains some of the most impressive stonework in the country, designed by such 16th-century Portuguese masters as Diogo de Arruda and Diogo de Torralva. The genius behind the ornate 16th-century Plater-esque doorway, however, was the Spaniard known in Portugal as João do Castilho. The ornate, archivolted doorway pays tribute to the Virgin and Child, who are flanked by some of the clergymen and saints who spoke and wrote most about them: Pope Gregory and Saint Jerome to the right, and Saint Ambrose and Saint Augustine to the left. The portico has weathered the centuries well, thanks to a carved pallium that acts as a stone awning. Unfortunately, a Renaissance cloister built next door obscures part of the beauty of this magnificent doorway.

The religious nerve center of the monastery, the Neo-Byzantine **charola** (rotunda), is distinguished by eight pillars that support a two-story octagonal structure crowned by a cupola; it was designed after the Holy Sepulcher in Jerusalem. Knights of the Order are said to have heard mass inside the rotunda mounted on horses. After it was damaged by lightning, King Manuel had the *charola* restored with Manueline flair. (The *charola* is once again undergoing extensive restoration work, and scaffolding has concealed some of its beauty. However, a pictorial display of the area under restoration can be admired at the entrance of the rotunda.) The **main cloister**, the 16th-century Claustro dos Felipes, was built during the reign of King João III. Legend has it that João was so upset when his father, Manuel, married Leonor, the woman João loved, that he disavowed his father's cherished Manueline style and looked elsewhere for inspiration. Historians point out, however, that Portugal's Golden Age was winding down, the exuberant Manueline style that characterized it in decline anyway.

Philip II of Spain is said to have been crowned king of Portugal in the main cloister in 1581, after he took advantage of Portugal's disastrous campaign in Morocco. The tiny holes in the pavement around the fountain, which was designed by Diogo de Torralva and used to be fed by an aqueduct, capture excess water and channel it into an underlying cistern. There are also several rooms under the cloister where initiation rites were carried out by the monks and where the luckless souls suspected of heresy were tortured during the Inquisition. The tomb of Baltasar de Faria, who introduced the Inquisition to Portugal during the reign of João III, is discreetly hidden in the upper terrace of the northeastern ablutions cloister.

From the terrace of the cloister of Santa Bárbara (which is reached by a spiral staircase in the main cloister) you can admire the magnificent **Manueline window** sculpted by Diogo de Arruda. The window, with its array of natural and maritime motifs, is considered not only the best example of Manueline art in Portugal, but also the most allegorical tribute to the Portuguese discoveries. Ropes, anchors, masts, shells, driftwood, nets, and even the Old Man of the Sea are carved in the stone of the window, and the artichokes lining it are a reminder that the Portuguese navy used them as a source of vitamin C to combat scurvy. The British Order of the Garter and the Golden Fleece, bestowed on Prince Henry the Navigator (his mother was Philippa of Lancaster), are represented by a chain and a ribbon encircling the two turrets flanking the window. Also carved in the window are the royal emblems of Manuel I (a blazon and armillary sphere) and the Cross of the Order of Christ, the two powers that made the Age of Discovery possible. Classical music concerts are held in July on the monastery grounds. The Convento is open daily except holidays.

Around in Tomar

Tomar proper was built near the ruins of the Roman city of Nabancia (from which the river Nabão derived its name). Laid out in the form of a cross by Prince Henry the Navigator, its medieval quarter, with the **praça da República** at its center, is located on the west bank of the river and still retains much of its flavor and charm. Here you will find the former palace of King Manuel I (now converted into the town hall) and the 15th-century **Igreja de São João Baptista**, which has a Flamboyant door and pulpit carved by French artisans and two paintings by the 16th-century Portuguese master Gregorio Lopes: one of the Last Supper and the other Salome's presentation of the head of Saint John the Baptist to King Herod. Of the two, the latter is richer in color and better preserved. Lopes, a court painter, is known for his love of detail as well as his realist touches.

On the north end of the tiny square, at number 41, you can shop at **Artlantida** for blue-and-yellow tiles and pottery with floral, medieval, and Templars motifs. The work in this store, which is open weekdays in the late afternoon, is produced by a women's cooperative lodged in a former convent on the southern edge of town.

The lavish **Tabuleiros festival** is held in the square every two or three years for four days during the first fortnight of July. With roots in an ancient fertility festival dedicated to the goddess Ceres, it was co-opted in the 14th century by the Brotherhood of the Holy Spirit—the latter founded by Queen Isabel as a means of gathering donations for the poor. (Queen Isabel was later canonized as Saint Elizabeth of Portugal.) The festival is an impressive affair, punctuated daily by sumptuous parades, including horse and chariot cavalcades along streets paved with flower tapestries on religious and medieval motifs. In 1991 symposia were presented on the Portuguese discoveries and the Brotherhood's role in them.

The festival's highlight is the *tabuleiros* march, in which young women dressed in white parade around the streets carrying on their heads *tabuleiros* (platters) of bread that are often as tall as they are. These *tabuleiros* consist of some 30 loaves of bread threaded onto rods attached to wicker baskets decorated with paper flowers, leaves, and stalks of wheat.

Sometimes the platters are topped off by a dove. The bounty was symbolically offered to the Holy Spirit as represented by the dove, the symbol of universal fraternity espoused by the Brotherhood. At night the *tabuleiros* are exhibited in the park below the monastery, which is illuminated with colorful displays of light. The festival is also celebrated in Brazil, the Azores, and Portuguese communities in North America. The next festival is tentatively scheduled for 1994.

If you miss the festival, the next best thing is to visit the **Galeria Risco** curio shop at rua Silva Magalhães, 12, where miniature *tabuleiros* are offered for sale. The shop, installed in a quaint two-story town house, also sells small copies of the town's waterwheels and paintings of the old quarter and the Convento de Cristo by local artists. Rua Silva Magalhães runs north from the praça da República.

Just a block south of the praça da República, at rua Dr. Joaquim Jacinto, 73, is the synagogue, now a museum named after Abraham Zacuto, King João II's court astronomer and historian. It is the only well-preserved vestige of medieval Jewish worship in Portugal. Used briefly in the 15th century by the Jewish community in Tomar before the Royal Edict of 1496 ordered the Jews and Muslims to convert to Christianity or leave Portugal, it subsequently served as a prison, a storehouse, and a cellar. It was finally acquired in 1923 by a Polish Jew, Samuel Schwarz, and was given to the state. The rectangular building, with its marble pillars and vaulted roof, now houses Hebrew tombstones and Jewish memorabilia from all over Portugal as well as gifts from Jewish organizations around the world. The water jugs lodged in the corners are an ancient method of soundproofing a room. Excavations in the house next door have uncovered the remains of a room where Jewish women took ritual baths. The museum is closed at lunchtime.

A five-minute walk south from the praça da República, via the rua da Infantaria 15, will bring you to the curious **Museu de Fósforos Aquiles de Mota Lima** (Match Museum), lodged in the cloisters of the former Convento de São Francisco facing the Varzea Grande fairground. The museum contains a valuable collection of more than 43,000 matchboxes from 104 countries assembled by its namesake between 1953 and 1980. Six rooms make up this unique collection, which boasts the world's largest and smallest matchboxes, a shawl decorated with 19th-century matchbox covers, a large set of German matchboxes graced with musical instruments, and a rare set of Russian ones that depict pre-Revolutionary actors. Aquiles de Mota Lima began collecting when he promised to help an

American friend with her hobby. What began as a casual favor soon became a passion. The courtyard and fairground in front of the convent are the site of a large annual artisan fair, held in late July, that attracts artisans from all over Portugal, including Madeira and the Azores.

Across the courtyard from the museum is the workshop of **Artlantida**, the women's pottery and tile cooperative, where you can admire work in progress. The workshop will take orders for reproductions. Its hours are weekdays 9:00 A.M. to noon and 3:00 to 6:00 P.M.

Farther east, a five-minute walk across the Ponte Velho on rua Marquês de Pombal, is the former **Convento da Santa Iria**, named after the beautiful nun (see the Santarém section, above). The riverside property is now privately owned. To visit its Renaissance chapel, apply for the key at the Turismo on avenida Dr. Cândido Madureira; Tel: (049) 32-20-22 or 32-26-02.

Northeast of the convent, at the end of avenida Dr. Cândido Madureira, on the eastern corner of the praça de Infante Dom Henrique, lies a lovely replica of a 16th-century patrician house built in 1936 to house the local tourism office. Today it is the home of the Comisão Municipal de Turismo (Municipal Planning Board), but it can be visited during working hours. An ornate Manueline portico, lined with Mudejar (Moorish-style) tiles, gives way to a large, wood-paneled salon decorated with antiques salvaged from stately homes and churches around Tomar. Photographs of 19th-century Tomar grace the walls while two life-size mannequins dressed in dark local peasant costumes welcome visitors. A life-size *tabuleiro* stands upright beside the female mannequin. The patrician villa next door, with its round, square, triangular, and tiled chimneys, offers a good sampling of Portugal's smokestack repertoire.

If you take avenida Dr. Cândido Madureira east, turn left at the traffic circle, and walk north on rua Everara, you will pass the formerly royal olive-oil presses, which continue to be powered by the Nabão river.

Some of the nicest views of Tomar can be had from the busy intersection at the northern end of rua Everara. The rua Serpa Pinto, popularly called *dos corredores* (racers) because of the horse races held on it during the Middle Ages, runs west from this juncture. It not only affords a spectacular vista of the Convento de Cristo but also contains several handsome, tiled houses. Bucolic scenes of the town and the river grace the glazed façade of a three-story building (number 23) on the left side of the street above a bookshop, while the geometric designs of the tiles on the building next door provide a more rational tone in harmony with the pharmacy on its ground level.

Farther down, at number 94, two tiled panels depicting the river and convent welcome you to the **Residencial União**, a quaint, family-run bed-and-breakfast inn with a Victorian look and a homey, Old World pace. All its 29 rooms are fitted with private baths, telephones, and television, and look out onto the street. The rates at this century-old establishment are another attractive feature for travellers on a tight budget. **Pensão Residencial Sinagoga**, tucked away on the quiet rua Gil Avô around the corner to the east, is a more modern but cozy alternative, with many comforts and regional decor. All 23 rooms have their own baths, and several look out onto a tiny cobbled street.

Directly east from the intersection, the Nabão river, spanned by the old, stone Ponte Velho and graced on the left bank by the former Convento da Santa Iria, is another of the scenic highlights of Tomar. Tomar's most picturesque eating establishment lies across the street from the convent, at Fonte do Choupo, 6. From this restaurant, **Bela Vista**, which is named for its view, you can capture in its entirety the beauty of historic Tomar to the west: the river, the old bridge and town, the impressive battlements of the Convento de Cristo, and a tiny, tree-lined island in the middle of the river. The restaurant is lodged on the ground floor of an old, whitewashed town house. In the summer ask to be seated in the stone-arched outdoor dining area, which is shaded by vines and large potted plants. House specialties are grilled trout and *frango à caril* (curried chicken). Service is somewhat slow, but the view and the relaxed atmosphere compensate. The adjacent **Nabão** restaurant is the next best choice. Its plain indoor dining room may not be as charming, but it provides sumptuous views and a fairly decent regional menu.

Parque Mouchão, a quiet corner of Tomar lined with aspen, poplar, and elm trees, is on a tiny island in the middle of the Nabão river that's connected to the west bank by a bridge. The entrance to the park is embellished by a huge wooden waterwheel of the Moorish style, the kind that was used for centuries to irrigate the area via a system of pottery buckets. The intimate and elegant **Estalagem de Santa Iria** on its north side has undergone a face-lift and opened its doors again to the public in the summer of 1991. Somerset Maugham lodged here when he visited Tomar. He apparently intended to stay only for a weekend but fell in love with the area and the inn and extended his visit to two weeks. The park's greenery and the old city, crowned by the Templars monastery, can be enjoyed to the fullest from the balconies of the south-facing rooms. The glass-enclosed restaurant and its popular verandah, which faces the garden, also afford panoramic views and a promising menu of international and regional fare.

Directly north of the island, on the west bank of the river overlooking Mouchão Park and facing the Convento de Cristo, is the **Hotel dos Templários**, an 84-room establishment with all the modern conveniences, including air-conditioning, curio shops, a hairdresser, game room, and outdoor swimming pool. (As this book went to press, a new annex was scheduled to open in June 1993, doubling the hotel's capacity and providing such amenities as a health club, a shopping arcade, a second restaurant, and an indoor pool.) The hotel's restaurant, which faces the river, has an extensive menu of both national and regional dishes, including such local specialties as *lampreia com arroz* (lamprey cooked in its own blood and wine and served on a bed of rice), *fatias de Tomar* (poached beaten egg yolks bathed in cinnamon syrup), veal scallops in Madeira wine sauce, and a rich *torta à Templarios* (almond-and-honey tart). For starters, you can nibble on *queijinhos de Tomar,* the snowy sheep cheeses that are a cottage industry of the region. These can be accompanied by a semi-dry Convento Tomar reserve white wine from the Adega Cooperativa de Tomar. Ask for Colheita Seleccionada, a minute part of the annual harvest that is given special nursing conditions during maturation. The Adega sells wine to the public and is located on the outskirts of Tomar at Algarvias, on the road to Torres Novas. To burn off some of the calories after dinner, climb the 365 steps that start beside the hotel to the **Capela de Nossa Senhora da Piedade**. From here you can admire Tomar, the river, the Templars convent on the hill, and, to the east, an old silk factory. Another way to enjoy the bucolic side of Tomar is to rent a rowboat, canoe, or paddleboat on the left bank and explore the tree-lined Nabão river.

For more adventurous fare, try **Chico Elias**, at Algarvias, half a mile southwest of Tomar on the road to Torres Novas. This country bistro is housed in a converted farmhouse, which stands alone on a ledge to your right as you turn a corner of the winding N 358. There is no sign, but the outside is gray and its iron doors are painted green. The restaurant is owned by Dona Ceu, a dynamic and imaginative cook whose creations include *feijoada de cara-cóis* (snail stew with sliced sausage and smoked ham), *coelho na abóbora* (rabbit stewed inside a gourd, cooked in a wood-fired oven, and served with rice), and reportedly the best *leite creme* (custard) in the region. Part of the secret behind the popularity of the latter is the old-fashioned iron pan that is heated in the wood-fired oven and used to brand and brown the caramel topping. Customers frequent Chico Elias for its food rather than its spartan decor, which consists of grapevine lamps, red-tiled floors, and benches. Reservations are a must; Tel: (049) 31-10-67; no credit cards.

For maps, directions, and general information on Tomar and the surrounding area, head for the new local tourism office on the corner of rua Serpa Pinto and rua Everaro (Tel: 049-31-30-95).

Nightlife is not the reason to visit Tomar. In town there is a choice between the subdued yet elegant ambience of the bar at the Hotel dos Templários and the turn-of-the-century **Cine Teatro de Tomar** (rua Infataria 15, 31), with its vintage hard seats and ancient piano from the silent-movie days. The theater is run by an eccentric octogenarian gentleman who shows original-language films with Portuguese subtitles and has filled the walls of his theater with color photographs of female stars. Be warned, however, that Cine Teatro sometimes shows off-color movies.

The trendy, music-loving crowd heads at night for the **Quinta Bar** on the outskirts of town. Live music by Portuguese and American folk singers brightens the weekends in the summer months. The cozy, pub-style establishment is housed in a converted country home some 7 km (4 miles) south of town. Take the N 110/IC 3 toward Lisbon for 6 km (3½ miles) and turn left onto the N 358-2 toward Castelo de Bode. The bar, with its Neo-Tudor beams and black wooden gate, is about 1 km (½ mile) down the road to your right.

The **Quinta da Anunciada Velha**, 3 km (2 miles) south of Tomar on the N 110/IC 3, is a rustic yet gentrified bed and breakfast owned by the counts of Tomar. Its entrance is marked by two white pillars, one of which carries the name in blue tiles. The property, a charming maze of architectural styles, goes back to the 12th century. It belonged to the Knights Templars and subsequently, until the 19th century, to the Order of Christ. In the main house the owners have set aside two rooms for guests, one with a private bath, both decorated with family heirlooms. The quaint, comfortable rooms have access to a terrace overlooking the property. Two self-catering apartments are also available to visitors, who enjoy the run of the property.

THE LOWER ZEZERE VALLEY

The damming of the lower Zêzere river has created the largest and one of the most enchanting man-made reservoirs in Portugal, one known for its pristine waters, abundance of fish, and sweet-smelling pine forests. Fishing and water sports are popular, particularly at **Castelo de Bode**, the crest of the dam at the southern end of the reservoir, 13 km (8 miles) southeast of Tomar via the N 110/IC 3 and N 358-2. In late 1992 the **Pousada de São Pedro**, which faces the dam and was originally built in the 1940s to house the engineers who worked on the massive project, closed for enlarging and upgrading. It is expected to reopen in the spring of 1993, when the number of rooms in the main building will have been doubled to 15; the less desirable seven-room annex will continue to handle the overflow. The pousada's main features are a fine restaurant and a terrace bar that overlook a valley lined with olive trees and mimosas below the dam. Pleasure cruises down the river are available on the *São Cristóvão,* a modern two-story ferry that leaves from the Castelo de Bode dock near the pousada. The two- and four-hour trips can be booked from the Hotel dos Templários in Tomar (Tel: 049-32-17-30; Fax: 049-32-21-91) or at any travel agency.

The **Estalagem Ilha do Lombo** is a charming, secluded island retreat in the middle of the river Zêzere, 16 km (10 miles) east of Tomar. (Unlike the pousada, it does not provide direct access to and unimpeded views of the river.) To get to it, leave Tomar on the N 110/IC 3 headed north toward Coimbra, then turn right at the second traffic light, and follow the signs to Serra and Ilha do Lombo. After Serra you'll arrive at a white house that serves as the post office, garage, and mainland dock for the inn, which is across from it. The modern inn itself—shaded by mimosas, blessed with the sweet perfume of orange blossoms, and by far the most romantic and delightful locale on the lake—has 17 large double bedrooms with red-tiled floors, ornate bamboo furniture, and balconies facing the water. There are two indoor restaurants and a poolside grill, as well as a rustic bar with a fireplace. Guests can explore the river by pedal boat or on the inn's ten-person craft, which looks like a small version of

the *African Queen*. Lodging reservations here and elsewhere in the area are a must in the summer season.

Farther upstream at Castanheira, 20 km (12 miles) east of
Tomar, is the modern **Estalagem do Lago Azul**, the third of
the Zêzere riverside hotels. The 20-room, air-conditioned
establishment has a boat-launching facility, a tennis court, an
outdoor swimming pool, a fine regional restaurant with a
view of the water, and a terrace bar, and is one of the stops
on the *São Cristóvão* cruise. The Lago Azul is run with
discreet efficiency by the owners of Tomar's Hotel dos
Templários. Take the N 110/IC 3 out of Tomar, turn right
onto the N 238 about 4 km (2½ miles) out of town, drive for
6 km (3½ miles), and veer right again toward Ferreira do
Zêzere and Castanheira. The *estalagem* is past these two
villages, about 10 km (6 miles) from the turnoff.

The **Estalagem Vale da Ursa** is a modern family-run inn on
the wooded banks of the Zêzere, 30 km (19 miles) northeast
of Tomar via the N 110/IC 3 and N 238. Its 12 airy bedrooms,
glass-enclosed restaurant, outdoor pool and tennis court,
and pine-and-marble bar overlook the lake some 165 feet
below. The inn has an excellent restaurant, too, featuring
such specialties as *sopa de peixe à Vale da Ursa* (a rich soup
containing both local river and ocean fish), *bacalhau
dourado* (creamed, baked dried salt cod), and *borrego na
caçarola* (lamb braised in an earthenware pot with onion
and tomato sauce). On Saturdays you can savor *maranhos,*
the inn's weekly haggis-like special, which consists of
sheep's belly stuffed with sausage, onions, mint, and other
herbs. The inn is near **Dornes**, a former Templars stronghold with a medieval tower and church that crown a tiny
peninsula overlooking the Zêzere to the north.

FATIMA

The religious sanctuary of Fátima, which lies 30 km (19
miles) west of Tomar via the N 113 and N 356, toward Leiria
and Batalha, is the largest ecclesiastical complex dedicated
to the worship of the Virgin Mary in Portugal as well as one
of the most famous Catholic shrines in the world. Situated in
the Cova da Iria hollow, where the Virgin is said to have first
appeared to three young shepherds—Francisco, Jacinta, and
Lúcia—on May 13, 1917, calling for peace in a world beset
by a terrible war, the shrine attracts hundreds of thousands
of faithful every year. (Subsequent monthly visits by the
Virgin in the form of cosmic phenomena were witnessed by

a growing number of pilgrims, until she made her final appearance on October 13, 1917.) Francisco and Jacinta died young, but Lúcia, the only one with whom the Virgin had actually conversed, continues to live a cloistered life as a nun in a Carmelite convent in Coimbra.

Legend has it that Mary handed Lúcia three letters foretelling the future. The Three Secrets of Fátima, as they have come to be known, are guarded under lock and key in Vatican vaults. The first two predictions, concerning the spread of Communism and its demise, and the culmination of World War II in a flash, believed to be the atomic bomb, have come to pass. The third secret has never been revealed. There is speculation that it may have to do with the end of the world, although some say it predicted the 1981 attempt on the life of Pope John Paul II. In 1991 the pope visited Fátima and prayed in thanksgiving to the Virgin for sparing his life, although perhaps his visit was also to acknowledge the fulfillment of the prediction that Communism would fail. Of equal symbolic significance was the subsequent visit by the patriarch of Moscow.

In 1930 the Church acknowledged the importance of the site by establishing the **shrine of Our Lady of Fátima**. Today the faithful camp out in the concrete esplanade in front of the shrine and hold all-night vigils by candlelight. Many show their fervor by walking on their knees to the shrine, which consists of a huge esplanade dominated by a Neoclassical basilica that contains the tombs of Jacinta and Francisco. The neighboring **Museu de Cera de Fátima** (Fátima Wax Museum), on rua Jacinto Marto, tells the religious story of Fátima in 28 scenes. Also within walking distance of the shrine is the clean and simply furnished **Hotel Dom José**, with a reputable restaurant to suit the austere needs of pilgrims.

The town of **Ourém**, 14 km (8½ miles) northeast of Fátima via the N 356, is tied to Fátima's name and history by legend. The story goes that in the 12th century Gonçalo Hermingues, known as the Traga Mouros (Moor Devourer), captured a Moorish woman named Fátima on a military expedition, falling in love with her and marrying her after she converted to Christianity and changed her name to Ouriana. They lived on his large estate, which he named Fátima, and which included the land around the present-day shrine. When his bride died, the former Traga Mouros became a monk.

High on a hill overlooking the town is an imposing medieval **castle**, which is open to visitors. The castle belonged to the counts of Ourém until the 15th century, when King João II seized it and gave it to a court favorite.

SOUTH OF TOMAR

The **castle of Almourol** is one of the scenic wonders of the Ribatejo. Built in the 12th century by the grand master of the Templars order, Gualdim Pais, over the ruins of a Roman fortress, it sits in timeless splendor on a tiny island in the middle of the river Tagus between Constância to the east and Vila Nova da Barquinha to the west. The island and its fortifications, mentioned by Strabo in a travel chronicle more than 2,000 years ago, have always been the stuff of books and legends. In Francisco de Morais's epic romance *Palmeirim de Inglaterra,* the British Crusader Palmeirim fights the giant Almourol for the hand of the beautiful Polinarda. Just as Palmeirim is ready to give in, another giant named Dramusiando comes to his aid and slays Almourol.

The castle itself, surrounded by ten circular towers that command a wonderful view of the hilly and verdant countryside, is said to be haunted by the daughter of the Christian mayor of Almourol and her Moorish lover, who eloped, leaving the girl's father to die of grief. Excavations on the island have unearthed Roman artifacts and coins as well as the remains of a tunnel that is believed to have linked the castle to the shore.

To get to Almourol from Tomar take the N 110 and N 358-1 to Constância, where you turn right at the bridge onto the N 3 and head toward Vila Nova da Barquinha. After a little over 3 km (2 miles), turn left at the sign for Castelo de Almourol and drive another kilometer or so to the river, where you'll have a fabulous view of the castle. You can visit it and/or circle the tiny island by boat during daylight hours.

Constância

Were it not for a paper mill operating on the south bank of the river, Constância would be one of the most picturesque towns in the Ribatejo. Its whitewashed houses and narrow cobbled streets lined with purple bougainvillaea climb the slopes of a hilly embankment where the Zêzere river flows into the Tagus. Cedar and olive trees dot the landscape, and colorful painted boats line up at the town's steep dock. It was here that the great Portuguese poet Camões was exiled from the court between 1547 and 1550 for falling in love with a lady-in-waiting to the queen. Today his statue graces a square facing the two rivers at the western end of town at the end of the avenída das Forças Armadas. Beside it is a luxurious, cool garden named after Camões, with plants and trees from places he visited in his travels (closed Mondays). Nearby, a plaque indicates the now-ruined house by the water where the author of Portugal's epic poem *Os Lusíadas* is believed to have lived during his stay here. It was also from Constância that the duke of Wellington launched his successful campaign against the French at Talavera during the Peninsular War.

The 19th-century **Palácio de Constância** (also known as Casa o Palácio), which once sheltered Queen Maria II on one of her tours of the region, is now a bed and breakfast 11 months of the year (closed in December). Guests are offered a choice of four rooms furnished with Portuguese antiques and have access to a large Victorian-style drawing room with fireplace, self-service bar, and card tables. The second-floor landing is graced by a painting of a priest by the 17th-century Spanish master Zurbarán, and there's a private chapel lined with tiles and marble down the hall. Some 200 yards east of the town hall there is a sign to the palace pointing to the left. The road becomes narrower and takes you directly to the gate of this property.

The **Falcão restaurant** next door, rua Luíz de Camões, 33A, is one of the area's best and is frequented by the town's businesspeople and resident artists. The restaurant, like the palace, is owned by the aristocratic Falcão family, which may account for the smart decor. The cooking is mainly country, with Ribatejano delicacies such as snowy *queijinhos do céu* (sheep cheeses) and firm *tigeladas* (egg custards) complementing its extensive fish menu. Wild game dishes such as partridge and rabbit are served during the fall hunting season. The pièce de résistance of the menu, however, is the *bife à pedra,* a succulent steak cooked and served on a red-hot stone. Closed Tuesdays. The other pleasant dining choice in the area is **Restaurante Cristina**, located 6 km (3½ miles) east of Constância on the main road (N 3) to Abrantes. Its fine kitchen, which serves up such regional delicacies as *maranhos,* attracts landowners from the area and businesspeople from Abrantes. Red-tiled floors, leather chairs, wood beams, decorative tiles, and local pottery provide a pleasant environment, while a large vitrine laden with a cornucopia of cakes and puddings reminds you to leave room for dessert.

Constância has not had only unwilling artists like Camões in residence, but also the 20th-century poet and actor Vasco de Lima Couto. His house, which adjoins an antiques shop at largo Azevedo Machado, 2, has been converted into a museum and contains his writings and theater memorabilia as well as a collection of modern Portuguese paintings (open afternoons). José Ramoa Ferreira, who runs the museum and its adjoining antiques shop, owns the tiny town's art gallery at rua Luíz de Camões, 28, west of rua Falcão. Ferreira is a talented art scout who exhibits some of the best of Portugal's modern regional and national artists. Constância is also known for its colorful *minas* (cloth-and-cane dolls) and miniature wooden riverboats. These can be admired and acquired at the new Câmara Municipal, a postmodernist structure on the main road to Abrantes across from the town's GALP gas station.

Constância is also known for its annual Festa da Senhora da Boa Viagem, which takes place on Easter Monday. The colorful feast is dedicated to the fishermen and boatsmen of the area, who bring their vessels to the edge of town to be blessed. Fireworks light up the sky at night, and the fairground above the river is invaded by the pleasant aroma of food cooking on charcoal stoves.

Abrantes

Recent development has marred the former beauty of Abrantes, 16 km (10 miles) east of Constância, but not the spectacular view of the area from its hillside **fortress** on the north bank of the Tagus. The Romans named the city Aurantes (Golden) because of the gold that washed onto the sandy banks of the river here. In the Middle Ages Portuguese kings made it the bulwark of their southern line of defense during the Christian Reconquest, and General Junot and the future duke of Wellington both made it their headquarters (in 1807 and 1809, respectively) during the Peninsular War.

Today Abrantes is best known for its delectable *palha de Abrantes,* the egg-thickened almond paste that is sprinkled with "thread eggs," the hardened strands of beaten egg yolks that are called *palha* (straw). The pastry cook at the **Hotel de Turismo** not only is an accomplished *palha* cook, but also whips up other Ribatejo sweets. The hotel's air-conditioned restaurant, with its fine vistas of the town and countryside, provides the ideal atmosphere in which to sample these sweets. The 15th-century **Igreja de Santa Maria do Castelo**, next to the fortress, serves as the temporary quarters of the city museum. Inside, the Gothic tombstones of Lopo de Almeida, the second count of Abrantes, and his wife, and a 15th-century statue of the Virgin and Child are among the more interesting pieces in the collection. Closed Mondays.

The town of **Sardoal,** 11 km (7 miles) north of Abrantes on the N 244-3, is known for its mineral waters, picturesque stone-carved squares, and elegant manor houses, and is one of the last unspoiled, traditional Ribatejano towns. The **Igreja de Santiago e São Mateus** contains a collection of seven religious paintings by an unknown 16th-century artist who signed his work only with the initials M.N., and is thus called the monogram painter or the Mestre de Sardoal. (M.N. also appears in other church work in the southern village of Montemor.) He was a master of the brush who managed by skillful strokes to convey a lyrical mysticism in his subjects. The paintings have figured in major Portuguese and European exhibitions and will probably be moved to a regional museum sometime in the future.

THE EAST BANK
OF THE TAGUS

Crossing to the opposite bank of the Tagus at Abrantes, you follow the N 118 southwest over the flat, fertile Ribatejo plain past farming towns and fields irrigated by the river. The **Casa dos Patudos** at **Alpiarça,** 48 km (30 miles) southwest of Abrantes, contains the fabulous art collection of Republican statesman José Relvas, who lived there. Among the treasures decorating his 19th-century manorial home are a fine sampling of Portuguese masters going back to the 15th-century "Primitives," paintings by Spanish greats such as Zurbarán and Murillo, and many other fine works by accomplished European artists. The collection also includes rich Flemish tapestries and Portuguese and Oriental carpets from the 17th to the 19th centuries, as well as china and porcelain from Europe, China, and Japan. The 18th-century *azulejos* (decorative tiles) in a room adjoining the dining room were originally from the convent of Santo António in nearby Chamusca. The museum is on the southern outskirts of town and is open Wednesday through Sunday and some holidays. Call before visiting; Tel: (043) 543-21. Alpiarça is also known for its sweet muscatel wines and its reed chairs.

The neighboring town of **Almeirim** is considered the dining room of the Ribatejo. It is here, for example, that *sopa de pedra* (stone soup) is believed to have originated—or at least to have been perfected. According to legend, after a mendicant monk was refused a meal by the people of the village, he played to their curiosity and gradually tricked them into providing him with the ingredients for a delicious "stone soup" by starting to boil a pot of water with a stone in it. As they doggedly demanded to know what else went into the soup, the monk would oblige by revealing another ingredient, which the townspeople would then supply.

Today there are several restaurants in the vicinity of the bullring that serve the soup (which typically contains kidney beans, macaroni, *chorizo,* and a variety of vegetables) in addition to a variety of other delectables. Success has not altered the rustic look of the oldest and most venerated of these, **O Toucinho**, rua do Timor, 20, but it has allowed the owners to open an annex next door. You enter the former through a busy kitchen where the smell of bread baking in a wood-burning oven provides a welcoming reception. In the restaurant itself, waitresses cater to your needs in small rooms furnished simply with wooden benches and tables. Apart from its mouth-watering *sopa de pedra,* O Toucinho specializes in grilled meats such as *rinzada de borrego* (lamb ribs) and large steaks. Customers can also choose between the simple house wine or the better-quality Quinta da Alorna whites, produced just up the road. The more spacious annex in the neighboring square is decorated with bullfight pictures. The restaurant is closed on Thursdays; Tel: (043) 522-37.

The tiny **Museu Etnográfico** is housed in the Casa do Povo nearby on the southern side of the rua de Coruche between the bullring and the town center. In it you will find the full range of Ribatejo folk culture, from household items to traditional dress. There is a nice, shady garden on the grounds.

During the 15th and 16th centuries Almeirim was a hunting retreat for the royal family, which built two now-defunct palaces here. Today, in addition to its *sopa de pedra* and wines, Almeirim is known for its leather goods, tin work, and iron stoves. Its sweet yellow melons, sold at roadside stalls, are also much admired. There are several shops in the town center flanking the praça da República and the gardens where you can find these items. (The square is to your right as you enter town.) The **Chico Leonor** antiques shop is located at rua Manuel Andrade, 13, in front of the post office. Here you can find Victoriana from the town houses and estates of the region, as well as large carved wardrobes of oak and chestnut, chandeliers, and Arraiolos rugs. It's interesting to visit the town on market day, the first Sunday of every month.

The 19th-century **Palácio da Alorna** estate is about half a mile south of Almeirim on the road (the N 118/IC 3) to Salvaterra de Magos. The wine cellars of this sprawling complex are open to the public, and its semi-dry Quinta de Alorna wine should not go untasted. The estate, which was built for the countess of Junqueira, is one of the last of its size and splendor to be built in the region.

From Almeirim you have a choice of routes back to Lisbon. The fastest is via Santarém and the A 1/IP 1 *auto-estrada*. Or you can continue south on N 118/IC 3 along the east bank of the Tagus through rich cattle country until you join the N 10/IC 11 and cross the river to Vila Franca de Xira, where you meet the A 1/IP 1 to Lisbon.

If you are in the region during September, however, you might want to stay on the east bank and visit the former fishing village of **Moita do Ribatejo**. The town, which is situated in the southwestern corner of the *charneca*, celebrates a lively annual pilgrimage called the Romaria de Nossa Senhora da Boa Viagem (Our Lady of the Good Journey). This colorful event, which takes place from the second Saturday in September until the following Wednesday, includes bull-running in the streets, bullfights, a colorful fair, and the blessing of the fleet by local priests.

The three-hour drive to Moita do Ribatejo takes you first, on the N 118/IC 3, through the large bullfighting estates and cattle farms around Salvaterra de Magos. After Samora Correia, the alluvial flats of the Tagus Nature Reserve, covered with grassland and wildflowers, do justice to the area's nickname—*mar da palha* (straw sea). Egrets, flamingos, and storks are common in these parts bordering the Tagus estuary. Continuing on the IC 3, you make your way toward Alcochete on the estuary past salt pans exploited since Roman times, and then past cork factories at Montijo and canals with the last remaining wooden Tagus sailing vessels.

Up to the middle of the century, before bridges connected the north with the south of the Tagus, an armada of these lovely painted boats was the only link between the two banks of the river. Some of the last shipbuilding facilities can be sighted at the entrance to the dock at Moita do Ribatejo. From the quay you can peer at Lisbon looming majestically across the water to the northwest. Several watermills dot the horizon to the west. The watermills, which were built over the marshes to harness the energy from the tidewaters, are mostly idle now. From Moita do Ribatejo you can make your approach to Lisbon from the south, crossing the Ponte 25 de Abril. Follow the signs to Lisbon and get on the A 2/IP 1 *auto-estrada*.

GETTING AROUND

The major cities on this route are linked by train and buses from Lisbon. Trains to the major Ribatejo towns of Vila Franca de Xira, Santarém, Tomar, and Abrantes leave frequently from the Santa Apolónia train station located by the waterfront at the eastern end of the city below the Alfama quarter. The service is regular and inexpensive. For information, Tel: (01) 888-4025. Buses to these destinations depart several times a day from the terminal at avenida Casal Ribeiro, 18B, a short cab drive northwest of Lisbon's center; Tel: (01) 54-54-39. Rodoviária Tejo is the regional bus company. The main terminal in Tomar is at Varzea Grande (Tel: 049-31-27-39); express buses to Lisbon leave from here. The buses are modern and comfortable. There are also daily bus tours of the Ribatejo, which can be booked at travel agents.

The best way to tour the region, and at your own pace, is by car. All the major international car-rental companies have offices at Lisbon's international airport and the major hotels. Give yourself three to five days to take in all the sights. Bridges cross the river Tagus at Vila Franca de Xira, Santarém, Chamusca, and Abrantes. The newly completed *auto-estrada* runs at first mainly along the west bank of the river Tagus to Santarém before heading inland, passing near the shrine of Our Lady of Fátima in the northwestern corner of the region. The rest of the Ribatejo's roads are fairly well marked and paved, but be prepared for delays in farm areas, where tractors and trucks share the road with smaller vehicles. It takes on average three hours (without stops) to drive the 135 km (84 miles) from Lisbon to Tomar via the more scenic route outlined in our chapter.

ACCOMMODATIONS REFERENCE

Rates given are projected 1993 prices for a double room, double occupancy. Price ranges span the lowest rate in the low season to the highest in the high season. Unless otherwise stated, rates include Continental breakfast. As prices are subject to change, always double-check before booking.

▶ **Casa dos Cedros. Azóia de Cima,** 2025 Alcanede. Tel: (01) 80-09-86. 10,000$00 (does not include breakfast). Open March through October.

▶ **Estalagem Ilha do Lombo. Serra de Tomar,** 2300 Tomar. Tel: (049) 37-11-08 or 37-11-28; Fax: (049) 37-14-03. 12,500$00–16,500$00.

▶ **Estalagem do Lago Azul. Castanheira,** 2240 Ferreira do Zêzere. Tel: (049) 36-14-45; Fax: (049) 36-16-64. 11,300$00–16,500$00.

▶ **Estalagem de Santa Iria.** Parque de Mouchão, 2300 **Tomar.** Tel: (049) 31-33-26; Fax: (049) 32-10-82. 9,500$00–13,500$00.

▶ **Estalagem Vale da Ursa. Vale da Ursa,** Cernache do Bonjardim, 6100 Sertã. Tel: (074) 995-11; Fax: (074) 995-94. 8,500$00–11,800$00.

▶ **Hotel Abidis.** Rua Guilherme de Azevedo, 4, 2000 **Santarém.** Tel: (043) 220-17. 6,000$00–7,000$00.

▶ **Hotel Dom José.** Avenida Dom José Alves Correia da Silva, 2495 **Fátima.** Tel: (049) 53-22-15; Fax: (049) 53-21-97. 8,000$00.

▶ **Hotel dos Templários.** Largo Cândido dos Reis, 1, 2300 **Tomar.** Tel: (049) 32-17-30; Fax: (049) 32-21-91. 7,800$00–16,000$00.

▶ **Palácio de Constância** (Casa o Palácio). 2250 **Constância.** Tel: (049) 992-24. 11,500$00.

▶ **Pensão Residencial Sinagoga.** Rua Gil Avô, 31, 2300 **Tomar.** Tel: (049) 31-67-83 or 31-67-84; Fax: (049) 32-21-96. 8,600$00.

▶ **Pousada de São Pedro. Castelo de Bode,** 2300 Tomar. Tel: (049) 38-11-59 or 38-11-75; Fax: (049) 381-176. 9,700$00–18,000$00.

▶ **Quinta da Anunciada Velha.** Cem Soldos, 2300 **Tomar.** Tel: (049) 34-52-18; Fax: (049) 32-13-62. 9,000$00–13,000$00. Closed December through February.

▶ **Quinta de São Sebastião.** 2630 **Arruda dos Vinhos.** Tel: (01) 950-1340. 9,000$00–10,500$00.

▶ **Quinta Vale de Lobos. Azóia de Baixo,** 2000 Santarém. Tel: (043) 42-92-64; Fax: (043) 42-93-13. 10,000$00–13,000$00.

▶ **Residencial União.** Rua Serpa Pinto, 94, 2300 **Tomar.** Tel: (049) 31-28-31; Fax: (049) 32-12-99. 4,500$00–5,500$00.

Pousadas can be booked through ENATUR, Avenida Santa Joana Princesa, 10, 1700 Lisbon, Portugal; Tel: (01) 848-1221 or 848-9078; Fax: (01) 80-58-46. But it is easier to make reservations through a travel agent. In the United States and Canada, pousadas can be booked through Marketing Ahead, 433 Fifth Avenue, New York, NY 10016; Tel: (212) 686-9213; Fax: (212) 686-0271.

Manor houses can be booked directly or through the manor-house associations—ANTER, P.I.T., PRIVETUR, and TURIHAB—listed in Useful Facts. Most of the houses belong to one or more of these associations, but because membership rosters change frequently we haven't attempted to spell out the associations for each house. Readers are advised to contact the manor-house associations for their current listings.

In the United States and Canada, it is possible to reserve rooms in P.I.T. manor houses through E & M Associates, 211 East 43rd Street, Suite 1404, New York, NY 10017; Tel: (212) 599-8280; Fax: (212) 599-1755.

THE ALENTEJO

By Jean Anderson

For travellers hurtling from Lisbon south to the Algarve or east to Madrid, the Alentejo is that endless stretch of cork oaks and olives that takes forever to cross. It seems as broad and flat as the Australian Outback or the Texas prairie—and just as boring, because the main roads slice across plowed ground, bypassing everything of interest.

How can tourists in a hurry know that cached about these red-brown plains are dolmens, menhirs, and cromlechs that predate those of Brittany? Or that there are tumbles of Roman ruins? Or medieval walled towns so white they might be icebergs off course? Or rambunctious country fairs and festivals?

How can they know that the provincial capital, Evora, was once a cultural center, with artists and writers in residence from as far afield as Paris? That the sugar-cube town of Arraiolos, piled up on its castle hill, is famous the world over for its gros-point tapestries and rugs?

How can fast-track travellers know that this is the land of the potter, the weaver, the wood-carver? That it's a place where shepherds, rather than stand idly by their flocks, whittle willow branches into cooking spoons or clip weeds into topiary? A land where women still kneel occasionally on riverbanks to do the family wash, where girls stroll home from the village well bearing plastic water jugs atop their heads, where cooks don't stint on garlic, onions, and olive oil? Of course, they can't. The Alentejo (meaning, literally, "across the Tagus" and pronounced allen-TAY-zhoo) doesn't flaunt its charms the way the Algarve does. And its allure—nothing more than basic, unspoiled Portugal, where life eases along at a slower tempo—is more subtle than seductive. About the only thing the tourist barreling across the Alentejo discovers is that it's B I G. It is in fact Portugal's biggest province, sprawling from the Algarve border 280 km (174 miles) north to the upper reaches of the Tagus river and Beira Baixa, rubbing up against Spain all along the way—for centuries a source of friction.

The Alentejo, in short, occupies nearly a third of the Portuguese mainland, and it isn't all cork oaks and olives. Ever since Portugal's entry into the European Community seven years ago, the winds of change have been blustering across these prairies with increasing ferocity. Groves of centuries-old olive trees are being axed to make room for bigger crops of wheat, and portable irrigation systems 100 feet long are creeping across these new fields of grain like giant centipedes. There are even tobacco patches here and there, and acres aflame with sunflowers. Tractors are exiling teams of oxen to pasture, pickup trucks are replacing donkey carts, and TV antennas are beginning to sprout from the lowliest cottages. The Alentejo has at long last joined the 20th century. Still, it remains, along with the Trás-os-Montes, Portugal's most unspoiled province.

MAJOR INTEREST

Museum town of Evora
Tapestry town of Arraiolos
Dolmens, menhirs, cromlechs, and the Escoural
    painted cave near Arraiolos
Market town of Estremoz
Pottery towns of Redondo and São Pedro de Corval
Ducal palace at Vila Viçosa
Fortified town of Elvas
Medieval walled towns of Monsaraz, Castelo de Vide,
    and Marvão

The Portuguese themselves rarely spend time in the Alentejo. Hunters come out in autumn to shoot rabbit and quail; but most Portuguese, being sun worshipers, prefer to vacation somewhere along their 500 miles of Atlantic shore or at Madeira. And you can scarcely blame the Portuguese hoteliers for assuming that most foreign visitors are beach buffs, too; doubtless they are. At any rate the Algarve, Cascais and Guincho west of Lisbon, and even the northerly Minho beaches, where the Atlantic runs cold, don't lack for modern

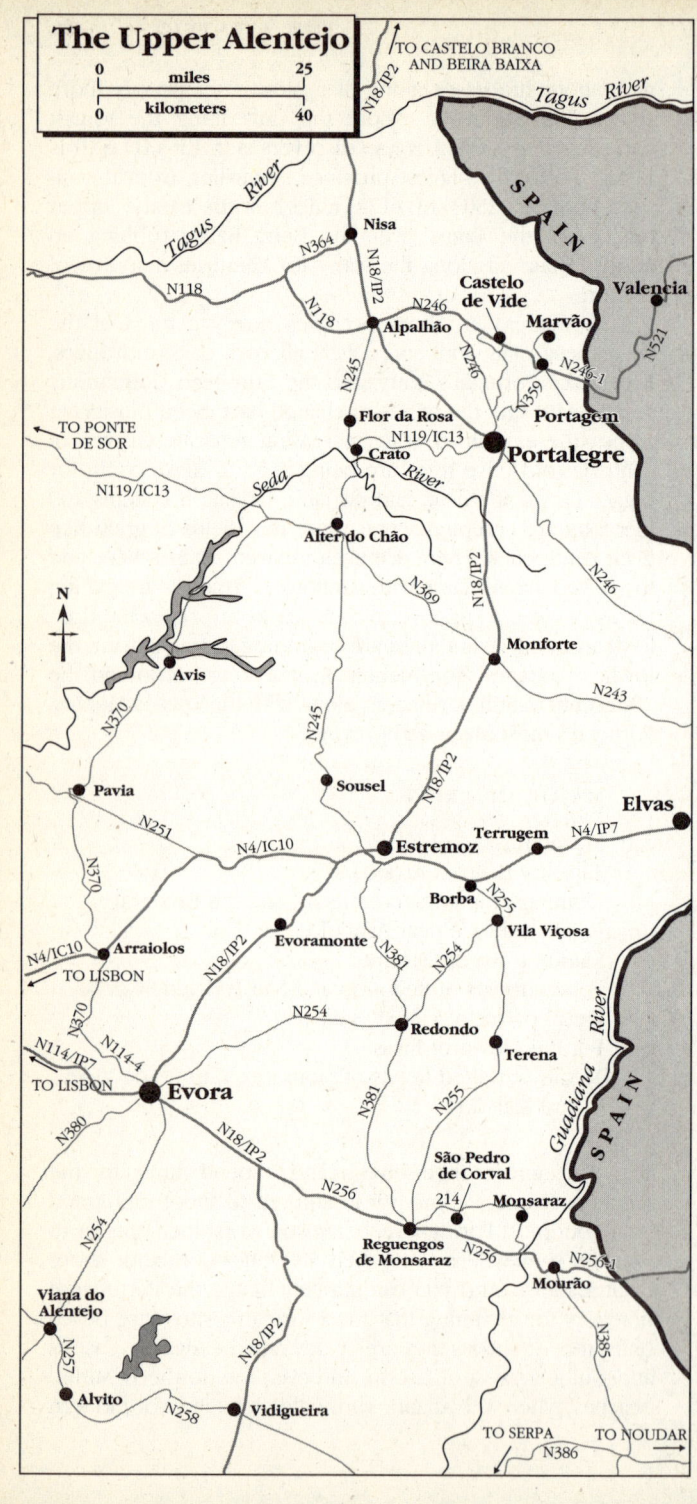

The Upper Alentejo

miles 0 — 25
kilometers 0 — 40

TO CASTELO BRANCO
AND BEIRA BAIXA

Tagus River

SPAIN

Valencia

Nisa

N364

N18/IP2

N118

N118

N246

Castelo
de Vide

Marvão

Alpalhão

N245

N246

N359

N246-1

Portagem

TO PONTE
DE SOR

Flor da Rosa

N119/IC13

Crato

Seda River

N119/IC13

Portalegre

Alter do Chão

N369

N18/IP2

N246

N

Avis

N245

Monforte

N370

N243

Pavia

Sousel

N18/IP2

Elvas

N251

N4/IC10

Estremoz

Terrugem

N4/IP7

N370

Borba

N255

Arraiolos

N18/IP2

Evoramonte

N381

N254

Vila Viçosa

N4/IC10

TO LISBON

N370

N254

Redondo

Terena

Guadiana River

N114/IP7

N114-4

Evora

SPAIN

TO LISBON

N380

N18/IP2

N381

N255

N254

São Pedro
de Corval

214

Monsaraz

N256

Reguengos
de Monsaraz

N256

Viana do
Alentejo

N257

N256-1

Mourão

Alvito

N258

Vidigueira

N385

TO SERPA

TO NOUDAR

N386

resort hotels. In fact, you could consider them overbuilt. The Alentejo, though, has been forsaken, and that may very well be its salvation, although the shortage of good hotel rooms doesn't make it easy for visitors. The lesson here: Make sure that your hotel reservations are confirmed before you set foot in the Alentejo, because otherwise you may find yourself stranded with no place to lay your head.

Choosing an Alentejo Base

With the Alentejo possessing so few first-class hotels, it isn't practical to move from place to place, staying in a different area every night, as you might do elsewhere. It makes far more sense here to pick a central home base from which you can make day trips, setting out in a new direction each morning. Distances are short enough within the visitor's Alentejo for easy circle tours that won't leave you exhausted at day's end or rushing to make it home before dark. In fact, the Alentejo's narrow, unlighted blacktops are *dangerous* to drive at night, because there are donkey carts creaking along in utter darkness—not to mention motorbikes, decrepit trucks, and cars with headlights missing and sometimes no reflectors or taillights at all.

Fortunately, two of Portugal's most palatial *pousadas* (government-run inns) couldn't be more centrally located. In the provincial capital of Evora, about one and a half hours east of Lisbon, there's the 32-room **Pousada dos Lóios**, occupying a 15th-century convent (its rooms may be cell-size, but they're blessed with big marble baths). Scarcely a 40-minute drive to the northeast of Evora, the even more luxurious 33-room **Pousada da Rainha Santa Isabel** (a 13th-century castle crammed with honest-to-God antiques) crowns the old walled town of Estremoz, on the N 4/IP 7, the main Lisbon–Madrid highway. Ten of its rooms were added late last year, as was a swimming pool. Manager Luís Abilio, one of the ablest in the pousada network, supervised the construction and decoration of the new one-of-a-kind rooms, furnishing them with the antique chairs, chests, and tables that have crowded the pousada's second-floor halls since it opened more than 20 years ago.

There's more good news. The **Pousada de São Miguel** opened in November 1992 just outside the sleepy country town of **Sousel** (soo-ZELL) just 18 km (11 miles) north of Estremoz, and is as convenient an Alentejo headquarters as either Estremoz or Evora. The pousada, a blindingly white, modern-as-tomorrow inn built from the ground up, is

Mooresque in design, a cubistic hilltop sprawl cascading down precipitous slopes. Geared especially to hunters (there are even kennels for hunting dogs), the Pousada de São Miguel offers 28 double rooms (all with private marble baths) and four suites. The furnishings are contemporary and the scheme throughout is a restful one of creams and woodsy greens. All rooms are blessed with sun-drenched balconies and see-forever views. There are acres of public space, too: a vast split-level dining room overlooking miles of Alentejo plains, a swimming pool, a bar properly snug and dark, and a cavernous lobby barrel-ceilinged in Roman brick (its centerpiece, a stuffed boar in a glass case, may offend animal rights activists). This welcome new pousada is rated C Superior.

A fourth appealing pousada, the **Pousada de São Gens** at Serpa in the south, perches high above a sea of plains. It's country rustic rather than regal, contemporary rather than historic, and it recently has been refurbished top to bottom. There are 16 well-proportioned rooms (plus two suites) with ceilings domed in the Moorish manner. Each has its own individually controlled air-conditioning, whopping balcony, and gleaming tile-and-marble bath. There's nothing fancy about the furnishings, but the regional wooden bedsteads, desks, and chairs, and the snowy cotton *colchas* (counterpanes) and draperies in calico florals are altogether pleasing.

There's a dedicated manager at the São Gens, an energetic young man named Domingos Lameiras, whose training ground was the lavish Pousada da Rainha Santa Isabel in Estremoz. Lameiras has done much to upgrade the São Gens (it's now ranked Category C), driving, for example, all the way to Lisbon to find the exact lamp needed for a particular corner of the bar or lobby. He's working with the pousada chef, too, trying to improve the quality of cooking. Other pluses at the Pousada de São Gens are its swimming pool, its eager-to-please staff (those at the grander Estremoz and Evora pousadas can be icy), and its utter peace and quiet. Its biggest disadvantage, indeed its only drawback, is its location—at the very bottom of the Alentejo area of greatest interest.

Evora, for example, lies 107 km (66 miles) to the north-west of Serpa and Estremoz some 153 zigzag km (95 miles) north. So if you stay at Serpa you must add an extra hour and a half or two of driving just to reach those points of interest lying north of Evora or Estremoz. Still, with the pousadas in these two towns so often booked up, it's good to know that the one at Serpa is now vastly improved. Besides, the little town of **Serpa** is worth a look: a moldering castle of Moorish origin (the Museu Arqueológico is inside with showcases full of Paleolithic, Neolithic, Roman, and Moorish shards), a great granite wall surmounted by an aqueduct of Romanesque arches, broad village streets planted with oleander and citrus, and paper-white houses roofed in red tile.

A second newly spruced-up pousada must also be included, and that's the 16-room **Pousada de Santa Luzia** at Elvas near the Spanish border, which turned 50 last year (it was the first pousada opened). The dining room here, specializing for the most part in Portuguese dishes, is terrific. Not for nothing do tour buses crowd the parking lot. The bedrooms at this pousada have been nicely redecorated and the bathrooms updated, but the pousada's location is against it. It not only lies 85 km (53 miles) northeast of Evora but also smack-dab on the busy N 4/IP 7 with 16-wheelers, buses, cars, and motorbikes roaring by 24 hours a day. This may be Portugal's only pousada with neither a view nor a building of historic interest.

The little country-rustic **Pousada de Santa Maria** in the mountaintop walled town of Marvão (always a great favorite among honeymooners and those seeking a tranquil retreat) has just reopened after being closed 14 months for renovation and enlargement. A few years ago the Portuguese government bought a block of historic town houses across the street from the original pousada and has painstakingly redesigned and restored them, adding 14 beautifully furnished bedrooms and 14 gleaming tile-and-marble baths. The project doubled the size of the old pousada and catapulted it into the C Superior category. But before you rush to make reservations you should know that the Pousada de Santa Maria is tucked into the northern reaches of the Upper Alentejo—hardly practical for our solely Alentejo strategy (it's about a two-hour drive north of Estremoz and 45 minutes farther from Evora).

If you stay at Marvão, you may be interested to know that there's quite a cache of megaliths some 25 km (16 miles) northwest near the dam called Barragem de Póvoa (signs point the way off the N 246). **Nisa**, 12 km (7½ miles) north of Alpalhão on N 18/IP 2 is famous for its terra-cotta jugs and platters, studded with tiny white marble chips, and for its appliquéd felt work. The Nisa Turismo, facing the market square in the middle of town, hands out the names and addresses of the workrooms that can be visited, along with a little map pinpointing their locations.

While we're on the subject of new projects, we must mention the new three-star, 114-room **Evorahotel** about a mile west of Evora on the road to Lisbon. This modern hotel/ conference center (with restaurant, bar, health club, squash and tennis courts, and swimming pool) is undistinguished-looking and "plastic modern," with one shoebox-shaped room after another. But the Evorahotel will definitely ease things for Alentejo travellers and take some of the load off Evora's Pousada dos Lóios, which can scarcely cope with the excursion buses chugging up to its front door to disgorge knots of tourists for one- and two-night stands.

What will also help, though in a smaller way, are two new Alentejo jewels, both centrally located. First, there's the lordly, just-opened **Convento de São Paulo Hotel** shelved on a slope of the Serra de Ossa some 10 km (6 miles) north of the pottery town of Redondo, halfway between Evora and Estremoz. Converting this huge monastery, parts of which date back to the 11th century, into an up-to-the-minute, four-star luxury hotel is surely the most ambitious project undertaken in the Alentejo since the castle at Estremoz became a pousada.

Here, however, the driving force is not the Portuguese government but an energetic Lisbon engineer named Henrique Leotte, whose family has owned the Convento de São Paulo monastery for 150 years. Leotte and his wife, Júlia, began renovating the old family property two years ago (with advice and assistance from the Espírito Santo Foundation in Lisbon, whose mission is to preserve the architectural and decorative arts of old Portugal).

When finished, the Convento de São Paulo Hotel will have 27 rooms; the first 12 opened just this past December and the balance are to be ready by summer 1993. All have been painstakingly renovated so that none of the old monastery's character has been lost (gleaming white plaster walls, floors of terra-cotta, authentic antiques). But there are marble-and-tile baths, too, and direct-dial room phones as well as radio and TV. Best of all, these rooms aren't as monk's-cell-size (or as dark) as those at Evora's Pousada dos Lóios, which also began life as a monastery. There are two cloisters at the Convento de São Paulo Hotel, two exquisite chapels (the larger will be used for small conferences, the smaller for weddings). The miles (it seems) of hallways and grand stairs groined in the Manueline manner are lined with rare 16th- and 17th-century blue-and-white *azulejos* (50,000 of them in all, several of them signed pieces, which add up to Portugal's finest private collection of glazed tiles).

There's more. The Convento de São Paulo has two dining rooms (one formal, one informal), a hillside swimming pool and sunning terrace, and an elevator (praised be!), for the monastery is built on many levels and its ceilings vault nearly out of sight. To come: tennis courts, riding, biking, mountain hikes, an indoor pool, and, if Leotte has his way, a rustic nine-hole golf course.

"My wife and I travel a lot, and we like the philosophy of small hotels," Leotte said at the Convento de São Paulo last fall. "We want to make it like an extension of the house [he and his wife live at the monastery] and give our guests the Portuguese style of living. But, at the same time, we want to be very professional." (To that end, Leotte raided the Ritz Intercontinental in Lisbon for key staffers.) From what we've seen, the Convento de São Paulo is a winner.

Another winner is the spanking new, elegantly rustic **Horta da Moura** at the foot of the perched medieval town of Monsaraz 56 kilometers (35 miles) southeast of Evora. This is a working farm (vineyards, olive and orange groves, peach orchards, sheep, bees, and a cheese-making plant). For guests there are six light and airy double rooms and eight suites, all done up in the solid-comfort, Alentejo style of a country gentleman's *quinta* (estate): darkly beamed ceilings, roughly plastered white walls, terra-cotta floors topped by Arraiolos needlepoint carpets, hand-tooled wooden furniture, and, in some instances, wood-burning fireplaces big enough to roast oxen. There's no shortage of activities either: billiards, swimming, hunting, riding—either on your own or at Horta da Moura's riding school. And, for those who would like to learn more about Portuguese farming, there's even the chance to pitch in and help do the chores.

There are also five top-notch bed-and-breakfast manor houses that are centrally enough located in the Alentejo to make handy tour bases. The first, **Quinta do Monte dos Pensamentos**, is a folk-art-filled country gentleman's retreat with four guest rooms (private but not *en suite* baths) located 1½ km (1 mile) west of Estremoz within full view (but mercifully not within earshot) of the N 4/IC 10. The mistress of the manor is Rosemary Leitão, an Englishwoman who was married to the late Reuben Leitão, one of Portugal's most famous modern writers, and who now runs the place with her son, Cristovão Tomás Bach Andresen Leitão.

The second manor house is the more sumptuous **Casa de Peixinhos** (circa 1611) on the southern edge of Vila Viçosa, 18 km (11 miles) southeast of Estremoz. Owners José and Maria de Lourdes Passanha have lavished millions of

escudos and untold hours on turning a stately family property into what may be Portugal's most luxurious B and B.
Each of the six bedrooms (no two alike) is filled with
antiques (or skillful reproductions), lush French fabrics, and
Portuguese ecclesiastical art. The decor is so stylish that a
summer 1992 issue of *Casa & Jardim* (the Portuguese *House
& Garden*) devoted 12 four-color pages to Casa de Peixinhos. The beds, moreover, are good and firm, and the outsize
baths, elegantly done up in tile and marble, rival those at the
Ritz in Lisbon. Casa de Peixinhos's only shortcoming is that it
serves nothing more than breakfast. So for dinner the
Passanhas send their overnighters into Vila Viçosa to the
cheerful little **Ouro Branco**, a good regional restaurant at
Campo da Restauração, 42 (across the street from the town
soccer field) that dishes up plenty of lusty Alentejo soups,
stews, and casseroles.

They also direct them to the map-dot of Terrugem, 13 km
(8 miles) east of Borba on N 4/IP 7 to Júlia Gaspar Vinagre's
unexpectedly plush **Restaurante A Bolota** (Tel: 068-65-61-52
or 65-61-58), where the menu is both polyglot and sophisticated. The chick-pea soup, studded with diced carrots, celery, and dots of *chouriço* (peppery, garlicky sausage), comes
to the table in a little cork bucket just like those the shepherds carry; the gratinéed homemade pasta with puréed
spinach and wild oregano is truly special, as are the pork
scallops creamed with Elvas plums and red Borba wine. "We
like to give things our special taste," says Senhora Vinagre, a
psychologist/interior decorator turned restaurateur. And that
A Boleta surely does, in the pleasantest of surroundings.

Finally, the Passanhas may dispatch their guests to the tiny
castle town of **Terena**, 15 km (9 miles) south, to dine
indoors or out at Susana Bianchi's **Miga's** (rua Direita, 28), a
restaurant occupying two ancient village houses that opened
early in 1991. The place drips with charm: terra-cotta tile
floors, whitewashed walls, fireplaces, rough country furniture. The cooks—"just village housewives"—know how to
grill chops to order and whip up a hearty *migas* (stir-fry of
yesterday's bread, garlic, bits of pork and sausage).

Susana Bianchi and her husband, Arnaldo Aboim, also
own **Casa de Terena**, a 300-year-old manor house where you
can stay in supreme comfort. It's located a couple of blocks
up the main street (rua Direita) from the restaurant and
scarcely 100 yards from the 13th-century castle that crowns
the town. While Casa de Peixinhos is plush, Casa de Terena
is cozy: a living room with a barreled brick ceiling and
roaring hearth, an entry hall floored in a mosaic of black-

and-white marble chips, iand an imaginative mix of furniture (everything from wicker coffee tables to crudely carved wooden benches to Victorian wing chairs upholstered in velvet). The six bedrooms are simply but gracefully furnished (all have TV), and the baths, if not as opulent as those at Casa de Peixinhos, are nonetheless up to the minute.

Since the 1992 *Berlitz Travellers Guide to Portugal* was published, a fourth fine country house (with swimming pool) has begun taking paying guests, and it sits in rolling plains in the very shadow of Terena. It's the tastefully renovated 200-year-old farm home of Britisher Anthony John Dubery and his young family, a sprawling complex of red-roofed, low white buildings called **Herdade Dom Pedro**. There is a small house for rent (with living room, two bedrooms, kitchen, and bath) plus three large double rooms in the main house. And by late 1993 Dubery expects to have made four additional rooms out of the stables. Although Herdade Dom Pedro, like most of Portugal's other manor houses, is a B and B, you can arrange to take lunch and/or dinner here, too. A good thing, because Herdade Dom Pedro, hidden in a maze of rutted dirt roads, isn't the easiest place to find, especially after dark. *Note:* If you stay at Casa de Terena or Herdade Dom Pedro, you will be about 20 minutes farther from the sights of Evora, Estremoz, and assorted points north than if you stay at Casa de Peixinhos in Vila Viçosa.

The fifth and final manor house, **Quinta dos Prazeres**, lies 41 km (25 miles or about 35 minutes) due south of Evora at Alvito, another of the Alentejo's many castle towns. The owner, Romana Gertrudes da Silva de Almeida Goes, has turned a series of farm outbuildings into pleasant quarters for overnight guests. There are four rooms and two suites, all with beautifully tiled private baths. There's also a huge lounge with bar, television, and fireplace, and, just outside, a small swimming pool. This quinta, located on the outskirts of town, boasts a tower built in 1494.

Alvito is a lively market town with a 15th-century quasi-Moorish castle (now being converted into a pousada) and a 16th-century parish church paved inside with impressive 17th-century tiles. But history buffs may be more interested in **São Cucufate**, a little-known Roman ruin buried in the cork orchards 17 km (11 miles) east of Alvito on N 258. Just before the hamlet of Vila de Frades, a historic marker on the left directs you to swing off the blacktop N 258 and onto a skinny, patchy tarmac road. After jouncing some 200 yards along it, you round a bend and burst upon what's left of an imposing Roman villa of red brick. Even though archaeologists are clearly excavating, the site is wide open, deserted more often than not, and you can stroll at leisure about this surprisingly extensive collection of foundations, tumbled walls, and arches.

Baixo Alentejo

Whoever said "There's no shade in the Alentejo" must have had the southern half of it in mind, the Baixo, or Lower, Alentejo. You will cross it in about two hours if you are driving north on the N 2 from Faro in the Algarve toward Evora or Estremoz (at Castro Verde the N 2 becomes the IP 2). Except for rows of eucalyptus parading along highway shoulders, there's almost nothing to filter the sun that burns down without mercy on this old granary of Rome. There are gnarled cork oaks here and there, and the occasional spiky aloe or fiery burst of wild poppies, but there's little to shield the boulder-strewn fields or seas of grain billowing north to the town of Beja and beyond.

There isn't much in this monotonous brown stretch to keep you from hurrying on to the Alto (Upper) Alentejo, which *does* offer plenty of interest. You may wonder as you look at the map, however, about that long stretch of western Alentejo Atlantic coastline sweeping north from the Algarve border all the way to the Tróia peninsula (for the latter, see Day Trips from Lisbon). There are occasional secluded crescents of sand tucked at the base of high ocher cliffs between Odeceixe on the Algarve/Alentejo border and the pin-neat white village of **Porto Covo** some 60 km (37 miles) north.

With its weathered fishermen lounging on scarlet park benches, its plane trees pruned into umbrellas, and its flowery central plaza, Porto Covo is as picturesque as any movie set. Astonishingly, just in the last year, northern European tourists have homed in on this little place in the sun. Its pocket plaza and main street are now cordoned off—pedestrians only. Sidewalk cafés are overtaking the streets, and a sandy track has been cut down to the beach so you no longer need to negotiate the tricky set of stone steps hacked into the cliff.

The Lower Alentejo beaches are often difficult to reach, and the Atlantic pounding in upon them is apt to be both cold and ferocious. North of Porto Covo the Alentejo shore flattens and is lined much of the way with spartan hotels and bungalows that are used, for the most part, by Portuguese families of modest means.

If you'd like to explore these windswept beaches for a day or so on your way to your Upper Alentejo headquarters from either the Algarve or Lisbon, there's a kitschy (some say charming) castle-inn at the old Phoenician stronghold of Vila Nova de Milfontes at the mouth of the Mira river just 16 km (10 miles) south of Porto Covo. The waterfront stone **Castelo de Milfontes** is privately owned, and its eight guest rooms are often filled with friends and relatives of the owner, an elderly widow named Dona Margarida de Castro e Almeida. Still, if you make reservations well in advance you will be able to stay here. The two choicest rooms are in the *torre* (tower) because they have *en suite* baths and huge rooftop terraces overlooking the sea.

As for the Upper Alentejo, you'll be pressed to see as much of it as you'd like in five days. The best possible place to begin your tour is Evora, the provincial capital, of which one native son wrote: "No other town in Portugal but Evora was able to tell me with purity and beauty that I am Latin, Arabian, Christian, Peninsular, and Portuguese." How better to summarize all the different peoples who have had a hand in shaping the Evora of today?

EVORA

Prehistoric man was the first to come Evora's way, how long ago no one knows, although he has left plenty of dolmens, menhirs, and other monuments scattered about for archaeologists to ponder. The first people of influence here were the Romans. From the second century B.C. to the fifth century A.D., Evora, Caesar's Liberalitas Julia, was a powerful seat of Roman Lusitania. The Visigoths followed, but they left little mark even though they occupied the area throughout the sixth and seventh centuries.

Next came the Moors, who captured Evora in 714 and held it until 1166. It's their presence that lingers everywhere. Later the kings of Portugal made this little Alentejo hill town the royal seat of preference. João I, father of Prince Henry the Navigator, went so far as to proclaim Evora Portugal's second town (after Lisbon). During the Renaissance some of Europe's finest sculptors, artists, and writers settled in and made Evora, for a time at least, the Portuguese Montmartre. Evora fell to Spain toward the end of the 16th century and slid into a lengthy decline that continued even after it regained its independence in 1663. It was at the foot of the old Roman temple here, however, that 20th-century rebels met to plot the Flower Revolution of 1974 (see the Chronology).

Today Evora is a sophisticated town of 45,000, an educational and cultural center, Portugal's fifth most important town (after Lisbon, Porto, Coimbra, and Guimarães). And, now that UNESCO has named it a World Heritage site, it has spiffed itself up. All of the broken street lights along praça do Giraldo have been replaced, all of the gaps in the intricately mosaicked black-and-white sidewalks have been filled in, and all the walls have been scrubbed clean of political graffiti. The townspeople have even repainted their houses, fringed their windows with geraniums, and hung out the welcome mat for all who would come this way.

As you approach Evora from the west or south—which you will if you're coming from Lisbon or the Algarve—you see it pyramiding up above the cork orchards like a giant pile of sugar cubes, blinding in its whiteness against the blue, blue Alentejo sky.

The best plan is to aim right off for the **Pousada dos Lóios**, letting the pousada directional signs (a little house with smoke coming out the chimney) guide you past the medieval town walls, then up through a maze of narrow cobblestone streets to the top of the town and the second-century Roman temple standing there. The pousada faces the temple, and if you arrive early enough in the day (before late afternoon) you should find a parking place in this broad square, maybe even at the inn's door. (See Choosing an Alentejo Base, above, for more on this pousada.)

Your next stop should be the Turismo on the west side of praça do Giraldo in the city center, a four-block stroll downhill from the temple along rua 5 de Outubro, to pick up a city map outlining fast, medium, and slow tours. It lists—awesome thought—18 major points of interest, and every local chauvinist can no doubt recommend twice as many. Not for nothing is Evora called the Museum Town. More than half of its attractions, however, are churches, so unless ecclesiastical architecture is an obsession you can skip all but three houses of worship, which we will discuss. If prehistory is a particular interest, by all means buy *Roteiro do Megalitismo de Evora,* a four-color pamphlet sold at the Turismo that describes the major menhirs, dolmens, and cromlechs scattered about the cork orchards near Evora. It is available in Portuguese only but so profusely illustrated with photographs, diagrams, and detail maps that it's invaluable even if you speak nothing more than English.

Evora deserves at least a full day. You'll find that the most sensible way to stroll—and this is a walking town if there ever was one—is to start at the highest point, the **Roman temple** dedicated to the goddess Diana and plenty impressive even though it covers about as much ground as a tennis court, and work your way down. (Afterward, if you can't face climbing back uphill to the pousada, you can grab a taxi at any of the town's many cab stands. Although nearly every cab is a Mercedes, fares are so cheap you can't help wondering how the driver makes a living—10 to 15 percent tips gratefully accepted.)

Only 14 of the temple's original columns still stand, and even fewer (12) of the Corinthian capitals, which are carved from Estremoz marble. Given the temple's history—it was bricked up at one point and used as an armory, then an abattoir—you're surprised to see so much of it left. Its latest threat: tourists scrambling up its eroded stairs for a closer look. The best angle for photographs is from the northwest corner looking back through the skeletal columns toward the pousada and the adjoining chapel of the **Convento dos Lóios**.

This early-15th-century chapel is private, the property of the dukes of Cadaval, but a custodian unlocks its massive wooden door each morning and afternoon. Unlike so many dour, dank, and dusty Portuguese churches, this one is bathed in light, especially in the morning, when the sun slants through high round windows, firing the gold altar to radiance and illuminating walls paved in early-18th-century blue-and-white tiles that depict the life of Saint Lawrence Justinian.

Your next stop should be the **Museu de Evora**, just around the corner from the chapel and the pousada on largo do Conde de Vila Flor. It too faces the Roman temple. An archbishop's palace during the 16th and 17th centuries, the museum wraps around a central courtyard that's strewn with Roman relics and, in amongst them, a jarring collection of modern Portuguese sculpture in the creamy beige and pink marbles of Estremoz and Borba. But better to have them here than out scattered around the base of the Roman temple, as they were for years. The stone-floored arcade around the courtyard and the rooms that open off it are filled with massive marble sarcophagi, busts, and bits and pieces of sculpture from various periods back to Roman times. The two most important are probably the broken bas-relief (bottom half only) of a Roman vestal virgin in a gauzy, billowing skirt, and a rather severe Gothic Virgin at her prayers.

Up a flight of stairs is a gallery, its walls hung with the work of the 15th- to 17th-century artists—Portuguese, Italian, and Flemish—who painted in Evora. Recently renovated, the rooms, with their polished floors of rare wood, white walls, and well-hung paintings, are a pleasure to stroll. In the old days a gnome of a man shuffled you through, pointing out art and air-conditioners with equal pride. Today you can move along at your own pace (do pull aside the large front gallery's curtains for a different perspective of the Roman temple).

Portuguese art takes some getting used to; you can't help wondering if these early painters all preferred dark palettes or if the canvases are just long overdue for a good cleaning. Probably a bit of both. At any rate, their mood is somber, even macabre when the subject is one of Christianity's gorier moments. Two notable exceptions: the 13 panels (late-15th-century Flemish) that chronicle the life of the Virgin (perhaps the museum's finest work), and a surprisingly graceful Nativity painted by Frei Carlos, a monk who lived at the **Convento de Nossa Senhora do Espinheiro**, 4 km (2½ miles) northeast of town. When we drove out last fall to see its Renaissance-Baroque church, this 15th-century monastery stood locked—and derelict.

Your next stop should be the *Sé* (Cathedral) directly behind the museum on largo do Marquês de Marialva (its mismatched conical towers soar above the museum courtyard). To reach it, leave the museum, turn left, and walk right around the museum building. En route, note (on your right) the mansion on the opposite side of the broad leafy square in front of the Sé. This long, low, white building, with trim the color of curry powder, is where Vasco da Gama retired after his triumphant voyages to the Indies. He would scarcely recognize his old home today, so often has it been altered and enlarged (today it is a school). The building's other claim to fame (or rather, infamy) is that it served as Evora's court of the Inquisition.

The **cathedral** is a brooding granite pile that took 64 years to build (from 1186 to 1250). What distinguishes it, however, is the way its soaring stone columns and vaulted ceilings have been pointed with chalk-white mortar—not exactly restful or conducive to meditation. The **cloister**, which you must ask to see, is altogether peaceful, a Gothic haven. But the cathedral's high point (quite literally) is its **treasury**, tucked away up a twisting stair in one of the towers. To wander from case to case marveling at the jewel-encrusted miters and reliquaries is to see at first hand what the wealthy English dilettante and frequent visitor to Portugal William Beckford had in mind in

1787 when he wrote, "Gracious goodness! The Roman Catholic religion is filled with fine stage effects!" But the glitter of the vestments, crosses, and croziers pales beside the delicacy of the 13th-century ivory Virgin, whose body opens in triptych to reveal the nine most important episodes of her life. Somewhere along the way she lost her head, and the wooden replacement doesn't begin to match the elegance of the ivory torso.

Three of Evora's best restaurants are within easy walking distance of the cathedral. The first choice, **Fialho**, at travessa das Mascarenhas, 14, is also the farthest away, but you can hoof it in ten minutes. With your back to the cathedral walk straight ahead down rua 5 de Outubro to praça do Giraldo, a distance of four not very long blocks. Turn right and follow the arcaded sidewalk to the end of the square, then continue straight ahead along rua João de Deus seven short blocks to a small park. About halfway along the north side of the park you'll come upon a little alley that shoots off to the right. This is travessa das Mascarenhas, and to find Fialho you need only walk one block in.

By most accounts Fialho is Portugal's best provincial restaurant. Gabriel Fialho, whose father started the business 50-some years ago, now presides over the kitchen, while his brother Amor greets guests out front. A salty little blue-collar *tasca* (bistro) when it first opened, Fialho is decidedly white-collar today, a hangout for businesspeople, where the portions are whopping and the prices reasonable. The place buzzes with the conversation of local scholars who've come to discuss the ways of the world and linger over such specialties as *sopa de panela* (a layered soup of sausages, chicken, bread, and fresh mint), partridges braised with cabbage, or any one of Gabriel's robust pork dishes.

Second choice is **O Aqueduto** at rua do Cano 13A, some four blocks closer. Don't follow rua João de Deus all the way to the end as you do when heading for Fialho. Instead, when you're three or four blocks along it, look sharp for signs on the right pointing to O Aqueduto. Follow them up one long, steep block. The restaurant is a series of small, white rooms with arched doorways leading from one to another, and has terra-cotta tiled floors throughout. The menu, for so inland a town, is surprisingly long on seafood—grilled shrimp or prawns, rice with shellfish or monkfish, *cataplana* (pork, clams, ham, and sausage braised in a garlicky tomato sauce). But there's also a wonderful selection of meat, and, in season, game (everything from partridge to javelina). As restaurants go, O Aqueduto is new (it opened in 1984), but already its Alentejo recipes have been featured at Portugal's great Festival Nacional de Gastronomia in Santarém.

If you feel like a less ambitious walk, **Cozinha de Santo Humberto**, just half a block downhill from praça do Giraldo at rua da Moeda, 39, is another excellent choice—and also a favorite for local businesspeople. It's a few steps down from the narrow cobbled street (this used to be Evora's Jewish quarter), and with its arches, vaulted ceilings, and terra-cotta tile floors it has the look of an old Moorish house. The chef, Joaquina Maximino, is famous for her lusty homemade soups, but most of all for her *migas,* an Alentejo classic that is nothing more than a scramble of pork, garlic, and crumbles of yesterday's bread. (It's a lot better than it sounds.)

If you're wondering what wines to order at any of these restaurants—indeed, at any Alentejo restaurant—by all means try some of the excellent local labels. The best table reds are Navegante Vidigueira Vinho de Mesa Tinto (an Alentejo *cooperativa* wine for which no vintage is given), Tapada de Chaves 1982, Borba Vinho Tinto Reserva 1976 or 1984, Herdade do Esporão 1986 or 1990, Quinta do Carmo 1985, and Terras de Xisto 1990, an incredibly smooth and well-balanced wine from Redondo. As for whites, you won't go wrong with Cartuxa (car-TOOSH-a) Vinho Branco Colheita 1989, or with Reguengos de Monsaraz Regia Colheita or Vidigueira, both 1987.

After lunch return to praça do Giraldo (note the huge 16th-century marble fountain, for which a Roman arch was sacrificed), walk to the south end of the square, then follow rua da República two blocks downhill to the **Igreja de São Francisco**. Just one block along, at rua da República, 81, you'll find another terrific little Evora restaurant that you may want to keep in mind for another day. It's **Restaurante Típico Guião**, run by the Guião family, and its narrow street-level, tile-floored, folk-art–trimmed dining room is nearly always packed (as is the big back room, which caters to tour groups). Guião's food is nothing if not gutsy and *garlicky,* with pork and fish predominating.

Though the church is a splendid example of Moorish-Gothic style for which the finest architects and artisans of the day pooled their talents, the main attraction here (if that's the right word) is the ghoulish **Capela dos Ossos** (Chapel of Bones). Its walls and columns supporting the frescoed barrel ceilings are entirely covered with human skulls and leg and arm bones—to induce piety, it's said.

Next, retrace your steps about 100 yards along rua da

República, turn right onto rua Miguel Bombarda (also called antiga rua dos Infantes) for two blocks, where the road forks, then bear left on rua da Misericórdia past the Igreja da Misericórdia (by all means step inside to have a look at its early-18th-century wall tiles depicting the life of Christ), then follow this street of splendid 16th- and 17th-century façades two long blocks to **largo da Porta de Moura**, a broad, treeless rectangle with a spherical fountain of white marble (circa 1556) at the south end. There are additional landmarks here: on the northwest corner, the early-16th-century **Casa Soure** (private) topped with the curious conical dome so characteristic of Evora, and, catercorner across the square beyond the fountain, the **Casa Cordovil** mansion (also 16th century, also private) with a delicate portico of horseshoe Mudejar (Moorish-style) arches.

Speaking of arches, on your wanderings around Evora you may have noticed snatches of a high, arched **aqueduct** around the edge of the old city walls. It looks Roman but is in fact a public works project put up by João III in the 16th century. It was—and is—an architectural masterpiece, an attraction so important that Camões, Portugal's beloved epic poet, mentioned it in his *Lusiads,* the story of Vasco da Gama's triumphant voyages of discovery: "Noble Evora," Camões wrote in the 16th century, "the seat once of the rebel Sertorius, famous now for the royal aqueduct with its hundreds of imposing arches. . . ."

Where you go next depends on whether you've had your fill of architecture. If you have, retrace your steps to rua da República and the praça do Giraldo, then, on your way back up to the pousada, browse the craft shops lined up on both sides of **rua 5 de Outubro**, Evora's "boutique row." Here you can see all of the Alentejo's famous handicrafts: rustic pottery, fancily painted wooden chests and chairs, cork ice buckets, and little copper coffeepots just like the one the waiter brings to your breakfast table each morning.

If, on the other hand, you're game for more sightseeing, leave the Porta de Moura square by way of rua Conde de Serra da Tourega, and walk two long blocks northeast to the largo do Colegio. Dead ahead lies the 16th-century **Jesuit University** (now a part of the University of Evora). The walls inside are covered with what may be Portugal's rarest collection of 16th-, 17th-, and 18th-century *azulejos,* some of them, as befits a Jesuit setting, depicting the lives of the saints. The school's classical **cloister**, with its arching double colonnade, is Evora's—indeed, one of Portugal's—most beautiful.

The fortress set high on the hill directly across largo do

Colegio from the university is the **Palace of the Counts of Basto** (private). This medieval castle built on Moorish and Roman foundations was the Evora residence of the kings of Portugal, and it is where Catherine of Bragança retreated after the death of her husband, Charles II of England. To return to the pousada, simply follow largo do Colegio as it arcs uphill (the back of the pousada is directly above you; the weathered stone walls separating it from the Palace of the Counts of Basto are part Roman, part Visigothic).

It's a steep uphill hike back to the **Pousada dos Lóios**, so you'll no doubt be ravenous by dinnertime. In summer you will dine in the glassed-in cloister (the granite doorway to the adjoining chapter room, all slender twisted columns, horseshoe arches, and delicately carved borders, is as fine an example of Luso-Moorish architecture as you're likely to see in Portugal). In cold weather breakfast, lunch, and dinner are served in the old monks' refectory, a long, narrow room with high vaulted ceilings, velvet draperies the color of ruby Port, and floors tiled in terra-cotta.

You can't help wondering how those 15th- and 16th-century monks would view today's dining room, where crystal sparkles, silver gleams, and candles softly flicker. Or what they would think of a menu sprinkled with French classics. You may be tempted to order steak Béarnaise, but you'll fare better with such Portuguese dishes as *sopa à Alentejana* (egg-and-bread-thickened garlic-coriander soup) and *porco à Alentejana* (paprika-rouged chunks of pork braised in the regional wine with baby clams, still in the shell). Don't fail to try one of the superb local sheep cheeses: the little nutty ivory-hued rounds for which Evora is famous or, better yet, the big and biting Beja, blushed with paprika. Some Portuguese actually prefer it to *queijo da serra,* Portugal's "Queen of Cheeses," which comes from the Beira Alta, farther north.

ARRAIOLOS
AND ANCIENT DOLMENS

If you haven't bought the booklet that the Evora tourist office sells pinpointing the locations of the menhirs and dolmens in the immediate area, you should do so before setting out on this leisurely daylong outing; otherwise you'll never be able to locate them. Moreover, the booklet contains photographs and diagrams of almost every historic site, so you can decide which ones interest you most.

Arraiolos

You should probably begin your tour at Arraiolos, 22 km (14 miles) north of Evora via N 114-4 and N 370, 46 km (29 miles) west of Estremoz via N 4/IC 10, and about 20 minutes longer from Vila Viçosa, also via N 4/IC 10. The Oriental-style rugs you've been seeing all over Portugal are made in this spic-and-span white town, where almost every door and window is framed in cobalt blue "to keep the evil spirits away." (Originally, perhaps, but today these brightly painted borders are more apt to be purely for show.)

All of the important *fábricas* (rug workshops) are lined up along the main street of this essentially one-street town (there are little alleys shooting off at odd angles but only one straight, drivable street stretching from one end of Arraiolos to the other). For rugs, you need only look for the *tapête* signs. The typical arrangement is a store out front and *fábrica* directly behind. **Fábrica Kalifa**, **Condestável**, and **Calântica** are just three of the shops you'll pass along this four- to five-block stretch. Many doors are left open, or at least ajar—a sign of welcome.

Most shopkeepers will gladly show you through their workrooms, especially if you've bought something—even a small pillow cover. Do ask, because you've never seen anything like these dimly lighted ateliers, piled to the rafters with rainbows of yarn. And you've never witnessed such frenzied activity. Women draw themselves into circles of six or eight to work on a single giant rug, spread from lap to lap. As they stitch in flowers, birds, geometrics, and yards and yards of background, their fingers fly over acres of stiff hemp with stunning speed, usually to the beat of rock 'n' roll twanging out of some little transistor radio tucked away in a corner. Even so, the work is so painstaking that it takes an experienced embroiderer three weeks to complete one square meter of tapestry.

If you have any intention of buying an Arraiolos rug, this is the place to do so, because you'll beat the prices of Lisbon by about 15 to 20 percent. Most of the Arraiolos shops, moreover, will pack and ship whatever you buy.

One early English fan of these intricately cross-stitched carpets, according to Dame Rose Macaulay, was that rich 18th-century aesthete William Beckford. On his way from

Lisbon to Spain, she writes in *They Went to Portugal* (1946), Beckford stopped at Arraiolos "to lay in a stock of bright carpets for his journey, lest he should find himself in an uncarpeted room; in the Estremoz posada he spread them all round his bed, they made a flaming, exotic appearance and protected his feet from the damp brick floors."

How did this tiny village tucked away in the cork orchards get into the rug business? And why are the motifs so distinctly Oriental? Historians believe that Alentejo women first learned the art of rug making from the Moors, who lived in these parts for more than 400 years and whose entourages usually included plenty of talented rug weavers. But the manufacture of carpets and the development of the designs so characteristic of Arraiolos today probably date back to the early 16th century, after Vasco da Gama returned from the East with piles of Persian carpets.

Before long these vividly patterned floor coverings became the rage among Portugal's rich and royal, many of whom lived nearby at Evora. This turn of events wasn't lost on savvy Arraiolos craftsmen, who decided that they could make a little money by copying them. There were plenty of sheep to provide wool. There was no shortage of plants from which bright natural dyes could be extracted, no shortage of skilled needleworkers. And, most important, no shortage of potential customers. It had to be a lucrative business. And 400 years later it continues to be one.

If you'd like to see some choice early Arraiolos carpets, follow the main street to the very heart of town (no more than four or five blocks) and the little treeless square where the village elders hang out and where the Turismo and Câmara Municipal (Town Hall) stand shoulder to shoulder. There's an eye-popping tapestry exhibit on the second floor of the town hall (one flight up). The 18th- and 19th-century embroideries hung on these walls are far more finely worked than the rugs made today.

This would be an excellent day for a picnic, and at any little *tasca* or grocery along the main street you can pick up the makings: a loaf of bread, a chunk of cheese, a plastic bag of olives, a bottle of wine, and perhaps a *paio,* the plump, smoky, dry-cured sausage bound up in string for which Arraiolos is also famous. For your alfresco lunch you might simply drive uphill to the grounds of Arraiolos's 14th-century **castle**.

Dolmens

Alternatively, you might head for any town exit; you'll be in the countryside in minutes and will have no difficulty finding a peaceful spot for your picnic. Afterward, you can spend the afternoon working your way from dolmen to menhir to cromlech to cave. Four major prehistoric sites cluster in the cork orchards to the south and west of Arraiolos and Evora, the farthest no more than 60 km (37 miles) away, and most of them much closer. These include the **Gruta do Escoural** (Escoural Cave), with its crude wall scribblings (still under archaeological investigation, the site is locked behind a chain-link fence, but there's a resident custodian who will let you in and tour you through the cave for a moderate tip); the **Cromlech and Menhir of Almendres** (an entire ring of standing stones); the **Dolmen of Zambujeiro**, which at 20 feet is the largest dolmen yet found on the Iberian Peninsula (the shards and crude tools found here are now on display at the Museu de Evora); and the **Dolmen-Chapel of São Brissos** (a red-tile-roofed, whitewashed chapel built around a dolmen). To find any of these remote sites, however, you must consult the Turismo booklet called *Roteiro do Megalitismo de Evora.*

You'll be in cork country as you search for these Stone Age relics, and there's an almost biblical quality about this landscape, where trees misshapen as scarecrows dance over the horizon. Cork oaks are the Upper Alentejo's single most important crop, providing as they do more than half the world's supply of cork. These evergreen oaks look a lot like the olive trees that often grow among them. But you *can* tell the two apart. Cork oaks have pricklier, greener leaves and their tops are flat, almost as if a crop duster had come flying low across the plains, shearing every cork in its path. It takes 40 years for an oak to produce good cork, which explains the old Alentejo saying: "If you plant for yourself, sow a vineyard; if you plant for your son, put in an olive tree; but if you are thinking of your grandson, it's a cork oak you want."

The oaks are stripped of their bark (cork) every nine years; the job is done between May and September by methods developed generations ago. Using sharp, elongated axes, men slit the bark vertically down each side of the trunk and large lower limbs. They then pry the cork away in halves or quarters, leaving a trunk so raw, so red it looks mortally wounded. But soon the rust red dulls to cinnamon brown, then chocolate, then inky black. All of this before a new layer of cork begins to grow. It's quite a show: hills and hills of cork, in different stages of development. In spring they parade across fields of wildflowers—yellow, red, purple, blue. If you squint, it's easy to imagine that someone has covered the cork orchards with Arraiolos's finest carpets.

Another interesting side trip from Evora is Evoramonte on the road (N 18/IP 2) to Estremoz; see the section on Vila Viçosa and Elvas side trips that follows the Estremoz section, below.

ESTREMOZ AND THE POTTERY TOWNS

If you'd like to see the Alentejo's liveliest country market at high-octane pitch, you should begin on a Saturday morning. That's when farmers converge on Estremoz—46 km (29 miles) northeast of Evora via N 18/IP 2, then N 4/IP 7—from every direction. Suddenly its main downtown square becomes a two-acre cacophony of rabbits, chickens, ducks, and geese, of mopeds, pickups, and two-wheeled donkey carts. If it's cheese or sausage you seek, chewy loaves of stone-oven bread, hand-carved wooden spoons, or even a cutaway sheepskin cloak like the ones the shepherds wear, this is the time to come. And the earlier the better, if you want to make it to the pottery towns south of Estremoz before they close, at 1:00 P.M. (Some of the savvier shops and potteries now stay open until 6:00 or 7:00 P.M. in summer and early fall.)

If, on the other hand, you merely want to pick up a few pieces of pottery at the Estremoz market, any day will do, because the ceramics stands stretching along the south side of the square are permanent installations. What they sell are the primitive plates and platters of Redondo, a pottery village about a half hour south of Estremoz; the somewhat more refined hand-painted earthenware of São Pedro de Corval (a half hour farther south—see below for both); stacks of the rustic terra-cotta jugs and pots made everywhere in the Alentejo; and platoons of *bonecos* (festive clay figurines), for which Estremoz is famous. The crudely shaped, garishly painted *bonecos* sold at the market average anywhere from 1,400$00 to 2,000$00 (about US $10 to $14), but artists' signed pieces, available at the pousada and atelier behind the Museu Municipal de Estremoz, fetch much higher prices.

Estremoz

The market is only one of Estremoz's attractions. Facing the east side of the main downtown square, the Rossio, directly opposite the market, there's the funky little **Museu Rural** on the ground floor of the town hall, a touching, if eclectic collection gleaned, it would seem, from local outbuildings and attics. These vintage farm and kitchen implements, and the bright provincial costumes, are the essence of the Alentejo, even today.

There's an even better exhibit at the Museu Municipal de Estremoz, inside the 17th-century walls at the top of the old town (see the description below). To reach it follow the pousada signs, which will lead you up through steep rocky streets barely wide enough to swing a Honda to the 13th-century castle (now a pousada) that presides over Estremoz. The houses squeezed in here are white, squintingly so— their snowy marble lintels and windowsills, scrubbed to high glare, will bounce your light meter's needle right off the top of the scale. There's every reason for Estremoz to call itself the White City Where Marble Shines.

As you nose your car uphill to the castle-pousada you're likely to see women out with paint buckets and mop-handled brushes, inky figures in widow's weeds and crumpled pork-pies of black felt, applying yet another coat of whitewash. These *donas de casa* no sooner finish painting a row of houses than they begin all over again. It's what psychiatrists might call obsessive-compulsive behavior. An old Alentejo joke about it may not be entirely apocryphal: It seems that a hunter once hung his gun at a café door, grabbed a bite inside, then came outside to discover that, while he'd been eating, his gun had been whitewashed along with the rest of the house.

There's plenty of space to park beside the Pousada da Rainha Santa Isabel, but be a bit wary of the children begging for escudos and cigarettes, even though their eyes are soulful enough to melt the stoniest heart—and be sure to lock car doors, windows, and trunk. If you aren't staying at this, the most palatial of Portuguese pousadas, have a quick look inside its marble halls before popping across the square to the municipal museum. Also ask the man at the reception desk if you can see the locked room where Rainha Santa Isabel is said to have died. He will more than likely direct you to a little house across the square, number 7. The lady of the house has the key to the beloved queen's chamber, which is approached through fancily grilled wrought-iron gates and a little tile patio at the northwest corner of the castle where, like as not, village youths are practicing their *futebol*. The queen's room, up three flights of steps, is a little chapel now, and the blue-and-white *azulejos* lining its walls chronicle the miracles performed by this 13th-century saint.

If you're staying at Estremoz in the **Pousada da Rainha Santa Isabel**, or in one of the recommended manor houses nearby (see Choosing an Alentejo Base, above), you'll certainly want to dine in the pousada's dining room. It is positively princely, two banquet-size rooms with high-vaulted ceilings, massive antique armoires, and a menu practically identical to that of the pousada at Évora (see above). Thanks to several recent study trips to France and Japan, the pousada chef has refined his skills and is now turning out dinners that are a match for the decor. Much of the credit goes to the energetic pousada manager, Luís Abilio, who has also had the great good sense to use his wife's old family recipes for a pastry cart full of *doces de ovos* (egg sweets). They're trundled to your table, and you won't go wrong ordering the *sopa dourada* (golden soup, a cinnamon-spiked egg-yolk custard strewn with cubes of toast or cake) or *toucinho do céu* (bacon from heaven, a translucent egg-and-pumpkin tart so sweet it sets your teeth on edge).

To many visitors, it's surprising that Estremoz, a largely agricultural town, should possess a municipal museum of such cultural clout. The street-level galleries of the **Museu Municipal de Estremoz** showcase an exuberant procession of little clay *bonecos*—shepherds holding suckling lambs, peasant women balancing baskets of eggs on their heads, cavalrymen dressed up like Napoleon, and, of course, hundreds of saints, the most popular of all being Rainha Santa Isabel, who stands straight and tall with an apron full of roses. Legend has it that this queen's goodness irked King Dinis. He scolded his wife repeatedly about giving so much to the poor, but she went right ahead. Once he nearly caught her distributing bread to the homeless, but when he demanded to see what she had hidden in her apron, the loaves had turned to roses.

The Museu Municipal de Estremoz has an upstairs, too, full of antique weapons and agricultural and culinary implements; but most interesting of all are the model Alentejo rooms.

If you cross the museum's rear courtyard, a clutter of broken Roman columns and capitals, you'll find sculptors at work in a little atelier. They are the Ginja brothers, Arlindo and Afonso, who transform brown blobs of Alentejo clay into faithful replicas of the *bonecos* in the museum. Most of their output goes into museums and museum shops, but they do keep a few pieces on hand to sell to visitors who happen their way. A couple of years ago you could have bought one of these polychromed clay figurines for 2,700$00 to 4,000$00 (US $19 to $28), but their price has escalated (and the value of the U.S. and Canadian dollars declined). Today a 6-inch *boneca* of Rainha Santa Isabel will set you back about 17,000$00 (US $120), and a 16-inch one, signed by the artist who made it, as much as 90,000$00 (US $630). Still, there is a way to beat the inflated prices—by buying unpainted *bonecos*. In many ways they are nicer than the painted figures, and they cost only a fraction as much.

If you aren't dashing on to see the potteries at Redondo and São Pedro de Corval, drive back down to the north side of the market square for lunch at the **Aguias d'Ouro** (rossio Marquês de Pombal, 27). The ground-floor *tasca* will be bedlam, a high-decibel, shoulder-to-shoulder mob of townsmen and farmers in from the country. What you want is the bigger, quieter upstairs restaurant, which is subdivided into a series of cozy, informal dining rooms, most of them paneled in blond wood and floored in herringbone parquet. This is a strictly white-tablecloth operation, and chef João Maria Serrano Grasina, a 15-year veteran at Aguias d'Ouro, ranks as one of the Alentejo's best cooks. He concentrates on *cozinha tipo da região* (typical regional cooking), and his specialties include *arroz de faisão* (wild pheasant braised with rice— meltingly tender except for the occasional piece of buckshot), a porridgy sweet-sour game soup thickened with crumbles of bread, and a bubbling *feijão dobrada* (earthen casserole of white beans, sausages, and tripe redolent of fresh coriander).

The Pottery Towns

You'll have to leave before lunch if you want to see the pottery of **Redondo**, a distance of 25 km (16 miles) south of Estremoz on N 381. Although housing developments are springing up west of the town, Redondo remains a backcountry hamlet of treeless streets and one-story houses snoozing under the fierce Alentejo sun. Its raison d'être is pottery, and the buildings you see emblazoned with plates are shops, sometimes with attendant *olarias* (potteries). At any one of them you can buy classic Roman water jugs, *tachos de barro* (rectangular clay casseroles), and whole sets of tableware with motifs so primitive they border on the childish. The stuff is absurdly cheap—and extremely fragile.

On the northeastern outskirts of Redondo on the road to Vila Viçosa (N 254) there's a well-stocked new *artesanato* (craft shop) called **Olaria Pirraça** that's open all day, every day. Despite its name, it sells not only the local pottery but also the work of regional weavers, woodworkers, and cabinetmakers. And on the road from Reguengos de Monsaraz to Monsaraz (a skinny blacktop numbered 214), you'll find **Tear** on the right-hand side just as you leave Reguengos. This association of regional artists and craftspeople sells everything from handwoven rugs and hand-painted Alentejo furniture and mirrors to the bold, bright pottery of São Pedro de Corval.

The more skilled potters at **São Pedro de Corval** are as likely to turn out a fancifully painted beanpot or candlestick as a plate or platter. This little town is no more than a half-hour drive from Redondo, 28 km (17 miles) via N 381 south to Reguengos de Monsaraz, then 8 km (5 miles) east on 214 toward Monsaraz. Most maps don't even show it, but you'll recognize it easily enough by the giant amphoras set by the side of the road (some of them even have *olaria* lettered on them). You don't need an appointment to visit any of the little potteries here. A cheerful *bom dia* (good day) or *boa tarde* (good afternoon) will usually get you inside to watch potters bending over their wheels, to see kilns being loaded, and, almost needless to add, to buy. Most of these potteries have a "seconds" room, where it's often possible to unearth a treasure or two among the throwaways.

The majority of São Pedro de Corval *olarias* are right on highway 214 (the estrada de Monsaraz), but there are a good many on rua do Jardim, too, which bisects it in the middle of town. Two of the best—**Olaria Guimarães e Velho** and **Olaria José Faisco Cartaxo**—are on that part of rua do Jardim that shoots north from route 214. Turn left and you'll find them lined up, along with several other potteries, on the very first block.

Between São Pedro de Corval and the perched walled town of Monsaraz, 8 km (5 miles) straight ahead to the east, there are several important Stone Age sites, among them the **Menhir of Outeiro**, an 18-foot monolith so impressive it was used to illustrate the term *menhir* in a French book on prehistoric Brittany, and the **Menhir of Bulhoa**, a simple phallic shape covered with inscriptions. To help you locate them in these boulder fields, the Turismo at Monsaraz (see below) has mimeographed a little diagram pinpointing seven major megalithic sites in the immediate area. Ask for the "Mapa dos Monumentos Megalíticos do Concelho de Reguengos."

Monsaraz

Few tourists are on to Monsaraz, a tiny Moorish town set on a jut of rock above the Guadiana river and the Spanish border. A good thing, because once tourists crowd into its sleepy streets, once they begin scrambling over the ramparts of its 13th-century **castle** built by Dom Afonso III and Dom Dinis, Monsaraz will slip forever out of its time warp. Halfway along stony rua Direita (the main street that extends from the town gate to the castle) you'll come upon the 16th-century Igreja Matriz (Parish Church)—worth a quick look—and directly beside it an 18th-century pillory.

The local Turismo (largo Dom Numo Alvares Pereira, 5) stands at right angles to the church, but it's one long flight up weathered stone stairs. It hasn't much to offer other than a little folder on the town (in English as well as French and Portuguese) and the flier on the megalithic monuments. No matter. The main attraction is Monsaraz itself, the rows of 16th- and 17th-century town houses with Gothic doorways and coats of arms, the women who gather in a patch of shade to talk and embroider, the children who play in a wedge of sunlight, and, not least, the 360-degree vistas down across the Alentejo plains from this fortified town that towers 1,060 feet above them.

Although Monsaraz could always claim a few salty cafés where locals and knapsacking northern European tourists hung out, most travellers preferred to pick up some cheese, bread, and wine, and picnic in the fields below town. **Casa do Forno**, on rua de São Tiago just 30 yards downhill from the town square and Igreja Matriz, has now changed that. Opened less than three years ago in an ancient town house, it's an elegant restaurant worthy of Lisbon—all terra-cotta tile floors polished to a low sheen, gleaming white walls, massive bouquets of flowers, and a prodigious menu of such Alentejo specialties as garlic-coriander soup and pork and clams, magnificently prepared by Mariana Ramalho, a Monsaraz cook of rare talent.

Another of the Alentejo's imposing megalithic sites, a place where fertility rites are believed to have taken place, can be found in the valley on the back side of Monsaraz. If you're interested in tracking it down, you must wind down the mountain's southern slope on the road toward Mourão (route 214 south). About 3 km (2 miles) beyond the foot of the mountain, in stubby fields to the right, you'll find the **Cromlech of Xarez**, a 12-foot phallic menhir surrounded by 50 standing stones arranged in a square. It's just off the main road, and visible, too. Still, lest you miss it, it's best to consult your trusty Turismo leaflet.

As you continue several kilometers farther south along the Guadiana, route 214 will intersect N 256. A right turn onto this major highway will bring you back to Reguengos de Monsaraz in less than 20 minutes. All that remains now is to pick up the route you want to follow back to your home base in Evora, Estremoz, or Vila Viçosa (for which see the following section). None is more than an hour away.

If you're travelling about the Alentejo between April and October, when the sun sets no earlier than 7:30 P.M., if you aren't "castled-out" by now, and if you're game for several more hours of exploration, there's a castle town deep in this back-of-beyond that nearly no one knows about. It's **Noudar**, and to reach it you'll cross some of the most elemental landscape you're likely to see in Portugal.

From the intersection of routes 214 and N 256 below Monsaraz, where you would have turned right toward Reguengos de Monsaraz to return to your Alentejo home base, Noudar is easily accessible. Elbow left instead, cross the Guadiana into Mourão, then pick up N 385 and whiz 24 km (15 miles) south to Amareleja. A left here onto N 386 will bring you, after 27 backwoodsy kilometers (17 miles) to Barrancos astride the Spanish border.

Barrancos crowns a hill, and just as you near the top there's a filling station and a fork in the road. Bear left—away from town and the Spanish border. Then twist along this skinny blacktop 11 km (7 miles) farther. It plunges uphill and down, crosses a river, and ultimately gives way to dirt. But press on through the cork orchards. Though dusty, the road is good—and Noudar is not the mythical place you're beginning to suspect that it is.

At long last you see it, isolated on a promontory, a tower rising above high wraparound ramparts of granite. This is Noudar, an ancient castle haunted by a Moorish serpent-maiden (or so a complicated legend of unrequited love would have you believe). As you stand on the castle mount with your back to the twists and turns of the Rio Ardila far below (it forms the border here with Spain), Noudar's battlements look impenetrable. They aren't. To the left, maybe 50 meters up from a tiny car park, you'll find the main gate and, once you're inside it, a forgotten village sprawled across stubbly fields among groves of ash.

Archaeologists are excavating and stabilizing the site, but you're free to roam. And to let your imagination slip backward over time to 1167 when Gonçalo Mendes da Maia, "The Fighter," captured Noudar from the Moors, then to 1283 when Alfonso X of Castile presented it, together with the towns of Serpa and Moura, to Portugal. The occasion was the marriage of his favorite daughter, Brites, to the Portuguese king, Afonso III. Possession of Noudar ricocheted back and forth between Portugal and Spain for centuries, however, and by the 1700s it had begun to dwindle into a ghost town. The last Noudarites climbed down from their hideaway on the heights in 1893, never to return. A ghostliness lingers about this forgotten border town today despite the ring of workmen's hammers. *A word of caution:* Watch your step. There are wide-open dungeons scattered about the castle grounds—no fences, no warnings—and any one of them is big enough to swallow you up.

To return to Mourão, then to your Alentejo home base in Evora, Estremoz, or wherever, merely retrace your steps. Depending on how long you linger at Noudar, the excursion will take three to four hours.

VILA VIÇOSA AND ELVAS

This easy day trip will take you across the central part of the Upper Alentejo. If you're starting out from Evora, you must drive northeast to Estremoz (N 18/IP 2, then N 4/IP 7). If you leave early enough (no later than 8:30 A.M.) there will be time to snake up the mountain to **Evoramonte** (17 km/11 miles) before Estremoz on the N 18/IP 2, a medieval castle town in the clouds that is visible from both Evora and Estremoz.

Evoramonte's **castle**, cloverleaf in design, has recently been plastered over with a hideous ivory-colored preservative that gives it the appearance of a stage set. But it's real, all right, a proper 14th- to 17th-century castle built on Roman-Moorish foundations that has earned a place in Portuguese history books. Here, in 1834, Crown Prince Pedro defeated his younger brother, Miguel, ending the ten-year Miguelist War—a destructive civil war also known as the War of the Two Brothers, which opposed the liberal factions in Portugal to the absolutist Miguel, who abrogated the constitution. Miguel signed his abdication at the Convention House just below the castle on Evoramonte's only street and agreed to exile. A plaque marks the spot.

Today the castle has been turned into a small museum that chronicles the history of this little sky-high town and the castle itself. From its top the whole of the Alentejo spreads out below you, a rumpled counterpane of browns and greens sprinkled with paper-white villages and *montes* (country estates).

Evoramonte itself is a backward village, a chalky row of houses with a chapel at one end and the castle at the other, all of them wrapped in massive crenellated stone ramparts, parts of which date back to the 14th century.

To reach Vila Viçosa from Evora you needn't go into the town of Estremoz. The road that N 18/IP 2 runs into a bit to the northeast after Evoramonte, the N 4/IP 7, sweeps around to the south of it on its way to the Spanish border. Just 15 minutes east of Estremoz there's a wide fork in the road, the right prong angling southeast to **Borba**. Take it. This country boom town has two claims to fame: its creamy pink marble and its robust red wine. And, as some collectors have discovered, Borba is one of the best towns in Portugal for antiquing. There are shops all along your way, some marked with giant copper caldrons, others by sidewalk clutters of bric-a-brac. You'll have no trouble spotting them. Nor should you have any difficulty finding a place to park.

Vila Viçosa

Your destination, however, is Vila Viçosa, 5 km (3 miles) southeast on N 255, a much bigger town of broad streets and esplanades planted with orange and lemon trees that in spring send their heady scent clear across town into the marble quarries beyond. (The combination of intensely perfumed air and marble dust is sometimes enough to activate the most latent allergy.)

Although a moldering 13th-century castle greets you as you enter Vila Viçosa (inside its walls are a tiny white village, a scatter of Roman ruins, and a lovely 16th-century church), the real reason for visiting is the **Paço Ducal** (Ducal Palace), the country seat and summer residence of the Braganças, Portugal's last ruling dynasty. It was begun in 1501, not finished until 100 years later, and as long as the Braganças owned it was forever being changed and enlarged. Today the palace occupies more than half the town, if you include all the outbuildings, topiary gardens, and the *tapada* (walled chase), which alone measures 18 km (11 miles) around. It's quite a spread, and most visitors are duly impressed. But not Joseph Baretti, an Italian critic who toured the place in 1760. "The furniture is rather mean than old," he scoffed, "and there are a hundred houses in Genoa incomparably better."

Not likely. It's true that the palace's façade, an extensive three-story sprawl of marble, has the austerity of an office building. Or maybe a barracks. But the immense macadam square (Terreiro do Paço) fronting the palace is partly to blame. It may once have been the scene of bullfights and rambunctious festivals, but today it resembles a parking lot.

What you see inside, however, is nothing if not regal, and you sense it the instant you step inside the cool, polished marble entry. You must join a guided tour, alas, to see the quarters upstairs, and even though you are hurried through these elaborately tiled, muraled, draped, and furnished rooms you'll find that an hour has elapsed by the time you are led down to the ground-floor royal kitchens (a blinding battery of copper), then out again into the sunshine.

You will leave the Paço Ducal with mixed impressions: of faded Aubusson carpets and Gobelin tapestries desperately in need of repair, of ornately inlaid marble tables, of showery crystal chandeliers, of pastel silk-lined bedrooms, of biblical wall panels worked out in tiles of Delft blue (these, it turns out, *were* designed by a Dutchman). You'll sense that ghosts wander these lonely corridors at night and that closets rattle with family skeletons (only natural, given the number of deaths and murders that took place here).

But most of all you will come away from this particular palace touched by the artistry of King Carlos's sketches and watercolors. As someone once commented, "What a pity he had to waste time on being a king!" Indeed. One wintry day in 1908, after travelling from Vila Viçosa to Lisbon, King Carlos and Crown Prince Luis Filipe were assassinated as they arrived at Lisbon's big waterfront praça do Comércio, better known as Black Horse Square or Terreiro do Paço.

For manor-house accommodation at Vila Viçosa, see Choosing an Alentejo Base, above.

Elvas

Once you've seen as much of Vila Viçosa as you'd like, retrace your steps through Borba to N 4/IP 7, then drive 28 km (17 miles) east to the fortified border town of Elvas, where you can lunch at the **Pousada de Santa Luzia** (on your right as N 4/IP 7 nears the main town gate). This casual little place won't win any prizes for decor (beamed ceilings that look prefab, and bare, off-white walls), but who cares? The food is first-rate and the menu usually includes a little of everything that makes Alentejo cooking the most Portuguese of the Portuguese: *sopa de grão* (thick chick-pea soup greened with shreds of spinach), *ensopado de borrego* (garlicky lamb-and-bread stew warmed by red peppers), *pezinhos de porco de coentrada* (braised pig's trotters with fresh coriander), and *torta laranja* (rolled orange torte), to name only four of the specialties that appear on the menu with some regularity.

The pousada modestly calls its dining room "one of the best restaurants in Europe." That's stretching it, but no one can deny that it does have one of the Alentejo's—one of Portugal's—best country kitchens. This is the place to enjoy the plump green olives for which Elvas is famous, also the place to pick up a little wooden box of the local sugarplums. These glacéed jade-green figs and plums, sold at the pousada desk, make a delightful K ration to keep in your car as you prowl the Alentejo.

After leaving the pousada, turn right onto N 4/IP 7 and drive a few meters uphill to the main gate of Elvas (a left turn at a busy intersection). Elvas is one Portuguese town that's more appealing from afar than it is up close. The city center seems completely overwhelmed by the mighty 17th-century ramparts that enclose it; in fact, the sun rarely reaches the narrower alleys and back streets. Even at high noon some parts of town are so dark you feel you should wipe away the shadows. Still, it's worth your while to spend a half hour navigating Elvas's web of streets, if only to get a sense of this old Moorish bastion, one that remained in Muslim hands 100 years longer than Lisbon. You can walk the battlements, and for your trouble you'll be rewarded by wide-angle views into Spain. You can also clamber about the hulking **Moorish castle**, which continues to dominate the town.

But most people find the high-striding **Amoreira Aqueduct** directly west of town far more impressive. To reach it, return to the main city gate, drive right onto N 4/IP 7 and head west toward Estremoz. No sooner have you passed the pousada and begun to arc down a long hill than you will see this architectural triumph, an ancient wall of arches three and four tiers high, dwarfing rows of eucalyptus as it marches across the plain into town. Like the aqueduct at Evora, it looks Roman—and its foundations are Roman— but the aqueduct itself was built much later, between 1498 and 1622. The citizens of Elvas paid for it themselves, and it still brings them water.

As you reach the bottom of the hill you'll see a little district road veering off to the right, toward the aqueduct. If you take it, you can drive right under those towering arches. The track turns to dirt here, but if you persist and follow it 200 or 300 yards uphill, you will get the town and aqueduct in the correct perspective—and in the proper light. The late-afternoon sun will have turned the aqueduct's old weathered stones to gold and sidelighted each white house inside the ramparts of Elvas.

From here you can make your way back to your home base, either the way you came or once again opting for any alternative route headed the right way. All secondary roads are well marked and well paved, and you're never more than a few miles from some little village.

Castelo de Vide and Marvão

Whatever your home base—Evora, Estremoz, Vila Viçosa, or farther afield—you can easily tour these two medieval walled towns in a single day, even though the jaunt will lift you out of the rolling prairieland and into the São Mamede and Marvão mountains of the northern Alentejo. From Estremoz it will take you about two hours to reach Castelo de Vide, from Vila Viçosa about 20 minutes longer, and from Evora about 40 minutes more, because in each case you must first drive to Estremoz (northeast on N 18/IP 2 from Evora and west on N 4/IP 7 from Vila Viçosa). From Estremoz it's a more-or-less straight shot 54 km (33 miles) north via N 18/IP 2 to Portalegre, the first town of consequence on the road to Castelo de Vide.

This road has just been straightened and widened, and it's often heavily travelled by trucks. The highway arcs around the west end of the not-very-attractive industrial city of Portalegre (best known for its finely woven tapestries), so you miss the inner-city gridlock. But you must watch carefully as you reach the town's northern fringes, so as not to miss the right turn onto N 246 to go north the last 22 km (14 miles) to **Castelo de Vide**.

If you want a breath-catching view of this old Roman spa, a white town of red-roofed cubistic houses jumbled up the slopes of a castle hill, keep an eye out as you near Castelo de Vide for a blacktop turning off to the right. Signposted "Sa. da Penha," this narrow road climbs onto a great green shoulder of mountain directly opposite town, crests at the little chapel of **Nossa Senhora da Penha**, then winds back down to join N 246-1 directly east of town, a distance, in all, of about 6 km (3½ miles). There are lumberjacks on these heights slashing their way through forests of chestnut, pine, and eucalyptus, and it's said that one of them places a candle in the chapel window each night so that it shines over Castelo de Vide, bright as an evening star. The chapel itself is about a three-minute hike up above the road via stairs and well-marked paths. But it's the *view* that's worth the climb. If you follow the forest road down the eastern flank of the mountain you'll find *miradouros* (lookouts) providing panoramas over a town that is unquestionably one of Portugal's prettiest.

Castelo de Vide doesn't disappoint up close, either, at least once you make your way through the modern sprawl of apartment blocks up to **praça Dom Pedro V**. You can park here while you explore the rest of the town on foot. The square itself is rimmed by fine 17th- and 18th-century mansions, but the focal point is surely the towering church of **Santa Maria** (more impressive outside than in, because it's strangely barn-like). The **Judiaria** (old Jewish ghetto) ascends from the square to the castle on tilting, twisting cobbled alleys past dozens of low white houses, each of which, it seems, is entered by a Gothic doorway and festooned with pots of geraniums.

For some reason, the **castle** was built outside the original town walls. Its keep belongs to the 12th century, and the castle (finally completed in 1327, although it was begun much earlier) is now little more than a shell. It was here, in the 13th century, that arrangements were made for the marriage of King Dinis and Dona Isabel of Aragón, who, as Rainha Santa Isabel, became one of Portugal's most adored queens.

While at the castle, climb the crumbling ramparts for a kestrel's-eye view down over town. And don't fail to stroll through the old town gates into a white, geranium-splashed village that has scarcely changed since the 16th century. About 20 yards along the only street, a narrow cobbled climb, you'll find a tourist office on the left with a desk of brochures up front and women busily embroidering linens in a back room. Ask here to visit the little chapel of **Nossa Senhora da Alegria** (Our Lady of Joy) located some 30 yards farther uphill. The Turismo representative, who speaks presentable English, will summon the keeper of the keys, and this village woman will escort you to the chapel and unlock its weathered wooden door. You'll be glad you took the time and trouble because the walls of this Lilliputian church are paved with stunning 17th-century polychrome tiles.

Marvão, just 12 km (7½ miles) east of Castelo de Vide via N 246-1 and practically on the Spanish border, is an even more startling walled town that grips a 2,838-foot pedestal of granite (this town was the Herminius Minor of the Romans). As you approach from the west, Marvão looks impregnable, little more than an outcropping of rock. But a road twists around behind this mighty hulk, sweeps through the old 13th-century gate, and clambers uphill to the castle.

Near the village of Portagem, where you begin your hairpin climb up to Marvão, was the ancient Roman town of Medobriga (now called São Salvador da Aramenha), for archaeologists a major dig. The important Roman relics unearthed here, however, have all been transferred to the Museu Nacional de Arqueologia e Etnologia at Belém just outside Lisbon. At Portagem itself, there remains a four-arched, gray stone Roman bridge that's remarkably well preserved.

Instead of aiming for Marvão's castle right away, head for the beautifully renovated **Pousada de Santa Maria**, once again following the pousada signs. The pousada's dining room, an informal, glass-walled aerie high above green patchwork plains, welcomes day-trippers. A good thing, too, because it is hands down this region's best restaurant. Home-cooked provincial food is what you'll get here—lusty soups and stews—and, if you're lucky enough to snare a window table, a view that sweeps halfway across Portugal, or so it seems.

After lunch stroll up along the cramped, rough stone streets of this essentially 16th- and 17th-century town to the **Igreja de Santa Maria** (a whitewashed, granite-trimmed church that now houses both the Turismo and the splendid heavy-on-Roman-relics collection of the **Museu Municipal de Marvão**), then on to the 13th-century **castle** directly beyond. Many of the houses along the way are fitted with lacy window grilles, and most façades are hung with canary cages or pots of red and pink geraniums. It won't take you ten minutes to reach the castle from the pousada. There's not much here except high, walk-around battlements from which you can see, it's said, all the way north to the Serra da Estrela, a distance of 100 km (62 miles), and as far west as the great rocky scarp of Palmela directly south of Lisbon—if, of course, the air is clear. But even in less-than-perfect weather you can gaze for miles across the Alentejo plains and over the mountains into Spain. (On damp early-spring or late-fall days, when fog wraps around this town like great billows of muslin, you'll be lucky to see as far downhill as the pousada.)

Nowhere is it written that you must return to your home base exactly the way you came. In fact, it's better to cover new ground. A quick glance at any detailed map of Portugal will show there are many alternate routes. If, for example, you're headquartered in Estremoz or Vila Viçosa, you can backtrack to Castelo de Vide and then, instead of returning to Portalegre, continue straight ahead on N 246 to the crossroads at Alpalhão, where you can turn right on N 18/IP 2 to go up to Castelo Branco in the Beira Baixa (see its separate chapter) or left on N 245 for the 70-km (43-mile) drive south to Estremoz. The overall distance back south is approximately the same as the route you drove north, and the bonuses include the massive fortified monastery at **Flor da Rosa** (destined to become a pousada), the old Moorish town of **Crato**, and, just 12 km (7½ miles) west of Alter do Chão on N 369/N 119 (the road to Ponte de Sor), a six-arched **Roman bridge** that still spans the Seda river.

Anyone with a passion for horses will be interested to learn that the **Coudelaria de Alter**, one of Portugal's important stud farms, lies just 3 km (2 miles) northwest of Alter do Chão on an unnumbered country road (but there's no shortage of signs to point the way). Originally founded by Dom João V some 250 years ago, the farm is now a government "zoological station." And the high-prancing Lusitanian stallions housed in its flashy orange-and-white barns can be visited—even petted.

If you're Evora-bound, you can follow this same route as far as Alter do Chão, then angle southwest, then south across the cork orchards via N 369 and N 370. You will zigzag along the river Seda passing the walled town of **Avis**, which clings to a crag above a mirroring lake (Henry the Navigator's father was master of Avis before he became João I), then **Pavia** (note the tiny white chapel of São Dinis built into a giant Stone Age dolmen), then Arraiolos of rug fame (there won't be time to stop now), and finally Evora.

Both return trips are easy back-road runs that rarely fail to produce some colorful bit of serendipity: a merry country wedding, for example, a Gypsy caravan, or a carnival come to town, with old-fashioned carousels being hurriedly assembled in some cornfield.

GETTING AROUND

Although there is frequent train and/or bus service to Evora and Estremoz, it makes no sense to use public transportation, because once in the Alentejo you'll need a car to get around and these aren't so easily rented in these remote parts. So the best plan is to get your car in Lisbon, where all major rental firms maintain offices both in town and at the airport. What you'll need is a very compact car that can squeeze through medieval gateways, not to mention the networks of sinewy streets inside them.

Evora couldn't be easier to reach. It's a fast two hours (144 km/90 miles) east of Lisbon if you head south to Setúbal via the *auto-estrada,* then right-angle east toward Espanha (Spain) on routes N 10/IP 1, IC 11, N 4, and N 114/IP 7. If you're based in Estremoz, you've another half hour to drive on N 18/IP 2, and, if in Vila Viçosa, still another 15 to 20 minutes, mostly on the N 4/IP 7.

ACCOMMODATIONS REFERENCE

Rates given are projected 1993 prices for a double room, double occupancy. Price ranges span the lowest rate in the low season to the highest in the high season. Unless otherwise stated, rates include Continental breakfast. As prices are subject to change, always double-check before booking.

▶ **Casa de Peixinhos**. 7160 **Vila Viçosa**. Tel: (068) 984-72 or 988-59. 15,000$00. Closed for the month of August and December 15 through January 15.

▶ **Casa de Terena**. Rua Direita, 45, **Terena**, 7250 Alandroal. Tel: (068) 451-88 or 451-32; Fax: (068) 451-55. 9,500$00.

▶ **Castelo de Milfontes**. Largo Brito Pais, 7555 **Vila Nova de Milfontes**. Tel: (083) 961-08. 20,000$00; tower rooms, 22,000$00. Includes breakfast, lunch, and dinner for two.

▶ **Convento de São Paulo Hotel**. **Aldeia da Serra,** 7170 Redondo. Tel: (066) 994-15; Fax: (062) 99-91-04. For reservations, contact Praça do Principe Real, 32-1°, 1200 Lisbon; Tel: (01) 347-3874. 14,500$00–27,000$00.

▶ **Evorahotel**. Quinta do Cruzeiro, Estrada Nacional 114, 7000 **Evora**. Tel: (066) 73-48-00; Fax: (066) 73-48-06. 12,100$00–13,900$00.

▶ **Herdade Dom Pedro**. **Terena**, 7250 Alandroal. Tel: (068) 451-37. 10,500$00; the small house with living room, two bedrooms (one tiny), kitchen, and bath, 25,000$00 per week.

▶ **Horta da Moura**. **Monsaraz**, Apartado 64, 7200 Reguengos de Monsaraz. Tel: (066) 552-54, 552-06, or 551-52; Fax:

(066) 552-41. 10,000$00–18,500$00; suites, 18,000$00–29,500$00.

► **Pousada dos Lóios.** Largo Conde de Vila Flor, 7000 **Evora.** Tel: (066) 240-51 or 240-52; Fax: (066) 272-48. 15,400$00–25,200$00.

► **Pousada da Rainha Santa Isabel.** Largo Dom Dinis, 7100 **Estremoz.** Tel: (068) 226-18 or 226-94; Fax: (068) 239-82. 15,400$00–25,200$00.

► **Pousada de Santa Luzia.** 7350 **Elvas.** Tel: (068) 62-21-94 or 62-21-28; Fax: (068) 62-21-27. 9,700$00–18,000$00.

► **Pousada de Santa Maria.** Rua 24 de Janeiro, 7, 7330 **Marvão.** Tel: (045) 932-01, 932-02, or 935-02; Fax: (045) 934-40. 12,800$00–20,000$00.

► **Pousada de São Gens.** 7830 **Serpa.** Tel: (084) 537-24 or 537-25; Fax: (084) 533-37. 9,700$00–18,000$00.

► **Pousada de São Miguel.** 7470 **Sousel.** Tel: (068) 521-94 or 523-28. 12,800$00–20,000$00.

► **Quinta do Monte dos Pensamentos.** Estrada da Estação do Ameixial, 7100 **Estremoz.** Tel: (068) 223-75 or (01) 396-7906. 10,000$00–11,000$00.

► **Quinta dos Prazeres.** Largo das Alcaçarias, 7920 **Alvito.** Tel: (084) 481-70 or 482-61, also (01) 342-8575, 342-5133, or 849-6071; Fax: (084) 484-69. 9,900$00–10,500$00.

Pousadas can be booked through ENATUR, Avenida Santa Joana Princesa, 10, 1700 Lisbon, Portugal; Tel: (01) 848-1221 or 848-9078; Fax: (01) 80-58-46. But it is easier to make reservations through a travel agent. In the United States and Canada, pousadas can also be booked through Marketing Ahead, 433 Fifth Avenue, New York, NY 10016. Tel: (212) 686-9213; Fax: (212) 686-0271.

Manor houses can be booked directly or through the manor-house associations—ANTER, P.I.T., PRIVETUR, and TURIHAB—listed in Useful Facts. Most of the houses belong to one or more of these associations, but because membership rosters change frequently we haven't attempted to spell out the associations for each house. Readers are advised to contact the manor-house associations for their current listings.

In the United States and Canada, it is possible to reserve rooms in P.I.T. manor houses through E & M Associates, 211 East 43rd Street, Suite 1404, New York, NY 10017; Tel: (212) 599-8280; Fax: (212) 599-1755.

THE ALGARVE
THE SOUTH COAST

By Marion Kaplan

Marion Kaplan spent 20 years in Africa as a freelance photojournalist working for Time *and* National Geographic, *among other magazines. In Portugal after 1980, she contributed to such publications as* Reader's Digest *and the* New York Times. *Now based in France, she is the author of* Focus Africa *and* The Portuguese.

Of all Portugal's regions the Algarve, in the south, is the paradox: a Mediterranean tempo on an Atlantic shore, a Christian people in an Islamic context, a sea-washed corner of Europe that has the spicy scent and intense light of Africa. At Cabo de São Vicente you can stand at O Fim do Mundo (the End of the World), as fearful mariners once called the southwesternmost point of all Europe, yet it was here that a new world opened through the vision of Prince Henry the Navigator.

Contradictions multiply. The modern Algarve, brutally marked by excessive and ugly building, is rimmed by dazzling clean beaches. Some reach emptily to eyespeck distances, others—west of Albufeira to Lagos—are snug buccaneer coves. Red sandstone cliffs and sea-sculpted rocks provide shelter and character. Off Faro and Olhão are true desert island idylls—Barreta, Culatra, Armona—that even summer vacationers and campers cannot crowd.

You can eat dull, tourist-packaged fodder and sizzling fresh seafood. You can shop in malls and superstores or buy a copper pot from the man who made it. You can nibble almond sweets relished by Moors centuries ago and sip a cocktail in a swank hotel. You rarely have to gamble on the weather—a long, dry summer and broad patches of winter sunshine add up to more than 3,000 hours of annual sunshine—but you can try your luck in three casinos (glamorously new and enlarged at Vilamoura, at Praia da Rocha, and at Monte Gordo).

You could be overwhelmed by high summer's crowds and traffic—and by January's outburst of almond blossom, by flamboyant Baroque art in more than 60 churches, the enduring stones of ancient forts and castles, by wildflowers in quiet places, wild birds in sprawling wetlands. Golfers, in this disparate landscape, can strive for a birdie of their own on 13 challenging courses.

In the Algarve you can meet country folk who have never seen the sea; fishermen who knew the rigors of codfishing in the Grand Banks off Newfoundland; clever farmers profiting from exotic fruit and horticulture; poets; lacemakers; basket weavers; cartwrights; colonies of retired, restless, or shrewdly investing expatriates from England and Western Europe; and time-share touts and drug peddlers.

MAJOR INTEREST

Superb coastline of diverse sandy beaches
Historic towns and areas (Faro, Loulé, Silves, Lagos,
    Sagres and Cabo de São Vicente, Tavira)
Hill towns and mountain vistas

Faro
Old quarter

Palácio dos Condes de Carvalhal at Estói
Roman ruins at Milreu

West of Faro
Albufeira, popular beach resort
Fishing port of Portimão, good shopping and restaurants
Lagos, for history, the harbor, and continuing charm
Sagres, symbol of discovery
Land's end at Cabo de São Vicente

East of Faro
Tavira, with its historic churches
Hamlets and fishing villages
Vila Real de Santo António, on the border with Spain

The Hill Towns
Scenic drives that link typical villages
Arab castle at Silves
Caldas de Monchique spa

Reviewing high-rise resort towns sprung from modest fishing villages, dusty chaos, and maladministration, the Portuguese press sighs for a paradise lost—forgetting, for a brief, rare moment, the dramas of Algarve history and the power of change. In former times Phoenicians came to trade, Carthaginian armies camped, Romans laid roads—their presence still conspicuous, most notably at Milreu near Estói. Then came Vandals and Visigoths.

In A.D. 711, with newfound religious fervor, Berbers and Arabs came bursting across the straits from Africa. The impact of the Moors on the Algarve for more than five centuries is palpable and inescapable, from the name itself—*al-Gharb,* "the western land"—to the artful filigree chimneys on low, plainspoken houses, to the widespread growing of oranges and figs and almonds. It is in the *Algarvio*'s sweet tooth, in people's faces, in their fatalism. What has gone, though, is all but the shadow of the civilization, of the philosophy and fine building, that Yemenis brought to their Iberian capital—Xelb, or Chelb, today's Silves.

Physically, the Algarve is a land apart. Measuring a little over 160 km (99 miles) from east to west, it is cut off from the vastness of the Alentejo by a barrier of windswept mountain ranges, the Serra do Caldeirão (Caldron), the Serra de Monchique (the highest, at 2,960 feet), and, west of Monchique, the Serra de Espinhaço de Cão (Dog Spine). Broad stretches remain an unpopulated wilderness. By the fastest, central route north of Albufeira, via Ourique and Setúbal (a large stretch of it N 264/IP 1), Lisbon is less than four hours' easy drive.

The Algarve, despite lack of foresight, urban sprawl, and builders' greed, has much that is worth seeing, and its pleasures are manifold. Setting and climate mean a predictable variety of water sports—sailing, windsurfing, deep-sea fishing from Vilamoura or Portimão, small-boat trips to translucent grottoes (near Lagos and Albufeira), cruises up the Guadiana river from Vila Real de Santo António or on the Ria Formosa between Faro and Olhão, and Algarve-wide swimming and sunbathing. Caution is required against a strong sun, an occasional undertow (not all beaches have lifeguards), an overattentive gigolo, petty thieving (leave nothing in a car), and choice of beach. Topless is commonplace;

some beaches are favored by nudists. Along the N 125, or close to it, from near Tavira in the east to near Lagos in the west, are several water parks. Their serpentine slides and competing attractions make them popular with families and teenagers. You can even find performing dolphins at the Zoomarine theme park near Guia, north of Albufeira. Theme parks, importing lavishly from faraway worlds, are the Algarve's fastest-invading trend.

There are many fairs in the summer months—a sardine festival at Portimão, seafood at Olhão, *doces* (sweetmaking) at Lagos. But if you happen to miss, say, Tavira's Feira da Boa Morte (Fair of the Good Death) at the beginning of August, you can be sure that at any time of year there are fairs across the Algarve as well as regular, well-attended markets (among them at Estói the second Sunday of each month and Loulé every Saturday). Markets are held in the morning; fairs and festivals, especially on weekdays, tend to be liveliest in the evening.

The Algarve's concentration on tourism might lead you to suppose that a frenetic life is led by all. In fact, farming is still a way of life for some 30,000 *agricultores* in a population of around 325,000. And if three-quarters of the *litoral* (coast) is now urbanized, a normal, rural, entirely Portuguese life is led across a very large proportion of the land.

Head from the *litoral* into the *barrocal,* the limestone hills, and up into the *serra* (mountains), and you will see a true, untainted southern Portugal where poverty precludes fine restaurants or fancy shops. Village cafés provide at the least a *papo seco* (bread roll) with cheese or smoked ham; some serve simple meals; all have mineral water, coffee, wine. Tiny, dark *tabernas* will sell you a glass of red wine from a barrel, a perfectly drinkable *vinho tinto,* for a few escudos.

The echoes of the past as well as the bland diversions of the present give today's Algarve its character. To explore it, slicing the map in four is practical: the center (Faro, nearby towns, and the resorts to the west as far as Portimão); west of Portimão to Lagos, Cabo de São Vicente, and wilder shores; from Faro east toward Spain (Tavira and the salt flats, marshes, and farms bordering the Guadiana river); and inland, from Alcoutim in the east to Silves and the heights of Monchique beyond. The four regions are remarkably different in mood and scenery. Distances are short and accommodation plentiful, the best hotels between Faro and Lagos. English is widely spoken in the resort areas along the coast.

(Faro, the first city discussed below, is shown on the map of the eastern Algarve, the chapter's second map.)

The Food and Wine of the Algarve

Catering to the wide-ranging taste of multinational tourism, many Algarve hotels and restaurants tend toward broad-based menus of classic cooking. In the Algarve you will find French cuisine, Chinese, Indian, and Indonesian restaurants, Scandinavian, Dutch, and German-owned establishments. You can eat prawns *piri-piri,* in the peppery Mozambique manner, drink and eat in English-style pubs. Portugal's own robustly distinctive dishes are sometimes not featured at all.

Yet the essence of Algarve food is its fish—grilled, fried, charcoal-broiled, boiled—and shellfish. From the lagoons come clams, razor clams, cockles, and oysters from private nurseries. (Portuguese oysters traditionally were among Europe's best.) Prawns, crab, lobster, and crayfish are all available, but truer Portuguese dishes are the local *arroz de lingueirão* (rice with razor clams), *bifes de atum* (fresh tuna steak), *sardinhas grelhadas* (grilled sardines, by the plateful), *caldeiradas* (fish stews), *lulas de caldeirada* (stewed squid), *sopas de peixe* (fish soups), and the Algarve's own savory oddity, *amêijoas e porco na cataplana* (clams steamed with lean pork and spicy sausage, smoked ham, onions, tomatoes, and herbs in lidded woks like flying saucers of copper or stainless steel; some recipes exclude the pork and meats). A certain drama attends the serving of a *cataplana,* borne sealed to the table. Its lid is unfastened before your eyes with a conjuror's deftness and—*hey presto!*—this unlikely casserole appears, gently steaming, good to the eye, and wonderfully appetizing.

Desserts include one version or another of almond cake, *pudim flan,* like crème caramel, or the more mountainous, though much lighter, *pudim Molotov* (source of the odd name unknown, although wags like to suggest that, before the 1974 revolution, it was called *pudim Salazar*). The best *doces* (sweets) are to be found in *pastelarias,* pastry shops where you can also get a coffee: white-covered *morgados,* foil-wrapped Dom Rodrigos, and fanciful marzipan sweets— tinted flowers, fruits and vegetables, odd fish and plump piggies, all miniature sculptures of the confectioner's art. Artful, too, are the figs dried, pressed, and stuffed with nuts; for once no sugar is added. The basis of most *doces* is almonds, eggs, sugar, and, quite often, pumpkin of the type called *gila* or *chila.* At fairs you will see puffball doughnuts fried to order and sprinkled with cinnamon; they are called *farturas,* which means "abundance."

Regional wines here have a modest reputation compared with Portugal's best and at times, because of the climate, have a higher alcohol content. In the realigning of former demarcated areas to fit the European Community's standards, the Algarve has emerged with four "determined" areas of quality-controlled wines: Lagos, Portimão, Lagoa (still the largest), and Tavira (the smallest). Quality is variable, with price and label some guide to caliber. House wines, sometimes but not always local, are usually drinkable and cheap. Even unassuming restaurants stock good national wines—*vinhos tintos, brancos,* the light and pleasant *vinhos verdes* from the green north, and *rosadas,* or *rosés,* markedly less sweet than the popular export, good *aguardentes* (brandies), as well as local bottles of obscure origin. Up in the hills, too, you will find a powerful firewater, *medronho,* distilled from the miniature strawberries of the arbutus tree. Don't do more than taste it if you are driving, but you will find a bottle, even if you don't care to keep it against winter chills, much appreciated by older Algarvios (the young prefer beer; Portugal makes a very good one called Sagres).

FARO

Faro has been the seat of authority in the Algarve since the 16th century, when the diocese was transferred from Silves, and formal capital since 1756; its historical importance is expressed in the sighs of its citizens and in the quiet cathedral square lined with orange trees in the old town. A pleasant and unpretentious city wrapped around a small harbor, modern Faro, a meld of many low town houses with standard taller blocks, has the market, shops, showrooms, and modest hotels of normal commerce. Recently opened is the city's first new hotel in years. Modern, comfortable, close to the airport, the **Hotel Dom Bernardo** is a practical base in Faro, its Jacuzzi suite probably the only one for miles around. Nearer Faro airport, the well-known French Ibis chain has opened a **Hotel Ibis**, one of their first in Portugal. Both hotels offer a city location and good, basic values; neither claims a soothing setting for a lazy vacation.

In the central **rua de Santo António**, a cheerful cobbled walkway of promenade cafés and shops, you can buy such Portuguese products as pewter, ceramics, copperware, linens, and shoes, and at the harbor end stop at the artfully decorated **Café Aliança** on the praça Dr. Francisco Gomes. Once a dairy, it has the verve and style of Lisbon's antique cafés and is open from early morning to after midnight every day of the year. Low-level industry discreetly operates in the town's outskirts—a cork factory and marble works are here. A commercial quay awaits the easing of bureaucratic restrictions on ferry routes to Tangier and Spain.

Still marked on the city map is an old Jewish cemetery; behind a high wall opposite the gates of Faro hospital, it is untended and derelict, a reminder that it was in Faro, in 1487, that a Jew, Samuel Gacon, printed the first book, or incunabulum, in Portugal—the Pentateuch. Books figured prominently in the trophies sacked from the city in 1596 by the earl of Essex, whose attack, during the 60-year period Portugal was ruled from Spain, was an act of war by Queen Elizabeth I's navy on Spain's King Philip II. Faro was burned to the ground; its books—the library of the bishop—went to the newly founded Bodleian Library at Oxford.

Faro has experienced fire and earthquake, the assault of Napoleonic armies, the cut and thrust of civil war. The Romans were here—Faro probably was their Ossonoba, although Faro's name has Arab origins. Some of the oldest stones of all—and some eye-catching gargoyles—may be seen along with Roman busts, an exquisite mosaic, paintings, furniture, ceramics, and fine tiles in the **Museu Arqueológico Lapidar Infante Dom Henrique**. Its rooms line the two-story cloister of the Renaissance convent of Nossa Senhora da Assunção, Faro's most elegant building, in the old quarter's praça Dom Afonso III, just behind the cathedral.

The *vila-a-dentro* (inner town) lies beside the sea within steps of modern Faro. Parts of its old walls still stand, and you can enter and leave through three archways. Beyond the Jardim Manuel Bivar (shaded gardens beside the harbor) and only a few paces from the tourist office is the 18th-century **Arco da Vila**, adorned with a statue of Saint Thomas Aquinas and capped with a stork's nest. A cobbled road leads directly to the cathedral square, belfry starkly outlined on the 13th-century **cathedral** tower, the old bishop's palace to the right. Styles mix: Romanesque, Gothic, Renaissance—and restoration. The cathedral grew from the 1271 church of Santa Maria, built from a mosque that itself, it is thought, was imposed upon Christian stones. Inside (mornings only) you can see an impressive organ, ornate gilt and tiled Gothic chapels, and, in the chancel, chairs that came, along with a bishop's prerogative, from Silves.

Of the old town's two other gates, the narrow Porta Nova has an inviting antiques shop on the inner side, a railway line, jetty, and the lagoons of Faro on the outside. From the grander Arco do Repouso, to the right of the museum, you can bear right and head across a large space, a fairground at times, to the 17th-century São Francisco church whose *convento,* in a common echo of the anticlerical urges of 1834, is now a barracks. Depicted on the church's 18th-century tiles is the life of Saint Francis of Assisi. (If the church is closed, as it often is, take comfort in the graceful tower and arches decorating the former Palácio Belmarço, now a labor court, as you return.)

Among Faro's other churches, the **Igreja do Carmo**, opposite the main post office and unfortunately framed by apartment blocks, presents a façade that is pure Baroque. Tucked behind it (access through the church) is the Capela dos Ossos (Chapel of Bones), which contains 1,245 skulls wall to wall and arched across the ceiling, the remains of monks— and others, surely—from the church graveyard. As at Evora's ossuary, a grim reminder of mortality is fixed above the door. In the **Museu Etnográfico**, in the district assembly building beside the fountain at the top of rua de Santo António, are collected enduring examples of Algarve culture. You can see culture in the making through a pillared arcade beyond the car park in the square, where *cataplana*-maker Armando da Luz has his workshop in the tiny house where he was born. The **Museu Maritimo**, in the port captain's offices overlooking the small harbor, presents a display of ship models and marine methods, including life as it was in the days of the great tuna traps, the classic and bloody "bullfight of the sea."

There are gentler pleasures, if you wish, in a cruise of the **Parque Natural da Ria Formosa**, a major European wetlands area for migrating birds. You can take a lagoon bird-watching expedition, including seafood lunch on an island, with bird enthusiast José Vargas (Tel: 089-213-76) or Isabel Vicente at Animaris, Lda. (Tel: 089-80-68-40; Fax: 089-80-66-86). In the lagoon the islands are low and flat, channels curving out toward the outlying long, thin **Ilha da Barreta** with its sea-facing, gleaming sand beach.

Behind the cathedral, occupying the ground floor of an old stone house, is the little *restaurante* Cidade Velha (reservations advised; Tel: 089-271-45); its *lombo de porco* is a filet of pork stuffed with dates and walnuts in a wine sauce. There are numerous more informal establishments serving good seafood—among them the cavernous, high-beamed **Dois**

Irmãos (Two Brothers), founded 1925, on the largo Terreiro do Bispo; out on Praia de Faro (Faro Beach), **Alcatruz** (Tel: 089-81-72-36), to the left of the causeway after the camping site; and, to the right after the causeway, the **Roque** (Tel: 089-81-78-68), on the shore of the luminous lagoon. Extremely popular for good food at low prices is **Casa José de Matos** (Tel: 089-81-73-94) on the left-hand side of the road near the Roque. For Sunday lunch especially, go early to avoid standing in line.

Estói

A short distance inland, some 12 km (7½ miles) north of Faro just off the N 2, lies the village of Estói, dominated by its parish church, a Neoclassical reconstruction on 16th-century foundations. Down the road to the left is the 18th-century faded pink **Palácio dos Condes de Carvalhal**, its charm only a little diminished by long closure and attendance by a single loyal gardener. The municipality of Faro, which purchased this small-scale "Queluz of the South," is beginning to refurbish the palace's 28 rooms, but the palace gardens alone—all that you can presently visit—are a work of ebullient art with their stone stairways, numerous busts and statues (of Portuguese poets, statesmen, Greek and Roman goddesses), superb tiles, fountains, and follies.

The Roman ruins of **Milreu** are on the western outskirts of Estói. With many of its treasures already removed to Faro's archaeological museum, to Lisbon, Lagos, and elsewhere (and further digging to be done), what may be seen are some fine mosaics—among them of fish in perfect still life—parts of columns, baths, kitchens, pale tokens of patrician villa life. The largest structure, a temple, became a Visigothic basilica in the third century.

At Estói, you are only 6 km (3½ miles) from the haute cuisine of **La Réserve,** for some years at the very summit of Algarve restaurants. Close to the village of Santa Bárbara de Nexe, 9 km (5½ miles) from Faro, the restaurant (Tel: 089-902-34; advance booking essential) is situated in the eight-acre gardens, with pool and tennis court, of the **Hotel La Réserve**. A member of the Relais & Châteaux group, with prices to match its exclusive status, the hotel accommodation consists of 12 air-conditioned studio suites and eight duplexes, each with separate living room, large verandah, and minibar. (No credit cards accepted.)

Just 3 km (2 miles) west of Santa Bárbara is the soothing peace of the **Quinta de Benatrite**, the single classical Algarve member of Portugal's government-sponsored manor house scheme. An oasis of calm on six rural acres, the gracefully restored *quinta*—the home of Mrs. Yvette Farquharson Oliver—caters to no more than six people. Mrs. Oliver maintains the tranquil country-house mood with furnishings mainly of 19th-century Portuguese and 18th-century English provenance. Probably older still is the barrel-vaulted ceiling of a guest suite. Unlike most manor houses, the quinta will serve meals on request (to guests only) and takes pride in its wide-ranging international cuisine. The quinta also has a swimming pool. For travellers seeking a country-house lunch or dinner, there is the English-owned-and-managed hotel **Monte do Casal**, 3 km (2 miles) from Estói on the Moncarapacho road; the cuisine, mainly French, features such house specialties as smoked quail mousse, and sorbet between the first and the main course; reservations advised (Tel: 089-915-03). The hotel, in its quiet setting, has four double rooms, five suites, terraces where hot and cold canapés are served, a garden, and a swimming pool.

WEST OF FARO

As you head west from Faro on the main east–west highway, N 125 (or from the airport, which is 8 km/5 miles west of Faro), you have the Atlantic to your left and, in a while, the rugged limestone hills called the *barrocal* on your right. Some 10 km (6 miles) west of Faro the road divides. The N 125-4 leads to the crafts town of Loulé, 8 km (5 miles) to the northwest, while the N 125 carries on west toward Portimão.

About 11 km (7 miles) out of Faro on N 125 and close to the seductive pleasures of nearby resorts is **São Lourenço**, home to a happy conjunction of Portuguese heritage and modern accomplishment in its small church's exuberant golden high altar and massed blue-and-white tiles, the 1730 work of Policarpo de Oliveira Bernardes, and, below the church on the short approach road, a cluster of cottages that open into the Centro Cultural de São Lourenço. There is always good art on display, by living Portuguese and foreign artists. Concerts and other cultural events are held here, too.

Shortly after São Lourenço is the bypass for **Almancil**, a town of no distinction except for its appealing local pottery products in muted colors (the pottery, or *olaria*, is on the N 125 near the Vale d'Eguas turning). Almancil is important only as an expanding business and shopping center, with restaurants serving the 1,680-acre resort complex of **Quinta**

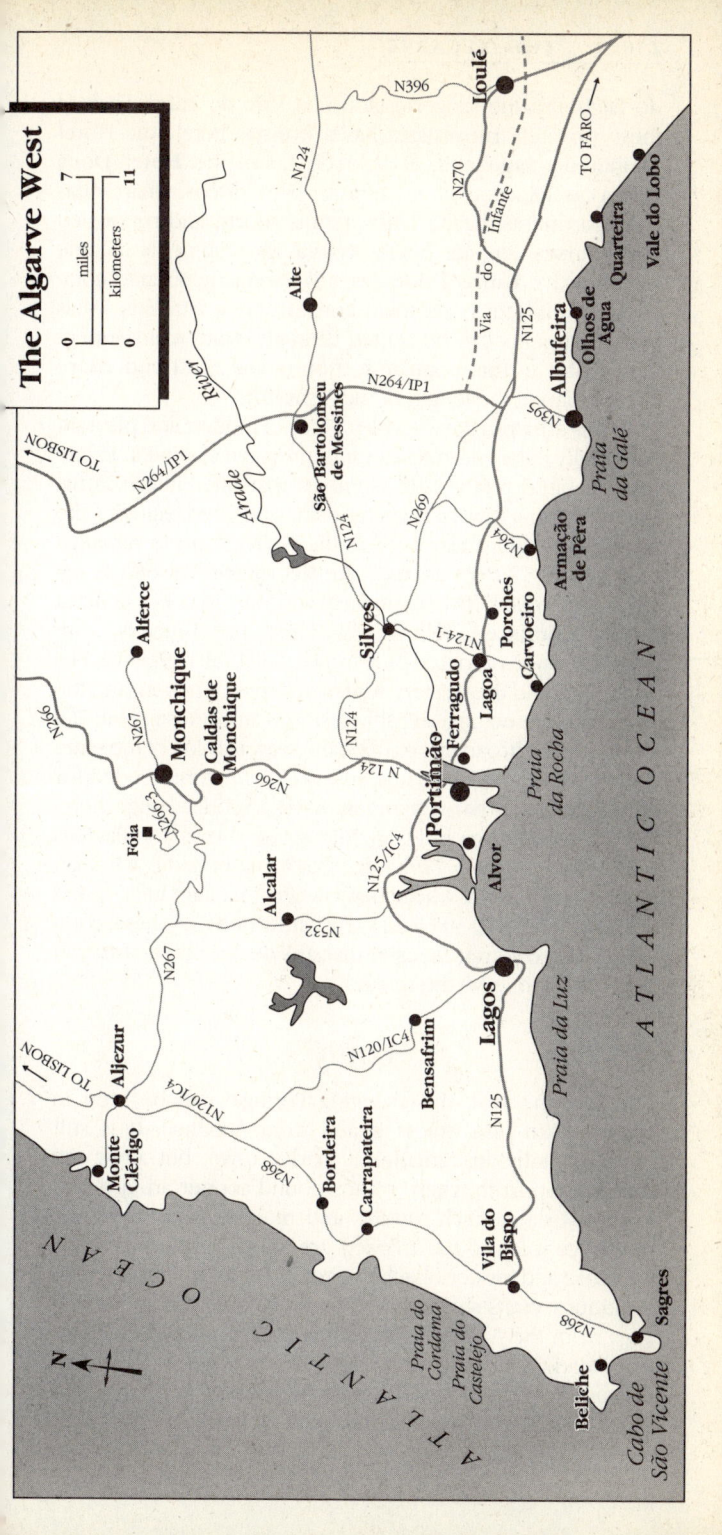

do Lago and the longer-established **Vale do Lobo**. Each of these privately run estates has a five-star hotel (the **Hotel Quinta do Lago** and, at Vale do Lobo, the **Hotel Dona Felipa**), a selection of restaurants, bars, discos, smart villas and apartments, health clubs, tennis courts, and renowned **golf courses**. Smaller nearby coastal developments include the attractive **Dunas Douradas**, a Norwegian-operated complex of well-built villas, town houses, and apartments. Villas and apartments can be rented through estate management year-round in this popular section of the coast and, more cheaply, along the length of the Algarve.

In this area you have a wide choice of modest and pleasant essentially Portuguese restaurants. Or you may dine in exemplary if often costly establishments that offer international menus leaning toward French cuisine and often featuring the region's excellent fish, such as the **Golfer's Inn** in Almancil (Tel: 089-39-57-25), **Casa da Torre-Hermitage** (Tel: 089-39-43-29) on the road between Almancil and Vale do Lobo, **Xenia** at Dunas Douradas (Tel: 089-39-63-47), **Les Lauriers**, with French cuisine prepared by a French chef (Tel: 089-39-72-11), tucked behind the western Almancil bypass junction, and the **Pequeno Mundo**, in a stylishly restored farmhouse some 760 yards along a broad dirt road on the seaward side of the same junction (Tel: 089-39-98-66); reservations recommended for all. Even beach bar-restaurants have a modish edge here, notably **João Passos** and **Gigi**. **Julia's**, too, always popular, has risen from humble *barraca* (shack) to become a stylish seashore restaurant whose new owners maintain Julia's good cooking (Tel: 089-39-65-12). The attractions of these complexes are so comprehensive that, as Vale do Lobo boasts, you never have to leave the resort.

Loulé

The old, the real, the changing Portugal can be seen in Loulé, 4 km (2½ miles) inland from Almancil. It is still predominantly an agricultural market town, but along the *avenida,* up from where smiths pound copper artifacts and leatherworkers stitch saddles and mule tack, up from the quirky cupolas of the market, are shops displaying costly furniture and modern kitchens. You'll see a camera shop and boutiques, crafts shops that sell multicolored rag-and-cotton rugs from the Alentejo, intricate wicker work and furniture from Madeira, locally made earthenware pottery and ceramics, and baskets of esparto grass in a variety of shapes and sizes. Beside the market, **Barracha** is bright with copper

gewgaws, copper pots, *cataplanas*. Gervásio's hardware
store is deep and dark, with a range of stock to outdo a Sears
catalogue. At Pagapouco, literally "pay little" and similar to a
low-key Woolworth's, the racks and counters are bright with
cheap merchandise. The echoing shop next door, the air
thick with fierce, competing odors, sells animal feeds, fertiliz-
ers, charcoal for cooking, and *cal* (lime) for whitewashing.

The narrow back streets behind the market hold evidence
of Loulé's Moorish origins. The castle, under its 1940s battlements and tourist polish, incorporates the walls of the Moors
and Roman relics. Early Portuguese kings passed by on
historic journeys. The town won its charter in 1266; its first
fair and the parish church also date to the 13th century.

Loulé, like all Portugal, is adapting to new times. Next to
an old stone courthouse in the winding streets behind the
market is a tasteful art gallery. You can get a good haircut or
see a new movie at the Charlot commercial center. The
three-star **Loulé Jardim Hotel**, with the look of a traditional
town house, has opened in the peaceful praça Manuel de
Arriaga; it has a rooftop pool. You'll get a comfortable room
with bathroom, and breakfast, at astonishingly low cost at the
Residencial Ibérica on avenida Marçal Pacheco (the road to
and from Faro). You can eat rustically at several small restaurants, enjoy French provincial cooking at the little **Aux Bons
Enfants** on rua Engenheiro Duarte Pacheco, around the
corner from the post office (reservations advised; Tel: 089-
620-96), or choose from a more wide-ranging menu at the
Avenida, just above the town-center roundabout (Tel: 089-
621-06). At the congenial **Musikefesta**, 3 km (2 miles) from
Loulé at Areeiro on the Almancil link road, you have live
music (on Thursdays, Fridays, and Saturdays), an attractive
menu—try the swordfish steak in cream sauce—and, that
most rare thing in Portugal, piping hot plates (Tel: 089-39-59-
78). Nearby, at the **Churrasqueira da Goncinha** (Tel: 089-41-
36-99), you'll find Portuguese families indulging in good
grills at good prices. The restaurant is open on Sundays, and
English is spoken.

Pause for a beer in the stately **Louletano**, a café-bar down
from Loulé market, and you will see a photo on the wall of
poet and local hero António Aleixo. The south, as much as
anywhere in Portugal, has a taste for poetry and a love of
legend. You may well hear the tale of the Algarve's winter
snow, a once-upon-a-time story of a Moorish prince who
wooed and won a northern princess. Pining for the snows of
her homeland, the fair lady became wan and hollow-eyed.
No gifts the king could shower on his beloved cured her

melancholy. Fearing a fatal decline, the loving husband ordered great groves of almond saplings to be planted that, come January, bloomed and blanketed the land with blossoms. Seeing the gleaming snowfield, the princess soon recovered—and the almond blossom appears, unfailingly, year after year.

The Algarvio's life is built upon the rhythms of nature, the seasons, the holy days. The high point of the year is carnival, and Loulé's is the merriest in the south. Carnival erupts in February with rollicking parades and floats, masks and monsters, the grotesque and the comic, girls in tights, mocking boys, dancing in the streets, nights of drinking and revelry. As this is Portugal, not Rio, passions are moderated, accidents few, the violence negligible. Lent is silence, relatively, broken by Easter.

On Sunday afternoon two weeks after Easter, pilgrims gather in Loulé to watch the ceremonial return of the town's patron saint, Nossa Senhora da Piedade, to her sanctuary in the 16th-century chapel on a high hill outside town, beside an unfinished, misconceived, flying saucer of a church. (On Easter Sunday she is brought, with little ceremony, to a town church.) This *romaria* (pilgrimage) of the Mãe Soberana (Sovereign Mother), the prime religious procession in the Algarve, dates to the 16th century. While it is an honor for townsfolk to take part, it is also something of a strain: The Lady is heavy, the hill high. Tradition demands that her bearers maintain a steady pace. One year, it is said, one of them dropped dead in his tracks and was borne along, onward and upward, with the image—for a man of faith surely a righteous deliverance.

At the marina complex of **Vilamoura**, 10 km (6 miles) west of Almancil along the N 125 (or by an access road off the N 396, immediately west of Quarteira), you are in a shrewd banker's blueprint, approved in 1966 and transformed thereafter into a 4,000-acre self-contained tourist city-state of hotels (among them the nine-story, angular-edged **Vilamoura Marinotel** looming above the marina, the ten-story **Hotel Atlantis**, and the step-roofed **Hotel Dom Pedro Marina**), apartments, villas, golf courses, swimming pools, riding stables, a casino, cinema, art gallery, fitness centers—all that's needed to support the pleasure principle. You can eat Portuguese cuisine, a steak, or, at the **Bamboo**, good Chinese (Cantonese) food. Or you could dine at the glossy new **casino** (from 8:30 P.M.), take in the show, play a little blackjack, roulette, *banque française*, baccarat, craps, bingo, or the slot machines. (A passport is obligatory; jacket and tie are not.) In the nearby 1,000-berth marina rest boats and yachts that have sailed the Atlantic, around the world, or merely along the coast for a beach-bar lunch. Yet Vilamoura, too, has vestiges of the ancient past, Roman, Visigothic, and Arab—neatly encapsulated in a small settlement, **Cerro da Vila**, with a museum beside it (ring the bell for entry).

Immediately west of Vilamoura (follow the signs on the secondary road N 1289-1, between the N 125 and the sea) lie the long beach and red cliffs of Falésia, setting of the (nine-hole) **Pine Cliffs Golf and Country Club**, a tastefully designed resort complex with the new 215-room **Sheraton Algarve Hotel**, which is nowhere more than three stories high. With all the amenities, comfortable rooms, and luxurious suites of the best Sheratons, it provides the ambience of a secluded, Moorish garden village within a costly, well-planned property development.

West again, about 4 km (2½ miles) farther on the same small road linked to the N 125, is **Olhos de Agua**, a fisher-men's beach that still determinedly retains its working grace despite the press of tourism on the hills behind. Here you have reached the first of the characterful beaches with odd rock formations that stretch west along the Barlavento (the windward, western Algarve). Some are well hidden, others famous—like São Rafael and Castelo west of Albufeira, and a cluster at Lagos. All have a name, sometimes only in local slang. Olhos de Agua, for example, means, literally, "eyes of the water," and on the boats' painted prows are bright eyes galore. Portuguese fishermen, as superstitious as sea people everywhere, cannot tell you the origin of the eyes, only that they help them see the fish. **La Cigale** (Tel: 089-50-16-37; reservations recommended) is a pleasant restaurant to the right of the beach, with a terrace view of the bay. In Albufeira, to the west, an extra pair of eyes might help you find parking.

Albufeira

Continuing west on N 125 and turning south on N 395 brings you to Albufeira, which used to be called the St-Tropez of the Algarve for a casual elegance that has been crushed by construction. But the town is still an immensely popular beach resort, crowded in summer. Albufeira lies, like Sa-lome in her seven veils, within a ring of broad new—and some not-so-new—roads. Directional signs point to *na-scente,* east side, and *poente,* the west side of the town; a one-way system is helpful, to a point. If you're driving, park at the first legal space for a walkabout. A good informal restaurant, **A Ruina**, specializing in fish and shellfish, is comfortingly situated right on and, in the nature of its several levels, above the fishermen's beach at the wharf called Cais Herculano (best access is from the eastern entry to town; reservations advised; Tel: 089-51-20-94).

The old Albufeira is small and hilly but walkable. The Romans called it Baltum and built defenses; the Arab name was al-Buhera (Castle on the Sea). There's not much of a castle to see now, though it's easy to imagine that the tunnel that links a "walking" street to the main beach has had its share of drama. Besides the 16th-century Misericórdia chapel, pleasant sights include the narrow terraces of fishermen's cottages, the beaches, and the grottoes nearby. The main square, pedestrians-only largo Engenheiro Duarte Pacheco, is lined with shops, cafés, and restaurants. There are more restaurants along the hilly streets, some with terraces overlooking the sea. For the freshest of fish, on praça Miguel Bombarda are **O Cabaz da Praia** (Tel: 089-51-21-37) and, right next door, **O Dias** (Tel: 089-51-52-46); reservations recommended for both.

Albufeira is only one of many towns in the Algarve where the English preserve their homely traditions as barkeepers, but **Sir Harry's Bar**, in the town center, is notable as being among the oldest established. English snacks are served along with English-style tankards of beer, over which, following an ancient custom, you may toast England's alliance with Portugal, unbroken since 1373.

Of the hotels, the **Hotel Boa Vista**, with a pool, is situated on the upper west side of town. The **Hotel Rocamar** sits above the beach at cliff level, and the sturdy **Hotel Sol e Mar**, with an indoor pool, is an old favorite where an elevator takes you from reception at the top to the beach below. Albufeira also has several self-catering "aparthotels." Among them, on a hill on the western side of town with a view to the sea, is **Apartamentos Albufeira Jardim**, with more than 470 apartments as well as swimming pools, tennis courts, a supermarket, and other facilities.

A beacon of elegant dining in the area is **O Montinho do Campo**, offering fine French cuisine in a gracefully converted farmhouse in built-up Montechoro on the eastern outskirts of Albufeira; Tel: (089) 51-39-59. Some 7 km (4 miles) west of Albufeira on the local coast road, the restaurant of the little German-owned cliff-top hotel **Vila Joya**, on Praia da Galé, also features haute cuisine prepared by Austrian chefs whose desserts are celebrated; Tel: (089) 59-17-95. Booking at both establishments is essential. You should book early, too, if you want to stay at Vila Joya, which has only 13 double rooms and two suites. (Like some restaurants, it closes for a few weeks during winter.) Its setting above a pretty beach, its pool tucked discreetly below the cliff, and its Moorish decor—the waiters even wear baggy 1,001-nights trousers—have made for continuing popularity among a mainly German clientele. Farther west of Albufeira at Porches, just off the N 125, you will find O Leão de Porches, serving good international food under antique wooden beams. You might try the medallions of pork in a fig, apple, and cream sauce. Tel: (082) 523-84; closed Sundays.

Porches is a major center for pottery. On the N 125, with Portimão ahead, you have on your right, on the brow of the hill, the Olaria Pequena, where Scottish potter Ian Fitzpatrick makes sophisticated pieces and tiles in modern designs. Less than one kilometer ahead on the left is a big *olaria* that features highly stylized glazed designs on terra-cotta plates, pots, vases, and tiles based on regional styles in brilliant emerald, turquoise, and cobalt blue, revived by the late Irish artist Patrick Swift, among the first foreigners to settle in the Algarve.

Between Albufeira and Porches on the lower coastal road, successfully guarding its tranquillity and privacy from the nearest resort town, grossly overgrown Armação de Pêra just to the east, is the delectably imaginative development of Vilalara. Set on 11 acres (with 14 gardeners), Vilalara is a luxurious village of apartments and suites, no building higher than two stories, with six tennis courts and three groups of swimming pools—fresh, seawater, and thalassotherapy health center. Through its discreet architecture and lush gardens with purling streams, pools, and waterbirds, the complex retains a profound sense of harmony uniting clifftop, gardens, and—down steps cut into the cliff—a secluded beach below. The restaurant offers international and Portuguese dishes, including some of the better-known recipes, allegedly 365 in all, for the Portuguese national passion, dried, salt cod—a fish, by the way, that is traditionally accompanied by red wine; reservations advised (Tel: 082-31-49-10).

Continuing west, back on the N 125, you have the unassuming town of Lagoa to your right, best known as a wine producer and, increasingly, for its mid-August fair of handicrafts, agriculture, commerce, and industry. Off to the left is Praia do Carvoeiro, a once-pretty fishing village with extensive villa development on the cliffs on either side and clusters of rock-framed sandy coves below (the pools and tunnels of **Algar Seco** are still compelling after dramatic reshaping in a winter storm). Of the 30 or so restaurants here, the cliff-top **O Castelo** is a long-standing favorite (Tel: 082-35-72-18); closed Mondays. A few more kilometers on the N 125 bring you to Portimão.

Portimão

The Roman name for Portimão was Portus Hannibalis. The Carthaginian Hannibal is believed to have founded the pleasant little town of **Alvor** on the shores of a lagoon to the southwest. In recent years Portimão, the biggest port and population center on the Algarve coast, has been bursting its bounds. But if, in its environs, you may still see the villages of Calvário and Purgatório, no longer must you suffer the miseries of slow-moving traffic. Now a striking new bridge leaps the Arade river. West of Portimão you cannot fail to see some of the massive construction that has grotesquely scarred approaches to Portimão's famous beach resort, **Praia da Rocha**, but at least the great, splendid beach itself has survived the assault. The harbor, too, is changing and expanding to meet a future as an international ferry port even as its distinguished mainstay, the fishing fleet, faces uncertainty.

Yet exploring Portimão is worth the effort. You will still see brightly painted trawlers though, as most now must use modern facilities away from the old waterside, you'll no longer be able to watch the juggler's trick the fishermen used to perform when, perfectly balanced, they tossed sardines ashore in brimming baskets as emptied baskets were tossed back. At the alfresco waterside restaurants below the eastern access bridge, you can still eat grilled sardines by the plateful. You could go to sea yourself on a deep-sea fishing or sailing trip, to coastal grottoes, or up the Arade river toward Sagres. (The tourist office in the largo 1° de Dezembro can provide information.) Across the harbor, on the Ferragudo side, is the picture-postcard Forte de São João, for years the home of Joaquim José Coelho de Carvalho, a diplomat, lawyer, and poet who died in his castle on the Arade in 1934 at the age of 82 (much of what you see was built early this century). Below it is a fine beach, Praia Grande, with good windsurfing and other water-sport facilities.

Portimão itself successfully juggles work with play, daily commerce with cosmopolitan shopping, fishing and food production (including a local wine) with friendly restaurants all over town. Its own 16th-century fort, Santa Catarina at Praia da Rocha, has been transformed into a peaceful viewpoint and terrace for refreshments. The central **rua do Comércio** is the main walkers' street, lined with the shops of the town's daily commerce; the **rua Santa Isabel** and its neighbors, to the right just after praça Visconde de Bivar if you enter the town from the N 125 bridge, is quieter and more elegant. Here you can find a cool art gallery and antiques, Vista Alegre porcelain and crafts, marzipan sweets and pastries, Charles Jourdan shoes and stylish boutiques.

Among varied restaurants in the neighborhood is the tasteful, calm **Casa de Jantar** on rua Santa Isabel, 14–16, reservations recommended; Tel: (082) 220-72. You can get a beer or wine and a plate of seafood at any of several *cervejaria* restaurants. **Alfredo's**, at rua Pé-da-Cruz, 10, is a good in-town place for a fish dinner; Tel: (082) 831-02. The best eating in the area—its fish, shellfish, and duck renowned—is **A Lanterna**, at the road junction of Parchal with Ferragudo on the eastern side of the bridge as you approach Portimão; Tel: (082) 239-48.

Past the unattractive access road to Ferragudo on the estuary's eastern side you'll find Ferragudo village, still maintaining its intrinsic charm despite much new building above it, and, up a rough road signposted Praia Pintadinho, a new German-owned and -oriented hotel, the **Casabela**. Attractively designed with Moorish features, the 52-room hotel has a terraced pool, tennis court, and grand views across the estuary. Most hotels near Portimão are at Praia da Rocha: the stately **Hotel Algarve** still very comfortable, the little **Hotel Bela Vista** in its lordly manor house determinedly holding its own, the **Hotel Oriental** a glamorous Moorish-style aparthotel of 85 studios around an atrium of fountains and gleaming mosaic tiles. At Praia da Rocha, too, adjoining the Tarik Hotel, where you may dine, is a **casino**; informal dress is accepted but you should remember to bring your passport.

WEST
TO THE END OF THE WORLD

The coast west of Portimão is marked by caves and coves, then the long beaches of Alvor and Meia Praia framing the entrance to the **Alvor lagoon**. For golfers the area's prime attractions are Sir Henry Cotton's craftsmanship at the **Penina Golf and**

Resort Hotel, 5 km (3 miles) west of Portimão on the N 125/IC 4, and the **Palmares course** to the west and south behind Meia Praia, where designer Frank Pennink included five sand-dune links in his scheme. For others it is the comforts of the **Hotel Alvor Praia** on the Praia dos Três Irmãos or the impressive swimming pool shaped into the clifftop at neighboring **Prainha**, a villa-and-apartment complex of many years' standing with an estimable terrace restaurant, **O Búzio** (reservations recommended; Tel. 082-45-85-61), whose menu blends classical Portuguese with international cuisine.

The N 125/IC 4, on its westward progress, passes close to a megalithic necropolis at **Alcalar**, where a dig progresses slowly. To get there, head inland on the N 532, a small signposted road off the N 125/IC 4 just to the east of the Penina Hotel entry. After 4 km (2½ miles) you are at a rough crossroads. Take the narrow tarmac road to the right and almost immediately the fenced track to the left. The track leads directly to the dig, within about 100 yards.

Back on the N 125/IC 4 you will see signs pointing to the village of Mexilhoeira Grande (where there's a striking parish church, Renaissance with a Manueline portal and Baroque art inside) and an inland dam engagingly named Barragem da Bravura (Dam of Courage) that has helped add rice growing to the Algarve's more familiar orange and almond orchards and hillsides of fig and carob. These are quiet places. Lagos, 19 km (12 miles) west of Portimão, a town of crucial importance to Portugal's great discoveries, a harbor and resort now, has liveliness and, in summer, holiday crowds.

Lagos

Lagos was a hive of activity in Roman times—then it was called Lacobriga. Moors overcame its walled defenses with little difficulty and expanded its trade. It was from Lagos that three sons of King João I and his English queen, Philippa, sailed to North Africa in 1415 to conquer the Moorish citadel of Ceuta, an eminently successful expedition that led one of them, the Infante Dom Henrique (Prince Henry the Navigator) to consider further projects. The small, swift ships to carry them through were built in Lagos. The town grew, and from 1578 until much of it was destroyed in the 1755 earthquake, Lagos was the capital of the Algarve. It was soon rebuilt, however. In 1797 Lord Nelson moored in its harbor. English poet Robert Southey was arrested here, in 1801, as a vagabond. He had failed to pay a courtesy call on the town's head magistrate, having been seduced by the town's pleasant air, attractive buildings, and gorgeous beaches, as vacationers still are today.

Here you can see the past, real and remembered. Pieces of old walls stand, as does a handsome, restored **Forte do Pau da Bandeira** with its tidy drawbridge and royal coat of arms. Beside the long promenade of the avenida dos Descobrimentos a darkly gleaming Prince Henry sits forever gazing out to sea in a great square, behind him the arcades of the old slave market (used now as an art gallery). The compact and engaging **Museu Municipal**, a few steps farther back from the sea, contains Roman mosaics, the city charter (1504), coins, and ethnic artifacts. The museum records in its collection of vestments what all Portugal remembers: the departure in 1578, after a last mass in Lagos, of the foolish young King Sebastian to his defeat and death in the Battle of Alcácer-Quibir in North Africa, which led in 1580 to a 60-year usurpation of Portuguese autonomy by Spain. A cult grew in those years around the conviction that King Sebastian had survived—and so he has, in the Lagos town center, in the striking statue by sculptor José Cutileiro.

There are some fine churches in Lagos, the **chapel of Santo António** beside the museum the most celebrated for its extravagantly carved and gilded woodwork, all but the ravishing painted ceiling predating the 1755 earthquake. The **Santa Maria**, at the corner of the square behind Prince Henry's right shoulder, has a worthy statue of the town's patron saint, São Gonçalo, who was born a few steps away. Set in the gray stone wall close to the seaport side of the church, a restored part of 16th-century fortifications, is a Manueline window from which, it is said, King Sebastian made his last address to the people of Lagos.

The market is always vibrant on workday mornings, the cheerful, tiled **Gilberto** at rua das Portas de Portugal, 85, among many restaurants in the area specializing in fresh fish. Most tourist development is on the outskirts of the town, leaving the center of small, stone, whitewashed or painted houses and cobbled streets agreeably unembellished. Crafts traditions are strong—you can buy handmade copper and whimsical marzipan and fig sweets. To the south are resplendent beaches and the bizarre rock formations called the **Ponta da Piedade**—sea-eroded arches, craggy shapes, and translucent grottoes you can get to on foot (many steps in the cliff) or more comfortably by small boat from Lagos.

In summer Lagos has an animated nightlife of discos and

boîtes. Cheerful open-air restaurants sprawl across walkways and pavements. For classier cooking and a more soothing setting there is **O Galeão**, rua da Laranjeira, 1 (reservations advised; Tel: 082-76-39-09), or **Alpendre** at rua António Barbosa Viana, 17 (Tel: 082-76-27-05).

For accommodation there is the **Hotel de Lagos**, with its own pools and nearby beach club and tennis courts, situated a short walk from the town center. Good food and value are available at the unpretentious little restaurant **O Alberto** behind the hotel on largo Convento Senhora da Gloria (Tel: 082-76-93-87); as at the two more elaborate restaurants mentioned above, its kitchen is open to view. Right by the harbor, with views out to sea, is the four-story **Albergaria Marina Rio**, its top floor a large sun terrace and swimming pool, heated in winter. A town house *residência* with Old World charm is **Albergaria Caza de São Gonçalo**; another choice for accommodation, just outside Lagos beside the popular little Praia da Dona Ana, is the dated but comfortable eight-story **Hotel Golfinho**. The 12-acre resort Vilabranca is brand-new; located 1 km (½ mile) southwest of Lagos toward Porto de Mós, it is only 5 km (3 miles) from the Palmares golf course. With a number of apartments and cottages, the resort, private and family-run, is focused around the adjoining **Vilabranca Hotel Club**, several small white buildings with blue-framed windows. A few pleasant rooms-with-breakfast and suites are available in the area's private homes, government-approved like the manor house accommodation widespread in the north. Above the beach at Praia do Pinhão is the **Casa do Pinhão**, and, to the east of Lagos, 3 km (2 miles) from the Palmares golf course (1 km on the tar road from Odiáxere), Henry and Margarida Swain welcome guests to their **Quinta da Alfarrobeira**, a farmhouse with three double rooms, an annex apartment for two to four people, and a pool.

As you keep on the westbound route out of Lagos you will see signs pointing to the small beach resorts of Praia da Luz (7 km/4 miles from Lagos), Salema, and Burgau. Each has its rentable villas and apartments and a selection of restaurants but is rarely crowded. At the Praia da Luz crossroads, look for the right turn leading to the Herdade do Funchal, an estate of spacious villas where artist-potters Jorge and Janet Mealha have their workshop. Follow tiled signs to the **Casa dos Oleiros**—it's down a lane away from other houses; on weekends phone first (Tel: 082-76-09-63). In Praia da Luz, **Darcy's** restaurant at rua da Praia, 14, serves informal dinners from a sophisticated menu, offering a pretty garden patio in summer and a dining room with a log fire in winter; reservations advised (Tel: 082-78-91-40).

Sagres and Cabo de São Vicente

From Lagos it is 33 km (20 miles) west and southwest to Sagres, then another 6 km (3½ miles) to Cabo de São Vicente (Cape St. Vincent). The road from Lagos to "the end of the world" (after Vila do Bispo it becomes the N 268) is winding, the land with each mile more wind-tossed and stern. Even in sunshine here the shepherds often wear their protective sheepskin tailcoats; you, too, can buy good, astonishingly cheap wool sweaters at the very gates of the cape fortresses.

The village of **Raposeira**, just to the east of Vila do Bispo, is noted for its **parish church** and the **Nossa Senhora de Guadalupe chapel**, thought to have been built originally by Templars in the 13th century. Here in the 1400s Prince Henry the Navigator rented lodgings while building his Vila do Infante, the headquarters for his enterprises, at the cape. Village rumor has it, too, that in Raposeira the ascetic prince, governor of the Order of the Cross of Christ, knew the love of a fair lady.

To this day scholars argue about what precisely occurred at Sagres and Cabo de São Vicente. Where 19th-century historians wrote of Prince Henry's great nautical school at Sagres, current thinking tends to a much looser gathering of mathematicians, cartographers, navigators, and shipbuilders. It did not help that in 1587 Sir Francis Drake, to the Portuguese nothing more than dastardly pirate, raided the coast—his enemy being the Spanish rulers of Portugal—and sacked the Vila do Infante. The earthquake of 1755 erased what was left. Even the precise site of the prince's residence is unknown. You can only believe, inside the Sagres **fortress** walls, that it must surely have been here.

Sagres point, exposed to wind and sea and sky, is the understated symbol of a heroic era of discovery. Within the Sagres fortress, its walls rebuilt in the 18th century and afterward, few buildings remain, one of them perhaps the chapel of Prince Henry's day. The long, low building beside the *rosa dos ventos* (compass rose) has been transformed from youth hostel to museum-cum-conference center, its unimaginative appearance in this magical place a matter of some controversy. The great *rosa dos ventos* itself, around which you can visualize students of navigation, is of uncertain ancestry; 20th-century restorers provided its present appearance. The town of Sagres on the southern horn of the promontory is small and windswept, its houses low and sturdy. A small harbor provides shelter for fishing boats.

Yet on this gaunt peninsula, you are on the legendary *promontorium sacrum* of the Romans, and a site sacred to early Christians as the resting place of the bones of the fourth-century martyred Saint Vincent—until, guarded by ravens, they were taken in 1173 to Lisbon (he is Lisbon's patron saint). Prince Henry found the inspiration here to demand feats of exploration from his sea captains. A young Columbus survived a wreck off this coast; Lord Nelson won his reputation off the same coast in the 1797 Battle of Cape St. Vincent.

At **Cabo de São Vicente**, on the promontory's western horn, 6 km (3½ miles) from Sagres across a wind-blasted heath, where you can see from within the cape's fortress walls the breakers crashing on tall cliffs and the rock throne of Saint Vincent below the lighthouse, you have reached the southwesternmost point of Europe, the ancient mariners' end of the world.

On this wild headland, where myth meets reality, much is left to your imagination. You may also extend your view—of great cliffs, of foolhardy fishermen perched on rocks, and of a stream of passing ships—if you are willing to climb 70-odd spiraling steps within the lighthouse to the rim of the great lamp whose 80-km (50-mile) ray of light guides modern mariners. (A marine facility, it's not always open to the public.) Once a monastery stood here and, before that, the chapel that held the bones of the saint.

In Sagres there are several fine beaches, among them the small Praia do Tonel and the broader Praia da Mareta with its flat sands and handy beach bar-restaurant, **O Telheiro**, serving good fresh fish; (Tel: 082-641-79). Down by the harbor, with a view across the Baleeira bay, another informal restaurant, **A Tasca**, is popular with tourists (Tel: 082-641-77 or 644-26). The days of cheap lobster and crayfish are gone, but here at least you are at the source.

A powerfully dramatic setting in the area for a meal or a bed (there are only four rooms) is the **Fortaleza do Beliche**, a modestly priced annex to the Sagres *pousada* (government-run inn), inside its own stone fortress walls perched above craggy cliffs and the sea close to Cabo de São Vicente (Tel: 082-641-24). The **Pousada do Infante** itself, at Sagres, has a quiet, airy position set back from a cliff and comfortable rooms with balconies. Very pleasant, too, and excellent value, is the sea-facing **Hotel da Baleeira** with a seawater swimming pool and a tennis court.

The grandest beaches, stunning and wild, are on the west coast to the north—the entire *litoral,* the **Costa Vicentina,** being a protected area. There are relatively few roads in the Algarve southwest, but you can reach the southern beaches on tracks from a minor road, N 1256, just west of Beliche, which lies between Sagres and the cape. From Vila do Bispo a 5-km (3-mile) narrow tar road gets you more easily to Praia do Castelejo. Just south of Castelejo, a rough road leads to **Torre de Aspa,** a 512-foot cliff, the area's highest; a small building, a derelict customs post, is a conspicuous landmark. As you approach Castelejo, a wide unpaved road bears right to **Praia do Cordama** (or Cordoana—the spelling varies) where, in summer, you will find a few campers—German vacationers predominate along this wild coast—and a beach bar providing refreshments and a simple meal. Sandy tracks lead to other dramatic, and usually deserted, beaches, although the Portuguese have a name for every single one.

Easily accessible on the western coast is the great dune-backed beach at **Bordeira,** close to Carrapateira, 14 km (8½ miles) from Vila do Bispo. On the north–south N 268, 34 km (21 miles) from Vila do Bispo, you will come to **Aljezur,** a small town founded by Arabs, still with its Arab name, its castle—stark ruins now—the very last to be taken in his sweep across the Algarve by Dom Pedro Peres Correia, master of the Order of Sant'Iago. Seven km (4 miles) to the west, up a steep, winding road—watch for the signpost—is the captivating seashore village of **Monte Clérigo.** Its back to stern, dark cliffs, it offers a bay of contrasting pleasures: the vast Atlantic shimmering from turquoise to blue to purple; a smooth, gleaming beach for sunbathers; and, when the standard northerly breezes are blowing, dramatic, rolling waves to delight a surfer's heart. The southwest triangle of main roads—linking Lagos with Vila do Bispo (and Sagres some 10 km/6 miles to the south), Vila do Bispo with Aljezur; and Aljezur, via Bensafrim on the N 120/IC 4, with Lagos—makes an agreeable round-trip tour.

EAST OF FARO

The character of the coast east of Faro, with its marshes and salt flats, is entirely different from that to the west. To Algarvios, this is the Sotavento, the leeward coast. Not only is the

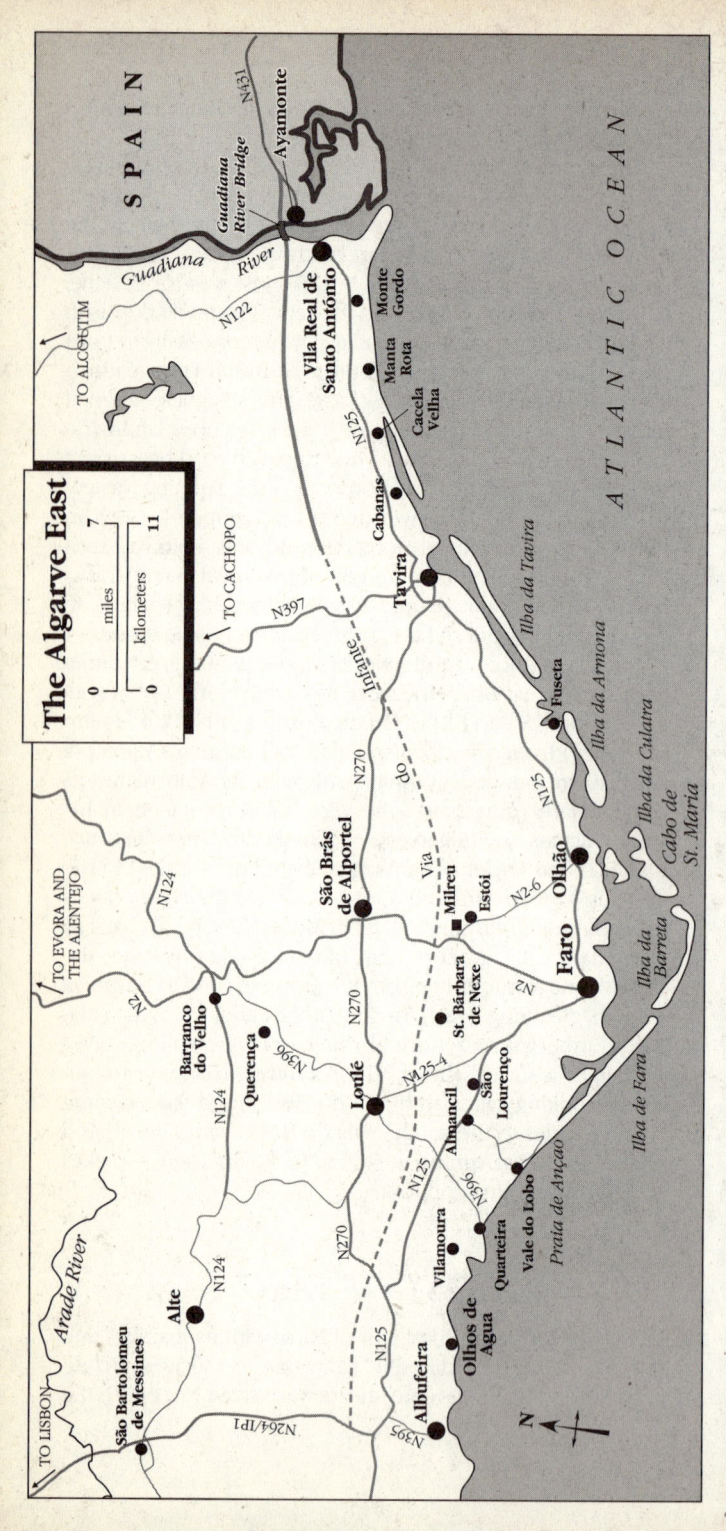

Sotavento in the lee of prevailing northerly winds, but a barrier reef keeps the ocean in some places a short boat ride away. The reef extends from Ançao beach west of Faro to just west of Manta Rota, a few miles from the Spanish border. It is the central feature of the 18,400-hectare (45,000-acre) **Parque Natural da Ria Formosa**, a wetlands zone of crucial importance to migrating birds. An unusually heavy winter rain can briefly turn lagoons an earthy red as suddenly engorged streams wash down to tidal traps. But most of the year, from such places as Cabanas, a fishing harbor and modest resort 5 km (3 miles) east of Tavira, or the tiny village of Cacela Velha (another 5 km to the east), you can see aquamarine colors in shallow lagoons, the crisp white border of ocean-facing beaches paler than those to the west, and the blue Atlantic beyond—an ever-changing vista that the windward Barlavento cannot match. You will find, too, that the Sotavento seawater is perceptibly warmer.

Yet the east has never been chic. By no coincidence its first golf course is only now in preparation. Tourism presses relatively lightly—most hotels (and a casino) are in mundane Monte Gordo, 50 km (31 miles) east of Faro and just 3 km (2 miles) west of Vila Real de Santo António and the Guadiana river frontier with Spain. In or near Tavira, a town of considerable charm and grace, there are no distinguished hotels, although you will find a selection of *pensões* in town and a few tourist villages and apartments for rent along the coast—the **Quinta do Caracol** on the western outskirts of Tavira has seven self-contained apartments, a pool, and tennis court. The **Eurotel Tavira**, within the Quinta das Oliveiras beside the N 125 about 2 km (1¼ miles) from Tavira, with swimming pool and tennis court, has taken on a new look with fresh paint; the spacious air-conditioned rooms have the feel of mini-suites. On the riverfront in Vila Real, with nearby Seville's Expo '92 as catalyst, the little, out-of-date **Hotel Guadiana** was transfigured to shining gem, its Neoclassical beauty and decor brought glossily to life.

A conjunction of an unravaged coast, of the wetlands park, of quiet farms and little-changed villages inland, the contrasts of ocean and river, and the cutting edge of history give the Sotavento its own indelible, low-key character. Of course there have been, and will be, changes. **Olhão**, an important fishing port 9 km (5½ miles) east of Faro, now has a computerized fish auction. Yet the cubist houses with their flat roof terraces that give the town its distinctive appearance are still home to hardy fishermen; the cobbled streets and market on the seashore drive, avenida 5 de Outubro, still have a traditional character; and the Baroque **parish church**, dating to 1698, still affords a panoramic view from the bell tower (take the steps through a door on the right-hand side of the church). At the back you will see a little chapel with wax ex-votos where fishermen's wives light candles and say prayers to Nossa Senhora dos Aflitos (Our Lady of Suffering). Olhão has a record of heroic resistance in the Napoleonic invasion, and when the French were forced to withdraw from the Algarve, a 17-meter boat crewed by Olhão men sailed the Atlantic in 1808 to carry the news to Portugal's exiled ruler, prince regent Dom João (later King João VI) in Rio de Janeiro. Prizes were handed out, medals struck, and Olhão's name (it means "big eye") expanded to Vila de Olhão da Restauração (Olhão of the Restoration).

In the summer months Olhão's principal attractions are out to sea: the beaches of the off-lying islands of **Armona** and **Culatra**. There is a year-round ferry service, intensified between June and September 30. The ride to Armona takes 20 minutes, to Culatra about 30 minutes, to Farol (at the western end of Culatra) 45 minutes. (Check at the pier east of the market by the GALP service station or at the Turismo in the municipal building.) The islands, very popular with youngsters, campers, and naturists, with bars and restaurants but no motorized traffic, have ample room for perfect isolation and privacy.

Fuseta, 11 km (7 miles) east of Olhão—the N 125 still the main coastal highway—is a small echo of Olhão. Here, too, a summer ferry takes vacationers to the offshore beach. Fuseta also has a particular distinction: Look at the lined faces of the elderly men you see—many of these Fusetans are the *lobos do mar* (sea wolves) who sailed each year to the cod banks of Newfoundland in the four-masted trawlers, *bacalhoeiros,* so admired by Captain Alan Villiers. Another 12 km (7½ miles) to the east, after the small town of Luz de Tavira (with a Renaissance church, its Manueline side portal virtually on the highway), you will come to Tavira itself.

Tavira

Admired by many travellers (James Michener among them) more than any other town in the Algarve, Tavira has among its merits a setting that links river with sea and island beach, a ruined castle that played a crucial role in Portuguese history, churches numerous and luminous, a distinctive architecture, bright boats old and new—and, above all in the context of the modern Algarve, the absence of ugly growth.

You can excuse the temporary bridge rushed into service when a support of the town's famous bridge, 17th-century with Roman origins, collapsed in 1989 in unusually heavy winter rains; all other town-center architecture is subject to close municipal control, rarer in Portugal than you might think.

In Tavira you will see well-proportioned houses topped by pyramidal Roman-tiled roofs. On the riverside road to the pier, across the water to your left, a derelict boatyard is all that remains of the celebrated tuna traps and the appalling "bullfight of the sea" in which the huge struggling fish were gaffed from foaming nets. (The last trap was abandoned in 1972.) The past is more fittingly preserved in the stones of the **castle walls**, from which you can see the river, called Gilão in Tavira, Séqua upstream, and the Ribeira de Alportel beyond that, as well as the town's tiled roofs and some of its distinguished churches. (The district total, Turismo might tell you, is 27; there are 18 in town, many closed. The tourist office, in the heart of town in a new building on rua da Galeria, just up the steps from the town hall and facing the Misericórdia church, will probably give you a map that lists nine. There is often a note on church doors to announce when Sunday mass will be held.)

The three-naved **Misericórdia church**, the Algarve's finest example of Renaissance art, has a portal from the 1540s, and panels of *azulejos* (decorative tiles), angels, and gargoyles. Concerts, not religious services, are held here. The **church of Santa Maria do Castelo** (open afternoons), built on the ruins of a mosque, encapsulates the town's dramatic past. Although much of what you see was rebuilt after the 1755 earthquake, in this church are the tombs of Dom Paio Peres Correia and the seven Christian knights whose slaughter by Moors he avenged in his capture of the town in 1242. Here, too, King João I knighted his sons after their conquest of Ceuta. The oddly shaped **Igreja das Ondas**, a trapezoidal fishermen's Church of the Waves dating to the 16th-century reign of King Manuel the Fortunate, is unfortunately usually closed. In the **Carmo** church—the key (*chave*) is kept opposite the church—you can observe the extravagant decoration of the dome and the splendid 18th-century chairs of the choir. The chapel of **Nossa Senhora da Consolação**, with 17th-century polychrome tiles, is usually open. In the chapels of **São Paulo** (if the church is open) you can see elaborate Baroque carvings.

All of these churches (and more) can be found in a gentle wander of the town. The castle, as well as Misericórdia and the tourist office, is up easy steps across the road from the town hall. There is some parking space in the town center. Close by, the long-established **Imperial** restaurant on the riverside rua José Pires Padinha offers typical Portuguese cooking; (Tel: 081-223-06). Farther downriver is the stone-decorated **O Caneção** (Tel: 081-819-21); specialties include *canja do mar* (seafood broth), *arroz de marisco* (shellfish and rice), *cataplana de tamboril* (described as monkfish hot-pot), and *perna de borrega à Tavira* (leg of lamb). The **Avenida**, at the corner of travessa Zacarias Guerreiro as you walk up the rua da Liberdade, is quieter, among its special-ties *espetada de tamboril* (monkfish on a spit); Tel: (081) 811-13. For dinner only, alfresco on the river's eastern bank, you might try the **Beira Rio**, which offers good international cuisine; Tel: (081) 231-65. And if you are yearning for a juicy steak, hot dogs or burgers, chili or a salad, you'll find them at **Lawns American Restaurant**, at 16 avenida Mateus Teixeira (Tel: 081-32-42-87), a little way behind the town hall. It's right next door to **Uncle Sam's** bar, which is open from 7:00 P.M. to early morning.

A good beach on Tavira island is reached by ferryboat from the pier beyond the salt flats. The oddly named Homem Nu (Naked Man) is another, more isolated, beach. In summer a minitrain with a quaint engine makes minitrips across the lagoon (or you can walk) across a footbridge at Pedras d'El Rei, a resort on the outskirts of **Santa Luzia**, a fishing village just west of Tavira.

East of Tavira, at **Cabanas** (note the elegant simplicity of the Conceição de Tavira parish church façade soon after you turn off from the N 125), you can rent a terraced apartment right on the lagoon (**Apartamentos Turísticos Cabanas Ria**, with a flower-filled atrium), walk across to a magnificent beach at low tide—or watch the clamdiggers do just that—and catch a fisherman's boat across the shallow lagoon at high water.

Along this stretch of coast you can get delicious oysters (sometimes lightly steamed to open the shell), cockles, whelks, clams, and razor clams. You can eat them straight from the sea, in modest restaurants where paper tablecloths are de rigueur, like the little **Restaurante Pedro**, near the fishermen's beach in Cabanas; across from the pump and 16th-century parish church in the tiny fort village of **Cacela Velha** (its big moment was when a force landed there in 1833 during Portugal's War of the Two Brothers); or—keep an eye out on the small coast road for the sign—at the beachside restaurant **Costa** at Fábrica, where *arroz de lingueirão* (rice and razor clams in an herby tomato sauce) is popular with the Portuguese families who flock to the Sotavento in summer (Tel: 081-95-14-67).

At **Manta Rota**, a small holiday resort a few kilometers east, the lagoons make way for open sea and vast sandy beaches. **Monte Gordo** is the easternmost beach resort, its long, pale strand the lure for a few high-rise apartment blocks, a casino, restaurants, souvenir shops, and hotels, including the pleasant four-story seashore **Hotel Vasco da Gama** with a pool and garden terraces, and the eight-story **Hotel Alcazar** with a large pool and Oriental touches to its decor. Far higher (16 stories), broader, and brasher is the new **Aparthotel Neptuno**, a huge building with a roofline stepped like a giant's stairway, three swimming pools, shopping center, sports facilities, and health club. Another new aparthotel, in a tasteful, low-key (three-story) style, is the **Aparthotel Montesol**. As along the rest of the coast, beach bar-restaurants are popular—**Jopel**, next to the casino, offers good cooking in an agreeable, airy setting.

Five kilometers (3 miles) to the east of Manta Rota (by an inner duneside road or the N 125) is **Vila Real de Santo António**, a fishing port and frontier town on the shores of the Guadiana river—and longtime ferry port facing Spain. Now open 6 km (3½ miles) upriver is an eye-catching bridge, its two tall towers and wings of cables sharply conspicuous against a quiet landscape. By this new road link with Spain, Vila Real is bypassed, yet it is a town of considerable interest.

The particular distinction of Vila Real de Santo António is that, after the 1755 earthquake, Portugal's great statesman, the marquês de Pombal, adapted the elegant classical grid plan devised for Lisbon to this Algarve town. Vila Real rose again in an astonishing five months, neat, clean, stylish, and focused around a central square paved in a radiating sunburst design. The shops in town are often full of Spanish housewives from Ayamonte across the river buying up Portugal's good, cheap linen. On the waterfront a short walk downriver from the prettily refurbished Hotel Guadiana, **António Mendonça**'s restaurant has a range of shellfish and fresh fish (avenida da República, 65; Tel: 081-430-89). You will see on many menus *bife de atum* (tuna steak), almost invariably deliciously cooked in an onion-and-tomato-based sauce, from fish caught nowadays out at sea as far away as the Azores.

From Vila Real it is only 4 km (2½ miles) inland on the N

122 to **Castro Marim**, a small town rising from salt flats and marshland, dominated by a grandly historic **ruined castle**, a fort, and a striking church. In the 14th century, before its transfer to Tomar, the Order of Christ was headquartered here. The huge walls of the castle built by King Afonso III allow a bird's-eye view of the one-story town houses with their singularly harmonious architecture and the flatlands stretching to Spain. On a hill facing Castro Marim sits the squat Forte de São Sebastião, built by King João IV in the mid-17th century to defend his newly restored throne.

The national parks service has a weekday facility here and can provide information on the Sapal de Castro Marim, a protected wetland area beside the river.

A feature for nature lovers are two former customs posts converted to tourist accommodation. The two **Centros de Acolhimento**—one called Seixo (pronounced SAY-show), the other Rocha—can each hold six people. The simple, stone-terraced houses are equipped with kitchens, bathrooms with hot and cold water, and linen. You need to take only your own food and drinking water. Seixo—the beds here are three double-tiered bunks in a single room—is on a rise with broad views of frontier Portugal and Spain. Rocha, with regular beds and separate bedrooms, is right at the river's edge. The new bridge astride the Guadiana distracts hardly at all from the peace of this wetland, particularly lovely in winter and spring.

From Vila Real you can take a riverboat cruise up the Guadiana, which along its lower stretch forms the border with Spain. Or a pleasant drive north (38 km/24 miles) from Vila Real on the N 122 takes you to **Alcoutim**, a river town of some charm with a Renaissance church, flowing lines of red rooftops, and a ruined castle. A quiet and beautiful 19-km (12-mile) riverside drive (1063) joins the N 122 just south of Odeleite. In Alcoutim there is a tourist information office just below the main square. A 30-room *estalagem* (inn), with a youth hostel behind and the river stretching gloriously in front, has been quietly developing. Restaurant meals are available, and refreshments are served by the cafés in the small town square. A few steps down, overlooking the river, **O Soeiro**, a snack-bar restaurant, has cozy and clean upstairs dining rooms. In **Azinhal**, on the way north, about 13 km (8 miles) from Vila Real, black-clad women still make real lace, *renda de bilros,* the old-fashioned way with bolster and bobbins; at Odeleite, 8 km (5 miles) farther on, men weave baskets with split cane. If the 20th century seems remote in the unpretentious eastern Algarve, you will nonetheless observe that virtually every little house, though it may lack running water, has television. And everyone you might engage in conversation has an opinion on current affairs, which include significant changes in this quiet world. Golf courses are coming, and, on the banks of the Foupana, a tributary of the Odeleite, a 560-acre wildlife reserve and safari resort is being created. At its heart will be the luxurious Hotel Lobo Ibérico. The rare Iberian wolf (*lobo*), once common across wild hills and heathland, will be back in the Algarve.

INLAND: THE HILL TOWNS

The Algarve is a great deal more than a coastal strip. Inland terrain (the hills of the *barrocal* and the *serras*) has been little touched by tourism. The more widely you explore—and on the tarmac roads, even where these are poorly maintained, no slope, no route is daunting—the stronger will be the contrasts with overgrown coastal resorts. Even the new homes of returned emigrants are startling in villages that seem rooted in an ancient landscape. Distances seem greater than they really are. Seasons change the colors. Away from people, trees take on another personality. The arbutus, flowering in winter, is the Algarve mistletoe. You will see hosts of great, evergreen carobs, the *alfarrobeira,* its biblical crop of long black beans (they sustained John the Baptist in the desert) having many uses to industry. Lowland orange groves, almonds, and figs make way for upland cork oaks, pine, and the strongly scented eucalyptus. You will see irrigation by *nora,* a waterwheel chain of buckets, and by electronically controlled sprinklers. And in spring you will see hillsides of white and pink rock roses, fields of wildflowers, an enchanting wild Algarve an easy drive from high-rise horrors in unendearing empires of concrete.

Inland towns and villages, too, have a character astonishingly different from that of the communities beside the sea. You will find people in the cobbled village of **Cachopo**, in the sparse rolling hills 40 km (25 miles) north of Tavira (on a winding N 397), who have never seen the sea. Who, they might ask, would tend their animals if they went? Cachopo is also situated on the Algarve's innermost east–west road, the N 124 that extends from just near Alcoutim in the east, past

Silves to Portimão, a circuitous route with long, repetitive stretches. A place to pause might be **Querença**, a hilltop village 8 km (5 miles) south of that road, after a turn about 8 km west of the crossroads village of Barranco do Velho. Querença's village square is dominated by a plump white church with Baroque interior features. Beside it, the village bar, café, and restaurant has good local cooking. (Via the N 396, Querença is only 10 km/6 miles from Loulé.)

The better, shorter, and more scenically varied east–west road is the N 270 linking Tavira with São Brás de Alportel, Loulé, and the coast near Albufeira. In São Brás there is the hilltop country house **Pousada de São Brás**, and, in the Casa da Cultura António Bentes, a modest **Museu Etnográfico** displaying Algarve traditional costumes. Already linking with the N 270 in the east and the more southerly N 125 are stretches of a new trans-Algarve expressway, the IP 1 (also called the Via do Infante), linking Spain to Sagres. Planned to relieve the pressure of traffic on the busy coastal N 125, it runs roughly parallel to it but a short distance inland. The 1993 objective: completion as far west as Guia, close to Albufeira.

On the farther inland N 124, 47 km (29 miles) from remote Cachopo—though, like Querença, reached more easily from Albufeira or Loulé—you will find, 24 km (15 miles) northwest of Loulé, in a setting remarkably different from the desolate eastern hills, the small hill town of **Alte**. A contest in the 1930s awarded Alte the title of the Algarve's most typical village, though passing time has inevitably imposed changes. One kilometer from the white houses rising steeply on the hillside are streams, small waterfalls, and trees. Favorite picnic places for visitors are at the nearby tree-shaded Fonte Grande. Here, carved in stone, and on tile panels along the short poet's walk steps away at Fonte Pequena, are the lyrical verses of village poet Cândido Guerreiro (1871–1953), their serenity predating the afflictions of tourism. Also within walking distance, *típico* restaurants overlook the less-than-sparkling Ribeira de Alte. In summer the Fonte Pequena restaurant arranges "medieval" banquets and folklore evenings (Tel: 089-682-29). The town's richly adorned parish church, part of it dating to the 16th century, has a Manueline portal and masterly *azulejos* of several styles from the early 18th century. If you prefer natural to church vaults, there is a stalagmite cavern, the *igrejinha* (little church) or Gruta das Soidos (Cavern of Noises—bat noises), a drive of 3 km (2 miles) above Alte and then a short walk on a rough track.

Silves

Of inland towns much the most historic (and handiest) is Silves, situated only 7 km (4 miles) north of Lagoa or a winding 20 km (12 miles) if you take the N 124 west of Portimão. Silves is dominated by its **castle**, marking the Moors' hold on Portugal for five centuries beginning in 711. The red sandstone has also more than once reminded historians of blood spilled in the 1189 siege of the Muslim citadel by brutish Crusaders serving King Sancho I. Two years later the Moors were back; only in the middle of the 13th century were they finally driven from the Algarve.

You can walk the castle walls and enjoy the gardens, the great cistern, and the view. Cramped streets will remind you of an Arab souk, but it is hard to see Silves as the Yemenite-built city Xelb, or Chelb, which one historian described as "ten times more remarkable for the opulence and sumptuosity of its buildings than Lisbon"; that cosmopolitan capital of southern Iberia was also praised by the Arab traveller Idrisi for its elegance and culture. The Arade river, once home to a fine port and shipyard, is now a shallow stream, the old Roman bridge across it replaced with a newer one. The cathedral, steps below the castle, its power shorn when the bishopric went to Faro in 1579, has but a modest architecture, Gothic transept, chancel arches, and its dignity. Even the remains of King João II, buried here after his death at Alvor in 1495, were removed a few years later.

Yet treasures more ancient have returned, to a brand-new **Museu Municipal de Arqueologia**, built over a deep Moorish well in the old town on rua da Porta de Loulé, just inside the great red stone archway. Among items displayed are pieces from the long era of Moorish grandeur. You may drive right to the castle and cathedral but will see more of old Silves by walking up through its narrow streets.

Silves has a modern life—shops, a cork factory, modest restaurants with Portuguese cooking, chicken barbecued with a hot *piri-piri* sauce (a cheap local favorite at restaurants by the Roman bridge). For shellfish at good prices, head for **Rui,** a cheerful *restaurante marisqueira* (specializing in seafood) at rua Comendador Vilarinho, 23, down the hill from the archway and fountain (Tel: 082-44-26-82), or Rui's new and expanded *marisqueira* in his brand-new four-star hotel, the **Albergaria Solar dos Mouros** (Tel: 082-44-31-06). Just across the Arade river, with a stunning view of the town and castle, it is the first modern, air-conditioned hotel in Silves. In March Silves holds a national citrus fair celebrating its successful centuries of orange growing; at the annual July beer festival you can taste, within the castle, the local beers accompanied by the celebratory sounds of fellow beer drinkers, folk music, pop, and rock. You might like to bear in mind that fairs everywhere are public and free. Large festivals usually demand an entry fee; village *festas* are less commercial and more fun.

Monchique

For many visitors, inland Algarve means a trip to Monchique, a drive west and north from Silves of 28 km (17 miles) on the N 124 and N 266. The route takes you past farms and vineyards up into forests of cork oak, olive, pine, sweet chestnuts, acacias, arbutus, and the inescapable eucalyptus. At 6 km (3½ miles) below the town, tucked into a valley, is southern Portugal's only spa, **Caldas de Monchique** (open June 1 to October 31). Its hot springs have aided sufferers from rheumatism and respiratory and digestive problems since Roman times (though not poor dropsical King João II, who died at Alvor shortly after taking the waters). Rooms with bathroom are available at the thermal establishment's pousada-operated **Centro de Repouso**, a four-story modern block beside the bottling plant, or you can stay a few steps up the hill in the **Albergaria Velha**, also government managed, which has a restaurant and tree-shaded cobbled esplanade. Small shops animate the tiny town. Under the brick cathedral roof of **O Tasco**, or at log tables outside, you can order a smoked-sausage roll and buy a glass of wine or a draught beer. In a little marbled hall a few steps down the hill you can drink— free—glasses of the Monchique water.

Monchique has its worthy churches, as well as a ruined Franciscan monastery, **Nossa Senhora do Desterro**, that you can climb up to. For many, however, the town's attraction is as a crafts center. Shops smelling of pine and dry grasses are to be found on the approach and in the small town itself, one of them expanding into a spacious emporium. Quite a few carpenters and basket weavers, as well as quarrymen, foresters, pig-breeders, and small farmers, earn a living up in these mountains. The Serra de Monchique, with its cooler climate, is also a favorite retreat for foreign residents.

At **Fóia**, 8 km (5 miles) above Monchique, you are at the Algarve's highest point: 2,960 feet. Fóia itself is no more than a broad, bald mound supporting an unsightly clutter of low buildings and tall aerials making the most of an unrestricted sky. The compensating view, on a clear day, extends across the green hills of Portugal and out into the Atlantic. On the upper roads are several popular restaurants with open-air terraces. You might try the **Estalagem Abrigo da Montanha**, a chalet whose name means mountain shelter, with verdant terraces, accommodation above them, and good regional cooking. The stone that you see being cut across the valley is granitelike syenite. Another mountain retreat is **Mons Cicus**, down a lane to your left as you approach Fóia, a modern building with broad verandahs, two swimming pools, hard-surface tennis courts, and rooms from whose terraces the view grandly encompasses earth, trees, a distant sea, and sky.

Just below Monchique, if you take an eastward turn on N 267 and drive 8 km (5 miles) to Alferce, you will be on the wilder slopes of **Picota** (2,540 feet) with a view that has been described as among the most beautiful in Portugal. (Paved roads leading upward off this route soon become rough dirt tracks.) From Alferce you can return to Silves on N 1073, a minor road that leads to the village of Fornalha and south through a quiet river valley to rejoin the N 124 close to Odelouca. Or, to head west, 3 km (2 miles) below the turning to Alferce as you leave Monchique is the westbound road N 267 that takes you smoothly down a winding 29 km (18 miles) through forests and farmland via Marmelete to the west-coast town of Aljezur.

GETTING AROUND

Faro is the main airline gateway to the Algarve, served by international airlines, TAP Air Portugal, and, as Portugal's denationalization policies take hold, smaller Portuguese airlines. Air Columbus competes in chartering. At a price, you could call up an air taxi (from a Piper Cherokee 6 to a Falcon 20 or helicopter) from Avialgarve (in Lisbon, Tel: 01-848-1365; Fax: 01-849-6895; in Faro, Tel: 089-50-15-17; Fax: 089-50-13-14). TAP Air Portugal's fleet includes Boeing 727s, 737s, Lockheed L1011s, the A310 Airbus; the regional airline, Linhas Aereas Regionais (LAR), makes use of much smaller aircraft. From Lisbon to Faro on a regular TAP flight is 35 minutes, by smaller aircraft a few minutes more. Tourist travel also includes numerous charter flights, mainly from British airports directly to and from Faro. High-season flights are often fully booked.

By car, the most direct route south from Lisbon to Faro is across the big Tagus river bridge (signs say Sul-Ponte), toward Setúbal (which you bypass) on the motorway, then a new stretch past Alcácer do Sal to Grândola, both towns now also bypassed, where an expressway takes you past Ourique on the N 264/IP 1 to near Albufeira, a run of just over 300 km (190 miles). Other routes—the twisting, bending, old and time-worn N 2 north of São Bras de Alportel, lined with eucalyptus and arbutus, or the western N 120/IC 4 passing rugged heathland, farms, and dune-edged beach at Carrapateira—are freer of traffic. But, if you drive, take nothing for granted. These roads are travelled by fast predatory cars, slow painted carts drawn by mules in gorgeous, gaudy harness, and scream-ing motorbikes.

From Spain there are several road entry points north of the Algarve. In the Algarve the road route has been vastly improved by the opening in 1991 of the long-awaited bridge across the Guadiana, 6 km (3½ miles) north of the ancient frontier towns Vila Real de Santo António in Portugal and Ayamonte in Spain. The drive from Seville to Faro is now comfortably under three hours. The train station at Vila Real de Santo António is within steps of the ferryboat immigra-tion post. Ferries, their future uncertain, continue to make the 30-minute crossing from 8:00 A.M. to 8:30 P.M.

Trains, part of the national network, traverse the length of the coast from Vila Real do Santo António to Lagos—their prime disadvantage being that most stations are outside town. The journey from Vila Real to Faro (both with in-town stations) provides stunning sea views invisible from the road. From Lisbon, trains leave south of the river at Barreiro after a ferry ride from the big central praça do Comércio (which *Lisboetas* call Terreiro do Paço), price included in the train ticket. Forget the slow trains. A *rápido* train takes about four hours to Faro. Tunes (12 km/7½ miles north of Albufeira) is the Algarve main rail junction. The railways also offer excursions, among them the *Comboio Azul* (Blue Train), which will take you from Vila Real de Santo Antonio (or Faro) to Porto and back over a weekend.

Buses provide service on all major and most minor roads—timetables are usually available at each city terminus of the old Rodoviária Nacional (now a private regional bus company called Eva Transportes). Tour companies, includ-ing Mundial Turismo, run coaches twice a day from Lisbon to and from the Algarve; travel time is about four hours to the main terminus at Ferreiras, near Albufeira. The coaches let passengers off at other main centers. Excursions can be booked from most hotels.

To catch the full flavor of the Algarve, to make your own discoveries, going by car—especially now that two major new bridges (near Vila Real and near Portimão) and new roads have immeasurably eased travel from Spain to the west—is the simplest way to travel. Rental companies are numerous and competitive; if you must come in high summer, *not* the best time to explore unless you adore heat and are ready to risk holiday crowds, it's best to book well ahead.

ACCOMMODATIONS REFERENCE.

Rates given are projected 1993 prices for a double room, double occupancy. Price ranges span the lowest rate in the low season to the highest in the high season. Unless otherwise stated, rates include Continental breakfast. As prices are subject to change, always double-check before booking.

▶ **Albergaria Caza de São Gonçalo**. Rua Cândido dos Reis, 73, 8600 **Lagos**. Tel: (082) 76-21-71; Fax: (082) 76-39-27. 8,000$00–13,500$00. Closed November through April.

▶ **Albergaria Marina Rio**. Apartado 388, 8600 **Lagos**. Tel: (082) 76-98-59; Fax: (082) 76-99-60. 6,000$00–15,500$00 (sea view).

▶ **Albergaria Solar dos Mouros**. 8300 Silves. Tel: (082) 44-31-06; Fax: (082) 44-31-08. 6,000$00–8,000$00.

▶ **Albergaria Velha**. 8550 **Monchique**. Tel: (082) 922-04 or 922-05; Fax: (082) 939-20. 5,300$00–7,500$00.

▶ **Apartamentos Albufeira Jardim**. Cerro da Piedade, Apartado 2101, 8200 **Albufeira**. Tel: (089) 58-69-72; Fax: (089) 58-69-77. One-bedroom apartment: 4,785$00–19,250$00.

▶ **Apartamentos Turísticos Cabanas Ria**. Avenida 28 de Maio, 38, **Cabanas**, 8800 Tavira. Tel: (081) 204-64 or 203-35; Fax: (081) 206-88. Studio apartment: 3,500$00–8,200$00.

▶ **Aparthotel Montesol**. Rue de Ceuta. 8900 **Monte Gordo**. Tel: (081) 51-11-36; Fax: (081) 51-16-99. Two-person apartment: 6,000$00–12,000$00.

▶ **Aparthotel Neptuno**. Apartado 66, 8900 **Monte Gordo**. Tel: (081) 51-19-81; Fax; (081) 51-15-51. Two-person apartment: 8,000$00–20,000$00.

▶ **Casa do Pinhão**. Praia do Pinhão, 8600 **Lagos**. Tel: (082) 76-23-71; Fax: (01) 858-3144. Double room: 13,000$00; suite: 14,000$00.

▶ **Casabela Hotel**. Vale da Areia, **Ferragudo**, 8400 Lagoa. Tel: (082) 46-15-80; Fax: (082) 46-15-81. 12,000$00–23,000$00 (sea view).

▶ **Centro de Repouso, Estabelecimento Termal das Caldas de Monchique**. 8550 **Monchique**. Tel: (082) 922-04 or 922-05. 3,750$00–4,500$00.

▶ **Centros de Acolhimento**. Reserva Natural de Sapal do Castro Marim e Vila Real de Santo António, Castelo da Vila, 8950 **Castro Marim**. Tel: (081) 53-11-41; Fax: (081) 53-12-57.

Seixo: per person: 600$00; for the house: 3,600$00. *Rocha:* double room: 1,950$00; for the house: 3,900$00.

▶ **Dunas Douradas.** Sitio do Garrão, Apartado 164, 8135 **Almancil.** Tel: (089) 39-63-23 or 39-62-97; Fax: (089) 39-63-71. Two-bedroom apartment: 6,250$00–28,000$00 (discounted for one couple).

▶ **Estalagem Abrigo da Montanha.** Estrada da Fóia, 8550 **Monchique.** Tel: (082) 921-31 or 927-50; Fax (082) 936-60. 9,000$00–12,000$00.

▶ **Eurotel Tavira.** Quinta das Oliveiras, 8800 **Tavira.** Tel: (081) 32-50-41; Fax: (081) 32-55-71. 7,000$00–12,500$00.

▶ **Fortaleza do Beliche.** 8650 **Sagres,** Tel: (082) 641-24; Fax: (082) 642-25. 9,800$00. Closed November 15 to end of December.

▶ **Hotel Alcazar.** Rua de Ceuta, 8900 **Monte Gordo.** Tel: (081) 51-21-84; Fax: (081) 51-22-42. 8,500$00–20,000$00.

▶ **Hotel Algarve.** Avenida Tomás Cabreira, **Praia da Rocha,** 8500 Portimão. Tel: (082) 41-50-01; Fax: (082) 41-59-99; in U.S. and Canada, Tel: (800) 223-5652; in U.K., Tel: (0800) 28-93-92. 14,500$00–36,000$00.

▶ **Hotel Alvor Praia.** Praia dos Três Irmãos, **Alvor,** 8500 Portimão. Tel: (082) 45-89-00; Fax: (082) 45-89-99; in U.S. and Canada, Tel: (800) 448-8355. 20,600$00–27,800$00.

▶ **Hotel Atlantis.** Apartado 210, 8125 **Vilamoura.** Tel: (089) 38-99-77; Fax: (089) 38-99-62. 17,500$00–38,000$00.

▶ **Hotel da Baleeira.** 8650 **Sagres.** Tel: (082) 642-12; Fax: (082) 644-25. 5,000$00–15,000$00.

▶ **Hotel Bela Vista.** Avenida Tomás Cabreira, **Praia da Rocha,** 8500 Portimão. Tel: (082) 240-55; Fax: (082) 41-53-69. 16,000$00–23,000$00.

▶ **Hotel Boa Vista.** Rua Samora Barros, 20, 8200 **Albufeira.** Tel: (089) 58-91-75; Fax: (089) 58-88-36. 10,000$00–22,500$00.

▶ **Hotel Dom Bernardo.** Rua General Teófilo da Trindade, 20, 8000 **Faro.** Tel: (089) 80-68-06; Fax: (089) 80-68-00. 12,650$00–13,800$00.

▶ **Hotel Dom Pedro Marina.** 8125 **Vilamoura.** Tel: (089) 38-98-02; Fax: (089) 31-32-70. Double room or junior suite: 16,000$00–27,000$00. More expensive senior suites: 31,000$00–48,000$00; double Jacuzzi suite: 50,000$00 to 75,000$00. Continental breakfast not included.

▶ **Hotel Dona Felipa.** Vale do Lobo, 8136 **Almancil.** Tel: (089) 39-41-41; Fax: (089) 39-42-88; in North America, Tel: (800) 225-5843. Double room: 32,100$00–46,600$00. Two-person junior suites: 40,950$00–59,400$00; deluxe suites: 72,850$00–106,000$00.

▶ **Hotel Golfinho.** Praia da Dona Ana, 8600 **Lagos.** Tel: (082) 76-99-00; Fax: (082) 76-99-99. 6,500$00–23,000$00.

▶ **Hotel Guadiana.** Avenida da República, 8900 **Vila Real de Santo António.** Tel: (081) 51-14-82; Fax: (081) 51-14-78. 8,000$00–11,000$00; two-person suite: 10,000$00–15,000$00.

▶ **Hotel Ibis.** N 125, Marchil, 8000 **Faro.** Tel: (089) 80-67-71; Fax: (089) 80-69-30. 8,000$00 (breakfast not included).

▶ **Hotel de Lagos.** 8600 **Lagos.** Tel: (082) 76-99-67; Fax: (082) 76-99-20. 12,000$00–25,400$00.

▶ **Hotel Oriental.** 8500 **Praia da Rocha.** Tel: (082) 41-30-00; Fax: (082) 41-34-13. Two-person apartment: 12,000$00–35,000$00.

▶ **Hotel Quinta do Lago.** 8135 **Almancil.** Tel: (089) 39-66-66; Fax: (089) 39-63-93; in North America, Tel: (800) 448-8355 or (800) 237-1236. Double room: 36,000$00–48,000$00. The hotel also has suites; the daily charge for the Presidential Suite, with its own swimming pool: 110,000$00–180,000$00.

▶ **Hotel La Réserve. Santa Bárbara de Nexe,** 8000 Faro. Tel: (089) 904-74; Fax: (089) 904-02. Studio suites: 28,000$00–40,000$00; duplexes: 30,000$00–44,000$00.

▶ **Hotel Rocamar.** Largo Jacinto d'Ayet, 8200 **Albufeira.** Tel: (089) 58-69-90; Fax: (089) 58-69-98. 6,500$00–15,500$00.

▶ **Hotel Sol e Mar.** Rua José Bernardino de Sousa, 8200 **Albufeira.** Tel: (089) 58-67-21; Fax: (089) 58-70-36. 10,000$00–20,000$00.

▶ **Hotel Vasco da Gama.** Avenida Infante Dom Henrique, 8900 **Monte Gordo.** Tel: (081) 51-13-21; Fax: (081) 51-16-22. 10,000$00–20,500$00.

▶ **Loulé Jardim Hotel.** Praça Manuel de Arriaga, 8100 **Loulé.** Tel: (089) 41-30-94; Fax: (089) 631-77. 7,000$00–8,500$00.

▶ **Mons Cicus.** Estrada da Fóia, 8550 **Monchique.** Tel: (082) 926-50; Fax: (082) 926-70. 10,000$00–15,000$00.

▶ **Monte do Casal.** Cerro do Lobo, **Estói,** 8000 Faro. Tel: (089) 915-03; Fax: (089) 913-41. Double room: 13,200$00–18,500$00; suite: 14,950$00–$26,500$00. Closed approximately December 8 through February 8.

▶ **Penina Golf and Resort Hotel.** 8502 **Portimão.** Tel: (082) 41-54-15; Fax: (082) 41-50-00; in North America, Tel: (800) 548-2323; in U.K., Tel: (0296) 43-28-61, Fax: (0296) 813-91. 26,500$00–45,000$00 (includes all sports fees plus buffet breakfast).

▶ **Pousada do Infante.** 8650 **Sagres.** Tel: (082) 642-22; Fax: (082) 642-25. 12,800$00–20,000$00.

▶ **Pousada de São Brás.** 8150 **São Brás de Alportel.** Tel. and Fax: (089) 84-23-05. 9,700$00–18,000$00.

▶ **Prainha.** Praia dos Três Irmãos, Apartado 25, Torralta, 8500 **Portimão.** Tel: (082) 45-85-61 or 45-87-51; Fax: (082) 45-95-69. Double apartment: 4,600$00–24,700$00.

▶ **Quinta da Alfarrobeira.** Estrada de Palmares, Odiáxere, 8600 **Lagos.** Tel: (082) 79-84-24. Double room or apartment: 6,000$00–10,000$00.

▶ **Quinta de Benatrite.** P. O. Box 17, **Santa Bárbara de Nexe,** 8000 Faro. Tel. and Fax: (089) 904-50. Double room or suite: 15,000$00.

▶ **Quinta do Caracol.** São Pedro, 8800 **Tavira.** Tel: (081) 224-75; Fax (081) 224-75. Apartments for double occupancy: 8,000$00–10,000$00; each extra bed: 1,500$00.

▶ **Residencial Ibérica.** Avenida Marçal Pacheco, 157, 8100 **Loulé.** Tel: (089) 41-41-00 or 41-53-30. 5,500$00–6,500$00.

▶ **Sheraton Algarve Hotel and Resort.** Pine Cliffs, **Praia da Falésia,** 8200 Albufeira. Tel: (089) 50-19-99; Fax: (089) 50-19-50; in U.S. and Canada, Tel: (800) 325-3535; in U.K., Tel: (0800) 35-35-35. Double room: 35,700$00–53,000$00; three types of suites: from 65,000$00–110,000$00 for the Diplomatic Suite.

▶ **Vila Joya. Praia da Galé,** Box 120, 8200 Albufeira. Tel: (089) 59-17-95; Fax: (089) 59-12-01; in Germany, Tel: (89) 649-3337; Fax: (89) 649-2636. Prices quoted are for half board—breakfast and dinner. Double room: 56,000$00–71,000$00; junior suite: 71,000$00–84,000$00.

▶ **Vilabranca Hotel Club.** P. O. Box 499, 8600 **Lagos.** Tel: (082) 76-99-24; Fax: (082) 76-75-58. 9,500$00–14,000$00.

▶ **Vilalara.** 8365 **Armaçao de Pêra.** Tel: (082) 31-49-10; Fax: (082) 31-49-56. Junior suites: 23,500$00–38,750$00; two-bedroom/two-bath apartments: 40,250$00–67,750$00; three bedrooms and three baths: 55,500$00–97,000$00.

▶ **Vilamoura Marinotel.** 8126 **Vilamoura.** Tel: (089) 38-99-88; Fax: (089) 38-98-69; in North America, Tel: (800) 448-8355. 19,800$00–38,500$00.

Pousadas can be booked through ENATUR, Avenida Santa Joana Princesa, 10, 1700 Lisbon, Portugal; Tel: (01) 848-1221 or 848-9078; Fax: (01) 80-58-46. But it is easier to make reservations through a travel agent. In the United States and Canada, pousadas can be booked through Marketing Ahead, 433 Fifth Avenue, New York, NY 10016. Tel: (212) 686-9213; Fax: (212) 686-0271.

Manor houses can be booked directly or through the manor-house associations—ANTER, P.I.T., PRIVETUR, and TURIHAB—listed in Useful Facts. Most of the houses belong to one or more of these associations, but because membership rosters change frequently we haven't attempted to spell out the associations for each house. Readers are advised to contact the manor-house associations for their current listings.

In the United States and Canada, it is possible to reserve rooms in P.I.T. manor houses through E & M Associates, 211 East 43rd Street, Suite 1404, New York, NY 10017; Tel: (212) 599-8280; Fax: (212) 599-1755.

BEIRA LITORAL

WEST CENTRAL PORTUGAL

By Marion Kaplan

The stout and stony midsection of Portugal, known collectively as the Beiras, is the historic core of the nation. Individually, they are three: on the Atlantic coast, the Beira Litoral, wrapped around the spirited city of Coimbra, and the two inland provinces of Beira Alta and Beira Baixa (the adjectives mean "upper" and "lower"). Here, nearly a thousand years ago, Portugal took root, flourished, and formed national borders that are virtually the same today. Yet it's an area less travelled than other regions. Geographically—even, in some ways, culturally—it's locked between the capital, Lisbon, to the south, and Portugal's second city, the northern port of Porto. And, sadly for the traveller, there has been a dearth of decent hotels.

Now at last things are on the move. You'll find comfortable accommodation, vastly improved roads, telephones that work. You will also still find, steps from the smooth highways, the true essence of old Portugal: towns and villages that have retained their traditions along with their ancient stone buildings, as well as a courteous people with strong family feeling. You'll see an underpopulated landscape of dramatic beauty and, removed from a world in perpetual tension, you will experience a rare sense of security.

Underpopulated? Not, certainly, in Coimbra, rising impressively from the northern bank of the Mondego River. Crowds throng the old streets, pavement hawkers shout their wares—peaches, panties, lottery tickets, fish—traffic presses from all sides, students pack the ancient university. Here, above all, you'll discover the essential Portugal.

The Beiras were part of the county of Portugal that Alfonso VI of León and Castile re-created between the Minho and Mondego rivers at the end of the 11th century, and in the next century (1139) Coimbra became the capital of the newly established kingdom of Portugal.

Coimbra is still the largest and most historically important city in Beira Litoral, but is only one reason to visit the region. The coastal (*litoral*) section is so candescent the tourist authorities call it the Costa de Prata—the Silver Coast. It is not clear if they are referring to the sheen of its waves, the shimmer of its sands, the gleam of the glassware of Marinha Grande and the porcelain of Vista Alegre, or the glint of the drying fish and the salt pans of Aveiro—all dazzling attractions along the coast tarnished only occasionally by ugly buildings and expanding commerce. For despite periodic editorials of protest in Coimbra's newspaper, *As Beiras,* development in Beira Litoral is hardly as extensive as in other parts of the country, and condominiums are not yet a major player in the province's centuries-old struggle with the shifting shoreline.

Nor should your visit be restricted to the coastline. Just inland are four mountain ranges: the Serra da Lousã east of Pombal in the south, the foothills of the Serra da Estrela east of Coimbra, the Serra do Caramulo in the northeast, and the Serra da Gralheira north of Aveiro, south of the Douro. The gray stones of their castles and hamlets and the green pines of their forests could tell tales of the bloody battles of both the Reconquest and the Peninsular War. Instead, in these great open spaces, you'll hear only a sweeping silence.

MAJOR INTEREST

Castelo de Leiria
Spectacular mountain scenery and bucolic charms of the Serra da Lousã
The romantic and historic university city of Coimbra
Roman excavations of Conímbriga
The fairy-tale forest of Buçaco
The canals and monuments of Aveiro
Natural and folkloric sights of the lagoon Ria de Aveiro

Your journey could begin in the south of the Beira Litoral with Leiria. After a visit to its castle you might head west for a

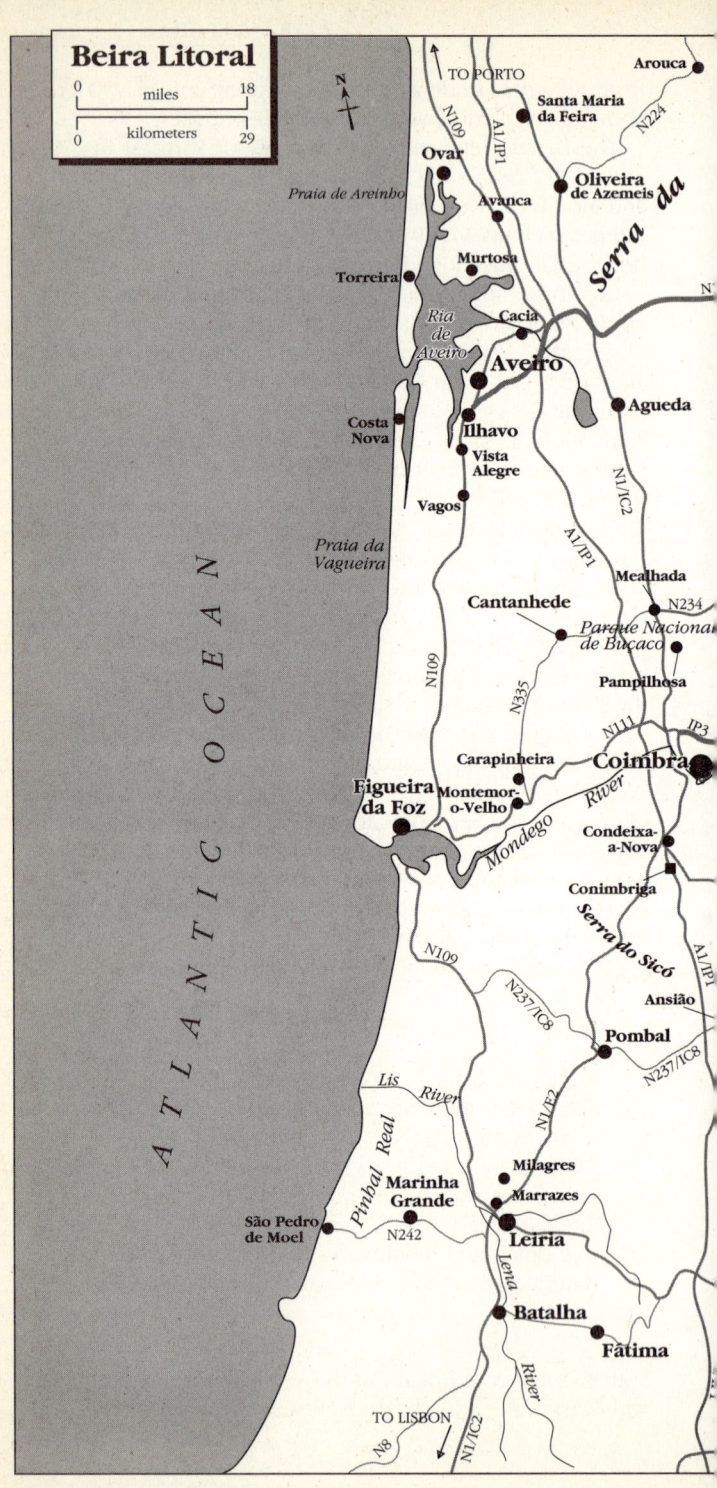

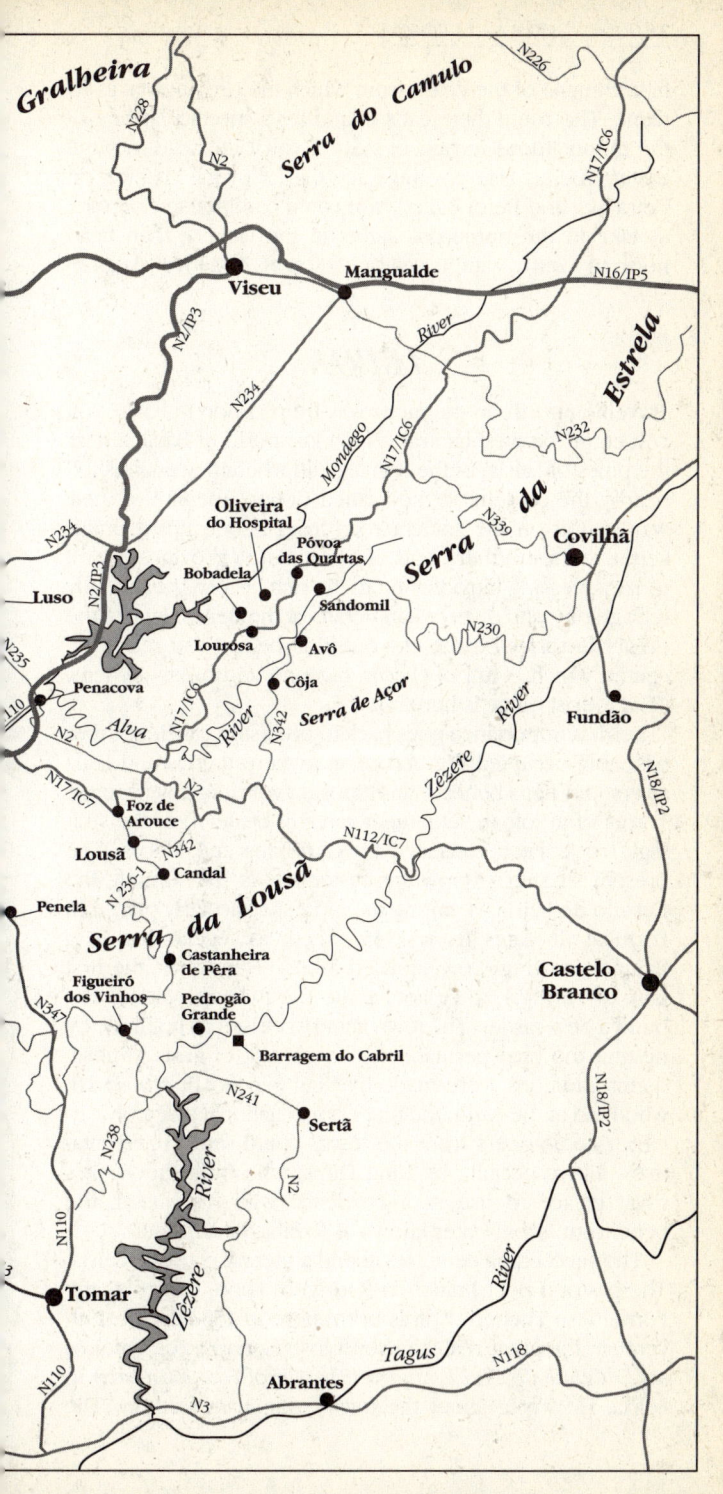

first glimpse of the coast, from which the province takes its name. The route then leads inland for a spectacular hint of the mountainous terrain in store if you later head into the eastern Beiras (for coverage see the following chapter, on Beira Alta and Beira Baixa). You could continue to Coimbra, to take in the numerous sights in the vicinity, then head north to Aveiro, with its celebrated canals and lovely lagoon.

LEIRIA

Travelling north on the motorway from Lisbon to Porto, you will enter the west central region just north of Batalha near the pines of Leiria, as the Romans did when they established nearby the settlement they called Colipo, the site of their way station on the ancient road from Lisbon up to Braga. Leiria, at the northern end of Estremadura province, is still today a pleasing introduction to the rich history, flat and hilly topography, and diverse handicrafts of the Beiras. Ignore the dreary factories on the city outskirts before you reach the center, which is full of charm, pigeons, and pretty gardens. (The tourist office is here, too.)

Leiria's importance goes back to prehistory; ancient tribes probably occupied the choice site where the Lis and Lena rivers join here beneath an imposing volcanic outcropping. Traces of a Roman settlement can still be seen on the strategic rock, later contested by Christians and Moors. The present structure sprawling custodially at the summit, the **Castelo de Leiria**, is among the most spectacularly placed in Portugal. It dates from 1135, when, as legend has it, a flapping, cawing crow signaled Afonso Henriques, the first king of Portugal, to recapture the site from the Moors and build a new castle. (The town later expressed its gratitude by nesting the bird permanently on its coat of arms.) Subsequent additions were made by King Sancho II, Afonso III, who held at the castle the first *Cortes* (national assembly), to which commoners from the towns could send representatives, and especially by King Dinis, who built the castle's royal palace to use as a residence with his queen, the beneficent Isabel (later known as Rainha Santa Isabel).

The succeeding centuries added a literary patina to Leiria. The pastoral poet Francisco Rodrigues Lobo, known as the Portuguese Theocritus, was born there in 1580. In the 19th century, the great realist novelist José Maria Eça de Queirós set *O Crime do Padre Amaro* (*The Sin of Father Amaro*) in Leiria. He wrote about the town's dominant feature: "The castle ruins stand out with a grand historic air, silhouetted against the sky and enveloped in the evening by the circling flight of owls."

Most of the owls have been driven away, however, for in recent years town fathers have taken to illuminating the castle at night, when it stands out golden against the black sky. Regardless of the hour, the castle is always the principal attraction of this trim, prim little district capital. You can drive up to its great portal. Inside, you'll have a splendid view of the surrounding countryside. Within its granite walls, too, are the remains of the 15th-century church of **Nossa Senhora da Pena,** its open roof and Gothic windows framing the sky. The royal palace is in better condition, and from its loggia there are fine views of the town. Best of all, however, is to climb up the creaky wooden stairs to the top of the keep; on a clear day the sweeping panorama extends as far south as the monastery of Batalha (see Day Trips from Lisbon) and west to the sea. Also westward lies the pine forest King Dinis planted to stabilize the land and furnish wood for the ships of Portugal, aptly described by early-20th-century Portuguese poet Afonso Xavier Lopes Vieira as "a green and whispering cathedral, where the light plays hide-and-seek." You may see local children doing the same in the grounds of the castle, while their older siblings exchange whispers and kisses between the battlements.

You may want to picnic on the castle grounds, but you can enjoy almost as panoramic a view with a lunch of such regional specialties as *morcelas de arroz* (black pudding with rice), local sausages, *brisas do Lis* (a sweet made of eggs and almonds), and *bolo do pinhão* (a cake made with pine nuts) at the **Hotel Eurosol restaurant,** rua Dom José Alves Correia da Silva.

If you are interested in shopping for crafts (baskets, coverlets, glassware, and pottery), you'll find them gathered in the district capital's shops from the surrounding area. Leiria's other sights include a 16th-century cathedral in praça Rodrigues Lobo, a square grandiloquently presided over by a statue of the 17th-century poet, and a provincial art museum and library in the town hall. Most interesting, though, is the 16th-century **Templo de Nossa Senhora de Encarnação** on a hill opposite the castle. The tiny chapel is the first of a number of pilgrimage spots, each celestially sited at the top of lofty staircases, that you will encounter as you work your way northward in Portugal.

If you care to stay, Leiria has several hotels, among them the new and entirely modern **Hotel Dom João III** and the

19th-century, four-story **Albergaria do Terreiro**, with a beautifully proportioned classical façade incorporating framed windows and iron balconies; rooms, though, have TV and air-conditioning. Both hotels are centrally located.

West to the Atlantic

An excursion into the **Pinhal Real**, King Dinis's pine woods, where you can watch the light play hide-and-seek on the trees and the sandy soil and where you will breathe in the scent of resin, can be conveniently combined with a trip to **Marinha Grande**, west from Leiria on N 242. The town developed in the 18th century when the marquês de Pombal permitted an Englishman, William Stephens, to cut down some of the king's trees to expand a glass factory he had purchased and establish the Real Fábrica de Vidros (Royal Glass Factory). Left to the state by William's brother, the Fábrica—later a factory and school—made fine crystal by the old methods for many years. The government's recent decision to close the famous factory, for entirely modern reasons of cost inefficiency, met with widescale mourning. There were hopes it would reopen. What did open in this bustling glass (and plastics) molds-making town, shortly before the tears and lamentations over the Stephens closure, is the attractive **Hotel Cristal** with an excellent restaurant, **O Vitral**. On the wide-ranging menu you'll find *pato à bigarade* (duck with bitter orange), good steaks, and *cherne com molho de anchovas,* a turbot-like fish in anchovy sauce.

Some 10 km (6 miles) farther west through the forest of pines, you will sight the Atlantic at the popular beach resort of **São Pedro de Moel**. Outside the high-season months of July and August, it's quiet, clean, and very pretty. Above the beach, with a bar and restaurant providing panoramic views, is the **Hotel Mar e Sol**. Its modern but modest seaside accommodations are also among the nicest on this stretch of the Costa de Prata. For more mountainous terrain, you might head northeast toward the Serra da Lousã, a preview of the spectacular pine-covered mountains characteristic of so much of the Beiras.

INTO THE SERRA DA LOUSA

If it's lunchtime when you start off on this leg of the journey, you might stop at the restaurant **Tromba Rija** (Tel: 044-320-72 or 324-21; reservations necessary for dinner; closed Sundays and Monday lunch) in the town of Marrazes, just north of Leiria. As its name, which means "hard snout," implies, regional dishes of roast pig, cured ham, and pork sausages are its specialties. Another restaurant with character is O **Cardápio do Visconde**, the former wine cellar of Marrazes's Quinta do Amparo (Tel: 044-81-27-14). Postprandial sightseeing is just up the country road to the northeast at **Milagres**, a tiny late-Baroque church filled with marble as well as *azulejos* (decorative tiles) lovingly depicting the miracles of a local resident's recovery after being injured in a fall from his donkey cart—an accident not unheard of here even today.

Heading northeast back on the main road, N 1/IC 2, you will soon spot **Pombal**, the town from which the influential minister Sebastião de Carvalho e Mello, known to posterity primarily for rebuilding Lisbon after the 1755 earthquake, took his title of marquês de Pombal before ending his years here in disgrace. (The town is said to have taken its name from the *pombos,* or pigeons, that once flocked around its castle.) Sacked during the French retreat in 1811 and more or less ignored from then on, Pombal has not fared much better than its marquis. Unless you are interested in surveying the Serra do Sicó and, beyond them, the Serra da Lousã from the top of its 12th-century **castle**, Pombal can easily be bypassed.

Turning east at Pombal onto N 237/IC 8, follow the twisting, panoramic road past Ansião (now N 237) to the mountains. Your next stop could be the hill town of **Figueiró dos Vinhos**, which has some fine 16th- and 17th-century monuments in the Igreja Matriz (Parish Church) and the convent of Nossa Senhora do Carmo. Farther east on a winding country road is the town of **Pedrógão Grande**, with its even older Igreja Matriz, dating from the 12th century. For sweeping views of the **Serra da Lousã**, continue on to the Barragem do Cabril, a nearby dam in the Zêzere river valley. Backtracking west and proceeding north on N 236-1, you will find one spectacular view after another as you wind through the attractive little town of Castanheira da Pêra and down past Candal with its fine roadside fountain.

The road (now N 236) then drops sharply down to **Lousã**, a stately town set in thick woods that has long attracted artists and architects, who have embellished it with fine 18th-century houses, a Renaissance misericord (hospice), and the rambling **Castelo de Arouce**, made of flaking layers of the local stone. Legend has it that around 79 B.C. a certain King Arouce sequestered his lovely daughter, the princess

Peralta, and his treasure in the castle while he journeyed to Carthage to seek help against invaders. Like the castle, however, the legend is somewhat in tatters, since no one knows what became of king, princess, or treasure. Yet thousands of treasure hunters have taken their toll on—if not treasure from—the castle, as romantic a ruin as it is bizarre, for it is situated quite defenselessly at the bottom of the valley.

Continuing northwest on the still minor N 236, you will then approach Coimbra, passing first through the little town of **Foz de Arouce**, with its respectable 18th-century residences.

COIMBRA

Coimbra, beloved by its citizens and cherished by all Portuguese as a fount of *portugalidade,* for years has frustrated travellers hoping to stay comfortably, eat well, and see all there is to see in this ancient capital, birthplace of six of Portugal's first kings. For whatever reason, the lively university city suffered from a severe lack of decent hotels. The good news is that Coimbra's catching up. You still can't be sure of arriving to find an ample choice of accommodation, but at least there are now more and better hotels.

The **Hotel Tivoli** has opened up on the west side of the city, the **Hotel Dom Luís** is on the southern approach with a panoramic view across the Mondego to old Coimbra, and even the charming Belle Epoque **Hotel Astória** on the riverfront near the Santa Clara bridge was thoroughly refurbished in 1990. Outside the city, the **Casa dos Quintais**, a manor house with three rooms, garden, pool and view, is just to the south. (Dinner isn't served here; the difficult winding and hilly approach on narrow lanes might deter drivers who enjoy a cocktail and wine with their food.) With accommodation secured, you can relax and explore Coimbra's impressive sights.

Hans Christian Andersen, who visited Portugal in 1866 and had the proper imagination to appreciate the fantastical aspects of the city, wrote: "Coimbra is a place where one should stay not just a few days, but several weeks, live with the students, fly out to the lovely open country around, give oneself up to solitude and let memory unroll pictures from legend and song, from the history of this place." Few travellers have the time to linger and after a day or two of sightseeing, unless you have other projects there's no need to.

Coimbra was founded in prehistoric times, on the

Alcáçova hill above the Mondego river. It took its present name from the nearby Roman settlement of Conímbriga (see below), though its original Roman name was Aeminium. The Mondego, unlike the Tagus and the Douro, runs its entire course in Portugal, and has been so frequent a theme in Portuguese literature it is also known as O Rio dos Poetas (The River of Poets). Its university, founded in Lisbon in the 13th century and transferred to Coimbra, was the only one in Portugal until the beginning of this century. The purest Portuguese is still said to be spoken in Coimbra. Through the ages the city has attracted many of Portugal's most important religious, artistic, intellectual, and political figures, among them Portugal's epic poet Luís de Camões, Lisbon's beloved Santo António (Saint Anthony of Padua), the novelist Eça de Queirós, and the longtime dictator António de Oliveira Salazar.

Too bad that another essentially Portuguese characteristic in Coimbra, the horrendous traffic, is not as intangible as the pure search for knowledge. Entering the city from the south, via the N 1/IC 2 or perhaps the A 1/IP 1 motorway—both lead to the Ponte Santa Clara—you will probably have more than sufficient time to take in the view of the white-walled, terra-cotta–roofed city rising on the Alcáçova hill above you. Park, if you can, on avenida Emídio Navarro or in the lot (keep some coins for the meter) at the beginning of rua do Brasil.

The Upper Town

For an overview of the city head for the **university**, one of the oldest in the world, and so situated you can see it from almost anywhere. Though large academic institutions exist in Lisbon and Porto and others have been established throughout the country, when the Portuguese speak of the Lusa Atenas, or Lusitanian Athens, they are referring to the university at Coimbra. On foot, it is reached by negotiating the steep medieval street called Couraça de Lisboa up the Alcáçova hill—the Acropolis of Lusa Atenas—to praça de Dom Dinis, where a statue of King Dinis regally welcomes you. Contrary to what Camões wrote in *The Lusiads,* that "Dinis was the first to make of Coimbra a seat of learning and to induce the Muses to leave Mount Helicon for the gentle swards of the Mondego," the king actually founded the university at Lisbon in 1290. For years the two cities swapped the seat of the country's learning back and forth, until in 1537 it finally found a permanent home in Coimbra.

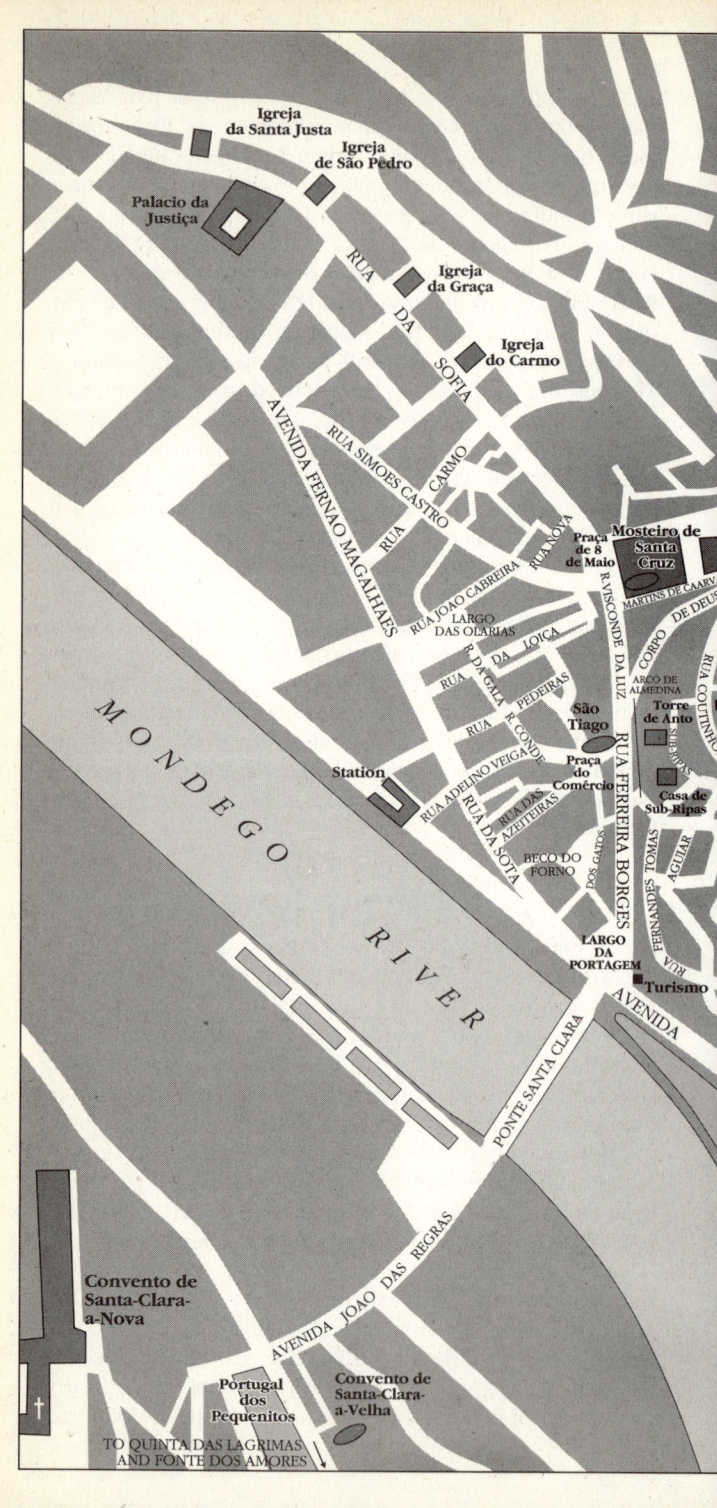

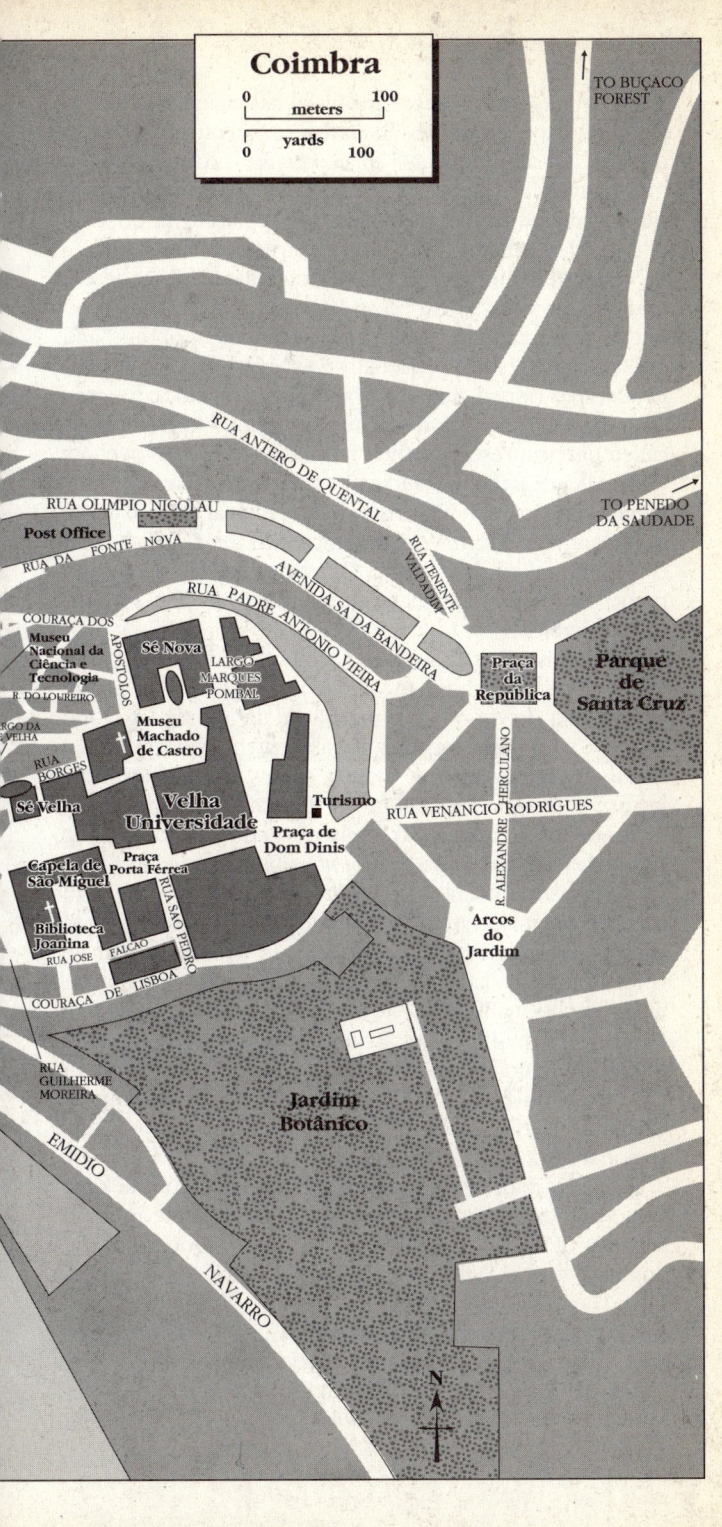

Coimbra

0 — meters — 100

0 — yards — 100

TO BUÇACO FOREST

RUA ANTERO DE QUENTAL

RUA OLIMPIO NICOLAU

Post Office

RUA DA FONTE NOVA

RUA TENENTE VALADIM

TO PENEDO DA SAUDADE

AVENIDA SÁ DA BANDEIRA

RUA PADRE ANTÓNIO VIEIRA

COURAÇA DOS APOSTOLOS

Museu Nacional da Ciência e Tecnologia

R. DO LOUREIRO

Sé Nova

LARGO MARQUES POMBAL

Praça da República

Parque de Santa Cruz

RGO DA VELHA

RUA BORGES

Museu Machado de Castro

Sé Velha

Velha Universidade

Turismo

Praça de Dom Dinis

RUA VENANCIO RODRIGUES

R. ALEXANDRE HERCULANO

Capela de São Miguel

Praça Porta Férrea

RUA SÃO PEDRO

Arcos do Jardim

Biblioteca Joanina

RUA JOSE FALCÃO

COURAÇA DE LISBOA

RUA GUILHERME MOREIRA

Jardim Botânico

EMIDIO

NAVARRO

N

The marquês de Pombal reorganized its academic structure when he expelled the Jesuits in the 18th century. Two hundred years later, Salazar—an economics professor at the university before he became dictator—reorganized its physical structure with the much-criticized replacement of some of the older buildings with modern structures.

Student life at the university is bohemian and steeped in tradition, as you can expect in Portugal. The students, who Andersen remarked a century ago "reminded us of Faust and Theophrastus," still occasionally wear black frock coats beneath capes ripped, they claim, with each romantic conquest. They also at times adorn themselves with colored ribbons called *fitas,* representing their faculties—red for law, yellow for medicine, light blue and white for sciences, dark blue for letters, and violet for pharmacy. Each May, near the end of the academic year, fourth-year students burn their ribbons in a ceremony called the Queima (Burning) das Fitas, the high point of a week of student celebrations equally popular with nonacademics.

Many university students in Coimbra live in the Alta, the city's upper reaches, in residences called *repúblicas,* groups of a dozen or so, usually from the same part of the country, who band together to take part in the rigors and revelry of academic life. Rigor comes as much in the lecture halls as in the seniority system on which the *repúblicas* are based; revelry takes place when the students sing serenades of *fado. Fado de Coimbra* became distinguished from its Lisbon counterpart in the first quarter of the 19th century. Its major local practitioner at the time, Augusto Hilário, established the Coimbra form by having a male voice sing the ballads—the lyrics usually mournfully romantic or intellectually witty—to the rhythms of the traditional 12-string Coimbra guitar. In the school year (other than during the Queima das Fitas), *fado* can be heard occasionally at the **Boémia** bar (rua do Cabido, 6) or regularly at **Trovador** (largo da Sé Velha, 15), which is also a fine regional restaurant; see more on it below.

From praça de Dom Dinis (where the statue of the king, some say justly, turns its back on the fortress-like modern faculties of arts, physics, and mathematics), proceed to the entrance to the **Velha Universidade** (Old University Building). The 17th-century Porta Férrea (Iron Gate) opens onto the Patio do Paço das Escolas, a dusty, car-filled courtyard where new students take part in ancient initiation rites. The jangly Baroque clock tower in front of you is affectionately known by the students as *a cabra* (the goat). It dates from the early 18th century and has become the symbol not only of the university but also of Coimbra, appearing on everything from ceramics to sugar packets throughout Portugal. The staircase to your right leads to the via Latina, a loggia so named because Latin was once the only language spoken by its thoughtful promenaders. The arcaded walk passes the Sala dos Capelos, where degrees are conferred beneath an ornately painted ceiling and the watchful eyes of the kings of Portugal, whose portraits line the walls. It then leads to a terrace with a lovely view of the lower city and the Mondego. Upstairs are more ornate chambers—the Reitoria (Rectory) and the Sala do Exame Privado, which has a portrait gallery of stern-visaged university rectors.

Returning to the courtyard, go past the clock tower and enter the **Capela de São Miguel**, where a Manueline portal leads to a sumptuous interior. The chapel's showpiece is a Baroque organ decorated with *talha dourada,* the gilded wood typical of the period throughout the Portuguese empire, when Brazil's mines filled the king's coffers. Of more local inspiration are the side altars, masterpieces of Coimbra Rococo.

Next to the chapel is the **Biblioteca Joanina**, built by King João V in the early 18th century, one of the most magnificent Baroque libraries in the world. Dom João's coat of arms hangs over the entrance, which leads to three huge halls embellished with chinoiserie, *talha dourada,* false perspective ceilings, *faux marbre* pilasters, and an inlaid marble floor. Though in such sumptuous company the thousands of books and manuscripts seem merely part of the decorative scheme, you'll be gratified to hear that they may be read and referred to by students.

A short walk down from the university at the largo da Feira is the **Sé Nova** (New Cathedral), which actually dates from the end of the 16th century. It is enough to admire its ornate façade, which echoes the luxury of the former episcopal palace across the street, and then visit the latter structure. The palace is now the **Museu Machado de Castro**, though its luxurious courtyards and loggias bespeak its former function more strongly. Named after an 18th-century Portuguese sculptor, the museum houses the country's finest collection of sculpture, an art with a long history in Coimbra. The collection begins with medieval sculpture, the highlight of which is a mace-bearing equestrian knight who heralds the way to the loggia for another splendid view of the city and river below. The collection continues in a wing on the other side of the loggia, which displays sculpture from the

15th and 16th centuries, when Coimbra's most influential school of sculpture flourished. Artists worked the soft white limestone from nearby Ançã that has mellowed into a pleasant nougat color beneath traces of its original polychrome paint. Another chosen medium was terra-cotta. French artist Philippe Houdart's *Ultima Ceia* (Last Supper) is perhaps the most compelling work in that or any medium in the museum. Before a background of bas-relief medieval architecture, life-size saints and Savior are portrayed with enticing individuality, down to the detail of Christ's closely cropped hair.

In addition to sculpture, the museum contains paintings, religious objects, tapestries, and coverlets—note the intricate embroidery from nearby Castelo Branco if you're planning to continue on to Beira Baixa and might like to buy a fine bedspread, a survival of the ancient craft seen here. Downstairs you can see what the structure was even before it became the bishop's palace: the dramatically lit, rough-hewn stones that are remnants of the labyrinthine foundation of Coimbra's Roman forum.

Down the street from the museum is the 12th-century **Sé Velha** (Old Cathedral). One of the finest Romanesque cathedrals in Portugal, it has a rich history. Sancho I and João I were crowned here, and Saint Anthony of Padua, who was born in Lisbon, was ordained here as well. The exterior, topped with battlements like a castle, is starkly medieval, though somewhat warmed by the Renaissance north door by João de Ruão and the Baroque lantern turret. The austere interior contains a number of tombs and a noteworthy Flemish altarpiece. Stairs off the south aisle lead to a Gothic **cloister** where, on a quiet day, you may hear the strains of music from students practicing in the nearby conservatory. At night the scene is enlivened by *fado* from **Trovador**, a restaurant serving trout, codfish, kidney, and other regional dishes in an upscale rustic setting.

From the cathedral, a cobblestone walk and steps lead down the rua de Sobre-Ripas, to the **Casa de Sobre-Ripas**, a Renaissance palace with doors and windows carved in the Manueline style. This exuberant decorative style, which flourished in the early 16th century under King Manuel I, is Portugal's most original contribution to architecture. It is characterized by intricately carved knots, nets, shells, anchors, and other Portuguese nautical themes.

As told by various Portuguese writers, a local legend has it that the palace was the scene of the murder of Maria Teles, wife of Inês de Castro's eldest son, João. Maria's sister, the jealous Queen Leonor, convinced João that his wife was being unfaithful to him and that he should have married the queen's daughter. João rushed home and stabbed Maria, prompting his disgrace and eventual exile from Portugal. The murder supposedly took place in 1379, while the palace was not built until 1547, so the tale has its detractors; but it does exemplify the kind of legend that is so much the fabric of Coimbra.

On the same street is the **Torre de Anto**, a medieval tower where Symbolist poet António Nobre lived briefly in the last century. These days, not words but objects are crafted here; the tower is occupied by the **Casa de Artesanato da Região de Coimbra**, a government-sponsored handicrafts center where you can purchase such specialties as hand-painted ceramics, metalwork, wools, and linens. Under the tower is the **Colegio Novo**, an attractive Renaissance cloister.

More steps lead to the Arco de Almedina, a 12th-century city gate and vestige of the Moorish presence (*medina* being Arabic for "city"). Through it is the Baixa, the lower, flat part of the city that stretches along the right bank of the Mondego, where the citizens of Coimbra go about their daily life.

The Lower Town

If the long walk from the university has worked up your appetite, you can easily take care of it in this part of town. *Tascas*—inexpensive restaurants much frequented by students and often indicated only by a laurel branch above the door—line rua dos Gatos and rua da Sota. One of the better ones is **Zé Manel**, beco do Forno, 12, a boisterous hole-in-the-wall that serves an extensive Portuguese menu including *sopa de pedra* (a hearty country soup), *chouriços na brasa* (grilled sausages), *bacalhau no forno* (baked cod), and an assortment of grilled meats in a characteristic Coimbra setting, decorated with rusty bells and defunct clocks as well as a boar's head and a portrait of Coimbra *fadista* Augusto Hilário.

Praça do Comércio, the square extending near the 12th-century church of São Tiago, marks the beginning of the commercial part of Coimbra. Many shops here and especially on the street a block in the direction of the Upper Town (rua Ferreira Borges and its continuation, rua Visconde da Luz and rua da Sofia) sell regional crafts as well as locally produced clothing and footwear.

Just ahead off rua Visconde da Luz is the **Mosteiro de**

Santa Cruz, one of Portugal's most historic buildings. Saint Anthony of Padua studied in this monastery, and it contains the tombs of the country's first two kings, Afonso Henriques and Sancho I. Other noteworthy features of the church are the Renaissance pulpit and the carved wooden stalls in the choir, upstairs. A door in the south transept leads to the sacristy, where among other paintings you should note *Pentecostes* (The Pentecost) by Grão Vasco, an important Beira painter whose work you will find more of in the town of Viseu in the Beira Alta. From here another door leads to the **Claustro do Silencio**, a Manueline cloister containing bas-reliefs of the Passion based on engravings by Dürer. In one corner is the oval Capela de São Teotónio, which houses the tomb of Saint Theotonius (prior of the monastery during the 12th century) and other relics. Upstairs are more choir stalls, decorated in *talha dourada* with scenes from the adventures of Vasco da Gama.

Farther along is rua da Sofia, the Street of Wisdom, so called because it was once lined with theological colleges. You'll soon see the **Igreja do Carmo**, a 16th-century church containing 18th-century paintings of clerics whose grim robes and grand headgear serve as reminders that Coimbra, along with Lisbon and Evora in the Alentejo, was a seat of the Portuguese Inquisition.

If your interest in wisdom is piqued, continue along rua da Sofia to visit the remains of representative theological colleges of the Igreja da Graça, the Igreja de São Pedro, and the Igreja da Santa Justa. Feeling overwhelmed by antiquity? You'll also find in this area, on rua dos Coutinhos, a small part of the collection of the **Museu Nacional da Ciência e Tecnologia** (National Science and Technology Museum)—so overcrowded, its director once complained, that less than 8 percent is on display here and in its other buildings. Among the excitements of modern technology: the biggest collection of IBM computers in Europe. Otherwise, this is the part of town to appease not so much your quest for wisdom as your sweet tooth. Coimbra's traditional pastries—*arrufadas* (puff pastries), *queijadas* (cheese tarts), and custard tarts called *manjares brancos*—are all featured in such places as the **Santa Cruz Café**, next to the former monastery of the same name back at praça de 8 de Maio.

Across the Mondego

The Ponte de Santa Clara—you can drive across this modern bridge—leads to more historic monuments of Coimbra on the western side of the river. The first, partially restored after centuries of flooding of the Mondego, is the Gothic former **Convento de Santa Clara-a-Velha**, founded under the patronage of Isabel of Aragón, wife of King Dinis. She is also remembered for the Miracle of the Roses, when bread and gold she was distributing to the poor were suddenly transformed into flowers as the king inquired disapprovingly about her activities. The miracle, along with her numerous other charitable acts of founding hospitals, orphanages, and homes for fallen women, led to her canonization as the Rainha Santa, the Queen Saint.

Another evocative ruin in the vicinity is the **Quinta das Lágrimas** (Villa of Tears), a key set piece in the love story whose heroes are Pedro I and his Galician mistress, Inês de Castro. In the garden of the *quinta* in 1355, Inês was murdered (by courtiers who feared she would have too much influence on the Portuguese throne), and a spring gushed forth on the spot. "The nymphs of the Mondego were long to remember, with sobbing, the dark dispatch," wrote Camões in *The Lusiads,* "and their tears became a spring of pure water, that remembrance might be eternal. The fountain marks the scene of her earlier happiness, and is still known today by the name they gave it, Fonte dos Amores. Lucky the flowers that are nurtured from such a source, its name telling of love." Inês de Castro was originally buried at Santa Clara-a-Velha, but her body was transferred to Alcobaça (see Day Trips from Lisbon for Alcobaça and for a variant of this tale).

Rainha Santa Isabel was also once entombed at the old convent, and her Gothic sepulcher was moved to the **Convento de Santa Clara-a-Nova**, built up the hill in the 17th century, when a second tomb was added for good measure. Though now used in part as an army barracks, the church may be visited to see the tombs, the polychrome wood panels depicting the lives of Saint Francis and Rainha Santa Isabel, and the adjacent Renaissance cloister.

Nearby is **Portugal dos Pequenitos**, where the essence of Portugal is delightfully distilled in a park containing child-height replicas of the most important architectural monuments in the country, plus examples of domestic architecture from throughout Portugal and the former Portuguese empire. True to its name, it is popular with youngsters; it also provides a charming crash course in Portuguese architecture for grown-ups. On this side of the river, too, you'll find you're close to **Real dos Canas**, a new restaurant that quickly acquired cohorts of Coimbra fans for its good Portuguese food and the view across the Mondego that they never tire of (Tel: 039-81-48-77; closed Wednesdays and holidays).

Other Sights in Coimbra

Before you leave Coimbra, there are a few outdoor places in the Upper Town that merit a visit—and where you can picnic if you want. The **Jardim Botânico**, near the university, devised by the marquês de Pombal, is one of the nicest formal gardens in Portugal. Above it is the **Parque da Santa Cruz**, lavishly planted with flora from throughout the former empire, and above that is the **Penedo da Saudade**, a promenade offering a panorama of the city and the river below. If you would like to take in the view while at table, try the nearby restaurant **Piscinas**, rua Dom Manuel, which serves traditional Portuguese cuisine.

THE COIMBRA AREA
South of Coimbra

The excavations of Conímbriga, which are well signposted, lie a few miles south of Coimbra, a mere 10 km (6 miles) on the motorway, then a brief drive past **Condeixa-a-Nova**, an appealing town with its own little Manueline church, some nice cafés in its main square, and the **Estrela factory**, which produces and sells hand-painted ceramics.

The site of **Conímbriga**, occupied since prehistory, was of interest to a number of peoples, including the Suevi invaders from the north, who conquered the town in the fifth century and provoked the inhabitants (Visigoths) to move to present-day Coimbra. By the second century B.C. the Romans were constructing a magnificent city with fountains, fine mosaics, gardens, and an aqueduct. Digging began around the turn of this century; Conímbriga is now the most extensively excavated Roman site in Portugal.

A section of the same ancient road that once connected Lisbon and Braga leads visitors from the entrance past the so-called Casa das Fontes (House of the Fountains), where re-created fountains plash and numerous mosaics depict simple geometric motifs or hunting and mythological characters. The road then leads to the town gate. Off to the right are the aqueduct and excavations of the forum and important public buildings; to the left is another sumptuous villa, the Casa de Cantaber (House of Cantaber), filled with ornamental pools in which skeletons were found during excavation and remain in situ. To see a third villa, walk back around the wall. By the parking area you'll find a modern museum displaying ancient artifacts from the site and also a series of fine equine mosaics recently relocated from Torre de Palma, a Roman villa being excavated near Monforte, northeast of Estremoz in the Alentejo.

A convenient coda to the excursion could be the town of **Penela**, a few miles farther southeast on N 347. One story relates that it was given its name during the Reconquest, when Moorish guards left their post at the town castle and the Portuguese entered, declaring, "Courage! We have a foot inside!" (*o pé nela*); others argue that the name is merely a diminutive of *penha*, the Portuguese word for "rock" or "bluff." Whatever the origin of its name, both theories take into account the main feature of the fortified village, its 11th-century **castle**—a well-placed structure whose views of the surrounding countryside are only enhanced by the weathering of the old structure.

Just 4 km (2½ miles) west, on a minor road, you'll find tiny **Rabaçal**. There too excavations have turned up a fine Roman house. For many people Rabaçal's charm lies in its tasty cheese, made from the milk of sheep and goats. And, if you're there at the end of September, you'll find a fine fair celebrating a harvest you might not expect: walnuts.

West of Coimbra

Another castle lies 29 km (18 miles) west of Coimbra at **Montemor-o-Velho** on a site occupied since Roman times. You'll get there on the relatively quiet N 111, a pleasant drive past rice paddies along the north bank of the Mondego river virtually parallel to the fast-growing IP 3, which will end at the port of Figueira da Foz. Montemor's fortifications date from the 11th century, though the present **castle** is predominantly a 14th-century structure built on the Mondego as part of the line of defense for Coimbra. The pale stone castle is largely in romantic ruin, and kestrels hovering above it maintain vigilance and add a medieval air. The best dining option in the area is **Ramalhão**, rua Tenente Valadim, 24, Montemor-o-Velho, which has an excellent regional menu that changes with the seasons.

Continuing west along the Mondego to its mouth on the Atlantic, you will reach **Figueira da Foz**, a brash and breezy town famous for its esplanades, discos, gambling casino (rua Bernardo Lopes; passport required for admission), bullfights, and expansive beach—all of which make it especially appealing to Spaniards from landlocked Salamanca due east. The pleasures of Figueira da Foz are much less cultural than in so many other towns, but it does sit on a spectacular stretch of the Costa de Prata. If the sight inspires you to want to see real silver, you'll find some at the **Museu Municipal Dr. Santos Rocha** (rua Calouste Gulbenkian), which houses an extensive archaeological collection that includes ancient silver coins. The other notable institution in Figueira, the palace-museum **Casa do Paço**, is decorated with thousands of Delft tiles salvaged from a Dutch shipwreck—a change, if you have absorbed a wealth of Portuguese architecture, from Portugal's own *azulejos*.

East of Coimbra

The slopes of the mountainous Beiras come quickly into view on the panoramic drive inland toward the **Serra da Estrela**. Spectacular forest and mountain scenery leads to a series of villages that seem to have been judiciously planted for a traveller's delight, but you'll need a large-scale map to find quite a few of them. A good initial routing would be to start on the IP 3 to the north of Coimbra then, after some 28 km (17 miles), take the right turn toward Arganil on the N 17-2 (which meets in about 10 km/6 miles the N 17/IC 7). If you continue a little farther you'll come to **Arganil** and the country road N 342. The small town of Arganil has a modern and comfortable *residencial* (bed and breakfast), **Hotel São Gens**, a pleasant base for this quiet area (they'll tell you where to eat).

To understand the character of this rural world, drive up the hill at Arganil to the sanctuary at the top; in the chapel you'll see an oddly dressed Christ Child—a Menino Jesus whose silver-topped stick and dapper tricorne hat derive from the defeat of Napoleon's forces. Then drive northwest on the N 342. You'll come to the pleasing small towns of **Côja** and **Avô**, which seem isolated from the outside world (they aren't, of course: television aerials betray a closer encounter than you might suppose). In Avô, on the banks of the Alva river, a tributary of the Mondego, you'll see the ruins of a castle and many surviving granite houses. In Côja look for the small sign to Porta de Balsa and then, in the heart of the bald-headed **Serra de Açor**, the tiny valley-deep, slate-roofed village of **Piódão**, a strange cluster of schist houses and an icing-sugar church, and you will hardly believe you are half a day's drive from animated Coimbra—or, perhaps, in Portugal at all.

Near Avô, a good map will help you find **Lourosa**, noted for its tenth-century Mozarabic church—the style of architecture that blends Christian and Moorish themes. (*Moçarabes* were Christian subjects of the Moors and tolerated by them.) **Bobadela**, to the northeast, has a Roman arch and a parish church with an inscription sweetly describing this serene place as *splendissima civitas.*

Oliveira do Hospital, a few kilometers east of Bobadela, is another town of ancient Roman origin, though as its name implies it was bestowed on the Order of the Hospital of Saint John in Jerusalem in the 12th century. One such knight can be seen in the tomb of Domingos Joanes in the Capela dos Ferreiros, in the parish church. Above it is a *cavaleiro* on horseback, much like the knight in the Museu Machado de Castro in Coimbra. **São Giao**, in the foothills of the Serra da Estrela (though not on the map—watch for the sign on N 17/IC 6 for the turnoff between Piaches de Alva and Sandomil), has an elaborately decorated Baroque church known as A Catedral das Beiras (The Cathedral of the Beiras).

You'll find appetizing food—in ample portions—in nearly every small town. A more sophisticated lunch of Portuguese specialties such as *truta com presunto* (trout with ham) and *ensopado de cabrito* (a casserole of kid and bread) and robust red Dão wine is available just 4 km (2½ miles) from Oliveira do Hospital at the **Pousada de Santa Bárbara**, Póvoa das Quartas, a modern inn perched dramatically at the edge of a valley in invigorating isolation. If the mountain air entices you into spending the night, or perhaps several, at the gateway to the Serra da Estrela (see the Beira Alta chapter, below), these are the most comfortable lodgings in the vicinity.

North of Coimbra

The magical forest of the **Parque Nacional de Buçaco**, and the madly fanciful Palace Hotel sheltered inside it provide a remarkable conjunction of experiences. You'll find lush nature in the old forest's dark thickets, grandly theatrical architecture in the hotel, richly colorful history wherever you look, and the true joy of knowing that here you can dine deliciously and drink superb wines. To get to this small realm of fantasy, head north from Coimbra on the A 1/IP 1 motorway; turn after a quick 11 km or so (7½ miles) toward Mealhada; turn left at the T-junction and follow the signs for Luso (route N 234); and from there signs will direct you to turn right up a steep mountain road that leads to the gates of the forest. The **Palace Hotel do Buçaco**, a Neo-Manueline extravaganza built at the turn of the century on the privileged site of the Buçaco monastery in the heart of the forest, provides luxurious accommodations fit for a king—literally. It was conceived as a hunting lodge for the Portuguese royal family but constructed as a hotel, where Portugal's last king, Dom Manuel II, tasted love—and scandal—before he was forced into exile.

The domain of monks since the sixth century, the hilly, sylvan enclave of Buçaco (sometimes spelled Bussaco) once enclosed numerous hermitages as well as the carefully cultivated indigenous and imported trees that are still flourishing. In 1810 it was the scene of the Peninsular War's Battle of Buçaco, in which Wellington's troops were pitted against the French on what the duke famously referred to as the "damned long hill" of Buçaco. The French were driven downhill and continued south to sack Coimbra, and the "valoroso e glorioso Duque de Wellington," as the Portuguese call him, emerged victorious. A few years later, when religious orders were suppressed in Portugal, the Carmelite monks were expelled from the forest (though some two dozen were later allowed to return to the monastery), which was taken over by the state and planted with even more trees. Today hundreds of species thrive in the forest beside moss-covered paths and religious monuments.

You can obtain a map of the forest at the Palace Hotel. It will show you the way through the paths to the old gates touched by history and legend. A papal bull once banned women from entering the monks' domain, yet a gate was carved for the queen. Those who cut down the sanctified trees did so on pain of excommunication. A strenuous path climbs past chapels containing terra-cotta sculptural representations of the Stations of the Cross to the **Cruz Alta**, where there is a museum devoted to the battle, as well as one of the most sweeping panoramas in the entire region.

There is much to see outside the hotel: the protected remains of the Carmelite church with its odd pebbled walls and cork doors, where the Iron Duke himself spent seven days in the sanctuary of a monk's cell; the great tile panels portraying bloody battle; the terraces and trim gardens. Inside you'll find the decorative touch of major artists and fine furniture in splendid vaulted rooms; theatrical whimsy, too, in the electric eyes of the armored knight on the great ornamental staircase.

The Palace Hotel can provide a regal meal of Portuguese classics and regional cuisine in its baronial dining halls— the chef de cuisine, Manuel Lourenço, has worked at the hotel for 40 years. Here you can also taste some of Portugal's most distinguished wines, including the eminent vinhos Buçaco themselves. A special occasion? Try a 1958 *tinto* (at 18,000$00) or the fine 1975 (at 8,000$00). For a contrast, head back to **Mealhada**, known throughout Portugal for its *leitão assado* (roast suckling pig). So many restaurants in the neighborhood loudly promote their *leitão,* you might suppose that was all they served. In fact, there's usually a menu of many other offerings. Among the best of these regional restaurants are **Couceiro dos Leitões** (on the southern side of the Mealhada main junction) and **Restaurante Meta** and **Restaurante Típico** on the north side. But in both directions you'll find others as good. To drink, you might like a robust Bairrada red or a light white Mealhada wine. There's a well-stocked wine shop, **Garrafeira Couceiro**, on the right on largo dos Chafarizes just as you enter the Mealhada main street.

Here, you are only 6 km or so (about 3½ miles) from Curia, a resort and spa with hotels ranging from the simple to the super-deluxe. The waters, it's claimed, are good for such health problems as rheumatoid arthritis, high blood pressure, kidney stones, gout, diseases of the digestive system, and more (in a watering season from April 1 to October 31). For the entirely healthy (and well-off) there's pure escape in the elegance of the truly grand **Grande Hotel da Curia**, recently refurbished throughout, or the exquisitely art nouveau **Curia Palace Hotel**. Alternatively, at Vacariça, about 4 km (2½ miles) from Mealhada (or Luso), the sprawling 18th-century manor house **Solar da Vacariça** has modern and attractive self-catering apartments, peaceful lawns, tennis court, and a pool. And if you're there on a Saturday morning, you'll find, back on the main road, a cheerful, crowded market beside the little church.

AVEIRO

The Rota da Luz (Route of Light) is how they've dubbed the area around Aveiro, an important port and enthralling little city on the northern coast. You'll soon see why. The brilliant light, glowing beaches, a generous sun, gleaming canals, gaudily painted boats, shining salt pans, a misty lagoon, whitewashed houses. All of these illuminate an area with its own steadfast individuality and charm. You'll be pleased to know, too, that there is a broader range of accommodations here than anywhere else in the province. Choices include the

Hotel Pomba Branca, built as a villa in the 1930s and recently refurbished, in the heart of Aveiro; **Quinta do Paço da Ermida**, a 17th-century manor house overlooking the porcelain factory and museum of Vista Alegre a few miles south of town; **Hotel João Padeiro**, a comfortable roadside inn a few miles to the northeast in Cacia; the **Pousada da Ria**, a modern inn built right on the edge of a lagoon north of Aveiro near Murtosa; and the **Pousada de Santo António**, built in 1942 as one of Portugal's three original *pousadas* (government-run inns) and remodeled in 1985, on a still-tranquil spot some 20 km (12 miles) east of Aveiro in Serém, just off the old N 1. (If you go there on the motorway, take the Albergaria-a-Velha exit heading toward Agueda. But *don't* go to Agueda, the district capital; that road leads away from the pousada.) In the Rota da Luz area outside Aveiro are other handsome old or brand-new hotels. The helpful tourist office in Aveiro, now in a charming canal-side building at rua João Mendonça, 8, will provide maps and information.

Because of its canals, the Portuguese are fond of calling Aveiro the Amsterdam or Venice of Portugal. The architecture, a pleasing mix of Baroque, art deco, and art nouveau, and simpler but more colorfully painted structures, gives Aveiro its own strong character, though as Andersen justly observed, "there is nothing here except the gondola-shaped boats to remind one of the capital of the Adriatic." He was referring to the *barcos moliceiros,* wooden boats once used to gather seaweed for fertilizer. Dramatically high-prowed and vividly painted with primitive motifs, the boats are so unusual that they actually bring to mind less Amsterdam or Venice than the ancient Phoenicians, said to have settled the area. *Moliceiros,* many restored by returning emigrants, are the pride of a summer regatta called the Festa da Ria, at which both the most beautifully decorated boat and the winner of the race are given a prize.

The rest of the year, a few still-working *moliceiros* and the salt-gathering *saleiros* go about their business on the canals of Aveiro, an important port until it silted over in the 16th century. The Canal Central, with its handsome mansions, and the Canal de São Roque, flanked by piles of salt drying in the sun and reached by passing through a quarter of brightly painted fishermen's houses, are reminders of Aveiro's prosperous past and continuing traditions of the present as a major fishing port.

At the height of Aveiro's affluence a local school of sculpture flourished, and the ornately carved art on display in its museum and churches is the main attraction on dry land.

Before seeing the art, however, try the equally sculptural *ovos moles,* crisp barrel- or seashell-shaped pastries stuffed with a sweet and succulent egg jam. Places to sample them are **Confeitaria Peixinho**, on rua da Coimbra (which also stocks the local version of the puff pastries called *arrufadas*) and **Pastelaria Rossio** just down the street from the Turismo.

You might then proceed to the visual riches of the town, beginning with the stately façades of the Câmara Municipal (Town Hall), across the canal from the Turismo, and, to its left, the *azulejo*-covered Igreja da Misericórdia. Nearby is the cathedral of São Domingos, which, among its splendors, houses the tomb of Catarina de Atalide, the object of much literary affection as Natércia in Camões's sonnets. Across from the cathedral is the **Museu de Aveiro**, housed in the former Convento de Jesus. In 1472 Joana, daughter of King Afonso V, left her palace for the convent, where she died. Some 200 years later she was beatified as Santa Joana Princesa, patron saint of Aveiro, and shortly afterward received her multicolored marble tomb—a confectionery showpiece of Portuguese art—in the lower chancel. Other highlights are the tomb of Dom João de Albuquerque, the *talha dourada* decorations of the chancel, the *azulejos* of the refectory, and the compelling, 15th-century *Retrato de Santa Joana* (Portrait of Santa Joana) in the painting gallery.

A short walk would bring you to the *azulejos* and *talha dourada* of the Igreja das Carmelitas. Then you could cross the **Canal Central** for a close-up look at Aveiro's main sources of income: fishing and salt production. At the Mercado do Peixe, active in the early morning, you can watch cod, eel, and other creatures being snapped up by the local housewives who aren't married to fishermen. The little canal running off the market leads to the colorful octagonal Capela de São Gonçalo, the scene of the annual winter Festa de São Gonçalinho, during which sweet cakes are rained down on an appreciative crowd of celebrants. Beyond the chapel, along the **Canal de São Roque**, are the colorful fishermen's houses. On the other side of the canal, reached by a humpbacked bridge, are the salt pans, where piles of sodium chloride glisten in the sun.

Back past the cathedral and the museum on the other side of the Canal Central is **Cozinha do Rei**, the restaurant in the Hotel Afonso V, where you can sample the catch of Aveiro's fishermen with the local specialties of appetizers of *mexilhões à moda de Aveiro* (mussels in a spicy sauce made with garlic and bay leaves), followed by *caldeirada de enguias* (eel stew). Look for local food in other restaurants in the old district, just beyond the largo do Rossio, bounded by the Canal das Pyrâmides, the Canal de São Roque, and the Cais dos Mercantes.

Ria de Aveiro

Though Aveiro may not quite qualify as the Venice of Portugal, the lagoon called the Ria de Aveiro, stretching north of the city, surpasses its Venetian counterpart in subtle natural beauty and intimate glimpses of an ancient livelihood. The best way to see it is to take the boat trip sponsored between June 15 and September 15 by the tourist office (Região de Turismo da Rota da Luz; Tel: 034-236-80). A motorboat takes you past the salt pans, past the port of Gafanha, where the cod is dried, through the lagoon, past the resort and dunes of São Jacinto, to the beaches at the fishing villages of Torreira and Areinho. The boat moors at Torreira between noon and 3:00 P.M. With transport arranged, you might lunch at the **Pousada da Ria**, whose restaurant serves the local version of *caldeirada de enguias* and other eel dishes prepared in a variety of ways, as well as meat dishes. Or you could eat more simply but very well at the restaurants in Torreira (a short walk takes you from the lagoon to a broad beach and the ocean). One good restaurant is in the handy **Estalagem Riabela**.

Taking you serenely past sand dunes, salt marshes, pines, a wildlife refuge, islands, and boatmen at work in the large, cargo-carrying *mercanteis,* the swan-necked *moliceiros,* as well as smaller boats like the fishing *bateiras,* the day-long trip is an enthralling experience. The lagoon can also be explored by driving from Aveiro north to Murtosa, or vice versa, along the coastal route—but be sure to go with a map. The roads reach into and around the lagoon but, with a sea opening between São Jacinto on the northern arm and Barra on the southern, you cannot encircle it. You'll find to the north, too, if you go to the beach at Furadouro, yet another lovely example of the Aveiro area's colorful range of working boats: the *meia-lua,* or half moon—its actual shape. And if you're on the beach when they head for shore over the surf, you'll see teams of oxen waiting to haul the boats from the water. The men may well have attended one of Portugal's modern fishing schools but old ways, along with the classical boats, survive.

THE AVEIRO AREA

On the coast south of Aveiro are a number of resort towns. The one with most character is **Costa Nova**, which boasts beaches on the ocean and the lagoon as well as houses boldly striped in white-and-blue, white-and-green, and white-and-red. From there you might enjoy the coastal drive down to Praia da Vagueira, from where, if you head inland and then north onto N 109 at Vagos, you will reach the famous porcelain and glass factory **Vista Alegre**. While much of the art of Aveiro is folkloric, the porcelain of Vista Alegre is the last cry in sophistication. Even if shopping is not on your itinerary, the factory is worth visiting. It resembles a stage set for a Portuguese version of *Carmen,* complete with sultry workers having a smoke under the poplars in the main square. The factory can be visited only by appointment, and then only the painting area; Tel: (034) 32-23-65. No appointment is necessary to see the fine museum of porcelain and glass (closed Mondays) or to purchase the merchandise in the factory shop (open daily).

Farther north on N 109, at Ilhavo, is the **Museu Marítimo e Regional**. Examples of *moliceiros* and other local folkloric and sea memorabilia are displayed along with an extensive collection of shells. Should they serve to stimulate your appetite, there is a restaurant back in Costa Nova specializing in shellfish, **A Marisqueira.**

The towns north of Aveiro hold other specialized surprises. Avanca, on N 109, has a small museum dedicated to António Egas Moniz, who won a Nobel Prize in medicine in 1949. Farther north off N 109 is the *azulejo*-rich town of **Ovar**, which gave its name to Portugal's fishwives, called *varinas,* who can still often be seen here in their country costumes, perhaps eating the eggy local version of *pão de ló* (sponge cake). Other ethnic garb and a large selection of Portuguese pottery are on display in the Museu Etnológico, hinting at the strong sense of tradition in Ovar evidenced during its Carnival and Easter festivals. The museum also has a section devoted to Joaquim Guilherme Gomes Coelho, whose realistic novels of country life in 19th-century Portugal, written under the pseudonym Julio Dinis, still delight readers of Portuguese.

Northeast of Ovar just off the N 223, at **Santa Maria de Feira**, is a fanciful castle with pointed turrets. The surrounding town is lovely in its own right. For more art and fine scenery, travel farther east from Santa Maria de Feira—older maps will use its former name, Vila da Feira, dropped when it was promoted from *vila* (town) to *cidade* (city)—on N 327 and N 326 or, from Vale de Cambra, on N 224 in a valley of the Serra da Gralheira to **Arouca**. There a Baroque monastery contains the mummified remains of Princess Mafalda, daughter of Sancho I, in an elaborate silver casket. The monastery also has a huge church filled with Baroque painting and sculpture, and a museum noted for its Portuguese primitives. If you're returning to Aveiro down N 224 from Arouca, the **Estalagem São Miguel**, at Parque de La Salette in Oliveira de Azemeis on the N 1/IC 2, is a fine place to stop for a meal of shellfish and other regional specialties.

GETTING AROUND

The abundance of small communities off the main public transportation routes, especially in the mountainous inland area, makes a car the best way to get around in Beira Litoral. Rodoviária Beira Litoral, the leading bus service, serves virtually all the larger places. Coimbra, Figueira da Foz, Aveiro, and Ovar have centrally located stations served by Caminhos de Ferro (CF), the national railway service; Leiria's station is accessible to the town only by taxi. Except for Coimbra and Aveiro, these towns are not yet served by fast trains. Tourist offices in Leiria, Jardim Luiz de Camões, Tel: (044) 327-48; Coimbra, largo da Portagem, Tel: (039) 238-86; and Aveiro, rua João Mendonça, 8, Tel: (034) 236-80, Fax: (034) 283-26, can provide current schedules for local transportation to the smaller destinations.

In Coimbra the Queima das Fitas is celebrated each May, the Festas da Rainha Santa in July. In Aveiro the Festa da Ria takes place in July and August, and the Festa de São Gonçalinho in January. Ovar's celebrations of Carnival and Easter are movable feasts.

ACCOMMODATIONS REFERENCE

Rates given are projected 1993 prices for a double room, double occupancy. Price ranges span the lowest rate in the low season to the highest in the high season. Unless otherwise stated, rates include Continental breakfast. As prices are subject to change, always double-check before booking.

▶ **Albergaria do Terreiro**. Largo Cândido dos Reis, 17, 2400 **Leiria**. Tel: (044) 81-35-80; Tel. and Fax: (044) 351-90. 8,000$00–9,000$00.

▶ **Casa dos Quintais**. Carvalhais de Cima-Assafarge, 3000 **Coimbra**. Tel: (039) 43-83-05. 8,000$00.

▶ **Curia Palace Hotel. Curia**, 3780 Anadia. Tel: (031) 51-21-31; Fax: (031) 51-55-31; in U.S. and Canada, Tel: (800) 528-1234. 12,000$00–18,000$00. Closed November through March.

▶ **Grande Hotel da Curia. Curia**, 3780 Anadia. Tel: (031) 51-57-20/29; Fax: (031) 51-53-17; in U.S. and Canada, Tel: (212) 686-9213. 10,000$00–20,000$00.

▶ **Hotel Astória**. Avenida Emídio Navarro, 21, 3000 **Coimbra**. Tel: (039) 220-55; Fax: (039) 220-57; in U.S. and Canada, Tel: (800) 528-1234. 13,000$00–17,000$00.

▶ **Hotel Cristal**. Rua de Leiria, 112, Embra, 2430 **Marinha Grande**. Tel: (044) 56-01-00; Fax: (044) 56-00-65. 8,700$00–10,500$00.

▶ **Hotel Dom João III**. Avenida Herois de Angola, 2400 **Leiria**. Tel: (044) 81-25-00; Fax: (044) 81-22-35; in U.S. and Canada, Tel: (800) 528-1234. 9,250$00–12,000$00.

▶ **Hotel Dom Luís**. Quinta da Varzea, 3000 **Coimbra**. Tel: (039) 44-25-10; Fax: (039) 81-31-96. 12,700$00–20,000$00.

▶ **Hotel João Padeiro**. Rua da República, 13, **Cacia**, 3800 Aveiro. Tel: (034) 91-13-26; Fax: (034) 91-27-51. 7,400$00–8,000$00.

▶ **Hotel Mar e Sol**. Avenida da Liberdade, 1, **São Pedro de Moel**, 2430 Marinha Grande. Tel: (044) 59-91-82; Fax: (044) 59-94-11. 7,500$00–12,000$00.

▶ **Hotel Pomba Branca**. Rua Luis Gomes de Carvalho, 23, 3800 **Aveiro**. Tel: (034) 225-29 or 260-39; Fax: (034) 38-18-44. 9,800$00–12,500$00.

▶ **Hotel São Gens**. 3300 **Arganil**. Tel: (035) 229-59; Fax: (035) 231-23. 5,200$00–6,800$00.

▶ **Hotel Tivoli**. Rua João Machado, 3000 **Coimbra**. Tel: (039) 269-34; Fax: (039) 268-27; in U.S. and Canada, Tel: (800) 223-5652. 16,000$00–18,000$00.

▶ **Palace Hotel do Buçaco**. Buçaco, 3050 **Mealhada**. Tel: (031) 93-01-01; Fax: (031) 93-05-09; in U.S. and Canada, Tel: (212) 686-9213. 24,000$00–30,000$00.

▶ **Pousada da Ria**. Torreira, 3870 **Murtosa**. Tel: (034) 483-32; Fax: (034) 483-33. 9,700$00–18,000$00.

▶ **Pousada de Santa Bárbara**. Póvoa das Quartas, 3400 **Oliveira do Hospital**. Tel: (038) 522-52; Fax: (038) 505-45. 9,700$00–18,000$00.

▶ **Pousada de Santo António**. Serém do Vouga, 3750 Mourisca do Vouga. Tel: (034) 52-32-30; Fax: (034) 52-31-92. 9,700$00–18,000$00.

▶ **Quinta do Paço da Ermida**. 3830 **Ilhavo**. Tel: (034) 32-

24-96. 10,000$00–14,000$00. Closed November through March.

▶ **Solar da Vacariça**. Vacariça, 3050 **Mealhada**. Tel: (031) 93-94-58. 8,950$00–$12,100$00.

Pousadas can be booked through ENATUR, Avenida Santa Joana Princesa, 10, 1700 Lisbon, Portugal; Tel: (01) 848-1221 or 848-9078; Fax: (01) 80-58-46. But it is easier to make reservations through a travel agent. In the United States and Canada, pousadas can also be booked through Marketing Ahead, 433 Fifth Avenue, New York, NY 10016; Tel: (212) 686-9213; Fax: (212) 686-0271.

Manor houses can be booked directly or through the manor-house associations—ANTER, P.I.T., PRIVETUR, and TURIHAB—listed in Useful Facts. Most of the houses belong to one or more of these associations, but because membership rosters change frequently we haven't attempted to spell out the associations for each house. Readers are advised to contact the manor-house associations for their current listings.

In the United States and Canada, it is possible to reserve rooms in P.I.T. manor houses through E & M Associates, 211 East 43rd Street, Suite 1404, New York, NY 10017; Tel: (212) 599-8280; Fax: (212) 599-1755.

BEIRA ALTA AND BEIRA BAIXA

EAST CENTRAL PORTUGAL

By Marion Kaplan

After the generally flat and open terrain of the Beira Litoral, Beira Alta and Beira Baixa (pronounced BYE-sha) unfold majestically and mysteriously. These most mountainous provinces in Portugal comprise several mountain ranges rippling southward from the Douro river down to the Tejo, or Tagus: the Serra de Montemuro just south of the Douro river, the Serra da Arada to their southwest, the Serra do Caramulo west of Viseu, the Serra da Estrela, grandest of all, east of Coimbra, the Serra da Lousã southeast of Coimbra, the Serra da Gardunha to the east of the Lousã and south of the Estrela, as well as the serras of Leomil, Lapa, and Marofa north of the Serra da Estrela, and the little wilderness of the Serra da Malcata to the east.

Against this mountainous backdrop strewn with boulders and covered with pines and eucalyptus (with the occasional errant palm rising defiantly), many peoples left their marks in and on the abundant local granite. Prehistoric tribes built many dolmens, some of which remain near Fornos de Algodres. The Romans turned a Celtic settlement at Idanha-a-Velha into a thriving town called Egitania, which became the capital of the Gothic kingdom. They also constructed a mysterious structure called Centum Cellas near the present-day town of Belmonte. You'll see again and again the name Viriato

313

(also written as Viriathus), the Lusitanian rebel who for 15 years led the resistance to the Romans. Moors left mosques. Kings built castles. Later, a more stable population put up the Baroque churches and residences outlined in crisp granite contours that so characterize the landscape today, only to have their efforts spoiled by Spanish, French, and English troops. Those varied legacies in this spectacular mountain setting are the roots of a self-assured society with its own fixed traditions. The peace of this world is broken only for *festas*. You won't meet hordes of travellers. That, perhaps, is part of the appeal of this granite backbone of Portugal.

MAJOR INTEREST

Rugged terrain of the Serra do Caramulo
Art and architecture of Viseu
Precipitous sightseeing in Lamego
Fortified castle towns near the Spanish border
Pastoral vistas and grand landscape of the Serra da Estrela
Granite villages of Monsanto and Idanha-a-Velha
Jardim do Antigo Paço Episcopal (formal gardens at Castelo Branco)

Its rich history notwithstanding, a timeless pastoral quality persists in the Beira Alta and Beira Baixa. In the late 15th and early 16th centuries it inspired the fantastic backgrounds in the paintings of Viseu painter Grão Vasco Fernandes, who became one of Portugal's most famous artists. Around the same time it provided a fitting setting for the plays of Gil Vicente, court dramatist to Manuel I and João III and the father of Portuguese drama.

Though for most outsiders the mountain area's famous passes are stunning, they do require vigilance if you are driving. The road accident statistics for Portugal are shockingly high and, despite an intensive nationwide campaign against drinking and driving, you might bear in mind that Portugal has about the highest per capita wine consumption in Europe. The greatest seasonal road hazard is snow, which falls patchily between December and March and can render the roads impassable. The rest of the year you are likely to come upon a number of other hazards: Cows, sheep, goats, and their owners make regular roadside appearances; small barrages of orange peels suddenly shoot from a speeding vehicle; trucks and buses the size of small houses loom unexpectedly on the horizon or in the rearview mirror.

The route proposed here begins in the Beira Alta (*alta* means "upper," which in this case is northern) at the Serra do Caramulo, northeast of Coimbra and east of Aveiro. After travelling the wild landscape, you might pause in the town of Viseu (just east of the Serra do Caramulo), then head north to the town of Lamego, almost at the Douro river. Then you could cut across to the southeast almost to the Spanish border to Almeida, until a few years ago so far off the beaten track that it gave rise to a Portuguese expression for big-heartedness— *alma até Almeida* (literally, "a soul as far as Almeida"). With the *pousada* (government-run inn) there as a base, you can comfortably explore the fortified castle towns along the Spanish border. Then the route continues southwest to the Serra da Estrela, the heart of the Beira mountain ranges, for a dramatic drive through the highest terrain in Portugal. With a dip east toward the remarkable stone villages of Monsanto and Idanha-a-Velha in the Beira Baixa (*baixa* means "lower," in this case southern), you could end your exploration in Castelo Branco, in a bishop's bizarre garden of clipped hedges and sly Baroque sculptures that include the ranks of Portuguese kings.

SERRA DO CARAMULO

From the coast around Aveiro, you might start inland on the broad highway N 16/IP 5 in the Viseu direction, with fine views to the left and right. One approach to the Serra do Caramulo looms up marked large on a brown road sign; the southward turnoff leads you onto a narrow, rattling road in marked contrast to the smooth highway. Just after the turnoff, though, in about 2 km (1¼ miles), you may see a minuscule sign marked **Reserva da Loendros**. One of Portugal's smallest protected areas, it exists solely to guard a rare rhododendron (*R. ponticum*) that flowers a vivid mauve in May and June. As the road rises (no road numbers appear) up the slopes of the serra 24 km (15 miles) toward Caramulo, reassuringly signposted from time to time and with occasional hamlets where you can stop for a coffee or ice cream, you may feel that the scent of eucalyptus, the imposing forested slopes, snug villages, and misted horizons make the rough ride worth it—and the road does improve.

Caramulo, a former spa town, displays its affluence at the **Museu do Caramulo**, some 200 yards from the town's well-marked roundabout and housed in an institutional-looking building from the Salazar era. (The dictator was born in

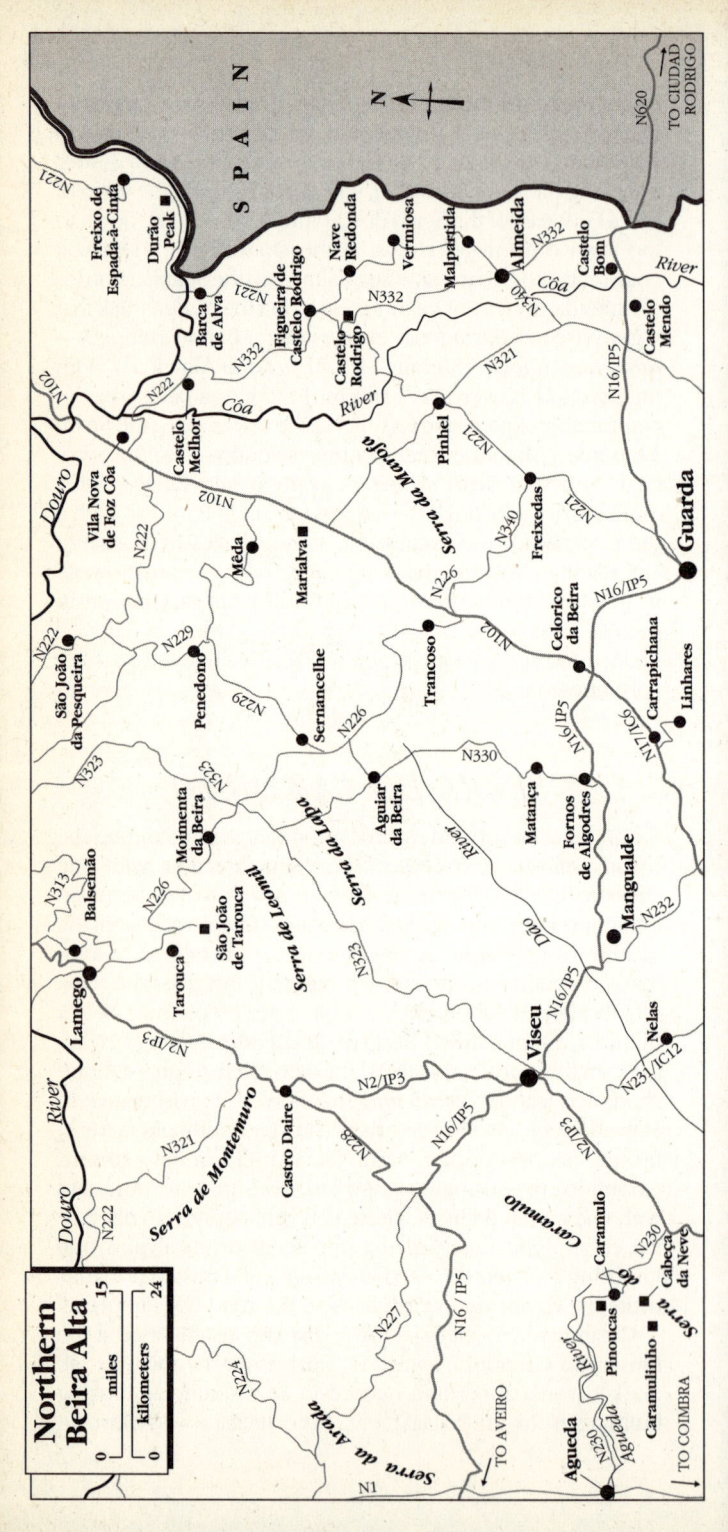

Northern Beira Alta

miles 0 — 15
kilometers 0 — 24

Vimieiro, a village near the Beira Alta town of Santa Comba Dão.) The museum contains an eclectic collection of vintage cars and modern art. An 1899 Peugeot in working order is on display, along with Salazar's Mercedes (in fact, he much preferred his Buick), Rolls-Royces, Bugattis, and many others. The art collection consists of works by Picasso, Dalí, and other modern masters. More specifically Portuguese in subject and authorship are the 16th-century Tournai tapestries, made for Manuel I, depicting Portuguese navigational exploits, and a few examples of the Viseu School of painting. The museum is open daily, except for Mondays in winter.

Caramulo once had 18 sanatoriums for lung disease, and indeed, your first few breaths of fresh mountain air may well entice you to stay. The best accommodations are at the modern, Salazar-era **Pousada de São Jerónimo** outside town a few kilometers downhill, perched over the Besteiros valley. Its restaurant serves such specialties as *sopa de abóbora* (pumpkin soup), *bacalhau con natas* (creamy cod), *borrego assado* (roast lamb), and *vitela estufada à camponesa* (a hearty veal stew). This could also be your introduction to the wines of the nearby Dão region. Reds such as Meia Encosta and Porta dos Cavaleiros are the most characteristic, but such whites as Fundação go well with the lighter fare. Wines of the Udaca cooperative are very pleasant, too.

You could also feast on the local produce. A loaf of some thick crusty bread, a bottle of Dão wine, a few thin slices of *presunto* (air-cured ham), and a *queijo da serra* (mountain ewe's-milk cheese) make a picnic as fine as any elegant meal. (*Serra,* as *queijo da serra* is known locally, is the most famous of Portuguese cheeses. In season from October to May, it has a runny, creamy quality reminiscent of Brie; in the warmer months it is preserved in cheesecloth with a mixture of red pepper and olive oil, and dries to a harder consistency.) One excellent high spot for a picnic is **Caramulinho**, 5 km (3 miles) southwest of the town. There, a desert landscape strewn with glistening granite boulders provides an intriguingly surreal setting where you might expect spacemen to ramble out of the rocky terrain. Another highland is the nearby **Cabeça da Neve** (4 km/2½ miles from Caramulo), where the views incorporate more recognizably earthly features such as rock-strewn pastures, wild foxglove, mountain villages, and the town of Viseu.

VISEU

The road below Caramulo, N 230, meets, via small roads from Campo de Besteiros or Tondela a little farther downhill, the fast N 2/IP 3 to Viseu, the most important town in the Beira Alta. Because of the forests that surround it, Viseu is sometimes called the City of Green Pines. Often the city is damp with rain, bleak with sharp winds, discouragingly gloomy. Because it's poorly signposted, it's not easy to find the artistic treasures within the venerable gates that define the old section in the center of town and keep modern Viseu at bay. The choice of hotels in Viseu is extremely limited. Accommodations in the area (characteristically isolated, though not sparing on comfort) can be found at **Casa de Rebordinho**, a broad granite manor house reached by driving some 5 km (3 miles) south of Viseu toward Nelas on N 231/IC 12 and then following the road toward Vila Chã de Sá another kilometer or so. In the heart of Viseu proper is the **Hotel Grão Vasco**, which provides the comparatively urban attractions of a bar, pool, and pleasant restaurant on grounds within walking distance of the main sights. There are several small restaurants here in the old town.

The hotel is named after one of Viseu's favorite sons and Portugal's most famous painter, Vasco Fernandes. Better known as Grão Vasco (Great Vasco), he was the master of a school of painting that flourished in Viseu during the 16th century. A remarkably well-appointed museum, the **Museu de Grão Vasco**, which features Vasco and the Viseu School, is the main feature of a visit to the town. You can park your car in the square called **Adro da Sé**, in front of the cathedral. (If it's Tuesday, when a bustling farmer's market and crafts fair takes place in the square, park near the Hotel Grão Vasco or the square known as praça da República, or the Rossio, and walk through the 15th-century gate called Porta do Soar to the Adro da Sé.) The museum is in the Paço dos Três Escalões, the former bishop's palace, a granite building that abuts the cathedral on the north side of the square. The top floor houses the museum's collection of religious paintings by Grão Vasco and other members of the Viseu School.

While Portuguese painting is not ranked very high in art history, the examples in this museum are exceptional. Their naturalism, gentle light, detailed drapery, and fantastic landscape backgrounds show the influence of Flemish painting that began with the artist Jan Van Eyck's diplomatic mission to Portugal in 1428/1429 and was nurtured by Portugal's commercial ties with northern Europe. When the Viseu School paintings were made, a century after Van Eyck's sojourn, those northern qualities had taken firm root in Portuguese soil and intermingled with indigenous motifs. Grão Vasco is best represented in the museum by *São Pedro* (Saint Peter), considered his masterpiece. That work is said to have been painted in reaction to a similar altarpiece his younger rival, Gaspar Vaz, made for the monastery in the nearby village of São João de Tarouca (see below). The two artists' Christs can be compared in the museum, though, where Vasco's *Calvário* (Calvary) and Vaz's *Cristo em Casa de Marta* (Christ in the House of Martha) and *Ultima Ceia* (The Last Supper) are all on display. On the same subject are 14 panels depicting scenes from the life of Christ, originally part of the cathedral altarpiece, now separated and displayed individually in their own room. *Adoracão dos Reis Magos* (The Adoration of the Magi) contains one of the school's most original Portuguese touches: The recent discovery of Brazil caused the African king Balthazar to be portrayed as an exotic South American Indian, a feathered headdress replacing his crown.

Modern, some contemporary, paintings by Portuguese artists are exhibited on the floor below. Also of interest on the ground floor is the 14th- to 16th-century wood statuary and sculpture made from the soft stone quarried from the Ança region of the Beiras.

Around in the Town

Most of Viseu's considerable architectural merits are within the Cidade Velha (Old Town), in the immediate vicinity of the museum. The Adro da Sé square itself is bracketed by the **Igreja da Misericórdia** to the west and the *Sé* (Cathedral) to the east. The Misericórdia is a distinctive set piece for the square as well as one of the best examples of the Baroque in all of Portugal. Its greatest beauty lies in the white stucco façade outlined in straight and curved contours of gray granite; the interior is dull by comparison.

The Sé, on the other hand, should be explored in depth. It is dedicated to Santa Maria, who shares honors with Saint Theotonius, the patron saint of the diocese of Viseu. His tomb is in Coimbra; his statue stands above the door of the cathedral's 17th-century granite façade. Inside you'll find a vault carved in stylized knots, an ornate altarpiece made of *talha dourada* (carved and gilded wood), *azulejos* (decorative tiles) in the north chapel, a sacristy with an intricately painted ceiling, a small museum of sacred art, and a cloister containing more *azulejos.* A new and startlingly modern altar in the transept, polished granite and steel in a pyramidal design, has aroused much controversy.

Viseu's other sights are all a pleasant stroll from the Adro da Sé to nearby streets lined with stately old residences, many of which are decorated with elaborate windows. Leading south off the square is rua Dom Duarte, named after the Portuguese king who was born in Viseu in 1391, in a stone building adorned with the finest Manueline window in the city 100 yards down from praça Dom Duarte. Off the praça runs rua Augusto Hilário, so called for the father of Coimbra *fado* singing, who was born in the small house marked with a commemorative plaque.

Both rua Augusto Hilário and rua Dom Duarte lead to **rua Direita**, which, along with its fine 15th-century houses, is the main center for Viseu's many crafts shops. Black-and-red pottery, basketwork, textiles, and metalwork are all produced locally and celebrated in late August and early September during the Feira de São Mateus, an annual fair established centuries ago by decree of Dom Dinis. (The Pavilhão de Artesanato da Assemblea Distrital, the district crafts office, in campo da Feira de São Mateus, has more information about the fair and Viseu's crafts.) Another regional specialty, the quality *queijo da serra,* is also for sale in shops on and around the street.

If architecture interests you, head over on the rua da Arvore to largo de Santa Cristina and the **Igreja do Carmo**, with its *talha dourada* and *azulejos,* then have a look at the houses south of rua Direita on rua dos Andrades. There are more on rua da Senhora da Piedade, back toward the cathedral and on the way to the Igreja de São Bento, which has the most striking *azulejos* in Viseu. If cheese interests you more than architecture, head west off rua Direita to rua Formosa, on which is the Mercado, a large covered market, where there is an abundance of *queijo* and other local produce.

Just ahead of the market is praça da República, or the **Rossio**, the town square around which life in Viseu revolves. It is elaborately paved, planted with lime trees, and flanked by a large *azulejo* wall. On its south side is another church decorated with *azulejos* and *talha dourada,* the Igreja dos Terceiros de São Francisco, and to the north is the **Casa Museu Almeida Moreira**, the formerly private collection of

primarily decorative arts that belonged to the original director of the Museu de Grão Vasco.

Viseu's most ancient place is the **Cava de Viriato**, supposedly once a secret cave and now a park on the north side of
the Pavia river. There the Roman Decimus Junius Brutus set
up a camp in 138 B.C. Local legend has it that the last stand of
the Lusitanian rebel Viriato occurred in Viseu, an event
commemorated by a romantic bronze-and-granite monument on the spot. Another legendary local event, the grant-
ing of Pavia water rights to on the feast day of São João, June
24, the millers of the nearby hamlet of Vil de Moinhos due to
the intervention of Saint John, is still celebrated in a procession called the Cavalhadas de Vil de Moinhos. Each year on
the feast day of São João, June 24, the millers, mounted on
horseback, lead a parade of dancers, musicians, and floats
through Viseu to the saint's chapel in suburban São João da
Carreira to express their gratitude.

Year-round, at the Grão Vasco hotel restaurant and the
smaller **Trave Negra** restaurant (rua dos Loureiros, 40), you
will find such local specialties as *cabrito assado* (roast kid)
and *trutas abafadas* (trout marinated in vinegar and oil), best
accompanied by a red or white Dão wine such as the one
called—what else?—Grão Vasco. Viseu also offers a rich
basket of eggy desserts called *castanhas doces,* which translates as "sweet chestnuts." They have nothing to do with
chestnuts, however, but everything to do with sinful amounts
of sugar and egg yolks. Decorated variously with almonds or
cherries or unadorned, they can be sampled in the restaurants or in such pastry shops as **Popedoce** at rua Direita, 128.

If you find Portuguese architecture a pleasure, you might
want to make a 17-km (11-mile) detour east on the N 16/IP 5
to **Mangualde** before moving on. Finest among its noble
residences is the Palácio dos Condes de Anadia, on the main
street. The palace, among the four or five most distinguished
in the country, is privately owned and still inhabited. Most of
the time it's closed to the public. Queries, or appeals to
enter, may be made through the **Hotel da Senhora do
Castelo** beside the hilltop sanctuary at Monte da Senhora a
few kilometers east on the old Guarda road. The hotel is a
large, old-fashioned establishment; its restaurant, **Solar
Beirão**, serves regional food, and here—if the palace is
closed to you—the mountains of Portugal lie open to all
eyes. The Dão valley, source of some of Portugal's superb
red wines, lies northeast of Mangualde.

LAMEGO

Leaving Viseu, head north through the rocky and forested terrain on N 2 (a section of this road is classified as IP 3). Just after Castro Daire, a delightful and unassuming little town 34 km (21 miles) from Viseu whose name bespeaks its origins as a Roman camp, the landscape opens up to a magnificent and ruggedly wild panorama of the Serra de Montemuro, rising off to the west. It's a thrilling approach across a great rocky heath, patched in spring with brilliant yellows and mauves, to Lamego, another town of ancient origin 33 km (20 miles) farther north, and one of the liveliest towns in the region. With Graeco-Celtic and Roman beginnings, Lamego acquired national stature as the place where Portugal's first *cortes* (national assembly) supposedly met in 1139 to recognize Dom Afonso Henriques as the nation's first king. Its grace-and-favor status diminished little in the subsequent centuries. Today, though, Lamego presents a largely Baroque face.

A prosperous town in the hills just to the south of the Douro valley, Lamego makes for a pleasant stopover on a tour of the Beiras or on the way north. You might stay at **Vila Hostilina**, a restored 19th-century farmhouse above Lamego with views of the town and the surrounding countryside, including its own vineyards and orchards, or you might enjoy the 19th-century **Hotel Parque**, set in gardens next to the famous pilgrimage church, the **Santuário de Nossa Senhora dos Remédios** on a hill above the town. (Obligingly, the church clock is silent after 9:00 P.M. until early morning.) Wherever you decide to stay, keep walking shoes handy: There are many steps to overcome to see the points of interest, as well as riverside walks if you want.

The church is a good place to begin your visit, since besides being Lamego's most important landmark it offers excellent views of the town and the outlying region as far as the Douro to the north. Its staircase, less elaborate than the one at Bom Jesus outside Braga, is its most prominent feature. Each September 8 thousands of the devout ascend it on their knees during the Festa de Nossa Senhora dos Remédios, a three-day celebration that includes many other sacred and secular events, from religious processions to rock concerts. This variety appears again in the amazing array of embellishments—fountains, statues, *azulejos,* chapels—awaiting you as you make your way up the nearly 700 steps. (If you're no penitent pilgrim, you can descend from the Hotel Parque without suffering, and you may drive to the hotel.) The fantastic display reaches its climax at the last landing before the top, the largo dos Reis, where grandiose Baroque motifs and imposing authority figures appear almost folksy, owing to the naïf treatment. The church itself is quite anticlimactic after the staircase, but the view and your sense of virtue will remedy any disappointment.

Down in town is the Sé, the tower of which dates from Romanesque times. The rest of the cathedral is a mixture of a Gothic and Renaissance exterior (as is its lovely cloister, reached from within) and an 18th-century interior. Across from the Sé, in the 18th-century former Paço Episcopal, or bishop's palace, on largo de Camões, is the **Museu Nacional de Lamego**, another rich provincial museum, which preserves a variety of relics from Lamego's history as far back as the Romans and contains an extensive assemblage of decorative and religious art. There are many *azulejos* here from demolished structures in the vicinity, and two unusual 14th-century statues worth mentioning, both depicting the Virgin pregnant with child and given the intriguing name of Nossa Senhora do O. Innocently enough, the name of this Lady of O, as Ann Bridge and Susan Lowndes recount in *The Selective Traveler in Portugal,* "comes, in part, from the seven antiphons in the Office of the days before Christmas, all of which begin with O."

Other interesting examples of the *genius loci* are ornate chapels from the monastery once attached to the town church of Chagas, as well as a number of paintings of the Viseu School, including scenes of the life of Christ by Grão Vasco and his beguiling altar panel *A Criação dos Animais* (The Creation of the Animals). Other highlights come from outside the Beiras: a collection of 16th-century Flemish tapestries on classical and mythological themes, and a series on the life of Oedipus.

The bishops weren't the only ones who lived in such luxury: Have a look at the 17th- and 18th-century town houses next to the museum. There are more on rua da Pereira, which also leads to the 16th-century Igreja e Convento de Santa Cruz, as well as the 17th-century Igreja do Desterro, the interiors of which are filled with elaborate decoration.

A street near the Desterro chapel becomes a pleasant path along the São Pedro de Balsemão river to the hamlet also bearing the saint's name. If your legs are still holding out, you might want to pick up some local ham, cheese, bread, and sparkling wine (if you're lucky enough to be in town on a Wednesday, there is a bustling outdoor food-and-crafts market held on the site called Recinto da Feira, right in the center of town) and follow the river about 3 km (2 miles) downstream (northeast). Your reward, at the bottom of the valley, is the tiny **Igreja de São Pedro de Balsemão**, said to be the oldest church in Portugal and second oldest in all Europe. Originally built as a basilica by the Visigoths in the seventh century, it was given a face-lift and a coffered ceiling in the late Renaissance. Inside, besides the seventh-century capitals on the columns, there is some interesting sculpture, including the tomb of Afonso Pires, a 14th-century bishop of Porto, and another very beautiful wooden statue of Our Lady of O. You can also make this trip entirely by car by heading 3 km (2 miles) in the direction of Tarouca and turning sharp left down to and through Balsemão village. A narrow tarred road takes you along the river valley to the little church. Only the last 50 yards or so is dirt track. Drive carefully: There's room for only one car on this two-way route.

Definitely worth visiting is Lamego's **castle**, the first of many you will come across in this part of the Beiras. To reach the castle, return to the museum and take the tortuous rua da Olaria, which becomes rua de Almacave and leads to the 12th-century Igreja de Almacave, the church where the legendary Lamego *cortes* met. The street continues past shops selling locally crafted baskets, wool blankets, and stockings to praça do Comércio, bordered by the walls and grounds of the castle. The keep dates from the 12th century, and along with the rest of the compound is well kept by *escoteiros,* the local boy scouts, which accounts for the exhibits of trustworthy scouting skills on display.

A pleasant place to lunch or dine is the restaurant in the Hotel Parque, **Nossa Senhora dos Remédios**. It serves the regional specialties of the Beiras and nearby Trás-os-Montes and Alto Douro as well as more local delicacies, such as the famous Lamego mahogany-hued *presunto,* made (as it is throughout Portugal) from pigs fed on chestnuts and/or cooked potatoes. It is eaten with melon and figs during the warmer months and appears year-round baked in a pastry crust as *bolo de presunto.* Other regional pies are *bolo de bacalhau,* made with dried salt cod, and *bolo de sardinhas,* with sardines. They offer a selection of gaudy sweets; their pudim Molotov, a vast, sweet soufflé, is as light as a bubble and quite delicious. A good wine is Santa Marta de Penaguião, from the Douro. The Lamego sparkling wine, Portugal's Champagne, comes in rosé and white—the *seco* is clear, dry, and prickly. If you'd like to taste it even closer to its source, the Turismo, avenida Visconde Guedes Teixeira, Tel: (054) 620-

05, can arrange visits to vineyards. Caves da Raposeira (Tel: 054-65-50-03) is the closest and the best known.

Southeast toward Almeida

A panorama of Portugal's history from the ancient Romans to the Peninsular War unfolds before you in the varied series of towns along the 138 km (86 miles) between Lamego and Almeida, a few miles from the border with Spain. Unfortunately, there's no such excitement in the restaurants en route, although every small town has some kind of restaurant, café serving refreshments, and grocery shop, often called *minimercado*. The first stop, 13 km (8 miles) from Lamego and then another 4 km (2½ miles) on a side road off N 226 in the direction of Tarouca, though not in the town itself, is **São João de Tarouca**, the site of Portugal's first **Cistercian monastery**, begun in the 12th century. In this tiny, tranquil village are amazing treasures: the great ruined monastery (one day to become a pousada), the church itself, with Saint John the Baptist above its portal, paintings that include the extraordinary 16th-century *São Pedro* (Saint Peter), attributed to Gaspar Vaz (and still sometimes to his rival Vasco Fernandes), glittering *talha dourada* with the gold-leaf style of Brazil, the early-18th-century frescoed ceiling, a 14th-century painted granite figure of the Virgin, the carved-wood choir stalls, the 4,709 blue-and-white Delft tiles in the sacristy (all different), an opulent organ, and a tomb containing the remains of Dom Pedro (who died in 1354), the bastard son of King Dinis who became count of Barcelos and was the author of *O Livro das Linhagens,* a medieval genealogical record of the nobility. And if you wonder how the modest villagers themselves regard their heritage, you should have been at the celebratory *festa* in the summer of 1992 when their prized *São Pedro* came home after a long absence for restoration.

Some 21 km (13 miles) farther ahead on N 226 is **Moimenta da Beira**, an agreeable town with some pleasing *azulejos* in the Mosteiro de Nossa Senhora da Purificação convent church. To find the church turn left after the GALP garage (on your right on the main road); it's on the right of the square you will reach in a couple of minutes. The Lady herself is at the left of the altar. You'll see two fine blue-and-yellow *azulejos*—and, outside, a small plaque that reads (in translation): "In this church made his penitence in May 1845 Manuel Pires, one of the last to be executed in Portugal according to the law." Next to these words it's recorded that 1968 marked the centenary of the abolition of the death penalty in Portugal. The Portuguese are proud of their humanitarian laws—the basis of provocative discussion in societies that still employ execution as penalty. If your own arguments have raised a thirst, you might want to pause here for a coffee or try the local white wine, Terras do Demo, with perhaps a hunk of *pão-de-ló* (sponge cake).

On the way to the next main town, Sernancelhe, you'll pass through the tiny hamlet of **Vila da Rua**. Go slowly so that you don't miss its roadside *pelourinho* (town pillory), its pillar topped by a series of carved human faces. On the way, too, you'll pass a little village with a memorable name. And unless some stern authority has demanded a repainting of the road sign, you might still find it daubed with the graffiti of a local wit. PENSO, it says in official letters; LOGO EXISTO, the spray paint adds. In English, "I think, therefore I am."

Sernancelhe (the word means "eyebrow") is 4 km (2½ miles) to the left off the N 226 beyond the village appropriately called Vila do Ponte for the bridge that crosses the Távora river in a rock-patched field. Sernancelhe has a visibly modern appearance, and you may have to ask directions to the ruined castle built by the Knights of Malta, with the eye-catching battlemented *casa do padre* (priest's residence) at its feet. Nearby is another striking *pelourinho* and several elegant residences.

A turnoff to the west on N 229 takes you to **Aguiar da Beira**, an ancient town with castle, medieval clock tower, Manueline *pelourinho,* and Romanesque church built on ancient Roman foundations, the Capela da Nossa Senhora do Castelo. Back at the intersection, the N 226 then leads to **Trancoso**, the first (and busiest) of many walled towns in this part of Portugal built up to protect the country from Spain. Spanish-Portuguese friction resulted in the battle between the two countries that took place in Trancoso in 1385, even though the town had been the site of the celebration of the marriage between King Dinis and Isabel of Aragón a century earlier. The worst skirmish you risk here today is with the town's heavy traffic, since Trancoso lies uncomfortably near a main highway. Battle your way through the modern town to the old city. Park at the gate and walk through the cobblestone streets to the castle—heavily fortified, as were so many castles in the region, by Dom Dinis—for a spectacular survey of the silent landscape surrounding the town. The daily life of Trancoso offers glimpses of the adaptation of modern business to ancient building—you might, for instance, pass the motorbike and cycle repair shop functioning in a handsome, pillared two-story granite house.

The N 226 (then the N 340) continues scenically southeast to the hamlet of Freixadas, where you turn left (north) onto N 221 for the castle town of **Pinhel**. Its **Museu Municipal**, in the former town hall on the praça de Sacadura Cabral, contains a few archaeological and religious relics that hint at the town's former importance as a Roman outpost and an episcopal seat. The faded grace of its churches and residences underscores the point that you have entered one of the least populated parts of Portugal. That fact becomes even more evident as you take N 321 (to the southeast) and N 340 (to the east and northeast) through arid terrain to Almeida, so before leaving Pinhel, you might want to buy a bottle of mineral water or the local wine (you'll see white igloo-shaped vats of it around town) for the trip.

Almeida

Almeida is a flat fortress town protected by ramparts in the shape of a six-pointed star. Though captured by the Spanish in 1762 and held by the French during the Peninsular War, the town is a peaceable place today, with a bandstand, pretty flower-filled gardens, tawny dogs running along the walls, and cows and horses grazing outside the gates. Inside is the **Pousada Senhora das Neves**, elegantly rustic with a polished wood and stucco interior. Because the pousada offers the best and almost only accommodations for miles around, in the high season you should book in advance for two or more nights' stay if you plan to explore the outlying region.

You might begin your tour with a walk around Almeida, along the ramparts built upon older foundations in the 18th century according to the system introduced by the French military engineer Sébastien Le Prestre de Vauban. Despite the new pousada, the town has an appealingly modest appearance. Its official buildings, churches, and residences are a pleasure to discover as you wander ramparts and streets at sunset, when local children play games in the streets and their parents sit and chat. Back at the pousada you can choose your dinner from among its Beira Alta specialties. *Sopa de peixe do Rio Côa* (fish soup), *trutas do Solar de Coelhosa* (trout), *lagueirada de bacalhau* (cod in one of its numerous recipes), and *ensopada de borrego à Beira* (lamb and bread stew) are often served with a fine selection of wines from the Dão and Douro valleys, or you might like to try the local wines from Pinhel and Figueira de Castelo Rodrigo.

CASTLES NEAR SPAIN

"Thou shalt make castels thanne in Spayne, / And dreme of joye, all but in vayne." The pertinent part of Chaucer's translation of Jean de Meun is neither the country (though it is near enough) nor the futility, but the joy of castle dreaming. This part of Portugal, with its remote location, barren terrain, sparse population—not to mention the castles themselves—is highly conducive to such fantasies. Here you are far from sprawling new towns and souvenir stands; most of the castles you will encounter on the loop north of Almeida, as well as farther south, stand in solitary, dream-like ruin.

The route proposed below allows for one long day's excursion. There's much to see. If you don't want too full a day, divide it in two. Head northeast on the country road to Malpartida, where the invading French troops fought a battle at the beginning of the last century. (Today's invaders are a rather more tame contingent of storks that roost on the region's roofs and in the fruit and vegetable plots in the warmer months.) The road then leads through the village of Vermiosa and past the man-made lake and dam of Santa Maria. Just beyond Nave Redonda, have a look at the **Convento de Santa Maria de Aguiar**, a former Cistercian monastery with a noteworthy Gothic church. Farther on is **Figueira de Castelo Rodrigo**, where you might want to stop at the Baroque Igreja Matriz to admire the gilded interior and the unusual upper-choir arch built of granite stones cut in interlocking S shapes. **Castelo Rodrigo**'s castle suffered from border skirmishes and is now in a state of exquisite ruin. Crumbling Gothic arches give way to ivy-covered towers, and ancient windows frame fantastic views of the surrounding countryside.

If you feel hungry in Figueira de Castelo Rodrigo, you might look into a bakery for *orelhas de dom abade* ("abbot's ears" cookies). An agreeable but long day's drive would take you north, on N 221, through the orchards of olive and almond trees and across the Douro river for a brief expedition into the Alto Douro. The highway leads to the little Douro river frontier town of Barca de Alva and on to the fortified town of **Freixo de Espada-à-Cinta**, the birthplace of the 16th-century navigator Jorge Alvares and the 19th-century poet Guerra Junqueiro. Under the watchful seven-sided tower built by Dom Dinis, the **castle** stands guard over the town, whose long name, Ashtree of the Belted Sword, is itself webbed in legends. Step into the Igreja Matriz, a Gothic church remodeled with Manueline details, to see a series of panel paintings attributed to Grão Vasco. Returning south on the N 221, you could turn to the right just a couple of kilometers out of town on the winding road that leads to the summit of the **Durão peak** for more spectacular views.

Retracing your route back across the Douro river to Figueira de Castelo Rodrigo, you could pick up provisions for a picnic along N 332 and N 222, leading northwest 20 km (12 miles) to **Castelo Melhor**, a village at the bottom of a conical hill around which are wrapped ruined medieval castle walls and a tower, with the summit of the hill rising above the walls. Beyond Castelo Melhor, as you drive west on N 222, you will be treated to dramatic vistas of terraced and contour plantings of vineyards and olive trees on the slopes above the Douro and Côa rivers, intermittently visible below. At **Vila Nova de Foz Côa**, 4 km (2½ miles) north of the intersection of N 102 and N 222, you may enjoy both a look at its Manueline church and a snack of its bountiful dried figs and almonds. A long, winding 42 km (26½ miles) west along N 222 brings you to the unassuming town of **São João da Pesqueira**; many of the Douro valley's grape pickers are hired from here for the crucial annual Port wine grape harvest. (With so many winding roads to drive, it's best to plan your own Port wine experiences for the day's end.)

From São João da Pesqueira, you could head south on N 222 and N 229 to **Penedono**, where the tiny golden **castle**, like a figment of Hollywood's imagination, is as elaborately crowned as the pillory at its entrance. Inside, you might note its interesting triangular plan and the extensive views from the top. (If it's locked, the key to the gate is at the café opposite.) A minor road, N 331, leads 25 km (16 miles) east via Meda to the main highway, N 102, where you travel about 8 km (5 miles) south to the turnoff on the right to **Marialva**, above whose charming village lie the extraordinarily impressive ruins of one of the most dramatically deserted of all the castle towns.

The N 102 leads farther south to the intersection with N 226 near Trancoso, where you turn left (east) for the zigzag route past Freixadas and Pinhel back to Almeida.

THE SERRA DA ESTRELA

If Almeida's proximity to Spain tempts you to cross the frontier, a fast dash of Spanish culture is right at hand in **Ciudad Rodrigo**, a fairly sizable town with an authentically Spanish castle and cathedral. (Don't forget your passport, and don't go on a Saturday, when a huge market of everything from potted chickens to pocket calculators in the Portuguese border town of Vilar Formoso creates considerable delays.

But if the silent landscapes and solitary spirit of the Beiras have made their mark upon you, you will find further delight south of Almeida in two tiny castle towns, Castelo Bom and Castelo Mendo, divided, on the map, by the speedy east–west IP 5, in fact accessible from it on minor roads that run underneath. (On the N 332 south of Almeida, you'll see a tiny track on the right that brings you—literally on a farm track—to the village of **Naves**, whose stone cottages and stone lintels above doors and stone steps to an open belfry seem worlds away from the fast traffic on the main highway. But use the highway for a better road to the little hilltop castle towns set like chess pieces on the stark and rugged terrain.) In **Castelo Bom** you'll see some new houses and many old ones of hand-hewn granite, outlines softened by bright flowerpots. You may hear the mellow chimes of the church clock enhancing the ambience of rural peace—and, you'll observe, poverty. At **Castelo Mendo**, you enter through an arched and towered gate guarded by two oddly headless prehistoric granite pigs—victims of a long-ago frontier war, someone might tell you with a smile. But now there's only amity—that's crisp-crusted Spanish bread the old ladies are buying from the travelling van. Up the street you'll come to the village's tall, hollow-topped pillory, a *pelourinho* as individualistic as any you have seen. Climb on up a few steps to the handsome ruins of a once-fine church and a tomb or two of war's human victims. Down where the street starts, look left and right, where two ancient faces observe each other with granite frowns.

South of Almeida, the superhighway N 16/IP 5 will take you swiftly the 39 km (24 miles) to **Guarda**, the highest city in Portugal and known as "the City of the Four Fs." *Fria, farta, forte,* and *feia* are Portuguese for "cold," "full," "strong," and "ugly." Tradition thus excuses not lingering in the busy town, though a stop at the Sé will soon dispel the last unkind remark at least. Like the French Gothic it was modeled on, the cathedral has flying buttresses and grim-faced gargoyles in local granite. Inside is a retable by João de Ruão, who made the monumental door to the Coimbra cathedral. Any lingering impressions of *feia* will disappear next door at the **Museu da Guarda** (located in the Antigo Seminário Episcopal) on General Alves Roçadas street, which contains an exhaustive survey of local archaeological artifacts and religious art. For lunch or dinner—good food and polished service—or an overnight stay, you'll find the sturdy, old-fashioned **Hotel de Turismo** in Guarda very pleasant.

From Guarda it's a short drive of about 26 km (16 miles) on the speedy N 16/IP 5 northwest—in June you'll see women selling cherries like strings of necklaces beside the road—to **Celorico da Beira**. Behind the southern end of the main street there's a useful staging post, the **Hotel Mira Serra**, with tasty regional cooking served in its restaurant—you might try their *lulas grelhadas* (grilled squid). If you stay the night, be sure to ask for a room as far away from the road as possible. The name of this hotel means "overlooking the mountains," and in truth you are not far away. But if you have time visit Celorico's lumbering castle, of pre-Roman origin, later Romanized, then refurbished by King Dinis in the 14th century and sacked by the Spanish in 1762. Building, and refurbishing, continues, you will see, in the little town's modern expansion. You might enjoy, too, another brief diversion, an easy country drive, to **Fornos de Algodres**, 9 km (5½ miles) west on the old N 16, parallel to the newer highway, and then a few kilometers up a steep hill to the plateau leading to **Matança** (a word that means "slaughter," usually of pigs before Christmas). The prime attraction of this route is a superb dolmen betwen Fornos and Matança—you'll see it on the left 6 km (3½ miles) from the main street of Fornos, standing alone in a field of wildflowers. (From this side, unkindly, the blue sign has its back to you.) As you return to Celorico, you'll have, heavy on the skyline, the massive bulk of the Serra da Estrela.

The road to the mountains from Celorico, N 17/IC 6, is signposted Gouveia, about 39 km (24 miles) south (and also Lisbon, rather farther south). The flow and shape of the land will soon tell you that you are among the serra's sprawling foothills. But you should allow a little time to turn left, 11 km (7 miles) from Celorico at the village of Carrapichana, to see **Linhares**. Like a living museum, with two keeps to catch the eye, it's a fortified village of remarkable beauty. Women here still do the family wash in a little stream trickling past the castle walls. History relates that Linhares was taken from the

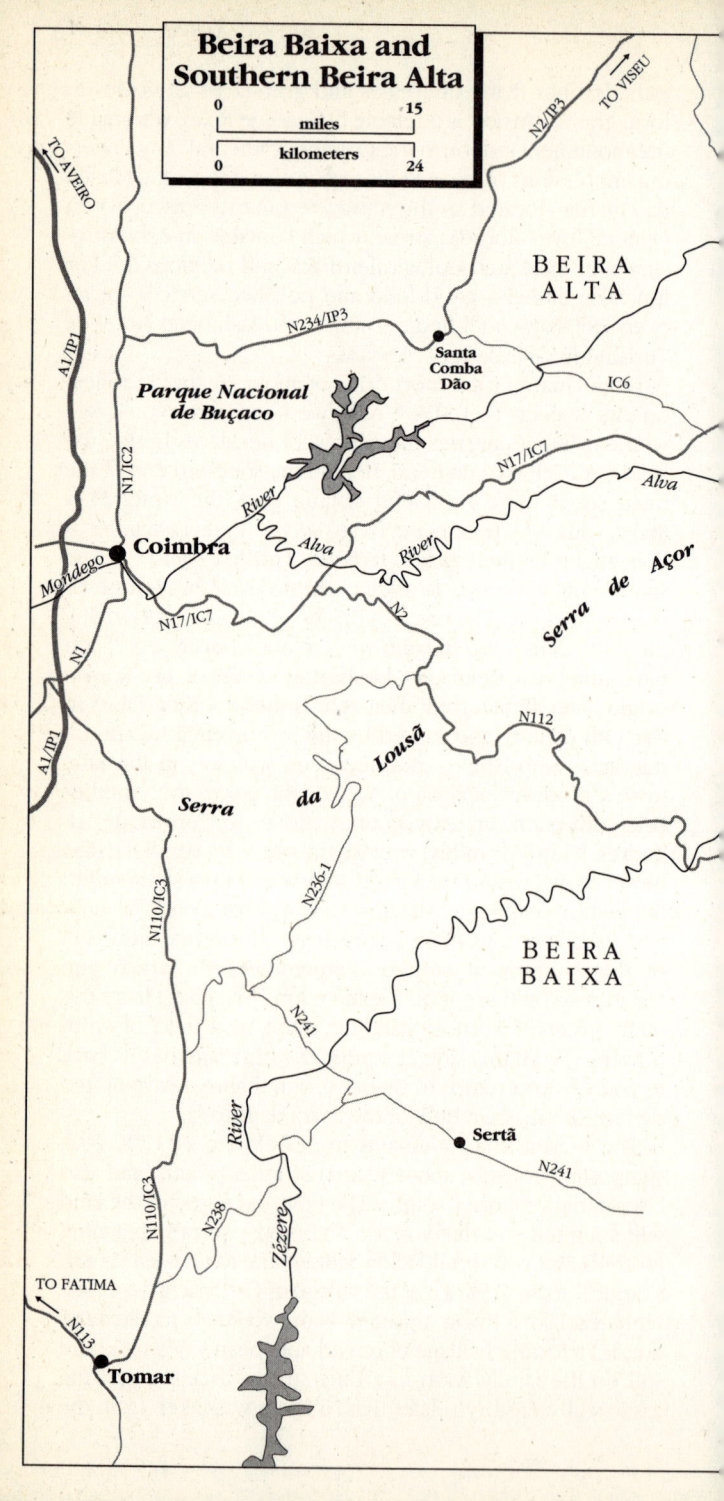

Beira Baixa and Southern Beira Alta

miles
0 — 15

kilometers
0 — 24

TO VISEU
N2/IP3

TO AVEIRO

A1/IP1

N234/IP3

BEIRA ALTA

Santa Comba Dão

IC6

Parque Nacional de Buçaco

N1/IC2

N17/IC7

Alva

River

Alva

Coimbra

Mondego

River

N2

Serra de Açor

N1

N17/IC7

N112

A1/IP1

Serra da Lousã

N236-1

BEIRA BAIXA

N110/IC3

N241

River

Sertã

N241

N110/IC3

N238

Zézere

TO FATIMA

N113

Tomar

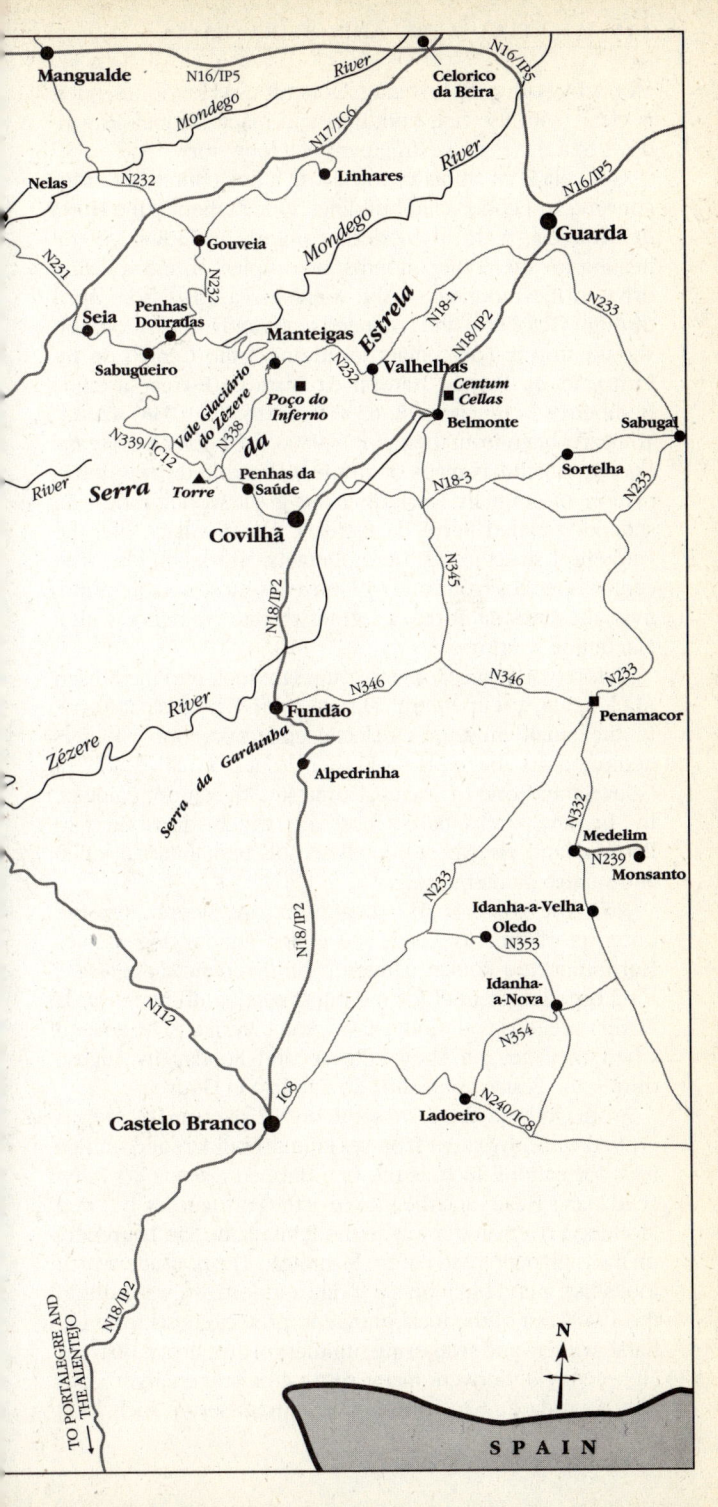

Moors by Portugal's first king, Dom Afonso Henriques, but it is clear from the fine buildings and many Manueline windows that this is only a fragment of a long story.

Gouveia is an attractive town with a fine church, a former convent, and good, solid buildings. One of them is the **Hotel de Gouveia**, with all modern comforts including central heating for the cooler months. If you plan on more than a drive in the mountains—the walking season is from April through October—and you need maps and information, you should stop at (or contact in advance) the **Centro de Informação do Parque Natural da Serra da Estrela**, avenida Bombeiros Voluntarios, 8, 6290 Gouveia; Tel: (038) 424-11. You can obtain from them, for 500$00, the book *Discover the Estrela,* which has maps of all the well-marked paths, information on animals (including the great woolly mountain sheepdog called Serra da Estrela), plants, village life, the geological structure of the mountains, and much else. The center operates from one of Gouveia's most notable buildings, the **Casa da Torre**, a former private residence with a Manueline window.

Before you leave Gouveia you might look into the **Museu Abel Manta**, just up the rua Direita behind the Casa da Torre. In the small museum's eclectic collection, one room is dedicated to the works of Abel Manta, a native son of Gouveia and one of Portugal's finest 19th-century painters. In the few works here (most are widely distributed in Portugal and elsewhere) you'll see his humanitarian touch and superb painter's eye.

Now the road, N 232, begins to rise steeply. On the outskirts of the city you'll see a sign announcing Montes Herminios, the Roman name for the mountain range. Here it's a breeding kennel for the big sheepdog. If the Serra da Estrela breed is your enthusiasm, you may like to be around when they are on show: the second Sunday in August, during the Festas do Senhor do Calvário in Gouveia.

From Gouveia, the drive south on N 232 toward Manteigas is filled with adventure. It passes granite boulders and strange rock formations such as the one dubbed *Cabeça do Velho* (Old Man's Head) and the source of the Portugueses' beloved Mondego river on the way to the **Pousada de São Lourenço**, on the high main road before Manteigas. The pousada, which looks like a combination ski lodge and fortress, was built in the 1940s out of the local granite to protect guests from the harsh winters and sweltering summers of the Serra da Estrela. (It recently underwent major restoration and enlargement.) The Pousada de São Lourenço restaurant serves such local specialties as *bacalhau* (dried salt cod), *truta* (trout from the hatchery at Manteigas just below), *cabrito à Serrana* (kid stew), and *queijo da serra*. Fish dishes go well with Castelo Rodrigo white wines, meat with Covilhã Reserva reds. After dinner, you might try the warming local brandy, Zimbro.

You'll find accommodations strikingly different from the pousada in **Sabugueiro**, well marked on your right some 8 km (5 miles) before the pousada and down a twisting 4-km (2½-mile) road. In this rustic picture-postcard of a village, rooms may be rented from **Casas do Cruzeiro**, a granite house in the heart of the village. There you may eat bread from the kitchen of the *patroa* (owner), mountain cheese from her larder, sausages smoked over her fire, and groceries from her small village shop. Her son, a doctor, had the idea of adapting gracious granite to the tastes of mountain enthusiasts. You can rent horses and saddles from Casas do Cruzeiro, a boat for the lakes and tarns, sleds for the snow, and skis and boots. Unless you, or someone with you, is a nondrinker, it's not a good idea to indulge in a grand dinner at the pousada: The road between the two establishments requires a clear head at all times.

Nearer the pousada, though, some 7 km (4 miles) from the Sabugueiro turnoff, you'll see a sign to **Penhas Douradas**, 1 km (½ mile) up the road. A resort area of sometimes rentable private houses and other accommodations, you'll find here modest bars and restaurants, including the **Caverna de Viriato** (Tel: 075-98-12-62), which also has rooms, and breeds the Serra da Estrela. Along with the mountain cheese, the dog is an emblem—and both, at their best, carry a high price. Be sure, if you buy one or other, that you have the real thing.

The Heart of the Serra da Estrela

From the Pousada de São Lourenço N 232 descends in switchbacks to **Manteigas**, a true mountain town whose older houses have wooden balconies. You can also find meals and accommodations in Manteigas. There are *residênciais* (bed and breakfasts), pensions, and the Albergaria Berne—though much cheaper, none has the grand situation of the pousada or the fey charm of Sabugueiro. Town crafts—textiles and leatherwork—are on display at the Centro Cívico, in the heart of town.

Only a short distance away, an easy drive, are several intriguing sights. You might like to buy bread, mountain cheese, and other provisions in Manteigas and head into the mountains. If you go south, toward Caldas de Manteigas and Torre, and turn left after 5 km or so (3 miles), in about 6 km (3½ miles) you arrive at a place called **Poço de Inferno** (Hell's Well), where a waterfall cascades deep into a gorge of the Leandros river. Back on the road to Torre, N 338, you'll be on one of the mountain's prettiest routes, where shepherds' thatched cottages and wildflowers adorn a tumbling stream. In this lovely **Vale Glaciário do Zêzere** you are near the source of a major Tagus tributary, the Zêzere and, moreover, in a glacial valley that excites geologists.

The road winds gently along the valley for more than 10 km (6 miles), then changes character as it rises steeply into bleak gray rock and climbs the few kilometers to **Torre**, the highest point (1,993 meters/6,539 feet) on mainland Portugal. (Pico, in the Azores, is higher.) You'll sometimes see the altitude given as 2,000 meters, which includes, it's said, the extra reach of the little tower at the top. The natural sights are splendid—the rugged outline, grand setting, black tarns, white heather—but the man-made intrusions at the broad, flat summit do not enhance the view, with the singular exception of the 23-foot sculpture by António Duarte of Nossa Senhora da Boa Estrela, carved into dark rock at Covão de Boi, just before the summit. Radar towers seem inescapable, but you may find a cheerful market of stalls or be pleased that you can get a coffee and refreshments of sorts in the very commercial snack bar. Seasons change everything: Between December and March, when snow conceals litter and tawdry building, the view is enchanting.

It's unlikely that you would come especially to Portugal for the skiing. To ardent and experienced skiers the slopes are of little interest. But if you cannot resist a snowy slope in the winter season, you'll find full information in **Covilhã**, down the mountain to the southeast 20 km (12 miles) or so from Torre. On the way down you'll pass the small ski resort of **Penhas da Saúde**. Of two ski runs in the area, Piornos has a 380-meter (1,247-foot) ski lift that can handle 460 skiers an hour, and the Covões de Loriga run has a 782-meter (2,566-foot) lift with a capacity of 450 skiers an hour. For additional information—also on the increasing range of manor houses in the region (ask for the *turismo de habitaçao* listings)—write to the **Região de Turismo Serra da Estrela**, Praça do Município, 6200 Covilhã; Tel: (075) 32-21-70, Fax: (075) 31-33-64.

Covilhã has a past that rather outshines its present. Founded according to legend in the seventh century by the Visigoth Julião, it was populated by Sancho I in the 12th century, saw the birth of explorer Pero de Covilhã in the 15th century and that of the mystic Heitor Pinto in the 16th, and became a cloth-producing town in the 17th. Its tradition as an industrial center continues today, and what you see is an animated town mixing commerce, university life, a revived Museu Têxtil, in the original factory founded by the marquês de Pombal, and a major market (a good place to buy mountain cheese). Of Covilhã's several hotels and numerous restaurants, you might like the central **Residencial Solneve**, on the main square, for a good, cheap room and regional cooking in its lower-level restaurant. The menu includes such dishes as *feijoada branco* (a white bean stew made with pork and sausages), *panela do forno* (the same meats mixed with rice), *trutas de escabeche* (pickled trout), and *batatas bebedas* ("drunken" potatoes, made with red wine). Try Covilhã and Fundão red and white wines with your meal. The restaurant also offers a broad array of desserts, including the delicious sugar-and-egg-yolk sweet called *barrigas de Perreira*.

Northwest from Torre to Seia, instead of east to Covilhã, a panoramic drive takes you across the entire breadth of the Serra da Estrela. Seia's pleasant houses and churches are memorable in their own right, but the tastiest souvenir of the Serra da Estrela, available here, might be *cabeça da velha*. Named after a local rock formation that resembles the head of an old woman (a short drive away up a country road), it is considered by some to be the best variety of *queijo da serra*. There are accommodations here, if you want, both manor houses and more rustic lodgings. The Turismo here or the larger office in Covilhã can advise.

From Seia the winding N 339/IC 12 leads you 11 km (7 miles) eastward to Sabugueiro; from there it's another 12 km (7½ miles) to the Pousada de São Lourenço.

THE BEIRA BAIXA

Take N 232 east of Manteigas to make a final crossing of the Serra da Estrela into the Beira Baixa. The Roman **Centum Cellas**, on the other side of N 18/IP 2 where N 232 ends, will give you a solid idea of just how ancient this part of Portugal is. The drive there, by contrast with the steep slopes and winding roads you have experienced in the serra, now eases into a gentle foray through forest and farms. Keep going some 24 km (15 miles) past Valhelhas until after you have seen the sign for Belmonte, on the right. You cross a river here, too—the broader, still lovely Zêzere. On the main N 18/ IP 2 you turn left and, almost immediately to your right (before the 2 km the sign says), you will see the square outline of Centum Cellas, also called the Torre de Colmeal. The original function of the ruin remains a mystery; one theory is that it was a Roman inn. If so, it was at least as well constructed as any present-day pousada, as its three stories of well-weathered granite still survive. Rather more likely, perhaps, it was a military structure, or even a fort. It stands there, stark, solitary, and mysterious in a field of broom sedge. But there's a cluster of modern houses just across the blacktop.

A series of enchanting castle towns follows. Just down N 18/ IP 2 from Centum Cellas is **Belmonte**, where there is a panoramic view of the area from the top of the castle wall built by Dom Dinis. Belmonte's name is famous as the birthplace of Pedro Alvares Cabral, the discoverer of Brazil in 1500. (The name Cabral is linked to the word "goat," which you will see in the stone crest on the little chapel.) Belmonte is socially intriguing, too: Here lives a small community of people who cling to their Middle Ages Jewish origin. South of Belmonte look for the N 345 in the direction of Caria, then turn left on N 18-3 toward Santo Amaro and bear left again for **Sortelha**, a stony village enfolded within a strikingly dramatic castle, its keep on a rocky spur, the *pelourinho* and village school just below. There are also a couple of unpretentious restaurants here, **O Celta** (Tel: 071-682-91) and **Restaurante Palmeiras** (Tel: 071-682-60), where you should find regional trout, rabbit, *cabrito,* and perhaps *javali* (wild boar) on the menu. In an ancient granite house in the heart of the old town inside the castle walls, there's also a delightful, dimly lighted, family-run restaurant called **Alboroque**. In its bare-floored, stone-walled, beamed-ceilinged upstairs dining room, you can order anything from grilled chicken to roast pork. And excellent they will be. The local wines from Covilhã and Fundão are cheap and good.

About 10 km (6 miles) to the east of Sortelha is well-signposted **Sabugal**, where you may still see the swallows that have converted loft space in the castle's deeply crenellated keep into a choice nesting spot. The exceptional expansiveness of the castle walls is perhaps due to the special attention King Dinis lavished on its rebuilding, for the formerly Spanish town became Portuguese only when he married Isabel of Aragón. The N 233 leads about 32 km (20 miles) south from Sabugal to the characterful town and castle of **Penamacor**. Within its walls, Catherine the Great's personal physician, António Nunes Ribeiro Sanches, was born to one of the Jewish families who once inhabited much of the region.

Such families flourished at **Monsanto**, 15 km (9 miles) south of Penamacor on N 332 and another 7 km (4 miles) east of Medelim. Today the town, which older Portuguese like to refer to as *a aldeia mais portuguesa do Portugal* (the most Portuguese village in Portugal)—it won a national prize for this odd honor in the Salazar era—is inhabited by elderly folk. Yet many affluent city dwellers are attracted to this singular village with its granite houses built among the boulders on its steep hill. It's worth the climb up (cars won't get this far) to the ruins of the castle to see what was once a Lusitanian *castro* (fortified village) and a vast panorama up to the Serra da Estrela and down to the town of Castelo Branco.

From Monsanto, it's a quiet drive in this plainspoken rural world to **Idanha-a-Velha**—back to Medelim (7 km/4 miles) then south about 9 km (5½ miles) to the haunting town that was once a Celtic village, then the Roman Egitania, and later the birthplace of Wamba, a Visigothic king. Tranquil as Idanha-a-Velha is now, there is an excitement in reading the messages in stone sent across many centuries, in and around the restored early-Christian basilica. (If it's closed, someone will almost certainly appear to let you in.) If you are in any of these unassuming Beira towns and villages at Christmas, you will see how ancient traditions endure in the great log fires each community lights—and maintains for days—in front of their church.

From Idanha-a-Velha you can get to Castelo Branco, the last stop on this suggested route, by heading south to Ladoeiro and west on N 240/IC 8 or, virtually equidistant (some 30 km/19 miles), west toward Oledo and Ponte de São Gens, then south on N 233 and IC 8.

Castelo Branco

Castelo Branco is the most important city in the Beira Baixa, yet its busy history of occupations and sackings has left little of interest to see today. What does remain can be surveyed from the Miradouro de São Gens, a lookout above the west side of town. Throughout its disturbances, Castelo Branco remained famous for its *colchas,* elaborately embroidered (and expensive) bedspreads that are on display (and for sale) at the **Museu Francisco Tavares Proença Júnior,** a regional museum (closed Mondays) housed in the Paço Episcopal (Bishop's Palace). Other noteworthy holdings of the museum include 16th-century Flemish tapestries and Portuguese primitive paintings.

Their sculptural counterparts are around the corner from the museum—note the pleasing pattern of the street's *calçadas* (cobbled pavement)—at the **Jardim do Antigo Paço Episcopal**, terraced gardens laid out in the 18th century. The trees, hedges, shrubs, and flower beds here are groomed with provincial formality. The real delights of the garden, though, are its statues. Pockmarked, moss-covered stone animals, apostles, fathers of the church, and kings of Portugal greet you at every step with a cartoon-like innocence and sagacity at once naïve and sophisticated. You might observe that the passionately disliked Spanish kings who ruled Portugal during the 60-year Hapsburg domination are depicted half the size of the rest.

The best accommodations in the area are at **Casa do Barreiro**, a distinguished manor house in the hill town of Alpedrinha about 40 km (25 miles) north of Castelo Branco on the N 18/IP 2. Also in Alpedrinha is another manor house, the solidly granite **Casa da Comenda**. Whether or not you have bought some Castelo Branco olive oil or cheese—its *cabreiro* is made from goats' milk, and the cheese known as Castelo Branco is a kissing cousin of *queijo da serra*—you might like to try the restaurant in the **Estalagem da Neve** on the southern outskirts of Fundão, a town some 10 km (6 miles) up a winding road to the north. You can also find accommodations either at the *estalagem* or its sister establishment, the **Hotel Samasa-Fundão**, in the town center. The *estalagem* restaurant serves regional specialties as well as the local dish of *lampreia* (lamprey eel), creamy dried salt cod (*bacalhau de natas*), and good Fundão red wine.

GETTING AROUND

The interesting small communities off the main public transportation routes here make a car the best way of getting around in Beira Alta and Beira Baixa. Rodoviária Beira Interior, the leading bus company, serves Viseu, Lamego, Guarda, Covilhã, and Castelo Branco. Viseu, Lamego, Covilhã, and Castelo Branco have centrally located stations served by Caminhos de Ferro (CF), the national railway service; Guarda's station is accessible to the town by bus and taxi. Viseu and Covilhã have small airports; Côja has a little aerodrome. Travel agents can arrange car rentals outside the major cities.

Turismo locations in Viseu (avenida Calouste Gulbenkian; Tel: 032-42-20-14), Lamego (avenida Visconde Guedes

Teixeira; Tel: 054-620-05), Covilhã (praça do Município; Tel: 075-32-21-70), and Castelo Branco (alameda da Liberdade; Tel: 072-210-02) can provide current schedules for local transportation to the smaller destinations.

In Viseu, the Cavalhadas de Vil de Moinhos is celebrated on June 24 and the Feira de São Mateus is held from August to September. In Lamego, the Festas da Nossa Senhora dos Remédios take place in September. In Gouveia, the Festa do Senhor do Calvário is on the second Sunday in August. In Monsanto, May 3 is cherished as the day of Santo das Cruzes; the *festa* is held on the first Sunday after May 3.

ACCOMMODATIONS REFERENCE
Rates given are projected 1993 prices for a double room, double occupancy. Price ranges span the lowest rate in the low season to the highest in the high season. Unless otherwise stated, rates include Continental breakfast. As prices are subject to change, always double-check before booking.

▶ **Casa do Barreiro.** 6095 **Alpedrinha.** Tel: (075) 571-20. 8,200$00.

▶ **Casa da Comenda.** 6095 **Alpedrinha.** Tel: (075) 571-61 or (01) 468-0708. 11,000$00. Open June through September.

▶ **Casa de Rebordinho.** Rebordinho, 3500 Viseu. Tel: (032) 46-12-58. 12,000$00–13,500$00.

▶ **Casas do Cruzeiro.** 6270 **Sabugueiro.** Tel: (038) 228-25; Fax: (038) 232-43. 6,400$00.

▶ **Estalagem da Neve.** 6230 **Fundão.** Tel: (075) 522-15; Fax: (075) 718-09. 10,000$00–11,000$00.

▶ **Hotel de Gouveia.** Avenida 1º de Maio, 6290 **Gouveia.** Tel: (038) 428-90; Fax: (038) 413-70. 9,800$00.

▶ **Hotel Grão Vasco.** Rua Gaspar Barreiros, 3500 **Viseu.** Tel: (032) 42-35-11; Fax: (032) 270-47. 14,000$00.

▶ **Hotel Mira Serra.** 6360 **Celorico da Beira.** Tel: (071) 726-04; Fax: (071) 733-82. 9,000$00–10,000$00.

▶ **Hotel Parque.** Santuário de Nossa Senhora dos Remédios, 5100 **Lamego.** Tel: (054) 621-05; Fax: (054) 652-03. 8,700$00.

▶ **Hotel Samasa-Fundão.** 6230 **Fundão.** Tel: (075) 712-99; Fax: (075) 718-09. 8,500$00–10,500$00.

▶ **Hotel da Senhora do Castelo.** Apartado 4, 3531 **Mangualde.** Tel: (032) 61-16-08; Fax: (032) 62-38-77. 9,000$00–10,500$00.

▶ **Hotel de Turismo.** 6300 **Guarda.** Tel: (071) 21-22-06; Fax: (071) 21-22-04. 14,800$00–16,000$00.

► **Pousada de São Jerónimo**. 3475 **Caramulo**. Tel: (032) 86-12-91; Fax: (032) 86-16-40. 8,000$00–18,000$00.

► **Pousada de São Lourenço**. 6260 **Manteigas**. Tel: (075) 98-24-50; Fax: (075) 98-24-53. 9,700$00–18,000$00.

► **Pousada Senhora das Neves**. 6350 **Almeida**. Tel: (071) 542-83 or 542-90; Fax: (071) 543-20. 9,700$00–18,000$00.

► **Residencial Solneve**. Rua Visconde da Coriscada, 126, 6200 **Covilhã**. Tel: (075) 32-30-01/2/3; Fax: (075) 32-30-01. 6,000$00.

► **Vila Hostilina**. 5100 **Lamego**. Tel. and Fax: (054) 623-94; 11,000$00–13,000$00.

Pousadas can be booked directly: contact ENATUR, Avenida Santa Joana Princesa, 10, 1700 Lisbon, Portugal: Tel: (01) 848-1221 or 848-9078; Fax: (01) 80-58-46. But it is easier to make reservations through a travel agent. In the United States and Canada, pousadas can also be booked through Marketing Ahead, 433 Fifth Avenue, New York, NY 10016; Tel: (212) 686-9213; Fax: (212) 686-0271.

Manor houses can be booked directly or through the manor-house associations—ANTER, P.I.T., PRIVETUR, and TURIHAB—listed in Useful Facts. Most of the houses belong to one or more of these associations, but because membership rosters change frequently we haven't attempted to spell out the associations for each house. Readers are advised to contact the manor-house associations for their current listings.

In the United States and Canada, it is possible to reserve rooms in P.I.T. manor houses through E & M Associates, 211 East 43rd Street, Suite 1404, New York, NY 10017; Tel: (212) 599-8280; Fax: (212) 599-1755.

PORTO AND THE DOURO VALLEY

By Ingeborg Lippmann
and Thomas de la Cal

Ingeborg Lippmann, a freelance photojournalist, was based in Africa and the Middle East for the New York Times *and* Time *magazine for twenty years, contributing to the* Christian Science Monitor, Newsweek, *and other publications as well. She has also covered much of South America. Over the past two decades she spent a few weeks each year covering Portugal, especially for the* New York Times *travel section. She now lives just outside Lisbon. Thomas de la Cal is the contributor for the Ribatejo, Minho, and Trás-os-Montes sections of this book.*

Called Portus-Cale by the Romans, Porto gave a name to a nation as well as to a world-renowned wine. From ancient beginnings at the mouth of the Douro river in northwestern Portugal, Porto grew into an important commercial city, and its inhabitants take pride in their reputation for industriousness. If you want convincing, walk along any of the city's shopping streets just before 9:00 A.M. and you'll find yourself wading in soapy water. Every morning before opening, shopkeepers scrub down the sidewalks in front of their establishments.

Commerce has ruled here since the time of the Phoenicians, who dropped anchor at the estuary and traded their wares for the metals mined in the interior. The gray pallor of

Porto's buildings matches the gray pinstripes of its merchants, and some of the city's most important monuments, such as its two steel bridges and its imposing stock exchange, are a tribute to their accomplishments.

Today Porto is undergoing urban renewal, spurred by a new artificial harbor on the Atlantic shore to the northwest. Old Porto, in and around the Penaventosa hill, on the right (northern) bank of the river, has been left to age slowly like a vintage wine. Here you will find a charming city where medieval quarters, Gothic steeples, Baroque spirals, handsome wooden boats, and colorful outdoor markets combine in a collage to be explored and savored like the blends of a fine tawny or ruby Port.

In less than an hour's drive east of Porto the terrain of this northern region, which stretches from the Atlantic Ocean to Spain, changes quickly from the humid, flat, populous industrial belt around the city of Porto, the Douro Litoral (Coastal, or Lower, Douro), to the dry, mountainous, and thinly populated interior of the Alto Douro (Upper Douro). Tucked away in the heart of this region lies the rugged and secluded Vale do Douro (Douro River Valley). Its soil and microclimate are ideal not only for the grapes that produce Port wine but also for travellers in search of scenic and vintage Portugal.

Despite their physical and climatic differences, the two Douros are joined historically and economically by the river, from whose golden complexion (*douro* means "golden" in Portuguese) they derive their name. The river's strategic importance—it links Portugal to Zamora and Valladolid in Spain and delineates Portugal's north—and the region's rich natural resources have over the centuries attracted traders, settlers, and armies who in turn have left their mark on its population, its food, and the land itself. Its people inherited the Celtic love of lore, the Phoenician savvy for commerce and maritime exploration, the Roman affinity for large urban projects, the Visigothic individuality and work ethic, the Suevic predilection for sausages, and the Moorish sweet tooth and terrace-farming techniques. And they have learned to live with the British, who have played an important role in the region's economy through the Port-wine trade for more than 250 years.

Our route starts with Porto, as the gateway to the region, and moves counterclockwise through the heart of the Douro.

MAJOR INTEREST

Porto

Sé (Gothic cloister and crypt of the bishops of Porto)
Medieval quarter of the Barredo
Museu de Arte Sacra (religious treasures)
Museu Guerra Junqueiro (Hispano-Arabic pottery and Flemish tapestries)
Eating and drinking in the waterfront quarter of the Ribeira
Igreja de São Francisco (gilt)
Palácio da Bolsa (Stock Exchange)
Baixa shopping district
Sweeping views of the city and environs from the Clérigos tower
Museu Soares dos Reis (Portuguese art masters)
Museu Romântico (and its Port-wine lodge, Solar do Vinho do Porto)
Jardim Botânico
Casa dos Serralves (modern art museum)
Port-wine lodges in Vila Nova de Gaia
View of Porto from the convent of Nossa Senhora da Serra do Pilar

Foz do Douro
Castelo de São João da Foz
Castelo do Queijo

Matosinhos
Igreja do Senhor Bom Jesus

The Douro Valley
Santa Maria de Cárquere priory near Resende
Sweeping views of Port country at Barrô
Peso da Régua Port-wine center
Annual grape harvest in vineyards near Pinhão
Alijó's Celtic ruins and manor houses
Mesão Frio view of the valley
Train tours of the Douro Valley

Amarante
Houses hanging over the Tâmega
Igreja de São Gonçalo
Arraial de São Gonçalo folk festival

The Food and Wine of the Douro

Fish is the staple of the coastal areas, while meat and sausages are favored by the people of the interior. Codfish, which Douro fishermen have been catching off Newfoundland since the 16th century, is particularly dear to the Litoral diet in its dried salt form, *bacalhau*. The Portuguese not only taught the world how to preserve the fish by salting but have also devised more than 365 ways of preparing it. *Bacalhau à Gomes de Sá,* named after a Porto restaurant owner, is a delectable baked cod, potato, and onion casserole garnished with eggs and olives. *Tripas à moda do Porto,* a spicy combination of beans, sausages, and tripe, was invented in the 15th century by ingenious Porto housewives after Prince Henry the Navigator requisitioned their meat to provision one of his armadas and left them to make do with the offal. Porto's citizens were eventually rewarded for their sacrifice when Henry's efforts to discover a sea route to the spice trade succeeded, some years after his death, in bringing to the city's larders a host of exotic spices and ingredients.

In the mountain and pastoral areas of the Alto Douro, *cordeiro* (lamb) and *cabrito* (baby goat) are popular meats, particularly braised lamb served with baked rice. Dark blood sausages, *morcelas,* are used widely in stews, while the more common garlicky pork *chouriços* are incorporated in soups and grilled as appetizers. River trout stuffed with golden brown *presunto* (air-cured ham) from Lamego or Chaves is an Alto Douro delicacy.

The people of the Douro share in the Portuguese affinity for egg-based and caramelized sweets—and have a sense of humor. Where else can you taste sweets with names like *barrigas de freira* (nun's tummies) and *testiculos de São Gonçalo?* The figs, oranges, and other fresh fruits of the Vale do Douro area are lower-calorie alternatives.

The Douro is one huge wine cellar. Apart from the famous fortified Ports, of which there are more than 150 varieties, there are also young, tart *vinhos verdes,* Douro reds and whites, *vinhos espumantes* (sparkling wines), and after-dinner spirits such as *bagaço,* Portugal's equivalent of grappa, and Cognac-styled *aguardente.*

Port is a fortified wine produced solely in the Douro river valley and its tributaries from a variety of grapes. The secret lies in its fortification process. When high-proof *bagaço* is added to young wines at the proper time, fermentation (the conversion of sugar to alcohol) is stopped to help maintain the sweetness and fruity flavor of the grapes. The process results in a unique wine with a rich color, a natural sweetness, and extraordinary longevity.

Port is named after the city of Porto, where it has traditionally been aged, bottled, and shipped. Before obtaining its present name, however, it was known variously as *vinho de embarque* (embarkation wine), on account of the way it was shipped by boat, and priest Port, because most of it came from monasteries. In 1986 the strict laws governing Port wine were changed. Now Port can be produced, aged, bottled, and shipped directly from any estate or by any grower in the Douro without having to pass through Porto.

There are several versions of how the making of Port came about. The most accepted theory is espoused by Nicolau de Almeida, in his seventies and master blender of the venerated Ferreira Port house; he believes that Port was produced by accident in 1820 when a change in weather yielded higher-than-normal sugar content in the grapes that stopped the fermentation process. The Anglo community in Porto, however, claim that it was a British subject by the name of Peter Bearsley who invented Port by chance one day when he added elderberry juice to his wine and found that it improved the wine's color and taste. The addition of some sort of brandy also helped maintain the freshness of the wines, some of which had not travelled well on the long sea journey to England.

Purists maintained that this barbarous practice adulterated an otherwise fine wine, but they waged a losing battle against the proponents of fortification. Their protests were not entirely in vain. The making of Port has improved since the early 19th century: Elderberry juice was abandoned; the fortification is now achieved by the use of the more refined and effective *bagaço* brandy (distilled from the hulls of crushed grapes), and the production and aging of the wine is carefully supervised by the government-run Port Wine Institute.

The process starts at the grape harvest each fall in the Douro wine region (the first demarcated region in the world, in 1756—a century before the French came up with the Appellation Contrôlée), which begins roughly 60 miles east of Porto and stretches along the river and its tributaries to the Spanish border. The grapes are crushed and stored in warehouses upriver at Peso da Régua and its environs for the winter, when the cool weather helps the lees settle. When fermentation reaches a desired point, brandy is added (roughly one-fifth of the wine volume), stopping fermentation within about 48 hours.

In the spring the new wine traditionally is transported to the shippers' lodges in suburban Vila Nova de Gaia, across the river from Porto, where it is allowed to mature. The wine is first kept in large wooden barrels called *pipas* for two to three years, while the lees continue to be drawn out. At the end of this period it is tasted and categorized. Some Ports continue to be aged in wooden barrels, others in bottles. The more common Ports, aged in barrels, generally are blended with other years' wines, which helps maintain the quality and standard of a particular brand, while the early bottled Ports normally come from a single harvest and are known as vintage Ports, or crusted Ports.

There are Ports for every occasion and taste. White Ports, which are the product of several types of white grapes and are blended, are aged in casks and come in sweet, dry, or extra-dry varieties. The last are light bodied and make an excellent aperitif. Ruby Ports are also blended, but are more full bodied, younger and sweeter, and serve as ideal dessert wines and mixers. Tawny Ports have been called the "Port man's Port" because of their mellow taste, which makes them suitable for all occasions. Some inexpensive tawnies are blended from ruby and white Ports, but the better-quality ones are often allowed to acquire their amber color and smooth flavor through the aging of blends of red wines in wooden barrels for seven to more than 40 years. It is expensive to maintain wines in a cask for a long time, so some older tawny Port can be more expensive than a bottle of vintage Port.

Vintage Port, however, is the queen of Ports. It is the product of an exceptional harvest. The unblended wine is normally bottled two years after the vintage, and matured for no less than ten years in the bottle. It is rich in color and full bodied. It is stored lying down to prevent the cork from drying out, and throws a heavy sediment, which explains why it is decanted. The next best thing to the vintage is the late-bottled vintage, or L.B.V., also the product of a fine vintage, which is allowed to mature longer in the cask before being bottled sometime from the fourth to sixth years of its age. The difference between the vintage and the L.B.V., however, is that the latter can be sold right after it is corked and does not need decanting. Another important vintage is *colheita* (also sometimes called Port of the vintage), which requires at least seven years in cask before bottling. Vintage, L.B.V., and *colheita* Ports are normally served as after-dinner drinks.

There is also a relative newcomer: single-vintage estate-bottled Port, a Port wine produced from the grapes of a single quinta, estate aged and bottled, then shipped from the quinta by the producer. Single-quinta Port *can* be a vintage, often is as good as a vintage, and generally is less expensive than a regular, blended, vintage Port.

The British, who made Ports fashionable throughout the world, have recently been surpassed by the French as the largest importers of Port wines (the French import mainly aperitif-type Port) but have increased their consumption of the finer vintage Ports. You can taste or acquire Port wine at the plush Solar do Vinho do Porto on the grounds of the Museu Romântico at the Quinta da Macierinha in Porto or at the wine lodges that line the dock at Vila Nova de Gaia across from the city.

The same grapes of the Upper Douro are used to produce unfortified table wines of note, such as Ferreira's superb red Barca Velha and Constantino's white Monopólio, and some of Portugal's best *vinhos espumantes,* such as the brut and *meio-seco* Raposeira bubblies. The latter are aged and fermented in cool, dank caves carved out of a mountain above the town of Lamego. Except during the month of August, the caves are open to visitors.

PORTO

At first glance, Porto is a city of gray buildings softened by red-tile roofs. The sober granite architecture of the financial district is almost forbidding until you step behind the façades—for example, into the sumptuous Salão Arabe in the Palácio da Bolsa (Stock Exchange). Explore the city on foot and you will come upon color and liveliness around every corner. Gothic elegance alternates with Baroque flair, while a few steps away tiny, ancient pastel houses—with laundry billowing in a riot of color from their balconies— miraculously stay in place on steep hillsides that plunge down to the river. This is the ancient and proud city that gave the nation not only its name but also its language, helped liberate Lisbon from the Moors, and produced Henry the Navigator. Its important contributions to the Portuguese nation and the working-class values and independent streak of its citizens make it the quintessentially Portuguese city. And although Porto, Portugal's second-largest city, may have lost some of its temporal power to its flashier rival, Lisbon, in the eyes of most of the nation it is still the hereditary guardian of all things Portuguese.

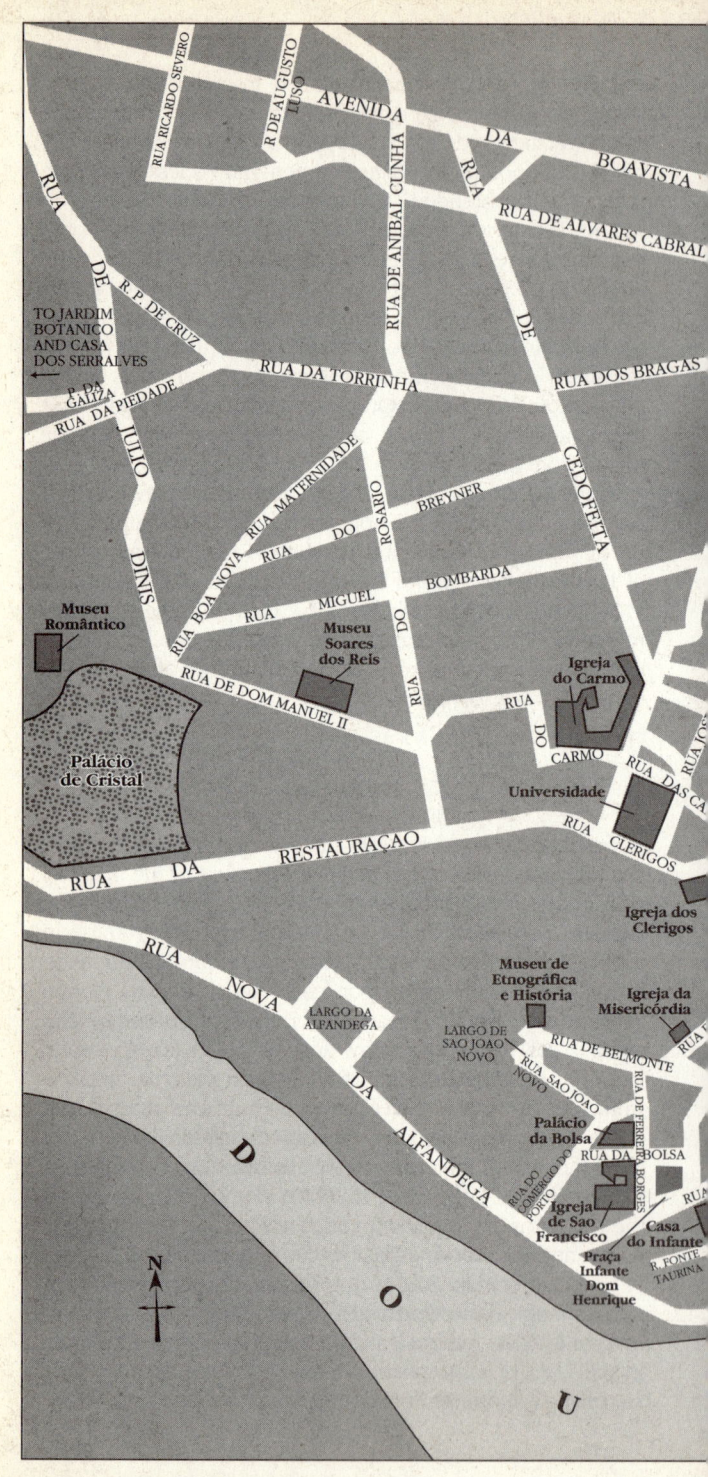

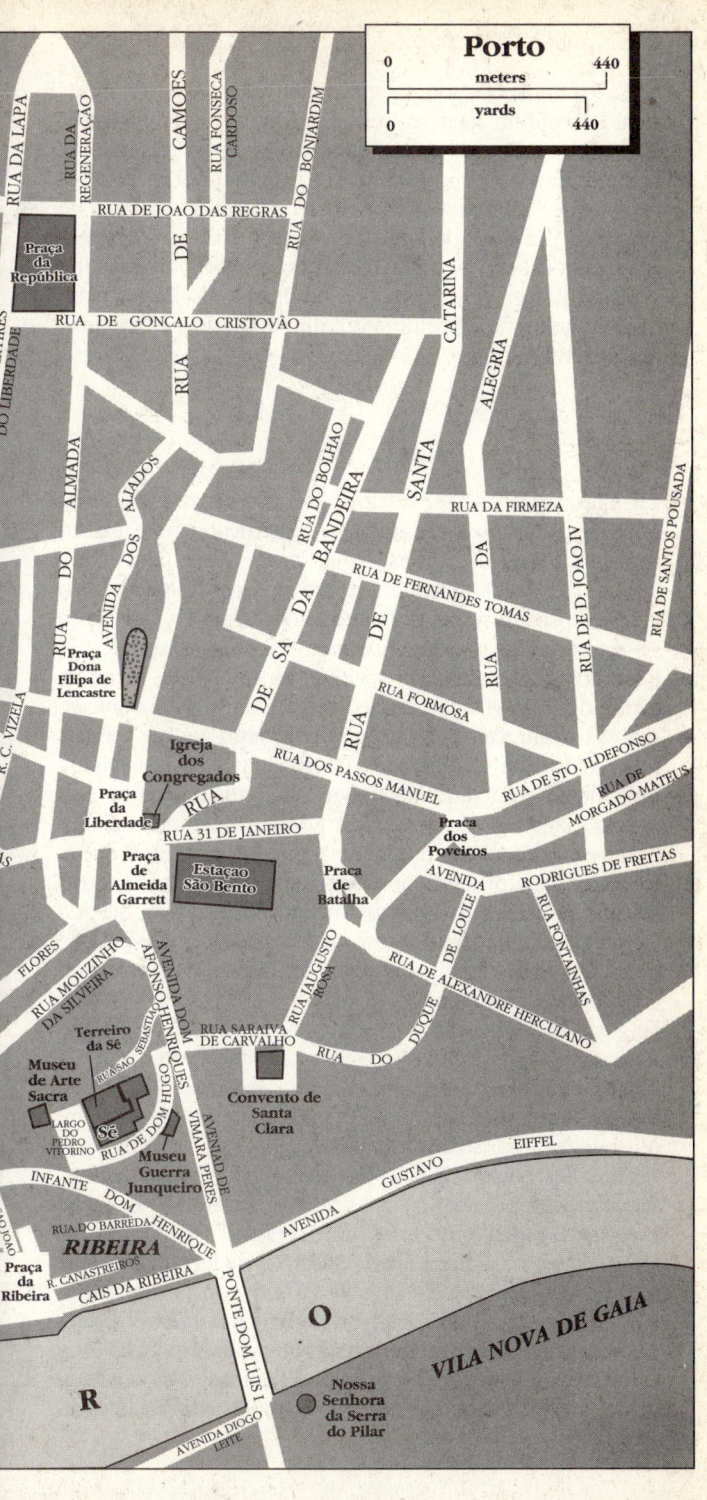

Porto, unlike Lisbon, is somewhat reluctant to flaunt its wealth in public. Its treasures lie hidden behind the ancient doors of granite palaces and museums, which house the art and antiques collections of the city's wealthiest merchants, and in the wines maturing in the cool cellars of its wine lodges at Vila Nova de Gaia. The narrow, cobbled alleyways and old houses of the working-class neighborhoods, and the stalls of flower vendors and fishmongers along the river, display the city's colorful side. Allow time to get to know Porto. Savor it slowly.

Early Porto

The Porto area has been inhabited for more than 3,000 years, but wars, earthquakes, and new construction have erased most of the signs of this early habitation. Some vestiges of pre-Celtic and Celtic civilization have been unearthed on Penaventosa hill, where the cathedral stands today, and can be seen in the Museu de Etnografia e História at largo de São João Novo. The Celtic or Celtiberian Lusitanians lived in fortified hill towns and carried out trading with Phoenician merchants attracted to the area's metal deposits. The hamlets ranged from the smaller *castros* (fortified villages) containing individual clans to *citânias* (towns) of up to 200 households.

Historians say that when the Romans finally conquered the area in the second century B.C., after a long, arduous struggle, they fortified the existing city on the right (north) bank and renamed it Portus. Across from it, on the left (south) bank, they built a new metropolis, which they called Cale. The twin cities came to be known as Portucale, and their dialect and name later served as the models for the language and the name of the new nation, Portugal. The Romans were replaced by the Suevi and the Visigoths in the fifth and sixth centuries A.D. (parts of the former Suevic wall can be seen near the cathedral); they, in turn, were vanquished by Moorish armies in 711.

Porto has always been in the forefront of Portuguese history. It was one of the first cities on the peninsula to shake off Moorish domination, in the 11th century. A Porto bishop, Dom Pedro Pitões, persuaded English Crusaders on their way to the Holy Land to help liberate Lisbon. Porto's merchants, equally resourceful and independent, were pioneers in championing civilian rule in the 14th century. By supporting the Crown against powerful nobles and bishops, they obtained in 1478 a royal decree barring the nobility from residing in their district. Their money and shipyards were used in Portugal's 15th- and 16th-century maritime exploration, and their fortunes, and those of the city, became tied to the new territories. In the 16th century, for example, the city was hard hit by its loss of the spice monopoly, but in the 18th century it became very prosperous through the development of the wine trade with England.

Napoleonic troops took Porto twice, in 1808 and 1809, but were finally expelled in 1809 by troops led by Sir Arthur Wellesley, the future duke of Wellington. The French invasions, however, sowed the seed of republicanism. In 1818 Porto Freemasons formed a liberal movement that spread to Lisbon and ended in 1820 in a constitution limiting the power of the Crown and terminating the Inquisition. This was followed by a civil war, won by the liberals, but only after Porto was besieged and bombarded during a year-long struggle. To pay off the huge war debt, the new government abolished the monasteries and sold off their holdings—which is why so many of these properties in Porto are owned today by private persons or the civil authorities.

The enterprising spirit of Porto's merchants ran free during the late 19th century. In 1876 Gustave Eiffel built a steel railway bridge (the Ponte de Dona Maria Pia) linking the right bank with Vila Nova de Gaia and the rest of Portugal to the south. This was followed ten years later by an impressive two-tier metal road bridge, the Ponte Dom Luis I, designed by Eiffel's disciple, Seyrig, which joins the upper and lower levels of Porto and Vila Nova de Gaia. (The Ponte de Dona Maria Pia has been declared a monument. A new concrete railway bridge next to it, the Ponte de São João, was inaugurated in July 1991.)

The beginning of the 20th century brought a new era of economic development and public works. The age-old problem of flash floods, which for centuries had devastated the lower part of the city and the Port-storage facilities at Vila Nova de Gaia, was finally solved with the damming of the Douro. A third bridge, the Ponte da Arrábida near the mouth of the river, completed in 1963, spans its 890-foot width in one single reinforced concrete arch and now carries the A 1/IP 1 highway, which connects with main routes on the north side of the river.

Today the economic emphasis has shifted away from the river to the seafront north of the river mouth, where such industries as fish canning, textile manufacture, furniture making, and ceramics are thriving. The old city and its Port wine have been left to age in peace.

The British and Porto

The British have traded with Porto (which they call Oporto) since the 14th century and have been a permanent fixture in the city since the 18th. At first they came to the river's mouth and traded cloth and codfish for Portuguese wine, honey, and fruit. Many of them eventually settled here and continued a brisk trade that was made official by the signing of the Methuen trade treaty between England and Portugal in 1703. The Douro replaced the Minho just to the north as England's main wine supplier, and the Port wine industry developed. The British wine exporters grew rich carrying out their business in the rua dos Ingleses (now called rua do Infante Dom Henrique) in Porto, and built their own Factory House (named after factors, or wine-buying agents, of the 16th century), where they held lavish parties. But life in Porto was not without its problems. The English Port merchants had to deal with the Inquisition (which among other things barred them from burying their dead in Portuguese soil), various attempts to break up their monopoly, Napoleonic invasion, a blight that nearly wiped out the vineyards, then fascism and revolution. Through their pluck and courage, and with occasional help from British forces, they have managed to endure.

The history of the Anglo community in Porto teems with colorful and resourceful characters. There was Scotsman George Sandeman, who arrived in Porto in 1790 with 300 pounds to his name and built it into a fortune and one of the largest of the Port houses. The future doyenne of the Delaforce Port house arrived in Portugal clinging to an empty barrel after a shipwreck. And there was the liberty-loving Richard Noble, who, whenever he saw a crowd fighting the police, would pick up his cane and lead the mob. There were also Renaissance men such as Joseph James Forrester, whose talents as an artist, surveyor, and cartographer were used to chart the Douro wine region and river, for which he was awarded a barony by the king of Portugal in 1855. He was also a Port purist who fought a bitter but losing battle with the British wine trade in Porto and London on the subject of adulteration. He drowned in his beloved Douro river in 1861, when his boat capsized in the dangerous Valeira rapids (now tamed by a dam). His two female companions, members of the Portuguese Ferreira Port dynasty, floated to safety, buoyed by their voluminous petticoats.

The descendants of those first Port merchants continue to thrive in Porto today. They remain English: They play cricket on Saturdays at their Lawn Tennis Club, swim at the Praia dos Ingleses near Foz, send their children to the British school of Porto, attend services at their Protestant church, and celebrate the Queen's birthday. And every Wednesday, as they have for more than 200 years, the male members of the British Association, some of whom trace their ancestry to the founding Port houses, meet at the Factory House to discuss business over lunch and Port. (They started meeting on Wednesdays because that was the day there was no delivery of mail from Britain, and they could therefore take their time over Port and cigars.) On the weekends they retire upriver to their quintas on the hills overlooking the Douro to oversee the maturing of the grapes.

Porto is a city of hills on the right (north) bank of the Douro. Its oldest and most photogenic quarters are situated three miles upriver from the estuary, in the southeastern corner of the sprawling city. The colorful waterside *bairro* (quarter) of the Ribeira is known for its street vendors and tiny bistros; the medieval Barredo quarter climbs the steep Penaventosa above it. At the summit, commanding a view of the city and its environs, is Porto's cathedral. The town of Vila Nova de Gaia, home of the Port wine lodges, lies directly across on the left bank. Porto and Vila Nova de Gaia are linked here by the two-tier Ponte Dom Luis I, a 19th-century metal bridge.

The center of Porto is a five-minute walk north from the cathedral via the avenida Dom Afonso Henriques, past the São Bento train station. At its center is the busy praça da Liberdade, which once served as the main northern entrance to the former walled medieval city; the 14th-century wall was torn down in the 18th century as the city grew northward. Remnants of the former two-mile wall can be seen above the Ribeira and in Miragaia, a picturesque area very near the Ribeira, running along the rua Nova da Alfândega and the Douro river. The area around the square is called the Baixa and serves as Porto's shopping and commercial district. Running north from it is the wide, elegant avenida dos Aliados, planted with flower beds and lined with outdoor cafés, restaurants, and banks and other businesses. Some of Porto's older hotels and pensions lie on the tiny streets and squares off it. At the top of the avenue is the imposing 20th-century city hall, flanked by the tourist and the main post offices. The city's modern hotels are located a ten-minute drive west of the Aliados on the avenida da Boavista, a modern thoroughfare that connects the city to the airport and Porto's beach suburbs of Foz and Matosinhos.

Porto is a walking, bus, and cab city. Most of its sights are contained in one main hub. Cars are best left at the hotels or in one of the few parking areas. Parking on the main thoroughfare, the avenida dos Aliados, is by meter.

Give yourself two full days to get to know the city. Make sure you wear comfortable walking shoes with rubber soles capable of handling the steep slopes and slippery cobbled streets. Most museums are open from 10:00 A.M. to noon and 2:00 to 5:00 P.M. Tuesday through Sunday (shops keep approximately the same weekday hours but are open on Saturday mornings only and closed Sundays), except for the Museu Romântico, Museu de Arte Sacra, the Museu Guerra Junqueiro, and the Museu de Etnografia História, which close on Sundays. Casa dos Serralves (the National Museum of Modern Art) is open from 2:00 to 8:00 P.M. Tuesdays to Sundays. The Museu de Arte Sacra can be visited by appointment only; call the cathedral (Tel; 02-200-8056 or 200-2678) to arrange a visit. The wine lodges can be visited Monday through Friday during the winter, and add Saturdays to their roster from June through August. The Sandeman, Real Vinícola, and Cálem lodges are open on Saturdays throughout the year.

The Cathedral

To the southwest of avenida Dom Afonso Henriques, at the top of the steep, wind-swept Penaventosa hill, stands Porto's cathedral, or *Sé,* where the parents of Prince Henry the Navigator, Philippa of Lancaster and João I of Portugal, were married in 1387, and where Henry was later christened. The Sé's foundations were laid in the 12th century, but many additions have been made over the ages to the original fortress-like Romanesque structure. Of note on the exterior are its elaborate Baroque doorway and elegant 13th-century rose window. The interior is rich in gold and silver. The 17th-century silver altar in the main chapel was painted over during the French invasions to conceal its splendor from marauding troops. Other items of note are a bronze relief of the baptism of Christ in the baptistry to the left as you enter the church; the crypt of the bishops of Porto, with a 17th-century gold-carved retable; and the 14th-century Gothic **cloister**, decorated with tiles depicting scenes from the Song of Songs in the Bible and from Ovid's *Metamorphoses.*

The tiny square on the north side of the Sé contains the

statue of Vimara Peres, who liberated the city from the Moors in 868. On Saturdays the square turns into the Vandoma flea market, where antique curios can be picked up at bargain prices. The Terreiro da Sé, the square in front of the cathedral, is the site of the former Baroque palace of the archbishops of Porto, which now serves as a municipal office building. It is an ideal spot from which to admire the picturesque Barredo and Ribeira quarters tumbling down to the river.

The Barredo

The tiny houses of this ancient *bairro* cling precariously to the steep slopes of Penaventosa, and since 1985 the city of Porto has been restoring some of the old structures. It is a miracle that so many of these homes have withstood earthquakes throughout the centuries. Segments of a sixth-century Suevic wall and a 12th-century addition stand directly below the northwestern corner of the Terreiro da Sé. A few steps south of the wall, at largo de Pedro Vitorino, is the **Museu de Arte Sacra**, which contains the religious treasures (plate, liturgical books, and vestments) that citizens of Porto were able to hide from Napoleon's troops, a valuable coin collection, and liturgical instruments (organs and stringed instruments such as lutes and guitars) from the 15th to the 19th century collected by Porto's wealthy bishops. Southeast of the museum at rua de Dom Hugo, 32, is the **Museu Guerra Junqueiro**, a lavish dwelling offering a glimpse of patrician life in Victorian Portugal. It contains some examples of the work of the satirical poet Guerra Junqueiro (1850–1923), as well as Hispano-Arabic pottery, Flemish tapestries, religious sculptures, and Portuguese furniture from the 16th century collected by the wealthy artist.

A maze of stone stairs, one of which is the Escada do Barredo (especially picturesque but best avoided at night), runs down from rua de Dom Hugo to the rua do Barredo, past homes festooned with colorful laundry billowing against the wind-like spinnakers. Like Lisbon's Alfama, this photogenic quarter is the scene of purse- and camera-snatchings, so proceed with caution.

The Ribeira

The quaint but crumbling waterfront quarter of Ribeira lies directly south of the rua do Barredo, and west of the Ponte Dom Luis I. This *bairro,* like the Barredo, has undergone some face-lifting since 1985. The quarter is crossed west to east by the cobbled cais (quay) da Ribeira, which contains the remains of the 14th-century Fernandina wall. Parts of the quay's thick wall have been converted into taverns and bistros from which you can gaze at the river, where wooden *rabelos* (square-riggers), loaded with wine kegs, are docked. These long, handsome vessels once carried the precious wine cargoes down the fast waters of the Douro to Porto. The **Taverna Bébobos** is a typical Ribeira tavern, where such simple regional fare as *sardinhas grelhadas* (grilled sardines) or a *caldeirada* (multifish stew) can be washed down with glasses of *vinho verde* drawn from a cask; closed Sundays.

The elegant and expensive **Casa Victorino**, at 44–48 rua dos Canastreiros, also in the Ribeira area, is very small—only seven tables—and specializes in fish. Although it's part of an old house and retains the granite block walls, the restaurant is air-conditioned. It's best to reserve; Tel: (02) 208-0668. Closed Sundays.

Housed in a former warehouse, **Downing Street** restaurant, at praça da Ribeira, 10, at the western end of the quay, has a third-floor dining room decorated with vintage photos of Porto and looks out onto the ancient cobbled square with its colorful renovated Ribeira houses. A house specialty is *arroz de tamboril* (monkfish and rice stew).

A Porta Nobre, Porto's newest and most genteel dining experience, lies a five-minute walk west, via rua Infante Dom Henrique, on the largo de São Francisco (on the western end of the Ribeira directly across the street from the Igreja de São Francisco). The restaurant, lodged in a newly refurbished, three-story riverfront house, has the look and feel of an English club and a balanced menu of Continental and Portuguese nouvelle cuisine. Crêpes and soufflés are house specials, served in all their flamboyant splendor by efficient waiters dressed in perfectly starched black tailcoats. Three dining rooms and two bars provide variety (two have views of the river) and a rich array of silver, china, silk, oak, and lace. This refined elegance tends to attract a mixture of old money and the new captains of industry from the Porto Stock Exchange, a two-minute walk north from the restaurant. Call and reserve a window table; Tel: (02) 200-1101.

Near the waterfront market at rua da Reboleira, 37, is the **Centro Regional de Artes Tradicionais**, with revolving displays of traditional handicraft techniques and the objects that result, from regions of Portugal and throughout the world. The shop on the lower level emphasizes Portuguese crafts.

The Ribeira is the setting for the city's most popular *festa,* the feast days of São João on the night of June 23 into all hours of June 24. The event is a pagan summer-solstice ritual, adopted by the Church, in which the population of Porto spends two nights of revelry consuming rivers of *vinho verde* and eating roast kid. Huge bonfires are lit to celebrate São João.

The Financial District

Porto's financial district lies a few steps northwest of the Ribeira square. At the juncture of the rua Infante Dom Henrique (formerly rua dos Ingleses) and rua de São João, above the square, you will encounter the four-story Georgian **Factory House**, which was built in the 18th century by British consul John Whitehead. The area in which it stands was once an elegant commercial center; now it is run-down and somewhat shabby. Behind the austere colonnaded façade of gray granite, however, is a richly decorated club where the young Wellington and his officers danced the night away in the early 19th century. Its well-stocked library is cared for by the wine families' historian. Entrance is barred to the general public, but you may catch a glimpse of the interior through one of its windows or the wrought-iron gate.

The rua Infante Dom Henrique runs west into the praça Infante Dom Henrique, dominated by a statue of the city's most famous son, Henry the Navigator. South of the square, on rua da Alfândega, is the **Casa do Infante**, popularly (but not by most historians) believed to be his birthplace. The 14th-century structure, which served as a customs house until the last century, has now been restored and converted into the city's historical archives and exhibition center. The southwestern corner of the palm-lined square houses the Gothic-style **Igreja de São Francisco**. The fact that it is next door to the stock exchange may explain why it has one of the richest and busiest interiors in Porto. Its walls, vaulting, pillars, and altar are covered with carved and gilded wood representations of animals, plants, and angels. The visitor's eyes are soon drawn to the 13th-century altar, where the simple granite statue of Saint Francis provides a respite from the dizzying display.

Porto's temple to business and financial enterprise, the **Palácio da Bolsa** (Stock Exchange) takes up most of the western side of the square. The exterior is solid and conservative, while its interior is more ostentatiously bold, rich in marble, stucco, and wood. The 19th-century Salão Arabe, with its arabesques and stained-glass windows, was inspired by the Moorish splendor of the palace at Granada. Built at the height of the Romantic movement, which captured the Portuguese imagination, it belongs more in a scene from *The Thousand and One Nights* than in a stock exchange.

Guided tours of the Bolsa are available (and are, in fact, the only way you can see its splendid rooms). The headquarters of the Association of Wine Exporters is also housed in the building, as a reminder of the role that wine has played in creating wealth for the city.

For a more down-to-earth experience, visit the **Museu de Etnografia e História** northwest of the Bolsa, at largo de São João Novo, a small but fine showcase of the traditional life of the Douro peasantry. An ancient wine press, peasant costumes and implements, and a weaver's workshop are on display, and regional handicrafts can be purchased. The museum is located in a former Jewish quarter, where some of Spain's most important Jewish families took refuge in the 15th century. Some of Porto's best jewelry shops are nearby, to the northeast toward praça da Liberdade, on rua das Flores. On the same street is the **Igreja da Misericórdia**, a 16th-century structure with an 18th-century Baroque façade, designed by Italian architect Nicolau Nasoni in collaboration with Portuguese engineer Manuel Alvares. A beautifully executed 16th-century painting is housed in the adjoining **Casa da Misericórdia** hospice owned by the same order that runs the church. The canvas, attributed to Colijn de Coter, has the Portuguese royal family present at the Crucifixion.

The Baixa

The Baixa (pronounced BYE-sha), around the praça da Liberdade, is the city's main shopping district. (Store hours in Porto run from 9:00 A.M. to 12:30 P.M. and 2:30 to 7:00 P.M. during the week, and from 9:00 A.M. to 1:00 P.M. on Saturdays.) Porto is not only Portugal's textile and leather center but is also esteemed for its intricate gold and silver filigree work, introduced by the Moors and perfected in the 17th and 18th centuries, when gold and silver began to pour in from the Portuguese colonies. **José Rosas & Cie.**, at rua Eugenio Castro, 282, deals in antique and secondhand jewelry; **Rosior**, on the neighboring rua da Cunha, at number 38, as well as at rua Eugenio Castro, 263, manufactures reasonably priced jewelry. On rua Cândido Reis, 18, behind the Infante de Sagres hotel, is the **Vista Alegre Showroom**, with a large selection of this fine china, as well as some Atlantis crystal.

There are no bargains in the antiques world of Porto, but interesting pieces such as Indo-Portuguese ivory-inlaid furniture do crop up at auctions at the **Galerias Vandoma**, at rua Mouzinho da Silveira, 181, which parallels rua das Flores. Good regional handicrafts can be found at the **Galeria de Artesanato**, rua Mouzinho da Silveira, 66A. East of praça da Liberdade is the rua de Santa Catarina, a pedestrian street known for its gift shops and fashionable clothing stores. The side streets that run into it also have their specialty shops. Leather and glassware can be purchased on rua 31 de Janeiro, while hand embroidery and linen are a century-old tradition at the **Casa dos Linhos**, at rua de Fernandes Tomás, 660. Clothes bargains and inexpensive regional handicrafts, such as wicker and pottery, are sold all day Monday through Friday and Saturday mornings at the colorful local market of **Bolhão** (rua de Sá da Bandeira), west of Santa Catarina. The larger **Bom Sucesso** market is a short cab ride northeast, at its namesake square.

The **Grande Hotel do Porto**, also on Santa Catarina, provides an opportunity for shoppers to stay in the thick of things. The former grande dame of Porto's hotels has had an extensive interior face-lift. The rooms are comfortable and clean, and all have satellite TV. These, along with the price, attentive service, parking facilities, and Belle Epoque restaurant (see the Dining section, below), help compensate for her not-so-splendid decor. Situated near the Grande is the **Majestic Café** (number 112), one of the oldest coffeehouses and landmarks of the city; it has been restored and declared a monument, under government protection. Its sculptured cherubs atop pilasters, its jasper pillars, and the finely carved wood here would make William Morris proud.

The area around praça da Liberdade and the wide avenida dos Aliados is also dotted with sidewalk cafés, pastry shops, and teahouses. **Arcadia**, at praça da Liberdade, 63, is one of the oldest pastry shops in Porto. Its Old World decor and Baroque-style pastries make it a temple of confectionery frequented by those with a sweet tooth.

Southeast of Liberdade

The tiled exterior of the **Igreja dos Congregados** brightens the praça de Almeida Garrett (named after Porto's romantic writer) southeast of Liberdade. The interior of the **São Bento** train station next door has an interesting collection of *azulejos* (decorative tiles) by the 20th-century master Jorge Colaço, combining Portuguese history and the evolution of the railway train. The capture of Ceuta (in North Africa) by João I in the 15th century is the centerpiece. Southeast of the square, off the avenida Dom Afonso Henriques at rua Saraiva de Carvalho, is the former **church of the Convento de Santa Clara**. The cross-fertilization of styles, from the Gothic, Manueline, and Renaissance stonework of its doorway to the Mudejar (Moorish-style) ceiling of its interior, will tax the keenest student of architecture. The panel of the Immaculate Conception by Joaquim Raphael is also worth noting in this small church, known for opulent touches that echo the rich past of the religious orders in Portugal.

West of Liberdade

The **Igreja dos Clérigos** with its **tower**, a Baroque structure built by Italian architect Nicolau Nasoni in the middle of the 18th century, dominates the skyline of its namesake street on a hill west of Liberdade. If you climb the tower's 240 steps you will be rewarded with a sweeping view of the sea to the west, Vila Nova de Gaia to the south, and the mountains to the east. Northwest of the Clérigos, past the book and pottery shops of the rua das Carmelitas, is the lovely palm-lined praça de Gomes Teixeira, with the 19th-century Fountain of the Lions, flanked on the south by Porto's university and by the tiled exterior of the 18th-century **Igreja do Carmo** to the west. The eastern exterior of the church is decorated with 20th-century *azulejos,* designed by Silvestro Silvestri, depicting the encounter between Christians and pagans on Mount Carmel, where the order was founded. The adjoining Igreja das Carmelitas and its monastic quarters have been turned into the barracks of the National Republican Guard (GNR).

The **Museu Soares dos Reis**, named after Portugal's most famous sculptor, is housed in the Carrancas palace (the residence of King Pedro IV during the siege of Porto) behind the neighboring Santo António Hospital, on rua de Dom Manuel II. The museum houses many of the late sculptor's works, including his famous *O Desterrado* (The Exile), which hauntingly exemplifies the Portuguese penchant for *saudade* (nostalgia). The museum also houses one of the nation's most complete collections of paintings by 15th- to 20th-century Portuguese masters, and contains valuable Limoges enamels and a sword belonging to the first king of Portugal, Afonso Henriques.

Porto's other great museum, the **Museu Romântico**, lies off the western end of rua de Dom Manuel II at rua de Entre Quintas, 220, in the 19th-century former Macierinha estate, where King Carlos Alberto of Sardinia spent his last days in exile. The building draws attention not only for its valuable collection of 19th-century European art and furniture but also for its basement **Solar do Vinho do Porto**, which offers more than 150 varieties of Port and a garden with a view of the river below. The bar is closed on Sundays.

Porto's Gardens

The Portuguese green thumb can be admired at several locations on the west side of the city. The gardens and man-made pond of the **Palácio de Cristal** exhibition center, at rua de Dom Manuel II, are the closest to the center and offer a cool haven and a good place to have a rest. The **Jardim Botânico**, farther west at rua do Campo Alegre, grows rare plants and trees from all corners of the former Portuguese Empire. (The garden is open weekdays from 2:00 P.M. till dusk; use bus line 35 or 37.) The other green space in Porto, the **Casa dos Serralves**, lies several miles farther west out in suburban Boavista. The sprawling estate, which belonged originally to the counts of Vizela, passed through several hands in the 19th and 20th centuries before being acquired by the state. The surprisingly modern mansion, at rua de Serralves, 977, houses the National Museum of Modern Art and is open Tuesday through Sunday from 2:00 P.M. till 8:00 P.M. It is a ten-minute bus ride (line 35) from the city center. The museum is devoted mostly to rotating exhibits; a recent one showcased the work of such modern masters of photography as America's Gordon Parks.

A new park, called the Parque da Cidade, is being created in northwest Porto, but it is not scheduled to open before the end of 1993.

Vila Nova de Gaia

Vila Nova de Gaia, across the Douro south of Porto, sits on top of a pre-Roman *castro* (fortified hamlet) and the former Roman settlement of Cale. It was made officially into a town in 1255 by King Afonso III and bequeathed to burghers and nobles to counteract the power of the bishops of Porto. It also suffered greatly over the ages from flash floods and is somewhat shabby and run-down. The town still serves as the vault for millions of bottles of Port maturing in the damp and cool cellars of some 60 wine lodges facing the river. Vila

Nova de Gaia was picked over Porto proper for practical reasons: Its north-facing location favors higher humidity and cooler air, which reduce the rate of evaporation of the wine in the cellars.

Cross the lower level of the Ponte Dom Luis I, by car or on foot, and turn right onto avenida Diogo Leite, which runs along the quay where the elegant rabelos are docked, to visit the wine lodges. Some of the best known are Sandeman, Croft, Ferreira, Graham, Dow, Taylor, Cálem, Cockburn (pronounced COE-burn), Barros, Fonseca, and Real Vinícola. The lodges offer guided tours in English, during which you can see the aging and blending process, sample their wines free of charge, and purchase bottles. All lodges can be visited weekdays except at lunchtime; the Sandeman, Real Vinícola, and Cálem lodges are open on Saturdays, and Real Vinícola on Sunday mornings in the summer.

Sandeman, at largo Miguel Bombarda, 3, is housed in a former 16th-century Jesuit convent beside the river. The 200-year-old company, whose symbol is a silhouette of a cloaked student from the university at Coimbra—wearing a Spanish sombrero, mark of the Spanish Sherry part of the house of Sandeman—has been acquired by Seagrams of Canada, but George Thomas David Sandeman (seventh generation) is the general manager of the house. The lodge has a small museum with tools and implements used in wine making that date back to the 18th century. The oldest section of the lodge has soft wooden stilts placed upright on the floor as a cushion to prevent damage to the oak barrels as they are rolled over them. The wood's texture is close to that of velour.

The Real Companhia Vinícola do Norte de Portugal, founded in 1889, is housed in a large estate at the eastern and upper end of Vila Nova de Gaia, at rua Azevedo Magalhães, 314. It produces both Port and *espumante*. To reach this lodge, cross the upper tier of the Ponte Dom Luis I and turn left at the third crossing, off avenida da República.

Several outdoor cafés on the esplanade by the river offer fine views of old Porto. The best picture-postcard view, though, is available at the former convent of **Nossa Senhora da Serra do Pilar**, which perches on a high promontory on the eastern corner of Vila Nova de Gaia overlooking the river. From the esplanade in front you can gaze down at the bridge, the old town, crowned by the Sé, and the remains of the 14th-century Fernandina wall to the north. The former convent has a round Renaissance cloister (the only one in Europe) and an unusual 17th-century barrel-vaulted roof. Its strategic importance has always attracted military attention. Wellington set up camp here in his campaign to oust the French from Porto, and liberal forces made it their headquarters during the civil war. The hill is once again a military headquarters, and only the church is open to the public.

Vila Nova comes alive every year on the second Sunday of January during the Festas de São Gonçalo e São Cristovão, which are more like a pagan fertility rite than a Catholic celebration. An image of São Gonçalo, known as the saint who helps women find husbands, discovered centuries ago in the river, is paraded through the streets by local boatmen accompanied by a phalanx of drummers. São Cristovão and São Roque are also honored, and gallons of Port and other wines are drunk, accompanied by phallus-shaped cakes. A more mellow time can be had all year round at the waterfront **Rabelo** *fado* house, at avenida Diogo Leite, 402, where dinner is accompanied by the soulful songs of Portugal's blues. The dim lights, ancient stone walls, and jugs of wine enhance the live performances by dark-clad singers till advanced hours of the morning.

The Foz and Matosinhos

The Atlantic coastal area west and northwest of Porto, from the Douro estuary to Matosinhos, is the city's mini-Riviera. Leave Porto by the river road (rua do Ouro) and follow it (5 km/3 miles) to the Foz do Douro (Mouth of the Douro), where the **Castelo de São João da Foz**, a former military prison, guards the entrance to the river. The 16th-century fortress was built on the site of a 13th-century Benedictine monastery despite protestations from the order. To placate the monks, the chancel of the former monastery was spared as part of the garrison's chapel, and can be visited. Our route then turns right (north) onto the avenida do Brasil, which parallels a palm-lined esplanade past the Praia dos Ingleses. The tiny, homey **Hotel Boa Vista** here occupies a small promontory overlooking the fort and the Foz. Its pub, rooftop restaurant, and small indoor pool and gym make it an attractive place to stay for travellers in search of a relaxed environment. The hotel is near some of the better Porto restaurants and fashionable discos.

The avenida do Brasil turns into the avenida de Montevideu, which is flanked to the east by seaside villas. One of these, now the **Dom Manoel** restaurant, at number 384, is among the area's best eating facilities, with an impressive fish menu, amusing decor, and air-conditioning.

The **Castelo do Queijo**, or **São Francisco Javier Fortress**, is right on the coast, 1 km (½ mile) down the road beside the praça de Gonçalves Zarco. The discoverer of Madeira, Zarco reputedly came from neighboring Matosinhos. The foundation of the 17th-century garrison contains an ancient sacrificial boulder used by Celtic Druids in the sixth century B.C.

Continue north to **Matosinhos** via the esplanada do Rio de Janeiro and the N 208. The former fishing village has grown tremendously in recent years following the construction of an artificial port and so has lost some of its charm to industry, but its waterfront restaurants continue to serve some of the best fish and shellfish in the region. The **Marisqueira Esplanada**, at rua Roberto Ivens, 628–638, has its own private vivarium. Here you can try mouth-watering *arroz de marisco, caldeirada de peixe* (fish stew), and *açorda de marisco* (coriander-spiked, bread-thickened shellfish stew into which raw eggs are dropped just before serving). *Broinhas de Leixoes* are a typical local honeycake dessert. A classy seafood restaurant, the **Conde de Leça**, located in a former private home at rua Pinto de Araujo, 110, has already won a prize for its *caldeirada,* a seafood dish similar to bouillabaisse.

Past the busy port of Leixoes, on a hill on the right before the *auto-estrada,* you will encounter the **Igreja do Senhor Bom Jesus** (better known as the Igreja do Senhor de Matosinhos), an 18th-century church containing a wooden statue of Christ on the cross that washed up on the beach in the tenth century. Legend has it that it is one of four carved by the disciple Nicodemus, destined for the four corners of the earth. The statue had lost an arm on its voyage. Fifty years after the statue's discovery, an old woman combing the beach for firewood found a wooden arm. When the arm would not ignite, she took it to the shrine, where it miraculously attached itself to the Nicodemus statue. A small 18th-century shrine on the beach marks the spot where she found the arm.

The Senhor de Matosinhos pilgrimage, in the first two weeks of June, is one of the liveliest and most colorful of its kind in the region, with singing, dancing, fireworks, and outdoor eating. The Baroque façade of the shrine is by the prolific Nicolau Nasoni. The ceilings of the nave and the chancel are covered by a sumptuous recessed panel depicting scenes from the Passion.

The return trip to Porto can be shortened by turning left at praça de Gonçalves Zarco by the Queijo fortress onto the avenida da Boavista. Avoid driving in the late afternoon on weekends during the summer months, however, or you may be stuck in bumper-to-bumper traffic with locals returning from a day at the beach. Trams, a convenient and leisurely alternative, can be mounted at stops along the route. The most popular itinerary runs mainly along the water from the largo de São Francisco to the Castelo do Queijo.

Staying in Porto

"Oporto has nothing to boast with respect to its hotels. Indeed I know of no city in Europe of this size and consideration that possesses so few," wrote a disappointed William Kingston in 1845. The situation was finally resolved a century later with the construction of the luxury **Hotel Infante de Sagres**, at number 62 praça Dona Filipa de Lencastre, just west of the avenida dos Aliados and several blocks northwest of praça da Liberdade. This elegant hotel has the look and feel of a stately town house with all the genteel touches and service of the Belle Epoque. Several members of the British royal family have stayed in the grand presidential suite, where the carved furniture, doors, and ceilings, crystal, and gold-colored chandeliers provide an opulent ambience. Standard doubles are far less princely, however; indeed there have been complaints about their smallness, darkness, and noisiness, particularly those rooms facing the praça Dona Filipa de Lencastre (savvy travellers insist on rooms overlooking the hotel's interior courtyard). The restaurant in the hotel is the most luxurious in the city, with a well-stocked cellar (see the Dining section, below).

Modern luxury chain hotels, with all the recreational amenities that go with them, have also made their appearance in Porto during the last few years. The 232-room **Hotel Méridien Porto** has a fine restaurant with a French menu and theme weeks featuring foods from various countries. Its discothèque is popular with businesspeople, and its conference facilities draw executives. The Méridien is situated in a modern neighborhood on the northwestern side of the city, ten minutes from the center by cab or bus, at avenida da Boavista, 1466. Its rooms, large, light, and quiet, are done up in restful schemes of beige, mauve, and slate. There's every modern amenity: TV, air-conditioning, minibars, direct-dial phones, even proper desks and sitting areas.

The **Hotel Sheraton Porto**, nearby and across the avenida da Boavista at number 1269, offers a heated indoor pool, a squash and health club and medium-size, shoe-boxy rooms, decorated, for the most part, in shades of brown.

Another five-star hotel in Porto is the **Tivoli Porto Atlántico**. Located off the avenida da Boavista in a choice residential area, it offers a relaxed and elegant atmosphere. Its Scandinavian-modern rooms, though small, are equipped with air-conditioning, satellite TV and video, and minibars. There are a restaurant and a bar, as well as both a heated indoor and an open-air pool, a health club, and conference rooms.

The latest luxury hotel, at rua de Serralves, 124 (even farther out of town near the *auto-estrada* and western terminus of the avenida da Boavista), is the five-star **Ipanema Park**. The hotel is sophisticated and elegant, and offers a health club, indoor and outdoor swimming pools, a restaurant, bars, and conference rooms.

We discuss the dowager Grande Hotel do Porto above, in the Baixa section.

Dining in Porto

When it comes to food, *Portuenses* can be reactionary in the extreme. Any variation on their centuries-old cuisine is viewed with suspicion, which explains why the menus in the restaurants and *tascas* (bistros) here tend to be of a sameness. But the food is flavorful and betrays some of its North African, Eastern, and New World influences.

The food and varied menu of **Portucale**, its penthouse view of the city, sea, and surrounding countryside, and its attentive service make it one of the most complete dining experiences in Porto and a local favorite. Its somewhat brash modern decor is compensated for by its mouth-watering dishes, which include lobster/rice stew, pheasant stuffed with almonds, wild boar, and a simply splendid version of Porto's traditional tripe dish that comes bubbling to table in its own terra-cotta casserole. This moderate-to-expensive restaurant, which occupies the 14th floor of an *albergaria* (modern inn) at rua da Alegria, 598, is a short cab ride northeast from the city center. Reservations are advised for lunch; Tel: (02) 57-07-17.

The **Restaurante Dona Filipa**, lodged in the Hotel Infante de Sagres (praça Dona Filipa de Lencastre, 62), is Porto's most elegant restaurant, frequented by the city's old guard. Its opulence—crystal chandeliers, wood-paneled mirrors, tapestries, and thick carpeting—is matched by its equally sumptuous food and vintage wine list, served by a phalanx of discreetly efficient black-tied waiters. The soufflés and flambées, with Port, are the trademark of the maître d', while the chef's artistry with desserts can be viewed on the pastry cart.

The **Grande Hotel do Porto** restaurant (rua de Santa Catarina, 197), with its stucco ceiling, topaz walls, velour curtains, and glass chandeliers, offers a less expensive fin-de-siècle alternative to the Dona Filipa. Guests have a choice of à la carte or prix-fixe dining.

The **Escondidinho**, a popular, down-to-earth establishment near the town center at rua dos Passos Manuel, 144, serves some of the city's best food of the Douro region. The atmosphere of this moderately priced, family-run establishment, which is a replica of a typical Douro country house, is relaxed and homey.

Posh new A Porta Nobre is discussed in the Ribeira section, above.

Nightlife in Porto

A good way to start the evening in Porto is by paying a visit to the Solar do Vinho do Porto wine bar (see above, in the West of Liberdade section). The **Mal Cozinhado** restaurant, at rua do Outeirinho, 13, on the western tip of the Ribeira dock, features regional folk dancing and music during the summer.

The Ribeira area also offers a more animated choice of music. **Postigo do Carvão**, a lively restaurant and piano bar frequented mainly by a young crowd, is housed in a former warehouse at rua Fonte Taurina, 26–34. **Aniki-Bobo**, next door, caters to jazz and folk-music lovers; food is not served and credit cards are not accepted.

Porto's chic crowd tends to head out toward the pubs and discos west of downtown. **Swing**, at praceta Engenheiro Amaro Costa, near the Palácio de Cristal, is frequented by Porto's young trendies, who like its combination of upstairs pub and downstairs disco. Sophisticated and well-heeled Portuenses frequent establishments in the affluent suburb of Foz do Douro, a ten-minute ride from the center, where pub-disco-restaurant combinations at Twins (mainly for the affluent middle-aged) and Greens are the latest craze. **Twins**, at rua do Passeio Alegre, 1000, is supposed to be a members-only club, but the rule is generally waived. The decor and menu are old-guard Continental. Meals are served Monday through Saturday. **Greens**, at rua Padre Luis Cabral, 1086, is less clubby and the cuisine more nouvelle. The restaurant is closed Saturday nights and Sundays.

The mayor's cultural office publishes a monthly calendar

of social events that can be picked up at the tourism office. It is written in Portuguese, but Turismo personnel or a friendly hotel concierge will translate for you.

THE DOURO VALLEY

The rugged Douro valley, scorching in summer and bone-chilling in winter, is spectacularly beautiful, especially when sunlight plays over its trees, vines, and rocks, gradually changing the deep shadows in the folds of the slopes to brightness. The river winds through narrow gorges, then flows broad and languid where the valley floor widens. In the upper valley, where the Port grapes grow, the steep schist slopes have been worked into an intricate, wavy pattern by the thousands of vineyards that hug the ground's contours. Small villages cling to the rising valley walls, and here and there images of stately pink or white quintas are reflected in the calm water of the river. The Douro's legendary fury—for centuries flash floods inundated the low-lying towns on its banks—has now been contained by ten dams, and the wooden *rabelos* that until recently carried the wine to Porto have been replaced by tour boats. Bed-and-breakfast establishments and inns have begun to sprout on the slopes and along the river's tributaries, and tours of the vineyards are becoming popular.

The grapes that produce Port wine are grown in the Alto Douro's demarcated wine zone, which begins 62 miles upstream from Porto and stretches some 2 miles south and 15 miles north along the river, all the way east to the Spanish border. The El Dorado for Port-wine vineyards, however, is a 13-mile strip between Peso da Régua and Pinhão, where the soil and climatic conditions are just right for the grapes. After Pinhão the landscape gradually becomes wilder and more primitive as the river snakes east toward Spain (see the Trás-os-Montes chapter for more details). There are few towns beyond Pinhão, and some of the barren hillside vineyards still show the scars of a 19th-century phylloxera plague that devastated the region's vines. American vines, nicknamed *americanos,* saved the day when their root stocks, immune to phylloxera, were grafted with the endangered domestic varieties.

But the region east of Porto is not only the domain of Port. The grapes of the region also produce some fine unfortified wines, such as the red Barca Velha and white Monopólio. And although the heart of *vinho verde* production is the

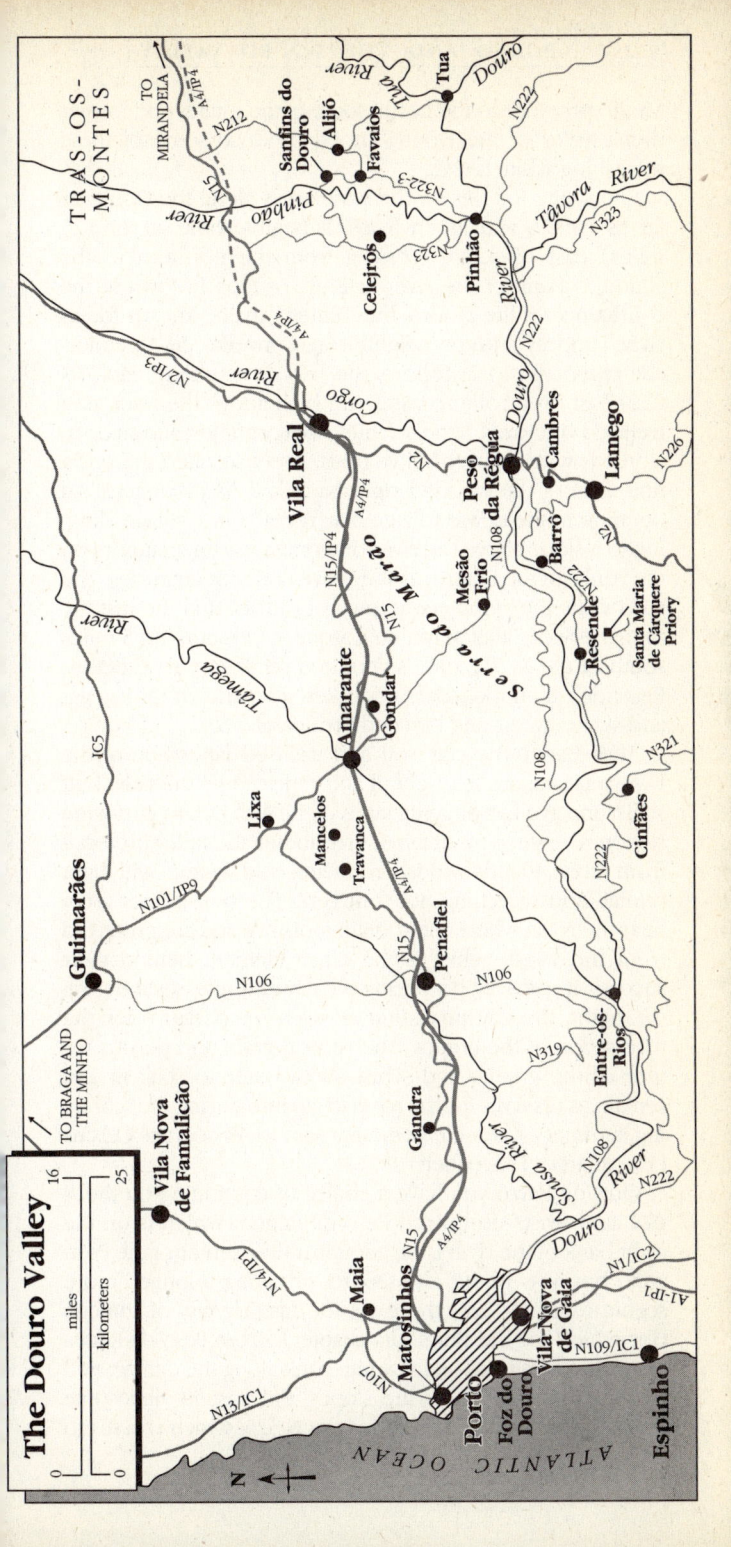

Minho province to the north, some of the estates and former monasteries of the Douro Litoral produce some of these refreshing white *verdes*.

Our route focuses on the wine areas along the Douro as far as Pinhão and its environs. It begins some 40 km (25 miles) east of Porto, crossing from the northern to the southern bank of the river at Entre-os-Rios (a town at the confluence of the Douro and Tâmega rivers, known for its river lamprey and the neighboring Convento de Alpendurada *vinho verde*). It follows the left, or southern, bank (N 222) east on a roller-coaster run high above the river, past trellised vineyards, handkerchief-size cornfields, and an occasional row or grove of olive trees. Every so often there is a fine vista of the wooded right bank and its mountains. An opening in the dense foliage may reveal a tiny village clinging to a slope above the river or women washing laundry on the banks of the Douro, as they have done for centuries. The road visits the *vinho verde* town of Cinfães and the historic monastery of Santa Maria de Cárquere (about 8 km/5 miles south of the N 222, on a signposted secondary road before Resende), then meanders on to Resende, known for its egg-and-sugar sweets and bed and breakfasts.

After Barrô, the clay soil and trellised landscape of the Douro Litoral are left behind and replaced by the pale, buff schist and ground-hugging vines of the Alto Douro Port-wine region. The steep mountains surrounding the valley protect it from moist Atlantic winds, producing cold winters with light rainfall and scorching hot summers. The best grapes grow near the river, where they obtain moisture and are protected from the wind. Schist is the other element behind their success. It gathers heat during the day and releases it during the night, thereby providing an even temperature for the maturation of the grapes. The vertical grain and porous nature of the granite and schist allow water to soak in and remain as reserves for the roots to tap into during the scorching summers when temperatures soar to 40 degrees Celsius (104 degrees Fahrenheit).

Outside Barrô you have a choice of continuing on the N 222 as it twists up toward Peso da Régua (which is on the right bank of the river), the administrative center of the Port-wine business in the Alto Douro, or taking a longer, more scenic route (N 226) there via the historic city of Lamego (for which see the Beira Alta chapter). From Peso da Régua the N 222 continues on the south bank along the demarcated region's most coveted vine slopes and past its handsome quintas. Our route briefly joins the N 323, which crosses to the right bank at Pinhão, the geographic center of the Port-wine region, climbs (N 322-3) a ravine to Alijó, known for its *pousada*'s (government-run inn) fine Douro cooking, and loops back to Pinhão on the N 323-1 and N 323 past granite medieval villages with views over vineyards spread out like a giant corduroy quilt.

After crossing back to the left bank at Pinhão, you backtrack on the N 222 and return to the right bank over a bridge near Peso da Régua, and climb on the N 108 west to Mesão Frio on the Serra do Marão, where you can continue toward Porto on the windy but scenic northern slopes of the Douro or veer right onto the N 101 and visit the enchanting resort town of Amarante, on the banks of the Tâmega. The wooded area around Amarante is littered with archaeological remains, Romanesque churches, and manor houses and offers swimming, fishing, and hiking opportunities. The town's Victorian teahouses, lodged on balconies over the river, and weekly outdoor *arraiais* (carnivalesque barn-style parties that go on to the wee hours) are other attractions. The tour ends on the N 15/IP 4 (which becomes the A 4/IP 4) back to Porto after stops at the tiny parish church of Travanca, and the Aveleda estate at Penafiel, where a walk in the semitropical gardens and a taste of its fine *vinho verde* provide a suitable finale to a Douro visit. The new IP 4 highway makes for less than a 30-minute drive from Amarante to Porto, but taking it means missing Travanca and the Aveleda estate at Penafiel. If you get on the A 4/IP 4 highway at Amarante, you can get off it at Penafiel, get on the old N 15 to visit Travanca and the Aveleda estate, then get back onto the A 4/IP 4 Penafiel for the short drive to Porto, unless you prefer the more sedate N 15 all the way to Porto.

Give yourself three to four days for a leisurely visit to the valley. The limited number of accommodations here makes it essential that you reserve your stay in advance. The best times to visit are either in April and May, when the valley is covered with wildflowers, or during the *vindima* (grape harvest) in late September and early October, when the grape leaves turn as bright as fall maples and the valley comes alive with activity and echoes with the songs of the grape pickers. Women and children pick the grapes, and the men carry baskets of them weighing over 100 pounds up and down dizzying slopes. Traditionally, the grapes were trodden in *lagares* (granite vats) by barefoot men to the beat of a drum or the wheeze of a concertina or an accordion. Although human labor has been replaced mostly by mechanical crushers (which purists say rob the wine of some of its taste), some of the large estates, such as Cálem's Quinta da Foz at Pinhão and Graham's Quinta dos Malvedos near Tua, still crush a small amount of their crop the old way for the benefit of tradition and tourists. Merry postharvest parties are held at the quintas, and wine is consumed liberally by all. Visits to the *vindima* can be arranged by travel agents and the Turismo staffs in Porto and Peso da Régua. It is possible to visit the valley by boat or train or a combination of the two (see Getting Around, at the end of the chapter).

Along the Douro River

Cinfães, 35 km (22 miles) east of Entre-os-Rios, surrounded by cornfields, olive groves, and trellised vines, is the area's commercial center for *vinho verde,* and a good spot to taste it. The light estate wine Quinta do Crasto is one of the area's finer "green" wines. Dom Afonso Henriques, the first king of Portugal, spent his early years in the town under the care of his godfather and tutor. The handsome Romanesque church of Santa Maria Maior, in Tarouquela (9 km/5½ miles west of Cinfães), belonged to a former Benedictine monastery founded in 1187.

The **Santa Maria de Cárquere priory**, off the N 222 east of Cinfães (about 8 km/5 miles southeast on a signposted secondary road before Resende) is a historic landmark. Legend has it that in 1109, on the summit of Montemuro, surrounded by rocky crests, the young Afonso Henriques was miraculously cured of a crippling deformity after his tutor, Egaz Moniz, was led to the site by the Virgin Mary in a dream. A Romanesque church and priory were constructed in honor of the event. The priory has since disappeared, but the church, which has been remodeled several times over the centuries, and the chapel crypt of the region's once-powerful lords of Resende provide a glimpse of the priory's former glory: a crenellated 11th-century tower, a Gothic chancel, an ornate Manueline façade, a colonnaded Romanesque doorway, an unusual Romanesque window supported by capitals of sculptured pelicans, and four sarcophagi with medieval inscriptions.

Resende is a tiny town some 26 km (16 miles) east of Cinfães, known for its sweet sugar-and-egg *cavacas* (straw hats) and its semisweet Casa de Rendufe *vinho verde,* which can be purchased at the *cooperativa* next door to the Casa de Rendufe. Several antiques-filled homes owned by members of the local aristocracy have opened their doors to bed-and-breakfast guests here. The **Casa de São Gens** is owned by country gentry with the famous explorer's name of Magalhães (Magellan). The 16th-century granite house, open year-round, boasts a fireplace that heats the entire building in winter (there are also electric heaters in the bedrooms) and a nice garden. Two double rooms are available: one with a private bath and a sofa where a third person can sleep, the other with a semi-private bath.

At Rendufe, 2 km (1¼ miles) beyond Resende on the road to Barrô, is the **Casa do Casal**, a rustic granite house surrounded by a garden with an excellent view over the Douro valley. Casa do Casal offers four double rooms and three bathrooms (not en suite). Breakfast only is served. For lunch and dinner, it's Cinfães or the simpler *tascas* in Resende.

The name of the 12th-century fortress church of **São Martinho de Mouros** alludes to the brief Moorish tenure in the area. Stories abound of Moorish treasures buried under rocks, fountains, and ruins in the surrounding countryside. The rural church, commanding a desolate hill pass, has an intricately carved stone tympanum. Its cool and airy interior contains the remains of primitive wall paintings depicting scenes of Saint Martin's life. The church lies less than one kilometer off the N 222, about 6 km (3½ miles) east of Resende.

Barrô, some 13 km (8 miles) northeast of Resende, clings to a high, wooded promontory with a sweeping view of the Douro valley and the Marão mountains to the north. The town is both the geological and official border between the Douro Litoral (Coastal Douro) and the Alto (Upper) Douro. From here on to the east the soil becomes drier and clay gives way to schist. Trellised vineyards begin to disappear, replaced by ground-hugging vines. From Barrô on lies the first demarcated wine zone in the world, stretching some 2 miles south and about 15 miles north along the river all the way east to the Spanish border. In 1756 a company formed by the marquês de Pombal to oversee production and fix prices in an effort to eliminate the British monopoly placed 325 granite posts as markers along the valley's borders. The company failed to break the British hold on the export industry but did succeed in setting standards and regulations. Today some of the original markers remain on the hillsides; others have been requisitioned by farmers for doorposts.

Six kilometers (3½ miles) east of Barrô you have a choice of routes to reach the Port country. You can either continue on the N 222 to Peso da Régua (13 km/8 miles) in the heart of Port country or turn right onto the N 226 for a slightly longer (23 km/14 miles) but more scenic journey via the bucolic and historic town of Lamego (see the Beira Alta chapter). If you decide on the former, you should first make a short 3-km (2-mile) detour on the N 226 to the **Miradouro da Boa Vista**, a lookout commanding some of the most sweeping views of the Douro valley, the town of Peso da Régua across the river, and the Marão mountains to the north.

Peso da Régua, the administrative center of the Port-wine trade of the Douro valley, lies 19 km (12 miles) northeast of Barrô on the north bank of the Douro. It is the starting point for the Linha do Corgo, the scenic train route that travels north to Vila Real in Trás-os-Montes, as well as one of the stops on the national railroad's Linha do Douro (see Getting Around, at the end of the chapter).

Although Peso da Régua lacks the architectural beauty and monuments of Amarante to the northwest, this is partly compensated for by the stark beauty of the river and surrounding countryside. It was from Peso da Régua, before the advent of the railway and the taming of the river, that the square-rigged *rabelos,* laden with wine barrels, set off on their perilous journey down the river to Porto. The boatmen eased the hazardous trip sometimes by dipping into the wine barrels and later topping them off with river water, much to the annoyance of the shippers. Today you can still catch a glimpse of these retired wooden ships soaking in the sun on the banks of the river.

Peso da Régua is the headquarters for the winegrowers' association. Their offices in the Casa do Douro contain a register of some 85,000 vineyards of the Alto Douro region, and the casa's entrance is lit up by a set of stained-glass windows depicting the production and history of Port. The Turismo beside the station, at largo da Estação (Tel: 054-228-46), will provide maps and other information on the region and help make arrangements for accommodations or arrange a visit to a vineyard.

The **Casa dos Varais** is a bed and breakfast housed in an elegant 18th-century home just across the river from Peso da Régua (opposite the railway station) on the road to Lamego, on the high ground above the left bank of the Douro. The house looks out onto terraced vineyards and the river, and is an ideal spot from which to enjoy the scenic flavor of the Port-wine valley. There are two double bedrooms and a private living room, decorated with antiques, open to guests. To get here from Peso da Régua, cross the bridge and take the N 2 toward Cambres and Lamego. Next door to Casa de

Varais is the **Casa Pingueis**, with three doubles with bath, living room, kitchen, and pool, for rent as one unit only. Casa de Varais and Casa Pingueis, which belong to the same family, are open from April 1 to October 30.

There are two good restaurants in Peso da Régua. The **Rosmaninho**, at avenida de Ovar, lote 3, offers tasty regional food and a good wine list. A bit farther away (drive 8 km/5 miles through old Régua on the road toward Loureiro) is the **Varanda da Régua**, open every day of the year, with a great wine list, good food, and a glorious view of the Douro valley (Tel: 054-247-49). The bistros of Peso da Régua also provide good regional food, such as *cabrito assado* (roast kid) accompanied by *arroz de forno* (baked rice), and trout stuffed with ham.

The best Port-wine vineyards start at Peso da Régua and stretch east along both sides of the Douro and its tributaries. The N 222 follows the left bank of the river east. The steep river slopes, which sometimes reach inclines of close to 90 degrees, have been intricately terraced by hand, stone by stone, with a skill and precision that would win the respect of Aztec stonemasons. Even the thin layer of dirt on which the vines grow had to be carried up, bucketful by bucketful. Some terraces date back to the 17th century, but the face of the Douro valley vineyards is rapidly changing with the introduction of *patamares* (two-row, "mechanizable" terraces without the old stone walls) and more and more vertical planting of vines, also to allow for mechanization at a later stage. The endless rows of steps sometimes lead to a whitewashed quinta of one of the Port-wine producers, crowning the slopes above the river. The trails on either side of the river and its banks were made by boatmen to pull their boats upriver on their return trips from Porto.

Pinhão, at the confluence of the Douro and Pinhão rivers, 22 km (14 miles) upriver from Peso da Régua, is the epicenter of the Port-wine vineyard area. It occupies a small strip of flat land on the right bank of the Douro. Behind it, the terraced mountains rise perpendicularly. Some of the major Port houses maintain storage houses beside the pretty train station, which is tiled with blue, white, and yellow panels depicting the Port-wine story. It is a sleepy town for most of the year, but, come the fall grape harvest, its population swells as grape pickers from the surrounding countryside congregate here. The intoxicating smell of wine fills the streets, and the canyon above the town echoes with the sounds of the *vindima,* which usually runs from the last week in September to the middle of October (but can be delayed or advanced depending on the weather conditions in a given year).

In Pinhão, on the riverside grounds of Quinta da Foz (owned by the Port house of Cálem) is the **Casa das Pontes**, which offers accommodation year-round. There are three single rooms and one double with bath. Reservations should be made in advance for September and October. A luxurious, restored 17th-century manor house run by the owners, the **Casa de Casal de Loivos**, has opened in the village of Casal de Loivos, 7 km (4 miles) above Pinhão. Take the very twisted N 322-3 between Pinhão and Alijó; about a kilometer outside of Pinhão there is a signpost on the right to Casal de Loivos. The Casa has eight double rooms with bath, an elegant living room, a pool, and possibly the best view over the Douro valley. Dinner and access to a very good wine list can be had on advance request.

The **Pousada do Barão de Forrester** at Alijó, a rustic town set on a high plateau 16 km (10 miles) north of Pinhão, offers comfortable accommodations and good food (for more on the pousada, see the section on Vila Real in the Trás-os-Montes chapter). The road from Pinhão (N 322-3) to Alijó twists along and climbs the terraced eastern side of the canyon above the Pinhão river. During the *vindima* you can stop your car and watch the picking from the road, and you may be invited to share a mug of wine with the pickers or a swig out of a bottle. The pousada, which is named after the Scot who mapped, and drowned in, his beloved Douro, is in a large house in the town's center. Opened in 1983, it has 11 comfortable rooms done up in bright fabrics and furnished with reproductions of antiques, a well-stocked Port bar, and a fine country restaurant (with a mural of grape trellises) serving some of the region's specialties, which include skillet-fried trout wrapped in tissue-thin slices of *presunto,* the Portuguese equivalent of prosciutto, *cabrito assado com arroz de forno* (kid baked en casserole with rice; to be ordered in advance), *cozido à Portuguesa* (meat, chicken, and vegetable stew), and *pudim de amêndoa* (almond pudding). The local wines are Alijó, Favaios, Sanfins do Douro, and Pegarinhos. If you are not satisfied with them, go on to the Douro-denominated reds and whites. The pousada can also arrange visits to the vineyards of Quinta do Noval.

An alternative to the pousada restaurant is the **Adega Típica do Souto**, Presandães, Alijó. The Adega is run by two brothers, who serve up good regional food. Ask them for a taste of their homemade muscatel wine, a treat they offer with great pleasure.

Alijó received its royal charter in 1226. Its origins are much older, as can be witnessed in the ruins of local Celtic *castros* (fortified Iron Age hill towns with ramparts and moats that were common in Portugal between 800 B.C. and A.D. 200) and in the Roman names of some of the neighboring towns such as Favaios (a bastardization of the Latin *flavias,* meaning "yellow"). The *castros* provide ideal spots for picnics and walks but are reachable only on foot, and some are difficult to find as they are located in vineyards. The pousada or the Câmara Municipal in Alijó should be consulted for information on the exact location of *castros* in the area.

There are several private *solares* (manor houses) of note in Alijó's town square and its adjoining streets that sport the coats of arms of several of the region's patrician families. Alijó's most striking feature is a large lime tree planted in 1856 that broods over the main square, provides shade during the blistering summers, and is an idyllic spot throughout the year at which to trade news and gossip. Alijó is the perfect place to get away from it all, eat good country cooking, sample the Douro's huge selection of wines, breathe fresh mountain air, and take a variety of long walks. Twice a year, during the annual fair (August 14) and the feast of São Martinho (November 11), the quiet is shattered by the sounds and merriment of a fairground, and the sky is lit up by fireworks.

You can return to Pinhão the way you came, or loop around some 30 km (19 miles) and visit the western side of the plateau, which offers more breathtaking views over the vineyards and a glimpse of primitive medieval villages where *carro duriense,* oxen-drawn wooden carts that look like Roman chariots, are sometimes still used.

For the loop, leave Alijó the way you came and drive 5 km (3 miles) to **Favaios**, a granite village that retains its medieval flavor. The town cooperative sells Favaios's sweet muscatel wine. From here, take the N 323-1 north past evergreens and small granite huts to Sanfins do Douro, given by King Dinis to his bastard son, Fernão Sanches, at the end of the 13th century. Southwest of Sanfins, at Sabrosa, which claims the birth of the famous explorer Ferdinand Magellan (scholars, however, place it in the Minho, although the Magellan family did own considerable land in the Sabrosa area), take the N 323 south and drive through vineyards scattered thick over the plateau. The descent to Pinhão is like a corkscrew and should be attempted during daylight hours only.

At Pinhão cross the Douro again to the left bank, follow

the N 222 to the Peso da Régua bridge, recross the river to the right bank, and follow N 108 west.

Mesão Frio sits high above the Douro, 12 km (7½ miles) west (on N 101) of Peso da Régua across a valley from the Serra do Marão, on the way to Amarante. The Marão mountains allow the Douro valley to enjoy a semi-Mediterranean climate by acting as a buffer against the cold Atlantic winds. The town's main street is lined with beautiful, old lime trees and 18th-century *solares*. Its Gothic parish church, with seven Romanesque tombstones, and the former Franciscan monastery of São Francisco, now converted into the town hall, adorn this street. A Baroque gate crowned by animals, the mansion's façade, and the iron-adorned fountain embellish the stately **Casa da Rede**, situated above the main road on the western outskirts of the town above the river. You can admire this private home, one of the region's finest, from the road. Mesão Frio has a new, modern hotel, the **Hotel Panorama**, on avenida Conselheiro Alpoim, that offers comfortable rooms, all with bath and television, and a restaurant. Ask for a room with a view of the valley and mountains.

At Mesão Frio you can either continue back to Porto on the N 108, which has stunning views of the river and the right bank, or turn north onto the N 101 toward Amarante, one of northern Portugal's most picturesque towns.

Amarante

A picture-postcard town with a dreamy enchantment to it, Amarante lies 25 km (16 miles) northwest of Mesão Frio on the wooded banks of the Tâmega on the border of Trás-os-Montes, the Minho, and the Douro Litoral. The wooden balconies and covered porches of its riverside homes and Victorian-style teahouses are reflected in the clear waters of the Tâmega and afford views of the town's monuments. The verandahs of the teahouses are ideal for watching youngsters, flocks of noisy geese, and fishermen while you sample the town's famous pastries.

The people of Amarante are known for their happy dispositions. *Amar* (love), the first part of the town's name, tells it all. Their patron saint is São Gonçalo, who finds husbands for unmarried women. The Romaria de São Gonçalo is a popular pilgrimage held on the first Saturday of June, when single women visit the **Igreja de São Gonçalo** to pray for husbands. The exterior loggia of the handsome 16th-century church is flanked by statues of four Portuguese kings who reigned during the time it was being built, while its interior contains the remains of the saint and an elegant 17th-century organ supported by Tritons. The church faces an 18th-century double-arched granite bridge, flanked by long obelisks and graced with semicircular platforms where courting couples woo and pedestrians pause to gaze at the river. In 1809 the town put up stiff resistance against Napoleonic forces on this bridge.

Other interesting sights include the church of São Pedro with its lively Baroque façade and nave decorated with early-17th-century *azulejos*. The Câmara (Town Hall) museum, located in the former 16th-century convent of São Gonçalo, adjacent to the church, houses the town's two *demônios* (a she-devil and a he-devil), believed to be holdovers from ancient devil worship; the two devils are not always on exhibit, but you can ask to see them in their storage place. A 19th-century bishop of Braga decided to dispose of the devils and sold them to an English buyer, but this caused such a local furor that they had to be returned. The museum houses a worthwhile permanent collection of paintings by Amadeo de Souza Cardoso, as well as modern works by local artists; open daily, except Mondays and holidays, 10:00 A.M. to noon and 2:00 to 5:00 P.M.

The Arraial de São Gonçalo (an *arraial* is a barn party) is held June 5 and 6 at the municipal gardens. For a small fee you can eat, drink, dance, watch folk dancing, and participate in a *marcha popular* led by *gigantes* (giants) of the forest, played by young men sporting huge heads made of glazed paper. The origin of the *gigantes* is lost in time, but they are believed to have some ties to northern European lore. The festivities are illuminated by lavish fireworks displays (the loud noise supposedly keeps away the devil).

The wooded area around Amarante has been likened to Germany's Black Forest, a similarity that may have attracted Germanic tribes such as the Suevi to it. Many remnants of pagan worship still exist here. Stone Age dolmens, early Iron Age *castros,* and unusual formations called *pedras baloiçantes* (balancing rocks) can be seen in the vicinity. The *castro* ruins of Carneiro (12 km/7½ miles southeast on N 101) and Candemil (14 km/8½ miles southeast on N 15) are two of the largest in the area. The country around Amarante is also graced with Romanesque churches. Freixo de Baixo (5 km/3 miles northwest on N 101) contains a 12th-century parish church with primitive frescoes; Mancelos (14 km/8½ miles west, off the N 211-1) has interesting carved tombs and a 12th-century church; Lufrei (3 km/2 miles north, off the N 312) has a Romanesque church, with a highly carved doorway, that has survived without much restoration; Gondar (6 km/3½ miles southeast, on the N 15) has both an ancient church and ruins of a former monastery.

There is trout fishing (permits can be obtained in Lisbon from the Direção-Geral dos Serviços Florestais e Agrícolas, at avenida João Crisótomo, 2628, and from local town halls); swimming, rowboats and paddleboats for hire (the latter are inexpensive and can be booked by the hour or day by your hotel) on the Tâmega; and hiking on trails around Amarante. There is also a superb camping area with a rustic restaurant beside the river on the outskirts of the town, at **Quinta dos Frades**. More information and maps on the region, its sights, and activities can be obtained at Amarante's local tourism office, located near the bridge on rua Cândido dos Reis.

Amarante's accommodations do not do justice to the pretty town. The somewhat dull, characterless **Hotel Navarras**, at rua António Carneiro, has a heated indoor swimming pool and dining facilities. The **Hotel Amaranto**, at rua Madalena, is a more modest alternative, with a panoramic view of the town from both its west-facing rooms and its restaurant. The **Casa Zé da Calçada** at rua 31 de Janeiro is a large town house with seven double bedrooms decorated with regional artifacts. Don't expect a manor house—it's a simple establishment—but the location helps compensate. It belongs to the **Zé da Calçada** riverside restaurant across the street, which is known throughout the Douro for its namesake, a casserole of dried salt cod and potatoes, and for regional specialties such as baked kid, and sugar, egg, and almond sweets like caramelized, peaked *foguetes* (rockets) and smooth, light *brisas do Tâmega* (Tâmega breezes). The wine list includes the local Quinta da Livração estate wine and the popular light Adega Cooperativa de Gatão. The pleasant Lailai pastry shop next door is also owned by the family.

Amarante's most colorful *tasca* is **Adega Kilowatt**, on rua 31 de Janeiro opposite the Lailai pastry shop. (Owner Domingus Calmante Teixeira's father worked with the electric company, hence the name.) Kilowatt has a superb selection of smoked and air-cured hams and *salpicão* (sausage) that can be served with the wine of your choice.

In the Marão mountains 25 km (16 miles) east of Amarante on the N 15 is the Pousada de São Gonçalo (see the section on Vila Real in the Trás-os-Montes chapter).

Having completed the northwestern and final leg of the tour of the Douro, take the N 15 back from Amarante. Drive 10 km (6 miles) northwest to Lixa and turn left. (The N 15 going northwest out of Amarante to Lixa is also the N 101/IP 9. If you stay straight on 101/IP 9 at Lixa instead of turning off toward Porto on the N 15 to the left, you'll come to Guimarães and then Braga in the Minho.) Before returning to Porto, get a final taste of vintage Portugal by visiting the Romanesque conventual church at **Travanca** off the N 15, with its splendid capital inscribed with dragons and its crenellated tower.

Then continue southwest on the N 15 to the leafy hilltop town of **Penafiel**, where you can enjoy a pleasant lunch at the modern **Restaurante Alvorada**, at praça Municipal, 59–61, and then stroll in the lush subtropical garden and taste the fine *vinho verde* wines of the **Quinta de Aveleda** outside the town off the road (signposted) to Porto; open Monday through Friday 9:00 A.M. to noon and 1:00 to 6:00 P.M. The sprawling garden is the estate's pièce de résistance, with dozens of varieties of flowers for all tastes and seasons. There are sweet-smelling yellow mimosas and acacias, which blossom in February; azaleas and hydrangeas that blaze with color through the spring; and begonias and araucarias in the summer. A 19th-century cottage, a duck pond with tiny thatched houses, wrought-iron bird cages, and granite-sculpted fountains will transport you to a more bucolic era. Of historical note at the Quinta de Aveleda are the remains of an ornate granite window said to have belonged to the palace where Prince Henry the Navigator was born, salvaged from ruins by the family and given a home on a tiny island in the main pond across from a delightful summer house. The ivy-covered, 17th-century main house (refurbished and expanded in the 19th century) and its private chapel can be admired from outside. The estate's wine facilities, lodged in the northwestern end of the property, include a wine-tasting bar and verandah with sweeping views of the vineyards, where some of the finer dry *vinho verde* whites such as Grinalda and the Adega Velha da Casa de Aveleda brandy (aged in *limousin* oak wood barrels) can be tasted. You can buy these items, as well as pottery and other regional crafts, at the estate's shop next door.

GETTING AROUND

With the completion in September 1991 of the last segment of a new four-lane toll road, the 317-km (197-mile) trip to Porto from Lisbon is an easy, three-hour drive. The highway, formerly the A 1/N 1 and now officially designated the A 1/IP 1, leads through pleasant scenery, bypassing industrial centers and offering exits at most places of interest to travellers, such as Fátima, Coimbra, Figueira da Foz, and Aveiro. The toll for driving the entire length is 2,590$00. Signposts (in Portuguese) warn of the scarcity of gasoline stations and service areas. Non-Portuguese-speakers take note: If you don't do so before leaving Lisbon, fill your tank at Aveiras de Cima; after that point there are no gas stations for 162 km (100 miles), until Mealhada.

Porto's new international airport, Pedras Rubras, is located at Moreira da Maia, 15 km (9 miles) northwest of the city. A taxi ride into town should run 3,000$00 to 4,000$00 with tip, depending on which part of Porto you are going to and the amount of luggage (make sure you agree on the fare with the driver before you get in). The number 56 bus connects the airport with the city center and the Campanhã railway station, at rua da Estação. The station, which is at the eastern end of the city, connects Porto internationally as well as with the Douro and the south of the country. The Trindade train station, on rua do Alferes Malheiro, across from the praça do Município, handles the trains to Guimarães and to Povoa de Varzim. The São Bento commuter station, at praça de Almeida Garrett, has a shuttle service to Campanhã station.

The Rodoviária Entre Douro e Minho, the leading bus company, at praça Dona Filipa de Lencastre, sells tourist passes for the city bus and tram system. The passes, good for four to seven days of unlimited travel, are worth buying only if you intend to use buses fairly often; Tel: (02) 31-24-59 or 200-6954. The company also runs half-day bus tours of the city called Porto Panorâmico with English-speaking guides. They tour the city and visit a wine lodge. The tours leave from praça Dom João I on Mondays, Thursdays, and Saturdays (Tel: 02-200-1109). Taxis can be caught at a cab stand at the southern end of the avenida dos Aliados.

Ferryboats tour the river, leaving on the hour from the quay at Vila Nova de Gaia, in front of Ferreira lodge. The 45-minute boat ride provides vistas of Porto and includes a visit to the Foz. The boat runs from 10:00 A.M. to 6:00 P.M. between May and October, except Saturdays.

Give yourself two full days to get to know Porto—and wear comfortable walking shoes. Also, pay a visit to the main Turismo at rua Clube Fenianos, 25 (open Monday through Friday from 9:00 A.M. to 7:00 P.M.; Saturdays 9:00 A.M. to 4:00 P.M.; Sundays 10:00 A.M. to 1:00 P.M.) to pick up its handy red pamphlet on the city, a map of Porto and its bus routes, and a miniguide with a short history of Port wine.

Several connecting scenic train routes range along the Douro; tickets can be purchased at the stations or through travel agents, as can tourist passes with discounts of 25 percent for one to three weeks' duration. (We recommend travelling first class, as second class can be pretty grungy.) Soft drinks, beer, and sandwiches can be purchased on these lines, but not meals.

The **Linha do Douro** begins at the São Bento station in Porto, follows the Douro through the heart of Port-wine country, and ends at Pocinho. Four trains make the four-hour trip every day. The journey can be broken up by stopping at important wine centers such as Peso da Régua or Pinhão. After Pinhão the terrain becomes wilder, and the river narrows. *Mortorios* (vine cemeteries) ravaged by the phylloxera plague of the 1860s and 1870s begin to appear, surrounded by abandoned stone villages.

The **Linha do Corgo** runs north from Peso da Régua along the deep gorge of the river Corgo to Vila Real, known for its Mateus rosé. The **Linha da Tua** runs from Tua, northeast of Pinhão, to Mirandela on the banks of the river Tua. (For these towns and areas, see the Trás-os-Montes chapter.) The diesel-engine train travels at a leisurely pace through Portugal's outback. (These were the routes for these two old train lines as we went to press; both have recently been shortened and may be further limited or discontinued in the future.)

A car is the best way to visit the interior, where many of the scenic and monumental attractions are off the main road and train lines. Cars can be rented at the airport or in Porto. The main-artery traffic around Porto, however, is horrendous and even dangerous. Expect long delays. Avoid night driving on the winding and poorly marked Douro roads.

There are one- and two-day package tours of the Port-wine region via boat and train. The best include wine tasting and lunch at a wine lodge at Pinhão. Trips can be booked through travel agents or Endouro, rua da Reboleira, 49, 4000 Porto; Tel: (02) 32-42-36 or 208-4161; Fax: (02) 31-72-60. There are several tour options. The one-day Douro Maravilhoso tour begins on the double-decker, 100-seat *Ribadouro* sightseeing boat (bar service on board), which cruises from Porto to Peso da Régua. Several dams en route are negotiated by locks. Breakfast and lunch are served on board. The return trip to Porto is by train in a first-class coach with bar service and guide. The two-day program begins with the same train ride to Peso da Régua. Lunch at Peso da Régua is followed by a tour via bus of the neighboring town of Lamego and the Murganheira Cellar, a local cooperative. After an overnight stay at Peso da Régua you return to Porto by boat, stopping for lunch at the former convent of Alpendurada.

ACCOMMODATIONS REFERENCE
Rates given are projected 1993 prices for a double room, double occupancy. Price ranges span the lowest rate in the low season to the highest in the high season. Unless otherwise stated, rates include Continental breakfast. As prices are subject to change, always double-check before booking.

▶ **Casa do Casal.** Rendufe, 4660 **Resende**. Contact Maria Ana Rooke Abreu Lima. Tel: (054) 977-23, (058) 94-12-06, or (01) 54-08-32. 7,300$00.

▶ **Casa de Casal de Loivos.** Casal de Loivos, 5085 **Pinhão**. Tel: (054) 721-49 or (02) 68-40-53. 13,500$00.

▶ **Casa Pingueis.** Cambres, 5050 **Peso da Régua**. Contact Lucia de Castro Girão. Tel: (054) 232-51 or (02) 617-4442. To be rented as a house (three double bedrooms, living room, kitchen, pool). For a period of more than 15 days, 26,000$00 per day; for a period of less than 15 days, 30,000$00 per day. Open April through October; closed during the Christmas and Easter periods.

▶ **Casa das Pontes.** Quinta da Foz, 5085 **Pinhão**. Tel: (054) 723-53 or (02) 39-40-41; Fax: (054) 723-54. 10,100$00.

▶ **Casa de São Gens.** 4660 **Resende**. Contact Maria Susana Pereira Magalhães. Tel: (054) 972-70. 5,000$00.

▶ **Casa dos Varais.** Cambres, 5050 **Peso da Régua**. Contact Lucia de Castro Girão. Tel: (054) 232-51 or (02) 617-4442. 10,500$00. Open April through October.

▶ **Casa Zé da Calçada.** Rua 31 de Janeiro, Cepelos, 4600 **Amarante**. Tel: (055) 42-20-23. 8,000$00–8,500$00.

▶ **Grande Hotel do Porto.** Rua de Santa Catarina, 197, 4000 **Porto**. Tel: (02) 200-8176 or 200-5741; Fax: (02) 31-10-61; in U.S. and Canada, Tel: (800) 528-1234. 10,500$00–13,200$00.

▶ **Hotel Amaranto.** Rua Madalena, 4600 **Amarante**. Tel: (055) 42-21-06 or 42-21-07; Fax: (055) 42-59-49. 5,600$00–8,300$00.

▶ **Hotel Boa Vista.** Esplanada do Castelo, 58, **Foz do Douro**, 4100 Porto. Tel: (02) 617-0588 or 617-1509; Fax: (02) 617-3818. 12,750$00–16,000$00 (sea view).

▶ **Hotel Infante de Sagres.** Praça Dona Filipa de Lencastre,

62, 4000 **Porto**. Tel: (02) 200-8101 through 8108; Fax: (02) 31-49-37; in U.S. and Canada, Tel: (800) 528-1234. 29,500$00–35,500$00.

▶ **Hotel Méridien Porto**. Avenida da Boavista, 1466, 4000 **Porto**. Tel: (02) 600-1913 or 600-1921; Fax: (02) 600-2031; in U.S. and Canada, Tel: (800) 543-4300. 25,000$00–32,000$00 (does not include breakfast).

▶ **Hotel Navarras**. Rua António Carneiro, 4600 **Amarante**. Tel: (055) 43-10-36; Fax: (055) 43-29-91. 6,000$00–10,000$00.

▶ **Hotel Panorama**. Avenida Conselheiro Alpoim, 525, 5040 **Mesão Frio**. Tel: (054) 992-36. 6,500$00–7,500$00.

▶ **Hotel Sheraton Porto**. Avenida da Boavista, 1269, 4100 **Porto**. Tel: (02) 606-8822; Fax: (02) 609-1467; in U.S. and Canada, Tel: (800) 325-3535; in U.K., Tel: (0800) 35-35-35. 24,650$00–35,350$00.

▶ **Ipanema Park Hotel**. Rua de Serralves, 124, 4100 **Porto**. Tel: (02) 610-4174; Fax: (02) 610-2809. 28,000$00–30,000$00.

▶ **Pousada do Barão de Forrester**. Rua José Rufino, 5070 **Alijó**. Tel: (059) 95-92-15; Fax: (059) 95-93-04. 8,000$00–12,300$00.

▶ **Tivoli Porto Atlántico**. Rua Afonso Lopes Vieira, 66, 4000 **Porto**. Tel: (02) 69-49-41; Fax: (02) 606-7452. 20,000$00–32,000$00.

Pousadas can be booked through ENATUR, Avenida Santa Joana Princesa, 10, 1700 Lisbon, Portugal; Tel: (01) 848-1221 or 848-9078; Fax: (01) 80-58-46. But it is easier to make reservations through a travel agent. In the United States and Canada, pousadas can be booked through Marketing Ahead, 433 Fifth Avenue, New York, NY 10016; Tel: (212) 686-9213; Fax: (212) 686-0271.

Manor houses can be booked directly or through the manor-house associations—ANTER, P.I.T., PRIVETUR, and TURIHAB—listed in Useful Facts. Most of the houses belong to one or more of these associations, but because membership rosters change frequently we haven't attempted to spell out the associations for each house. Readers are advised to contact the manor-house associations for their current listings.

In the United States and Canada, it is possible to reserve rooms in P.I.T manor houses through E & M Associates, 211 East 43rd Street, Suite 1404, New York, NY 10017; Tel: (212) 599-8280; Fax: (212) 599-1755.

THE MINHO
THE NORTHWEST

By Thomas de la Cal

The Minho, tucked away in the northwest corner of the country, between the Minho river and Spain to the north and the Douro province to the south, with the remote province of Trás-os-Montes to the east, is Portugal's Garden of Eden. Its rich soil, ample rainfall, and thermal springs keep it eternally verdant. Mists shroud its interior with mystery and give the land an aura of sublime peace.

Physically, the Minho has been likened to a huge amphitheater. The serras of Peneda, Gerês, and Padrela in the east form a semicircle facing west onto a stage where some of Portugal's most dramatic historical events—including the birth of the nation—took place, starring a mixed cast of Celtic, Germanic, Slavic, Spanish, and other Mediterranean peoples. The performances took place amid a vast array of natural settings—a luxuriant Atlantic coastline, green valleys, pristine lakes, and majestic peaks.

The personality of the people is as mixed and their imagination as fertile as their land. *Minhotos* inherited their warmth and their perpetual nostalgia from the Celts, who settled the area in the first millennium B.C., some of their poetic and artistic inspiration from Greek visitors of the Bronze and Iron ages, and their spirit of adventure from the Phoenicians (the Minho claims several renowned explorers). The Romans built roads, started the wine business, and passed on many of their superstitions, while the Suevi, a Germanic tribe, focused on hard work and small, independent landholdings. The Suevi controlled a large chunk of the Iberian Peninsula until forced to retrench by the Visigoths, who populated the

Minho's mountainous interior and gave the Portuguese language its Baltic sounds. The Moors left behind their taste for sweets and spices, enchanted castles and princesses. The Minhotos' independent streak—the Moors and Romans were never able to subjugate them—led to a secession from the kingdoms of León and Castile in the 12th century, and the establishment of the Portuguese kingdom.

The Minhotos' most impressive quality, however, is their ability to blend the northern work ethic with the southern *joie de vivre* without letting one dilute the other. Hard work has made their region one of the country's principal cattle-growing (mostly oxen), wine-producing, and textile-manufacturing centers. But the Minhotos can play with equal vigor, as evidenced in their all-night *arraiais* (barn parties) and their spirited folk dances, the *viras* and the *malhão*.

They are also extremely religious, but here too they have managed a graceful blend of opposites: Christian faith and pagan past. Minho *festas* (feast days) and *romarias* (pilgrimages) combine somber church ritual with carnival-like rites of spring. The ancient Mother Goddess religion, with its ties to fertility and the earth, has merged in the Minho with the cult of the Virgin. In some villages Mother Nature, the Minho's unofficial patron goddess, is worshiped with splendid flower pageants and parades.

Women have an important role in the region's economy. They tend the fields while the men work outside the country. Behind this arrangement are the traditional inheritance customs of the Minho: Small family plots are divided equally among all descendants, making the fragmented landholdings too small to support families. Minho women have also taken a role in politics. The region's history is filled with heroines such as Deu-la-Deu Martins, who outsmarted Spanish invaders in the 14th century, and Maria da Fonte, who led a revolt against state authority in the mid 19th century. Minhota beauty, legendary in Portugal, is displayed at its best during feast days, when the Minho women don their traditional costumes and intricate gold-filigreed jewelry.

While the past still lives in the Minho, "progress" is blighting its splendid Atlantic beaches with tacky resorts. Factory pollution is beginning to smudge the air of such ancient towns as Guimarães and Braga, and men, returning from their work stints abroad, are littering the countryside with gaudy copies of the houses they admired overseas. Minho hospitality, however, endures, as do pockets of rare natural beauty.

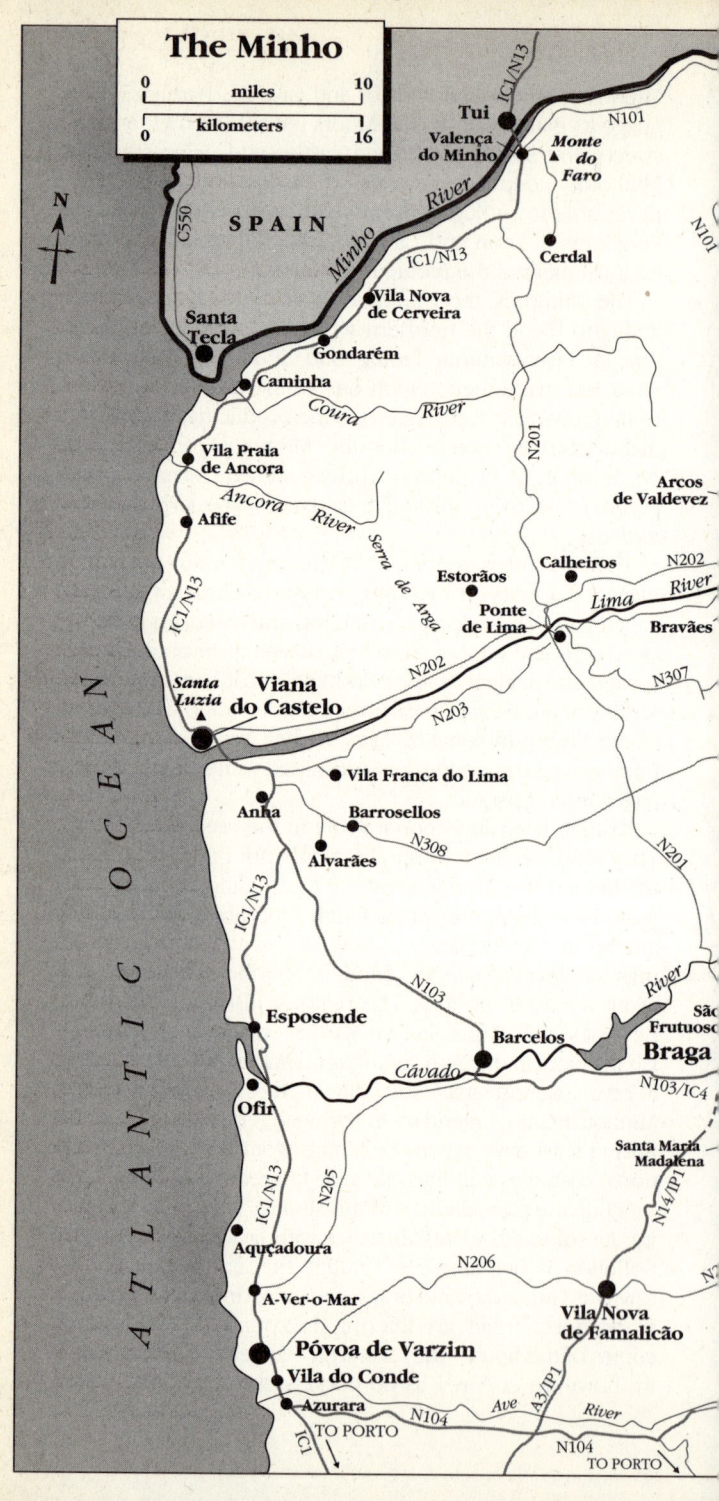

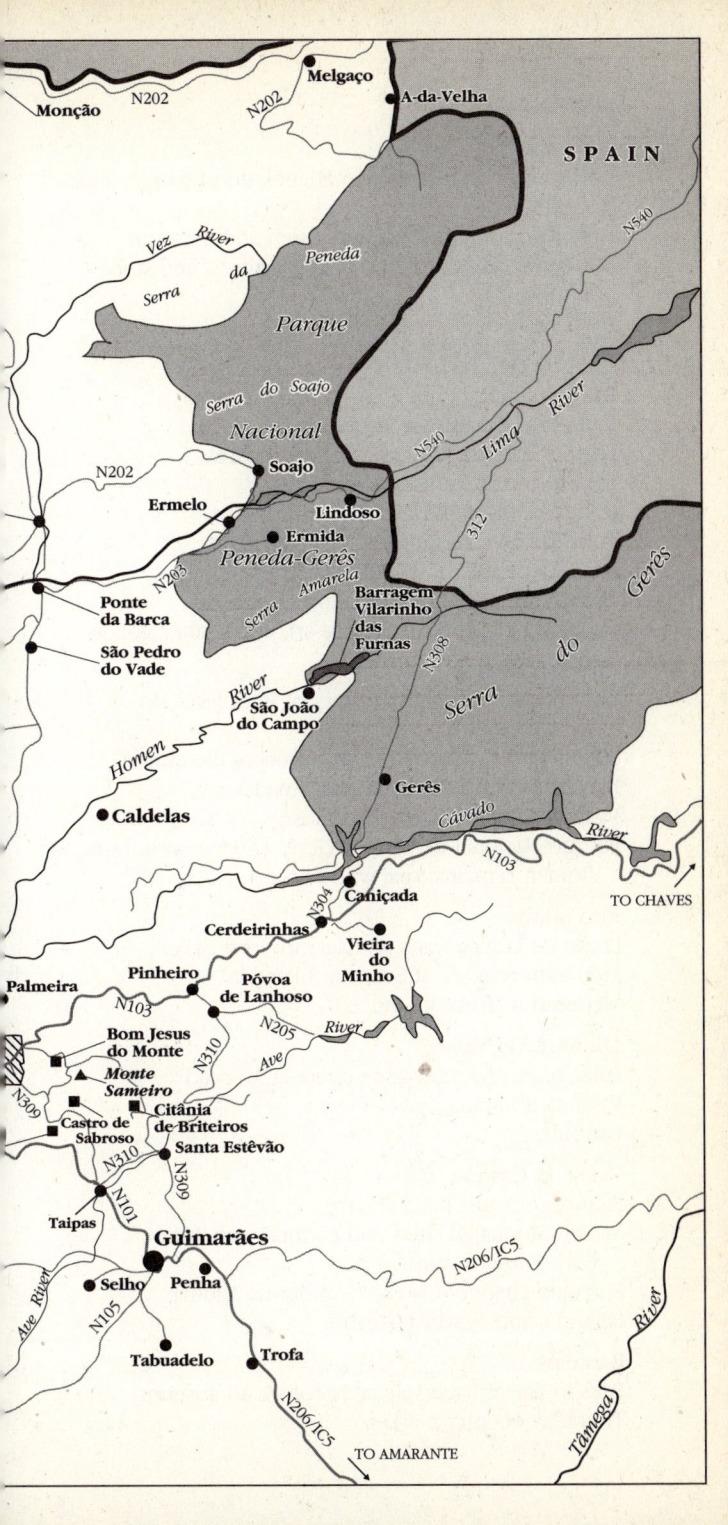

MAJOR INTEREST

Guimarães
Romanesque Igreja de São Miguel, ducal palace, and castle
Nossa Senhora da Oliveira church and museum
Museu Martins Sarmento (Celtic artifacts and stone sculptures)
Iron Age Citânia de Briteiros
Ancient Castro de Sabroso

Braga
Cathedral chapels and treasury
Former archbishop's palace and square
Palácio dos Biscainhos city museum
Jardim de Santa Bárbara
Torre de Menagem (Keep)
Baroque façade of the Casa do Raio
Holy Week festivities and annual wine fair
Shopping for crafts, religious art, and leather goods

The Braga Area
Baroque staircase at sanctuary of Bom Jesus do Monte
Santuário de Monte Sameiro's view of the Minho
Baroque church of Santa Maria Madalena
Visigothic chapel of São Frutuoso
Parque Nacional de Peneda-Gerês (hiking, swimming, Roman remains, spa, wild horses)

Alto Minho
Ponte de Lima's crafts and agriculture market
Mountain regions of Soajo and Peneda
Medieval fortress at Lindoso

Minho River Valley
Palácio de Brejoeira wine estate at Monção
Valença do Minho
Caminha

Viana do Castelo
Picture-postcard main square
Museu Municipal (tiles and earthenware, Indo-Portuguese furniture)
Baroque chapel of Nossa Senhora da Agonia
Festivals and flower pageants

Barcelos
Palácio Ducal (open-air archaeological museum)
Thursday country market

The Atlantic Coast
Beaches
Póvoa de Varzim (fishermen's *bairro,* woollen sweaters, and gold- and silversmiths)
Vila do Conde (lace-making school, annual crafts fair, Plateresque church doorway)

Food and Wine of the Minho

Minho dishes have a straight-from-the-farm flavor and a diversity commensurate with the region's topography. The substantial culinary repertory ranges from kid and lamb in the mountainous midriff to fresh trout and eel in the river valleys, from fish stews, cod, shellfish, and sardines in the coastal areas to pork, cured hams, and sausages, in the interior. The region's *caldo verde,* a thick potato-and-cabbage soup with a dash of olive oil and slices of sausage, is aptly named after the verdant countryside. (The cabbage is the emerald green, nonheading Galician cabbage, or collard.) *Sopa seca* (dry soup), an odds-and-ends dish invented by frugal housewives in mountain areas to recycle meats, vegetables, and bread, is a meal in itself. Leftovers are resuscitated with hot broth, seasoned with mint, layered into a terra-cotta casserole, and baked.

Other indigenous Minho specialties include the heavy, vinegary *rojões e sarrabulho à moda do Minho* (pork stew with maize dumplings) and the dark-meated *lampreia* (river eel), marinated and cooked in its own blood mixed with wine. Some lamprey dishes are curried. The latter spice, together with saffron, became popular in the 16th century after Vasco da Gama returned with ships laden with spices from India. Minhotos love lamprey so much that they make desserts in its image, using an intensely sweet egg-yolk custard poached in an eel-shaped mold—eyes, mouth, and teeth sculpted with icing.

Pork is a staple of the Minho diet. Nutritious meals of cooked potatoes, corn, chestnuts, and wheat are lavished on pigs throughout the year, in order to guarantee their flavor. Pork curing and sausage making are cottage industries. Every fall the pigs are butchered, hams are laid out to cure, and yards of casing are stuffed with blends of pork and spices to produce such popular sausages as *salpicão,* a pork tenderloin cured in dry wine, salt, and garlic, then smoked, or the dry, long, thin *linguiça,* consisting of chopped pork shoulder, garlic, and paprika. Sausages and hams make great appetizers and add consistency to stews like the hearty *cozido à Portuguesa,* a mélange of meats and vegetables.

Meals are accompanied by rich and crunchy *pão de milho* (corn bread) or the more traditional *broa,* a dense and chewy yeast-raised corn bread, and washed down with the region's *vinho verde,* named not for its color but for its relative youth and the green countryside. *Vinhos verdes,* reds and whites, young and fizzy, should be drunk during their first two years. The British call them "eager" wines on account of their effervescence. The best *vinhos verdes* are the estate whites such as Palácio da Brejoeira, Solar de Bouças, and Quinta da Aveleda. The vines grow and cling to trellises, telephone poles, and any other object they find, reaching heights of up to 150 feet. The trellising practice, which was introduced by the Romans, frees the precious ground soil for a second crop and prevents the grapes from overripening, so that they yield a medium-dry, crisp, low-alcohol beverage. A word of caution, though, about *vinho verde:* Because of its relatively high acid content, too much of it before going to bed may cause indigestion and/or wild dreams.

Give yourself a minimum of a week to explore the Minho. Our essentially circular coverage begins at the royal town of Guimarães, where it all started, moves next door to Braga, the religious capital of Portugal and a major center of Baroque art, and then turns northeast into the Peneda-Gerês national park. It veers west into the bucolic Lima river valley, studded with patrician estates; goes up through the Alto Minho; meanders along the fortress-lined Minho river valley, which borders Spain and gave the region its name; then heads south along the Atlantic coast to Viana do Castelo, the capital of Minho folklore. A short detour from Viana do Castelo southeast to Barcelos, the ceramic center of the north, is recommended before returning to the Minho's Atlantic coastline.

GUIMARAES

Guimarães, the cradle of the Portuguese nation, lies in a tree-studded valley surrounded by mountains 55 km (34 miles) northeast of Porto via the new, four-lane IP 1 and N 206 highways. These roads have helped clear a large bottleneck in the area, particularly the IP 1, which is expected to reach Braga by early 1994. A more scenic route, only 4 km

(2½ miles) longer, uses the N 105-2 and the N 105. However, avoid the latter during the morning and evening rush hours, as these roads are narrow and twisting, and you may end up choking behind a truck spewing carbon monoxide.

In the tenth century the Galician countess Mumadona Dias founded the monastery of Salvador do Mundo at Vimarenes, then a center of the growing county of Portugal. The town soared into prominence by being in the vanguard of the revolt (1118–1128) that shook off the yoke of Spanish domination. The liberator was the young Count Afonso Henriques, son of Henry of Burgundy and Princess Teresa (Tareja in Visigoth), bastard daughter of Alfonso VI, the king of León and Castile, who had acquired the region as part of her dowry in 1095. When Henry died in 1112, Afonso Henriques was a small child and Teresa became the ruler of Portugal, but she alienated her subjects by taking a Galician count as her lover and siding with the Leónese against her subjects' aspirations for autonomy.

When Afonso Henriques came of age, he led the Portuguese barons and religious leaders against the combined forces of his mother and her lover, defeating them in the bloody Battle of São Mamede on the outskirts of the city in 1128. The victorious Afonso Henriques, a giant of a man and a military genius as well, went on to liberate large tracts of Portugal from the Moors and proclaimed himself king of an independent Portugal in 1139. Papal recognition, however, did not come until 1179, after a hefty financial contribution was made to the Vatican.

Medieval Guimarães is re-created yearly on the first Sunday of August during the Festas Gualterianas, when the residents don period costumes and perform medieval plays. Guimarães is known for its handicrafts. Of particular interest are the *cantarinhas das prendas,* earthenware pots decorated with shiny mica, traditional dowry utensils in which young women place their valuables, such as gold and silver filigree, to present to their husbands when they marry. Lacy linens are made by the women in the lush hills south of Guimarães, particularly around the town of Trofa, 12 km (7½ miles) on the N 101/IP 9 toward Amarante, where they sell their work by the roadside.

The Town

Guimarães is two cities. By far the more charming is old Guimarães, full of churches, tiny cobbled streets, and medieval town houses and arches, which runs roughly from the largo da Oliveira at its center, northward up to the Colina Sagrada, the "Sacred Hill" and its monuments, tied to Portugal's beginnings. You can walk from the Oliveira square to the Colina in 15 minutes. Then there is dynamic modern Guimarães, south of the square, composed mostly of small business establishments, medium-size shoe and textile factories, and uninspired apartment blocks.

The divider of old and new Guimarães is the flower-lined alameda da Resistência ão Fascismo. The local Turismo is at the western end of this avenue, and Oliveira square is a block north of the fountain on its eastern end.

The Sacred Hill

The **Colina Sagrada** is dear to the Portuguese heart. It was in the **castelo** at the top of this hill that Afonso Henriques is believed to have been born. The castle's heavily restored tenth-century **Torre de Menagem** (Keep) and its eight surrounding towers were the inspiration behind the Portuguese coat of arms. On the green beside the castle's western ramparts is the tiny 12th-century Romanesque **Igreja de São Miguel do Castelo**, where he is said to have been baptized. The floor of the chapel, covered with gravestones of Portuguese nobles, reads like a Who's Who of Portuguese medieval nobility.

São Miguel is dwarfed by the giant building next door, the 15th-century **Paço dos Duques** (Ducal Palace) of Dom Afonso, count of Barcelos and first duke of Bragança. This Afonso, the bastard son of King João I, travelled extensively throughout Europe on diplomatic missions for his father and apparently acquired a taste for things northern, which explains the Burgundian "maison" architecture of the building. The third duke, Fernando, was beheaded by King João II, and the building was abandoned. The Braganças, a resilient and politically astute family, survived and returned to power in 1640, ruling Portugal until they were ousted by the Republic in 1910. In 1933 António Salazar had the old palace restored and converted into a presidential residence and **city museum**.

The palace contains something for everyone: an armory, Indo-Portuguese furniture, copies of French and Flemish tapestries of the 16th to 18th centuries, paintings by Portuguese, Italian, and Dutch masters, and a valuable collection of Persian rugs from the 15th to 17th centuries. There are several canvases attributed to the 17th-century painter Josefa de Ayala (better known in painting circles as Josefa de

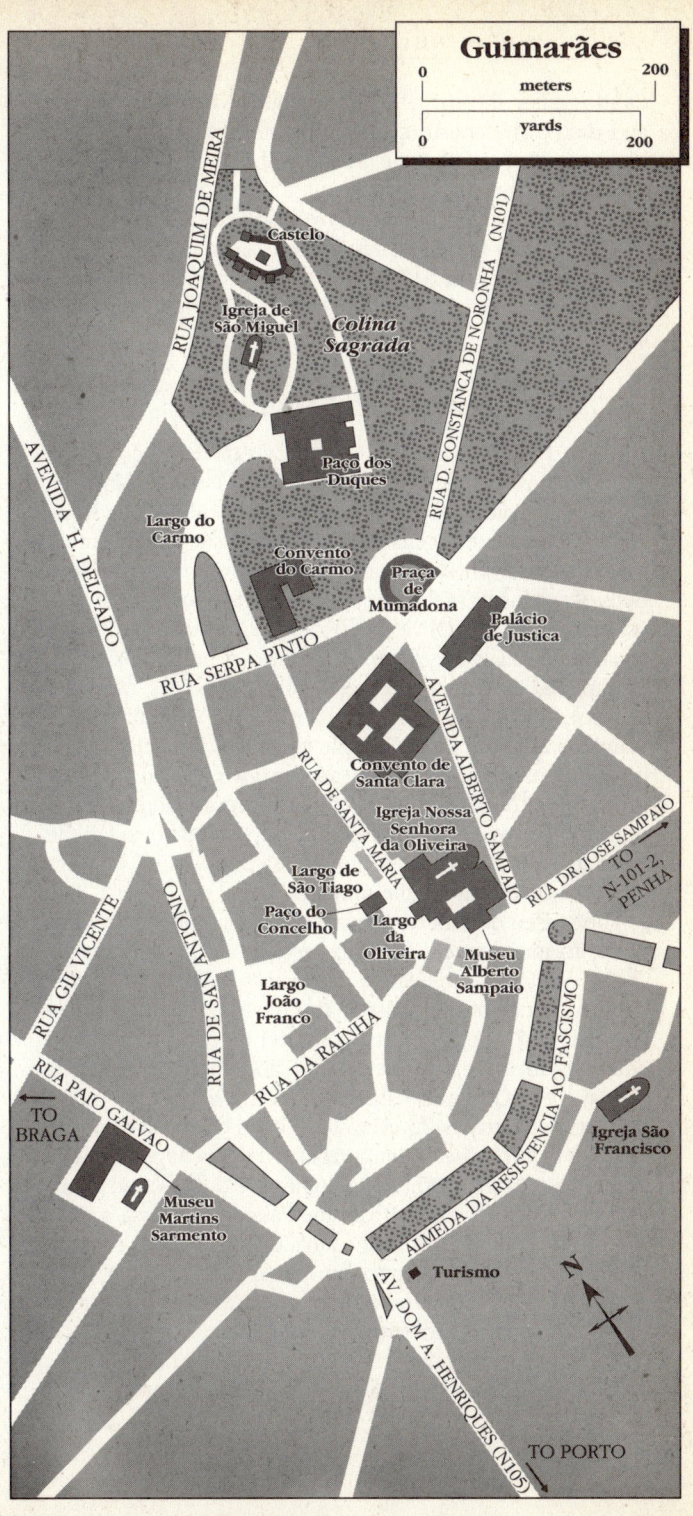

Guimarães

0 — meters — 200

0 — yards — 200

RUA JOAQUIM DE MEIRA

Castelo

Igreja de São Miguel

Colina Sagrada

RUA D. CONSTANÇA DE NORONHA (N101)

Paço dos Duques

AVENIDA H. DELGADO

Largo do Carmo

Convento do Carmo

Praça de Mumadona

Palácio de Justiça

RUA SERPA PINTO

AVENIDA ALBERTO SAMPAIO

Convento de Santa Clara

RUA DE SANTA MARIA

Igreja Nossa Senhora da Oliveira

RUA DR. JOSE SAMPAIO

TO N-101-2, PENHA

Largo de São Tiago

Paço do Concelho

Largo da Oliveira

Museu Alberto Sampaio

RUA GIL VICENTE

RUA DE SAN ANTONIO

Largo João Franco

RUA DA RAINHA

ALMEDA DA RESISTENCIA AO FASCISMO

RUA PAIO GALVAO

TO BRAGA

Museu Martins Sarmento

Igreja São Francisco

■ Turismo

N

AV. DOM A. HENRIQUES (N105)

TO PORTO

Obidos, after the town in Estremadura where she painted and died). The chestnut ceilings of its banquet and dining halls are shaped like the inside ribbing of a Portuguese caravel, in tribute to Portugal's maritime exploits.

To reach the hill by car, drive northeast up avenida Alberto Sampaio (which starts at the eastern end of the alameda da Resistência ão Fascismo), veer left at the end of this street onto rua Serpa Pinto, and take the first right onto largo do Carmo.

Largo da Oliveira

Directly south of the Colina Sagrada, via the largo do Carmo and the tiny cobbled rua Santa Maria, lies the largo da Oliveira, a typical medieval square lined with Gothic stone arches and somewhat shabby but distinguished 15th-century town houses with elaborate wrought-iron grilles. The iron bells of the tower of the **Igreja de Nossa Senhora da Oliveira** (Our Lady of the Olive Tree) on the eastern side of the square still toll as they have for centuries. Children play here unimpeded by cars, watched by their mothers from the square's outdoor café. Legend has it that the Visigoth warrior Wamba was asked by his people to be their king. Seeking a divine signal, Wamba drove an olive-wood staff into the ground and declared that he would become king only if it put forth leaves. Leaves did sprout and Wamba bowed to the inevitable—and centuries later Nossa Senhora da Oliveira was built on the site of the miracle.

The **Museu de Alberto Sampaio** is housed on the grounds of the former convent building next door. The only vestige of the original tenth-century monastery is the door on the eastern corner of the cloister. The museum contains priceless art and other objects collected from convents and churches in the area. The second floor holds a glittering display of ecclesiastical plate, including a portable silver triptych popularly believed to have been captured from the Spanish in the Battle of Aljubarrota in 1385 but apparently of Portuguese origin. Other highlights are a 35-pound silver cross carved with scenes from the Passion of Christ; a stunning 15th-century silver chalice inlaid with Limoges enamel; and a Manueline monstrance attributed to Gil Vicente, who, as well as being the father of Portuguese theater, was one of the most talented goldsmiths of his era.

The museum was the scene of a spectacular heist in 1975. Among the goods stolen were gem-studded crowns and a gold chain dating from the reign of João I that was made to stretch from the entrance of the town to the church. The thieves have apparently been identified, but the treasures have yet to be be returned.

Other highlights in the square include the handsome 14th-century **Padrão da Batalha do Salado** (a porch lined with saints carved in limestone by French masons) in front of the Igreja de Nossa Senhora da Oliveira and at the northwestern corner the **Antigo Paço do Concelho** (Old Town Hall), an elegant crenellated structure built over Gothic arches that now serves as the municipal library. The square, a pedestrian island, is the ideal spot to escape from the noise and fast pace of modern Guimarães, where new textile, tanning, and kitchen-appliance industries are replacing traditional crafts such as silver- and goldsmithing, hand embroidering, and linen weaving. The art of wine making, however, remains as strong as ever in the region. At the newly opened **Garrafeira Santa Maria** wineshop, on the western end of the square, enthusiasts can stock up not only on most Minho wines but also on Port and other Portuguese varieties.

Some of the spacious guest rooms and the elegantly rustic dining room of the **Pousada de Nossa Senhora da Oliveira** front the northeastern corner of the square. Several aristocratic town houses from the 15th to the 17th century were remodeled and joined together, decorated with fine reproductions of antiques, and staffed with hospitable Minhotos to re-create a medieval-style inn. If you are a light sleeper, however, be prepared to be kept up at night by the banter of teenagers hanging out under the arches of the old town hall.

In keeping with its medieval flavor, the inn's fine restaurant is housed in the kitchen of a former baronial residence. What makes it especially pleasant is its massive gray stone fireplace that is open front and back and can be enjoyed by diners on either side of it. The kitchen serves regional specialties and is known for its richly flavored *rojões à Minhota* (pork stew), served with pickled cauliflower and carrots. The pork is so tender it falls from the bones.

For a more intimate and romantic bistro, try the cozy **El Rei** restaurant behind the pousada, at largo de São Tiago, 20. This restaurant also serves as a gallery for area artists. Their paintings line the walls and can be purchased. The most popular lunch spot in town is the family-run **Jordão** restaurant, near the city center at avenida Dom Afonso Henriques, 55, with regional decor and food.

The Sarmento Museum

The **Museu Martins Sarmento** lies a few blocks west of the largo da Oliveira on rua Paio Galvão. Lodged partly in a Gothic cloister, the museum contains the findings of the 19th-century archaeologist Francisco Martins Sarmento, Portugal's Schliemann, who spent his life and fortune excavating the Iron Age cities of Briteiros and Sabroso, north of Guimarães. The collection includes coins, jewelry, and artifacts dating back to the Celts. Its two most interesting pieces are the Pedra Formosa, one of two large granite slabs from Briteiros, inscribed with human forms, which scholars believe could have been from entrances to Celtic crematoriums, and the ten-foot-high colossus of Pedralva. This latter freestanding statue, which was found in Monte de Picos in Pedralva, acquired by Sarmento in 1876, and moved to the museum in 1929, is so large that it took 24 oxen to move it. Some scholars think it was carved in the pre-Roman era. Others, arguing that it is too advanced for that period, believe it may have been executed in modern times.

Although the handsome 17th-century **Casa dos Pombais** manor house (west of the museum on the avenida de Londres) is surrounded by modern Guimarães, its thick walls and garden ensure its privacy and preserve its patrician heritage from the hustle and bustle outside. The two double rooms available to guests give onto the garden and are furnished with family heirlooms, such as carved oak beds and handwoven rugs. The grounds and two large salons are rented out for parties, so don't be surprised if you are invited to a wedding reception while staying at the house.

Outside Guimarães

The luxury **Pousada de Santa Marinha da Costa**, which lies 2 km (1¼ miles) east of the city center on the N 101-2, halfway up the Serra de Santa Catarina overlooking Guimarães and on the way to Penha (see below), is the ultimate in getting away from it all. The gardens of the former Augustinian monastery, which meander up the mountain behind the *pousada* (government-run inn), are irrigated by its freshwater springs. Guests can sleep in former monks' cells, in large suites decorated with antiques from the royal palace of Ajuda in Lisbon, or in a modern annex. A marble staircase lined with tiles designed by the 18th-century master Policarpo Oliveira Bernardes can be admired outside the drawing room. The marble pillars and arches of the old monastery kitchen provide a dignified backdrop for sumptuous dining. Recently remodeled by the state, the pousada has more than 50 double rooms and can accommodate large tour groups.

A breathtaking view of the region can be had from the top of the mountain (follow the signs indicating Penha) above the pousada. At the summit is a monument to Gago Coutinho, the first person to cross the southern Atlantic (1922) to Brazil in an airplane, and the 20th-century Santuário de Nossa Senhora da Penha, the patron saint of travellers. Small curio shops, cafés, and restaurants on the summit are popular with pilgrims visiting on weekends.

Travellers in search of the leisurely life of the region's country squires can find it in the ivy-lined **Paço de São Cipriano**, an 18th-century baronial manor house with an imposing crenellated tower, sprawling gardens, and a pool surrounded by trimmed box hedges. This lovely antiques-filled home, with five double bedrooms to let (three with private baths), is 6 km (3½ miles) south of Guimarães; detailed directions are given in the Turihab brochure. The sprawling estate, owned by the patrician, English-speaking Sotto Mayor family, is beside the parish church on the southern outskirts of this tiny village, and is open to guests from April through October. Two of the bedrooms have splendid king-size beds (one in iron and copper, the other in carved oak) surmounted by elaborate canopies, and breakfast is served in a 15th-century kitchen. The best time to stay here is summer, as the house has no central heating.

The **Casa do Ribeiro**, 7 km (4 miles) west of Guimarães at Selho, is a perfect example of an 18th-century manor house. It is solidly built in granite, contains its own chapel, and has the crest of the Ferras Pinto family carved in stone over an imposing gate. The two double rooms, one suite, and one single bedroom are furnished with antiques and look out onto forested hills. Your attentive hosts, who speak English, can direct you to local restaurants.

North of Guimarães

The Iron Age **Citânia de Briteiros** lies 11 km (7 miles) north of Guimarães on a hill overlooking the pristine waters of the Ave river. The 19th-century Portuguese archaeologist Martins Sarmento spent his adult life uncovering the secrets of this *citânia* (a pre-Roman or Roman fortified hilltop town), which is the largest of its kind in Portugal. The site, which was walled at one time and whose layout is reminiscent of ancient Mycenae in Greece, contains the remains of some 200 round, rectangular, and elliptical houses (some of which have been reconstructed, to the disdain of purists) and a large cistern. In the southwestern corner of the *citânia* lies an interesting granite slab that scholars believe may have had a part in a Celtic reincarnation ritual. The Romans are thought to have converted the crematorium into hot baths. The artifacts discovered on the site are displayed at the Martins Sarmento museum in Guimarães.

To get to Briteiros head north out of Guimarães on the N 101, turn right onto the N 310 at Taipas (known for its ancient Roman baths), and left at Santo Estêvão. (Beyond the *citânia,* north and west on the same road, N 309, are Monte Sameiro and Bom Jesus do Monte; see the Braga Area, below.)

The **Castro de Sabroso**, also excavated by Sarmento, can be seen from Briteiros on a hill to the west. It is smaller than Briteiros (only some 35 dwellings), and is believed to be the older of the two sites. Its walls are thicker and better joined than those at Briteiros. Sabroso stands on a hill above the tiny town of Cancela, and can be reached from Taipas by heading north on the N 309 toward Cristina de Longos. About 4 km (2½ miles) from Taipas, turn right and climb past Cancela to the top of the hill.

BRAGA

Braga, 22 km (14 miles) northwest of Guimarães on the N 101 and 7½ km (5 miles) north of Sabroso on the N 309, is Portugal's Eternal City, with perhaps more churches and saints per capita than Rome. At the height of Church power, the nuns and priests of Braga outnumbered laymen nearly two to one. For more than 600 years its archbishops were the lords of Braga, answerable only to the Pope. The nobility was barred from owning land inside the city's walls, where all business was centered around the needs of the Church. In the late 18th century, things changed: The medieval walls came down, the bourgeoisie moved in and diversified the economy, and the archbishops were forced to relinquish their administrative grip on the city.

Today industrial parks and shopping arcades have replaced churches and palaces on the builders' agenda, and new industries such as auto-accessory manufacturing thrive alongside the older candle-making and religious-artifacts crafts. For the first time since the Inquisition the Church is having to compete for parishioners with other religious sects, including Mormons and Jehovah's Witnesses.

The archbishop here continues to wield tremendous power as the religious and spiritual leader of Portugal. During Holy Week (the week before Easter), Braga's churches and street chapels are kept constantly lit by votive candles, and its religious shops are filled with a steady stream of pilgrims. It appears that the old adage "Porto earns, Lisbon spends, Coimbra studies, and Braga prays" still holds true.

Braga got its name from the Bracari, the name given by the Romans to the Goidelic (or Gaelic) Celts who settled it around 300 B.C. It received the seed of Christianity from the Romans, who conquered it and made it the hub of a network of roads. As the empire crumbled, the Suevi swooped down in 409 and ruled the city till 485, when they in turn were vanquished by the Visigoths. In 716 a Moorish army leveled Braga, and for the next 300 years Christians fought Moors for this strategic enclave. After its reconquest by Ferdinand I in 1040, it landed in the lap of Henry of Burgundy through his marriage to Princess Teresa of León and Castile.

In 1112, after Henry's death, Teresa handed over the city to Archbishop Maurice Bourdin, making him lord of Braga. The new ecclesiastical masters of Braga soon expanded their power, throwing their spiritual weight behind Dom Afonso Henriques in his successful bid to establish an independent kingdom. Large building projects were undertaken with the profits from the spice trade in the 16th century, under the auspices of the flamboyant archbishop Dom Diogo Sousa, who imported Biscayan artisans to work on the cathedral and added a Renaissance wing to the archbishop's palace. Gold from Brazil and the religious zeal fostered by the Counter-Reformation helped turn Braga into the center of Baroque art in Portugal during the 18th century. The bishops and their retinues dressed in satin and jewels and even had their own private orchestras—but trouble lay around the corner.

In 1790 the bishops were forced to give up their feudal title of lords of Braga to civilian authorities. In 1808 the city was overrun by Napoleonic troops, and the churches sacked. The final blow came in 1910, when Church properties were confiscated by the Republic and all temporal power was assumed by secular authorities. Although some properties were later returned, the bishops of Braga never recovered their former power.

A new building boom has pushed Braga beyond its old boundaries and spread it across the valley. The city's main artery, the avenida da Liberdade, which runs from the praça da República in the north to the river Este, is lined with banks and concrete office blocks and caters to the more temporal needs and pleasures of the new moneyed crowd.

The historic quarter, west of the praça de República, is fairly small and best done on foot. Park at the guarded municipal parking lot directly north of the cathedral, on the praça Conde de Agrolongo.

The Old City

The pedestrians-only **rua do Souto** is the conduit into this haven, which comprises most of the former domains of the bishops of Braga and is fairly concentrated. It begins in the tiny Barão São Martinho square, directly west of the praça da República, and runs west past some of the city's oldest and poshest shops and trendy outdoor coffeehouses crowded with shoppers and university students. It ends at the picture-postcard largo do Paço, the nerve center of the old city. The square is graced by a Flamboyant fountain and flanked by the former archbishop's palace to the north and the cathedral to the south. Most of Braga's other interesting sights are located in the vicinity of this square and require no more than a ten-minute walk. The rua Dom Diogo de Sousa picks up the westerly trajectory of the rua do Souto and ends at the 18th-century Porta Nova arch, the former western perimeter of the city.

Restaurant row is located directly outside the Porta Nova, in the tree-lined campo de Hortas.

The Cathedral

The *Sé* (Cathedral), off the rua Dom Diogo de Sousa, is Braga's centerpiece. Construction was begun in the 12th century under the patronage of Henry of Burgundy on the site of the sixth-century church of Santa Maria, which had been destroyed by the Moors in 711, and of an even earlier (A.D. 43) temple to the Egyptian goddess Isis. Over the centuries various archbishops left their mark on the Sé's architecture. The result is an interesting mélange of styles, from imported elegant Romanesque arching over the main entrance to Gothic arches in the portico, to a busy Baroque façade and imposing bell towers.

The courtyard of the Sé complex is lined with chapels. The Gothic **Capela dos Reis** on the south end contains the tombs of the founders of the cathedral, Henry and Teresa.

The **Capela de São Geraldo**, at the eastern end of the courtyard, is lined with 18th-century *azulejos* (decorative tiles) depicting the life of Braga's first archbishop, Saint Gerald. The **Capela da Glória**, next door, contains the beautifully carved tomb of Archbishop Gonçalo Pereira, the uncle of Nuno Alvares Pereira, the military genius behind the Battle of Aljubarrota. The courtyard and adjacent cloisters house several shrines to Nossa Senhora do Leite (Our Lady of the Milk), nursing the infant Jesus. The chapels are surrounded by wax and plastic breasts left by women asking the Virgin to bless them with ample milk.

The interior of the cathedral, though heavy and dark, contains several items of artistic merit. The 15th-century bronze tomb of the Infante Dom Afonso, one of Henry the Navigator's brothers, in the southwest wing exhibits its Flemish creator's flair for the ornate. The choir walls teem with representations of animals and plants from the New World.

The religious treasures of the cathedral, which date back to the tenth century, are stored in the **Museu de Arte Sacra** in the northwest wing. Of all the gold and silver exhibited, the silver monstrance of 18th-century Archbishop Gaspar de Bragança, son of King João V, is the most striking. It weighs nearly 19 pounds and is encrusted with 450 precious stones. There are guided tours of the treasury and the chapels (afternoons only in the winter).

Around the Cathedral

The **Chafariz do Largo do Paço** (or Bishop's Fountain, as it is popularly called) stands directly opposite the Sé in a peaceful cobbled square lined with arches. The picturesque square (depicted on Portugal's 500-escudo note) is a favorite meeting place for students from the neighboring university. The **Antigo Paço Episcopal**, the former archbishop's palace, on the north side of the largo do Paço, is composed of 14th-, 17th-, and 18th-century wings, and now serves as the city library and as the rectory of the university of the Minho. The library, which can be visited, houses more than 300,000 volumes, some dating from the ninth century. Its rarest documents are contained in the magnificent ivory-and-wood **Sala do Arcaz**. Special permission is required to visit the Sala do Arcaz, but documents can be requested and read in the wood-lined reading room. Also of interest is the entrance to the university rectory, whose walls display some fine examples of 17th- and 18th-century *azulejos*.

In keeping with tradition, the noble family who built the

17th-century **Palácio dos Biscainhos** had it erected outside the walls of the city of the archbishops, on the street bearing its name northwest of the Arco da Porta Nova, west of the Sé at the end of the rua Dom Diogo de Sousa. The two-story nobleman's palace, remodeled in the 18th century and now the city museum, shows something of the sumptuous lifestyle of the old Portuguese nobility.

East of the palace, in front of the 18th-century wing of the former archbishop's palace, is the **Câmara Municipal** (Town Hall), built in the late 18th century by André Soares, the most renowned Baroque architect of his time. Facing east toward the former archbishop's palace, the well-balanced building marks the turning point of political power in Braga.

The **Jardim de Santa Bárbara**, behind the former archbishop's palace to the east, is an oasis of tranquillity and beauty where more than 50 varieties of flowers bloom in elaborate designs. The all-purpose eatery **Lusitana**, at the southeast corner of the garden, is the ideal spot for a light lunch or tea. Patrons can nibble on *combinados* (combination platters) that might include Braga's hearty *frigideiras* (meat pies) and such *doces d'ovos* as *fatias de Braga* (spongey-sweet poached loaves of egg yolks sliced and submerged in cinnamon syrup).

If you want to burn off calories and get a bird's-eye view of the city, climb the steps of the 14th-century **Torre de Menagem** (keep), on largo de São Francisco. This imposing crenellated structure is the last of six towers that once guarded the city. Nearby, the Moorish-style filigreed wooden screens of the 16th-century **Casa dos Crivos**, at rua de São Marcos, are the last of their kind in Braga.

Between the Casa dos Crivos and the keep, the coffeehouse tradition is alive and well at the 19th-century **Café A Brasileira**, a favorite among the city's artists and intellectuals. Marble, copper, and glass fittings and ancient waiters in white livery provide a refined, Old World elegance. The trendier crowd frequents the smartly refurbished **Vianna** café and snack bar in the arcades in front of the tourism office at the northern end of avenida da Liberdade. Outdoor tables provide an ideal setting for people-watching during the day. At night the glass-and-iron sliding doors are closed, and live jazz and folk music provide ambience.

Another sign of the times is a new, multipurpose social venue at avenida da Liberdade, 747–767, housed in a converted theater, where people come to be part of the scene. The Art Deco–styled center, the brainchild of one of Regine's former lieutenants, has the sophisticated trappings of one of her Euro-chic clubs. Guests can dine and play billiards or a game of chess at the center's **T Club**, sip coffee or tropical cocktails at the spacious **O Nosso Café**, and dance the night away at **Trigonometria**.

The handsome iron- and stonework of the **Capela de Nossa Senhora de Conceição** (Our Lady of Conception Chapel) and the lacy Manueline work of the windows of the adjoining **Casa dos Coimbras**, in São João de Souto square, one block south of the rua do Souto by way of rua Francisco Sanches, were built in the 17th century. The two are privately owned but can be admired from the street. The exterior of the **Hospital São Marcos**, in the square to the south, has an amusing façade designed by the 18th-century architect Carlos Amarante, who lined the ledge of the roof with granite statues of the Apostles gesticulating madly.

The front of the 18th-century **Casa do Raio**, one block to the south in the street sporting its name, is considered one of the most beautiful and original examples of civil Baroque architecture in the country. In this palace André Soares, the designer of the town hall, brought together Portugal's tile, wood, and stone crafts in a voluptuous yet elegant composition.

Most of ancient Braga lies under the modern city, waiting to be unearthed. A few archaeological treasures have been discovered quite by accident. One of these, the **Fonte do Idolo** (Fountain of the Idol), at rua do Raio, 309, was uncovered by workers installing a sewage pipe. Behind an inconspicuous green gate and at the foot of some steps lies part of a collapsed altar believed to have been used in immersion rituals in a temple to the Lusitanian idol Tongenabiago. Latin inscriptions indicate that the Romans later adapted it for their own purposes.

Braga's religious passion reaches its height during Semana Santa (Holy Week), when the city is transformed into one huge temple of worship, as church icons and other treasures are paraded in streets lined with banners of ancient families whose ancestors fought to liberate Portugal from the Moors. The nights are spectacularly lit by thousands of the penitent carrying candles and by churches festooned with lights.

The Festas de São João in late June date back to pre-Christian times and the observance of the summer solstice. All-night parties are held in streets illuminated by raging bonfires, *vinho verde* flows freely, and the odors of roast pork and grilled sardines compete with the fragrance of burning wax and incense.

The third big event of the year here is the *vinho verde* fair, a week-long event held in the Palácio Municipal de Exposiçãos (Industrial Fairground). The region's main wine producers and smaller estate bottlers exhibit their wares and provide tastings. In 1993 the fair will be held from April 28 through May 1.

Staying in Braga

For a city with a constant flow of pilgrims, Braga's accommodations leave much to be desired, and finding a room in the city is *never* easy.

Some of the best hotels in the region and by far the best in the Braga area are in the cool and luxurious surroundings of the Bom Jesus sanctuary in the hills above Braga (see the Braga Area section, below, for details). The **Casa da Pedra Cavalgada**, a 19th-century villa at Palmeira on the northeastern outskirts of Braga, via N 101, offers traditional Victorian Portuguese ambience and decor. Two large double bedrooms and a large living room are available to guests, as are its small, well-kept grounds. No credit cards.

Dining in Braga

There are relatively few restaurants in the city. **Inácio**, across from the Arco da Porta Nova, is Braga's most popular and endearing restaurant. The family-run establishment is strictly a regional affair, with wooden beams and whitewashed walls covered with regional artifacts providing a rustic backdrop to such Minho delectables as wood-fired *cabrito no forno* (baked kid), *rojões à Minhota,* and the house specialty, *lampreia com arroz.* (Call ahead of time if you want to order this last, mouth-watering dish.) Owner Claudionor Sobral, an attentive host, keeps a well-stocked cellar with the best Alvarinho green wines. He also carries Solar das Bouças, a semisweet green wine bottled in neighboring Amares. Closed Tuesdays; campo das Hortas, 4; Tel: (053) 61-32-35.

The **Cantinho do Campo das Hortas**, down the street on the southwestern corner of the square, has made a reputation for its excellent food, attracting a large and loyal following of city officials, businesspeople, and clergy at lunchtime. Two tiny, cozy, and busy dining rooms have been fashioned out of a quaint working-class town house. The menu includes recommended daily specials, as well as several regional dishes such as a tender, mint-herbed *cabrito assado* (roast kid) that virtually melts in your mouth. Because there are no reservations, try to arrive before the 1:00 P.M. lunch rush.

For an elegant dinner, head for the neighboring hills of Bom Jesus (5 km/3 miles away) to the restaurant of the **Hotel do Elevador** (see below, in the Braga Area section). Its Old World decor, deferential service, and setting attract the elite of Portuguese society. Both the fixed-price and à la carte menus include regional and Continental dishes that are good value for the money. In Braga tradition, sweets are a heavy favorite here, particularly the chef's *bolo de amêndoa* (almond cake). Tiny eateries along the rua do Souto offer snacks throughout the day, as do more than 20 pastry shops. The city is known for its rich desserts. The *pudim à abade de Priscos* (abbot of Priscos pudding), named after a plump priest with an insatiable appetite, requires 15 egg yolks and a generous topping of caramel.

Shopping in Braga

Lace and embroidery, damask bedspreads, earthenware goods such as chestnut roasters, wicker and straw baskets, and religious art make up much of the cottage-industry output of Braga and its environs. Bargains can be obtained at the weekly Tuesday fair (ask for directions at the Turismo, on the southeast corner of the praça da República). The Turismo also carries many of these same goods at only slightly higher prices. The rua do Souto west of the square is Braga's fashionable shopping street, with boutiques and antiques shops and coffee and pastry shops. The religious artifacts industry is alive and thriving here. The **Casa Fânzeres**, at number 132–134, the oldest and most pictur-esque, specializes in the sale and repair of religious an-tiques.

Braga is also one of the country's main centers of leather goods. The **Sapatária Teresinha** and **Amorim**, at numbers 84 and 148, respectively, specialize in handmade shoes; **Herdeiros de Francisco José Ferreira**, at number 124, sells handbags, briefcases, and suitcases. The *viola Braguesa* or the *cavaquinho* guitar, which served as models for the ukulele, can be bought or admired at the top of rua do Souto at **Vadeca** (largo Barão São Martinho, 14). **Casa Eden**, across from the Santa Bárbara garden, at rua do Souto, 140, sells damask bedspreads and hand-embroidered linens.

THE BRAGA AREA

The hills to the east and south of Braga are covered with religious sanctuaries. The most spectacular is **Bom Jesus do Monte**, perched high in a wooded area amid grottoes and streams 5 km (3 miles) east of the city via the avenidas João XXI and João Paulo II. The 19th-century travel writer William Kingston called the site "a lovely prospect to excite the poet's muse, or the warmest adoration of the true worshipper of nature and of nature's God." The sanctuary's most striking feature is a monumental Baroque staircase, sculpted in stone and adorned with fountains and other waterworks.

You can drive up to the shrine, then walk down the stairs and return to your car at the top via a water-powered funicular that runs every 15 minutes; or you can leave your car at the bottom, climb the stairs, and take the funicular down. Either way, gaze up from the bottom to see how the granite sculptures form a giant chalice.

Most visitors prefer to stay up here while visiting Braga because the location offers a cool sanctuary from the heat and pollution that often engulf the plain of Braga below. The most exclusive and genteel accommodations are in the **Hotel do Elevador**, on the northwestern side of the square facing the sanctuary. Plush furnishings, attentive staff, an elegant restaurant, and large rooms with sweeping views of its gardens and the Braga valley make it a memorable place to stay. The recently refurbished **Hotel do Parque**, on a slope above the church, has been tastefully renovated without losing its turn-of-the-century flavor. The hotel has a paneled bar, a breakfast room, and club-styled salon, but no restaurant. (Lunch and dinner can be had a few steps away at the Elevador.)

The turn-of-the-century **Santuário de Monte Sameiro**, 4 km (2½ miles) south of Bom Jesus on the N 103-3, is known more for its breathtaking views of the Minho and its huge dimensions than for its architecture. Masses are held in a football-field-size courtyard below the church.

The shrine also attracts another breed of pilgrim, seeking a more earthly delight: the **Sameiro** restaurant, beside the church. The cook and owner of the restaurant, Maria da Conceição, has won several awards at regional and national competitions. House specialties, all cooked on wood-fired stoves, include baked lamprey and codfish in cream sauce. During the summer, river trout and kid from the surrounding area go well with the house's tart *vinho verde*. Maria will not divulge the secret behind her famous *tarta de chila* (spaghetti-squash tart), but Port and honey seem to be among its ingredients; the squash is candied to give it texture. Closed Mondays.

Four kilometers (2½ miles) southwest of Sameiro, on the thickly wooded slopes of Mount Falperra, is the **Igreja de Santa Maria Madalena**, one of the finest examples of stonework architecture in Portugal, designed by André Soares. You can also reach Falperra from Braga via the N 309 (5½ km/3½ miles). The tiny seventh-century **Capela da São Frutuoso**, 3½ km (2 miles) north of Braga off the N 201 on the way to Ponte de Lima, at Real, is one of the few remaining examples of Suevic Neo-Byzantine architecture left in Portugal. The ancient chapel, abandoned at the time of the Moorish invasion, was rebuilt in the 11th century. The simple beauty of its design clashes with the ornateness of the Igreja de São Francisco next door. To enter São Frutuoso, apply for the key from the chaplain at São Francisco.

PENEDA-GERES PARK

The spectacular alpine **Parque Nacional de Peneda-Gerês**, northeast of Braga, which stretches between Spain to the north and the river Cávado to the south, is a balm to nature enthusiasts, who are drawn to its 175,000 acres of forests, man-made lakes, rivers, waterfalls, and rocky ridges rising up to 5,075 feet. It is divided into several valleys by the serras of Soajo, Peneda, Amarela, and Gerês and by the Lima, Homen, and Cávado rivers. Annual precipitation in the region is considerable, and the bare granite summits of the horseshoe-shaped park are covered in snow during the winter. Slopes cascade down to the lush, deep-cut valleys abloom with Gerês iris and other colorful indigenous plants. The more remote areas house a varied wildlife, including roe deer, wolves, and wild Luso-Galician horses. Fishermen are attracted to the park's trout-brimming rivers; boat enthusiasts and windsurfers have several artificial lakes to pick from; hikers and mountaineers can spend days on man-made trails.

Vestiges of human habitation have been found in the area dating back 5,000 years, and the ancient artifacts can be reviewed in the ethnography museum outside the tiny village of São João do Campo (also called Campo de Gerês) on the western border of the park below the Vilarinho das Furnas dam. The southern side of this reservoir is lined with Latin-inscribed milestones belonging to the **Roman road** built by Emperor Vespasian.

The park is a one-hour drive northeast of Braga. Take the N 103 east to just past Cerdeirinhas, then turn left onto the N 304. After crossing the Cávado river past Caniçada, follow the N 308-1 off to the right and drive north 6½ km (4 miles) to Gerês. Organized tours of the park by bus, on horseback, or on foot can be booked through travel agencies or through Trote Gerês, Cabril, 5495 Borralha; Tel: (053) 65-92-92. Maps and itineraries are available at the rangers' lodge at the main entrance of the park just past Caniçada or at the Turismo in the spa town of Gerês (on avenida Manuel Francisco da Costa).

The most scenic and luxurious accommodations in the area are near the junction of the N 103 and N 304 on the hills directly south of the entrance to the park. The newly elegant **Pousada de São Bento**, on the N 304, 1½ km (about a mile) north of the junction, was named after a sixth-century saint who is reputed to have lived in a cave near the entrance to the park. It has the look and the modern comforts of a Swiss chalet and the relaxed atmosphere of a Portuguese home. Its glass-enclosed restaurant and outdoor verandah afford sweeping views of the magnificent Cávado river. The 30-room inn also has a small pool. Reservations should be made well in advance in summer.

An open-air market is held nearby at **Vieira do Minho** on alternate Mondays. To get to the market take the N 304 south for 1½ km (about a mile), turn right, and follow the N 304 east for another 5 km (3 miles). The market, where merchants share the field with farmers selling the region's beautiful, long-horned *barroso* oxen, is a good place to buy shag and wool rugs, linen, country bread and cheese, and beautifully carved *cangas* (ox yokes) with Celtic inscriptions (they make handsome headboards).

Gerês, located on the eastern edge of a gorge at the base of the Gerês mountain range, has been a spa since Roman times. This one-street town became a fashionable watering hole in the 18th century and now serves as the excursion and provision center for the park.

You can begin a popular one-day drive in the Peneda-Gerês park by climbing the wooded slopes directly north of Gerês along the left bank of the Gerês river gorge for about 10 km (6 miles) on N 308, past waterfalls and picnic areas. Turn left at the *albergaria* (hostelry) onto a dirt road and drive for 5 km (3 miles) through woods lined with Roman milestones (Emperor Vespasian's road) and moss-covered rocks. The Vilarinho das Furnas reservoir suddenly appears to your right. Underneath the waters of the placid man-made lake lies the town of the same name, which was sacrificed to make way for the dam (barragem). The reservoir is flanked on the north by the jagged, bald peaks of the Serra Amarela. If you are lucky you might catch a glimpse of the park's wild horses drinking in the lake at dawn or sunset.

Turn left at the first T-junction and drive 2 km (1¼ miles) on a paved road past the tiny village of **São João do Campo** (also known as Campo de Gerês) to the ethnography museum, with its traditional iron kitchen utensils, looms, spinning wheels, Celtic yokes, and farm implements, and a regional crafts store. Turn left onto another dirt road and drive several kilometers to the **Junceda Belvedere**, a rocky lookout point with a prehistoric feel and a spectacular view of the Gerês valley. To complete the semicircular tour, backtrack several kilometers and take another signposted dirt road southeast toward the Casa Abrigo da Bela Vista. The road meets the N 308 just above Gerês.

ALTO MINHO

The heart of the Minho, called the Alto Minho (Upper Minho), begins north of Braga in the hills enfolding the river Lima and stretches north to the Minho river. The Atlantic Ocean forms its western boundary and is the backdrop for Viana do Castelo, its administrative capital; the wild Soajo mountains, sandwiched between the Peneda mountains to the north and the Amarela mountains to the south, form the eastern border with Spain. The interior is dotted with elegant manor houses and granite *cruzetas* (crosses) threaded with grapevines and with tiny farms and wood and granite *espigueiros* (corn cribs) that resemble miniature Greek temples on stilts.

There is an idyllic look to this lush and soothing landscape that belies its turbulent past. The area surrounding the Lima river produced many of the knights who fought under Afonso Henriques to liberate the region from Spanish rule. Their descendants still live in their ancestral homes beside the Lima, and some rent out rooms to visitors. There are nearly 30 manor houses in the Alto Minho that take paying guests.

Ponte de Lima

This small town straddling the Lima, 33 km (20 miles) north of Braga on the N 201, has always beguiled visitors. The invading Roman legions were so enchanted by the river's beauty that they believed it to be the Lethe, the legendary river of forgetfulness, and refused to cross it until their general, Junio Bruto, swam across. In time they built a bridge, of which the last four arches on the right bank still stand.

During the early Middle Ages Ponte de Lima played a pivotal role in the border defenses of the Minho against the Moors. Today only vestiges remain of the defensive walls that once encircled the town. The 15th-century **fortress-palace** of the marquês de Ponte de Lima has been converted into the town hall, and the medieval **prison tower** has been turned into the town archives, with a tiny workshop to restore the city manuscripts, which date back to the 12th century.

The café-lined main square, cooled by a large Baroque fountain, is an ideal spot from which to admire the multi-arched bridge marching across the mirroring river, and, on the opposite bank, the white onion-domed bell tower of the **Igreja de Santo António da Torre Velha**.

The best times to visit Ponte de Lima are during the feast of São João in June; on Corpus Christi (late May or June), when the streets of the town are paved with colorful flower tapestries laid down by competing neighborhoods; and during the Feiras Novas (New Fairs) in mid-September. The latter presents the region's traditions in a colorful parade filled with historical pageantry and dress. The monuments are festooned with lights, and huge fireworks light up the night. All-night *desfolhadas* (corn-husking parties) are held at manor houses and farms, where singing, dancing, and drinking alternate with the husking. Ponte de Lima is also known for its colorful open-air market. Every other Monday since the Middle Ages the wide, sandy left bank of the river by the bridge has been transformed into a huge tent bazaar for all kinds of farm products, horses and oxen included, plus locally produced crafts such as hand-carved wooden furniture, tin lamps, linen, woollen blankets, glazed pottery, and wicker. Sardines are grilled on charcoal braziers and eaten with rich, moist *pão de milho,* accompanied by the fine local *vinho verde.* The Alvarinho grape, the most coveted of the green-wine stocks for its low acid content and high alcohol level, is said to have been grafted from several stocks in the nearby tiny town of Sá.

Dining in Ponte de Lima used to be limited to fairly simple meals at a few establishments on the riverfront. Now the **Churrasqueiria Tulha**, in rua Formosa east of the main square, has helped fill the gap. Pine and oak furniture and an indoor grill provide a warm and welcoming atmosphere in this restaurant, which is lodged in a converted grain-storage barn. The family-run establishment specializes in charcoal-grilled meat and fish and carries Paço de Cardido, a white estate-bottled *vinho verde,* as well as fine Ponte de Lima cooperative *verdes.* Closed Tuesdays.

For more ambitious fare, drive up the hill on N 307 (6 km/ 3½ miles) directly south of Ponte de Lima to the secluded **Monte Madalena** restaurant. You will be rewarded not only with glorious views of the town and the Lima valley but also with gracious service and creative, well-cooked regional dishes. The classically decorated establishment, with formally attired waiters, is a favorite of the local aristocracy and officialdom. House specialties include small game and river trout. Closed Mondays.

Manor Houses

Ponte de Lima and its environs, Minho's manor row, make the ideal base from which to explore the region. A group of manor-house owners have formed an association, TURIHAB, to handle reservations for most of the properties in the Minho; other similar organizations—ANTER, P.I.T., and PRIVETUR—handle the rest. TURIHAB shares its offices with the national Turismo on the praça da República (see the Useful Facts section for addresses and contact numbers for all four associations). The English-speaking TURIHAB personnel will help steer you to the manor houses, some of which are off the beaten track. If you write to the national Turismo at the same address, they will mail brochures and maps with walking tours of the region.

There are more than 20 manor houses in the borough of Ponte de Lima that offer rooms to guests. The newly restored **Casa de Crasto** is a mere half kilometer from the center of the town on the left side of the road to Ponte de Barca (N 203). This 17th-century manor house and its five large guest rooms are filled with heirlooms and 19th-century antiques. Guests have access to the grounds, which include a rose garden and vineyard. A long verandah runs along the front of the house, offering views of the estate and neighboring mountains. Most of the other manor houses are on the right (north) bank of the river opposite Ponte de Lima.

The secluded baronial **Casa do Outeiro** is about 2 km (1¼ miles) northwest of Ponte de Lima on the right bank. A tiny road (consult your Turihab brochure) leads to the crenellated entrance and chestnut-lined courtyard. The house, owned by the friendly, English-speaking Gomes d'Abreu e Lima family, has a warm, lived-in feeling, with three bedrooms to let, as well as a cozy Victorian parlor and a large, stately dining room where candlelight dinners are served. Guests can enjoy breakfast in a 16th-century kitchen equipped with a huge granite fireplace and wood stove, or on an adjoining terrace overlooking a dreamy garden and orchard.

The view of the Lima valley from the terraced gardens of the **Paço de Calheiros** (6 km/3½ miles northeast of Ponte de Lima) is one of the enticing features of this 18th-century manor. The home has been restored by the young, dynamic count of Calheiros. Available for rent are four double bedrooms with private baths in the main house, all facing the garden, plus six modern apartments with kitchenettes in the magnolia-lined courtyard. Guests have access to two large salons decorated with Portuguese antiques. The hospitable count, who traces his ancestry back to before the birth of the nation, may invite you to dinner or to visit his textile factory at Barcelos. Or you can play a round of tennis or simply lounge in the designer pool.

If you tire of the patrician ambience, a secluded and romantic experience can be had at the **Moinho de Estorãos**, a converted watermill on the banks of the tiny Estorãos river. The mill, beside an old Roman bridge 6 km (3½ miles) west of Ponte de Lima off the N 202, is equipped with all the amenities, including a large fireplace for intimate evenings. While you are out in this neck of the woods, take a peek at the magnificent **Solar dos Condes de Bertiandos** on the N 202 south of Estorãos, composed of two adjoining 18th-century buildings and an older crenellated tower from the 16th century. The large baronial home (which does not take in guests) is one of the most impressive of Portugal's manor houses.

East Along the Lima

The drive from Ponte de Lima east on the N 203 along the left bank of the river Lima is dotted with Minho estates, ancient watermills, granite homes with wooden balconies streaked with the colors of farm goods drying, and monasteries. The most striking structure is the early Romanesque **Igreja de São Salvador** at Bravães, 14½ km (9 miles) east of Ponte de Lima; its arresting doorways are carved with animal and geometric designs, vestiges of the magical and astral side of Christianity in the early Middle Ages. The interior contains the remains of Renaissance frescoes discovered during restoration work in the 1940s. The view of the town of **Ponte da Barca** and its solid 16th-century bridge, as seen from across the river on the right bank of the Lima 18 km (11 miles) east of Ponte de Lima, is one of the most pleasant in the Minho.

The baronial splendor and lineage of the **Paço Vedro de Magalhães**, 3 km (2 miles) southeast of Ponte da Barca, off the N 101 toward Braga, is equally impressive. The magnificent 18th-century estate belongs to the Corte Real e Lima family, which is blessed with a long line of explorers and statesmen; two Corte Real brothers explored part of the North American coast during the 16th century under a British flag. The property nestles in secluded woods surrounded by mountains. Its imposing portico is itself dwarfed by the family's baronial hall, its walls covered with paintings of the family's famous ancestors and sporting a standard of the lieutenant-general of the Order of Malta. The main hall is so large that at one time equestrian events were staged there. Three double bedrooms have been set aside for guests and are decorated with genteel elegance. The 18th-century **Casa da Agrela**, at São Pedro do Vade (on N 101 6 km/3½ miles from Ponte da Barca), is a smaller but equally pleasant alternative in the foothills of the Amarela mountains. Three rooms with garden views are available. Meals can be taken in patrician splendor; after dinner, Port is served in a cozy alcove lit by a log fire.

There are unfortunately no restaurants in the area to match the beauty and comfort of its manor houses. The **Adega Regional** restaurant in a converted farmhouse on the banks of the Vez river in **Arcos de Valdevez**, 5 km (3 miles) north of Ponte da Barca on the N 101, takes special pride in its trout and steaks. Guests have a choice of dining alfresco in a vine-covered courtyard or indoors surrounded by antique farm implements. The alternative is to drive to neighboring Ponte de Lima.

Ponte da Barca and Arcos de Valdevez both provide an entrance to the Peneda section of the Peneda-Gerês park, which is cut off from the Gerês area by the Serra da Amarela. The tourist information booth at the Ponte da Barca provides hiking maps of the park and information on where to rent rowboats to explore the river.

An enjoyable one-day drive (80 km/50 miles) through this part of the park includes both banks of the Lima river. The N 203 follows the left bank of the river all the way east to the 13th-century **fortress of Lindoso**, which was built by King Dinis to guard the pass where the Lima enters from Spain. Before Lindoso, about 10 km (6 miles) east of Ponte da

Barca, the road passes a turnoff to the right to **Ermida**, the site of several prehistoric dolmens.

Backtrack 11 km (7 miles) from Lindoso to the Ponte de Parada do Monte, cross the river, and head for the mountain village of **Soajo** on the N 304 (3 km/2 miles). Here, the *monteiros* (mountain people), known for their independence, have made a living for centuries by hunting. Under an arrangement with King Dinis in the 13th century they were allowed autonomy so long as they kept his court stocked with game and came to his aid during invasions. To cement the partnership, the king prohibited the nobility from taking residence in Soajo. They could spend no more time in the village, he ruled, than it took a piece of bread toasted at the end of a spear to cool down. This edict is said to be the origin of the unusual pillory in the main square: a triangular shape with a mischievous face carved in it held up by a long granite pole. (In general, kings bestowed pillories on towns as symbols of their right to dispense justice.) The cluster of *espigueiros* (granaries) mounted on a huge boulder here overlooking the barren peaks of Peneda are a symbol of the community, which owns them in partnership. Lively corn-husking parties with singing and dancing are held here during the fall harvest.

The **Casa do Adro** is a clean and functional inn in a typical 18th-century town house near the main square. It has singles, doubles, and suites, furnished in ordinary modern taste. The Casa do Adro's main attraction is the kitchen, in which guests are served breakfast facing a large granite chimney where game was once roasted. The two cafés near the square provide simple meals (rabbit and lamb, specialties of the area) and local color. From Soajo you can visit the dolmens at **Mezio**, 7 km (4 miles) west on the N 202 toward Arcos de Valdevez, which have shapes similar to those at Stonehenge.

To return to Ponte da Barca on the south bank of the Lima, follow the signs out of Soajo toward Ermelo, but make a left turn and cross the river before Ermelo. Then proceed west on the N 203 toward Ponte da Barca. Before reaching this charming village you will cross a pass dotted with primitive *brandas,* round rock shelters used by shepherds in the summer. To visit **Ermelo**, with its pretty Romanesque chapel and ornate Manueline pillory, you must leave your car and walk down a stone path worn by hundreds of years of use. Farther down the road you will pass *canastros,* round wicker containers with thatched roofs used to store grain.

The N 101 north of Ponte da Barca climbs to the spectacular

Serra da Bualhosa gorge, where whitewashed villages, onion-domed churches, and terraced farms cling to the steep slopes. On the other side of the pass lies the Minho river valley.

MINHO RIVER VALLEY

The Minho river and its narrow valley run east to west for about 96 km (60 miles) from Melgaço in the northeast to Caminha at the mouth, separating Portugal from Spain. They are flanked south and north by mountains: on the left bank (the southern, Portuguese side) by the high peaks of the Serra da Peneda and several other smaller ranges; and on the right bank by the equally impressive mountains of the Cordillera Cantabrica, in the Spanish province of Galicia. For centuries a series of forts, some still standing, guarded Portugal's northern frontier against invasion. Some of the forts have been converted into pousadas and tourist attractions. The Minho river continues to be a major source of lamprey in the spring and succulent *mexilhões* (mussels). The valley's eastern plateau still yields some of the most precious Minho wines, fermented from the Alvarinho grape.

The area around **Monção**, 39 km (24 miles) north of Ponte da Barca on the N 101, particularly the district around Pinheiros to the south, is considered the Mecca of *vinho verde*. The huge, 19th-century **Palácio de Brejoeira**, 5 km (3 miles) south of Monção on the N 101, produces what are considered to be the most outstanding—and most expensive—of the estate white *vinhos verdes* and *aguardentes,* with vines grafted exclusively from the Alvarinho stock. Part of its success can be attributed to its dowager owner and administrator, Herminia Silva D'Oliveira Pais, who personally oversees her wine production from vine to bottle. The sprawling mansion, modeled after the royal palace of Ajuda outside Lisbon, can be admired from the iron gates (and on the label of its bottles).

The former fortress town of Monção, on the banks of the Minho river midway between Melgaço and Valença do Minho to the west, is known for its courageous women. The first was Deu-la-Deu Martins, who saved the town in the 14th century from Spanish attackers. After months of siege, she flung the last of the town's bread over the wall, defiantly informing the Spanish that there was plenty more where that came from. The Spanish, believing the Portuguese had enough supplies to hold out indefinitely, lifted their siege. Her statue now stands in the main square. Inês Negra, another heroine, fought to retake Monção from the Spanish, also in the 14th century. King João I and his ally John of Gaunt, the duke of Lancaster (John's daughter married João and was the mother of Henry the Navigator), had been laying siege to the town for 50 days. Inês Negra challenged and defeated in combat a woman from the fortress, to settle the siege. The remains of the town's fortifications line the river facing Spain, a stone's throw away.

The **Casa de Rodas**, on the southeastern outskirts of Monção, is a beautiful example of 18th-century manorial Portugal, surrounded by pines and Alvarinho grape vineyards. Four bedrooms (two with private baths) are open to guests, who also have access to most of this elegant house furnished in fin-de-siècle style.

The 19-km (12-mile) ride west to Valença do Minho on the N 101 is very picturesque. The hills above the tiny medieval town of **Lapela** provide a magnificent vista of its crenellated keep, the river, and the majestic mountains of Galicia to the northwest. For an even more impressive view, drive to the summit of **Monte do Faro**, 7 km (4 miles) southeast of Valença do Minho. To get to this lookout point, turn left onto the N 101-1 toward Cerdal just before Valença, then turn left again toward Faro. From the chapel of Santa Ana here you can admire the Soajo and Peneda mountain ranges to the east, Galicia to the north, and the Minho river mouth to the southwest.

Valença do Minho

The double fortress town of Valença do Minho, overlooking Tui in Spain, epitomizes the once-violent nature of Luso-Spanish relations. From a hill above the Minho, Valença guards Portugal's northern border. Its double-walled 17th- and 18th-century defenses divide the old quarter into two crown-shaped precincts. The main entrance to the town is through the Porta da Coroada, a monumental doorway emblazoned with the coats of arms of the kingdom, and then through a covered passage. Despite its seemingly impregnable façade, Napoleonic troops were able to capture Valença in 1807 before being repelled by a combined force of British and Portuguese regulars. During the second Napoleonic invasion in 1809 the French bombed the town from Tui across the river, but that time the defenders held out.

Today the garrison town has been largely transformed into a bazaar and is one of the most welcoming, picture-postcard locales in the Minho. Many of the houses have been turned into shops selling such Portuguese handicrafts as linen, pottery, wicker, leatherware, tin and copper goods, peasant dresses, and colorful Portuguese scarves. The crafts shop connected to the Pousada de São Teotónio also provides a large selection of Minho folk art. Besides its shops, the old quarter is made up of quaintly cobbled streets, fountain-cooled squares, outdoor cafés, tiny whitewashed churches, splendid tile homes, and handsome town houses with ornate Manueline windows and crenellations.

The **Pousada de São Teotónio** is lodged on top of the bastion overlooking the river and the iron bridge that spans it, built by Gustave Eiffel in the late 19th century. The architect of this "California Modern" pousada made good use of the river view, incorporating it into most of the 15 bedrooms as well as the bar, terrace, garden, and restaurant. The restaurant serves quality regional food such as spicy lamprey, kid, and Valença's very own *enguias com toucinho* (eels with bacon). Try its hearty country vegetable soup, which carries the full variety of the Minho's produce, cooked a day in advance to allow the ingredients to blend.

Other dining spots in Valença include the **Parque**, a typical Portuguese bistro with colorful regional decorations, a warm and friendly staff, and a reputable grill. It is tucked away in the rua da Oliveira facing the western battlements of the southern polygon. **Monumental**, a lively bistro specializing in fish, is lodged literally inside the walls of the fortress at the main entrance of the town. **Fortaleza**, a new, whitewashed establishment at rua Apolinário Fonseca, facing the bridge and moat of the second fortress, is becoming a popular watering hole, drawing a mixed crowd attracted by its view of the battlements from a covered terrace, and its sweets and ice cream. Meals here are uninspired, however.

If you like vintage trains, head east for the railway station, outside the fortress perimeter, to visit the train museum, housed across the tracks from the stationmaster's office, east of the N 13 as you enter town. It contains a steam engine built in Manchester in 1875 by Beyer Peacock and an elegant salon car constructed in France for the Portuguese royal family.

Southwest to Viana do Castelo

The 27-km (17-mile) ride from Valença on the N 13/IC 1 southwest to Caminha is one of the most enchanting in the Minho. The rocky terrain, patched by pine forests and vineyards, gives way to a more mellow landscape tempered by the pastels of orchards and grain fields and riverside villages lined with Minho mansions. The river widens and the tiny islands of Boega and Amores appear.

The elegant **Pousada de Dom Dinis** in Vila Nova de Cerveira was built inside the ruins of a 14th-century walled town overlooking the Minho. Segments of the old castle and some outbuildings inside the ramparts have been converted into 26 rooms and three apartments with terraces, furnished with replicas of old Minho wooden furniture; two bars with views of the river; and a glass-enclosed restaurant where you can sample the area's tender *arroz de sável* (stewed rice and shad), curried or baked lamprey (in spring), *arroz de frango de cabidela* (chicken risotto), and *biscoitos de milho doce* (sweet corn wafers). The compound is peaceful: all stone, stucco, and oleander, surrounded by crenellated ramparts that are penetrated by a massive arched gate. The square glass box of a building that houses the restaurant detracts somewhat from this otherwise charming pousada.

The beauty and comforts of the region can be savored to their fullest at the **Estalagem da Boega**, a stellar inn perched on the terraced slopes above Vila Nova de Cerveira, on the road to Gondarem. The former estate offers a choice of accommodations, from motel-style apartments to five refurbished and coveted rooms in the mansion. The pièce de résistance is the tiled, coffered dining room, where traditional Minho meals are served with pomp and circumstance. Other attractions are a tiny cellar bar and a terraced pool surrounded by lawns and fed by a natural spring.

The **Kalunga**, one of the region's most panoramic terraced restaurants, clings to the mountain above the inn. The menu is pure Minho (grills are the house specialty), the wine is homemade, and the service is friendly and attentive.

At the mouth of the Minho and Coura rivers, **Caminha** faces the Portuguese fortress island of Insua in the estuary and the Spanish town of Santa Tecla on the right bank. It is said that the town was named Caminha because a sandbar often forms at the river's mouth, allowing people to walk (*caminhar*) from the town to the island. Over the centuries Caminha has undergone many vicissitudes on account of its strategic position, guarding the mainland from invaders, including the Vikings. Today it is largely a fishing and coppersmithing center. Its spotless main square is a mosaic of architectural periods, from the medieval crenellated **Torre do Relógio** (Clock Tower) to the elegant **Palácio dos Pitas**, with its ornate Manueline windows, to the 17th-century

Paços do Conselho (Town Hall). Nearby, the lovely panels of the wood-carved ceiling of the 15th-century **Igreja Matriz** (Parish Church) were apparently the work of a Mudejar (Moorish-style) artist. Outside on the northern wall there is a comical gargoyle of a man relieving himself, his derrière pointing at Spain.

Docelândia (sweetland), the area's foremost confectionary and deli, lies a few steps south at rua de São João, 32. Patrons can enjoy its delicacies in the petite interior salon or order to go. The sweets are made on the premises. South of the Caminha main square is the **Adega Machado**, a small, intimate bistro tucked away on the quiet rua Visconde Sousa Rego, tastefully decorated with tile, wood, and regional furniture. Its proximity to the sea and two rivers is evident in its menu, which includes shellfish, pickled shad, fleshy trout from the Coura river accompanied by a green parsley sauce and cured ham, and the house special, *tainha assada no forno* (baked mullet). Meat lovers can select the tender *cabrito assado* from the neighboring Serra de Arga.

From high ground at the southeastern end of Caminha, the **Quinta da Graça** overlooks the ocean to the west and the Coura and Minho rivers. The 17th-century manor accepts guests year-round, accommodating them in an ambience of Minho squiredom. There are three double rooms with private baths in the main house, and three apartments with terraces. There's also a pool and easy access to the river Coura for fishing, and it's a short distance (2 km/1¼ miles) to the beach.

After Caminha the N 13/IC 1 turns south and travels along the Atlantic **Costa Verde**, with its wide, sandy beaches (some ruined by tacky resorts) and fishing villages. The Praia de Moledo, 2 km (1¼ miles) south of Caminha, is the foremost beach of the Alto Minho, where the elite of the region hold court in the summer. Their expensive modern homes dot the pine woods fronting the long expanse of sand. Old fortresses and deserted beaches are becoming rare elsewhere in Europe, but you can still find them around these parts by veering off the main road.

VIANA DO CASTELO

This prosperous, busy coastal city is located on a plain on the right bank of the Lima river estuary. A popular tourist center, known for its colorful folk festivals, fireworks, and deep-sea fishing, Viana has a long history. Vestiges of human habitation dating back as far as the Stone Age have been uncovered on both the shore and the mountain. The Greeks and the Phoenicians visited it in the Iron Age, the Romans somewhat later, and all left their mark on the art and adventurous spirit of the people. Viana's name, some say, is actually a bastardization of Diana, the Roman goddess of the hunt.

In the 15th century Viana's sailors put their town on the world map: Gonçalo Velho colonized the Azores; João Velho charted the mouth of the Congo river; and João Alvares Fagundes mapped the banks of Newfoundland for Portuguese cod fishermen. The handsome Renaissance and Manueline buildings that grace the old quarter were constructed during this period. Viana merchants—many of them Jews forced to convert to Christianity who gravitated to Viana because it was more tolerant than other cities—also began to trade with the Hanseatic League and Great Britain, exchanging wine, fruit, cork, honey, and other produce for cloth and other finished goods. It was out of Viana do Castelo that the first Port wine was shipped to England. The wine trade and gold from Brazil helped fuel a Baroque building boom in the 18th century. Today Viana remains an important fishing community as well as a boat-building, pottery, and crafts center.

Boat tours explore the shore and river on Tuesdays and Saturdays; book them at the Avic travel agency, avenida dos Combatentes da Grande Guerra, 206 (Tel: 058-82-97-05). Walking tours depart from the Turismo, housed in a handsome 15th-century palace on the rua do Hospital Velho, near the praça da República. Palace tourist shops sell blue-and-white Viana ceramics, linen, copperware, gold and silver filigree jewelry, colorful regional costumes, now worn mostly on feast days (green or red for feast days, blue for mourning, black for brides to set off their gold filigree), multicolored peasant scarves, *palmitos* (sprays of artificial flowers), and handkerchiefs with hearts sewn on them, traditionally given by young maidens to their beaus.

The area in and around the delightful **praça da República**, north of the Turismo, contains the city's most impressive buildings and its best outdoor cafés, shops, and restaurants. At its center is the ornate 16th-century fountain designed by the master stonemason João Lopes the Elder, who crowned it with an armillary sphere representing the world to remind all proudly that it was a Minhoto, Fernando de Magalhães (Ferdinand Magellan), who proved that the world was round. Facing the fountain are several architectural jewels.

On the east is the 16th-century crenellated and arcaded **Antigo Paços do Conselho** (Old Town Hall), now an exhibition and cultural center. The Renaissance façade of the **Misericórdia Hospice**, designed by João Lopes the Younger, is an ode to Greece, held up by Athenian atlantes and caryatids. (The adjoining church contains important 18th-century *azulejos* by António Oliveira Bernardes and his son, Policarpo.) The Gothic portal of the **Igreja Matriz** (Parish Church), one block south of the square, pays homage to the merchants of Viana, who are shown being carried on the shoulders of the Apostles. Across from the Igreja Matriz, at rua do Poço, 16, is the new **Instituto da Juventude Viana do Castelo**, where young artists from the region show and sell their art. The center's café is also the meeting place for Viana's young artistic community.

West of the town center, toward the mouth of the river, on rua Manuel Espregueira, is the **Museu Municipal**, housed in the 18th-century former Maceias Barbosa family palace. The building has wonderful *azulejos* painted by Policarpo Bernardes, who, together with his father, led the Portuguese tile revolution to combat the Dutch influence in Portugal. The ground floor has coffered ceilings and exquisite Indo-Portuguese furniture. The museum holds a rare collection of 18th-century Coimbra glazed pottery, and many other items.

The castle of **São Tiago da Barra** lies several blocks southwest of the museum near the mouth of the river. The fortress, which can be visited, has undergone several adaptations over the centuries; inside is a quaint little chapel dedicated to Saint James.

Northwest of the castle, off rua de Monserrate, is the tiny Baroque **Capela de Nossa Senhora da Agonia**, which despite its name is the center of one of the most spectacular and lively feasts in Portugal. For three days, at the end of the third week in August, Viana becomes one huge festival, doing justice to its reputation as the country's folk-culture capital. The streets glitter with thousands of colorful lights and are spanned by hundreds of wooden arches decorated with colorful paper and ornamental flowers and ribbons. The squares are filled with choral folk groups, who perform the fast-paced traditional *viras* and *cana verde* dances. Towering *gigantones,* played by young men balancing on stilts and wearing large cardboard heads, enliven the crowds and inspire the awe of children. The city reeks with the tantalizing odors of sausages, pork, and sardines being grilled over coals in outdoor stalls. After the statue of Nossa Senhora da Agonia is paraded through streets paved with flower petals, then floated out to sea to bless the fishing fleet, the festival ends in a blaze of fireworks at the harbor.

The towns around Viana are also known for lavish spring flower pageants, bearing out the Minho's reputation as the garden of Portugal. The Festas da Senhora das Rosas are held in May in the neighboring town of Vila Franca do Lima. The women of the village weave intricate rose tapestries, which they carry on their heads. At the Festas dos Andores Floridos (also in May) in Alvarães, floats covered entirely with roses are drawn through streets carpeted with intricate flower designs.

Staying in Viana do Castelo

Viana has a fairly large and varied selection of accommodations. The most scenic is the **Hotel de Santa Luzia**, at the top of Monte de Santa Luzia, 4 km (2½ miles) north of the city. Its three suites and 52 rooms, refurbished in art deco style, echo a more relaxed and opulent era. Many of them command a grand view of Viana, its river, and the ocean. The food in the glass-lined dining room is mostly Continental. The hotel, owned by the government, provides on-the-job experience for future pousada employees and hoteliers, so the staff is young and eager.

The **Casa Grande da Bandeira**, at largo das Carmelitas, 488, is a 17th-century patrician town house with three spacious rooms in a quiet residential quarter in the eastern end of town. Guests share a large common room furnished with Victoriana and views of the house garden and Lima river. Owner Maria Tereza Majer de Faria is attentive and hospitable, and will provide touring suggestions.

The **Quinta do Paço D'Anha**, across the river, is one of the most luxurious of the area's manor houses. The sprawling property, at Anha, 3 km (2 miles) to the southeast of Viana, produces, bottles, and sells an esteemed white *vinho verde* named after it as well as its own *aguardente bagaceira* spirits. Guests have a choice of three independent houses— a former wine press, the estate's original grain-storage facility, or an ancient tool shed—that have been tastefully converted into spacious apartments, with their own living rooms, baths, wood-fired stoves, lounges, and kitchenettes. Each has access to a grassy courtyard facing the estate's vineyard and olive grove. If you happen to visit at the end of September or in early October, you may be invited to take part in the vine harvest and wine making and bottling at the quinta. A tour of the main house, filled with antiques collected mainly by the grandfather of the present owner, will give you an idea of the splendor and wealth that surrounded the Alpuim family, who owns the estate. Horseback riding is also available.

The **Solar de Cortegaça**, at Subportela on the north bank of the Lima river on the N 202, 9 km (5½ miles) east of Viana do Castelo, is another heraldic manor house, filled with heirlooms of the Abreu family. Of the three double bedrooms with bath, the tower suite is the most coveted, with windows on two sides and an elegant bath brightened by *azulejos*. The family cook will prepare special Minho dishes for guests, who partake under candelight, surrounded by heraldry in the family dining room.

Dining in Viana do Castelo

The **Cozinha das Malheiras**, lodged in the former stables of a Viana palace on rua Gago Coutinho directly south of the Paços do Conselho, is a posh restaurant frequented by city businesspeople. The scheme is pure white, with modern Portuguese art on the walls. The *arroz de marisco* (shellfish/ rice stew) is the highly rated house specialty. The kitchen also offers a variety of international, traditional Minho, and nouvelle Portuguese cuisine. Less sedate and more typical Minho fare, entertainment, and decor are available at **Os Três Potes**, housed inside a former bakery in a cul-de-sac on the beco dos Fornos, a two-minute walk southeast of the main square. Waitresses in Minho dress serve prix-fixe or à la carte meals. The English-owned establishment provides a sampling of Minho classics, including air-cured ham and other meats such as roast kid and *rojões*. Reservations are required in the summer, particularly on the weekends, when Minho folkloric shows are staged; Tel: (058) 82-99-28.

The **Casa D'Armas** is a waterfront restaurant lodged in a former armory, which may have something to do with its stiff medieval decor but does not detract from the fine presentation of tasty meals. Its extensive wine list includes white *vinho verde* from the neighboring Paço D'Anha estate. House delicacies include river salmon, veal with mushrooms in white wine sauce, and *torta de amêndoa* (almond torte).

A vine-clad outdoor dining room and solid reputation for Minho fare make **O Espigueiro**, 5 km (3 miles) south of Viana on the main (N 13/IC 1) road to Porto, popular with families on the weekends. It is about 300 yards off the road to your right and is signposted. The **Quinta do Santoinho** next door is the ultimate dining and party experience in the area, where all-night *arraiais* (parties) are held for tourists. For a fixed price, guests eat, drink, and dance to their hearts' content. There are even fireworks and *gigantones* to animate the party. Those who survive till the end are served a *champorreão,* a powerful punch of Champagne, *vinho verde,* beer, lemon, sugar, and ice. The parties are held Tuesdays, Thursdays, and Saturdays during August; Thursdays and Saturdays during May, June, July, and September; and Saturdays in October. Reservations for the event, which begins at 8:00 P.M., can be made in Viana at avenida dos Combatentes, 206 (Tel: 058-82-97-05) or at the quinta (Tel: 058-32-21-56).

Before leaving Viana, drive 4 km (2½ miles) north or take a seven-minute funicular ride (leaves on the hour in the morning and every half hour after 2:00 P.M.) from rua 25 de Abril to the summit of the wooded Monte de Santa Luzia, which served for centuries as a refuge in times of plague or invasion. From the tower of the Neo-Byzantine basilica known as the Santuário de Santa Luzia, a copy of Sacré-Coeur in Paris, there's a panoramic view of the Lima estuary and the southern Minho. Above the basilica and behind the Hotel Santa Luzia lie the ruins of an Iron Age city, which was later occupied by Romans and Suevi.

BARCELOS

The center of pottery making in the north—and home of the Portuguese good-luck symbol, the rooster—is Barcelos, on the right bank of the Cávado river 30 km (19 miles) southeast of Viana do Castelo via the N 13/IC 1 and the N 103 on the way to Braga. The cock became equated with good luck and justice, according to the legend, when a man on a pilgrimage to Santiago de Compostelo was accused of stealing silver and sentenced to death by hanging. As his last wish he requested an audience with the magistrate who had condemned him and was received as his judge was sitting down to a dinner of roast cockerel. Pointing to the dinner plate, the accused declared that the cockerel would proclaim his innocence. The judge laughed and had him led away but did not eat his meal. Just as the unfortunate man was being hanged, the cock stood up, crowed, and fell dead again. The judge rushed to the gallows and found the prisoner still breathing because the noose had failed to tighten around his neck. The **Cruzeiro do Senhor do Galo,** a 15th-century cross commemorating the event, stands on the esplanade beside the ruins of the palace of the count of Barcelos and first duke of Bragança, the **Palácio Ducal**, now an open-air museum. The esplanade looks down on a Gothic bridge that spans the steep ravine of the Cávado river.

Across from the palace, on the northwestern corner of the square, is the elegant 15th-century **Solar dos Pinheiros**, nicknamed Casa do Barbadão (the Bearded One) after one of its occupants. The southern tower has a relief of this Barbadão, a Jew, pulling at his beard, which he vowed never to cut after his daughter fell in love and bore a son to a Gentile out of wedlock. The Gentile happened to be King João I, who made his bastard son the first duke of Bragança. East of the house, on the largo do Município, stands the 13th-century Romano-Gothic **Igreja Matriz** (Parish Church), rich in gilt and carved capitals. Near the town center, to the northeast, is the octagonal Baroque **Templo de Senhor da Cruz**. The church is decorated with flowers and lights during the feast of the Cross (in 1993, May 1–3). Farther north, on the avenida dos Combatentes da Grande Guerra, is the former church of the Benedictine **monastery of Nossa Senhora de Terço**, filled with 18th-century *azulejos* depicting the life of Saint Benedict.

Barcelos's main attraction, however, is its pottery. A huge country **market** is held every Thursday in the campo da República, a large esplanade in the center of the town. At the fair, one of the most colorful in the country, you can pick up multicolored rag rugs, bags, fruit trays, wine holders and baskets made of rushes, lace, linen, and *cangas* (hand-carved ox yokes), in addition to pottery, at bargain prices. The terra-cotta pottery—figurative, decorative, and kitchen oriented—is produced in the surrounding countryside in small and medium-size workshops. Here, too, you'll find primitive figurines in paintpot colors, echoing the region's pagan past. The foremost proponent of this art was Rosa Ramalho, whose pregnant goats are said to have inspired Picasso. Rosa's granddaughter, Julia, has carried on the family trade. Her work, as well as other goods produced in the region, can be purchased in the medieval crenellated keep on the largo da Porta Nova, which has been converted into the local Turismo and regional crafts center.

Barcelos is also known as an antiques center. The **Casa das Antiguidades** on the pedestrian rua Duques de Bragança, a block west of the largo da Porta Nova, is the most prestigious shop and the place for china, silver, and Indo-Portuguese teak furniture inlaid with ivory.

The best restaurants in Barcelos are near the Turismo. The **Casa dos Arcos** is a tiny, comfortable establishment on the rua Duques de Bragança, with stone walls, thick wooden beams, and dim lighting. The medieval-style restaurant, which is popular with the city's intelligentsia, offers a fine selection of regional dishes such as *rojões* and *cabrito* and Barcelos's estate-bottled white Quinta do Tamariz and the tart Quinta da Portela. A few steps east of the Turismo is the simple and rustic **Muralha**, which serves good, wholesome food. More upscale, the **Bagoeira**, several blocks to the east, caters to the old guard, with traditional dishes and Victorian decor. This restaurant, on avenida Dr. Sidónio Pais, is a good place to try the region's *laranjas doces* (oranges stuffed with sweet pumpkin sauce) or *queijadinhas* (cheese, egg, and almond sweets) shaped like stars. But the more traditional place to taste these and other Barcelos sweets is the **Confeitaria Salvação**. This fifth-generation pastry shop and teahouse beckons from a pedestrian walkway west of the tourism office, at rua Dom António Barroso, 137–143. Dona Alice, the energetic owner, has created several house pastries, including her award-winning *barca cellus,* an almond, egg, and pumpkin sweet served in a miniature earthenware riverboat. (The delicacy and Barcelos itself were named after an early vessel that ferried people across the town's river; Phoenician sailors who visited the site called it *barc-ellus,* meaning "small boat.") Clients have a choice of a busy front parlor or a more intimate back room where Dona Alice exhibits her trophies and antique pastry-shop paraphernalia, and entices customers with the smells emanating from the pastry ovens next door.

The only accommodations of real elegance in the Barcelos area are at the British-owned **Quinta do Convento da Franqueira**, a former Franciscan monastery surrounded by 35 acres of pine woods and vineyards. There are two beautifully furnished rooms in the main house overlooking manicured gardens and a rustic swimming pool. Meals, available upon request, are served with the estate's own *vinho verde.* The property is located 4 km (2½ miles) south of Barcelos off the N 205 toward Póvoa de Varzim.

The **Casa do Monte**, 2½ km (1½ miles) north of Barcelos (signposted) off the N 103, is a two-story farmhouse with ivy-covered walls and neatly trimmed lawns. Its three rooms and two suites, furnished in a refined country style, overlook the gardens and a pine-studded valley. The atmosphere is relaxed and rural, and a tennis court and swimming pool are available on the grounds.

THE ATLANTIC COAST

Some of the most deserted and untamed coastline in the Minho stretches south from Viana do Castelo for some 24 km (15 miles) to Ofir along the N 13/IC 1. The road travels inland, curving gently around the patchwork of farms, pine forests, alluvial flats, and river mouths, providing occasional glimpses to the west of golden beaches and sand dunes dotted with shrubs.

As you drive, you'll come across several access roads to these unspoiled beaches, particularly the coastline between Amorosa and São Bartolomeu do Mar. The turnoffs to the beaches are marked by blue signs showing an umbrella and/or the word *praia* (beach). The wild coastline is interrupted momentarily at Ofir, where several nondescript hotels have been built along a fabulous golden strand that stretches south from the mouth of the Cávado river. After Ofir, known for its hand-knit bedspreads, which are sold along the roadside, the untamed beach landscape resumes. Don't be surprised to see seaweed (used by the local farmers as fertilizer) drying on poles and swaying in the wind alongside the daily laundry. You can see the rustic huts of the seaweed harvesters on the Praia de Santo André just outside Aguçadoura.

The landscape changes dramatically after Aguçadoura. Once-charming fishing and shipbuilding towns have been overtaken by tasteless summer resorts catering mainly to the people of Porto. Remnants of the past, however, continue to charm in defiance of the concrete and plastic onslaught. This is the case in the picturesque fisherman's district of **Póvoa de Varzim**, where women continue to mend the nets by hand and sell fish as they have done for generations, while men tend to the boats and the fishing. For centuries the people here practiced endogamy, permitting marriage only among members of the immediate community. The practice is dying off, but other customs remain alive, such as passing down the inheritance to the youngest son so that he can take care of his aging parents. Families continue to place their individual signs on their equipment and boats, a practice some scholars believe to be inherited from Scandinavian and other northern European fishermen, who populated the flat coast over the centuries, forming close-knit clans to safeguard their traditions and property.

The fishing community comes alive on August 14 and 15 during the feast of Nossa Senhora da Assunção, when the life-size statue of the patron saint is carried down to the beach to bless the fleet. The event is followed by a beachside *arraial* (party) and fireworks.

Of interest to shoppers here are the heavy wool fishermen's sweaters and the silver and gold creations fashioned and sold at the famous **Gomes** shop on rua da Junqueira behind the casino. You can watch the silversmiths working the metal behind a glass partition. There's also a liquor store, outside town on the N 13/IC 1 toward Porto, where Alberto Montenegro has collected more than 150,000 bottles to satisfy all tastes and pocketbooks.

The temple for fish and shellfish in the area, however, is highly regarded **Marinheiro**, at A-Ver-o-Mar, 2½ km (1½ miles) from the center of Póvoa de Varzim on the main road from Viana do Castelo. Large tanks hold a cornucopia of marine life for viewing and tasting. The popular *caldeirada dos poveiros* (rich fish chowder) that varies according to the day's catch was invented by the local fishing community.

The old quarter of **Vila do Conde** has also retained some of its past charm and beauty. The former maritime town occupies the right bank of the Ave river estuary, 3 km (2 miles) south of Póvoa de Varzim. It became an important shipbuilding center during the Age of Discovery, and continues to fashion wooden ships for the Portuguese cod fleet. You can still admire endless rows of cod being dried along the right bank of the river. In 1987 the town's yards completed a replica of the caravel that transported Bartolomeu Dias around the tip of South Africa and opened the way for Vasco da Gama's historic trip to India. The ship is now docked off Cape Town, South Africa, but you can inspect the shipbuilding facilities, where they still use tools from an earlier age, at the riverside Cais das Lavandeiras.

Lace making has also been a business here since the 17th century. This labor-intensive craft is taught at the **Escola de Rendas** (Lace School) at rua Joaquim Maria de Melo, 70, where *rendas de bilros* (bobbin lace) can be purchased. Portugal's largest **crafts fair** is held here during the last week of July and the first week of August, with artisans from every province participating. The feast of São João (June 23 and 24) is also a popular event, during which the town is spectacularly lit with bonfires, lights, and fireworks. The two days of partying end with a candlelit procession to the beach led by lace makers and other town women wearing typical Minho dress.

There are several buildings of note in Vila do Conde. The most impressive monument is the **Convento de Santa Clara** complex above the bridge. The chapel of its handsome 14th-

century Gothic church contains the intricately carved Renaissance tombs of its founders: Don Afonso Sanches, the bastard son of King Dinis, his wife, Dona Teresa Martins, and
their two sons. The 18th-century fountain in the center of the
close was fed by an aqueduct from the same period (parts
are still standing) that ran from Póvoa de Varzim and was
built with 999 arches (because the builders thought that
1,000 would have been too presumptuous and might have
offended God). The convent is now a rehabilitation center,
but there are guided tours of the church. The view of Vila do
Conde, lapped by the Atlantic to the west and the Ave river to
the east, is one of the finest in the area. The ornate
Plateresque doorway of the crenellated **Igreja Matriz** (Parish
Church), northwest of the Turismo (rua 25 de Abril) on rua
da Igreja, was fashioned by Biscayan stonemasons in the
16th century. The rope-shaped Manueline *picota* (pillory) in
front of the church on the praça Vasco da Gama, is a perfect
example of the symbol of justice personified by the pillories:
A hand holding a sword pointed upward at several carved
heads graphically explains the penalty for straying from the
law. The square, which retains some of its Renaissance
flavor, has fine views of the river and the convent of Santa
Clara to the southeast. The neighboring streets are dotted
with chapels and several houses with ornate Manueline
windows and doors.

The **Estalagem do Brasão**, near the Vila do Conde town
center, is a comfortable modern inn with 26 rooms and four
new suites, a bar, and a fairly good restaurant with egg-and-
sugar convent desserts, such as the soft, caramelized *pastéis
de Santa Clara*. The restaurant of the **Motel de Sant'Ana**, on
a small hill at Azurara across the river from Vila do Conde, is
the most popular dining spot in the area. It has all the
requisites: a view of the convent of Santa Clara, the river, and
old Vila do Conde, a fine Portuguese and international
menu, and good service. The rooms, however, are musty
and dreary, and should be avoided. Before leaving Azurara,
pause at its pretty 16th-century Manueline parish church, the
patron saint of which is Santa Maria-a-Nova, who is supposed
to bring happiness to wedded couples.

GETTING AROUND
The Minho is fairly well linked by train from Porto, which
has an international airport. The **Linha do Minho** runs from
Porto's Trindade station, up the coast past Vila do Conde,
Póvoa de Varzim, Barcelos, Viana do Castelo, and Caminha.
Vintage train tours from Viana do Castelo to Valença do

Minho unfortunately were suspended in 1992 but may resume in the summer of 1993. The tours featured 19th-century coaches pulled by steam engines and manned by crews in period costume. To find out whether these train tours will resume, contact the tourism office in Viana do Castelo, rua do Hospital Velho, 4900 Viana do Castelo. Tel: (058) 82-26-20; Fax: (058) 82-97-98. You can also catch commuter trains to Guimarães and Braga from the Trindade station in Porto.

Bus service between the towns is fairly good but, as you might expect, slow. The leading regional bus company, Rodoviária Entre Douro e Minho, and other smaller services operate out of the main bus depot in Braga on travessa da Praça do Comércio (Tel: 053-61-60-80; Fax: 053-61-60-90).

The best way by far to see the Minho is by car. The four-lane IP 1 from Porto to Braga is practically completed and has already helped clear a huge traffic bottleneck. The N 13/IC 1 from Póvoa de Varzim to Porto is now a newly completed four-lane highway that has eliminated another major traffic hurdle. At the height of the summer season, the N 13/IC 1 from the northern border at Valença do Minho to Póvoa de Varzim is busy with tourists and returning Portuguese guest workers from the north of Europe.

ACCOMMODATIONS REFERENCE
Rates given are projected 1993 prices for a double room, double occupancy. Price ranges span the lowest rate in the low season to the highest in the high season. Unless otherwise stated, rates include Continental breakfast. As prices are subject to change, always double-check before booking.

▶ **Casa do Adro. Soajo,** 4970 Arcos de Valdevez. Tel: (058) 673-27. 6,000$00–7,200$00. Closed November through December.

▶ **Casa da Agrela. São Pedro do Vade,** 4980 Ponte da Barca. Tel: (058) 423-13. 10,500$00.

▶ **Casa de Crasto. Ribeira,** 4990 Ponte de Lima. Tel: (058) 94-11-56. 10,300$00.

▶ **Casa Grande da Bandeira.** Largo das Carmelitas, 488, 4900 **Viana do Castelo.** Tel: (058) 82-31-69. 10,000$00–12,000$00.

▶ **Casa do Monte.** Barreiro, Abade de Neiva, 4750 **Barcelos.** Tel: (053) 81-15-19 or (02) 48-14-98. 7,000$00.

▶ **Casa do Outeiro. Arcozelo,** 4990 Ponte de Lima. Tel: (058) 94-12-06. 10,100$00.

► **Casa da Pedra Cavalgada.** Lugar do Assente-Palmeira, 4700 **Braga.** Tel: (053) 62-65-96. 7,500$00.

► **Casa dos Pombais.** Avenida de Londres. 4800 **Guimarães.** Tel: (053) 41-29-17. 11,000$00.

► **Casa do Ribeiro.** São Cristovão de Selho, 4800 **Guimarães.** Tel: (053) 53-28-81. 9,850$00.

► **Casa de Rodas.** Lugar de Rodas, 4950 **Monção.** Tel: (051) 65-21-05. 9,850$00. Open April through September.

► **Estalagem da Boega.** Quinta do Outeiral, **Gondarem,** 4920 Vila Nova de Cerveira. Tel: (051) 79-52-48 or 79-52-31. 9,800$00–10,500$00.

► **Estalagem do Brasão.** Avenida João Canavarro, 4480 **Vila do Conde.** Tel: (052) 64-20-16; Fax: 64-22-18. 7,300$00–10,500$00.

► **Hotel do Elevador.** Bom Jesus do Monte, 4700 Braga. Tel: (053) 67-66-11; Fax: (053) 67-66-79. 10,600$00–12,800$00.

► **Hotel do Parque.** Bom Jesus do Monte, 4700 Braga. Tel: (053) 67-65-48 or 67-66-07; Fax: (053) 67-66-79. 10,600$00–12,600$00.

► **Hotel de Santa Luzia.** Monte de Santa Luzia, 4900 **Viana do Castelo.** Tel: (058) 82-88-89; Fax: (058) 82-88-92. 9,700$00–18,000$00.

► **Moinho de Estorãos.** Estorãos, 4990 Ponte de Lima. Tel: (01) 921-3733 or (058) 94-15-46. 10,300$00.

► **Paço de Calheiros.** Calheiros, 4990 Ponte de Lima. Tel: (058) 94-71-64; Fax: (058) 94-72-94. 13,900$00–14,600$00.

► **Paço de São Cipriano.** Tabuadelo, 4800 Guimarães. Tel: (053) 48-13-37. 14,600$00. Open April through October.

► **Paço Vedro de Magalhães.** 4980 **Ponte da Barca.** Tel: (058) 421-17. 13,900$00. Open May through October.

► **Pousada de Dom Dinis.** 4920 **Vila Nova de Cerveira.** Tel: (051) 79-56-01; Fax: (051) 79-56-04. 15,400$00–25,200$00.

► **Pousada de Nossa Senhora da Oliveira.** Rua de Santa Maria, 4800 **Guimarães.** Tel: (053) 51-41-57; Fax: (053) 51-42-04. 12,800$00–20,000$00.

► **Pousada de Santa Marinha da Costa.** 4800 **Guimarães.** Tel: (053) 51-44-53; Fax: (053) 51-44-59. 15,400$00–25,200$00.

► **Pousada de São Bento.** Caniçada, 4850 Vieira do Minho. Tel: (053) 64-71-91; Fax: (053) 64-78-67. 12,800$00–20,000$00.

► **Pousada de São Teotónio.** 4930 **Valença do Minho.** Tel: (051) 82-42-42; Fax: (051) 82-43-97. 12,800$00–20,000$00.

► **Quinta do Convento da Franqueira.** Lugar de Pedrego, 4750 **Barcelos.** Tel: (053) 81-56-06. 9,850$00. Open April through September.

► **Quinta da Graça.** Vilarinho, 4910 **Caminha.** Tel: (058) 92-11-57. 9,850$00.

▶ **Quinta do Paço D'Anha. Anha,** 4900 Viana do Castelo. Tel: (058) 32-24-59. Apartment: 13,900$00.

▶ **Solar de Cortegaça. Subportela,** 4900 Viana do Castelo. Tel: (058) 97-16-39 or 94-29-39. 10,000$00. Closed November through March.

Pousadas can be booked through ENATUR, Avenida Santa Joana Princesa, 10, 1700 Lisbon, Portugal; Tel: (01) 848-1221 or 848-9078; Fax: (01) 80-58-46. But it is easier to make reservations through a travel agent. In the United States and Canada, pousadas can be booked through Marketing Ahead, 433 Fifth Avenue, New York, NY 10016; Tel: (212) 686-9213; Fax: (212) 686-0271.

Manor houses can be booked directly or through the manor-house associations—ANTER, P.I.T., PRIVETUR, and TURIHAB—listed in Useful Facts. Most of the houses belong to one or more of these associations, but because membership rosters change frequently we haven't attempted to spell out the associations for each house. Readers are advised to contact the manor-house associations for their current listings.

In the United States and Canada, it is possible to reserve rooms in P.I.T manor houses through E & M Associates, 211 East 43rd Street, Suite 1404, New York, NY 10017; Tel: (212) 599-8280; Fax: (212) 599-1755.

TRAS-OS-MONTES
THE NORTHEAST

By Thomas de la Cal

The region of Trás-os-Montes (Behind the Mountains) is as remote as its name implies. Cut off from the rest of Portugal by the Marão, Barroso, and Gerês mountains to the west and the Douro river to the south, and bordered on the north and east by Spain, the province is the country's Outback. Adding to its isolation are four mountain ranges—Alvão, Padrela, Nogueira, and Mogadouro—which run roughly north to south, dividing the province into high plateaus and deep-cut valleys. Trás-os-Montes was considered so remote in the 14th century that King Dinis, who wanted to secure his borders, had to give away land in order to get people to settle there. A string of fortresses was built along the frontier. The region became a hardship post for civil servants and army officers out of Lisbon and Porto and a haven for criminals and for political and religious exiles. Spanish and Portuguese Jews fled here from the Inquisition during the 16th century. Many of them were Marranos, or "New Christians," who ostensibly had converted to Christianity but continued to practice their Jewish faith in secret. Trás-os-Montes has given rise to a strong, self-sufficient population, including some of Portugal's most daring missionaries and explorers, and the long-lived house of Bragança, whose members are the pretenders to the Portuguese throne.

Winters are harsh here and summers blistering hot; the plateaus are covered with stunted vegetation, which supports the region's sheep, and crowned by massive rocky

437

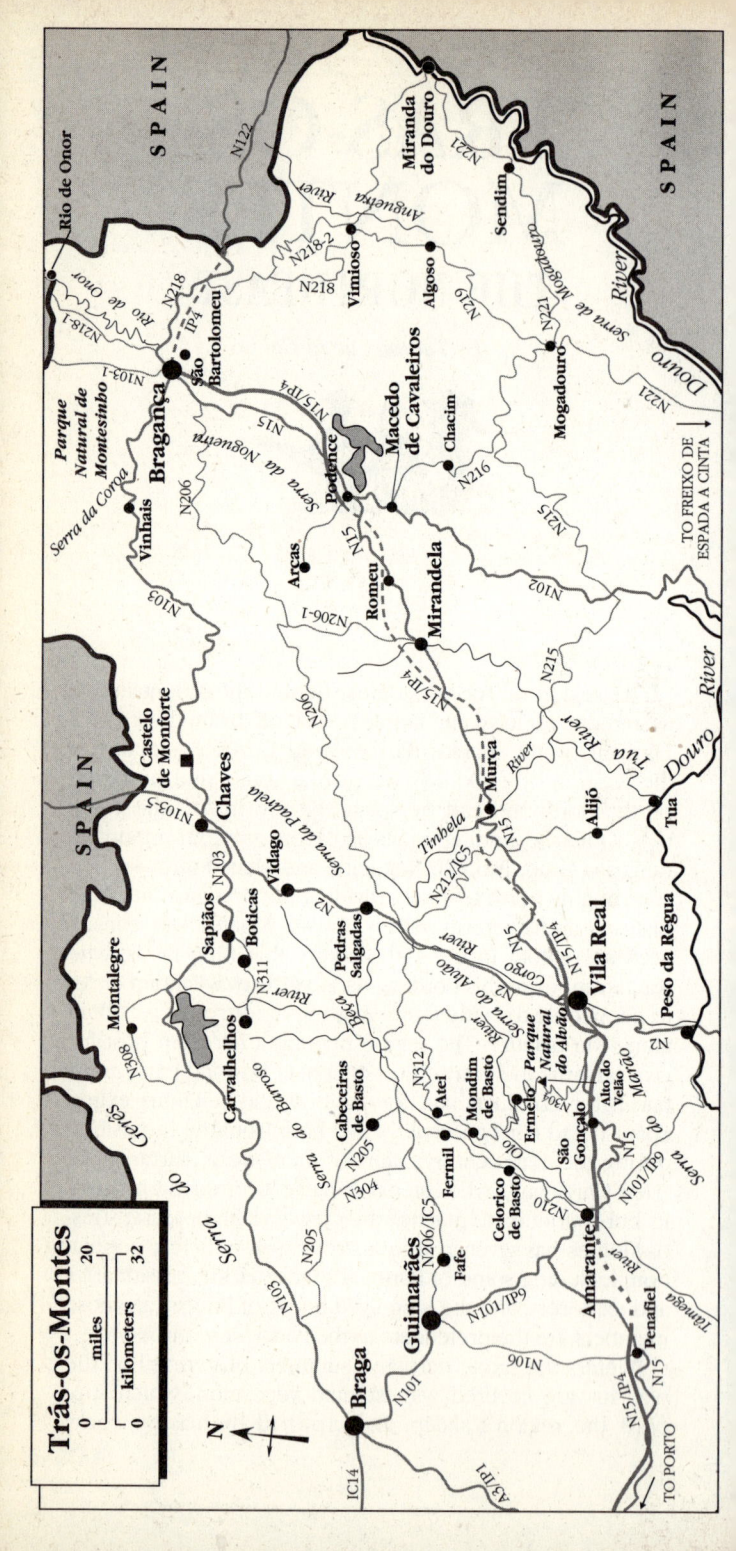

Trás-os-Montes

crests, while the valleys, gentler and more lush, support a mixed agricultural economy of corn, grapes, olives, figs, oranges, apples, and almonds. Commerce and agriculture are the staples of this thinly populated region, and industry is virtually nonexistent. The past is very much alive in unspoiled, self-sufficient communal villages of granite and schist, such as Rio de Onor at the northeastern border, where belief in *bruxas* (witches) and *curandeiros* (healers) is still a way of life. Some of these villages are so ancient that you will feel as though you are entering the Europe of the Middle Ages, possibly earlier. Here you will see women in black carrying large loads on their heads and men-and-ox teams tilling fields as they have done for centuries, and smell the sweet, yeasty aroma of bread baking in communal ovens.

Trás-os-Montes is ideal for those who want to get away from it all and enjoy simple, vanishing pleasures such as fresh, clean air and water, wide-open spaces, and unadulterated food. You can see Paleolithic art engraved on the walls of the Douro canyon, explore Celtic *castros* (fortified villages) more than 2,000 years old, and climb the battlements of the fortress towns lining the Spanish border. You can taste the waters of spas used since Roman times, ride horses, hunt partridge and rabbit on the plateaus and boar in the mountainous areas, watch rare birds on rocky crests, fish in pristine rivers and mountain streams, swim in crystal-clear lakes, hear ancient dialects, watch equally old and rare dances, and shop for handmade copper, tin, leather, linen, and woollen goods. The region also offers a variety of accommodations, from the efficient and comfortable state-run inns to cozy hunting lodges, elegant ancestral homes, and rustic rural houses of granite, schist, and wood. The choice is limited and not five-star, but it's wholesome, homey, and pure country.

The best time to visit Trás-os-Montes is during the mild seasons: spring, when the almond and chestnut trees bloom in the valleys, and early fall, during the grape harvest.

MAJOR INTEREST

Vila Real's Palácio Mateus

Environs of Vila Real (mountain villages of Serra do Alvão and Terra do Basto and manor house accommodations)

Romeu (granite village)

Miranda do Douro (museum, cathedral, and folk dances)

Bragança (museum, citadel, and Romanesque civic
    building)
Parque Natural de Montesinho
Chaves (museum, keep, spa, Vaubanesque fortresses,
    colorful verandahs)

Trás-os-Montes has been inhabited for thousands of years.
Stone Age markings adorn the Douro river canyon at
Mazouco, on its southeastern border with Spain. Celtic vestiges dot the landscape in the ruins of fortified hamlets and
rock carvings that were used by Druids and also live on in
the customs, religion, and folkways of the area, where ancient rites still celebrate birth, puberty, marriage, and death.
In some villages epic stories passed down from generation
to generation provide an oral record of peoples and events.
The Romans mined the region's gold quarries and tapped its
warm-water springs in the northwest near Chaves; the Suevi
from southern Germany settled the Trás-os-Montes valleys;
the Visigoths, another Germanic tribe, from the Baltic area,
gravitated toward its upper plateaus.

    Trás-os-Montes is slowly entering the 20th century. A ma-
jor highway, the N 15/IP 4 will traverse the region by 1997,
passing through Vila Real, Mirandela, and Bragança, to link
Portugal to Zamora in Spain. Stretches of the new highway
are already operating, namely those from Porto to Penafiel,
from Amarante to a few miles east of Vila Real, and from just
north of Macedo de Cavaleiros to Bragança. Plans are afoot
to start mining the large iron and coal deposits along the
Douro river and in the northeastern interior near Bragança.
Signs of modernity are also cropping up in remote villages
as new wings and television antennas burgeon on ancestral
homes.

The Food and Wine of Trás-os-Montes

The food of Trás-os-Montes is as simple, unpretentious, and
hearty as its people. The quality of its produce guarantees its
taste: The region is known for its potatoes and cabbages,
river trout, veal, lamb, kid, ham, and sausages. Garlic, paprika, and mint are the basic herbs and spices. *Sopa seca*
(dry soup) contains most of these ingredients, plus bread.
The various meats and vegetables that go into it are pre-
cooked, then doused with scalding stock, sprinkled with
mint, and baked before serving. Sausages are popular in
stews. *Azedo,* made of beef, pork parts, paprika, and hot
peppers, has been called the "king of sausages." *Alheira*

(spiced sausage) was invented during the Inquisition by Marranos to fool the Catholic population into believing they were eating pork. Instead, this sausage was made with chicken, rabbit, partridge, and bread, cleverly camouflaged by garlic, hot peppers, and paprika. (Pork was eventually added as the sausage made its way into the general population.) Mahogany-colored *presunto* (Portuguese prosciutto) from Chaves and Valpaços, another of the region's delicacies, can be served as an appetizer (with or without melon), stuffed in trout, or wrapped around the latter, then quickly sautéed.

Almonds and eggs are a major ingredient in Trás-os-Montes desserts. Together with pumpkin, they make up Murça's rich flan called *toucinho do céu* (bacon from heaven), said to have been invented by nuns, who named it after its heavenly flavor. (Lard or bacon fat may have been used in the original recipe.) A more common and traditional dessert is *tigela de marmelada,* a thick marmalade made from the region's sweet oranges, served in an earthenware bowl (*tigela*).

Pão (bread) is the staple of Trás-os-Montes, and one of its finest treats. It is normally baked at high temperatures in brick or stone ovens, which accounts for its thick crust and moist, chewy interior. The best-flavored breads are baked in wood-burning ovens, together with aromatic wildflowers that add to the aroma and taste. In some remote areas the bread is formed into symbolic shapes: Stars represent the sun, which provides light and warmth, and human figures work the soil with their hands. During winter feast days bread pyramids, or *charolos,* are built to signify harvest plenty. The bread, blessed by the village priest, is supposed to ward off sickness and evil spirits. Scholars believe the bread cult may be a holdover from the fertility rites of an ancient religion.

The route outlined below starts at Vila Real, near the eastern end of the Douro province. It tours highlights of the scenic Serra do Alvão to its north and the Terra do Basto plateau (sometimes called the Terras de Ribatâmega) to the northwest, before heading northeast on the N 15 toward Bragança. A southeasterly detour through almond and olive country also offers a view of the impressive Douro river ravine before it rises into Spain, and of tiny border towns like Miranda do Douro, renowned for its veal steaks, ancient dances, and unique Mirandês dialect. The Parque Natural de Montesinho and its communal villages can be explored from the walled city of Bragança in the far northeast before heading west (N 103) to the spa town of Chaves, famous for its Roman bridge, picturesque verandahs, and *presunto,* air-cured ham, which many connoisseurs rate higher than Italian prosciutto.

VILA REAL

Vila Real, the administrative and commercial center of southern Trás-os-Montes, is located at an altitude of 1,455 feet at the edge of a gorge at the juncture of the Marão, Alvão, and Padrela mountains and the Cabril and Corgo rivers, 50 km (31 miles) east of the eastern Douro town of Amarante, on the N 15/IP 4. A thriving agricultural center surrounded by apple, plum, and fig orchards, it is known primarily for its rosé wines, Borges & Irmão Port, earth-baked, silver-gray *olaria* (pottery), and hand-loomed *linho* (linen) from Argarez, all of which can be purchased at the Turismo, at avenida Carvalho Araújo, 94, or at the annual feast of Saint Peter (June 27 to June 29). The trick *bilhas* (water pitchers) are a popular gift item.

The *olaria* comes primarily from the neighboring town of Bisalhães, where holes in the ground serve as kilns. The kitchen and decorative pottery (pots, jugs, platters, etc.) is placed over coals, the hole is covered so that air cannot get in, and the ashes and smoke transform the clay into an ashen-gray color. The pottery is embellished with hand-carved flower patterns and geometric designs passed down from generation to generation.

Vila Real was built near the ancient sanctuary of Panóias (5 km/3 miles northeast of the city), where the Romans sacrificed animals and possibly humans to their gods. It was the seat of the counts of Vila Real, the Meneses, between the 15th and 17th centuries. Their rivalry with the other great Trás-os-Montes family, the Braganças, however, ended in tragedy in 1642 when the Meneses sided with the Spanish against the Bragança king of Portugal. The king, João IV, had the family rounded up, accused of attempted regicide, and executed. Part of the façade of their Renaissance palace is all that remains of this once-powerful dynasty.

Vila Real's strategic location at the juncture of the Douro province and Trás-os-Montes has helped it play an important role in the economy of the region. In 1895 it became the first town in Portugal to install electricity. Today it continues to grow and modernize, but its center maintains its old charm.

The main sights are contained on and along the cobbled **avenida Carvalho Araújo**. The **Sé** (cathedral), a former Dominican monastery built in the 15th century in Gothic style, has an unusual statue of the Virgin standing on top of a dragon. The Renaissance façade at number 19 is what remains of what is believed to have been the house where Diogo Cão, the 15th-century navigator who explored the Congo basin, was born. Farther west the monumental double staircase of the 19th-century Câmara Municipal (Town Hall), with its carved granite balusters and amphoras, welcomes visitors with Baroque flair. The view of the Corgo ravine from the esplanade behind the Câmara is impressive.

The **Palácio Mateus**, 3 km (2 miles) southeast of Vila Real, is one of the area's showpieces and its principal claim to fame. The Baroque façade, designed by Italian architect Nicolau Nasoni, is featured on the label of the rosé and other Mateus wines. Although the building is still a residence of the counts of Mangualde and Vila Real, parts of it can be visited. Its tiny, quaint museum contains, among other things, a collection of letters from 19th-century personalities such as Wellington, Talleyrand, and Metternich. It also displays a copy of a 19th-century illustrated edition of Camões's epic poem *The Lusiads;* the volume was part of a limited edition of 250 printed in France for the heir of the Mateus household. There are three immaculately manicured gardens with elaborate box-trimmed hedges at the southeastern corner of the palace. The Fundação da Casa Mateus sponsors classical music concerts and organizes guitar and music courses on the premises in August and September.

The palace can be visited daily but is closed at lunchtime. Unfortunately, wine tasting is not conducted on the grounds but in a modern bottling plant nearby (open until 5:00 P.M. in winter, 8:00 P.M. in summer; closed at lunchtime and on Saturdays and Sundays).

Vila Real proper is devoid of interesting restaurants and memorable accommodations, but its environs offer idyllic alternatives. The **Casa das Quartas**, a 16th-century manor house surrounded by orchards and vineyards on a wooded hill 4 km (2½ miles) east of Vila Real (off the N 15 to Murça), has three guest rooms with private baths. Guests can stroll in several levels of gardens of rose bushes, box-trimmed hedges, and fruit trees, play cards or watch television in comfortable sitting rooms elegantly furnished with patrician country antiques, or visit the private family chapel. Continental breakfast is served in your room or in the garden. The modern municipal sports complex nearby boasts an Olympic-size pool and tennis courts. Closed during the Christmas and Easter periods.

The **Pousada de São Gonçalo** is 900 meters (2,970 feet) above sea level in the serene solitude of the Marão mountains, 22 km (14 miles) west of Vila Real on the N 15/IP 4 toward Amarante. Its 15 rooms with private baths are somewhat small and uninspiring, but its views are breathtakingly rugged, and its restaurant offers the best of regional cooking. This is the ideal place to enjoy *trutas recheadas com presunto* (trout stuffed with smoked ham). The *pousada* (government-run inn) rests on a jagged cliff's edge like an eagle's nest, surrounded by the dark expanse of the Marão range.

The **Pousada do Barão de Forrester**, at Alijó, 40 km (25 miles) east of Vila Real on a bucolic, vine-covered plateau, also has good food and a full selection of wines. Its rooms are done up in bright fabrics and reproductions of antiques, and its dining room is decorated with murals of grape trellises. The friendly, English-speaking staff can arrange visits to the neighboring vineyards, where grapes are grown for some of Portugal's most famous Port wine.

Excursions from Vila Real

Retreats of great beauty and tranquillity near Vila Real are the **Parque Natural do Alvão** and the **Terra do Basto** (or Ribatâmega) plateau north and northwest of Vila Real. In the spring, the rolling countryside is awash in the color of thousands of wildflowers. During the winter, when its peaks are snowcapped, its valleys are dotted with *medas de palha,* corn stalks woven and positioned around poles to form shapes like upside-down cones, designed to force rainwater to run off quickly. The stalks are used as bedding for farm animals. Crystal-clear streams run through the area's pine-studded valleys, where thatched houses can still be seen. In the high passes the wind soughs over rocky crests, interrupted by the occasional shrill whistle of a shepherd calling his dogs or the tinkle of a goat's bell. A panoramic sweep of this rugged, rumpled region can be enjoyed from the heights of the **Alto do Velão**, 20 km (12 miles) northwest of Vila Real, on the N 304. You may spot eagles nesting above the waterfall at **Fisgas do Ermelo**, a natural site outside the tiny village of Ermelo, located farther up the road on the Olo river.

The sister towns of Mondim de Basto, Celorico de Basto, and Cabeceiras de Basto, all part of a powerful medieval earldom, obtained their names from a legendary Lusitanian warrior who fought bravely against the Romans. **Mondim de Basto,** past Ermelo (N 304), 44 km (27 miles) northwest of Vila Real, is a charming venue on the banks of the Tâmega river, with ancient cobbled streets and Romanesque and Gothic churches. **Celorico de Basto** (N 210), a bit farther downstream on the right bank toward Amarante, is lined with manor houses and guarded by an 18th-century castle. Northwest of Mondim, on the N 304, the imposing three-story **Casa do Barão de Fermil** lords it over the family's namesake ancestral village. The yellow villa has the lines of a French château and colonial trimmings, such as raised tiles on the edges of the roof, Chinese style. It is now a bed-and-breakfast operation with all the luxuries and trappings of a Portuguese country estate. Five bedrooms (three doubles and two suites with bathrooms) have been refurbished for guests, who can also enjoy the comforts of a spacious sitting room furnished with antiques, a large garden, and a small swimming pool. Continental breakfast is provided, and Dona Maria Fernanda Mourão, the hostess, will serve dinner if given notice in the morning or will steer you to the best bistros in the area for hearty mountain food. Closed during September and the Christmas and Easter periods.

The neighboring **Casa do Campo,** at Molares, about 2 km (1¼ miles) south on the N 210 toward Celorico de Basto, is a more stately, traditional Portuguese manor house, with its own private chapel, medieval tower, and crenellated battlements. Its grounds and bedrooms provide breathtaking views of the surrounding countryside, and its camellia garden is the envy of the region. Attentive owner Maria de Oliveira Matos Meirelles will serve meals in the family's baronial dining room, given prior notice. Guests can choose from among three double bedrooms decorated in a traditional style and a new Art Deco suite, with television and minibar. Four bedrooms, a common room, and a kitchenette are now available inside the tower. Guests have access to a new swimming pool surrounded by terraced vineyards.

The **Casa da Tojeira** is 13 km (8 miles) farther north of Fermil outside Arco de Baúlhe on the road (N 206) to Fafe. Behind its wooden door and granite-carved entrance staircase lies a splendid manor house with six double bedrooms. The present owners, a wealthy industrialist family, have given the house a face-lift and spared no expense in acquiring antiques for the redecoration. The north-facing verandah looks onto mountains and vineyards, while a modern, indoor swimming pool and sauna have been set into a knoll to the west of the house so that it won't clash with the estate's vintage ambience. (Use of these facilities requires payment of a modest fee.)

In the hamlet of Cabeceiras de Basto (N 205), 6½ km (4 miles) to the north of Arco de Baúlhe, the former **Convento de Refójos,** now a church, contains ancient ritualistic masks and a gilded organ supported by fauns. The ledges of the church's roof hold life-size granite statues of Saint Michael and the Twelve Apostles. A statue of Basto stands at the western end of the main square facing the former convent. **Atei,** across the Tâmega from Vila Nune (north on the N 312 from Mondim), has Roman ruins and a subterranean passage from the town to the banks of the river, believed to have been used as an escape route during sieges. The Basto area is known for its trout, its *cabrito assado no forno com arroz* (roast kid and rice), and its leather (belts), tin (lamps), and baskets, all of which can be bought at the local Turismo at Mondim de Basto, on rua Comendador Alfredo Alves de Carvalho (Tel: 059-384-79), or at the fair held at Mondim on the second and twenty-second of every month.

CENTRAL TRAS-OS-MONTES

The road northeast from Vila Real to Bragança (N 15) begins as a tapestry of pine trees, vineyards, olive groves, and fields of grain, and gradually gives way to an impressive lunar landscape. **Murça,** 40 km (25 miles) east of Vila Real, lies on a promontory above the Tinhela river ravine. Its famous *porca,* an Iron Age granite boar, stands in a bed of petunias in the main square. This curious animal is thought to have played a role in a prehistoric cult. Some scholars believe it may have been placed in fields to protect crops from evil spirits. During the political struggles of the 19th century the *porca* was painted blue when the conservatives won an election and red if the progressives were victorious. Murça is also known for its *toucinho do céu* flan and for its honey, sausages, and goat cheese.

Mirandela, 31 km (19 miles) east on the sandy banks of the river Tua, has a 16th-century bridge with 20 arches that was built on Roman foundations. It is also celebrated for its tin and wrought-iron work, such as pots and pans, stoves, and elaborate window grilles, which can be bought in shops lining the main street in front of the river. Mirandela has a lively annual crafts fair from the last week in July to the end of the first week in August. Eleven kilometers (7 miles) to the east is Jerusalém do Romeu, its rolling hills covered with olive and cork. The town was the seat of another great Trás-os-Montes noble family, the Távoras. In the 18th century, like the Meneses before them, the Tavora family sided with the Spanish against the Braganças, with tragic results; they were rounded up and executed by order of the marquês de Pombal. Their handsome palace, now the seat of the municipal government, dominates the town.

After Jerusalém do Romeu turn right for a short (2½-km/1½-mile) detour to the restored granite-and-shale village of **Romeu**, home of the region's most famous eating establishment. The **Maria Rita** restaurant, on the village's only street, is styled after a typical Trás-os-Montes patrician town house, with large dining rooms, stone fireplaces, and rustic furniture. The regional menu includes *sopa de alheiras,* a thick and spicy garlic soup loaded with *alheira* sausages, wild game, and asparagus. Whole turkeys, baby pigs, and lambs are cooked to order for parties who call in advance; Tel: (078) 931-34. House wines include homemade Romeu (red), Julieta (rosé), and Romeu (Port). Don't miss the **Museu de Curiosidades** next door, which contains 19th-century fire trucks, four Model-Ts, antique sewing machines, and musical and photographic equipment. The village, its restaurant, and the museum are owned by the patrician Meneres family, as is most of the outlying land and the neighboring rustic hamlets of Vila Verdinho and Vale de Couço.

Travellers can enter the inner sanctum of an aristocratic Trás-os-Montes family at the handsome **Solar das Arcas** in the small village of Arcas, northeast of Jerusalém do Romeu. (The road to Arcas is 13 km/8 miles east of Jerusalém do Romeu at the Podence turnoff; from there it is another 12 km to Arcas on a quaint but tiny secondary road.) Maria Francisca de Pessanha, the dowager matron of the clan, has opened her 18th-century home and working estate—one of the largest in Trás-os-Montes, surrounded by olive groves, poplar forest, and orchards—to lodgers, who have the choice of the elegant splendor of the main house (one double room in oak with bath and a four-poster bed, and access to a cozy living room with a large granite fireplace) or the rustic flavor of two apartments in typical country farmhouses. The latter have two double bedrooms each and all the amenities, including fireplace and kitchenette. Meals can be had, on request, in the charming dining room of the main house (the closest restaurant is 12 km/7½ miles away), and other activities, such as hunting, fishing, riding horses, and jeep tours of the estate, can be organized.

After Jerusalém do Romeu, as you continue northeast on N 15 toward Bragança, 53 km (33 miles) away, the trees begin to disappear and a barren landscape takes over, as you traverse some of the most thinly populated countryside in southern Europe. If you have enough time and prefer more architecture and human contact, veer right 9 km (5½ miles) east of Jerusalém do Romeu onto N 216, toward Macedo de Cavaleiros, for a longer, historic route (181 km/112 miles) to Bragança via southeastern Trás-os-Montes.

SOUTHEASTERN TRAS-OS-MONTES

Almost every town in southeastern Trás-os-Montes, no matter how humble, boasts a Romanesque, a Gothic, and a Baroque church or a blend of the three, and often a castle, or at least the remains of one. The castles were mostly built in the 14th century by Dom Dinis, Portugal's builder king, to protect the country's eastern border.

Macedo de Cavaleiros

Macedo de Cavaleiros, about 6½ km (4 miles) after the turnoff from N 15, is said to have obtained its name from two medieval knights adept at fighting Moors with *macedos* (maces). Another claim is that it was named after the Spanish nobleman Alváro Gil de Macedo, who once owned the region. With the Moors gone the sport has turned to game, and the weapons are rifles. The town continues to be a favorite of aristocrats from the north of Portugal, who maintain manor houses and hunting lodges within its limits. It is also known for its wicker baskets and crocheted bedspreads and activities including swimming at the Azibo dam and visits to the sanctuaries of Santo Ambrósio and Nossa Senhora de Balsemão in neighboring Chacim. The **Estalagem do Caçador**, lodged in the former town hall, is one of the region's finer privately owned inns. Its 25 bedrooms are all furnished with Portuguese antiques and handmade bedspreads and linen. The lodge's large salon contains a huge marble fireplace, leather chairs, elaborate gros-point rugs from Arraiolos, and hunting curios. Its dining room is traditionally Portuguese, with carved leather-backed chairs, hand-crocheted tablecloths, and elaborate silverware and china. Game dishes, prepared during the hunting season (September through February), include Port-marinated partridge and fricasseed hare; veal steaks stuffed with *presunto* are a year-round specialty. The cellar stocks the family estate-bottled Valperdinhas red wine. A rose garden and a marble-lined swimming pool are other attractive features. This moderately priced establishment, owned by a Porto publishing magnate, tends to fill up in hunting season, so if you plan to visit during the fall, you had better book well in advance.

The ruins of a 12th-century Templars fortress overlook the town of **Mogadouro**, 50 km (31 miles) southeast of Macedo on the N 216, which is known for its wood crafts (chairs, religious objects, and kitchenware), and its woollen (blankets and clothes) and leather goods (harnesses). In the early spring the Serra da Castanheira (northeast of Mogadouro on the N 219) is clothed in a white mantle of blooming chestnut trees.

Guarded by an imposing tower, **Freixo de Espada à Cinta** sits surrounded by millions of almond trees on a fertile plain in the southeastern corner of Trás-os-Montes, 45 km (28 miles) south of Mogadouro on N 221. There are several versions as to how the town obtained its unusual name of "Ash Tree with a Sword Around It." One account claims it came from a Visigoth nobleman named Espadacinta, another that it originated with Dom Dinis, who hung his sword on an ash tree here before resting in the shade. Yet another tale says the town was named after a valiant nobleman from León, whose coat of arms bore an ash and a sword and who defended Freixo against the Moors.

To encourage the settlement of this remote town 2½ miles from the Spanish border, Portuguese kings made Freixo a sanctuary for fugitives, giving selected condemned prisoners their freedom in exchange for living here. The town was given its charter in the 11th century, and King Dinis built its main fortifications in the late 13th century. It subsequently became a prosperous silk center, and is now known for its wines, woollens, oil, almonds, and fruits.

The seven-sided **Torre do Galo** (Cock's Tower), which offers a fine view of the almond-tree-studded valley, is the last survivor of four similar structures built by King Dinis. It stands beside the lovely **Igreja Matriz** (Parish Church), construction of which was begun in the 14th century and completed in the 17th. The famous Spanish Plateresque, or Neo-Manueline, architect João de Castilho, who was married to a woman from Freixo, added the Renaissance touches to the elegant Gothic doorway. The interior is rich and impressive, adorned with an elaborate wrought-iron pulpit, a wood-carved chancel, and a collection of 16 painted wall panels attributed to the 16th-century master Vasco Fernandes (Grão Vasco; see the Beira Alta chapter).

The best time to visit Freixo de Espada à Cinta is in the early spring, when the flowering almond trees transform the valley into a white bower. The **Quinta da Boa Vista**, a tourist development on the town's outskirts, consists of four independent houses, each with three airy bedrooms furnished with modern touches. There is a fairly good restaurant, a bar, a swimming pool, and tennis courts.

Take N 221 back toward Mogadouro for 10 km (6 miles), and turn right at the sign for **Mazouco**, where donkeys continue to be a major means of transport and some villagers still make their own sausage and cheese. Leave your car in the square and ask any of the locals to guide you to **O Carneiro** (The Sheep), a Paleolithic rock carving engraved on the steep canyon wall that drops precipitously down to the Douro river southeast of the village. Golden eagles, black storks, and Egyptian vultures still nest on the ledges and crannies of the tall cliffs of this gorge, which runs roughly north to south for 70 miles from Miranda do Douro to Barca de Alva.

Despite its small size, **Sendim**, on N 221 near the border (27 km/17 miles east of Mogadouro), boasts one of Portugal's most famous restaurants, **Gabriela**, a rustic, no-frills establishment in the town square. Alice, the cook and second-generation owner of the 70-plus-year-old restaurant, recently passed away and will be missed by those who enjoyed watching her preside over a huge open fire. Her legacy lives on with the family, who have vowed to maintain her standards and her mouth-watering *posta Mirandesa à Gabriela* veal steak. Alice's steak, cooked over a fire of grape and olive vines, earned her a Coq d'Or and the appreciation of countless diners.

Miranda do Douro

Miranda do Douro, perched above the Douro river and its ravine across from Spain, 22 km (14 miles) northeast of Sendim on N 221, was for centuries the linchpin in the string of fortified towns defending the northeastern border and the seat of an important bishopric. It grew prosperous from its trade with Spain under the rule of the powerful Távora grandees, and was the center of culture and religion of Trás-os-Montes during the Renaissance. During the 18th century, however, the persecution of the Távoras by the autocratic marquês de Pombal, who grew wary of their growing power,

a series of invasions, and the loss of the bishop's seat to Bragança plunged Miranda do Douro into a decline from which it is only now starting to emerge. A new border post, new road links to Spain, and the recent construction of a dam have all fueled its reemergence.

Miranda's 16th-century **cathedral**, rich in gold, houses the curious statue of the Meníno Jesus da Cartolinha, a baby Jesus sporting a top hat. It is said to represent a boy who miraculously appeared during a siege of the town by the Spanish in 1711 and led the Portuguese to victory. Little remains of Miranda's castle, which was destroyed during another Spanish siege in 1762, but its crenellated **Torre de Menagem** (Keep), the temporary headquarters of Wellington during the Peninsular War, still stands.

Miranda's culture and folklore are still thriving. It has its own dialect, Mirandês, a blend of low Latin, archaic Portuguese, Galician (northwestern Spanish), Spanish, and some Hebrew, which is still spoken and taught locally. The **Museu da Terra de Miranda** contains furniture and costumes of the region and archaeological artifacts, such as pre-Roman double-edged axes and spears, Celtic jewelry, Roman lapidaries, scales, and pottery, Moorish daggers, and carved stones from an old synagogue. During the Festas da Santa Bárbara (third Sunday in August) and the Romaria de Nossa Senhora do Nazo (early September) you can admire the town's ancient and colorful folk dances: the *pingacho* (rough ballet), the *Geribalda* (a round dance), and the *Mira-me Miguel* (a square dance); and watch its *pauliteiros* (stick dancers), men clad in white flannel shirts, aprons, and flower-covered hats who perform ritualized sword fights to the accompaniment of bagpipes, cymbals, and drums. The *pauliteiro* troupe is run by the energetic former priest of neighboring Duas Igrejas, the director of Miranda's museum, who is the self-appointed champion of Mirandês culture.

Miranda is known for its hooded, hand-embroidered brown woollen capes (*capas de honra*) and waistcoats, worn by the town's important men during ceremonies and feast days; its *facas de palacoulo* (knives with forks attached to them, used by the shepherds of the region); and its braised *posta à Mirandesa* (veal steaks), which can be tasted at the **Mirandes**, a rustic family-run restaurant. The **Pousada de Santa Catarina**, a simple 12-room inn 3 km (2 miles) northeast of Miranda do Douro (N 221), overlooking the dam, is decorated in spartan fashion but has nice views of the calm waters of the dam and across the plain of Zamora in Spain. The restaurant serves small game such as stewed partridge and rabbit during the winter hunting season, and Douro river trout wrapped in *presunto* and sautéed in butter. The area's garlicky *fumeiro* (smoked mixed sausage) is a savory appetizer.

NORTHEASTERN TRAS-OS-MONTES

The northeast is the outback of Portugal, known for its hardy, independent frontier folk; wild, untamed country; villages as old as recorded history; and Portugal's most resilient royal line. Bragança, its walled capital, is a testament to the will and bold pioneering spirit of its founding fathers and their descendants. The town is 87 km (54 miles) northwest of Mirando do Douro via the N 218; 245 km (152 miles) northeast of Porto via the N 15/IP 4; and only 30 km (19 miles) from the Spanish border.

Bragança

For a remote outpost in the northeastern corner of Portugal, the walled town of Bragança (known as Brigantia by the Celts and Juliobriga by the Romans) has left a decided mark on Portuguese history. The house of Bragança, founded by the bastard son of King João I in 1442, ruled Portugal from 1640 until 1910, when it was ousted by the Republic. The Braganças and the town took their name from the powerful Bragançôes warrior clan that ruled the area in the 11th and 12th centuries. The last of the Bragançôes, Fernão Mendes, married the sister of the first king of Portugal, Dona Sancha.

The town commands a high promontory on the barren slopes of the Serra da Nogueira 2,165 feet above sea level. Its medieval walls and citadel are among the best preserved in Portugal. It was a major rope-making and silk center in the 15th and 16th centuries, with an important community of Jewish merchants. Although the Inquisition forced many Jews to convert, some families chose to go underground and continue to practice their faith in secret. Copper (kitchenware), leather goods (jackets, belts, bags), woollen blankets, and basket weaving have replaced silk in the shops in the praça da Sé, the town's main square.

The citadel's **Torre de Menagem** (Keep) houses the town's military museum and memorabilia from the Spanish and Napoleonic wars, during which Bragança was occupied. The **Torre da Princesa**, beside it, once imprisoned Dona Leonor, the comely wife of the fourth duke of Bragança, Don

Jaime. She was locked up here by her husband, who could not bear that any other man should lay eyes on her. Dona Leonor and a lover were later murdered by the duke, after he had moved his court south to Vila Viçosa. The shaft of a medieval pillory in front of the castle is driven through a granite statue of a boar, believed to have formed part of an Iron Age cult. Some scholars believe that the boar, like Murça's *porca,* served as a talisman against evil spirits. The **Domus Municipalis**, a rare and beautiful example of an Iberian Romanesque civic building, lies at the southern end of the citadel beside the 16th-century church of **Santa Maria**. The pentagonal 12th-century structure has an elegant frieze of carved modillions lining its walls and a cistern underneath it. The building served as the meeting place of the *homens bons* (good men, the highest nonnoble class in Portugal), or city officials, and now offers a cool haven from the scorching summer heat.

Outside the citadel walls, at rua Conselheiro Abílio Beça, in the 18th-century palace of the bishops, is the **Museu Regional Abade de Baçal**. Its garden contains archaeological remains dating back to the Iron Age, and its two floors exhibit Trás-os-Montes furniture, tools, ancient coins, church plate and vestments, Indo-Portuguese furniture, and paintings. The abbot of Baçal (1865–1947) was a diminutive and energetic scholar who recorded in many volumes the history and customs of the region, including those of its Jews, who played a major role in the silk trade. The museum is closed at lunchtime and on Mondays and holidays.

Bragança gained prominence in 1780 when the bishop moved there from Miranda do Douro. His seat was installed in a heavy 16th-century Jesuit building in the praça da Sé. On the north side of the square is the **Solar Bragançano**, an intimate restaurant set in a former town house. Wooden ceilings, chandeliers, and Arraiolos rugs provide an Old World touch but don't affect the reasonable prices of this establishment frequented by Bragança's elite. House specialties are *cabrito branco à Montesinho* (white Montesinho kid), baked cod with boiled potatoes, and veal steak *solar* style, with egg and orange rinds. The region's semisweet *favalos* (muscatel) can be enjoyed with hors d'oeuvres of *alheiras* (spiced sausages) or Portugal's "queen of cheeses," *queijo da serra* (sheep cheese from the Beira Alta). **Lá em Casa**, on rua Marquês de Pombal, is an earthier alternative, with rustic regional touches in its pottery, copper, and ironware (closed Mondays).

A splendid view of Bragança's walls and citadel and of the

surrounding mountains can be had from the balconies of the 16 rooms and from the restaurant of the **Pousada de São Bartolomeu,** on a hill about a mile southeast of town. The inn also has a comfortable salon, with a huge stone fireplace and wood-paneled bar. Its charming restaurant serves both regional and international cuisine, and wild boar, partridge, and hare during the hunting season. The cook is also known for his *cozido à transmontana,* a hearty boiled dinner containing several meats and vegetables, and *feijoada à transmontana,* a good winter white-bean casserole containing pork, sausage, and pig's ears. The pousada is popular with business travellers throughout the year and tends to fill up, so book several months in advance.

The former monastery of **Castro de Avelãs** lies 5 km (3 miles) north of Bragança off the N 103 to Chaves. Little is left of the monastery, but its church is unusual in its brick construction as well as in its design, which incorporates three adjoining cylinders. This former Benedictine center of worship has Moorish and Romanesque touches and is believed to have been built in the 11th or 12th century. Abandoned in the 19th century when the religious orders were banned, it is now inhabited by doves.

Parque Natural de Montesinho

Wolves, foxes, and wild boars roam the 185,000-acre Parque Natural de Montesinho, between Bragança and the northern border with Spain, which contains some of the wildest bush country in Portugal. The park also comprises self-sufficient villages like Rio de Onor, where communal life and pre-Christian pagan rituals continue to be practiced. The natives still believe in the evil eye and *bruxas* (witches). This is one of the areas in which bread plays a major role in religious events: Between Christmas and Epiphany, the unmarried men in some villages, such as Sacóias and Varge (north on N 218-1), don hideous devil masks and "frighten" the women of the village into donating food and wine to the church. Villagers construct tall pyramids of bread, eggs, and sausages, called *charolos,* and take them to the church to be blessed and auctioned off, then ceremoniously eaten. The blessed bread is supposed to ward off sickness and evil spirits. It is also said to represent fecundity.

The village of **Rio de Onor** straddles the border with Spain in a fertile valley 24 km (15 miles) northeast of Bragança on N 218-1. Its citizens still own certain pastures in common, rotate chores, and have a democratic (albeit all-male) governing body. Two *mordomos* (stewards) are elected yearly to conduct town business. Not long ago the village owned a communal pair of shoes that men wore on their visits to the "big city" of Bragança. The rest of the year they went barefoot or wore wooden clogs. The village is a diplomatic anomaly: Half of it lies in Portugal, the other in Spain. Its inhabitants cross freely from one side to the other, share the same grocery store on the Spanish side, and have practiced endogamy (marriage only with members of the immediate community) for centuries. To reach Rio de Onor from Bragança (24 km/15 miles) take the N 218 east out of town, veer left onto N 218-1, turn right 2 km (1¼ miles) past the airport, and follow the signs to Rio de Onor.

West of Bragança

The N 103 west to Chaves (96 km/60 miles) from Bragança is a scenic route winding through oak and chestnut woods surmounted by the bare peaks of the *serras* (mountain ranges) of Montesinho and Coroa. Round, whitewashed *pombais* (pigeon houses), where pigeons are raised for eating, alternate with trout farms and cattle grazing on steep slopes.

The rugged beauty and life of the region can be sampled at the **Moinho do Caniço** bed and breakfast, converted from a windmill of wood and stone on the left (east) bank of the small, pristine Baceiro stream at Castrelos, 12 km (7½ miles) west of Bragança on the N 103. This two-room establishment is simply but tastefully furnished, and the property includes a brick bread oven and stone fireplace, the remains of the former milling station, a vegetable farm, and fruit orchards. (The mill is rented as one unit, not room by room.) A simple country restaurant is within walking distance. This is a perfect secluded base from which to take walking tours of the Montesinho park.

Vinhais and the remains of its 14th-century fortifications crown a high mountain pass overlooking a fertile valley planted with apple orchards 34 km (21 miles) west of Bragança. An important and wealthy monastic enclave up to the 19th century, when the religious orders were banished, Vinhais has lost some of its prosperity and glitter. Villagers have built homes inside the castle grounds, and chickens and goats run free in its former courtyard. The **Igreja de São Francisco**, atop a flight of steps off the main rua dos Frades, is a faded beauty today. Gone are its rich ceiling paintings, but the elaborate gilded altar and polychrome statues of saints survive. The church was originally part of a larger convent, which was divided during the religious turmoil of the 19th century in order to keep it from falling into private hands. Seminarians have since returned to the convent next door, renamed Encarnação. To visit the church, get the keys from the nuns, who live in a yellow house on the western corner of the courtyard. The pretty Visigothic **Igreja de São Facundo**, on the grounds of the cemetery in the valley below the town, has a fine exterior decorated with carved heads.

More contemporary wood carving, such as yokes for ox carts, wooden furniture, walking sticks, and kitchen utensils, can be obtained at the town's colorful biweekly market held on the ninth and twenty-third of each month (or the next day if a Sunday) at the soccer field, on the western corner of the town past the convent. Other items include the area's Pinheiro cream cheeses, woollen blankets, mountain boots, donkey and mule saddles, and other farming paraphernalia, sold by black-garbed Gypsies and other itinerant merchants. Peasants from the surrounding countryside park their donkeys and carts on the main street to visit the market.

THE ALTO TAMEGA

The wide, fertile valley of the upper Tâmega river, surrounding the town of Chaves, has always attracted settlers and invaders alike: the former for its rich soil, the latter drawn to its gold mines and because it represented a breach in the otherwise impregnable wall of mountains protecting the north from Spain. It is strewn with pre-Celtic, Celtic, and Roman remains, with thermal springs and spas.

Chaves

Chaves (the word means "keys") lies at the center of the Alto Tâmega valley. Several explanations are given for the origin of its name. One says it was named after the keys given to Nuno Alvares by João I, father of Prince Henry the Navigator, for his valiant service at the Battle of Aljubarrota in 1385, in which the Portuguese vanquished a much larger Spanish force. Another account claims the name was derived from "Flaviis," a bastardization of its earlier Roman name, Aqua Flaviae.

Chaves is known for its *presunto* and for its thermal springs. The Romans named it Aqua Flaviae and mined the gold and iron of the area. The Ponte Trajano, built in A.D. 104, turned the town into an important junction on the Roman road linking Braga to the south with the northern town of Astorga in Galicia, Spain. The bridge is still in use, but the rest of the Roman town lies under modern Chaves, waiting to be excavated. The last functioning Roman spa was demolished in the 17th century during the revolt against Spanish rule.

Most of the historic sites are in and around the medieval **praça de Camões**. The **Museu da Região Flaviense**, with objects depicting the life of the people in the region, is housed in a former 15th-century palace of the dukes of Bragança. It also contains an important collection of Roman coins from the first to the fourth century A.D., along with minting instruments. The adjoining **Museu Militar** is lodged in the town's 14th-century keep. The manicured gardens of the keep display archaeological remains dating back to the Iron Age, and its ramparts provide a sweeping view of the Tâmega and the surrounding countryside. You can gaze at the garden from **Dionisyos**, a bistro-style restaurant with both indoor and outdoor dining, located in the adjacent praça do Município.

The praça de Camões also contains an ornate Manueline *pelourinho* (pillory), a column, usually with an ornamental top, that kings bestowed on towns and villages, symbolizing the right to dispense justice; earlier versions also served as gallows. The lovely Romanesque doorway of the parish church beside it was uncovered during recent restorative work. The interior of the Baroque **Igreja da Misericórdia** next door is embellished with 18th-century *azulejos* (decorative tiles) depicting the life of Christ, attributed to the master tile painter Oliveira Bernardes.

Chaves is called the *cidade das varandas* because of the colorfully painted wooden verandahs on the eastern side of the square and the neighboring rua Direita.

On the eastern side of town are the two 17th-century Vaubanesque fortresses of São Francisco and São Neutel (neither open to the public). The curative waters at the health spa beside the river, at 73 degrees Celsius (163 degrees Fahrenheit), are said to be Europe's warmest. For something more filling, cross the Ponte Trajano to the left bank, turn left, and head down to the largo de São Roque. The tiny **Restaurante Campismo**, named after the camping area in front of it, a rustic family-run establishment, offers gracious service and fine cooking. Trout stuffed with the town's renowned *presunto* and *cabrito no churrasco* (spit-roasted kid) are specialties. The tart, somewhat cloudy house white wine goes well with fish. A more robust, dry red from neighboring Valpaços is also recommended. No credit cards accepted.

O Pote, a lively restaurant about a kilometer (½ mile) from the center of town on the main road to Spain (N 103-5), is a good place to try *bolas de carne* (minced beef balls in tomato sauce). Another treat is *pão de presunto,* a hearty bread baked with slices of the area's rich ham.

Chaves may boast about its food, but its accommodations are another matter. One might expect that one of its palaces or fortresses would have been converted to complement the charm of the old city. Instead, the pattern has been to build in flashy, modern provincial style. As an example, the newly opened **Hotel Aquae Flaviae** offers all the amenities of a chain hotel, including air-conditioning, pool, fine regional restaurant, even a piano bar, but fails to charm. It is, however, ideally located near the city's spa center on the riverfront.

Faustino and Filhos, one of the country's largest *tascas* (bistros), housed in a warehouse nearby at travessa do Olival, 12, is a good place to mingle with farmers and other local folk and taste regional wines, drawn from huge vats.

The neighboring town of Santo Estevão 7 km (4 miles) northeast of Chaves and 5 km (3 miles) from the Spanish border, helps ease the accommodations problem at Chaves. The **Quinta de Santa Isabel,** a 13th-century farmhouse of granite, wood, and stone, offers two doubles (one with bath) and one single, decorated in a country style, with access to a modern kitchen. The house was named after the saintly princess Isabel of Spain, who stayed overnight in the neighboring castle on her way to marry King Dinis of Portugal.

The imposing **Castelo de Monforte** lies off N 103 14 km (8½ miles) northeast of Chaves on a wind-swept promontory. The 14th-century structure was built by King Dinis around the remains of a Romanized Lusitanian *castro* to protect the Tâmega valley. It was used at different times as a prison and as a refuge for fugitives. From its ramparts you have a clear view of Spain and the mountains to the north and can gain a sense of the isolation and hard life of the frontier people. A cattle market is held outside the castle walls on the eighteenth of each month. To reach the *castelo* you must brave a bumpy but short (½-mile) dirt road. Visits are conducted from 3:00 to 6:00 P.M. daily.

Vidago

The spa town of Vidago, 17 km (11 miles) southwest of Chaves on the N 2, holds the key to accommodations in the area. The royal family frequented this spa and made it popular at the end of the 19th century. The **Vidago Palace Hotel**, the dowager matron of Trás-os-Montes hotels, closed its doors in the fall of 1992 and is undergoing a face-lift to restore some of its past luster and beauty. It is scheduled to reopen in July 1993. The Belle Epoque establishment was inaugurated in 1910 by Mauel II, the last king of Portugal, and became a watering hole for the aristocracy and high society. The complex, which sprawls across a lush park west of the train station, is surrounded by gardens, ponds, fountains, tennis courts, and a nine-hole golf course. The main building's public areas and its 128 rooms will be totally refurbished and redecorated with art deco flair. The pièce-de-résistance, the Doric-columned dining room, will retain its Old World charm and its waiters in white livery, while the posh Royal (Manuel II) Suite will continue to lord it over the manor.

The hotel's spa building is being transformed into a state-of-the-art health center, while the existing annex, tucked away behind the main building, will provide such amenities as outdoor swimming pool and disco. Leisurely, romantic afternoons can be spent rowing or strolling along a man-made pond populated with swans.

Outeiro Machado

Of all the archaeological remains that abound in the area around Chaves, the rock carvings outside Outeiro Machado may be the most interesting. The 165-foot-long granite boulder, carved by Neolithic artists with ladders, axes, and other symbols, is believed to have been used by Celtic Druids for sacrifices. Part of the stone was damaged when villagers, inspired by rumors of hidden gold, used dynamite to try to dislodge it.

To reach the stone head west out of Chaves on the Vale de Anta and Soutelo road, turn right at a yellow sign advertising "Arte Rupestre" (Rock Art) about 3 km (2 miles) out of Chaves, and follow the dirt road and signs for about 1 km (½ mile) to an open field. The boulder is easy to spot, right in the middle of the field.

The Serra do Barroso

The Serra do Barroso, centered some 50 km (31 miles) west-southwest of Chaves, is famous for its beautiful long-horned Barroso oxen and for its drinking waters. To get to Boticas, at the entrance of the *serra,* turn left (south) at Sapiãos onto N 311 from N 103, west out of Chaves. The people of Boticas are known for their curious practice of burying wine in the ground for a year. The custom began in the early 19th century, during the Napoleonic invasions, when the towns-folk decided to hide their wine rather than let the French soldiers consume it. Unearthing the wine after the French left, they discovered it had improved. They began calling the buried wine bottles *mortos* (dead), and the unearthing pro-cess *levantar um morto* (raising the dead). You can taste the wine at the vine-covered **Santa Cruz** restaurant, poised on a hill overlooking the Beça river. Large, succulent portions of braised beef, hare, and trout, plus moist country bread, are prepared in an open kitchen by village women. The look is pure country. Homemade sausages and ham are also served. No credit cards accepted.

For entertainment, and to improve their cattle stock, vil-lages in the vicinity compete during the summer in *chegas de bois,* pitting their champion bulls against each other. The bulls are treated like sports heroes, paraded with bands and given food by the cheering patrons, who goad them into battle. The fight ends when one bull gores the other to death or one turns and runs away. Women toss red handkerchiefs at the victor. At the end of the season the champion is rewarded by being put to pasture with the local cows.

The **Estalagem de Carvalhelhos** is a simple country inn set in the midst of woods, springs, and gardens in Carvalhelhos, 8 km (5 miles) west of Boticas on N 311. Its drinking water is among the best in the north, its restaurant's service is atten-tive, and the cooking is homey and country style. The moder-ately priced establishment, with 20 spacious double bed-rooms with bath, is open only from June through October.

The neighboring Iron Age *castro,* with its moat, double-walled perimeter, and circular homes, is one of the best-preserved in the country. You will find it at the end of a dirt road on the hill above the estalagem. Don't be surprised to see an occasional blond shepherd in the region; he is proba-bly a descendant of the Suevi, a Germanic pastoral people who populated the area in the fifth century A.D.

For maps and further information on the region, contact

the Turismo in Chaves at Terreiro da Cavalaria; Tel: (076) 210-29. The staff speaks English and is very helpful.

Montalegre rests 3,000 feet above sea level on a rocky promontory facing the Larouco mountains and Spain to the north, in the northwestern corner of the province, 43 km (27 miles) west of Chaves. The town, known for its tasty potatoes, is dominated by an imposing, heavyset castle, built by King Dinis in the 14th century over the ruins of a 13th-century fortress. The castle, which is composed of three towers and a keep and surrounded by a semicircular wall and battlements, has been extensively restored. Roman stones with Latin inscriptions, found in the surrounding area, are also exhibited in the courtyard. From the battlements you see a small stream spanned by an ancient stone bridge; women often do laundry on its banks.

The tiny church of **Misericórdia**, which stands in the main village square, has an elaborate three-layered gilt reredos, its columns adorned with carvings of acanthus leaves.

Montalegre is slowly emerging from the Middle Ages, with government money coming in to fund an agricultural research facility and to support a new army barracks. Right now, however, donkey carts with round wooden frames continue to be the main form of transport to border villages inside the rugged *serra* to the north.

GETTING AROUND

Major places in the Trás-os-Montes are fairly well connected by road, train, and plane. The best way to see the region, however, is by car, which has to be picked up in Porto or Lisbon; there are no agency rentals in the region. Linhas Aéreas Regionais (LAR) flies to Vila Real and Bragança from Lisbon and Porto. LAR reservations can be made domestically at Porto's airport (Tel: 02-948-3245; Fax: 02-948-9191) and the Lisbon airport (Tel: 01-848-0637; Fax: 01-849-9552), or through the national airline offices.

Two scenic train lines connect the region with the Douro valley and Porto. The **Linha do Corgo** runs from Peso da Régua on the Douro north through Port-wine country to Vila Real. The **Linha da Tua**, which has vintage wooden cars and seats, is the most scenic and rustic in all of Portugal. It starts at Tua, east of Pinhão in the eastern Douro, and runs northeast to Mirandela. The coal-fired steam engine has now been retired and replaced by diesel power. The train used to make a four-hour run to Bragança, but cost overruns recently forced the national rail company to shorten its reach by more than an hour. Passengers bound for Bragança now board buses at Mirandela that take them the rest of the way.

The Rodonorte bus company, at rua Guerra Junqueiro, 111 (Tel: 073-228-70; Fax: 073-249-82) services the region, while the Agência de Viagens e Turismo, Sanvitur, can book intercity express buses to major Portuguese destinations (Tel: 073-228-26).

Train tickets can be bought at the railway stations or through travel agencies. Tourist passes are available for one to three weeks' duration. These passes allow unlimited travel in any class at a low, fixed cost. Rail travel in Portugal is inexpensive, and first class is definitely worth the small extra cost. Children under 4 travel free on laps, and youngsters between 4 and 12 pay half fare. People 65 and over also pay half fare. Soft drinks can be purchased, and passengers bring snacks—or sometimes whole meals, complete with wine, which they are known to share. Advance booking is usually not necessary. Information on schedules and tickets can be obtained at Turismo locations and at the main train station of Campanhã in Porto; Tel: (02) 56-41-41 or 56-42-24.

ACCOMMODATIONS REFERENCE

Rates given are projected 1993 prices for a double room, double occupancy. Price ranges span the lowest rate in the low season to the highest in the high season. Unless otherwise stated, rates include Continental breakfast. As prices are subject to change, always double-check before booking.

▶ **Casa do Barão de Fermil.** Fermil, 4890 **Celorico de Basto.** Tel: (055) 36-12-11, 36-12-31, or (02) 68-07-78. 10,800$00.

▶ **Casa do Campo.** Molares, 4890 Celorico de Basto. Tel: (055) 36-12-31. 10,000$00–10,300$00.

▶ **Casa das Quartas.** Abambres, 5000 **Vila Real.** Tel: (059) 32-29-76. 10,300$00.

▶ **Casa da Tojeira. Arco de Baúlhe,** 4860 Cabeceiras de Basto. Tel: (053) 66-31-69; Fax: (053) 51-44-16. 12,400$00.

▶ **Estalagem do Caçador.** Largo Manuel Pinto de Azevedo, 5340 **Macedo de Cavaleiros.** Tel: (078) 42-13-54 or 42-13-56; Fax: (078) 42-13-81. 10,000$00–14,000$00.

▶ **Estalagem de Carvalhelhos. Carvalhelhos,** 5460 Boticas. Tel: (076) 421-16 or 421-50; Fax: (076) 421-74. 5,500$00–6,500$00. Open June through October.

▶ **Hotel Aquae Flaviae.** Praça do Brasil, 5400 **Chaves.** Tel: (076) 267-11 or 264-96; Fax: (076) 264-97. 9,000$00–14,300$00.

▶ **Moinho do Caniço. Castrelos.** Contact Arnaldo Cadavez, Avenida Abade Baçal, 5300 Bragança. Tel: (073) 235-77 or 259-52. For the mill as one unit, 9,000$00.

▶ **Pousada do Barão de Forrester.** Rua José Rufino, 5070 **Alijó.** Tel: (059) 92-92-15; Fax: (059) 95-93-04. 8,000$00–12,300$00.

▶ **Pousada de Santa Catarina.** Estrada da Barragem, 5210 **Miranda do Douro.** Tel: (073) 422-55; Fax: (073) 422-65. 9,700$00–18,000$00.

▶ **Pousada de São Bartolomeu.** Estrada de Turismo, 5300 **Bragança.** Tel: (073) 224-93; Fax: (073) 224-94. 8,000$00–12,300$00.

▶ **Pousada de São Gonçalo.** Serra do Marão, 4600 **Amarante.** Tel: (055) 46-11-13; Fax: (055) 46-13-53. 8,000$00–12,300$00.

▶ **Quinta da Boa Vista.** 5180 **Freixo de Espada à Cinta.** Tel: (079) 621-45. 6,500$00–9,800$00.

▶ **Quinta de Santa Isabel.** Santo Estevão, 5400 **Chaves.** Tel: (076) 218-18 or contact Lizette Chaves, Avenida Estados Unidos de America, 69, 2 Dto., 1700 Lisboa, Tel: (01) 849-4788. 7,000$00–8,000$00.

▶ **Solar das Arcas.** Arcas, 5385 **Torre de Dona Chama.** Tel: (078) 40-11-35. Double room: 13,900$00; apartment: 15,000$00.

▶ **Vidago Palace Hotel.** 5425 **Vidago.** Tel: (076) 973-56 or 973-57; Fax: (076) 973-59. 15,000$00.

Pousadas can be booked through ENATUR, Avenida Santa Joana Princesa, 10, 1700 Lisbon, Portugal; Tel: (01) 848-1221 or 848-9078; Fax: (01) 80-58-46. But it is easier to make reservations through a travel agent. In the United States and Canada, pousadas can be booked through Marketing Ahead, 433 Fifth Avenue, New York, NY 10016; Tel: (212) 686-9213; Fax: (212) 686-0271.

Manor houses can be booked directly or through the manor-house associations—ANTER, P.I.T., PRIVETUR, and TURIHAB—listed in Useful Facts. Most of the houses belong to one or more of these associations, but because membership rosters change frequently we haven't attempted to spell out the associations for each house. Readers are advised to contact the manor-house associations for their current listings.

In the United States and Canada, it is possible to reserve rooms in P.I.T manor houses through E & M Associates, 211 East 43rd Street, Suite 1404, New York, NY 10017; Tel: (212) 599-8280; Fax: (212) 599-1755.

MADEIRA

By Jean Anderson

*Andnow our course took us into regions and past islands
already discovered by the great Prince Henrique. First came
Madeira, so called from its many forests. This was the earliest
of the islands to be settled by Portugal and the best known to
fame. Although set on the very edge of the known world,
none of those beloved by Venus can outshine it, had it too
been hers she would quickly have forgotten Cyprus, Gnido,
Paphos, and Cythera.* (Camões, *The Lusiads,* 1572)

Could Portugal's epic poet have oversold the island of
Madeira? Not at all. Its effect, even in today's age of tourism,
is magical.

Some say that Madeira is a vestige of Atlantis, that
legendary—or maybe not so legendary—continent that vanished beneath the sea sometime before the dawn of history.
Certainly there's the look of legend everywhere about
Madeira, the otherworldliness of Shangri-la.

For João Gonçalves Zarco and Tristão Vaz Teixeira, two
of Prince Henry's able Portuguese navigators who sailed
here in 1420, this green, rumpled island was paradise
found—particularly after puny, barren Porto Santo just 25
miles northeast, where they'd been blown ashore a year
earlier with fellow navigator Bartolomeu Perestrelo.
Stranded on Porto Santo for weeks while they readied their
storm-battered ships for their return to Portugal, the explorers surveyed the southern horizon and the cloudbank that
always seemed to hover there. Did the Ocean of Darkness
lie just beyond? The end of the world? This was the early
15th century, a time when the Atlantic was still known as
the Green Sea of Gloom, when sailors, more superstitious

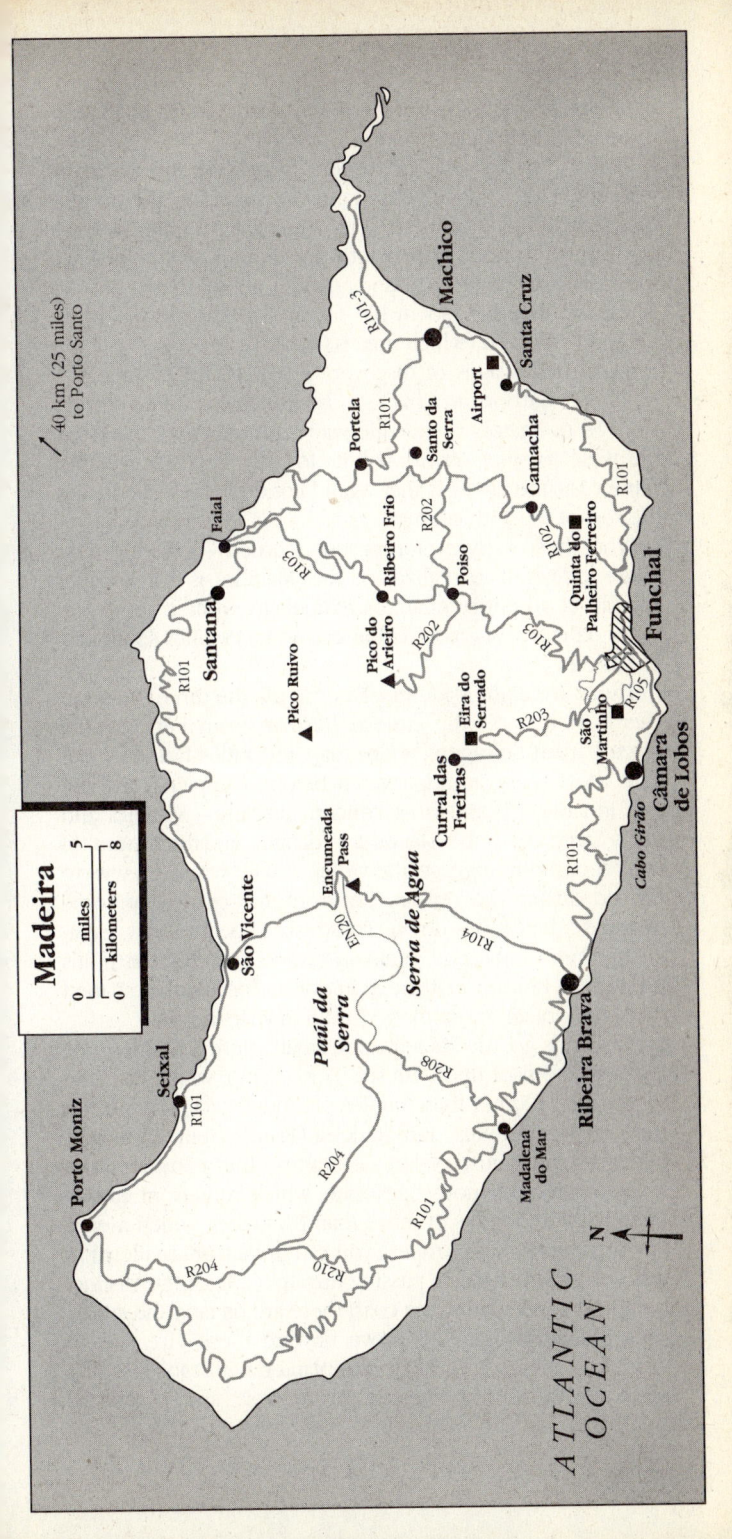

than scientific, believed in a flat earth, mermaids, and monsters of the deep.

The following year, on orders from their prince, who reasoned that land lay behind the shroud of fog, the navigators returned to Porto Santo to investigate. Cautiously they pushed south and slipped into the curtain of cloud. What they beheld, rising thousands of feet above them, was an island so majestic, so lushly forested that they promptly named it Madeira (which means "wood").

With the voyages of discovery just beginning, Madeira's sheltered harbor, at what is now Funchal, offered Prince Henry's navigators a strategic way station as they explored the west coast of Africa. And its forests provided valuable timber for the caravels that would conquer the seas during the rest of the 15th century.

What those early explorers soon learned—and most travellers today fail to realize—is that Madeira is not a single island but an entire Atlantic archipelago, located some 360 miles off the west coast of Morocco and 535 miles southwest of Lisbon.

There are eight Madeira islands in all: the three Desertas, clearly visible on the eastern horizon from Funchal, the three barren Selvagens, more than 150 miles farther south near the Canary islands (which belong to Spain), and the two inhabited islands that concern us here—Madeira and Porto Santo. All of the islands are volcanic, and their tumultuous topography suggests the violence with which they were heaved during the Tertiary Era from an ocean floor some two and a half miles down. These island peaks today, especially those of Madeira, seem so savage, so razor sharp, it's difficult to believe that the primeval holocaust that shaped them took place more than 30 million years ago.

As islands go, the Madeiras are small, mere volcanic chips that seem to float upon the sea. Porto Santo, which has little to brag about other than 6 miles of sandy beach, measures a meager 9 by 3 miles, and Madeira (Prince Henry's "bigger, better island") just 36 by 14 miles. But consider this: Madeira's mountainous backbone, which runs from east to west, rises to heights of more than 6,000 feet, which means that in 11 short km (7 miles) you can drive from sea level to crags above the clouds, passing through at least five distinct botanical zones. Along the coast there are banana and sugar-cane plantations; as you move upward these give way to vineyards, then scraps of garden planted with cabbages and potatoes, then misty forests of mimosa and *vinháticos*

(Madeira mahogany), and finally heathery moors reminiscent of Scotland.

Madeira itself offers just about anything else a body could want: plenty of posh resort hotels with pools as big as soccer fields (to compensate for the lack of sandy beaches) . . . remote country inns . . . major wine, wicker, and embroidery industries . . . a sophisticated capital (Funchal) with a casino and loads of good restaurants . . . storybook towns shelved high in the hills . . . a terrain so green, so creased by terraces it looks as if someone had draped the island with emerald corduroy . . . and, not least, balmy daytime temperatures that seem permanently stuck around 27 degrees Celsius (80 Fahrenheit)—at least along the south shore. In the mountains and on the north shore temperatures are always cooler, sometimes significantly so, and there's always more rain there, too, so it's best to carry a sweater and raincoat as you travel about the island.

MAJOR INTEREST

The capital city of Funchal
Madeira wine
Embroidery and other handicrafts
Mercado dos Lavradores (market) in Funchal
The great gardens
The volcano village of Curral das Freiras
The wicker village of Camacha
Pico do Arieiro and Pico Ruivo, Madeira's highest peaks
The thatched village of Santana
The south shore, especially the fishing village of Câmara de Lobos and the clifftop views from Cabo Girão
The rugged north shore
The drive around the western tip of Madeira
The high plateau of Paúl da Serra
The island of Porto Santo (for those who demand nothing more than a sandy beach to snooze upon)

Given the big-city gridlock of contemporary Funchal, not to mention the extraordinary complexity of the postage-stamp farms, vineyards, and irrigation ditches (*levadas*) hacked into Madeira's near-vertical slopes, it seems impossible that this island was uninhabited when Prince Henry's navigators claimed it in the 15th century. But the colonists sent to settle it and Porto Santo began with a blank canvas.

Prince Henry wasted no time developing the islands, especially water- and soil-rich Madeira. It's said that in their haste to clear the land the colonists set fire to the forests, which then smoldered for seven years. It may be so. At any rate, a rich ash was laid down in which cuttings of the Malvasia grape, imported from Crete, and shoots of Sicilian sugarcane quickly took root.

Within decades Madeira sugar and wine were both turning a profit. Just 30 years after Madeira was discovered, the Venetian explorer Cadamosto remarked on the quality of the island wine. And not so very much later Shakespeare mentioned it in *Henry IV, Part I*: "Jack," Poins asks Falstaff in act I, scene two, "how agrees the devil and thee about thy soul that thou soldest to him on Good Friday last for a cup of Madeira and a cold capon's leg?"

Both industries thrive today, but tourism is the big money machine. This isn't, as you might think, a jet-age phenomenon. Quite the contrary. Island tourism began more than 200 years ago, when fragile British ladies were sent down to winter in Madeira's sunny climes. At about the same time the British navy discovered that this palmy Atlantic island was a perfect spot for R & R and routinely put its sailors ashore here after months at sea.

In addition, Britons homeward bound from Africa or India believed that nothing could reacclimatize them to the cold, raw winters of home, even prevent consumption, like a few weeks on Madeira, so they began to break their journeys here. Some of them never left, which explains why you see so many blond, blue-eyed Madeirans.

A number of Scots and Englishmen, deciding that there were fortunes to be made in Madeira, relocated here, and to this day their descendants control much of the local hotel, shipping, bunkering, wine, and embroidery businesses. A little-known fact: Portugal very nearly handed Madeira over to England in 1661 as part of the marriage agreement between Catherine of Bragança and Charles II, but decided to hold back and play its trump card only if England demanded more in the way of a dowry from the Portuguese princess. England didn't (Catherine's dowry was the richest ever: 2 million cruzados, plus Bombay and Tangier), and so the Madeira islands remain Portuguese to this day, an autonomous entity with representation in the national parliament.

Even 200 years ago it didn't take long for word of Madeira's healthful climate to spread, and soon many of Europe's noble families, its princes of finance, even a few of its crowned heads, began building expensive *quintas* (estates) in and around Funchal. For a while during the 19th and early 20th centuries, Madeira was a watering hole every bit as fashionable as Baden-Baden and the French Riviera.

The island's place in the sun lasted longer than that of most stylish resorts, mainly because it was too difficult—and expensive—for Everyman to reach. But by the 1960s, when engineers finally managed to hack a landing strip into the side of a mountain on the eastern end of Madeira, the gilded set had already defected to exotic new dots on the map.

As might be expected, the winter-weary of Europe now whizzing down to Madeira aboard 727s and 737s from Lisbon—and charters from elsewhere—are more hip and less stuffy than their predecessors. But it's the island's 12-months-of-June climate that they seek, just as their forerunners did. They find it, as visitors always have, at Funchal, on the sheltered south shore, which is spared most of the "weather" blustering in from the north.

How much time should you allow Madeira? It all depends on your interests and, to some degree, your budget, because Madeira costs more than the rest of Portugal (except maybe for the resort complexes in the Algarve). In the old days visitors settled in for the winter. Even today winter remains the high season, from a social standpoint at least. You'll find it difficult to obtain rooms in Funchal during the Christmas/ New Year's and Easter holidays, because the "regulars" book months ahead of time, often reserving the same quarters year after year. But the weather changes little, so it really doesn't matter what time of year you come, although it's apt to rain around the spring and fall equinoxes.

Most travellers today spend about a week on Madeira, or maybe split a week between Madeira and Porto Santo. There's no question that a week will give you plenty of time to sunbathe, to "do" Funchal, and to see most of the rest of the island as well. However, although you may think that you can just whiz around an island that measures only 36 miles long and 14 miles wide, it's not so. On these narrow, twisting blacktops you can scarcely average 20 miles an hour. Nor would you want to drive any faster, because children and animals are forever popping onto the highway unannounced.

If you have nerves of steel and no trace of vertigo, the best way to see Madeira is by rental car. But if you're faint of heart you'll be better off in a car with driver (every hotel concierge is plugged into the network of local cab drivers who hire out for the day) or aboard one of the many island tour buses. These behemoths slam around the mountains with terrifying speed, ricocheting passengers from side to side, so be sure to keep Dramamine handy.

Every tour of Madeira should begin in the capital city of Funchal, which resembles nothing so much as a scaled-down Rio. It too sprawls around a crescent harbor and climbs a great green amphitheater of mountains at its back. Mini-Rio or no, Funchal is nonetheless a proper city with a population of about 120,000. Its sidewalks, like those of Rio, are worked out in intricate mosaics of black and white.

Your first Funchal stop should be the Turismo (Tourist Office) at avenida Arriaga, 18, the jacaranda-canopied main street. Here you can pick up free city and island maps, brochures, and details about all island excursions, including hikes along Madeira's mountaintop *levadas* (irrigation ditches). This office, by the way, may be the most efficient and helpful in all of Portugal. Its staff is large, English speaking, and knows Madeira and Porto Santo in detail.

Madeira Wines

Then step directly next door to the **Madeira Wine Company** (avenida Arriaga, 28), housed—or at least partly so—in a 16th-century Franciscan monastery. Many wineries today are all steel pipes, tanks, and ducts, but not this one. It's what you expect a winery to be: massive wooden beams strung with cobwebs, cool stone floors, and oaken vats of wine aging in a sort of perpetual twilight. In the old days you could just wander about the São Francisco wine lodges, but today the operation is far more organized. There are two well-thought-out tours with English-speaking guides offered on weekdays (at 10:30 A.M. and 3:30 P.M.). To join one, you need only show up at the reception area.

The São Francisco lodges aren't where the bulk of the Madeira Wine Company's wines are produced. Most of them, and this includes such well-known labels as Blandy's, Cossarts, Miles, Leacock's, and Welsh, are made in modern plants elsewhere around town. The São Francisco lodges are mostly for show, a place to introduce visitors to the four basic types of Madeira wine: pale dry Sercial; nutty, semidry Verdelho; sweet and mellow Bual; and the dessert-rich Malmsey (an Anglicization of Malvasia)—in a butt of which George, duke of Clarence (the brother of Edward IV and Richard III), was drowned in 1478 in the Tower of London. Or so the popular English schoolboy tale goes.

The Madeira wine industry, as we've already said, began shortly after Prince Henry the Navigator's colonists arrived on the island. But the wines didn't develop their complexity, their depth of character, their finesse until a couple of centuries later, and even then quite by accident. It seems that British schooners bound for the New World routinely called at Madeira to provision and, while there, took aboard casks of island wine (fortified with brandy to stop fermentation). The ships then proceeded to America, following the favorable trade winds through the South Atlantic and Caribbean, where the sun was so hot it melted the pitch in the ship's planking and, quite literally, cooked the wines. But instead of being ruined, the wines actually improved. They emerged from their steamy voyage smoother, richer, nobler than identical wines that had never left the island. And they aged better, too.

For a time, island wines were sent as ballast aboard ships to India just so that they would develop the longevity and slightly "burnt" taste that connoisseurs had come to expect of fine Madeiras. Today the tropical journeys are all simulated at the wineries. The wines are gradually heated in a process known as *estufagem* to temperatures as high as 49 degrees Celsius (120 degrees Fahrenheit). But the result is the same. This complicated process is explained as you tour the São Francisco lodges, as is the *solera* system, the topping off of older wines with carefully chosen newer vintages, which not only improves the quality of the wines but also ensures uniformity. Like most winery tours, this one ends in the tasting room, where you can sample—and buy—a variety of Madeiras.

Few places are easier to tour than Madeira, first, because Funchal is so compact and, second, because you can make easy day trips out of town, looping in a different direction each day. Although there are some points of historical interest, what makes Madeira special are its emerald-in-the-rough beauty; its equator-to-England botanical diversity; and its wine, wicker, and embroidery industries. It's a rich menu and you can pick and choose at leisure, alternating days in town with days in the country.

At the outset, you should spend a few days in Funchal relaxing, orienting yourself, and poking around in the city center. On another day you might head for the hills directly above Funchal to see the Jardim Botânico (Botanical Garden) and the oddity of Curral das Freiras, a hamlet built inside a volcano. You might spend part of another day on top of the island at Pico do Arieiro, catching en route the exotic gardens at Quinta do Palheiro Ferreiro and the wicker town of Camacha, then pressing on to Pico Ruivo, to the thatched village of Santana, or to the wide bay at Machico, where Prince Henry's navigators stepped ashore in 1420. The cliff-hanger, however, is the day-long drive around the western land's end at Porto Moniz. Along the way you can visit the fishing village of Câmara de Lobos, the lofty headland of Cabo Girão, the tumultuous north shore, and the brooding moonscape of Paúl da Serra (a high plateau on the western half of the island). Porto Santo, Madeira's satellite island, deserves another day or two—*if* you seek nothing more than sun, sea, and sand.

Staying on Madeira

Because Madeira is so small, there's no need to plan a complicated itinerary with shifting accommodations. All you need is a comfortable spot where you can lounge in the sun, a home base from which to make leisurely day trips about the island. Not surprisingly, Funchal offers the best choice of hotels, most of which line up on cliffs on the western edge of town. There's the huge, futuristic **Casino Park Hotel** (a trifle seedy at last look; it caters to tour groups), with floor shows and the on-grounds **Casino da Madeira** for those who like to live it up after dark (it was designed by Oscar Niemeyer, whose signature work is the Brazilian capital, Brasília); the smaller, posher **Hotel Savoy** (an architectural extravaganza that's part ancient Greece, part 20th-century Las Vegas); the towering **Madeira Carlton** (formerly the Madeira Sheraton), which, alas, is replacing the island touches that first made the hotel so appealing (beamed ceilings, terra-cotta floors, and roughly plastered white walls hung with local folk art) with bits of glitz and flash (strips of "fairy lights" in the elevators, for example); and the **Madeira Palácio** (opened 21 years ago as the Madeira Hilton). Located on a strip of condos, quick stops, and high-rise apartment blocks about halfway between downtown Funchal and the colorful fishing village of Câmara de Lobos some 9 km (5½ miles) west, this mod hotel with its glass, steel, and marble lobby bordering on high tech originally seemed cold and uninviting, but landscapers have worked miracles and softened the hard edges. The trees, shrubs, and birds of paradise here, so scraggly at first, have grown to jungle lushness and now effectively isolate the Madeira Palácio, its huge free-form pool, tennis courts, and sprawling seaside gardens from the ticky-tackiness of the overbuilt neighborhood. All 230 rooms and 23 junior suites, though shoe-box-shaped, are being completely redecorated in a toned-down scheme of peaches, pinks, maroons, and beige (much more attractive than the former splashy modern motifs). The baths are all new, too. Every room has its own big balcony, approximately half of them overlooking the ocean and the lofty green sea cape of Cabo Girão.

And then there is **Reid's Hotel**, a turn-of-the-century grande dame that reminds you of nothing so much as one of those elegant old Cunarders, somehow run aground—in Eden. Reid's roosts atop its own promontory and is very nearly swallowed up by ten acres of tropical gardens. There are secluded walks and lookouts hidden in this jungle of bougainvillaea, oleander, and hibiscus. Given Reid's elegance, its idyllic setting, and the guarantee of quiet, peace, and privacy, it's scarcely surprising that its guest list reads like a Who's Who. Winston Churchill came here to paint, George Bernard Shaw learned to dance here, the king and queen of Sweden visited recently, and down the years Reid's has welcomed too many kings and queens of the silver screen to count.

To celebrate its centennial in 1991, and, to do so in high style, Reid's closed for three months in the summer of 1990 and underwent massive renovation. Although many of the bedrooms in the Garden Wing were lushly redecorated with fine French fabrics and thick-pile carpets, and other rooms were enlarged into junior suites and gained private patios, the emphasis was on modernizing the public rooms. The once-stodgy main dining room has been spruced up (and lightened up), cozy alcoves have been tacked onto the bar, and the rooftop Grill (rechristened Les Faunes) has been extended out onto the terrace, nearly doubling the number of tables with panoramic views.

Les Faunes is Madeira's most elegant restaurant—no contest. The most glamorous, too, with its crisply contemporary scheme of ocean blue and white and its gallery of prints from Picasso's picaresque *Les Faunes* series. Most of the women diners come sweeping by in long dresses (or at least their cocktail best), the men in white dinner jackets. The mood is decidedly romantic: candles flickering in hurricane lanterns, tables sprigged with nosegays, and a good improvisational pianist, who plays, praised be, unamplified. More important, the food at Les Faunes is expertly prepared and exquisitely presented under the aegis of sous-chef de cuisine Leudiere Fabrice, who honed his skills at the famous Ferme St-Simeon in Honfleur, Normandy. He works in concert with executive chef André Bertron, who has worked at a number of distinguished hotels, most recently in Morocco.

The menu staggers, includes everything from freshly sautéed *foie gras* with vanilla and melon *confit* to roasted lobster with black truffles to *le plat végétarien*. What a long way Reid's has come from its days of bland, boring, British food. Much of the transformation is due to the on-the-ball German general manager, Peter Helmut Späth, who arrived in time to oversee the hotel's recent renovation and whip things back into shape. Reid's has never looked lovelier and its service (with staff to guest ratio of three to two), once again, is perfection.

There is even a new Reid's restaurant *outside* the hotel for those who don't want to get dressed to the nines night after night. Called **Villa Cliff**, it occupies an old villa perched atop the promontory directly west of Reid's; a pebbled walkway connects the restaurant and the hotel. The young chef here, José Acácio Afonseca, is Madeira-born, and the recipes he prepares seven days a week for lunch and dinner are sophisticated renditions of the regional dishes for which Portugal and Madeira are famous: *espada enrolada de vinho e alhos à madeirense* (little rolls of the island scabbard fish braised with garlic in white wine), *costeleta de porco com mel e laranja* (pork chops sauced with honey and orange), and, instead of a chariot load of sunny egg sweets, plenty of tropical island fruits. You can eat indoors or out (on a huge tiled terrace high above the sea). You don't have to stay at Reid's in order to lunch or dine at Les Faunes (Tel: 091-76-30-01) or Villa Cliff (Tel: 091-76-30-25), but you do need to reserve a table, and for one on the terrace you must call several days in advance.

If the five hotels mentioned so far (all five-star luxe), are too rich for your wallet, you'll be pleased to know that there are two pleasant new four-star hotels right on the water that offer every modern amenity (swimming pools, game rooms, restaurants, TV, etc.). One is the high-rising, 215-room **Hotel Baia Azul** about a half mile west of Reid's, a tour-group favorite with small, cheerful (if spartan) rooms, all with cream-colored marble baths and most with balconies. Farther west, beyond the Madeira Palácio, is the **Atlantic Gardens**, which calls itself a resort suite hotel. Built as a condo, this sprawling complex located, unfortunately, beside a Shell Oil tank complex, rents unsold one-bedroom efficiency apartments to overnighters. There are 55 rental units in all, each with a small bedroom, modern bath, and stylishly furnished, oversize kitchen/dining/living area opening onto a big seaside balcony.

If you'd prefer to stay somewhere cozier, you couldn't do

better than the barely finished **Quinta da Bela Vista**, a small five-star *estalagem* (privately run inn) set in lush gardens high above Funchal. In the main house (a 150-year-old mansion owned by Dr. Roberto Monteiro, whose brother runs the Estalagem Senhora de Guia at Guincho near Lisbon), there are four stately suites, some with fireplaces, all filled with family antiques. Then, set well back among the giant palms and jacarandas, there are two modern units designed to complement the old quinta; they bring the total number of rooms to 67. Other pluses: a swimming pool with sun terrace, bar, gym, Jacuzzi, and sauna. And, in the old house, one of Funchal's finest restaurants (some local gourmets rate it second only to Les Faunes at Reid's). Quinta da Bela Vista's affable young maître d'hôtel, Carlos Duarte Aveiro Freitas, earned his stripes at Reid's, as did chef João Fernandes. A graduate of Madeira's hotel school and only 28 years old, Fernandes already knows his way around a kitchen. Although the dining room is Old Madeira at its best (gold draperies, crystal chandeliers, and breakfronts agleam with heirloom silver), the menu is both modern and imaginative: sautéed, pâté-stuffed mushrooms served in a puddle of *beurre blanc,* pork medallions sauced with coriander, and avocado ice cream topped with the deepest, darkest "fudge sludge" imaginable.

Another Old Madeira quinta reborn as an inn (although not nearly so new or posh as the Quinta da Bela Vista) is the 41-room **Albergaria Quinta da Penha de França**, a garden-engulfed house located midway between the Casino Park and Savoy hotels (the rooms in the new wing are the choicest).

If you crave something outside the city and utterly away from it all, there are two little *pousadas* (government-run inns) in the clouds. The newer, and nicer, one is the 18-room **Pousada do Pico do Arieiro**, at the very top of Arieiro, Madeira's second-highest peak (5,939 feet), about a half-hour's drive straight up the mountain above Funchal. The more rustic 12-room **Pousada dos Vinháticos** perches halfway up Serra de Agua in the middle of the island; the views from it are absolutely mesmerizing. The bad news is that you are 39 km (24 miles) west of Funchal—a good hour's drive over hair-raising roads guaranteed to try both your nerves and your skill at the wheel. Under no circumstances should you drive them after dark.

FUNCHAL

You will find Funchal perfect for walking as long as you parallel the sea. Most of the main streets do. But the cross streets climb or drop at alarming angles, and unless you're fit, you'll soon be huffing and puffing.

In addition to Madeira wine, what interests most island visitors are the handicrafts. The best way to get a fix on them is to cross avenida Arriaga from the São Francisco wine lodges and stroll a block west to rua do Conselheiro José Silvestre Ribeiro. A right here and one short downhill block will bring you to the **Casa do Turista** (number 2). Don't be misled by the shop's name; its inventory is strictly top of the line. Inside this old admiral's house you will see the most intricately worked Madeira linens, the most handsome wicker baskets, and the finest tapestries, together with delicate china and crystal from the Portuguese mainland. There's quite a bit of folk art, too (costume dolls, hand-knit woollen helmets like those island farmers wear, fishermen's sweaters). Best of all, the shop will pack and ship anything you buy (not true of many island shops).

You have several options for lunch. You can pause at any of the little sidewalk cafés along the town's main street, **avenida Arriaga** (most are located a couple of blocks east, nearer the cathedral); you could buy some cherimoyas (a green, alligator-skinned tropical fruit the size of an apple with perfumey white flesh), bananas, and passion fruit in front of the big public garden on avenida Arriaga, then find a shady bench and picnic inside this block-square garden where black swans preen, water gardens trickle, and poinsettias as big as oaks bloom right around the calendar with no special consideration for Christmas.

Or you could walk west past the park toward the rotunda at the far end of avenida Arriaga, where a brooding bronze Prince Henry the Navigator sits above the clamor of traffic. Just one block beyond the public garden (and one block before the rotunda), rua dos Aranhas angles right and uphill. And about half a block along it on the right, at number 22, you'll come upon what many locals consider to be Funchal's best restaurant: **O Celeiro**—definitely the sort of place local businesspeople like to keep to themselves. Reservations are advised (Tel: 091-373-22).

You may have to wait to get in even if you've called ahead for a table because there are only two rooms, and an antique gristmill appropriates about half of one of them (the restaurant building was originally a granary). But you will be rewarded with first-rate island cooking: a tomatoey *sopa de peixe* (fish soup) made with *espada,* the delicious though undeniably ugly black scabbard fish that swims in local waters, or maybe a skewer of prawns, mushrooms, and sweet red peppers brought sizzling to table. You can order a *garafa* of the local *tinto* (red) or *branco* (white), but these are usually unpleasantly tannic, and you'll probably be happier with one of the fine table wines from the Portuguese mainland. Every good Madeira restaurant stocks them in abundance.

After lunch, stroll back east along avenida Arriaga past the wine lodges and tourist office to the Sé (Cathedral) looming above you. The cathedral was built at the end of the 15th century, and though it's said to be early Gothic in style with flourishes of the Manueline (an exuberant architectural form introduced by Manuel I that incorporates ropes, knots, spheres, and other nautical motifs to commemorate Portugal's great discoveries), it seems altogether tame compared to the tower of Belém and the Jerónimos monastery near Lisbon. In fact its façade—white stucco edged in brown basalt—is downright dour. But the interior is magnificent, especially the coffered cedar ceiling inlaid with ivory and the rows of lacily carved and gilded 17th-century choir stalls. It's an impressive setting for mass and for the concerts played here every June during the Madeira Music Festival.

From the cathedral it's three short blocks uphill along rua João Tavira to rua do Bispo. Turn right, mosey half a block along this shady street, and you'll find, at number 21 just across the street, the **Museu Diocesano de Arte Sacra**. Like so many Madeira museums, this one occupies an old palace, in this case the bishopric, which dates back to 1600. The collection of religious artifacts within positively glitters. Although some were rescued from village churches threatened by neglect or ruin, the more opulent, and certainly many of the paintings, are 15th- and 16th-century Flemish. There's good reason for this: In the early days, Madeira's most valuable export was sugar, a costly commodity often bartered for works of art. The Flemish were the master artists of the day, and, not so coincidentally, some of the people Prince Henry sent down to help colonize Madeira were Flemish (his sister, Isabel, had married Philip the Good, duke of Burgundy and ruler of Flanders).

Once you leave the museum, step around the corner into the broad, sunstruck **praça do Município** (Municipal Square), a sea of ocean-wave mosaics worked out in marble chips of black and white. It's dizzying to cross, but you should make your way to the west side of the square, if only to slip inside the **Colégio** church (begun in 1569 by the Jesuits but now home to the island's embryo university). This is an ornate church with a richly gilded retable (circa 1660) behind the high altar. That it has survived is a miracle, given the fact that this house of worship became a barracks after the marquês de Pombal banished the Jesuits in 1759 (see the Chronology at the end of the book).

From the Colégio it's a short uphill block or so along rua dos Ferreiros to the venerable **Pereira d'Oliveira wine lodge** at number 107. Compared to the Madeira Wine Company this is a small family operation, but d'Oliveira sells some singularly fine old Madeiras, such as an 1850 Verdelho. This is the place to buy a Madeira bottled in the year of your birth, or perhaps of your marriage, a wine to save and savor during a special celebration.

You might spend what's left of the afternoon walking through the oldest part of town—easy enough to reach from d'Oliveira. Simply return to the Colégio, walk one block east (left) along rua Marquês do Funchal to rua 5 de Outubro, then saunter six blocks downhill to **rua da Alfandega**. A right onto this narrow cobbled street will plunge you into Funchal of old. There are tinsmiths here, recycling oil drums into washbasins and water sprinklers. There are shops and *tascas* (bistros) galore, women pausing to chat with friends, men hanging out in little coffeehouses. It's all very "slice of life."

After six short blocks rua da Alfandega dead-ends into the imposing 16th-century **Palácio de São Lourenço**, a fortress-castle that served as the home of Madeira's military governors. Turn right here onto avenida Zarco and walk past the fort (not open to the public) two steep—but mercifully short—uphill blocks to Funchal's main drag, avenida Arriaga.

Turn left and make your way five blocks west past the rotunda to the swatch of greenery on avenida do Infante directly above the harbor. This is the **Parque de Santa Catarina**, where you'll find the pristine little **Capela de Santa Catarina**. Built in 1425 by Zarco, one of Madeira's discoverers, it is the island's oldest church, but it has been partially rebuilt at least twice, in the late 15th century and again in the 17th, each time so skillfully that it's impossible to tell what's original.

You might end the afternoon in high style by taking a proper English tea on the terrace at **Reid's Hotel**, at estrada

Monumental, 139, on the west end of town, from which there's a dynamite view across Funchal harbor. You don't have to be a hotel guest in order to pause here for tea; don't miss the *bolo de mel* (honey cake) if it's on the tea trolley. Or you could take tea instead at **Quinta Magnólia** across estrada Monumental from Reid's, then 100 yards uphill on rua do Dr. Pita. With its stately trees and tidy lawns, the quinta resembles nothing so much as a British country club, which in fact it was until the old British "regulars" either died off or stopped wintering in Madeira. Today the quinta is home both to an art gallery and to Madeira's hotel school, whose students are carrying on the English tradition of afternoon tea. They also serve lunch Monday through Saturday between 1:00 P.M. and 2:00 P.M. (but no dinner), and the menu changes daily to feature whatever was studied that morning. Quinta Magnólia's dining room is small, so if you'd like to lunch there you'll have to reserve a place; Tel: (091) 76-40-13. The bar, by the way, opens at noon.

Around the Mercado dos Lavradores

Begin another day in Funchal at the **Mercado dos Lavradores** (Workers' Market), near the foot of rua Brigadeiro Oudinot at the eastern end of Funchal. It's open every day except Sunday, but Friday morning is when it's at its busiest and best, so you may want to juggle your schedule in order to visit the market at prime time. With its flower sellers in red capes and full skirts striped in hot colors surrounded by acres of orchids and birds of paradise, with its pyramids of home-grown cabbages, tomatoes, bananas, and custard apples, with its baskets of *espada* and sardines, still streaming seawater, it is a photographer's dream.

Be sure to climb up one flight to the second-floor balcony, where small vendors in from the country sell braids of garlic, strings of *piri-piri* (the incendiary little Angolan red peppers slipped into so many island recipes), and huge orange wedges of winter squash. If you can weave your way through the booths to the railing, you'll be rewarded with a straight-down view of the market melee just below. It's a terrific photo op.

After leaving the market, climb two blocks up rua Brigadeiro Oudinot and cross the bridge over a bougainvillaea-shrouded ravine to the **Instituto do Bordado, Tapeçarias e Artesanato da Madeira** (Embroidery and Tapestry Institute of Madeira), at rua do Visconde de Anadia, 44. One flight up there's a charming little museum full of frothy eyelet-trimmed pinafores and petticoats, silken linens embroidered in stunning detail, and petit-point portraits of Prince Henry the Navigator, Pope Paul, and, of all people, Jacqueline Kennedy Onassis. The stitches are so fine, the shadings so delicate, you'd swear the portraits were done in pastels.

The Madeira embroidery industry was begun some 150 years ago by a young Englishwoman named Elizabeth Phelps, the daughter of Funchal wine shipper Joseph Phelps. She had long admired the needlework of Madeira country women, and in the 1850s, when the dreaded *oidium* blight that had already wiped out many of the vines in Europe began decimating island vineyards and impoverishing hundreds of small farmers, inspiration struck. If Madeira women could be taught to embroider fine linens with the designs beloved by the English, Miss Phelps reasoned, they could surely make enough money to help support their families in this time of crisis.

Working at first with a small group of women, Elizabeth Phelps taught them new stitches, and soon had them embroidering top-quality Irish and Belgian linens. On her next trip to London she showed samples of the Madeira embroidery to British friends, who snapped them up and begged for more. Soon Miss Phelps found a London agent for the Madeira embroideries, and the rest is history.

Even today, although the Institute exercises strict quality controls (only linens hand-embroidered on the island bear the little lead seal of authenticity), Madeira embroidery remains very much a cottage industry. As you drive around the island, you'll see groups of women and girls talking and embroidering—on mountainsides, in doorways, under grape arbors. Usually each works on a single item—a napkin, a tea towel, or a handkerchief—but sometimes a particularly skilled group will combine talents on a large tablecloth.

A block downhill from the Instituto do Bordado, Tapeçarias e Artesanato at **Patrício & Gouveia** (rua do Visconde de Anadia, 34) you can, if you ask, watch linens being stamped with the designs that will be sent out into the countryside to be embroidered, or finished linens being laundered, pressed, and packaged for sale in the company showrooms.

Funchal is chockablock with embroidery shops, but some of them are choicer than others. Patrício & Gouveia has a broad inventory of delicate table linens, many with intricate open work. If needlework is of particular interest, however, you should also visit two other top shops, each about a five-minute walk from Patrício & Gouveia. For tablecloths, placemats, tea towels, and handkerchiefs embroidered and appliquéd in bright colors, or gossamer white-on-white "shadow prints," stroll over to **Imperial de Bordados** at rua de São Pedro, 26, near the Colégio (ask to see the stunning tablecloth they made for Princess Grace of Monaco). For daintily embroidered pastel blouses and lingerie, simply walk downhill to the Sé and to **Teixeiras**, located directly across the street from it at rua do Aljube, 15.

The Quinta das Cruzes Area

Afterward, grab a bite at a sidewalk café (there's no shortage of them around the cathedral), then taxi up to **Museu das Cruzes**, at calçada do Pico, 1, about half a kilometer straight up from the public garden on avenida Arriaga. (You can walk, but it's a tortuous climb.) Most guidebooks tell you that this old quinta was the home of Madeira's discoverer, João Gonçalves Zarco, and that it was built in the 15th century. Well, most guidebooks are wrong. Zarco did build a home here, but the house you see today is 18th century. No matter: The reason you come to this quinta is not so much the house as the orchid greenhouses out back, the archaeological shards strewn about the grounds, which come down to us from the island's earliest settlers, and most of all the exhibits of 17th- to 19th-century Euro-Asian porcelains, paintings, and furnishings inside. It's an impressive collection, all gathered from island homes and churches, and it proves how sophisticated life was in this Portuguese colony two and even three centuries ago.

Zarco lies buried in the little tiled chapel of the 17th-century **Convento de Santa Clara**, directly next door to the Museu das Cruzes. Like so many island churches today, it's kept locked, so you'll have to ring the bell to get in. For a small contribution one of the nuns will put down her embroidery and show you through.

Just a block below the convent you'll find Madeira's newest museum, **Casa Museu Frederico de Freitas**. Opened only in 1987, the museum is housed in an 18th-century mansion that was the home of the prominent Funchal barrister for whom it is named. There is a new, double-height front gallery devoted to rotating exhibits (the island watercolors and etchings hung for the grand opening are still there, which prompted one local wit to call it "the permanent temporary show"), then, in the house itself, 12 showplace rooms of furniture, paintings, and artifacts, left exactly the way Dr. de Freitas arranged them. Still to come, a new wing to showcase his rare collection of *azulejos* (decorative tiles).

From the museum you can stroll down to the public garden on avenida Arriaga, about five blocks below, then make your way back to your hotel, either on foot or by taxi (there's a cab stand in front of the garden).

Dining in Funchal

For dinner, there is no shortage of choices in Funchal, but in each case you should call ahead for reservations. You might, for example, doll up and go to the **Quinta da Bela Vista** (Tel: 091-76-41-44) or to one of Reid's restaurants: **Villa Cliff** (Tel: 091-76-30-25) or **Les Faunes**, a rooftop restaurant with wrap-around windows, fabulous views of Funchal harbor, and classic French cuisine; Tel: (091) 76-30-01 (see Staying on Madeira, above). Or you might head for **Casa dos Reis** at rua da Penha de França, 6, just two blocks from the Casino Park Hotel and almost directly across the street from the Albergaria Quinta da Penha de França. The cozy upstairs-downstairs restaurant, all snowy linens and gleaming crystal, serves a mix of French, East Indian, and Portuguese special-ties: lobster crêpes, shrimp curry, or a real Madeira fish muddle made with plenty of garlic, tomatoes, and whatever the fishermen's nets have fetched up. Tel: (091) 251-82.

You might opt, instead, for the pretty, year-old, upstairs-downstairs **Restaurante Dona Amélia** (Tel: 091-257-84) a few steps away at rua Imperatriz Dona Amélia, 83, (all greens and creams with cascading ferns, terra-cotta floors, and wrap-around windows) that's already earned a reputation for its garlicky *gambas* (langoustines) and refined *espetadas* (shish kebabs Madeira-style). Dona Amélia's are juicily pink and meltingly tender because they're made of *filet mignon;* they come to table on chunky little skewers whittled out of bay laurel.

Or you might head for Dona Amélia's older, equally lovely sister restaurant, the ever-popular **Casa Velha** just down the block at rua Imperatriz Dona Amélia, 69, on the second floor of an old town house directly next door to the Casino Park Hotel. Artful still lifes of local fish, fruits, and vegetables greet you as you enter the main dining room (floors of terra-cotta, walls painted the color of country cream, a ceiling planked in brown wood). There's plenty of table-hopping here among both tourists and townsfolk, as well as in the airier glass-walled "greenhouse" just beyond, overlooking a small grove of banana and papaya trees. (Don't be surprised if you see the chef stroll into the grove, mid-meal, to hack off some ripe fruit for a dessert he's preparing. Talk about fresh!) Madeira classics are the specialty at Casa Velha, especially that ubiquitous black *espada* (scabbard fish), which might be churned into a silky mousse or flambéed with Madeira or Champagne. (Black of skin, snakelike of body, and fearsome of tooth, *espada* is blessed with surprisingly delicate, lean white flesh.) There are steaks galore, too, prepared half a dozen different ways. Tel: (091) 257-49. As for dessert, this restaurant, like many others in Funchal, is abandoning the artery-clogging island egg sweets in favor of lighter fruit salads and puddings.

The **Casino da Madeira**, a futuristic round building on the grounds of the Casino Park Hotel, is less than a five-minute walk from Casa Velha, Dona Amélia, or Casa dos Reis, so this might be the night to try your luck at roulette, blackjack, or the newest rage, bingo.

Another of Funchal's first-rate restaurants, **Solar do F**, at avenida Luís de Camões, 19, is only a few blocks from Reid's, the Savoy, the Madeira Carlton, and Casino Park hotels, and the Albergaria Quinta da Penha de França, so it makes a convenient choice for dinner (no lunch served). Because this old quinta is an indoor-outdoor restaurant, at least in warm weather, it's possible to dine either under the stars or in one of its elegant but understated rooms (a particular favorite is the former wine cellar, with ceilings barrel-vaulted in stone). Seafood's the main thing here, as befits an island restaurant, and much of it is grilled over open coals and brought sizzling to table. A house specialty to look for is the skewer of giant prawns and *espada,* green pepper, and tomato, a supremely succulent marine shish kebab. Tel: (091) 202-12.

You might do as the locals do and go down to **Caravela**, a casual harbor-view restaurant atop an office building at avenida do Mar, 15, that is famous for its ocean-fresh seafood. Tel: (091) 284-64 or 254-71. Or you might taxi to the old fishermen's quarter at the eastern end of the harbor to dine at **Romana**, an atmospheric spot at largo Corpo Santo, 15, with dark beamed ceilings and rough plaster walls hung with hand-painted plates. There are two menus at Romana, one French and one Portuguese; the Portuguese is the one to insist upon, because it offers such Madeira specialties as *carne de vinho e albos* (braised chunks of pork marinated with crisp white wine and garlic). Avoid the house dessert, a perfumy, stiffly set passion-fruit pudding, which one wit has dubbed "the Portuguese Jell-O." Tel: (091) 289-56.

Another dinner might be at a *restaurante típico* (folk restaurant) in the hills above town. **A Seta**, at estrada do Livramento, 80, is the best choice. It's too far to walk and too confusing a route to drive, so you should hire a taxi for the evening (not expensive). Then settle in for a hearty dinner of *espetada* (charcoal-grilled skewers of beef aromatic of garlic and bay leaves) and *bolo de caco* (chewy rounds of yeast bread baked on top of the stove on lava stones) accompanied by island-grown potatoes, yams, beans, and carrots fatter and sweeter than those produced anywhere else. But food is only one of A Seta's attractions. You'll be serenaded as you dine by *fado,* mournful ballads belted out here by a young *fadista* enveloped, like every proper female *fado* singer, in a voluminous black shawl. And when she takes her break, you'll be entertained by folk dancers in bright regional costume. It's all a bit touristy, true, but lots of fun. Tel: (091) 74-36-43 or 74-36-31.

If you're feeling ambitious, you might even drive 9 km (5½ miles) west of Funchal to the town of Câmara de Lobos to watch the sun set behind Cabo Girão from the second-floor dining terrace of **Coral**, a lively bar-restaurant located on a little waterfront square called largo da República. Its chef can prepare *espada* at least half a dozen different ways, all of them delicious. The special dessert here is a fresh banana pudding, but it isn't much better than Romana's passion-fruit number. Besides, it languishes all day on the unrefrigerated pastry wagon. Tel: (091) 94-24-69.

The Hills above Funchal

Madeira's luxuriant **Jardim Botânico** in the hills above Funchal is no more than a 15-minute drive from the city center up to the **Quinta do Bom Sucesso**, until 1936 the home of the Reid family (of Reid's Hotel). The house itself is now a little natural history museum with drawers of pressed flowers and cases of stuffed birds. The grounds were turned into a botanical garden and horticultural laboratory and opened to the public in 1960. With its flower beds and hothouses stair-stepping 450 feet up the side of a mountain and its near-aerial views of Funchal, Bom Sucesso is breathtaking. There are great blocks of color everywhere, so the effect is of an outsized, living Mondrian: hot red squares of salvia, bright yellow rectangles of ginger lily, intense blue ribbons of hydrangea. There are magnolias, too, and fern trees, even umbrella pines under which you can enjoy a simple lunch.

If you don't dawdle at the garden you'll have time to return to Funchal, head west out of town along avenida do Infante (route 101), then, just as you approach Reid's Hotel, turn right onto rua do Dr. Pita (route 105) and climb a couple of kilometers uphill past Quinta Magnólia to the stark black-and-white **Igreja de São Martinho**, which crowns a lonely pinnacle and is visible for miles.

Your destination is one of Madeira's curiosities, the village of **Curral das Freiras**, built inside the crater of an extinct volcano. The round trip will take you two hours because this is another daredevil drive. Once you reach São Martinho, edge right along route 105, and twist for a kilometer or so through the upper fringes of Funchal to **Pico dos Barcelos** (pause here long enough to enjoy the gull's-eye view of town).

Less than 2 km (1¼ miles) ahead, the road forks; turn left onto route 203 and follow it 12 km (7½ miles) to **Eira do Serrado**, the lookout at the top of the crater. Soon houses and vineyards give way to cool glades of eucalyptus, then clouds of hydrangeas, then deep pine woods.

You should reach the rim of the crater, 3,318 feet up, just as shafts of late-afternoon sun spill over it onto the houses far below, sprinkled up and down near-perpendicular slopes like white flower petals. According to the story all Madeira schoolchildren learn, the nuns from the Santa Clara convent in Funchal fled to this secret valley in the 16th century to escape the pirates pillaging the city (*curral das freiras* means "corral of the nuns"). In time, a tiny settlement developed here, but it was completely cut off. Not until 1959 was a road built down into the crater linking this little community with the outside world. Before then the only way in and out was by foot (or donkey) along a tortuous route. Although only 15 km (9 miles) from Funchal, Curral das Freiras is still more isolated than many towns on Madeira's remote western tip. It didn't get television until the mid-1980s.

When you're ready to return to Funchal, simply go back the way you came.

TO THE TOP OF THE ISLAND

A leisurely day's tour in the heights above Funchal might include a visit to Quinta do Palheiro Ferreiro, one of the island's dreamy gardens (by the end of 1993, part of this vast estate will be transformed into a par-71, 18-hole golf course, and within a few more years 150 villas and 70 condos will be scattered around the links). This outing might also include a pause at the wicker town of Camacha, and lunch 5,939 feet up at the very top of Pico do Arieiro, Madeira's second-highest mountain. (At 6,104 feet, Pico Ruivo is the loftiest, and it's clearly visible to the north from Pico do Arieiro.)

The route out of town is altogether confusing, because street names and highway numbers change often. The best plan is to ask your hotel concierge to mark your map, routing you through town the easiest way, then up into the hills to **Quinta do Palheiro Ferreiro**. It's only 8 km (5 miles) northeast of Funchal, but given city traffic it may take you half an hour to reach it. These gardens belong to the Blandy family, who also own Reid's Hotel and one of the major wine houses; the gardens are closed on Saturdays and Sundays.

The house at this estate is surprisingly modest, but the gardens are ravishing. They showcase hundreds of botanical exotics from around the world that coexist happily with Madeira's own spiky dragon trees and stately mahoganies. As you stroll the formal and informal gardens, passing arbors, reflecting pools, and pavilions, you'll see South African proteas, Japanese loquats, Mexican blood lilies, and New Zealand fern trees. The gardens were laid out by a French landscape architect in the 18th century for the first conde de Carvalhal. The Blandys bought the estate in 1884, and it was Mildred Blandy, the mother of today's owner, who began importing flowering trees, shrubs, and plants. Something blooms here nearly every day of the year. You're free to roam the gardens at your leisure; the house, however, is off limits. (Though Adam Blandy is building an 18-hole golf course and condo complex at Quinta do Palheiro Ferreiro, the gardens will remain intact.)

Camacha

On leaving the quinta, go right on the district road, which within a few miles dead-ends into route 102. Turn right again for a 4-km (2½-mile) run through misty woodlands to Camacha, headquarters of Madeira's wicker industry. This business was also introduced by the English, in this case by William Hinton and James Taylor. In Victorian times many wealthy British families built summer houses in the cool mountain village of Camacha and filled them with Italian wicker. Seeing all the willow and cane growing in the area, Hinton and Taylor decided to teach villagers to make the wicker furniture so popular in other parts of Europe. They could undercut the Italian prices and make a bundle. Quite so, and the business continues to boom today.

Most of the wickerwork is done behind closed doors in and

around Camacha, but if you visit in late spring you'll encounter whole families out on the slopes peeling willow shoots, which have been boiled in a tar bath to loosen the bark. You will also see osiers and young stalks of cane propped against fences everywhere, drying in the open air, masses of straw spread on rooftops under the down-pouring sun, and men loading bundles of each onto flatbed trucks for distribution to the weavers, most of whom freelance out of their own homes just as the embroiderers do. By fall everything will have been woven into chairs and baskets, which will be stacked up along miles of highway, awaiting pickup.

The best place at Camacha to see men weave osiers into baskets and cane into tables and chairs is in the basement of **Café Relógio**, a great barn of a shop facing the broad town square. Its inventory simply staggers: baskets and hampers of every conceivable size and shape, dog and cat beds, trunks and foot lockers, whole sets of porch furniture, all piled to the rafters.

Although Café Relógio is, as its name suggests, a restaurant as well as a shop, you'll fare much better if you push on to the new Pousada do Pico do Arieiro, less than half an hour away. To reach it, follow route 102 north out of Camacha, lined now by banks of hydrangeas and thickets of watercress. After a squiggly 8 km (5 miles), make a sharp left onto route 202, the road to Poiso and Pico do Arieiro, 15 km (9 miles) straight ahead (as straight, that is, as any Madeira road is likely to be).

The road climbs quickly, leaving behind foggy groves of pine and eucalyptus and soaring into the clouds. Soon you're on top of a great fleecy field pierced here and there by savage crags. You might be in an airplane. Animals range free on these hardscrabble heights, so you must watch for the occasional sheep and hog. There are even wild ponies scavenging about up here, although few people are lucky enough to glimpse them.

You couldn't pick a more panoramic spot for lunch than the **Pousada do Pico do Arieiro**. Or a better country restaurant. You can feast here on such Madeira specialties as fresh watercress soup, pork loin stuffed with garlicky sausage, even roast suckling pig. The pousada's architect has given the place the rustic look of a hunting lodge, then wrapped the lounge/bar/dining room—one vast sweep of space— with glass so that you won't miss any of the ever-changing roof-of-the-world drama just outside. A word of caution: The pousada manager is overworked and surly much of the time, and, depending upon his mood of the moment, he may refuse to seat you in the pousada dining room and direct you to the huge restaurant next door that caters to tour-bus groups. If you are firm, he will sometimes back down. His logic is that only pousada guests should dine at the pousada, so most lunches the place is empty.

After lunch, how you spend the rest of the day will depend upon your particular interests. First and foremost, however, you must climb 150 feet or so up to the lookout at the very peak of **Pico do Arieiro**. On a clear, cloudless day you can see **Pico Ruivo**, the granddaddy of them all, in full splendor to the north, and even the island of Porto Santo some 25 miles northeast. There's a well-marked trail leading from Pico do Arieiro to Pico Ruivo that crests Madeira's mountainous spine most of the way. It's three miles each way, not overly arduous; if you don't tarry, the round trip will take you about four hours—time enough to make it back to town before nightfall if you set out by 1:30 or 2:00 P.M. The hike is option number one, because it will lead you deep into Madeira's unspoiled interior as no highway can.

Santana

Option number two is to roller-coaster by car over to the thatched village of Santana on the precipitous north shore. You've only to retrace your steps from Pico do Arieiro to Poiso, then turn left onto route 103 and snake past Ribeiro Frio (there's a government trout hatchery in this valley) and São Roque do Faial to Degolada, where 103 dead-ends into route 101. A left turn onto this two-lane blacktop will send you careening along the cliffs to the village of Faial, then Santana. This sounds like a long drive, but in fact it shouldn't take even an hour. The total distance from Pico do Arieiro to Santana is barely 38 km (24 miles).

What's unusual about Santana are its brightly painted, thatched A-frames. "Munchkin houses," someone once called them, and there's no denying that they'd be quite at home in *The Wizard of Oz*. Giant nonheading cabbages grow in the yards of these fairy-tale houses, framed with sunny spills of nasturtium. Children, puppies, and kittens all tumble about the flower beds, and women sit in doorways embroidering linens that will one day cover dining tables thousands of miles away.

These cheerful thatched houses are unique to Santana, but no one can say when—or why—they were first built. Probably some clever Santanan figured that if the thatched triangular huts used to shelter livestock worked so well, then a larger version would do nicely for his family. It would be sturdy and furnish good protection from the wind and rain that blew down from the North Atlantic as well as provide a snug haven from the fog that so often hovered over Santana.

As for the houses' gaily striped façades, who knows? Madeirans do love color, as a glance at any home garden quickly proves. So very likely some inventive woman (it is the wife and mother who keeps the house freshly painted) decided to brighten the front of her house (and perhaps the sometimes gloomy north-shore days) with the primary colors she loved. Then friends and neighbors simply followed her lead. They are also, alas, now playing follow-the-leader when it comes to replacing the thatched roofs with corrugated tin and plastic.

Santana is just the place to poke around, trying first one side road, then another. You never know what lies around the next bend, but you can be certain it will be something trapped in an earlier time warp. Some of Santana's prettiest A-frames line the road that shoots downhill toward the sea, directly opposite the uphill turn to Pico Ruivo—a sharp right in the center of town.

To return to Funchal, you have only to double back to Poiso, then proceed straight ahead via route 103, winding down into town. The total distance is about 40 km (25 miles), and the return trip shouldn't take you more than 1 to 1½ hours.

Machico

Option number three would be to drive from Pico do Arieiro past Poiso to the intersection of 102, then, instead of turning south toward Camacha, bear north (left) and zigzag past Santo da Serra to Portela. A right turn here onto route 101 will bring you twisting and turning down the island's steep eastern flank to the little seaside village of Machico. This is not a lengthy drive—about 30 km (19 miles) in all— but you'd better allow at least three-quarters of an hour to negotiate all the hairpin turns.

It's at Santo da Serra that island developers are turning the old nine-hole hilltop course where Victorians used to duff about into a state-of-the-art golf center. Nine new holes were opened in October 1991, making the **Campo de Golfe da Madeira** 6,200 yards long and a par 72. There's a new clubhouse, too, with pro shop, snack bar, and restaurant. By the summer of 1993 nine more holes will be added, bringing the total to 27. In the words of its promoters, this new Madeira course will be "the most spectacular in Europe and one of the most exciting in the world." Still to come at Santo da Serra: a 150-room, five-star, luxury hotel overlooking the links, complete with health center, sauna, swimming pool, tennis courts, and riding stables.

Machico is where Prince Henry's navigators first came ashore in 1420, and where, legend has it, they found evidence of an earlier visitor. When Zarco and Teixeira beached their boat on Machico's gray gravel strand, the story goes, they found a crude wooden cross with a Latin inscription, which one of them translated: "Here came Machim, an Englishman, driven by the tempest, and here lies buried Anna d'Arfet, a woman who was with him."

The navigators had heard the story of Robert Machim, as had most of 15th-century Europe. But the tale of the star-crossed lovers had been just that—a tale. It seems that Machim, rather than marry the woman of high birth chosen for him, eloped aboard a ship bound for Spain with his true love, Anna d'Arfet. The ship was caught in a ferocious storm and blown far off course, and when land was at long last sighted the lovers begged to be put ashore. They were, at what is now Machico. Anna died a few days later, and, although ill and weak, Machim managed to give her a proper burial. He himself died shortly thereafter. This all happened about 75 years before the arrival of the Portuguese navigators. Or so it's said.

Today tourism is overtaking the little town of Machico. Pleasure boats mingle in the bay with fishing smacks, and tennis courts are encroaching on the shore. It's a pretty enough town, with broad streets and squares shaded by plane trees, and it boasts two churches worth a peek. First there's the **Capela dos Milagres** (Chapel of the Miracles) on the left, or north, bank of the river that bisects the village. Tristão Vaz Teixeira, whom Prince Henry had appointed governor of the Machico region (Zarco got Funchal), had the little church built early in the 15th century. It was destroyed by a flood in the early 19th century and had to be rebuilt. The second church, the 15th-century **Nossa Senhora da Conceição**, stands in the middle of town on a little square shaded by sycamores. Its distinguishing feature is the fancy portal donated by Manuel I, for whom Manueline architecture is named.

The return to Funchal is easy—you just follow the coast road (route 101) south past the airport at **Santa Cruz**, then continue on into town via the airport road. The drive will take you less than a half hour, because this is Madeira's best highway. In the last year alone, two high-flying bridges have replaced twists and turns through two deep gorges and trimmed 20 minutes from the airport–Funchal run. Time permitting, pause at Santa Cruz to see the mostly Gothic 16th-century church, one of the biggest and most architecturally impressive outside of Funchal—odd for a town that is no more than a dot on the map, and no one can explain just why it is here.

AROUND THE WESTERN TIP OF MADEIRA

Save this trip for a day when the sun is shining on the north side of the island—and check the weather report to make sure. You can't judge what's happening on the other side of Madeira by local weather because in Funchal's microclimate, the sun is almost always visible. On this day-long excursion you will hurdle Madeira's mountainous spine to explore the little-developed north shore, the steep slopes of which plummet into pounding surf past beaches so small they look like fingernail parings. Then you will move west along this inhospitable coast to land's end at Porto Moniz. The total distance is less than 160 km (100 miles), so depending upon how often you stop to "ooh" and "aah" you will be back in plenty of time for dinner. But you must set out by 8:00 A.M.

Leave Funchal via route 101 (avenida do Infante), passing hotel and condo row on the way west and continuing some 9 km (5½ miles) through banana plantations and vineyards en route to the aquatint fishing village of **Câmara de Lobos** (home of the restaurant Coral; see Dining in Funchal). Winston Churchill used to set up his easel on a little knoll above the horseshoe of black lava that cups the town. It was a good vantage point from which he could look down upon dozens of red, blue, and yellow boats careened on the shingle beach, brown fishing nets strung up like butterfly wings to dry, and squat, square white houses roofed in red tile that cling to the cliffs of Câmara de Lobos as if magnetized.

Things haven't changed much since Churchill's day. Toddlers still go skinny-dipping in the surf, older youths continue to dig for clams beneath boulders veloured with algae. And fishermen bring in boatloads of *espada,* the local catch that dominates island menus everywhere. There are even racks of cod drying in the sun and well on their way to becoming *bacalhau,* the dried salt cod beloved by every Portuguese.

The only recent development at Câmara de Lobos is the gaggle of children begging for escudos. They are hard to resist, especially when you look beyond the picture-postcard façade of this little town and see the primitive conditions in which many of them live. A policy that usually works is to hand the oldest child a 50-escudo coin, indicating that he is to share it with all of his friends. This generally sends the children scurrying off to make change. You can also refuse them with a stern "No," or, better yet, an emphatic German *"Nein,"* but you may feel like Scrooge for the rest of the day.

When you've seen as much of Câmara de Lobos as you like, continue west to Cabo Girão, which looms some 9 km (5½ miles) straight ahead. The scraggly vineyards you pass are said to be Madeira's best, and it seems miraculous that their grapes are juicy and sugary enough to produce any wine, let alone the noble Madeiras. You will see scraps of vineyard all along the south shore, demonstrating what a cottage industry wine making is on this island.

Cabo Girão, Europe's second-highest sea cape (after Norway's North Cape), rises 1,933 feet straight out of a roiling sea. As you stand at the little stone-walled lookout at its brink you'll be astounded to see, far below, postage-stamp gardens wrested from this almost perpendicular headland. You can't help wondering how on earth they are tended and watered. Punishing work, to say the least.

The view from the cape simply dazzles. To the left you can see Funchal, sparkling in the sun, and beyond it all the way to the eastern end of the island. Ahead to the south there's nothing but open ocean, and to the right more precipitous cliffs, matted with prickly pear and stalks of aloe. Never mind the little lizards darting here and there—they are completely harmless—but if you leave your purse or camera bag open, don't be surprised to discover that one of them has crawled inside.

Your climb toward the north shore begins at Ribeira Brava, some 13 km (8 miles) farther along, although it may well take you half an hour to reach it, because the highway switches back down the western flank of Cabo Girão at a pitch so steep you'll have to shift into second gear, maybe even first, to spare your brakes. You'll soon find yourself driving the Madeira way, honking just before each new curve to alert anyone just around it that a car is coming—a good policy.

Once in Ribeira Brava, cross the gravelly riverbed that cleaves this little town and turn right onto route 104. From here to São Vicente on the north shore it's 26 km (16 miles) and flat, at first, as the blacktop parallels the river. But soon you wind up, up, up past the little **Pousada dos Vinháticos** and into the puffy clouds that always seem to obscure Encumeada pass, then unwind on the downhill run to the north shore, plunging from misty groves of mahogany and mimosa to green slopes so tightly terraced that cows must be confined in *palheiros* (thatched huts) lest they gobble up precious crops or, worse, fall off the mountain.

The next 18 km (11 miles) are guaranteed to test both your driving ability and your cool, for the highway (route 101) is nothing more than a shelf hacked into bedrock. It lurches along high above the surf on its way to **Porto Moniz**, splashing through waterfalls and swooshing in and out of tunnels. Much of the way the road is scarcely one lane wide, so if a tour bus should come barreling around a bend toward you, either you or it will have to back up to the nearest lay-by to let the other pass. This is not a drive for the meek or the acrophobic.

By the time you reach the Porto Moniz area it will be noon, or maybe later. At any rate, it will be time to break for lunch. Old Madeira hands prefer to lunch at Seixal, the town directly before Porto Moniz. **Aquário** is their favorite restaurant in these parts; according to one Funchal hotelier, it serves the best grilled fresh tuna on the island. In Porto Moniz itself, you have two respectable, if not outstanding, restaurants from which to choose. They roost almost side by side on low lava cliffs overlooking this hamlet's main attraction: natural saltwater swimming pools. These are giant caldrons in a black lava flow solidified eons ago during Madeira's formative stages. Both restaurants, **Cachalote** and **Orca**, cater to tourbus groups, so the best plan is to pick whichever one looks emptier. Nondescript, modern eateries with glass windows gazing seaward, both are clean and efficient, and you won't go wrong at either ordering anything that swims.

The next leg of the tour will bring you across a high, barren moor of brutal beauty called **Paúl da Serra**. To reach it, take route 101 west out of Porto Moniz, although, in truth, the road hairpins skyward. After about 8 km (5 miles) a blacktop angles off to the left (route 204), and that's the road you want. The highway, at long last straight, runs for 22 km (14 miles) along Madeira's spine, where half-wild sheep graze amid bits of stubble.

This year, for the first time, there are two options for the return trip to Funchal, the most spectacular of which is the straight-ahead spin through clouds and razorbacks of EN 204 (a highway so new the tar's barely dry) that links the Paúl da Serra with Encumeada pass; from here, it's a matter of retracing your steps to Ribeira Brava, Cabo Girão, and Funchal. This is a wide road with broad, well-graded curves, but the road cuts are so fresh you must watch for falling rocks. The route's a thriller, all 18 km (11 miles) of it. And yet it's easier to drive than the old downhill spiral from Paúl da Serra to the south shore—quicker, too.

On the old route, as you aim south across the Paúl, tufts of green begin to push up through the pebbles, and blushes of heather appear. The road veers sharply right (it is now called route 208), then tightens into a corkscrew and plunges through 11 km (7 miles) of pines, eucalyptus, and vineyards to .ejoin route 101 on the south coast a few miles east of Madalena do Mar. You have only 14½ km (9 miles) to drive farther east to reach Ribeira Brava, where you took the Encumeada pass road earlier in the day. Then it's back to Funchal the way you came. You should make it home well before dark.

THE ISLAND OF PORTO SANTO

This low-slung, semiarid island located just 25 miles to the northeast of Madeira isn't for everyone. It's tiny—only 9 miles long and 3 miles wide—so unless you crave a lazy day or two on the beach you'll probably find little reason to make the 20-minute flight over from Madeira.

The island capital of Vila Baleira isn't much, either: a cluster of red-roofed white houses, a couple of churches, a few shops set about a square pebbled in black and white, which perches on low hills about two-thirds of the way along the shore, the point at which the strand narrows and arcs eastward toward the little rocky outcropping, Ilhéu de Cima.

Porto Santo's main claim to fame (other than its 6 miles of sugary beach) is the house where Christopher Columbus is said to have lived shortly after his marriage to the daughter of Bartolomeu Perestrelo, one of Prince Henry's navigators and the island's first governor. It's just off the main square, a rough stone building two stories tall with a walled garden where fuchsia-colored bougainvillaea seems to have run amok. For years the town fathers said that the house would "open soon" as a museum. At long last, it has. Called **Museu**

Casa de Colombo, the old house plus a new one directly next door are filled with exhibits pertaining to the life of Columbus: maps, papers, charts, ship designs and models, even life-size wax models of Columbus (poring over his logs) and his wife (standing by attentively). The museum is closed on Saturdays and Sundays.

A jumbo airstrip (used by NATO and the Portuguese army) stretches across the middle of Porto Santo, dividing the flatter agricultural west from the hillier east. The island's highest point, Pico do Facho, stands a mere 1,680 feet above sea level. There are some craggy cliffs along the northeast shore, but the island is for the most part a rolling checkerboard of wheat fields, vineyards, and small gardens where tomatoes, melons, and figs grow. Water is desperately short on the island, and high-tech, airplane-propeller-type windmills help pump what little of it is available. These are no doubt more efficient than the old, wooden, cloth-sailed variety that used to do the job, but they are nowhere near as picturesque. A few of the old windmills still remain (on a hill near the airstrip and at the village of Camacha), but these are mostly for show.

Although few Americans come to Porto Santo, Britons, Northern Europeans, and Madeirans flock over in summer to windsurf, sail, and sack out on the sand. Autumn belongs to the wealthy hunters who fly in to shoot rabbits and partridges, both of which outnumber people hereabouts.

Rabbits very nearly decimated this island once, all because Perestrelo had smuggled a pregnant doe rabbit aboard ship in Lisbon and released her in the Porto Santo wilds. By the time the colonists were ready to reap their first Porto Santo harvest, that one doe rabbit (and her first litter) had multiplied and remultiplied many times. In a matter of months rabbits had overrun the island, devouring everything in sight, including, alas, the colonists' carefully tended crops. His shortsightedness cost Perestrelo the governorship of Madeira; he got Porto Santo instead, rabbits and all.

Far and away the best place to stay these days on the island of Porto Santo is **Luamar**, a new suite hotel at Cabeço da Ponta at the southwestern end of the beach. This three- and four-story, U-shaped concrete-block complex was built a few years ago for time-sharers. Seventy of the units remain unsold, however, and these are now available to overnighters. The apartments are compact (bedroom, bath, combined kitchen/living/dining area with balcony), but they are pin-neat and trimmed in cheerful schemes of green, cream, and rose. The feeling throughout is one of lightness and airiness (even in the suites overlooking the highway that runs the length of the island). At street level there's a sweep of glassed-in lobby/lounge, a restaurant (breakfast only so far, although there are plans to serve three meals a day), and, just outside, a giant pool set on a terrace of candy-striped tile above the beach. Still to come: tennis courts, gym, and sauna.

Second best, although it has slipped noticeably of late, is the 97-room **Hotel Porto Santo**, on the beach about a mile southwest of Vila Baleira. Now managed by Trusthouse Forte, the hotel is rated four stars but deserves only three. The Porto Santo caters, for the most part, to bargain tour groups (primarily British, German, and Swiss), and the wear and tear shows in the stained carpets, scuffed furniture, and sloppily patched bathroom tiles. The food, alas, is dreadful—3,750$00 (about US $30) for a prix fixe dinner that features such "Portuguese classics" as *osso bucco, fettucine à Cristovão Colombo,* and peach strudel, most of them barely edible. This once-lovely little hotel needs a major overhaul, particularly the drab, shoe-boxey rooms, which cry out for fresh rugs, fabrics, and paint, all of them light and bright.

Third and last hotel choice? The 108-room, three-star, middle-of-town **Hotel Praia Dourada**, a modern barn of a place popular among knapsacking northern Europeans and budget tours. The rooms are clean, spare, uninspired, and, for so sunny an island, strangely dark. There is a basement restaurant, a lobby-level lounge and TV room, and a court-yard pool about the size of a badminton court. Porto Santo's glorious beach lies five minutes away at least, an unpleasant walk through streets abuzz with motorbikes.

As for food on Porto Santo, don't expect much. The island's three best restaurants are probably **Baiana** on rua Dr. Nuno S. Teixeira overlooking the main square, **Snack-Bar Marquês**, a long block downhill on rua João Santana, and, on the beach next door to the Porto Santo Hotel, **Restaurant/ Bar Mar e Sol**. All three serve pretty much the same thing: hearty homemade soups, *espada* (grilled, sautéed, or batter-fried), and grilled or fried pork chops. Desserts run to heavy, homemade cakes, fruit salads, and Olá (ice creams pre-fabbed on the Portugese mainland into a devastating array of splits, sundaes, and mousses).

Life barely creaks along on Porto Santo; in fact, it moves so slowly that not much seems to have happened since Columbus left more than 500 years ago. Bring a good book.

GETTING AROUND

Given the number of jets roaring in and out of Madeira's international airport today, it's difficult to believe that just 30 years ago there was no air service to the island. In those days Madeira-bound travellers flew to Porto Santo, then negotiated the last 25 miles by boat in what was usually a three- to four-hour pitch-and-roll crossing. Poor sailors would arrive at Funchal pea green—hardly the way to begin a vacation.

Then in the mid-1960s, engineers hacked out the side of a mountain on the eastern end of Madeira, shelved there a landing strip about the size of an aircraft-carrier deck, and TAP Air Portugal began jetting down from Lisbon. It is still the only scheduled airline serving Madeira.

For transatlantic passengers today, the easiest way to reach Madeira is still via Lisbon because TAP whizzes back and forth with near-commuter frequency; TAP's overnights from North America arrive in plenty of time to connect with the 8:01 A.M. to Funchal. If you're flying from Boston and don't mind breaking your trip for a day in the Azores, you can jet to Ponta Delgada on the island of São Miguel (about 4 hours east of Boston), then catch the following day's Ponta Delgada–Funchal flight; there are two nonstops each week (on Saturdays and Mondays) from Ponta Delgada to Madeira. There's also good service from Porto on the Portuguese mainland: five nonstops a week. The island of Porto Santo fares less well, with only two dead-of-night flights from Lisbon each week (and none from Porto or the Azores). The flying time to either Porto Santo or Madeira from Lisbon is 1½ hours; from Porto to Madeira, about 1¾ hours; and from Ponta Delgada about 2 hours.

With its rapidly expanding routes, TAP now links several large European cities with Madeira. There are, for example, three nonstops a week from London and Paris, one nonstop each week from Frankfurt, plus once- or twice-a-week jet service, direct but with one stop, between Madeira and Madrid, Milan, Rome, and Zürich. And, of course, there are charters zipping in from all over Europe (among them TAP's own subsidiary, Air Atlantis).

Madeira's airport has always had a reputation for being a "white knuckler," not only because its runway is so short but also because it perches far above the sea. Things have improved recently, thanks to the engineers who added 300 extra meters of runway on a trestle high above the ground that strides northward almost to the village of Machico. Although landings and takeoffs are no piece of cake, at least they don't seem as death defying as they once did. Even with the longer runway, the only large jets with engines and brakes powerful enough to make it are Boeing 727s and 737s. Madeira's dream of a jumbo jetport is expected to materialize in 1996, making it possible for widebodies to fly in nonstop from North America as well as from Europe. Will the island lose the remoteness and otherworldliness that have made it special all these centuries?

"Probably so," sighed one of the major island developers, who is at work on the 27-hole golf course, club, and hotel complex at Santo da Serra in the hills above the airport. This, plus the new 18-hole golf resort now being built by Adam Blandy at the family estate, Quinta do Palheiro Ferreiro, nearer Funchal, will no doubt spawn the building of even more new hotels and condos.

To ensure that paradise isn't forever lost, the Madeira Department of Tourism has just commissioned a study to determine how the island can best cope with the additional load of tourists. The results? Spread the season, making Madeira a year-round destination, and spread the business around the island. Develop small, low-rise tourist villages that capture the regional character. Will it work? Or will Madeira be disastrously overbuilt, like the Spanish Canaries directly south? Time will tell.

Aerocondor 19-passenger Dornier 228 turboprop planes make four Madeira–Porto Santo round trips each day between early April and late October; off season, service is less frequent. Either direction, it's a 20-minute hop gate to gate. For flight information and reservations while you are in Madeira, contact TAP Air Portugal at avenida Dr. António José de Almeida, 17, in downtown Funchal; Tel: (091) 39-210 or 301-51. Because these planes are so small, it's best to reserve a seat well in advance—and to arrive at the airport early.

You can also sail between Madeira and Porto Santo. Ask about schedules from the Turismo, at avenida Arriaga, 18, in Funchal. The crossing is often so rough that even old salts would rather fly. By the two sleek, new, 244-passenger catamarans *Independência* and *Pátria,* the trip takes one and a half hours under ideal conditions, longer in heavy seas. There is no service on Tuesdays. Cost of a Funchal–Porto Santo round trip: 7,000$00.

The company offering a broad assortment of excursions around Madeira is Intervisa, at avenida Arriaga, 30 (Tel: 091-283-44. You can also pick up excursion brochures by the handful at the Turismo and in the lobbies of all major hotels.

If you'd like to penetrate deep into the island's interior, getting well off the beaten track, you may want to consider one of the excursions offered by INVI SAFARI, at rua dos Murças, 43A (Tel: 091-229-21, 334-64, 295-85, or 332-38). For boat trips along the coast and out to the Desertas (three uninhabited islands within plain view of Funchal), contact Costa do Sol at the marina on avenida do Mar (Tel: 091-243-90 or 385-38).

If you prefer to see Madeira at your own pace, you'll find that many major automobile-rental companies maintain offices in town and/or at the airport. The car you want is a powerful little mountain goat that can climb Madeira's narrow serpentine roads without complaint. A big, bulky model simply won't do. And be sure to fill your car's gas tank before you set out on an excursion—you'll use a lot more gas than you'd think on the hills, and there are few filling stations outside the major towns.

To hire a car with an English-speaking driver you have only to ask your hotel concierge.

On Porto Santo the best way to get about is probably by taxi. Fares are cheap, the drivers know just where to take you, and there's little point in renting a car when you can see everything in a morning or an afternoon.

ACCOMMODATIONS REFERENCE
Rates given are projected 1993 prices for a double room, double occupancy. Price ranges span the lowest rate in the low season to the highest in the high season. Unless otherwise stated, rates include Continental breakfast. As prices are subject to change, always double-check before booking.

▶ **Albergaria Quinta da Penha de França**. Rua da Penha de França, 9000 **Funchal**, Madeira. Tel: (091) 290-87. 12,825$00–16,900$00.

▶ **Atlantic Gardens**. Apartado 261, Praia Formosa, 9003 **Funchal**, Madeira. Tel: (091) 76-21-11; Fax; (091) 76-67-33. 13,000$00–20,000$00.

▶ **Casino Park Hotel**. Rua Imperatriz Dona Amélia, 9000 **Funchal**, Madeira. Tel: (091) 23-31-11; Fax: (091) 23-20-76. 20,000$00–30,000$00.

▶ **Hotel Baia Azul**. Estrada Monumental, 9000 **Funchal**, Madeira. Tel: (091) 76-62-60; Fax; (091) 76-42-45. 13,750$00–26,000$00.

▶ **Hotel Porto Santo**. 9400 **Porto Santo**, Madeira. Tel: (091) 98-23-81; Fax: (091) 98-26-11. 14,450$00–15,950$00.

▶ **Hotel Praia Dourada**. Rua Don Estevão d'Alencastre, Vila

Baleira, 9400 **Porto Santo, Madeira.** Tel: (091) 98-23-15; Fax: (091) 98-24-87. 10,850$00–11,935$00.

▶ **Hotel Savoy.** Avenida do Infante, 9000 **Funchal,** Madeira. Tel: (091) 22-20-31 through 22-20-39; Fax: (091) 22-31-03; in North America, Tel: (800) 448-8355. 34,125$00–57,750$00.

▶ **Luamar Suite Hotel.** Cabeço da Ponta, 9400 **Porto Santo,** Madeira. Tel: (091) 89-41-21; Fax: (091) 98-31-00. 10,200$00– 13,100$00.

▶ **Madeira Carlton Hotel.** Largo António Nobre, P. O. Box 598, 9007 **Funchal,** Madeira. Tel: (091) 310-31; Fax: (091) 233-77; in North America, Tel: (800) 448-8355. 21,000$00– 43,000$00.

▶ **Madeira Palácio.** Estrada Monumental, P. O. Box 4614, 9058, **Funchal,** Madeira. Tel: (091) 76-44-76; Fax: (091) 76-44-77; in North America, Tel: (800) 223-5652. 24,000$00– 44,000$00.

▶ **Pousada do Pico do Arieiro. Pico do Arieiro,** 9000 **Funchal,** Madeira. Tel: (091) 301-10; Fax: (091) 286-11. 14,520$00–17,820$00.

▶ **Pousada dos Vinháticos.** Encumeada, Serra de Agua, 9350 **Ribeira Brava,** Madeira. Tel: (091) 95-23-44 or 95-21-48; Fax: (091) 95-21-48. 10,780$00–12,100$00.

▶ **Quinta da Bela Vista.** Caminho do Avista Navios, 4, 9000 **Funchal.** Madeira. Tel: (091) 76-41-44; Fax: (091) 76-50-90; in U.S. and Canada, Tel: (212) 686-9213, Fax: (212) 696-0271. Doubles 21,400$00–26,800$00; suites 40,000$00–45,400$00.

▶ **Reid's Hotel.** Estrada Monumental, 139, 9000 **Funchal,** Madeira. Tel: (091) 76-30-01; Fax: (091) 76-44-99; in North America, Tel: (800) 223-6800; in New York City, (212) 838-3110, Fax: (212) 758-7367. Double rooms: 38,300$00– 58,700$00; junior suites: 55,200$00–85,800$00; one-bed-room suites: 65,300$00–167,000$00, this last for the Chur-chill or George Bernard Shaw suite.

The pousadas of Madeira, now completely independent of ENATUR, the Portuguese government agency responsible for the operation of the mainland pousadas, are best booked directly or through your travel agent.

THE AZORES

By Marion Kaplan

Islands have their own peculiar allure, and the nine volcanic islands of the Azores (Açores in Portuguese, pronounced ah-ZOH-resh) lack for nothing in an intriguing history, a dash of legend, spectacular natural beauty, exuberant vegetation, and peaceable charm. Like green gems in the Atlantic, the Azores form an archipelago 400 miles long, from Santa Maria in the east to Flores and Corvo in the west. The wind-carved cliffs of these westernmost islands, from Portugal more than a third of the way across the Atlantic, mark—for navigators, for the Portuguese, for Professor J. H. Parry writing in *The Discovery of the Sea*—the true extremity of Europe.

The Azores, when first sighted by Portuguese mariners (the eastern islands in 1427, Flores and Corvo in about 1450), were uninhabited. So eager, in fact, was Prince Henry the Navigator to populate them that—through his sister, Isabel, married to Philip the Good, duke of Burgundy and ruler of Flanders—he offered land to Flemish farmers. The islands have been ports of call for seafarers for centuries.

Christopher Columbus paused at Santa Maria, the southernmost island, on his return to Spain after discovering the New World in 1492 (a mean story has it that he failed to pay his water bill). A few years later, Vasco da Gama, having discovered the route to India, delayed his triumphal return to Lisbon to take his sick brother to Terceira. Countless mariners—pirates, settlers, traders, ocean wanderers, and cheerful modern yachtsmen—have passed by since. So do vacationing emigrants, and tourists—in flights of four hours from New York or two hours from Portugal, to whom the islands belong, although their government is autonomous.

The islands have always meant different things to different

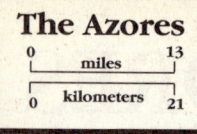

The Azores

0 miles 13

0 kilometers 21

Distances between islands are not to scale.

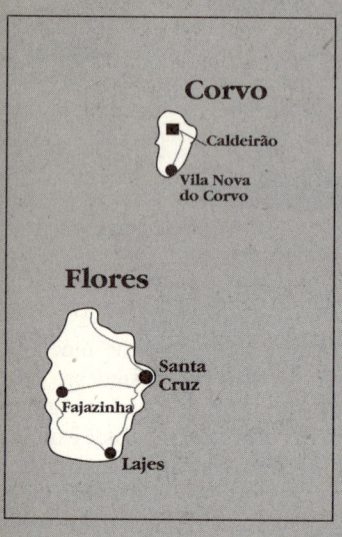

Corvo

■ Caldeirão

Vila Nova do Corvo

Flores

Santa Cruz

Fajazinha

Lajes

N

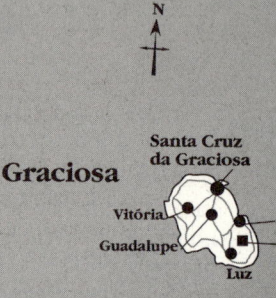

Graciosa

Santa Cruz da Graciosa

Vitória

Guadalupe

Luíz ■

↑ TO CORVO AND FLORES

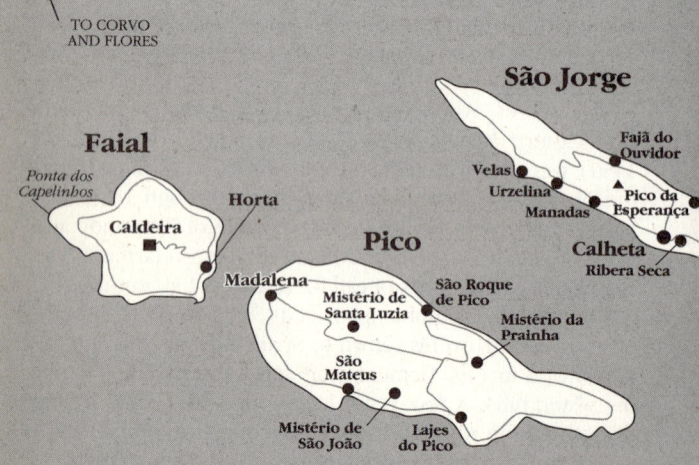

São Jorge

Fajã do Ouvidor

Velas

Urzelina

Manadas

▲ Pico da Esperança

Calheta

Ribera Seca

Faial

Ponta dos Capelinhos

Horta

Caldeira ■

Pico

Madalena

Mistério de Santa Luzia

São Roque de Pico

Mistério da Prainha

São Mateus

Mistério de São João

Lajes do Pico

ATLANTIC OCEAN

São Miguel

Ponta da Bretanha

Mosteiros

Capelas

Pico do Carvão

Caldeira das Sete Cidades

Ribeira Grande

Porto Formoso

Praia dos Moinhos

Nordeste

Achadinha

Furnas

Pico de Vara

Santa Bárbara

Lagoa das Furnas

Ponta Delgada

Agua de Pau

Vila Franco do Campo

Povoação

Praia

Caldeira do Enxofre

ATLANTIC OCEAN

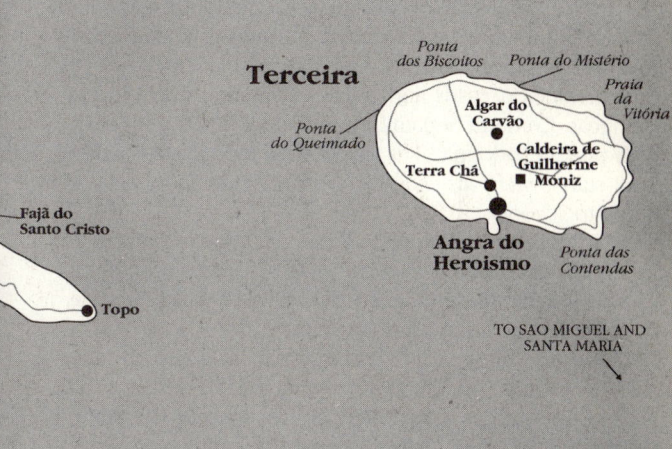

Terceira

Ponta dos Biscoitos

Ponta do Mistério

Praia da Vitória

Algar do Carvão

Ponta do Queimado

Caldeira de Guilherme Moniz

Terra Chá

Angra do Heroismo

Ponta das Contendas

Fajã do Santo Cristo

Topo

TO SAO MIGUEL AND SANTA MARIA

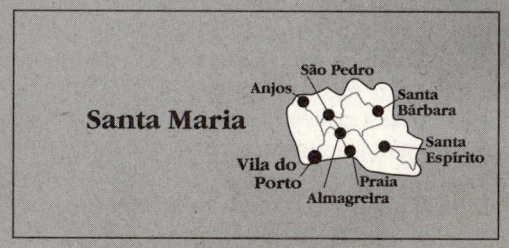

São Pedro

Anjos

Santa Bárbara

Santa Maria

Santa Espírito

Vila do Porto

Praia

Almagreira

people. Pirates, hungering for gold, never saw their extraordinary beauty. The settlers, who own tiny rock houses set in lava they have worked into soil and food, have felt terrible despair, intense need, deep love for their volcanic Eden. Sailors in sleek yachts and modest wooden boats come by the thousands; they like the islands' position, their modesty, their temperate landscape where sea legs can walk and walk.

Golfers have fine courses on São Miguel and Terceira to hit a birdie. You'll find tennis courts and people to play with, and keen divers to accompany you in underwater wonderlands. You can catch a trout in a well-stocked *ribeira,* or a swordfish, a shark, or tuna from the sea; these waters have given deep-sea fishermen record after record. (You'll probably eat a fair amount of *arbrótea,* which is turbot-like and tasty; its name translates as "forkbeard.") The island architecture pleases the eye, the farming is unusual—those hills mean the farmers take their milking stools and churns to the cows rather than herd them to the barn. You'll see horses and donkeys carrying four balanced churns, transporting corn, towing carts. You'll hear city sounds—the discos and pubs have arrived—and the tintinnabulation of cow bells.

You'll see thickets of trees, heathers, and ferns, and exquisite flowers that flourish in astonishing variety—50 of 850 species are exclusive to the islands. Come in April and May and you'll be wooed with azaleas. In August (when it seems that every relative of every Azorean is visiting, too) you'll still find privacy on roads and hillsides bursting with blue hydrangeas. Come in September and you'll find the hills alive with pink belladonna lilies, sweetly named, as a new school year starts, *meninas-vão-para-a-escola* (the little girls are going to school).

Whichever way you look at them, the great ocean and the green islands make a magical image. "Great green ships / themselves, they ride / at anchor forever; / beneath the tide," wrote John Updike in his poem "Azores."

Their greenness is due in large part to a certain atmospheric stability: A high-pressure area known to meteorologists as the Azores High often builds up over the central North Atlantic, heralding good weather for continental Portugal and the rest of Europe, and sustaining (with the warmth of the Gulf Stream and an ample amount of precipitation) the variety of vegetation. Much of the flora was imported from the far reaches of the Portuguese empire over the centuries and painstakingly cultivated into patchwork quilts of fields that are stitched together with lava fences, draped with hydrangeas. Don't go to the Azores expecting Tahiti, however, or even Madeira. Hard cinders rather than soft sands—there are few sand beaches—make up most of the islands' shorelines. Though the climate is technically subtropical, making possible that gorgeous variety and abundance of wildflowers and shrubs, you will enjoy the Azores most if you regard them as a rather weather-beaten greenhouse. Damp gusts more than occasionally come along, so travel with adequate rain gear year-round.

This metaphorical greenhouse is of the somewhat fussy Victorian variety. Politically conservative and proudly Roman Catholic, the Azoreans are as staunchly rooted in tradition as their islands are in the sea. The family unit remains strong; old-fashioned courtship rituals persist among the young; and *festas,* or religious ceremonies, take place around the calendar throughout the archipelago, as evidenced by the gaily decorated Pentecostal chapels called *teatros* or *impérios.* The Espírito Santo (Holy Spirit) cult is a power throughout the islands—and wherever Azoreans have emigrated.

Other features of the Azorean landscape are more earthly in nature, though they may not look it. Seismic activity has given rise to *caldeiras* (craters), *furnas* (caverns), and hardened lava flows that formed over inhabited areas and are philosophically named *mistérios* (mysteries). One topographical feature, the *laje* or *lage* (flat rock) is so common that a number of communities are named after it. These phenomena are as characteristic of the terrain as the brightly painted chapels and the Baroque churches chiseled out of black basalt, which provide an ornate backdrop for the folkloric events that reach their peak on the Day of Pentecost. In addition to religious festivals, different traditions of singing and dancing are followed concurrently on each island then, so if local color is your interest, Pentecost (early June) is the time to go.

If the constraints of tradition and the harshness of the land were responsible in varying degrees for massive waves of Azorean emigration (first to Brazil and later to the United States and Canada), those very factors now attract people to the archipelago. The vast majority of visitors are emigrants returning to their homeland. You'll hear at picnics at São Miguel's Furnas (where you can boil your four-minute egg in a fumarole or geyser) an easy mix of two languages in phrases spoken by all-American youth and older islanders ("Mãe, c'mon—vamos"). Others, however, have come to appreciate the colorful and luxuriant folklore and flora. One such recent visitor was the conservative U.S. author and critic William F. Buckley, Jr., who with uncharacteristic verbal leanness in his book *Atlantic High* called the Azores "quite simply . . . the most beautiful group of islands in the world."

MAJOR INTEREST

Volcanic crater lakes and hot springs of São Miguel

Architecturally and historically important town of Angra do Heroismo on Terceira

View of surrounding islands from São Jorge

Yacht port of Horta and volcanic landscape of Ponta dos Capelinhos on Faial

View of perfect volcanic crater of Pico from Faial

Magnificent flora and waterfalls of Graciosa and Flores

Religious and folkloric festivals of Espírito Santo (Pentecost) in all the islands

Their Atlantic setting, their green-eyed beauty, the hot breath of the volcanoes, the mix of sea mist and sparkling sun have wrapped the archipelago in eternal mystery. You'll encounter proponents of the view that the Azores are Plato's sunken empire, the lost continent of Atlantis (which Madeira also claims to be, but then both archipelagos belong to the Atlantic Ocean's restless "ring of fire"). You'll hear the opinion that these are the Forgotten Islands of the Romans. There's even an argument as to whether Diogo de Silves was the first Portuguese to arrive, or Gonçalo Velho Cabral, who, chroniclers reported, named the islands Açores for the goshawks he saw flying above them. The earliest extant document about the archipelago is a royal decree dated 1439 ordering that Santa Maria be populated. A similar decree regarding São Miguel dates from 1445. The settlers of the two easternmost islands came primarily from Estremadura, the Alentejo, and the Algarve. Population of the central group—Terceira, Graciosa, São Jorge, Faial, and Pico—was due in large part to Prince Henry the Navigator's Flemish connection. The islands, in turn, supplied Flanders with raw plant materials to dye its textiles. The westernmost two—Flores and Corvo— remained unsettled until the 16th century.

During the expansion of the empire, the Azores served as a stopping-off place for Portuguese navigators, who brought the wealth of the Americas and the India trade to the islands, especially Terceira. Like the rest of Portugal, the archipelago came under the domination of Spain during the Castilian usurpation, when Philip II of Spain invaded Portugal in 1580 and proclaimed himself King Filipe I. In the late 1820s and

1830s there arose the War of the Two Brothers, between two sons of King João VI: Dom Pedro, who stood for a liberal government under a constitutional monarchy, and his younger absolutist brother, Dom Miguel. Most of mainland Portugal supported Miguel. The independent-minded Azoreans supported the cause of Pedro and provided an unlikely power base for his eventual victory. (Poor Dom Pedro, who had been emperor of Brazil and king of Portugal, died of consumption only three months later.)

Emigration from the Azores then became the more powerful issue, much of it connected with the whaling industry. Melville wrote in *Moby Dick* how "no small number of these whaling seamen belong to the Azores, where the outward bound Nantucket seamen frequently touch to augment their crews from the hearty peasants of these rocky shores. . . . How it is, there is no telling, but Islanders seem to make the best whalemen." These emigrants eventually settled as far afield as New England, Canada, Brazil, California, and Hawaii, where communities of Azorean descendants continue their customary colorful celebrations of the feast of Pentecost.

The 19th century saw expanded commercial contact between the Azores and the outside world. In addition to supplying whalers, the islands exported wheat, flax, dye plants, wine, and oranges. Migration worked both ways. Early in the century, two enterprising Boston families, the Hicklings and the Dabneys, moved to São Miguel and Faial, respectively, to manage much of the export business (their descendants have since left the islands). Early in this century, the strategic importance of the archipelago made it a vital link in cable transmission, as well as a stopover for ships and, finally, aircraft. It provided the United States and Britain with strategic naval and air bases during both world wars and has remained an invaluable asset for NATO ever since, through the Lajes Agreement on use by the United States of the Terceira airbase, renegotiated from time to time. Islanders' resentment over long-unresolved issues of land ownership continues to this day.

Azoreans have always been conscious of their distinct identity, which goes beyond general insularity (*insularidade* in Portuguese) to specific Azoreanness (*açorianidade*), a term coined by Azorean writer Vitorino Nemésio to refer to the island's *Weltanschauung*. The islands' isolation has shaped the sensibilities of some of Portugal's greatest modern writers. The Azores have produced a large number of journalists, too. As Azorean scholar Onésimo T. Almeida has pointed out, "for the outsider it is astonishing to hear that the islands have had more than six hundred different newspapers throughout their history and today still publish seven dailies, one of which, *O Açoriano Oriental,* is the third oldest newspaper in Europe, seven weeklies, and four journals dedicated to works on literature, history, art, folklore and culture."

The islands, an autonomous region since 1976, print Azores stamps and proudly fly the flag of the goshawk and nine stars alongside the Portuguese banner. (In fact, you're more likely to see another bird indigenous to the islands with the less majestic name of *milhafre.*)

In the appealingly idiosyncratic Azores, each island additionally has its own sense of identity, not to mention superiority. For sightseeing, the islands of São Miguel, Terceira, and Faial are reasonably close to one another. A couple of days' stay in each will allow you to cover the most interesting ground in the Azores. If you have extra time at your disposal, however, do discover the charms of the other islands. Coverage begins with the eastern group of São Miguel and Santa Maria; moves on to the central islands of Terceira, Graciosa, São Jorge, Faial, and Pico; and ends with the western group of Flores and Corvo.

SAO MIGUEL

The largest and easternmost island in the Azores (it measures a maximum 65 km by 16 km, or just over 40 miles by 10 miles), crescent-shaped São Miguel has been inhabited since 1439. Today it has half of the archipelago's total population of about 250,000—and the best tourist facilities, including some starkly modern hotels. The nicest accommodation in town for the couple of nights you may need to explore the western portion of the island is at the **Hotel São Pedro** in the sizable city of Ponta Delgada (with a population of about 120,000, it is the largest in the archipelago). Built in the 19th century as the Hickling family town house, the hotel has a harbor view and preserves a Georgian air in its antiques-appointed rooms; its restaurant is described below. Almost as elegant, on the outskirts of town, is **Casa de Nossa Senhora do Carmo**, a 17th-century manor house that offers four rooms with baths, a tranquil garden, and meals on request.

By the sea in Vila Franca do Campo (25 km/16 miles east of Ponta Delgada) there is also the very attractive **Estalagem Vinha de Areia**, converted from an elegant residence (André

Malraux stayed here). Businesslike, modern, air-conditioned, and convenient is the **Hotel Açores Atlântico** in Ponta Delgada.

Ponta Delgada

Despite some unsightly modern construction, Ponta Delgada reveals enough of its history to make for a pleasant promenade. You can pick up a map at the tourist office on avenida Infante Dom Henrique near the stage-flat arches of the 18th-century town gates and proceed across the pavements decorated in black and white stones, reminiscent of Rio de Janeiro, to the waterfront. Walk along to **Forte de São Brás**, a fortress begun in the 16th century to defend the city against corsairs, then head away from the harbor and have a look at the religious buildings, the 18th-century **Igreja de São José** with its dark stone framing white surfaces, and the lavish interior of the 16th-century **Convento de Nossa Senhora da Esperança**. You'll pass two palaces, the 17th-century Conceição and the 19th-century Fonte Bela, and the 17th-century mermaid-covered, Baroque town house, Casa de Carlos Bicudo, as you make your way back past the town gates and the 16th-century Igreja Matriz de São Sebastião, the parish church, with its ornate Baroque and Manueline portals.

If you'd like a preview of the geometric-motif pottery you'll be seeing *in situ* in the villages of Lagoa and Vila Franca do Campo, stop into the **Casa Regional da Ilha Verde** (rua do Aljube, 6), a shop where local crafts are sold. From there, rua dos Manaias leads past the 17th-century Igreja de Santa Bárbara and the Paço do Concelho, the town hall, also from the 1600s. On the following street, rua João Moreira, is the **Museu Carlos Machado**, housed in the former convent of Santo André, dating from the 17th century and containing sections on Azorean natural history and folklore. One of the most unusual artifacts of island life on display is the *capote-à-capelo,* an extravagantly hooded cape worn by island women until just a few decades ago.

If the museum has piqued your interest in island culture, proceed to the **Livraria Nove Estrelas** at rua do Mercado, 35, where prints and English-language books about the Azores are on sale. Also on Mercado are the town theater and open-air market next to it. A cross street, ladeira da Mãe de Deus, leads to an overview of Ponta Delgada at the **Reduto da Mãe de Deus**, a 15th-century fortification where in 1944 an antiaircraft battery mistakenly fired on the plane carrying General Dwight D. Eisenhower home to the United States from North

Africa. Back down on the waterfront below it is the 17th-century **Igreja de São Pedro**, which houses the 18th-century *Nossa Senhora das Dores* (Our Lady of Sorrows), one of the finest sculptures in the Azores.

You might follow your stroll around Ponta Delgada with a meal at the **Hotel São Pedro** restaurant, on largo Almirante Dunn. It serves all the Azorean specialties, including *caldo azedo* (bean and potato soup), *couves solteiras* and *couves fervedouros* (cabbage soups), *polvo guisado em vinho de cheiro* (octopus stewed in local wine), *caldeiradas de peixe* (fish stews), *arroz de lapas* (limpets with rice), and *lapas de molho Afonso* (limpets in a spicy sauce). São Miguel is also famous for its beer. Try, too, if the hotel has it, the local *vinho de cheiro,* a strong red table wine. Besides the ubiquitous island sweets, one of the nicest desserts is a slice of the locally cultivated pineapple.

To see the other sights of São Miguel, you will need a car. The tourist office will tell you where to rent one. One popular diversion is a visit to a pineapple hothouse, the largest being **Estufas Agosto Arruda** just north of town. There you can see the plants in various stages of cultivation, sample the fruit and a liqueur made from the juice, and stroll around the carefully tended grounds with their good views of Ponta Delgada and the harbor.

From there the drive inland to the northwest leads to the panoramic mountain Pico do Carvão, and **Caldeira das Sete Cidades**, a volcanic crater that, according to legend, contains the remains of seven cities founded by the archbishop of Porto and six other bishops, who fled to the fabled island of Antilia to escape the Moors. Today it is the site of a small village and twin lakes, one blue and one green—formed, goes the tale, from the parting tears of a princess and her shepherd lover. Next to the blue lake, Lago Azul, are extensive gardens planted with flowering trees and shrubs, which will begin to give you an idea why São Miguel is known as the Ilha Verde (Green Island).

From here the scenic route continues northeast to the rocky terrain at Mosteiros and along the coast past a promontory called Ponta da Bretanha, a reminder of the Breton settlers who along with the Flemish are said to be responsible for the French pronunciation of "u" in São Miguel speech. Continue to the cliffside village of **Capelas**, the center of São Miguel's tobacco plantations; there, the hill called Morro das Capelas affords more sweeping views of the coast.

Your next stop could be the handsome town of **Ribeira Grande**, a center of the island's tea plantations. It has an extensive beach as well as a number of noteworthy monuments in its churches (the 16th-century Nossa Senhora da Estrela, the 17th-century São Francisco and Espírito Santo, and the 18th-century Nossa Senhora da Conceição) and a 16th-century town hall. Its regional restaurant is **O Fervedouro** (rua do Passal, 3); you might also want to make a detour to the village of Santa Bárbara for a regional meal at **Cavalo Branco**, on largo do Meio Moio, 23.

Heading toward the eastern end of the island on the southern coast road from Ponta Delgado, you'll pass a number of sand beaches before reaching the fishing port of **Lagoa**, noted for its very attractive, mainly blue-and-white pottery made from volcanic clay. The **Cerâmica Viera** dates its founding to 1862. Past the villages of Agua de Pau and Caloura, a pleasant resort where a modest motel has expanded to the long, low, and modern **Hotel Caloura** and underwater diving is popular, **Vila Franca do Campo**'s churches are worth stopping to see. The 15th-century **Igreja de São Miguel** boasts a beautiful Gothic portal and a marvelous interior containing Gothic arches carved with plant motifs and a relief titled *Souls in Purgatory;* its bell is the oldest on the island. The 18th-century **church of São Pedro** has an elaborate portal of its own and contains a statue of Saint Peter carved out of the creamy Ançã stone from the Beiras in mainland Portugal. The 16th-century **Igreja de Santo André** contains a lavish interior with *azulejos* (decorative tiles) and a paneled ceiling. The small port has its own simple beauty. You'll see bright boats with names like *Vai com Jesus* (Go with Jesus) and, in the cobblestone pavement in the town square, caravels in full sail. Offshore is a tiny island, Ilheu, with its own natural seawater swimming pool, reached by boat.

You may want to shop for more pottery before heading inland past the crater lake of Lagoa das Furnas to the town of **Furnas**. The most relaxing accommodations on the island are here at the **Hotel Terra Nostra**, where a couple of nights' stay will give you a pleasant sense of eastern São Miguel. The oldest part of the complex is called Yankee Hall, the summer home built by the Hickling family around a thermal spring in the 19th century. Later additions, including an art deco hotel with an excellent regional restaurant and a new wing, make it the closest thing the Azores has to a fashionable resort. Whether or not you stay here, be sure to visit the hotel's lush botanical garden, planted with vegetation imported to the Green Island from around the world, and ask to have a dip in its outdoor pool, which is filled with heated mineral water so replete with iron it looks like apricot juice.

Furnas gets its name from the *furnas,* or caverns, that were created by a volcanic eruption in the 17th century; in places it still stinks richly of sulphur. Today the hot ground is also used to cook *cozido de Lagoa das Furnas,* a regional dish of meats and vegetables steamed in a cloth bag buried in the earth. The **Terra Nostra** hotel restaurant serves it in style, as does the **Casa de Chá Terra Nostra**, with its great views of the crater lake (to check or order in advance, Tel: 096-543-43).

From Furnas the coastal drive will take you to the principal sights on this side of São Miguel, for which you might want to pack a picnic of *cabreiro* (goat's milk cheese) or some *queijo da ilha,* a local cheese made from cow's milk. Your first stop could be **Povoação**, a fishing village that grew up around the 15th-century Capela de Santa Bárbara, a chapel considered the first place of worship built on the island. To the north is **Pico de Vara**, the highest point on São Miguel (1,088 meters, or 3,569 feet), with excellent views. Nordeste, at the northeast corner of the island, offers an interesting 15th-century church, **Igreja de São Jorge**, with basalt pillars amid the wood carvings and statuary inside, and **Achadinha**, 12 km (7½ miles) to the west, also merits a stop to see the lavish interior of its 16th-century church, **Igreja de Nossa Senhora do Rosário**. The final point of interest on this part of São Miguel is **Porto Formoso**, where if you're in the mood for a swim you might want to try **Praia dos Moinhos**, one of the nicest little dark-sand beaches on the island. From there, an inland road leads back to Furnas.

SANTA MARIA

Santa Maria, the roughly rectangular (17 by 9½ km, or 11 by 6 miles), southernmost island in the Azores, is easily seen in a day's drive through quiet fields sparsely dotted with windmills and whitewashed low, cubic houses with red-tile roofs. The first island in the archipelago to be discovered, Santa Maria owes its distinctive architecture to the fact that its original settlers came from the Algarve. Columbus was another early visitor, said to have sent his men to give thanks in the 15th-century **Igreja de Nossa Senhora dos Anjos** in the fishing village of **Anjos** for deliverance from a shipwreck. Uncertain of who he was (a pirate?), the island governor briefly locked him up. Though the church is a reconstruction, it is still interesting from a historical point of view; and the village, a short drive north of the airport, makes a convenient first stop on your way around the island.

The next two places on your tour could be the interior villages of **São Pedro** and **Santa Bárbara**, the former with simple and ancient churches. The landscape is best appreciated at a lookout called **Miradouro do Espigão**, overlooking vineyards and the **bay of São Lourenço**. From here you can head inland to **Santo Espírito**, where the sights include whitewashed houses, windmills, the parish church with a Baroque façade in island stone, and the small **Museu de Etnografia**. West of it is the pleasant village of Almagreira, and, just south, the fishing port of **Praia**, which gets its name from the long beach. (Santa Maria, the only island in the Azores that is not volcanic in origin, is also the only one with golden sandy beaches.)

Farther west is the island's main town, **Vila do Porto**. Among its many monuments is the **Igreja de Nossa Senhora da Assunção**, built in the 19th century on the ruins of a 15th-century church. **Café Restaurante Atlantida** (rua Teófilo de Braga) is the place for a regional meal of *caldo de nabos* (a turnip soup), *sopa do Império* (meat stew), or just the local pastry, a sugar-coated cookie called *cavaca*, accompanied by a glass of the local *vinho de cheiro* or dessert wines called *vinho abafado* and *vinho bastardinho*.

The only accommodations on the island are here in Vila do Porto at the **Hotel do Aeroporto**, originally built when the U.S. Air Force constructed the airport in 1944.

TERCEIRA

The third (*terceira*) island in the Azores to be discovered, egg-shaped Terceira (29 by 17½ km, or 18 by 11 miles) is also the third largest. But culturally it is of primary importance, and its main town, Angra do Heroismo, is on UNESCO's World Heritage List because of its architectural and historical significance. For that reason, you may want to stay in Angra for the couple of days you'll need to see the town and drive around the island.

Settlement of Terceira began in about 1450, with immigrants primarily from Flanders, the Algarve, and the Alentejo. Initially agricultural, Terceira soon became an important stop for galleons from India and the Americas, attracting French, English, and Flemish corsairs, whose constant presence brought about the construction of the fortifications that are still an important part of the landscape in Angra do Heroismo. In 1474 the settlement of Angra became the seat of government and remained an administrative center of the Azores for more than three centuries. In 1534 it was given the status of a city—the first in the Azores—and the seat of a bishopric. When Philip II of Spain became king of Portugal in 1580, the Portuguese pretender Dom António took refuge on Terceira.

The Spanish, whose forces included the writers Cervantes and Lope de Vega, invaded the island the following year, initially with little success. The islanders won the Battle of Salga ingeniously by driving away the Spanish with wild bulls. Following more bloody fighting, however, the Spanish finally gained control in 1583. Francis Drake attacked in 1589–in these islands he was just another corsair. Sir Walter Raleigh and the earl of Essex commanded the fleet that attacked the Spanish here in 1597, hoping in their turn for a prize in Spanish gold. After the restoration of the Portuguese throne in 1640, the Spanish presence came to a violent end. Further struggles took place in the 19th century, when Angra became the seat of the liberal regency of Pedro IV. Because of its citizens' bravery at that time, Pedro's daughter, Maria II, extended the city's name to Angra do Heroismo (Bay of Heroism) at the suggestion of Almeida Garrett, the romantic poet and dramatist who spent his youth on Terceira.

Angra do Heroismo

Though much surviving from its past was damaged in an earthquake in 1980, Angra do Heroismo remains a pleasant town for a walk along orderly cobblestone streets lined with whitewashed stone buildings with terra-cotta tile roofs. The islanders are long used to outsiders, from passing mariners, planeloads of tourists who pop in and out, and Americans posted to the military base at Lajes, but accommodations are surprisingly modest. Your first choice might be the sturdy, three-star **Hotel de Angra** on the city's main square. Or you might like, among other possibilities, the **Residencial Beira Mar**, a clean and well-maintained establishment with some rooms right on the bay and one of the nicest restaurants in town. You might begin a look around on the rua Direita, where you can visit the 18th-century **Igreja da Misericórdia** to see paintings and sculptures dating from the same period. From there, rua do Conselheiro Jacinto Cândido leads to the **Palácio Bettencourt**, an extravagant private residence from the Baroque era, open to the public as the town library.

Across from it is the **Sé** (Cathedral), recently restored to a condition so pristine that it practically belies its 16th-century origins. Rua do Marquês then leads past the richly planted Jardim Municipal (City Park) to the 17th-century **Igreja do Colégio**, a Jesuit church whose lavish decorations include a very fine display of 17th-century Dutch glazed tiles, and the Palácio dos Capitães-Generais, the former palace of the military governors, now occupied by the regional government.

If you return to the park, you will pass the Paço do Concelho, the 19th-century town hall built where its 17th-century counterpart once stood. The **Museu da Angra** is nearby at the intersection of rua de São Francisco and the rua Chagas, in a former convent. It houses an unusual collection of 15th- to 20th-century weapons, religious paintings, and sculpture. Note especially the Flemish works, a reminder that Henry the Navigator appointed a Fleming, Jacome de Bruges, as Angra's first governor. A more extensive collection of art is housed privately at the **Casa Museu Francisco Ernesto de Oliveira Martins**, at rua de São Pedro, 200, for which an appointment is necessary (Tel: 095-232-88). For a final overview of the city, take rua do Pisão to the **Alto da Memória**, an obelisk erected to the memory of Pedro IV on the site of Angra's first castle.

The **Beira Mar** hotel restaurant (rua de São João, 1–5) serves local specialties such as *alcatra* (a beef pot roast especially popular during the Pentecost feasts), *alcatra de cherne* (made with grouper), *polvo guisado* (octopus stewed in wine), and *morcela* (a type of sausage). The island produces its own *verdelho* white wine as well as *queijo da ilha* cheese. Another regional restaurant serving the same specialties is **Adega Lusitania**, rua de São Pedro, 63–65.

Pick up a car and picnic provisions to see the rest of the island with its Algarve- and Alentejo-type houses, some with tall chimneys and flanked by characteristic conical wooden structures for drying corn. See someone up one of these tree-high wigwam racks, and you'll think he's building a castle of corn. In season the roads are lined with hydrangeas and roses, and the herds of cattle that are so important to the island's economy feed indolently in the green fields. (Terceira has its own running of the bulls, in which the beast is marginally restrained and controlled by a long rope. Called *tourada à corda,* it takes place during the Festas Sanjoaninas from about June 19 to 27.)

You might begin your island tour with a view of Angra and

the bay from Monte Brazil on the outskirts of town. Head inland from there for more views of Terra Chá, then over to Ponta das Contendas on the southeast corner of the island. Driving to the north coast, you could turn left to climb the Serra do Cume—and look down upon a breathtaking patchwork of fields with the sea to your left, an image in which the careful shaping of the land by the islanders coincides with ancient notions of a fabled Atlantis. Down again, you'll come to **Praia da Vitória**, a town named for its surprisingly unvolcanic and extensive sand beach. For a more unusual bathing experience, after a stop at Ponta do Mistério for a look at an otherworldly landscape, continue to **Ponta dos Biscoitos**, where volcanic rock formations make natural swimming pools popular with youngsters. Continue to **Ponta do Queimado** and walk across to its lighthouse—this quiet spot, and the forest called Mata da Serreta across the road, are agreeable places for a picnic. Head inland again to the natural beauties of the grottoes of **Algar do Carvão**, then move on to contemplate the mighty **Caldeira de Guilherme Moniz**, with its 15-km (9-mile) perimeter, the largest volcanic crater in the Azores. There are heather and ferns here. Bulls roam in a wild scented garden. You'll see wisps of steam in the air—more *furnas,* the eerie chimneys for unseen fires far, far below. In the great green space of the crater, where a mantling of trees is a modest edging for a giant's lawn, you have a potent reminder of the powerful forces that created the islands millennia ago—and in a 40-second frenzy in the New Year of 1980 almost destroyed Angra.

GRACIOSA

With more gentle slopes than the other islands, pear-shaped Graciosa (12½ by 8½ km, or 8 by 5 miles) lives up to its name, which means "gracious." Its terrain is dotted with flowers, waterfalls, and windmills that may have been built originally by the island's Flemish settlers, perhaps joined by people from the Beiras and Minho of mainland Portugal. A recent theory suggests that the first windmill appeared on the islands in 1818, installed by a Terceira priest. For the cupola-capped windmills common in Graciosa there are no certain explanations. Looking for origins, sources, reasons can suggest answers that lead only to fresh puzzles. For instance, when you see farmers bringing in their corn, hauled by cows in carts with woven bamboo sides and solid wooden wheels, questions arise on how it came to be—and who is adapting what? Some things seem familiar, though. Be there in September when grapes are harvested for wine, and that heady scent emanating from several dark *adegas* can only be fermenting must. This gracious island, a jewel in the ocean, a miniature cosmos with hardworking people, appeals to everybody. **Santa Cruz da Graciosa**, the town nearest to the airport, is especially interesting for its handsome black-stone churches as well as for its **Casa Etnografia da Ilha Graciosa** (rua Alexandre Herculano), a collection of wine-growing implements and other ethnological objects displayed in a former boat house. Other villages are **Vitória** (which houses some lovely Portuguese primitive painting in the 17th-century **Capela de Nossa Senhora da Vitória**), Guadalupe, Luz, and Praia. Small churches demonstrate the power of faith no less than grander ones. In singular touches—the precious panels, fresh flowers, exquisite lace-edged altar cloths—there is instant evidence of a fierce devotion.

One of the most fascinating aspects of the island is the volcanic crater called **Caldeira do Enxofre**, with a cavern where there are several still-active fumaroles. At its rim there are views of the four other islands of the central group. But you may descend, if you care to, the 182 stone steps into the dark and sullen interior. At a depth of some 100 meters, you reach the vaulted cavern with its sulphurous lake measuring a daunting 426 feet across by 50 feet deep. Small boys, unofficial guides, might escort you on the way, whistling cheerfully and tossing an occasional stone into black emptiness. It's recommended that you make the descent between 11:00 A.M. and 2:00 P.M., when shafts of sunlight illuminate the interior. You will learn that in the 19th century a Prince Albert of Monaco, a keen oceanographer who studied the Azores waters, was among the first to descend into this geologically unique cavern—by rope. Remarkable though the Enxofre *furna* may be, it is reassuring to return to leafy lanes and soft green fields.

Close by, at Carapacho, a spa of sorts was set up to take advantage of the rich variety of mineral waters. A swim in the translucent sea here would probably be as therapeutic. If you're making a circular drive, pause just west of Santa Cruz, close to the airport, to see the stone whale of Ponta da Barca—a great rock, a lighthouse, and yet another fine view.

Among Graciosa's lodgings is the **Residencial Santa Cruz**, with 20 modest rooms and home-cooked meals of seafood specialties on request. There's also the newer **Residencial**

Ilha Graciosa—both are in Santa Cruz. The local wines are dry and white—try Terra do Conde—and the sweeter *angélica,* a liqueur.

SAO JORGE

Updike must have had São Jorge (56 by 8 km, or 35 by 5 miles) in mind when he wrote about the "great green ships" of the Azores, for it sits staunchly in the middle of the central group like a vigilant, surfaced submarine. Yet, due to its lack of good harbors, its early settlement was spotty. Nevertheless, the island attracted corsairs from around the world, who may have thought it held riches like the gold and silver brought by galleons to Terceira. For poor São Jorge it was a dreadful irony and, as time passed, things got worse. The struggling settlers experienced one bad harvest after another, a series of shocks and eruptions that might have chased out to sea a less hardy and determined people. Isolation and misery eased at last with the building of two ports and finally, in 1983, an airport. Go there now and you'll find a small community spread thinly along the southern rim of their exquisitely beautiful island, busily engaged in fishing, preserving, and, above all, dairy farming (mainly from Herefords) and cheese making. The São Jorge cheese, *queijo de São Jorge* or often simply *queijo da ilha,* has won worldwide markets. It is made in several factories, is big and round (7 to 12 kg/15½ to 26½ pounds), a creamy yellow, solid, and deliciously savory.

Though São Jorge has some pretty villages—notably Velas, Urzelina, Manadas, Calheta, Ribera Seca, and Topo (where women everywhere make brightly colored *colchas,* or coverlets)—the island's main enchantments are scenic. One of its loveliest features are the **fajãs,** flat parcels of neat farmland spread like scatter rugs from cliff to cliff or snugly set in ravines by the sea. There's a string of them along the north coast from the Fajã do Ouvidor to the Fajã da Caldeira do Santo Cristo; a walk along northern São Jorge, with wonderful views of Graciosa and Terceira in the distance, is highly refreshing—especially when fueled by *queijo de São Jorge* and fresh island bread, often baked in ovens using hedgerow wood for fuel and brushed clean with heather. From the 1,053-meter-high (3,455 feet) **Pico da Esperança,** a mountain peak at the center of the island, you'll have views of the whole central group.

You could stay at the **Estalagem das Velas,** which makes up for its stark modern style not only with great views of the islands of Faial and Pico but also with home-cooked meals (on request) of the seafood specialties of the islands, including mussels, crab, and lobster.

FAIAL

Faial fans out irregularly from five sides of the **caldeira**, the volcanic cone in the center of the island (21 by 14 km, or 13 by 8½ miles). Its name is taken from its beech shrubs (*faias* in Portuguese), even though the most prominent plants here are the ubiquitous hydrangeas that prompted the writer Raul Brandão to christen Faial the Ilha Azul, or Blue Island.

Originally settled by the Portuguese, the island was later populated by the Flemish, who came here in search of fortune with their countryman Josse van Huerter, whose name was eventually corrupted into **Horta**, the name of the island's principal city and the only natural port in the Azores. Another prominent foreigner was John Dabney, appointed U.S. consul to the Azores in 1808 and whose family soon controlled the local whaling industry as well as the export of wine and oranges from the neighboring island of Pico. Further development came with Horta's role as a cable center linking Europe with North and South America, which brought foreign companies, such as Deutsch-Atlantische Telegraphengesellschaft and Western Union, to the island at the beginning of this century. The old Western Union compound is now the **Hotel Faial**, the social hub of upscale islanders. You'll find quieter accommodations at the **Estalagem de Santa Cruz**, in a restored 16th-century fort on the harbor across from the peak of Pico island. American actor Raymond Burr ran the place a few years ago before purchasing other property on the island.

Faial is accustomed to foreigners. Allied fleets had it as a friendly base in World War II. Early cross-Atlantic flyers and pilots of the first big aircraft paused here. For the grand Pan American "Clippers" in their day Horta was the natural stopover in the leap across the Atlantic. Not every American, however, has found Horta heavenly. Mark Twain, describing his 1867 stopover there in *Innocents Abroad,* wrote that the "community is eminently Portuguese, that is to say, it is slow, poor, shiftless, sleepy, and lazy. . . . The people lie, and cheat the stranger, and they are desperately ignorant, and have hardly any reverence for their dead."

Times have changed. Today the outsiders who call at Horta are mainly yachtsmen. In season you can find them at **Pete's Café Sport** at rua Tenente Valadim, 9, a scene straight out of the Spouter Inn in *Moby Dick*—and a lively introduction to Faial. Above it, Pete (whose real name is José Azevedo) recently opened a private museum to house his collection of scrimshaw, the traditional old whalers' craft of carving whales' teeth and bone.

Throughout the year you can see a modern artistic tradition at Horta's marina, where yachtsmen have applied their painting skills with varying degrees of success to cover the concrete walls with bright naïve paintings that are supposed to ensure safe passage. The marina is also the setting for Horta's annual **Semana do Mar** (Week of the Sea), a festival from the first to the second Sunday in August that features sporting events, crafts, music, and food. Horta (as well as Ponta Delgada and Angra) figures in several major sail events and races.

Horta's other cultural riches are more historical. In addition to the **Museu de Arte Sacra** with its displays of gilded carved wood, tiles, and religious paintings and sculpture, there is the **Museu de Horta**, which has an exhibit of scenes of Azorean life painstakingly executed in the unusual medium of fig-tree wood. The mostly Baroque Igreja Matriz de São Salvador, Igreja de São Francisco, Igreja de Nossa Senhora do Carmo, and Igreja de Nossa Senhora das Angústias, as well as the panoramic chapel called the Ermida de Nossa Senhora do Pilar, complete the city's major sights.

The relaxed atmosphere of Horta may encourage you to stay in the town, but there is another side to Faial, a raw and dramatic volcanic legacy. At the core of the island you almost know what to expect with a drive up familiar hydrangea-hedged roads to yet another *caldeira*—but, at its rim, nature surprises you with a double take. To your right, you go through a short tunnel to look 400 meters (1,312 feet) down into the green-carpeted crater, its scale and beauty undiminished by comparison with others you've seen. But emerge and look left (southwest) and you face the stunning outline of **Pico**, the peak on the island of the same name that is Portugal's tallest mountain. Perhaps it's wearing a cardinal's hat of a cloud, telling islanders that rain and wind are on the way. A gentle sunset, with pink-tinged cloud, only enhances the striking beauty of the setting. Close to the *caldeira,* rising to Faial's highest point (at 1,043 meters or 3,422 feet) is the mountain, which lacks the nobility of Pico. Its name doesn't help: Cabeço Gordo, or Fat Head mountain.

But go west, too, to see the awesome image of volcanic power at **Ponta dos Capelinhos**, the site of the volcanic eruption that began in September 1957 and rumbled on until October 1958. This was a powerful earth movement that came, not from a mountaintop but from the sea. At first a small island, Capelinhos joined Faial as a new bleak wasteland of a cape, a dune of lava dust that contrasts as startlingly with the soft green vistas of the islands as does the stark black basalt you see elsewhere. A lighthouse here is half-buried in the lava of the dead landscape, and a small museum displays documentation on the eruption.

There is village community life, human creativity in art and music, the pleasant conviviality of the boats in the harbor, and nature's fearsome crafting of volcanoes. Spend a little time on the island, go fishing, go slowly, walk, look, and listen—to the rock music of the Horta discos, and the echoing sighs of long-gone whaling men.

Horta has several pleasant places to pass the evening. To eat, it's hard to beat the notable restaurant of the **Estalagem de Santa Cruz** on rua Vasco da Gama, with the sea beside you.

PICO

"The isle of Pico has its name from the peak or high mountain upon it, which is frequently capt with clouds, and serves the inhabitants of Fayal nearly the same purpose as a barometer." So wrote George Forster in *A Voyage Round the World* in 1777.

The peak, the highest in Portugal at 2,351 meters (7,714 feet), has a shape so pure and graceful that, like a Mount Fuji lost at sea, it's hypnotic. For many it's the principal reason for visiting the island of Pico (42 by 15 km, or 26 by 9 miles), especially since blight killed off most of the vines that once produced the *verdelho* wine served as far away as the tables of the czars. To climb the mountain—in summer only—you should go with a guide. (Contact the tourist office in Horta on Faial, on rua Vasco da Gama; Tel: 092-222-37.) You will normally climb to caves in the afternoon, sleep in them overnight, rise at 2:30 A.M. and climb until 5:30 A.M. for a dawn view down Pico and across to Faial, Terceira, Graciosa, and São Jorge, from behind whose long, thin spine you can watch the sun rise. It takes two or three hours to descend.

If you're not a climber but would just like a pleasant day trip from Faial, cross the channel from Horta (Vitorino Nemésio's novel *Bad Weather in the Channel* immortalized the crossing in literature) for a closer look at Pico. Don't let that title put you off. The weather is often clear and sunny;

launches packed with islanders and their well-wrapped bundles make several trips each way every day from Horta to Madalena on Pico, a distance of 5 nautical miles. You can arrange a half-day or full-day trip with a taxi directly, or through an agency—Ornelas is one (see Getting Around). A drive along Pico's perimeter would take you through towns and villages interspersed with stark lava wastelands, the *mistérios*. Heading south from the entry port of Madalena, you'll pass the village of Candelária in an area of orchards and vines, and the **Mistério de São João** on the way to **Lajes do Pico**.

In Lajes you are in the island's first town, where settlement began about 1460. The Ermida de São Pedro, the island's first church, once roofed with thatch, is here, its window and door in perfect symmetry. Stark white and edged with black, it echoes the style of many much rougher black-and-white basalt cottages that you'll see on the island. There's now a **Museu dos Baleeiros**, a whaling museum, installed in the old boathouse on rua da Pesqueira. Scrimshaw is on display, from paper knives to handsome sailing boats, items carved from both whalebone and whale teeth. At the café you can get a coffee or try the island wine, *cavaco,* which tastes like a strong cider.

From Lajes, take the inland road through the little lake district to see more dramatically bleak phenomena at **Mistério da Prainha**. The road leads you to the port of São Roque, where *cachalotes,* small sperm whales, only a few years ago were brought up the slipway, greasily carved into great chunks and rendered into blubber and bone. (Here, it was the closing of the islands' last factory when one owner died that stopped the whaling, rather than any EC ruling.) Whatever you think of whaling, to the islanders the men who went out in canoes to harpoon the whales were—and are—heroic figures. They are there still, dreaming, yearning, recalling the days when whaling was *o pão dos pobres,* the poor man's bread (only the boat captain profited: he owned the teeth), and perpetually awaiting the call to the boats.

You could drive west along the north coast, dotted by the village life of boats, the land, the wall-enclosed vines, the church. How charming it all looks, and how picturesque, but every inch of the way you will see evidence in these villages of the long, hard labor that transformed volcanic rock to cottage wall, to a windproof hedge, to soil that fosters productive cultivation. You could either complete the circuit or return the same way, heading across the base of the peak to **Mistério de Santa Luzia** before returning to Madalena for the boat back to Horta. If you fancy staying on Pico island, you'll find the **Hotel Caravelas** in Madalena comfortable. Additionally, São Roque, Lajes do Pico, and Madalena each have a modest *pensão*.

FLORES AND CORVO

"At Flores in the Azores Sir Richard Grenville lay," begins Tennyson's famous poem about the English privateer's fateful encounter with the Spanish fleet off the island in 1591. Such stories of violence (there is another one about the Confederate *Alabama,* equipped by the British in the Azores, which wreaked havoc among Union ships off Flores during the American Civil War) illustrate that sea charts and island geography were well advanced, human ambition and greed sadly predictable, and nothing at all about the natural beauty of the little island. The flowers that gave **Flores** its name flourish all year round on the island, which receives twice as much rain as São Miguel, though if you come in summer what you'll see most are the sky-blue hydrangeas that rule elsewhere. Even the fussy Twain was eventually pleased: "It seemed only a mountain of mud standing up out of the dull mists of the sea," he wrote. "But as we bore down on it the sun came out and made it a beautiful picture—a mass of green farms and meadows that welled up to a height of fifteen hundred feet, and mingled its upper outlines with the clouds. . . . It was the aurora borealis of the frozen pole exiled to a summer land!"

On this pineapple-shaped island (17 by 12½ km, or 10½ by 8 miles) **Santa Cruz**, the main town, is located on the east coast. You'll find its **Museu Etnográfico**, a small museum in a former monastery with a collection illustrating the island's agrarian, fishing, and religious activities, at praça Marquês de Pombal, and there are two interesting churches, the 17th-century Igreja de São Boaventura and the 19th-century Igreja de Nossa Senhora da Conceição. Other places to see are the village of **Fajãzinha**, picturesquely located near the waterfall of Ribeira Grande, and the numerous chapels, water mills, and waterfalls around the island. Also of interest are the island's rock formations, especially the **Enxaréus grotto** and the **Rocha das Bordões**, a great striated basalt cliff in the southwest—both best seen from a boat. If you include in your trip a look at the islet of **Monchique**, you will have joined the estimable company of mariners who have navigated to the westernmost point of Europe. In Santa Cruz you could stay at the **Residencial Vila Flores**.

On Flores you should be able to persuade a local boat-man to make the crossing to **Corvo**, the northernmost, smallest (6½ by 4 km, or 4 by 2½ miles), and, for our purposes, last of the Azores, inhabited by only a few hundred people who speak an archaic form of Portuguese. Azoreans say there are several accents in the islands, all different from mainland Portugal. In any language, you will find someone to help you arrange a boat to sail around the tiny island. In any case, visit the village of **Vila Nova do Corvo**, known locally as Corvo, which prides itself on being the smallest town in Portugal (population 300), and whose dignity was much offended when mainland newspapers turned the island's first road accident, between its one car and one of a few motorbikes, into a comic item. From Corvo, you could walk—or perhaps hitch a ride on a tractor—to **Caldeirão**, Corvo's extinct volcano. Inside is a crater lake with nine tiny islands, lightly said to be a microcosm of the Azores themselves.

GETTING AROUND

TAP Air Portugal, the Portuguese national airline, flies from Lisbon directly to São Miguel, Terceira, and Faial in about two and a half hours, and from Boston directly to São Miguel in about four hours Direct charter flights are often available from such travel agencies as Azores Express (199 South Main Street, Fall River, MA 02721, Tel: 800-762-9995 or 508-677-0555); Suntrips (2350 Paragon Drive, San Jose, CA 95131, Tel: 800-444-7866 or 408-432-1101); and Lawson Tours (2 Carlton Street, Toronto M5B 1J2, Canada, Tel: 416-977-3000).

Within the archipelago, SATA Air Açores (main office: avenida Infante Dom Henrique, 55; 9500 Ponta Delgada, São Miguel; Tel: 096-223-11) flies among all the islands except Corvo, using a fleet of British Aerospace turboprops. The islands are spread out: It takes about 40 minutes to fly from São Miguel to Terceira; another 30 minutes from Terceira to Faial; and about 25 minutes from Faial to Graciosa. Space is limited and overbookings are not infrequent, so be sure to confirm your reservations and arrive at the airport at least an hour before departure time.

Passenger boats and smaller craft sail to all the islands. Current schedules are available from the Ornelas Travel Agency (avenida Infante Dom Henrique, 41, 9500 Ponta Delgada, São Miguel, Tel: 096-253-79) and government tourist offices (avenida Infante Dom Henrique, 9500 Ponta Delgada, São Miguel, Tel: 096-257-43; Airport, Santa Maria, Tel: 096-863-55; Terreiro dos Cavales, 47, 9700 Angra do Heroismo,

Terceira, Tel: 095-233-93; rua Vasco da Gama, 9900 Horta, Faial, Tel: 092-222-37).

On individual islands, the most flexible means of transportation is a car. Tourist offices have information about renting them as well as motorcycles and bicycles.

For what's going on when and where, check with Turismo on your arrival. They keep a printed calendar of *festas* and happenings that includes the main religious holidays (look for any of the Espírito Santo processions, the most numerous and important) as well as sail events, car racing, music concerts, ballet, golf and tennis championships, gastronomy gatherings, and bullfights. Every tiny village has its saint's day with a procession and celebration. A selection of the main *festas* includes: Carnaval in February or March, the Easter cycle—religious feasts that take place between Lent and the feast of the Sacred Heart—and Pentecost celebrations that last to the end of summer and are mainly connected with the strong cult of the Espírito Santo (Holy Spirit). A number of other celebrations also occur regularly.

On São Miguel the Procissão do Senhor dos Enfermos (Procession of Our Lord of the Infirm) takes place the first Sunday after Easter in Vale das Furnas; the Santo Cristo festival the fifth Sunday after Easter; the Procissão do Trabalho (Procession of Labor) in Vila Franca do Campo the Sunday following May 8, and the Festa do Senhor Bom Jesus da Pedra the last weekend in August in Vila Franca do Campo; there are special ceremonies throughout the island called Véspera de Reis (Vespers of the Kings) on January 6 and Cantorias das Estrelas (Singing of the Stars) on February 2.

On Santa Maria, the Festa de Santo Amaro takes place January 15 in Almagreira and the Festas da Vila August 15 in Vila do Porto. On Terceira, the *tourada à corda* (running of the bulls) kicks off the bullfight season, which begins in May and takes place throughout the summer, alternately in Angra do Heroismo and Praia da Vitória. On São Jorge, the Festa de São Jorge happens in Velas in April, and a procession takes place the first Sunday in September in Fajã do Santo Cristo.

On Faial the Nossa Senhora das Angústias festivities are celebrated in May; the Festa de São João takes place June 24; the Semana do Mar from the first to the second Sunday in August; all in Horta. On Pico, the eventful Festa de Bom Jesus takes place in São Mateus on August 6, and the Semana dos Baleeiros is in Lajes do Pico the last week of August; there is a small grape harvest the second week of September at Madalena. On Corvo, the leading festival, the Festa da Padroeira (patron saint), takes place on August 15. Flores

celebrates its Festa do Emigrante in Lajes the second weekend of July, but, as in other islands, the Festas do Espírito
Santo predominate.

ACCOMMODATIONS REFERENCE

*Rates given are projected 1993 prices for a double room,
double occupancy. Price ranges span the lowest rate in the
low season to the highest in the high season. Unless otherwise
stated, rates include Continental breakfast. As prices are
subject to change, always double-check before booking.*

▶ **Casa de Nossa Senhora do Carmo.** Rua do Pópulo de
Cima, 220, Livramento, **Ponta Delgada**, 9500 São Miguel. Tel:
(096) 322-48. 11,200$00–14,400$00.

▶ **Estalagem de Santa Cruz.** Rua Vasco da Gama, **Horta**,
9900 Faial. Tel: (092) 230-21; Fax: (092) 229-40. 12,300$00–
15,000$00.

▶ **Estalagem das Velas.** Velas, 9800 São Jorge. Tel: (095)
426-32; Telex: 82725 ESTVEL P. 8,000$00–9,500$00.

▶ **Estalagem Vinha de Areia.** Vila Franca do Campo, 9680
São Miguel. Tel: (096) 531-33; Fax: (096) 525-01. 10,000$00–
13,000$00.

▶ **Hotel Açores Atlântico.** Avenida Infante Dom Henrique,
Ponta Delgada, 9500 São Miguel. Tel: (096) 62-93-00; Fax:
(096) 62-93-80. 12,500$00–17,000$00.

▶ **Hotel do Aeroporto. Vila do Porto,** 9580 Santa Maria.
Tel: (096) 862-11; Fax: (096) 865-34. 7,200$00–8,000$00.

▶ **Hotel de Angra.** Praça Velha, **Angra de Heroismo,** 9700
Terceira. Tel. and Fax: (095) 270-41. 11,000$00–12,400$00.

▶ **Hotel Caloura.** Agua de Pau, **Lagoa,** 9560 São Miguel.
Tel: (096) 932-40; Fax: (096) 936-11. 9,900$00–14,700$00.

▶ **Hotel Caravelas.** Rua Conselheiro Terra Pinheiro,
Madalena, 9950 Pico. Tel: (092) 62-25-00; Telex: 82696
AHOTEL P. 9,500$00–12,000$00.

▶ **Hotel Faial.** Rua Consul Dabney, **Horta,** 9900 Faial. Tel:
(092) 221-81; Fax: (092) 221-89. 9,500$00–14,950$00.

▶ **Hotel São Pedro.** Largo Almirante Dunn, **Ponta Delgada,**
9500 São Miguel. Tel: (096) 222-23; Fax: (096) 62-93-19.
11,500$00–14,400$00.

▶ **Hotel Terra Nostra.** Rua Padre José Francisco Botelho,
Furnas, 9675 São Miguel. Tel. and Fax: (096) 543-04.
11,500$00–15,500$00.

▶ **Residencial Beira Mar.** Rua de São João, 1–5, **Angra do
Heroismo,** 9700 Terceira. Tel: (095) 251-89; Fax: (095) 259-
99. 5,900$00–7,900$00.

▶ **Residencial Ilha Graciosa.** Avenida Mouzinho de Albuquerque, **Santa Cruz**, 9880 Graciosa. Tel: (095) 726-75; Telex: 82683 REGRAC P. 7,000$00–8,000$00.

▶ **Residencial Santa Cruz. Santa Cruz da Graciosa**, 9880 Graciosa. Tel: (095) 723-45; Fax: (095) 728-28. 4,500$00–5,200$00.

▶ **Residencial Vila Flores**. Travessa de São José, 9970 **Santa Cruz**, Flores. Tel: (092) 521-90; Fax: (092) 526-21. 4,500$00–6,000$00.

CHRONOLOGY OF THE HISTORY OF PORTUGAL

Prehistory

Portugal's long and rambunctious history began in Paleolithic times, perhaps half a million years ago. Chellean and Acheulian hand axes have been unearthed near Lisbon, together with tools and weapons shaped of flint and bone (some of these are on display in the ethnological museum next door to the Jerónimos monastery in the Lisbon suburb of Belém). According to *Past Worlds: The Times Atlas of Archaeology,* there have been significant finds up and down the west coast of Portugal between the Algarve-Alentejo border and Coimbra in the Beira Litoral, some 185 miles to the north. But the most exciting discovery is the most recent: In the early 1960s a small painted cave was found in the Alentejo, 80 miles southeast of Lisbon.

- **18,000–13,000 B.C.:** The bull, horse, and hybrid figures crudely drawn on the walls of the Escoural Cave (9 miles south of Montemor-o-Novo and 25 miles west of Evora) may not be as extensive as those at Lascaux in France or Altamira in Spain, but they may be even older and they certainly give some notion as to the manner of man who roamed these red-brown plains before the dawn of recorded history.

- **4000–1500 B.C.:** Megalithic culture flowers in Portugal, particularly around present-day Evora in the Alentejo. This cult of standing stones, of stone gods, then spread north to France and Britain—or so archaeologists now suspect. Clusters of dolmens, menhirs, and chromlechs (areas marked off by stones) still exist throughout the Alentejo. Elsewhere in Portugal the major megalithic sites are the splendidly preserved Dolmen de Barrosa near the Minho seaside resort of Ancora, and, in Trás-os-Montes just northwest of Chaves, the great rock at Outeiro Machado, upon which early Neolithic artists have left more than 350 carvings—axes, ladders, even human faces.

Migrations and Invasions

- **1100–600 B.C.:** Phoenicians trade along the south and west coasts of Portugal, establishing the post of Alisubbo (now Lisbon), then moving as far north as Nazaré and Aveiro. The people of these two fishing towns claim to be descended from the Phoenicians, and certainly the design of their boats—flat bottoms and high, turned-up prows—is pure Phoenician. Next came the Carthaginians (Phoenicians who had settled in North Africa near Tunis in the ninth century B.C.) and then the Greeks, each sailing out of the Mediterranean through the Straits of Gibraltar, then moving west along the Algarve coast before rounding the land's-end promontory of Cabo de São Vicente and following the rugged shore north to Lisbon.

- **700–600 B.C.:** Invasion and occupation by the Celts, who build fortified towns on hilltops throughout the northern half of Portugal. The major remaining sites (Portugal's oldest settlements) are Citânia de Briteiros and Castro de Sabroso, southeast of Braga in the Minho province. At the larger, more impressive Briteiros, two houses (circular structures of stone) have been reconstructed, the better to show what life was like in this Celtic town. There was a public water system here, a well-laid-out street plan, even an escape tunnel leading down to the river Ave hundreds of yards below. Celtic ornaments, implements, and painted pottery recovered at the site can be seen in Guimarães at the Museu Martins Sarmento (named for the 19th-century archaeologist who excavated these sites). While Celts were taking over the north of Portugal, the Iberians, possibly from North Africa, occupied the south but unfortunately left few traces.

- **535 B.C.:** The Carthaginians settle at Cádiz, dominating the region until 206 B.C., toward the end of the Second Punic War.

Roman Portugal

At the time of the Second Punic War (218–201 B.C.), the Lusitanian people, of largely Celtic origin, populate the land. The Romans drive out the ruling Carthaginians in 206 B.C. but don't reach the westernmost part of it (what is now Portugal) until some decades later. During their 600-year occupation the Romans build extensively throughout Portugal: temples, roads, aqueducts, and cities, the wealthiest city being Conimbriga (second century B.C.–A.D. 468), not far south of today's Coimbra. Now being excavated, Conimbriga sprawls across a field. There are colonnaded streets, reflecting pools, fountains, and intricate mosaics worked out in chips of red, white, and black marble.

Iberia's best-preserved Roman temple stands in Portugal, too: the little Corinthian temple of Diana at Evora (second century A.D.).

- **197–179 B.C.:** The Lusitanian War rages between the Romans and the Lusitanians, the warlike Celtic tribes and other peoples already occupying what is now Portugal, and at the end of it Lusitania becomes a part of the Roman province of Hispania Ulterior.

- **154–139 B.C.:** Lusitanian resisters try to oust the Romans. Their leader, a valiant warrior named Viriathus, or Viriato ("The Man with the Bracelets"), is today a Portuguese national hero of epic proportion.

- **138 B.C.:** Romans kill Viriathus at Viseu, smash the resistance, and begin colonizing Portugal in earnest. Local resistance continues for more than 100 years.

- **61–45 B.C.:** Julius Caesar manages to subdue the restive population of Hispania Ulterior. In 60 B.C. he establishes a provincial capital at the Roman seaport of Olisipo (Lisbon) and begins building towns at Santarém, Evora, Elvas, and Beja. Caesar also turns the Alentejo into "the granary of Rome" (it remains Portugal's breadbasket today).

- **27 B.C.–A.D. 212:** Under Augustus (and the Pax Romana) Iberia is almost wholly Romanized. The old Hispania Ulterior is split into two provinces: Baetica (now Andalusia) and Lusitania (most of Portugal plus the modern-day Spanish provinces of Extremadura and Salamanca). Portugal north of the Douro river later becomes part of the Roman province of Gallaecia.

- **A.D. 200 onward:** The Christianization of Portugal begins, and bishoprics are established at Braga, Lisbon, Evora, and Faro.

Visigothic Portugal

The fifth century sees the decline of the Roman Empire in Iberia as the Germanic Suevi, Vandals, Alans, and Visigoths sweep in from the north and east. At first the Visigoths respect the Roman Order, but by the end of the sixth century they rule Iberia themselves from their powerful seat at Toledo.

- **409:** The first wave of barbarians—Vandals, Alans, and Suevi—cross the Pyrenees into Spain, then, in time, move westward to Portugal. Only the Germanic Suevi, sometimes called Swabians, who settled between the Roman city of Portus (Porto) on the Douro and the Minho river farther north, and the Visigoths, who ultimately ruled Portugal, left their mark. Although Visigothic ruins are scattered over much of Portugal, the only Suevic relic of significance is the seventh-century Byzantine church of São Frutuoso at Braga in the Minho.
- **410:** Suevi kingdom of Gaellica is founded north of the Tagus river.
- **414–418:** Visigoths arrive and drive out the Vandals and the Alans, eventually into Africa. The Suevi mingle and merge with the locals.
- **474:** End of Roman rule in the Iberian Peninsula after the Battle of Tarraco (modern Tarragona, Spain).
- **585:** Led by King Leovigild, the Visigoths suppress the Suevi and annex Seuvic territory to their kingdom of Toledo.
- **586 onward:** Now ruled by King Recared, the Visigoths become Roman Catholics and begin persecuting Spanish and Portuguese Jews.

Moorish Portugal

When they first call on North African Muslims to help them defeat the Visigoths, few of the native peoples living on the Iberian Peninsula dream that the Moors would overrun it, then rule large parts of it for more than 500 years. Or that they would change the very look of their land and leave imprints—architectural, agricultural, and otherwise—that are still clearly visible. The *azulejos* (decorative glazed tiles) that face so many Portuguese buildings today were introduced by the Moors, for example, as were the tall filigreed chimney pots and giant water wheels still in use in the Algarve (itself an Arabic word meaning "the west"), the arcaded streets, the fountain-splashed courtyards, and the water gardens so characteristic of Portugal.

- **711:** A Visigothic faction supporting King Witiza appeals to North Africa for help in defeating the imperious, intolerant Visigoths. The Moors cross the Straits of Gibraltar into Spain and begin their conquest of Iberia.
- **716:** Braga, the former Suevic capital, falls to the Moors.
- **717:** All of Iberia is in Moorish hands except for the mountainous far north. The Visigoths, still in control of Asturias in north-central Spain, begin the Christian Reconquest of Arab-held peninsular lands.
- **722:** The north of Portugal is reclaimed from the Moors as far south as Porto, which changes hands several times over the next three centuries.
- **868:** As part of the attempt to reconstitute a Christian kingdom, the soldier Vimara Peres briefly holds Porto and builds a castle at Vimarenes, a town later known as Guimarães and often called the Cradle of Portugal.
- **931:** The beginnings of a dynasty of the counts of Portugal under Count Hermengildo Gonçalves (popularly known as Count Mendo) and his wife, the Countess Mumadona Dias.
- **945:** Mumadona founds the monastery of Salvador do Mundo on the site of the present-day church of Nossa Senhora da Oliveira in Guimarães.
- **968:** The counts repel a Viking invasion of the northwestern part of the peninsula. The Vikings weaken the Moors in the south.
- **1035 onward:** The rise of Castile under Ferdinand I. He reconquers Coimbra in 1064, by which time Mumadona's dynasty is in complete decline. In the reconquered areas, Christians replace Muslims as the dominant class, but the new sovereigns retain some Muslim religious, secular, and economic institutions.
- **1092:** The Moors lose Porto for the last time.

The Dawn of Portuguese Nationhood

- **1095**: Santarém and Lisbon fall to the Moors. Alfonso VI, king of León and Castile, marries his daughter Teresa to the French knight Henry of Burgundy, who had fought so valiantly against the Moors. He dubs Henry earl of Portucale.
- **1109**: The Spanish kingdom of León and Castile makes Portucale an independent county within its realm.
- **1111**: Birth of the earl of Portucale's first son at the castle of Guimarães. Named Afonso Henriques, he will become the first king of Portugal.
- **1112**: Henry dies. Teresa governs but arouses hostility because of her fruitless interventions in León.
- **1128**: At the urging of local barons, young Afonso Henriques revolts against his mother, defeats her forces at the Battle of São Mamede at Guimarães, and seizes control: the first decisive step toward the formation of the Kingdom of Portugal.
- **1139**: Afonso Henriques declares Portucale independent of the Spanish kingdom of León and Castile and proclaims himself King Afonso I.
- **1143**: Portugal's independence recognized by León.
- **1147**: Afonso marches south from Porto and, with the help of Crusaders, drives the Moors from all lands as far south as the Tagus, including Lisbon and Santarém.
- **1179**: After half a century of squabbling between León and Castile and Portugal, Rome recognizes Afonso as king of the "sovereign and independent state of Portugal."
- **1185–1223**: Afonso's successors in the Burgundian dynasty, Sancho I and Afonso II, work to consolidate and unify Portugal south along the coast. During this period the Knights Templars and the Knights Hospitalers, military orders founded earlier in Palestine, extend their activities to Portugal, as do the Knights of Calatrava, founded in Castile in 1156. The Portuguese branch of the Order of Santiago is also founded.
- **1249**: Afonso III recaptures Faro in the Algarve, and the last of the Moorish forces leave Portugal. Afonso III reigns until 1279, restricting the power and privileges of the Church and including commoners in the Cortes (the legislative body).
- **1256**: Lisbon is named capital of Portugal.

- **1279–1325:** The reign of Dinis I. This forward-thinking king unifies Portugal, institutes programs of economic and agricultural reform, founds the Portuguese navy, and builds 50 fortresses along the Spanish border (among them the hilltop castles at Estremoz, Marvão, and Monsaraz). He also negotiates the Treaty of Alcañices (1297), forcing Castile to honor Portugal's boundaries, and founds a university at Lisbon (1290). Later moved to Coimbra, it is Continental Europe's second-oldest university (after Bologna).

The Age of Discovery

Troubles with Castile (now separate from León) continue. When Fernando I, the last of the Burgundian-dynasty kings, dies, power passes to his widow, Leonor Teles, who marries their only child, a daughter, to Juan I of Castile, with the condition that the Portuguese throne pass to her unborn grandson. But the people rise up and name as regent and defender of the realm João, Grand Master of Avis (a bastard son of Pedro I, known as "the Just").

- **1385:** In April João ascends the throne as João I, the founder of the Avis dynasty. In August he defeats the Castilians at the Battle of Aljubarrota.
- **1386:** João I signs the Treaty of Windsor with England, which ensures "an inviolable, eternal, strong, perpetual and true league of friendship, alliance and union."
- **1387:** João I marries Philippa of Lancaster, daughter of John of Gaunt, further cementing Portugal's ties with England.
- **1394:** Infante Dom Henrique (Prince Henry the Navigator), the third son of João I and Queen Philippa, is born in Porto.
- **1415:** Conquest of Ceuta, on the North African coast, marking the beginning of Portuguese expansion.
- **1419:** Prince Henry goes to Sagres and Cabo de São Vicente in the Algarve to found his school of navigation, remains of which can still be seen.
- **1419–1425:** Portugal colonizes the Madeira islands, discovered late in the previous century.
- **1431–1432:** Portugal claims the Azores, discovered in the late 14th century.

- **1433**: João I dies, and Prince Henry's oldest brother, Dom Duarte, ascends the throne.
- **1434–1435**: Portuguese navigators round Cape Bojador on the west coast of Africa.
- **1436–1437**: Prince Henry leads an attack against Tangier but is defeated.
- **1438**: Prince Henry returns to Sagres and the voyages of discovery.
- **1444**: Portuguese navigators reach Cape Verde; slave trade begins at Lagos in the Algarve.
- **1445–1457**: Portuguese forces push farther down Africa's west coast, reaching Senegal, Gambia, and the Cape Verde Islands.
- **1458**: The king of Portugal commissions Venetian cartographer Fra Mauro to draft a new map of the world incorporating all of Prince Henry's discoveries.
- **1460**: Prince Henry dies at Sagres at the age of 66.
- **1469**: Vasco da Gama is born.
- **1482**: Portuguese navigators reach the mouth of the Congo river.
- **1484**: King João II refuses to finance the voyages of a Genoese explorer who had served Prince Henry and married the daughter of one of his navigators. His name: Christopher Columbus. (A controversial new theory holds that Columbus was not Italian but Portuguese.)
- **1488**: Portuguese explorer Bartolomeu Dias rounds Africa's Cape of Good Hope.
- **1492**: Columbus, sailing under the Spanish flag, discovers the West Indies.
- **1494**: Portugal and Castile sign the Treaty of Tordesillas, which grants to Castile all discoveries west of a mid-Atlantic meridian (370 sea leagues west of the Cape Verde Islands) and to Portugal all discoveries east of it, which includes Brazil (historians believe the Portuguese already had some inkling of its existence at the time of the treaty).
- **1495–1521**: Reign of Manuel I (Prince Henry's great-great nephew) and the flowering of the exuberant architectural style named for him. The best examples of Manueline architecture are the tower of Belém and the Jerónimos monastery near Lisbon, the famous "rope" window at the Convento de Cristo at Tomar, and the cloister and "unfinished chapels" at the great

cathedral at Batalha, which Prince Henry's father began building to commemorate Portugal's victory over Castile at Aljubarrota. Prince Henry lies buried here together with members of his immediate family.

- **1496:** Expulsion of the Jews from Portugal, following their expulsion from Spain in 1492.
- **1497–1498:** Vasco da Gama leaves Lisbon for the East Indies, rounds the Cape of Good Hope, arrives at Mozambique, then sails on to India.
- **1500:** Portuguese navigator Pedro Alvares Cabral discovers Brazil (see also 1494, above).
- **1510:** The Portuguese annex Goa on the southwest coast of India after failing to conquer Calicut.
- **1515:** The Portuguese control the Indian Ocean.
- **1519–1521:** Magellan, a Portuguese said to have been born in the landlocked province of Trás-os-Montes, sails east from Sanlúcar de Barrameda, Spain, in the service of the king of Spain, to circle the globe. He is killed in the Philippines, but one of his captains completes the round-the-world voyage in 1522.
- **1521–1557:** Reign of João III, who, married to a sister of Charles V, fell under Castilian influence. Portugal, now heavily in debt because of its voyages of discovery, suffers a decline.
- **1524:** Luiz Vaz de Camões, Portugal's great epic poet, is born in Lisbon. Vasco da Gama dies.
- **1536–1558:** The Portuguese Inquisition is at the height of its power.
- **1557:** The Portuguese open a trading post at Macão in China.
- **1572:** *The Lusiads,* Camões's epic poem immortalizing Portugal's voyages of discovery, is published in Lisbon.
- **1580:** Camões dies in Lisbon.
- **1638:** C. M. Kopke, a German living in Porto, founds the first Port wine company. It still bears his name and is the most distinguished house in the Barrios Almeida group.

The Spanish Domination

In 1580, with Portugal impoverished and its army destroyed by the Moroccans at Alcácer-Quivir, Philip II of Spain pounces, annexing not only mainland Portugal but also such colonies as Madeira. When he denies Dutch ships entry to

Lisbon to load spices from the Portuguese islands in the East, they sail on to the Indies and soon not only shut the Portuguese out of the spice trade but also seize such valuable possessions as the Moluccas, São Tomé (in the Gulf of Guinea off the west coast of Africa), Angola, and Brazil. Under the three Philips, II, III, and IV, Spain dominates Portugal for 60 years. At the end of Spanish rule in 1640, Portugal is little more than a backward province. There is much emigration, to Brazil, England, the African colonies, and North America.

The Rise of the House of Bragança

Outraged by the crushing taxes levied to finance Spanish wars, the nobles of Lisbon rebel. Led by the duke of Bragança and aided by the French, the Portuguese regain their independence.

- **1640–1656**: João, duke of Bragança, rules newly liberated Portugal as João IV. Wars with Spain continue. During João IV's reign Portugal regains Brazil, Angola, and São Tomé (since 1975 the independent African Republic of São Tomé and Principe).
- **1662**: Catherine of Bragança, sister of Afonso VI, marries Charles II of England (it is for her that New York City's borough of Queens is named). The British finance the defense of Portugal.
- **1668**: After a long series of wars and invasions, the Treaty of Lisbon is signed, and Spain at last recognizes Portugal's independence.
- **1703**: The Treaty of Methuen is signed with Britain, allowing Portuguese wines to be sold in Britain and British woollens in Portugal, whereupon the Portuguese textile industry collapses.
- **1706–1750**: The reign of João V. Portugal once again grows rich and powerful thanks to the discovery of gold and diamonds in Brazil. Many of the country's most resplendent buildings are built, including the palace at Mafra, the summer palace at Queluz just outside Lisbon, and the Baroque library at Coimbra (by most accounts, the world's most beautiful library because of its painted ceilings and rare gilded and inlaid woods).
- **1755**: The great earthquake and fire destroy most of Lisbon and kill more than 30,000 people. With the blessing of José I, the marquês de Pombal redesigns

the city and Lisbon becomes a town of leafy squares and broad boulevards lined with buildings four and five stories tall.

- **1755–1777**: José I all but hands the throne to the rigid and tyrannical marquês de Pombal, who tries, among other things, to throw off the English yoke and make Portugal economically independent. He also expels the Jesuits because they have become too powerful.
- **1756**: Port-wine-growing region demarcated (100 years before France's *appellation contrôlée*).
- **1777–1792**: José I dies, Maria I (The Mad) ascends the throne, and the marquês de Pombal falls from grace. Most of Pombal's reforms are rescinded; the Jesuits return to Portugal.
- **1792**: With Maria I now deranged, João VI becomes regent.

The Peninsular War

Because of its great alliance with Britain, Portugal is drawn more or less unwillingly into the Napoleonic Wars; as a result, battles are fought on her soil that terribly devastate the country.

- **1793**: Portugal joins Britain in its struggle against Napoleon.
- **1801**: Portugal loses Olivenza to Spain.
- **1807**: Junot's French troops invade Portugal. The Portuguese royal family flees to Brazil.
- **1808**: Wellington arrives with detachments of British soldiers to fight the French.
- **1810**: Wellington scores the decisive victory against the French by winning the Battle of Buçaco just north of Coimbra.

The Decline and Fall of the Monarchy

- **1811**: The French are driven out of Portugal into Spain. With the Portuguese royal family still in exile in Brazil, British General William Carr Beresford governs newly liberated Portugal.
- **1815**: Brazil is now a kingdom united with Portugal. João VI prefers to reside in Brazil.

- **1817–1820**: Weary of British rule, Portuguese liberals rise up repeatedly, only to be quelled by British soldiers.

- **1820–1821**: A new liberal Portuguese constitution is drafted and approved by the Cortes, which confirms João VI king of Portugal. He returns from Brazil with Queen Carlota and their younger son, Miguel. Crown Prince Pedro remains in Brazil. The king agrees to the terms of the new constitution; Queen Carlota and Prince Miguel do not and are exiled.

- **1822**: Pedro declares Brazilian independence rather than return to a constitutional Portugal.

- **1825–1834**: João VI dies and Crown Prince Pedro, now emperor of Brazil, is proclaimed king. Pedro refuses to return to Portugal and vows, instead, to pass the crown to his baby daughter, Maria da Glória, and to let his younger brother, Miguel, serve as regent until she comes of age. Prince Miguel agrees, but soon after assuming power he reneges, abolishes the new constitution, and returns to the absolutist ways. Crown Prince Pedro, deposed as emperor of Brazil, returns to Portugal to find that his brother has seized the throne. The Miguelist Wars follow, until Pedro defeats Miguel once and for all at Evoramonte. Pedro IV no sooner gains power than he dies. His daughter, Maria da Glória, now 15, succeeds him as Maria II.

- **1836**: Maria II marries Duke Ferdinand of Saxe-Coburg-Koháry, a cousin of Queen Victoria's consort, Prince Albert.

- **1837–1907**: Unrest continues with repeated power plays among the liberals and conservatives. An anticlerical movement leaves many great monasteries derelict.

- **1861–1869**: Under King Luis I, liberals and conservatives serve in office in turn, in a system called rotavism.

- **1908**: King Carlos I is assassinated in Lisbon along with Crown Prince Luís Filipe. Carlos's second son ascends the throne as Manuel II.

- **1910**: To save Portugal from civil war, King Manuel abdicates, retreats to England, and remains there in exile until his death in 1932. The Republic is born on October 5.

The Republic of Portugal

The young republic struggles to restore order and a sound economy, but with little success.

- **1916**: Portugal joins the Allies and declares war on Germany.
- **1917–1922**: The war leaves Portugal financially depleted and minus much of its manpower. This is a period of postwar chaos—economic, social, and political.
- **1926**: A military coup overthrows the government and General António Carmona soon emerges as Portugal's new president; he remains in office until his death in 1951.
- **1928**: Dr. António de Oliveira Salazar, an economics professor from the university at Coimbra, is named finance minister; he quickly balances Portugal's budget and helps restore political order.
- **1932 onward**: Salazar becomes prime minister and within a year masterminds the organization of the New State, which gives him the powers of a dictator.
- **1939–1945**: Portugal remains neutral during World War II but allows Great Britain and the United States to build air bases in the Azores.
- **1949**: Portugal is an original member of NATO.
- **1961**: Portugal loses its colony of Goa to India.
- **1968**: A freak accident incapacitates Salazar (his deck chair collapses and he suffers irreversible brain damage). His successor, Marcelo Caetano, continues the rigid Salazar policies, including an unpopular war with the African colonies.
- **1970**: Salazar dies.
- **1974**: On April 25 the military seizes power in a virtually bloodless coup now known as the Flower Revolution (soldiers march through Lisbon with red carnations stuck into the barrels of their guns). Portugal veers sharply toward the left as Communists and Socialists gain strength at the polls. Communism is especially popular among the farmers of the Alentejo, who work the vast estates of absentee owners for very little pay.
- **1974–1975**: Portugal's African colonies of Angola, Mozambique, Guinea, São Tomé, and the Cape Verde Islands gain independence, and more than 500,000 refugees flood into Lisbon. Because of a housing

shortage, the leftist government domiciles them in worker-run tourist hotels (even the Ritz is commandeered).

- **1976 onward:** A new constitution is adopted. Political power struggles continue among rightists, centrists, and leftists, but gradually a more stable coalition government is stitched together. General António Eanes is elected president.
- **1986:** Dr. Mário Soares, a Socialist, is elected president. Portugal joins the European Community.
- **1991:** Soares is reelected for a second (and final) four-year term as president. The history of Portugal and its cultural heritage are honored at EUROPALIA 91, in Belgium.
- **1992:** Portugal serves as president of the European Community.
- **1993:** Portugal begins gearing up for the ASTA (American Society of Travel Agents) World Travel Congress, which Lisbon will host in the autumn of 1994. The convention is expected to bring 5,000 to 7,000 travel industry leaders to Portugal from around the globe. This will be the first time Portugal has hosted an ASTA Congress; as a result, travel to Portugal is expected to boom from 1993 on throughout the 1990s.

—Jean Anderson

INDEX

Abano, 120
Abrantes, 193
Abside, 102
Achadinha, 512
Adega Kilowatt, 382
Adega Lusitania, 515
Adega Machado: Caminha, 423;
  Lisbon, 96
Adega Regional, 417
Adega Regional de Colares, 129
Adega do Saloio, 123
Adega Típica do Souto, 378
Ad Lib, 98
Adro da Sé, 318
Aguiar da Beira, 326
Aguias d'Ouro, 225
Albergaria Caza de São
  Gonçalo, 260, 277
Albergaria Marina Rio, 260, 277
Albergaria Quinta da Penha de
  França, 475, 499
Albergaria Residencial Josefa de
  Obidos, 137, 157
Albergaria Senhora do Monte,
  87
Albergaria Solar dos Mouros,
  273, 277
Albergaria do Terreiro, 288, 310
Albergaria Velha, 274, 277
O Alberto, 260
Alboroque, 338
Albufeira, 253
Alcalar, 258
Alcântara Mar, 98
Alcatruz, 247
Alcobaça, 141
Alcobaça Restaurant, 125
Alcoutim, 270
A Aldeia, 84

Aldeia Saloia de José Franco,
  132
Alentejo, 12, 15, 16, 18, 20, 200,
  202 (map)
Alfa Lisboa, 84
Alfama, 8, 57, 58 (map)
Alfredo's, 257
Alga-Mar, 151
Algar do Carvão, 516
Algar Seco, 256
Algarve, 10, 239, 249 (map),
  264 (map)
Alhandra, 169
Alijó, 379
Aljezur, 263
Almancil, 248
Almeida, 327
Almeirim, 194
Alpendre, 260
Alpiarça, 194
Alte, 272
Altis, 83
Alto da Memória, 515
Alto Minho, 413
Alto Tamega, 456
Alto do Velão, 444
Alvito, 209
Alvor, 256
Amarante, 380
Amazónia Hotel, 88
Amérigo Francisco Marques,
  Livreiro Antiquario, 103
Amoreira Aqueduct, 232
Amoreiras Shopping Center, 99
Amorim, 409
Ana Salazar, 99
Angra do Heroismo, 514
Aniki-Bobo, 369
Anjos, 512

Antiga Casa Maritima, 146
Antigo Paço do Concelho, 399
Antigo Paço Episcopal, 405
Antigo Paços do Conselho, 425
Antiquariatum, 102
António Madeira, 102
António Mendonça, 269
Apartamentos Albufeira Jardim, 254, 277
Apartamentos Turísticos Cabanas Ria, 268, 277
Aparthotel Magnoliamar, 154, 158
Aparthotel Montesol, 269, 277
Aparthotel Neptuno, 269, 277
Aparthotel de Tróia, 154, 158
Apeadeiro Restaurante, 117
Aquário, 493
O Aqueduto, 215
Aqueduto das Aguas Livres, 75
Arcadia, 361
Arcos de Valdevez, 417
Arco da Vila, 245
Arganil, 302
Armona, 266
Aroeira—Clube de Campo de Portugal, 147
Arouca, 310
Arrábida Peninsula, 17, 19, 150
Arraiolos, 219
Artesanato Regional Português Arameiro, 100
Artlantida, 182, 184
Atei, 446
Atelier Fotográfico de Carlos Relvas, 177
Atlantic, 82
Atlantic Gardens, 474, 499
Atlantis: Cascais, 116; Lisbon, 100
Aveiro, 305
Avenida Arriaga, 476
Avenida Carvalho Araújo, 443
Avenida da Liberdade, 56
Avenida Palace Hotel, 83
Avenida Restaurant: Loulé, 251; Tavira, 268
Avis, 236
Aviz, 90
Avô, 302

Azambuja, 169
Azeitão, 152
Azenhas do Mar, 130
Azinhal, 270
Azores, 20, 501, 502 (map)

Bachus, 92
Bagoeira, 430
Baiana, 496
Bairro Alto, 67
Bairro Alto Discotheque, 98
Baixa: Lisbon, 54, 98; Porto, 360
Baixo Alentejo, 210
Bamboo, 252
Baralto, 94
Barcelos, 428
Barracha, 250
Barredo, 357
Barreto & Gonçalves, 101
Barrô, 375
Basílica da Estrela, 70
Batalha, 142
O Batel, 117
Bay of São Lourenço, 513
Bazar do Parque, 114
O Beco, 149
Beco do Chão Salgado, 78
Beira Alta, 20, 313, 316 (map)
Beira Baixa, 313, 332 (map), 337
Beira Litoral, 12, 18, 282, 284 (map)
Beira Mar, 515
Beira Rio, 268
Bela Vista, 185
Belém, 11, 14, 75, 109
Belmonte, 338
Benard's, 66
Benfica, 18
Berlengas, 136
Bertrand's, 66
Biblioteca Joanina, 295
A Bilha—Artesanato e Turismo, 99
Bobadela, 303
Boca do Inferno, 118
Boémia, 294
Bolhão, 361
Bom Jesus do Monte, 14, 410
Bom Sucesso, 361

Aux Bons Enfants, 251
Bonjardim, 92
Borba, 230
Bordeira, 263
Bota Alta, 93
Braga, 402
Bragança, 452
A Brasileira, 66, 95
Bussaco Forest, 20
O Búzio, 258

Cabanas, 268
O Cabaz da Praia, 254
Cabeça da Neve, 317
Cabo Espichel, 151
Cabo Girão, 492
Cabo da Roca, 120
Cabo de São Vicente, 262
Cacela Velha, 268
Cachalote, 493
Cachopo, 271
Cacilhas, 146
Café Aliança, 245
Café A Brasileira, 406
Café Creme Piano Bar, 97
Café Nicola, 56, 95
Café Relógio, 487
Café Restaurante Atlantida, 513
Café-Restaurante Martinho da
  Arcada, 92
Calântica, 219
Caldas de Monchique, 274
Caldeira do Enxofre, 517
Caldeira de Guilherme Moniz,
  516
Caldeirão, 524
Caldeira das Sete Cidades, 510
Camacha, 486
Câmara de Lobos, 491
Câmara Municipal, 406
Caminha, 422
Campo da Feira, 174
Campo de Golfe da Madeira,
  489
Campo Pequeno, 73
Canal Central, 307
Canal de São Roque, 307
O Caneção, 268
Cantinho do Campo das Hortas,
  408

Cantinho da Várzea, 130
Caparica, 146
Capela do Fundador, 143
Capela da Glória, 405
Capela dos Milagres, 490
Capela de Nossa Senhora da
  Agonia, 425
Capela de Nossa Senhora de
  Conceição, 407
Capela de Nossa Senhora da
  Memória, 140
Capela de Nossa Senhora da
  Piedade, 186
Capela de Nossa Senhora da
  Vitória, 517
Capela dos Ossos, 216
Capela dos Reis, 404
Capelas, 510
Capela de Santa Catarina, 478
Capela da São Frutuoso, 411
Capela de São Geraldo, 405
Capela de São João Baptista, 69
Capela de São Miguel, 295
Capela do Senhor dos Passos,
  170
Capelas Imperfeitas, 144
Capuchos, 127
Caramulinho, 317
Caramulo, 315
Caravela, 483
Carcavelos, 110
O Cardápio do Visconde, 289
Carmo, 267
O Carneiro, 450
Carolina do Aires, 147
Cartaxo, 169
La em Casa, 453
Casa do Adro, 418, 434
Casa da Agrela, 417, 434
Casa das Antiguidades, 429
Casa dos Arcos, 430
Casa D'Armas, 427
Casa de Artesanato da Região
  de Coimbra, 297
Casa d'Avó, 172
Casa do Barão de Fermil, 445,
  462
Casa do Barreiro, 340, 341
Casabela Hotel, 257, 277
Casa dos Bicos, 54

Casa do Campo, 445, 462

Casa Canada, 99

Casa do Casal, 375, 386

Casa de Casal de Loivos, 378, 386

Casa dos Cedros, 176, 197

Casa de Chá Terra Nostra, 512

Casa Cisterciense, 142

Casa dos Coimbras, 407

Casa da Comenda, 340, 341

Casa da Comida, 91

Casa Cordovil, 217

Casa de Crasto, 415, 434

Casa dos Crivos, 406

Casa Eden, 409

Casa Etnografia da Ilha Graciosa, 517

Casa Fânzeres, 409

Casa do Forno, 227

Casa Grande da Bandeira, 426, 434

Casa do Infante, 359

Casa de Jantar, 257

Casa José de Matos, 247

Casa do Leão, 60, 91

Casa Leonel, 100

Casa dos Linhos, 361

Casa Macario, 101

Casa da Misericórdia, 360

Casa do Monte, 430, 434

Casa Museu Almeida Moreira, 320

Casa Museu Francisco Ernesto de Oliveira Martins, 515

Casa Museu Frederico de Freitas, 481

Casa de Nossa Senhora do Carmo, 508, 526

Casa dos Oleiros, 260

Casa do Outeiro, 415, 434

Casa do Paço, 302

Casa dos Patudos, 194

Casa da Pedra Cavalgada, 408, 435

Casa de Peixinhos, 207, 237

Casa da Pergola, 117, 156

Casa Pingueis, 377, 386

Casa do Pinhão, 260, 277

Casa do Poço, 137, 157

Casa dos Pombais, 400, 435

Casa das Pontes, 378, 386

Casa das Quartas, 443, 462

Casa dos Quintais, 290, 311

Casa Quintão, 101

Casa do Raio, 407

Casa de Rebordinho, 318, 341

Casa da Rede, 380

Casa Regional da Ilha Verde: Lisbon, 101; São Miguel, 509

Casa dos Reis, 482

Casa do Relógio, 137, 157

Casa do Ribeiro, 401, 435

Casa de Rodas, 420, 435

Casa de São Gens, 374, 386

Casas do Cruzeiro, 335, 341

Casa dos Serralves, 363

Casa de Sobre-Ripas, 296

Casa Soure, 217

Casa da Tapada, 128, 157

Casa dos Tapetes de Arraiolos, 101

Casa de Terena, 208, 237

Casa da Tojeira, 445, 462

Casa da Torre, 334

Casa da Torre-Hermitage, 250

Casa do Turista, 476

Casa dos Varais, 376, 386

Casa Velha, 482

Casa Victorino, 358

Casa Zé da Calçada, 382, 386

Cascais, 17, 115

Casino da Madeira, 472, 483

Casino Park Hotel, 472, 499

O Castelo, 256

Castelo de Arouce, 289

Castelo de Bode, 188

Castelo Bom, 330

Castelo Branco, 339

Castelo de Leiria, 286

Castelo Melhor, 329

Castelo Mendo, 330

Castelo de Milfontes, 211, 237

Castelo de Monforte, 458

Castelo dos Mouros, 127

Castelo de Palmela, 148

Castelo do Queijo, 366

Castelo Rodrigo, 328

Castelo de São João da Foz, 365

Castelo de São Jorge, 60

Castelo de Sesimbra, 151

Castelo de Vide, 233
Castle of Almourol, 191
Castro de Avelãs, 454
Castro Marim, 270
Castro de Sabroso, 402
Cavalo Branco, 511
Cava de Viriato, 321
Caverna de Viriato, 335
O Celeiro, 476
Celeiro dos Frades, 142
Celorico de Basto, 445
Celorico da Beira, 331
O Celta, 338
Central Bazaar, 124
Central Restaurant, 178
Centro de Arte Moderna, 73
Centro Cultural de Belém, 78
Centro Equestre da Lezíria
    Grande, 168
Centro Regional de Artes
    Tradicionais, 358
Centro de Repouso,
    Estabelecimento Termal das
    Caldas de Monchique, 274,
    277
Centros de Acolhimento, 270,
    277
Centro de Turismo e
    Artesanato, 99, 101
Centum Cellas, 337
Cerâmica Artistica Isabel
    Garcia, 100
Cerâmica de Bicesse, 114
Ceramicarte, 116
Cerâmica Viera, 511
Cêrca Moura, 61
Cerro da Vila, 253
Cervejaria da Trindade, 68
Chafariz do Largo do Paço, 405
Chapel of Santo António, 259
Chaves, 456
Chiado, 65, 98
Chico Elias, 186
Chico Leonor, 195
A Choupana, 114
Church of the Convento de
    Santa Clara, 362
Church of Santa Maria do
    Castelo, 267
Church of São Pedro, 511

Churrasqueira da Goncinha,
    251
Churrasqueiria Tulha, 414
Cidadela, 115
Cidade Velha, 246
La Cigale, 253
Cine Teatro de Tomar, 187
Cinfães, 374
Citânia de Briteiros, 401
Ciudad Rodrigo, 330
Clara, 92
Claustro Real, 144
Claustro do Silencio (Coimbra),
    298
Cloister of Silence (Alcobaça),
    141
Clube de Empresários, 92
Clube de Golfe da Penha Longa,
    121
Coconuts, 117
Coimbra, 290, 292 (map)
Côja, 302
Colares, 129
Colégio Church, 478
Colegio Novo, 297
Colina Sagrada, 396
Comida de Santo, 93
Condeixa-a-Nova, 300
Conde de Leça, 366
Condestável, 219
Confeitaria Peixinho, 307
Confeitaria Salvação, 430
Conímbriga, 300
Constância, 191
Convento dos Capuchos, 147
Convento de Cristo, 180
Convento dos Lóios, 213
Convento de Nossa Senhora da
    Esperança, 509
Convento de Nossa Senhora do
    Espinheiro, 214
Convento de Refójos, 446
Convento de Santa Clara:
    Funchal, 481; Vila do Conde,
    432
Convento de Santa Clara-a-
    Nova, 299
Convento de Santa Clara-a-
    Velha, 299
Convento da Santa Iria, 184

Convento de Santa Maria de Aguiar, 328
Convento de São Paulo Hotel, 206, 237
Conventual, 91
Copo de Três, 97
Coral, 484
Corvo, 524
Costa, 269
Costa do Estoril, 108
Costa Nova, 309
Costa Verde, 423
Costa Vicentina, 263
Couceiro dos Leitões, 305
Coudelaria de Alter, 236
Covilhã, 336
Cozinha das Malheiras, 427
Cozinha do Rei, 307
Cozinha de Santo Humberto, 216
Cozinha Velha, 122
Crato, 236
Cristo Rei, 146
Cromlech and Menhir of Almendres, 221
Cromlech of Xarez, 228
Cruz Alta: Coimbra, 304; Sintra, 127
Cruzeiro do Senhor do Galo, 428
Cucos, 133
Culatra, 266
Curia Palace Hotel, 305, 311
Curral das Freiras, 485

Darcy's, 260
O Dias, 254
Dionisyos, 457
A Doca, 146
Docelândia, 423
Dois Irmãos, 246
Dolmen-Chapel of São Brissos, 221
Dolmen of Zambujeiro, 221
Dom Fernando, 83
Dom Manoel, 365
Dom Manuel I, 88
Dom Pepe, 111
Domus Municipalis, 453
Dornes, 189

Douro River, 17
Douro Valley, 17, 19, 370, 371 (map)
Downing Street, 358
Dunas Douradas, 250, 278
Durão Peak, 329

Eduardo Azenha, 131
Eira do Serrado, 485
Elevador da Bica, 68
Elevador da Gloria, 67
Eloy de Jesus, 101
Elvas, 231
Embaixada, 83
English Bar, 114
Enxaréus Grotto, 523
Ericeira, 131
Ermelo, 418
Ermida, 418
Escola de Rendas, 432
Escondidinho, 369
Escorial, 92
O Espigueiro, 427
Estação Zootécnica Nacional, 169, 176
Estalagem Abrigo da Montanha, 275, 278
Estalagem da Boega, 422, 435
Estalagem do Brasão, 433, 435
Estalagem do Caçador, 448, 462
Estalagem de Carvalhelhos, 460, 462
Estalagem do Convento, 137, 157
Estalagem Ilha do Lombo, 188, 198
Estalagem do Lago Azul, 189, 198
Estalagem Muchaxo, 120, 156
Estalagem da Neve, 340, 341
Estalagem Riabela, 308
Estalagem de Santa Cruz, 519, 521, 526
Estalagem de Santa Iria, 185, 198
Estalagem São Miguel, 310
Estalagem Senhora da Guia, 119, 156
Estalagem Vale da Ursa, 189, 198

Estalagem das Velas, 518, 526
Estalagem Vinha de Areia, 508, 526
Estói, 247
Estoril, 10, 111
Estoril Casino, 113
Estrela Factory, 300
Estremadura, 8, 11, 104, 133, 134 (map)
Estremoz, 223
Estufa Fria, 71
Estufa Quente, 71
Estufas Agosto Arruda, 510
Eurotel Tavira, 265, 278
Evora, 211
Evorahotel, 206, 237
Evoramonte, 229

Fabrica de Cerâmica Constancia, 100
Fábrica Kalifa, 219
Fabrica da Sant'Anna, 100
Factory House, 359
Faial, 519
Faianças Artísticas Bordalo Pinheiro, 138
Fajãzinha, 523
Falcão Restaurant, 192
Faro, 244
Fateixa, 111
Fátima, 13, 189
Les Faunes, 473, 482
Faustino and Filhos, 458
Favaios, 379
Feira da Ladra, 64
Feira Nacional do Cavalo, 178
Fénix, 86
Ferrari, 101
O Fervedouro, 511
Fialho, 18, 215
Figueira de Castelo Rodrigo, 328
Figueira da Foz, 301
Figueiró dos Vinhos, 289
Fisgas do Ermelo, 444
Flores, 523
Flor da Rosa, 236
Fóia, 274
Fonte do Idolo, 407
Formosinho, 150

Fornos de Algodres, 331
Fortaleza: Peniche, 135; Valença, 421
Fortaleza do Beliche, 262, 278
Forte Dom Rodrigo, 117
Forte do Pau da Bandeira, 259
Forte de São Brás, 509
Fortress of Lindoso, 417
Four Seasons, 113
Foz de Arouce, 290
Foz do Douro, 365
Francisco Ramos, 101
Freixo de Espada-à-Cinta: Beira Alta, 329; Trás-os-Montes, 449
Funchal, 476
Furnas, 511
Furnas Lagosteira, 118
Furusato, 114
Fuseta, 266
O Fuso, 135

Gabriela, 450
Galeão, 99
O Galeão, 260
Galeria de Artesanato, 361
Galeria Luis Serpa, 103
Galeria Risco, 183
Galeria São Mamede, 103
Galerias Vandoma, 361
Gambrinus, 91
Garrafeira Couceiro, 305
Garrafeira Santa Maria, 399
Gerês, 412
Gigi, 250
Gilberto, 259
Girassol, 83
Golegã, 177
Golfer's Inn, 250
Gomes, 432
Gouveia, 334
Graciosa, 516
Grafieira, 97
Grande Hotel da Curia, 305, 311
Grande Hotel do Porto, 361, 369, 386
Greens, 369
Gruta do Escoural, 221
Grutas de Mira de Aire, 143
Grutas de Santo António, 143

Guarda, 330
Guimarães, 13, 394, 397 (map)
Guincho, 17, 119
Gulbenkian Foundation, 72

Helena Simões Ferreira, 102
Helio, 99
Herdade Dom Pedro, 209, 237
Herdeiros de Francisco José
  Ferreira, 409
Holiday Inn Crowne Plaza, 84
Holiday Inn Lisboa, 84
Horta, 519
Horta da Moura, 207, 237
Hospital São Marcos, 407
Hot Clube de Portugal, 98
Hotel Abidis, 176, 198
Hotel Açores Atlântico, 509, 526
Hotel do Aeroporto, 513, 526
Hotel Albatroz, 118, 156
Hotel Alcazar, 269, 278
Hotel Algarve, 257, 278
Hotel Alif, 88
Hotel Alvor Praia, 258, 278
Hotel Amaranto, 382, 386
Hotel de Angra, 514, 526
Hotel Aquae Flaviae, 458, 462
Hotel Astória, 290, 311
Hotel Atlântico, 113, 156
Hotel Atlantis, 252, 278
Hotel Baía, 117, 156
Hotel Baia Azul, 474, 499
Hotel da Baleeira, 263, 278
Hotel Bela Vista, 257, 278
Hotel Boa Vista: Albufeira, 254,
  278; Foz do Douro, 365, 386
Hotel Caloura, 511, 526
Hotel Caravelas, 523, 526
Hotel Carlton, 86
Hotel Central, 124, 157
Hotel Continental, 86
Hotel Cristal, 288, 311
Hotel Dom Bernardo, 244, 278
Hotel Dom João III, 287, 311
Hotel Dom José, 190, 198
Hotel Dom Luís, 290, 311
Hotel Dom Pedro Marina, 252,
  278
Hotel Dona Felipa, 250, 278
Hotel do Elevador, 409, 410, 435

Hotel Estoril-Sol, 114, 156
Hotel Eurosol Restaurant, 287
Hotel Faial, 519, 526
Hotel Foz Praia, 139, 157
Hotel Golfinho, 260, 279
Hotel de Gouveia, 334, 341
Hotel Grão Vasco, 318, 341
Hotel Guadiana, 265, 279
Hotel do Guincho, 120, 156
Hotel Ibis, 244, 279
Hotel Infante de Sagres, 367,
  386
Hotel João Padeiro, 306, 311
Hotel de Lagos, 260, 279
Hotel da Lapa, 83
Hotel Lisboa, 85
Hotel Lisboa Plaza, 85
Hotel do Mar, 151, 158
Hotel Mar e Sol, 288, 311
Hotel Méridien Porto, 367, 387
Hotel Mira Serra, 331, 341
Hotel Navarras, 382, 387
Hotel da Nazaré, 139, 157
Hotel Oriental, 257, 279
Hotel Palácio, 113, 156
Hotel Palácio dos Seteais, 128,
  157
Hotel Panorama, 380, 387
Hotel do Parque (Bom Jesus do
  Monte), 410, 435
Hotel Parque (Lamego), 322,
  341
Hotel Pomba Branca, 306, 311
Hotel Porto Santo, 496, 499
Hotel Praia Dourada, 496, 499
Hotel da Praia Norte, 136, 157
Hotel Pullman Lisboa, 85
Hotel Quinta do Lago, 250, 279
Hotel La Réserve, 247, 279
Hotel Rex, 88
Hotel Rocamar, 254, 279
Hotel Samasa-Fundão, 340, 341
Hotel de Santa Luzia, 426, 435
Hotel São Gens, 302, 311
Hotel São Pedro, 508, 510, 526
Hotel Savoy, 472, 500
Hotel da Senhora do Castelo,
  321, 341
Hotel Sheraton Porto, 367, 387
Hotel Sol e Mar, 254, 279

Hotel dos Templários, 186, 198
Hotel Terra Nostra, 511, 526
Hotel Tivoli: Coimbra, 290, 311;
   Sintra, 124, 157
Hotel da Torre, 88
Hotel de Turismo: Abrantes,
   193; Guarda, 331, 341
Hotel de Vale de Lobos, 131,
   157
Hotel Vasco da Gama, 269, 279
Hotel Veneza, 87
Hotel Village Cascais, 118, 156

Idanha-a-Velha, 339
Igreja do Carmo: Coimbra, 298;
   Faro, 246; Lisbon, 68; Porto,
   362; Viseu, 320
Igreja dos Clérigos, 362
Igreja do Colégio, 515
Igreja da Conceição Velha, 54
Igreja dos Congregados, 361
Igreja de Encarnação, 66
Igreja da Graça, 173
Igreja dos Grilos, 149
Igreja de Jesús, 148
Igreja do Loreto, 66
Igreja da Madre de Deus, 64
Igreja de Marvila, 172
Igreja Matriz: Barcelos, 429;
   Caminha, 423; Golegã, 177;
   Mogadouro, 449; Sesimbra,
   151; Viana do Castelo, 425;
   Vila do Conde, 433
Igreja da Misericórdia: Angra
   do Heroismo, 514; Chaves,
   457; Porto, 360; Viseu, 319
Igreja de Nossa Senhora dos
   Anjos, 512
Igreja de Nossa Senhora da
   Assunção: Atalaia, 179;
   Cascais, 116; Vila do Porto,
   513
Igreja de Nossa Senhora da
   Nazaré, 140
Igreja de Nossa Senhora da
   Oliveira, 398
Igreja de Nossa Senhora do
   Pópulo, 138
Igreja de Nossa Senhora do
   Rosário, 512

Igreja das Ondas, 267
Igreja de Santa Catarina, 66
Igreja de Santa Clara, 175
Igreja de Santa Iria, 175
Igreja da Santa Luzia, 61
Igreja de Santa Maria: Marvão,
   235; Obidos, 138; Sintra, 126
Igreja de Santa Maria da
   Alcáçova, 173
Igreja de Santa Maria do
   Castelo, 193
Igreja de Santa Maria Madalena,
   411
Igreja de Santiago e São
   Mateus, 194
Igreja do Santíssimo Milagre,
   174
Igreja de Santo André, 511
Igreja de Santo António da Sé,
   63
Igreja de Santo António da
   Torre Velha, 414
Igreja de São Facundo, 456
Igreja de São Francisco: Evora,
   216; Porto, 359; Vinhais, 455
Igreja de São Gonçalo, 380
Igreja de São João Baptista, 182
Igreja de São Jorge, 512
Igreja de São José, 509
Igreja de São Julião, 149
Igreja de São Mamede, 130
Igreja de São Martinho, 485
Igreja de São Miguel, 511
Igreja de São Miguel do
   Castelo, 396
Igreja de São Pedro: Palmela,
   148; Peniche, 135; Ponta
   Delgada, 510; Torres Vedras,
   133
Igreja de São Pedro de
   Balsemão, 324
Igreja de São Roque, 68
Igreja de São Salvador, 416
Igreja do Seminário, 172
Igreja do Senhor Bom Jesus,
   366
Ilha da Barreta, 246
Imperial de Bordados, 481
Imperial Restaurant, 268
Inácio, 408

Instituto do Bordado, Tapeçarias e Artesanato da Madeira, 479
Instituto da Juventude Viana do Castelo, 425
Intermobilia, 102
Ipanema Park Hotel, 368, 387
Isto e Aquilo, 116

Jardim do Antigo Paço Episcopal, 340
Jardim Botânico: Coimbra, 300; Funchal, 484; Lisbon, 69; Porto, 363
Jardim da Estrela, 70
Jardim de Santa Bárbara, 406
Jardim Zoológico, 74
Jesuit University, 217
João Padeira, 117
João Passos, 250
João Trindade Antiquario, 103
Jopel, 269
Jordão, 399
José Medeiros, 132
José Rosas & Cie, 360
Judiaria, 234
Julia's, 250
Jumbo, 116
Junceda Belvedere, 413

Kalunga, 422

Lagoa: Algarve, 255; Azores, 511
Lagos, 258
Lajes do Pico, 522
Lamego, 322
A Lanterna, 257
Lapela, 420
Largo da Oliveira, 398
Largo da Porta de Moura, 217
Largo das Portas do Sol, 61
Laurentina, 94
O Leão de Porches, 255
Les Lauriers, 250
Lavores, 101
Lawns American Restaurant, 268
Leiria, 286
Lennox Country Club, 113, 156
Linha do Corgo, 385, 461
Linha do Douro, 385

Linha do Minho, 433
Linhares, 331
Linha da Tua, 385, 461
Lisboa à Noite, 96
Lisboa Sheraton Hotel and Towers, 84
Lisbon, 8, 11, 16, 18, 45, 52 (map)
Lisbonense, 99
Livraria Campos Trindade, 103
Livraria Nove Estrelas, 509
Lorenco & Santos, 99
Loulé, 250
Loulé Jardim Hotel, 251, 279
Louletano, 251
Loures, 133
Lourinhã, 135
Lourosa, 303
Lousã, 289
Luamar Suite Hotel, 495, 500
Luís L. Leal, 102
Lusitana, 406

Macedo de Cavaleiros, 448
Machico, 489
Madeira, 16, 17, 19, 20, 464, 465 (map)
Madeira Carlton Hotel, 472, 500
Madeira House, 99
Madeira Islands, 11
Madeira Palácio, 472, 500
Madeira Wine Company, 470
Mafra, 131
Majestic Café, 361
Mal Cozinhado (Porto), 369
O Mal Cozinhado (Santarém), 175
Mangualde, 321
Manta Rota, 269
Manteigas, 335
Mar e Sol, 136
Mare Viva Restaurant, 79, 146
Marialva, 329
Maria Rita, 447
Marinha Grande, 288
Marinheiro, 432
A Marisqueira, 309
Marisqueira Esplanada, 366
Martinho da Arcada, 95
Martins and Costa, 101

Marvão, 20, 235
Matança, 331
Matosinhos, 366
Mazouco, 450
Mealbada, 18, 305
Menhir of Bulhoa, 226
Menhir of Outeiro, 226
Mercado dos Lavradores, 479
Mercado da Ribeira, 54
Méridien, 82
Mesão Frio, 380
Mezio, 418
Michel, 60, 91
Miga's, 208
Milagres, 289
Milreu, 247
Minho, 12, 13, 15, 20, 388, 390
   (map)
Miradouro da Boa Vista, 376
Miradouro do Espigão, 513
Miranda do Douro, 450
Mirandela, 446
Mirandes, 451
Misericórdia Church: Lourinhã,
   135; Montalegre, 461; Obidos,
   138; Peniche, 136; Tavira, 267
Misericórdia Hospice, 425
Mistério da Prainha, 522
Mistério de Santa Luzia, 522
Mistério de São João, 522
Mogadouro, 449
Moimenta da Beira, 325
Moinho do Caniço, 455, 463
Moinho de Estorãos, 416, 435
Moita do Ribatejo, 196
Mónaco, 109
Monastery of Nossa Senhora de
   Terço, 429
Monção, 419
Monchique: Algarve, 274;
   Azores, 523
Mondim de Basto, 445
Monsanto, 339
Monsaraz, 227
Mons Cicus, 275, 279
Monserrate, 19, 127
Montalegre, 461
Monte Cara, 93
Monte do Casal, 248, 279
Monte Clérigo, 263

Monte do Faro, 420
Monte Gordo, 269
Monte Madalena, 415
Montemor-o-Velho, 301
O Montinho do Campo, 254
Monumental Restaurant, 421
Mosteiro dos Jerónimos, 77,
   109
Mosteiro de Santa Cruz, 297
Mosteiro de Santa Maria, 141
Mosteiro de Santa Maria da
   Vitória da Batalha, 143
Mosteiro de São Francisco, 175
Motel da Piscina, 130, 157
Motel de Sant'Ana, 433
Municipal Gallery of Visual
   Arts, 149
Muralha, 430
Murça, 446
Museu Abel Manta, 334
Museu de Alberto Sampaio, 398
Museu da Angra, 515
Museu Arqueológico Lapidar In-
   fante Dom Henrique, 245
Museu Arqueológico de São
   João de Alporão, 172
Museu Arqueológico de São Mi-
   guel de Odrinhas, 131
Museu de Arte Popular, 14, 76
Museu de Arte Sacra: Braga,
   405; Horta, 520; Porto, 357
Museu do Automóvel Antigo,
   109
Museu de Aveiro, 307
Museu dos Baleeiros, 522
Museu do Brinquedo, 125
Museu do Caramulo, 315
Museu Carlos Machado, 509
Museu Casa de Colombo, 494
Museu de Cera de Fátima, 190
Museu da Cidade: Lisbon, 73;
   Setúbal, 148
Museu do Conde de Castro
   Guimarães, 116
Museu das Cruzes, 481
Museu de Curiosidades, 447
Museu Diocesano de Arte
   Sacra, 477
Museu Escola de Artes De-
   corativas, 61

Museu de Etnografia, 513
Museu de Etnografia e História, 360
Museu Etnográfico: Almeirim, 195; Faro, 246; Santa Cruz, 523; São Brás, 272
Museu de Evora, 213
Museu de Fósforos Aquiles de Mota Lima, 183
Museu Francisco Tavares Proença Júnior, 339
Museu de Grão Vasco, 318
Museu da Guarda, 331
Museu Guerra Junqueiro, 357
Museu de Horta, 520
Museu de José Malhõa, 139
Museu Machado de Castro, 295
Museu da Marinha, 77
Museu Maritimo, 246
Museu Marítimo e Regional, 309
Museu Martins Correia, 177
Museu Martins Sarmento, 400
Museu Militar, 457
Museu Municipal: Lagos, 259; Pinhel, 327; Viana do Castelo, 425
Museu Municipal de Arqueologia (Silves), 273
Museu Municipal Dr. Santos Rocha, 302
Museu Municipal de Estremoz, 224
Museu Municipal de Marvão, 235
Museu do Município (Obibos), 138
Museu Nacional de Arqueologia e Etnologia, 77
Museu Nacional de Arte Antiga, 55
Museu Nacional do Azulejo, 64
Museu Nacional da Ciência e Tecnologia, 298
Museu Nacional dos Coches, 78
Museu Nacional de Lamego, 323
Museu da Região Flaviense, 457
Museu Regional Abade de Baçal, 453

Museu Regional de Arqueologia e Etnologia (Setúbal), 149
Museu Romântico (Porto), 362
Museu Rural, 223
Museu Rural e do Vinho, 170
Museu São Rafael Pequeno, 138
Museu Soares dos Reis, 362
Museu da Terra de Miranda, 451
Musikefesta, 251

Nabão, 185
Naves, 330
Nazaré, 139
Nisa, 205
Nossa Senhora da Alegria, 234
Nossa Senhora do Cabo, 151
Nossa Senhora da Conceição, 490
Nossa Senhora da Consolação, 267
Nossa Senhora do Desterro, 274
Nossa Senhora de Guadalupe Chapel, 261
Nossa Senhora da Pena, 287
Nossa Senhora da Penha, 234
Nossa Senhora dos Remédios, 14, 324
Nossa Senhora da Serra do Pilar, 364
O Nosso Café, 407
Noudar, 228

Obidos, 137
Odeleite, 270
Odrinhas, 130
Oeiras, 110
Olaria Guimarães e Velho, 226
Olaria José Faisco Cartaxo, 226
Olaria Pequena, 255
Olaria Pirraça, 226
Olhão, 265
Olhos de Agua, 253
Oliveira do Hospital, 303
Ondaparque, 147
Orca, 493
Ourém, 190
Ouro Branco, 208

Outeiro Machado, 459
Ovar, 309

Paço de Calheiros, 416, 435
Paço Ducal, 230
Paço dos Duques, 396
Paço de São Cipriano, 401, 435
Paços do Conselho, 423
Paço Vedro de Magalhães, 417, 435
Padrão da Batalha do Salado, 399
Padrão dos Descobrimentos, 76, 109
Palace of the Counts of Basto, 218
Palace Hotel do Buçaco, 303, 311
Palácio da Alorna, 195
Palácio Bettencourt, 514
Palácio dos Biscainhos, 406
Palácio da Bolsa, 359
Palácio de Brejoeira, 419
Palácio dos Condes de Carvalhal, 247
Palácio de Constância, 192, 198
Palácio de Cristal, 363
Palácio Ducal, 429
Palácio dos Marqueses de Fronteira, 74
Palácio Mateus, 443
Palácio Nacional (Sintra), 125
Palácio Nacional da Ajuda, 79
Palácio Nacional de Mafra, 131
Palácio Nacional de Queluz, 122
Palácio da Pena, 126
Palácio dos Pitas, 422
Palácio de São Bento, 70
Palácio de São Lourenço, 478
Palmares Golf Course, 258
Palm Beach, 117
Panorama Room, 84
Pap'Açorda, 91
O Parafuso, 146
Parque Eduardo VII, 71
Parque Florestal de Monsanto, 74
Parque de Marinha, 119
Parque Mouchão, 185

Parque Nacional de Buçaco, 19, 303
Parque Nacional de Peneda-Gerês, 20, 411
Parque Natural do Alvão, 444
Parque Natural de Montesinho, 454
Parque Natural da Ria Formosa, 246, 265
Parque Natural das Serras de Aire e Candeeiros, 143
Parque Restaurant, 421
Parque de Santa Catarina, 478
Parque da Santa Cruz, 300
Parreirinha, 96
Pastelaria de Belém, 78
Pastelaria Bénard, 95
Pastelaria Ferrari, 95
Pastelaria Oliveira, 144
Pastelaria Rossio, 307
Pastelaria Sala de Cha Versailles, 95
Pastelaria Suíça, 56
Pátio Alfacinha, 96
Patrício & Gouveia, 480
Paúl da Serra, 493
Pavia, 236
Pavilhão Chines, 97
Pedrogão Grande, 289
Pena, 126
Penafiel, 383
Penamacor, 338
Penedono, 329
Penedo da Saudade, 300
Penela, 301
Penhas Douradas, 335
Penhas da Saúde, 336
Peniche, 135
Penina Golf and Resort Hotel, 257, 279
Peninha, 127
Pensão Residencial Sinagoga, 185, 198
Pensão Residencia Santa Maria da Arrábida, 150
Pensão Ribamar, 139, 158
Pequeno Mundo, 250
Pereira d'Oliveira Wine Lodge, 478
O Pescador, 117

Peso da Régua, 376
Pete's Café Sport, 519
Pico, 520, 521
Pico do Arieiro, 488
Pico dos Barcelos, 485
Pico da Esperança, 518
Pico Ruivo, 488
Picota, 275
Pico de Vara, 512
Pine Cliffs Golf and Country Club, 253
Pinhal Real, 288
Pinhão, 17, 377
Pinhel, 327
Piódão, 302
Piriquita, 124
Piscinas, 300
Pitta, 99
Planetário Calouste Gulbenkian, 78
Poço de Inferno, 336
Pombal, 289
Pombalino, 84
Ponta dos Biscoitos, 516
Ponta dos Capelinhos, 520
Ponta Delgada, 509
Ponta da Piedade, 259
Ponta do Queimado, 516
Ponte da Barca, 417
Ponte de Lima, 413
Ponte 25 de Abril, 145
Popedoce, 321
Porches, 255
Porta Branca, 93
A Porta Nobre, 358
Portas do Sol, 173
Portimão, 256
Portinho da Arrábida, 150
Porto, 17, 349, 350 (map)
Porto Covo, 210
Porto Formoso, 512
Porto Moniz, 493
Porto de Mós, 143
Porto Santo, 11, 494
Portucale, 368
Portugal dos Pequenitos, 299
Postigo do Carvão, 369
O Pote, 458
Pousada do Barão de Forrester, 17, 378, 387, 444, 463

Pousada do Castelo, 137, 158
Pousada Castelo de Palmela, 148, 158
Pousada de Dom Dinis, 422, 435
Pousada do Infante, 262, 279
Pousada dos Lóios, 203, 212, 218, 238
Pousada do Mestre Afonso Domingues, 144, 158
Pousada de Nossa Senhora da Oliveira, 399, 435
Pousada do Pico do Arieiro, 475, 487, 500
Pousada da Rainha Santa Isabel, 203, 224, 238
Pousada da Ria, 306, 308, 311
Pousada de Santa Bárbara, 21, 303, 311
Pousada de Santa Catarina, 451, 463
Pousada de Santa Luzia, 205, 231, 238
Pousada de Santa Maria, 20, 205, 235, 238
Pousada de Santa Marinha da Costa, 400, 435
Pousada de Santo António, 306, 311
Pousada de São Bartolomeu, 454, 463
Pousada de São Bento, 412, 435
Pousada de São Brás, 272, 280
Pousada de São Filipe, 149, 158
Pousada de São Gens, 204, 238
Pousada de São Gonçalo, 444, 463
Pousada de São Jerónimo, 317, 342
Pousada de São Lourenço, 21, 334, 342
Pousada de São Miguel, 203, 238
Pousada de São Pedro, 188, 198
Pousada de São Teotónio, 421, 435
Pousada Senhora das Neves, 327, 342
Pousada dos Vinháticos, 475, 493, 500

Povoação, 512
Póvoa de Varzim, 431
Praça de Camões, 457
Praça do Comércio, 51
Praça Dom Pedro V, 234
Praça Luís de Camões, 66
Praça do Município, 477
Praça da República: Tomar, 182;
    Viana do Castelo, 424
Praça dos Restauradores, 56
Praia, 513
Praia do Carvoeiro, 255
Praia do Cordama, 263
Praia das Maçãs, 130
Praia dos Moinhos, 512
Praia da Rainha, 147
Praia da Rocha, 256
Praia da Vitória, 516
Prainha, 258, 280
Primorosa de Alvalade, 98
Príncipe Real, 70, 86
Procópio, 97

Queluz, 19, 122
Querença, 272
Quinta da Alfarrobeira, 260,
    280
Quinta da Anunciada Velha,
    187, 198
Quinta de Aveleda, 383
Quinta d'Avenida, 85
Quinta da Bacalhôa, 153, 158
Quinta Bar, 187
Quinta da Bela Vista, 475, 482,
    500
Quinta de Benatrite, 247, 280
Quinta da Boa Vista, 450, 463
Quinta do Bom Sucesso, 484
Quinta do Campo, 141, 158
Quinta da Capela, 129, 157
Quinta do Caracol, 265, 280
Quinta da Cardiga, 178
Quinta do Convento da
    Franqueira, 430, 435
Quinta das Encostas, 111, 157
Quinta do Fidalgo, 144, 158
Quinta dos Frades, 382
Quinta da Graça, 423, 435
Quinta das Lágrimas, 299
Quinta Magnólia, 479

Quinta da Marinha Aldeamento
    Turístico, 119, 157
Quinta de Monserrate, 129
Quinta do Monte dos
    Pensamentos, 207, 238
Quinta do Paço D'Anha, 426,
    436
Quinta do Paço da Ermida, 306,
    311
Quinta do Palheiro Ferreiro,
    486
Quinta dos Prazeres, 209, 238
Quinta de Santa Isabel, 458, 463
Quinta do Santoinho, 428
Quinta de São José, 133, 158
Quinta de São Sebastião, 169,
    198
Quinta de São Tiago, 128, 157
Quinta das Torres, 152, 158
Quinta Vale de Lobos, 176, 198
Quinta do Vinagre, 129

Rabaçal, 301
Rabelo, 365
Ramalhão, 301
Ramiro Leão, 99
Raposeira, 261
Real dos Canas, 299
Redondo, 225
Reduto da Mãe de Deus, 509
Refúgio da Roca, 120
Regionalia, 114
El Rei, 399
Reid's Hotel, 473, 478, 500
Resende, 374
Reserva da Loendros, 315
Reserva Natural do Estuário do
    Sado, 154
La Réserve, 247
Residência Inglêsa, 87
Residencial Beira Mar, 514, 526
Residencial Ibérica, 251, 280
Residencial Ilha Graciosa, 517,
    526
Residencial Santa Cruz, 517,
    527
Residencial Solneve, 337, 342
Residencial União, 185, 198
Residencial Vila Flores, 523, 527
Restaurante Alvorada, 383

Restaurant/Bar Mar e Sol, 496
Restaurante A Bolota, 208
Restaurante Campismo, 457
Restaurante Castiço, 175
Restaurante Cocheira Alentejana, 94
Restaurante Cristina, 192
Restaurante Dona Amélia, 482
Restaurante Dona Filipa, 368
Restaurante Meta, 305
Restaurante Palmeiras, 338
Restaurante Pedro, 268
Restaurante Porto de Santa Maria, 119
Restaurante a Primavera, 95
Restaurante São Caetano, 96
Restaurante 33, 92
Restaurante Típico, 305
Restaurante Típico Guião, 216
Restaurante à Tipoia, 93
Restaurante Várzea de Colares, 130
Ria de Aveiro, 308
Ribatejo, 12, 13, 18, 160, 162 (map)
Ribeira, 357
Ribeira Grande, 511
Rio de Onor, 454
Ritz Grill, 82, 93
Ritz Intercontinental, 82
Rocha das Bordões, 523
Romana, 483
Romeu, 447
Roque, 247
Rosior, 360
Rosmaninho, 377
Rossio: Lisbon, 55, 98; Viseu, 320
Rota do Vinho, 169
Rua da Alfandega, 478
Rua Augusta, 99
Rua do Comércio, 257
Rua Direita, 320
Rua 5 de Outubro, 217
Rua Frederico Arouca, 116
Rua Santa Isabel, 257
Rua de Santo António, 244
Rua do Souto, 404
Rui, 273
A Ruina, 254

Sabugal, 338
Sabugueiro, 335
Sagres, 261
Saisa, 111
Sala do Arcaz, 405
Sameiro, 410
Santa Bárbara, 513
Santa Cruz: Flores, 523; Madeira, 490
Santa Cruz Café, 298
Santa Cruz da Graciosa, 517
Santa Cruz Restaurant, 460
Santa Engrácia, 64
Santa Justa Elevador, 68
Santa Luzia, 268
Santa Margarida Beach, 150
Santa Maria, 512
Santa Maria de Cárquere Priory, 374
Santa Maria Church: Bragança, 453; Castelo de Vide, 234; Lagos, 259
Santa Maria de Feira, 309
Santana, 488
Sant'Anna Factory, 100
Santarem, 170
Santa Rufina, 100
Santiago, 151
Santo Espírito, 513
Santos & Nascimento, 99
Santuário de Monte Sameiro, 410
Santuário de Nossa Senhora dos Remédios: Lamego, 322; Peniche, 136
São Bento, 361
São Cucufate, 209
São Francisco Javier Fortress, 366
São Giao, 303
São João do Campo, 413
São João da Pesqueira, 329
São João de Tarouca, 325
Sao Jorge, 518
São Julião da Barra, 110
São Lourenço, 248
São Martinho de Mouros, 375
Sao Miguel, 508
São Paulo, 267

São Pedro, 513
São Pedro de Corval, 226
São Pedro de Moel, 288
São Pedro de Sintra, 123
São Tiago da Barra, 425
São Vicente de Fora, 63
Sapa, 123
Sapatária Teresinha, 409
Sardoal, 194
Sarmento, 101
Sarmento Museum, 400
Sé: Angra do Heroismo, 515;
   Funchal, 477; Guarda, 330;
   Lamego, 323; Lisbon, 63; Vila
   Real, 443; Viseu, 319
Secla, 139
Semana do Mar, 520
Sendim, 450
Senhor Vinho, 95
Sé Nova, 295
Sé Velha, 296
Sernancelhe, 326
Serpa, 205
Serra de Açor, 302
Serra da Arrábida, 145
Serra do Barroso, 460
Serra do Caramulo, 315
Serra da Estrela, 20, 302, 330
Serra da Lousã, 289
Sesimbra, 151
A Seta, 483
Seteais, 127
Setúbal, 148
A Severa, 96
Sheraton Algarve Hotel and Re-
   sort, 253, 280
Shrine of Our Lady of Fátima,
   190
Silves, 273
Sintra, 19, 122
Sir Harry's Bar, 254
S. Miguel, 140
Snack-Bar Marquês, 496
Soajo, 418
O Soeiro, 270
Solar, 102
Solar das Arcas, 447, 463
Solar Beirão, 321
Solar Bragançano, 453
Solar dos Chavões, 170

Solar dos Condes de
   Bertiandos, 416
Solar de Cortegaça, 427, 436
Solar do F, 483
Solar dos Pinheiros, 429
Solar de São Pedro, 123
Solar da Vacariça, 305, 312
Solar do Vinho do Porto, 69,
   363
Sortelha, 338
Sousel, 203
Springfellows, 98
Sua Excelência, 91
Swing, 369

Tabuleiros Festival, 182
Tagarela, 116
Tágide, 90
Tapada de Mafra, 132
A Tasca, 262
Tasca do Manel, 94
O Tasco, 274
A Tasquinha, 140
Tavares, 90
Taverna Bébobos, 358
Tavira, 266
T Club, 407
Tear, 226
Teatro Nacional Dona Maria II,
   56
Teatro de São Carlos, 66
Teixeiras, 481
O Telheiro, 262
Templo de Nossa Senhora de
   Encarnação, 287
Templo de Senhor da Cruz, 429
Terceira, 513
Terena, 208
Terra do Basto, 444
Terra Nostra, 512
Timpanas, 96
Tivoli, 82
Tivoli Jardim, 85
Tivoli Porto Atlántico, 368, 387
Toca do Cabóz, 131
Tomar, 179
Torre, 336
Torre de Anto, 297
Torre de Aspa, 263
Torre de Belém, 76, 109

Torre das Cabaças, 173
Torre do Galo, 449
Torre de Menagem: Braga, 406;
    Bragança, 452; Guimarães,
    396; Miranda do Douro, 451
Torre da Princesa, 452
Torre do Relógio, 422
Torres Vedras, 133
O Toucinho, 195
Tourist House, 100
Trancoso, 326
Trás-os-Montes, 12, 17, 19, 437,
    438 (map)
Travanca, 383
Trave Negra, 321
Os Três Potes, 427
Tricana, 93
Trigonometria, 407
Tróia, 153
Tromba Rija, 288
Trovador, 294, 296
Tulhas, 125
Tun Fon, 94
Twins, 369

Uncle Sam's, 268

Vadeca, 409
Vale Glaciário do Zêzere, 336
Vale do Lobo, 250
Valença do Minho, 420
Van Gogo, 117
Varanda, 82
Varanda do Oceano, 147
Varanda da Régua, 377
Vasco da Gama Aquarium, 109
Vasco da Gama Restaurant, 85
Vela Latina, 109
Velha Goa, 94
Velha Universidade, 294
Vestal Faianças de Alcobaça, 142

Via Augusta, 99
Viana do Castelo, 423
Vianna, 406
Vidago, 459
Vidago Palace Hotel, 459, 463
Vieira do Minho, 412
Vilabranca Hotel Club, 260, 280
Vila do Conde, 432
Vila Franca do Campo, 511
Vila Franca de Xira, 166
Vila Hostilina, 322, 342
Vila Joya, 254, 280
Vilalara, 255, 280
Vilamoura, 252
Vilamoura Marinotel, 252, 280
Vila Nogueira de Azeitão, 152
Vila Nova de Foz Côa, 329
Vila Nova de Gaia, 363
Vila do Porto, 513
Vila Real, 442
Vila Real de Santo António, 269
Vila da Rua, 326
Vila Viçosa, 229
Villa Cliff, 474, 482
Vimeiro, 135
Vinhais, 455
Viseu, 318
Vista Alegre, 100, 309
Vista Alegre Showroom, 360
Vitória, 517
O Vitral, 288
Viuva Lamego, 100

Xairel, 102
Xenia, 250

York House, 86

Zé da Calçada, 382
Zé Manel, 297
Zurique, 87